THE MODERN
CORPORATION
AND AMERICAN
POLITICAL
THOUGHT

DATE DUE

Scott R. Bowman

THE MODERN CORPORATION AND AMERICAN POLITICAL THOUGHT

Law, Power, and Ideology

The Pennsylvania State University Press
University Park, Pennsylvania

Library of Congress Cataloging-in-Publication Data

Bowman, Scott R., 1949–
    The modern corporation and American political thought : law,
    power, and ideology / Scott R. Bowman.

        p.   cm.
    Includes bibliographical references and index.
    ISBN 0-271-01472-5
    ISBN 0-271-01473-3 (pbk.)
    1. Corporations—Political aspects—United States. 2. Corporation
law—United States. 3. United States—Politics and government—20th
century. I. Title.
HD2731.B64 1996
322'.3'0973—dc20   94-45439
                                                                         CIP

It is the policy of The Pennsylvania State University Press to use acid-free paper
for the first printing of all clothbound books. Publications on uncoated stock
satisfy the minimum requirements of American National Standard for Information Sciences—Permanence of Paper for Printed Library Materials, ANSI Z39.48–
1992.

For my parents,
**Sharon S. Bowman and
Robert E. Bowman**

Contents

Preface

This book is about the power exercised by the modern large corporation. In addition to analyzing corporate power within its institutional setting, I explain how economic, legal, political, and ideological factors have contributed to its socially comprehensive character. To that end, I trace the evolution of corporate enterprise in the United States as reflected in American political thought and law, analyze the (internal) organization of corporate power and the (external) exercise of this power in the marketplace and politics, and explore issues pertinent to the global spread of transnational corporations. In arguing for a theoretical position that significantly revises current approaches, I also address debates concerning the nature of class conflict in American society.

I must confess that I did not originally intend this work to have such a wide compass. It is the product of an intellectual odyssey that began with relatively limited objectives, but then took numerous detours and added new dimensions before finally arriving at its destination. Originally, I set out to analyze conceptions and theories of corporate power in American political thought and political science and to assess their analytical and ideological significance within specific historical settings. My research eventually led me to other disciplines—history, law, sociology, economics—that contained a wide range of studies concerning the modern corporation. I discovered that, in the great majority of cases, social scientists did not seek to integrate, or even discuss, analyses outside their own disciplines or areas of specialization. This is unfortunate, considering the affinities that many of the studies from different areas share. Our knowledge of the corporation could be substantially advanced through efforts to synthesize this storehouse of information. Intrigued with the possibilities that such a synthesis might yield, I decided to take some preliminary steps in that direction.

As I expanded the scope of my project considerably, my initial objective of examining theoretical aspects of corporate power continued to guide my research and analysis. Adopting a transdisciplinary perspective did not in itself solve theoretical problems, but it did help to clarify them. The strengths of one area of scholarship often highlighted the weaknesses of others. Through this method of study, I gradually developed an approach that gave some shape to my theoretical interests.

Recounting the entire process here would most likely tax the reader's patience, so I shall mention only its major features.

My study of the historical origin and development of corporate enterprise in the United States convinced me that important aspects of the contemporary debate about corporate power had been misconceived, or at least had not been adequately informed by a knowledge of American history. As my investigations focused on understanding how corporate capitalism had transformed the marketplace from an arena of competitive struggle to a largely cooperative environment, and on how decisions of judges and political leaders had affected this dramatic change, I realized that I needed to delve deeper into the legal foundations of American capitalism. Through this inquiry, I came to understand the fundamental importance of judge-made and statutory law in structuring and regulating power relationships—an issue, I discovered, that had not been adequately analyzed by students of corporate power. My legal and historical research had provided me with a fresh perspective on theoretical questions. Most important, it had yielded insight into what I have since defined as the political (or nonpecuniary) nature of corporate power.

I then sought to integrate my ideas about legal change and the growth of corporate enterprise with my earlier research on corporate power in American political thought. This undertaking suggested to me a method for interpreting the evolution of liberalism in the twentieth century in light of the works of several political thinkers. As I pursued this task, I came to understand better how the growth of the large corporation had influenced ideological developments in the twentieth century, and especially how liberal ideas had been revised to justify the rise and consolidation of corporate power. At the same time, I attempted to pull the various strands of my research together within a historical and conceptual framework that could explain the growth of corporate power with reference to its two dimensions: internal (within the enterprise) and external (in society at large). By this circuitous route, I returned to my point of departure. On the basis of critiques of various works, I was able to clarify the theoretical tasks that I had been struggling with from the outset, and then to develop an alternative to current theoretical and conceptual approaches to corporate power.

This book draws on knowledge from various disciplines and fields, including history, law, political science, political theory, institutional economics, and sociology. I have made a concerted effort to use these materials in a synthetic, rather than eclectic, fashion. In this respect, the historical themes are intended to provide the common thread that is necessary to achieve a measure of coherence.

My hope is that this work will contribute to the growing interest in the political study of the corporation. The subject of corporate power has not received the attention it merits. Recent contributions to this area of scholarship notwithstanding, there is a great need for more research on empirical and theoretical aspects of corporate power. In the past, this burden has not been shouldered equally among disciplines in the social sciences. For several decades, historians, sociologists, and economists have taken the lead in examining the social and political significance of the modern corporation. By contrast, these matters have suffered relative neglect at the hands of political scientists.

Having leveled this accusation, I should amend it by pointing out that, some years ago, it was a political scientist, Richard L. Sklar, who impressed on me that corporate power posed novel challenges for students of political science. As both my mentor and my colleague, his theoretical perspectives on power and other issues profoundly influenced my thinking throughout the course of the intellectual meanderings I have described. His critical assessments of this project, at each stage from beginning to end, have been uniformly beneficial and deeply appreciated. I shall forever be indebted to him for the inspiration that he has provided, for the knowledge that he has imparted through his teaching, and especially for the theoretical insights that helped me fit together the pieces of my own theoretical puzzle. As it happened, his study of the impact of transnational corporate power in developing nations, and my examination of the development of corporate power in the United States, brought us, by different paths and for different reasons, to the same theoretical problem—or, as he put it, we had been looking at this problem "through opposite ends of the telescope." He had the "wrong end" of the telescope, which meant, of course, that I had the better view. But we agreed that we were observing the same phenomenon. Although fortuitous, this meeting of the minds was entirely logical. I was even more gratified when I discovered exactly how the solution he had devised for this theoretical conundrum could be adapted to my own work.

A special acknowledgment is also due Martin J. Sklar, whose studies of the Progressive Era greatly influenced and clarified my thinking about corporate capitalism, corporate liberalism, the development of antitrust law, and broader issues of social theorizing. I am beholden to him as well for his careful and thoughtful reading of an earlier version of this manuscript. His comments and suggested revisions were indispensable in helping me to improve and sharpen many aspects of my argument. I am also in the debt of several scholars whose criticisms, suggestions, and observations, on all or portions of this book, were of immense value. They include David Becker, Donald Brand, Irving Louis Horowitz, John H. M. Laslett, Jeffrey Lustig, Paul Mattick Jr., Carl Parrini, and Duane Smith.

I would especially like to thank Sandy Thatcher, Director of Penn State Press, for taking an avid interest in this project. His extraordinary professionalism and patience have made my tasks much easier. And I must acknowledge a profound debt to Peggy Hoover, Senior Manuscript Editor at Penn State Press, whose superb editing greatly improved the quality of the book. I also wish to acknowledge the excellent work of the following students who, under the auspices of the UCLA Student Research Program, aided me with various research tasks during the final stages of preparing the book: Tim Medcoff, Iona De Guzman, Sheryl Greene, and Steven Smelser. Finally, I wish to express my deepest gratitude to all of my family, and to Eve Sklar, for unwavering support, and to extend a very special thank-you to my mother, Sharon S. Bowman, and to my wife, Suzanne, for their exceptional contributions in helping me to complete this project.

Chapter 1

CORPORATE POWER

> *Concepts such as legitimacy, authority, power, and constitutionalism have now entered deeply into the discussion of the modern business corporation. Nevertheless, this approach exposes a serious dilemma. On the one hand, the corporation is today an intrinsic part of the economy and society. It is the dominant way of doing business and of producing and distributing most of the goods by which men live and earn their living. Its organizations reach deep into the patterns of daily life for millions. . . . On the other hand, the existence of the modern corporation does not accord with long-standing conceptions of political organization, and no theory exists by which it can be reconciled with such conceptions.*
>
> —Grant McConnell, 1966

1. INTRODUCTION

Corporate power persists as one of the great enigmas of political science. A complex phenomenon possessing economic, legal, political, and social significance, corporate power does not lend itself to facile description or to conventional methods of political analysis. Nor are there convenient historical analogies that might offer guidance in disclosing the inner principles of this mysterious force. The American business corporation is largely an indigenous creation. It has come to embody the sort of practical genius that Americans are famous for—a capacity to exploit new opportunities and to adapt to changing exigencies even while assiduously planning the next venture. Since the early decades of the nineteenth century, the fate of industrial capitalism in the United States has been inextricably bound up with the growth of corporate enterprise.

Throughout the history of the republic, the corporation has served as the primary agency for economic development and expansion, at home and abroad. The corporation in America, however, is not now, nor has it ever been, an economic device pure and simple. It was born in political turmoil, in a time when corporations were regularly granted monopoly powers and exclusive privileges and just as regularly decried as engines of tyranny. Corporate enterprise evolved from that stage only to become a more potent means of exercising control over the American economy and polity.

In the present era, the large business corporation is at once a legal entity (a fictitious and immortal person possessing rights and obligations), an enterprise chartered by government and subject to the rule of law, a joint-stock company that earns dividends for its stockholders, and an economic, political, and social institution through which power is exercised internally (within the enterprise) and externally (in society at large). This abbreviated description, however, only scratches the surface of the subject matter. Every aspect of corporate power—in the economy, the law, politics, and society—contains its own set of issues and analytical problems.

Corporate power poses unprecedented theoretical challenges for political scientists. It defies rigid disciplinary boundaries just as it eludes academic preconceptions of social reality rooted in ideological doctrine. The political study of the corporation, therefore, cannot be fitted neatly into any one of the discrete realms of the academic division of labor or their various subdivisions. Such a study, in brief, requires a transdisciplinary approach that can account for the complexity of corporate power in terms of the development of corporate capitalism in the modern era.

Nearly a century ago the large corporation, as we know it today, first appeared as a solution to the ills of the competitive marketplace. As the strategy of combination supplanted competition, corporations began to consolidate through various means, or simply to gobble up their competitors in rapid fashion. By 1904, the first great merger movement of corporate capitalism had utterly transformed the structure of the American economy and set in motion the corporate reconstruction of American society. The dawn of a new century had ushered in the age of corporate power. Although students of the corporation have since amassed considerable evidence of corporate domination at home and abroad, we have yet to devise a political theory of the business corporation that can fully comprehend the dimensions of corporate power. It is the aim of the present study to examine the reasons for this state of affairs and to suggest how it might be remedied.

Unconventional subjects call for unconventional methods and approaches. Several related objectives determine the scope and content of this work. The major analytical and theoretical tasks may be summarized as follows: (1) to analyze the liberal justification of corporate power in American law and political thought; (2) to critique leading conceptions of corporate power in American law, political thought, and social science; (3) to examine the role of law in facilitating economic and social change and in structuring relationships of control; (4) to propose a transdisciplinary approach to the study of corporate power; and (5) to evaluate current justifications for the rise of transnational corporate power.

At different stages in the development of capitalism in the United States, liberal ideology has been revised and adapted (through the law and political thought) to justify the rise and the consolidation of corporate power. Corporate enterprise could not have secured its extraordinary legal privileges or achieved ideological acceptance so readily without assuming the guise of personhood in a market economy. The accommodation of the corporation (a collective form of enterprise) to the individualist precepts of Anglo-American law stands as one of the salient achievements of nineteenth-century American jurisprudence. In the twentieth century, corporate citizens and statesmen have joined entrepreneurial actors in the theater of economic life. Both the legal edifice of corporate power and its ideological justification in the law have been built on legal and moral conceptions of the corporate individual. However, the personification of the corporation comprises only one aspect of a comprehensive ideological revisionism during the modern era. In the law, as in political theory, the corporate reconstruction of American society is justified with reference to the premises of a revised laissez-faire liberalism, the "corporate liberalism" that arose during the social movement of corporate capitalism in the Progressive Era. Consequently, my analysis of the liberal justification of corporate power entails an examination of the relationship between ideology and social change; it also involves the study of specific ways in which ideological beliefs have been revised to reconcile the world view of liberalism with the exigencies of the corporate order.

The precepts of liberal ideology, in both its classical and revised forms, have shaped ideas about corporate power in American law, political thought, and social science. By examining the ideological content of conceptions of corporate power, we may distinguish the elements that have explanatory value from those that serve primarily a moral purpose. While this method of ideological critique will be applied to other (nonliberal) approaches, it has special relevance for liberal analyses. By and large, the most influential theoretical ideas about corporate power, including crucial analytical distinctions, have been shaped fundamentally by liberal beliefs or ideals. A considerable portion of my analysis of the concept of corporate power, in American legal theory, political thought, and social science, will be devoted to demonstrating the limitations that these enduring ideological assumptions have imposed on political theories of the corporation.

Heretofore, theoretical studies in analytical and sociological jurisprudence have not adequately conceptualized the relationship between the coercive and ideological aspects of the law in liberal-capitalist societies. Jurisprudence, in the main, does not address the complexity of power in the modern world. It lacks an analytical conception of power that can account for relationships of control rooted in the law. Nor has political science produced a conception of power that can incorporate or synthesize the study of coercion in jurisprudence. Both disciplines fail to analyze the interrelationship between ideology, power, and the law. This aspect of my analysis has relevance for understanding how legal reasoning that embodies ideological doctrine may be employed to justify and legitimize power relationships. It also provides insight into how the law structures relationships of control through general principles. Indeed, I make the argument that a political theory of the corporation must be based on an analytical approach that conceptualizes corporate power in terms of relationships of control structured and regulated by law. My analysis of the law of corporations, antitrust law, and constitutional law establishes the foundation for this claim.

An approach to corporate power elaborated in this work unfolds, in a synthetic fashion, through systematic analytical criticism of concepts of corporate power in American law, political thought, and social science; through an analysis (historical in scope) of the interrelationship between corporate power, ideology, and the law; and through an examination of the empirical dimensions of corporate power. On the basis of these factors, and with special focus on the critiques of liberal managerial theory and conventional Marxist class analysis, I make the case for a revised class analysis that can explain the socially comprehensive character of corporate power, including the significance of corporate domination for liberal-democratic political institutions, and that can account for the restructuring of relationships of control through the law to effect the consolidation of that power. This approach is based on a historical interpretation of the rise and consolidation of the corporate-capitalist order that takes as its focal point the corporate reconstruction of American society during the Progressive Era. It is a central premise of this study that one can discover the keys that unlock the mysteries of corporate rule, within the enterprise and throughout society, only by conducting a careful study of its origins, not by ignoring its historical development or by abstracting corporate power from its social context in order to analyze its components.

With this approach in mind, I venture again into the past to better understand the future development of corporate capitalism. In the final chapter, I use the writings of numerous influential individuals in the corporate and academic domains to construct an emergent ideological justification of transnational corporate enterprise. The task of understanding the global political implications of the claims of the transnational ideologists, I argue, may be aided by a knowledge of the rise and consolidation of corporate power in the United States. In order to predict the future of corporate capitalism, we must first decipher its past. This most recent and perhaps greatest theoretical challenge posed by the global spread of transnational enterprise manifests the need for a theory that can comprehend the development of corporate capitalism in terms of the historical relationship between liberalism, class, and corporate power. The proof of this contention is the substance of this work.

2. CORPORATE POWER AND AMERICAN LIBERALISM

Since the birth of the United States, social critics have linked the analysis of corporate power with its deleterious implications for American politics and society. Motivated by a profound skepticism of the putative social benefits of corporate enterprise, and wary of the antidemocratic tendencies of concentrated power within the business corporation, this long-standing political conception of the corporate device has inspired the periodic resurgence of American antimonopoly sentiment in its various stages from 1781 to the present.

Monopoly power in the mercantilist era of the early nineteenth century developed out of different economic circumstances than did the monopoly power of the trust builders at the century's close. At all times, however, the antimonopoly critique of corporate power, and the political and moral recommendations it produced, took shape within the premises of liberalism, the dominant ideology of American society. In the aftermath of the legal and political accommodations of the Progressive Era and the New Deal period, antimonopoly sentiment has been largely contained and legitimized through the public regulation of enterprise. Nevertheless, it survives in various forms and on many political fronts outside of courtrooms and regulatory commissions. It has been muted but not silenced. Corporate power, rather than the inequities or social ills of capitalism in general, has posed the greatest challenges to American political activists and has inspired the most significant efforts of liberal reform. The study of the concept of corporate power in American law and political thought therefore entails examining a vital political tradition that has been the source of both critical analysis and ideological justification.

To understand better the significance of the American liberal tradition for corporate power, we must briefly examine the components of classical liberal ideology. The ideological beliefs that are generally agreed to constitute classical liberalism are derived primarily from the works of seventeenth- and eighteenth-century European, mainly British, political philosophers and economists.[1] Liberalism first developed as a progressive, if not radical, ideology that served to justify the interests and political objectives of the rising capitalist class, or bourgeoisie. At its core, classical liberalism contains an affirmation and defense of the freedom and rights of the individual whether they be political, religious, or pecuniary. It is the last of these for which liberalism offered the strongest defense, and understandably so, since it sought to justify an economic system that was premised on contractual relations between individuals. To the classical liberal mind, government is a necessary evil. It exists to preserve the rights of the individual, to maintain order; yet government must also be formally constrained in the exercise of its power lest it overstep its rightful authority. Because individuals will abuse power, a "government of laws, not men," must be established. Thus, as liberalism supplanted monarchist doctrines of absolutism, the ideal of the rule of law emerged as a basic principle of the liberal-capitalist order.

The liberal's distrust of centralized power finds expression not only in the concepts of limited government and constitutionalism but also in the related idea of balance. The concept of balance in political theory— whether conceived as a just ordering of classes by inherent capacities, as a means of ameliorating class conflict and preventing revolution, or as a mechanism whereby power checks power to ensure republican government—antedates liberalism by several centuries. Numerous political thinkers, including Plato, Aristotle, Polybius, Machiavelli, Harrington, and Montesquieu, formulated influential conceptions of social or political balance pertinent to their specific theoretical objectives.[2] Whereas the ancient Greek and republican conceptions of balance presume that social harmony and stability are necessary for attaining the good of the whole (polis or republic), the classical liberal conception of social balance endeavors to protect the liberty of the individual by allowing the laws of the market to operate freely. As society becomes self-regulating, thereby permitting greater freedom for the individual, the responsibilities of the citizen and statesman in establishing and maintaining social balance diminish correspondingly. An automatic balance or harmony displaces a contrived balance, just as the liberal conception of the individual good displaces the ancient conception of the common good.

The liberal interpretation of social balance derives in part from classical political economy and its underlying conceptual distinction between politics and economics. For Adam Smith, the founder of this school, economic activity represented the realm of freedom, the sphere in which the pursuit of self-interest, subject to the natural laws of the marketplace, yielded socially beneficent and efficient results. On the other hand, the realm of politics or government, being subject to the artificial and often abusive laws of human beings, was by nature coercive. The task, as Smith conceived it, was to severely delimit the role of government in order to preserve the realm of freedom and social efficiency. Hence, the very notion of power in the economic sphere suggested that the laws of the marketplace had been tampered with or abused from without, as the classical theory of monopoly clearly indicates. When combined with a sturdy individualism and a historic fear or distrust of centralized power, the Smithian conception of social balance, based on the separation of state and society, was destined to become an article of faith for the American liberal.[3]

A product of both the Enlightenment and the Reformation, classical liberalism also contains a conception of history as material progress—a partly economic, partly religious view that identifies industry and acquisitiveness with the social good and heavenly rewards. As Harold Laski observed, liberalism quite clearly constitutes "the philosophy of business civilization."[4] Laski's statement holds as true for American liberalism as it does for its European counterpart. Although it initially imported from abroad, American liberalism has been shaped by native conditions and predispositions. It cannot be adequately understood apart from the colonial experience and its emphasis on self-determination and religious freedom.[5] The staunchly individualistic tenor of American liberalism, exemplified by the avid belief in the rights of property as well as in other individual rights or liberties, no doubt derives in part from the pre-Revolutionary American experience. Furthermore, American liberalism contains a version of material progress that is peculiarly its own—namely, the doctrine of the open frontier, economic expansion, unlimited opportunity, and upward mobility—in short, the American promise.

The triumph of liberal ideology in the United States, however, was not foreordained. Americans were not of one ideological mind before or after the Revolution. Class, regional, and religious differences strongly influenced political beliefs and objectives. In pamphlets, newspaper articles, and speeches, Revolutionary leaders and activists invoked republican and liberal ideals to forge a cross-class ideological consensus.[6] Lockean liberalism served one purpose during the Revolution and quite another in its aftermath. Indeed, there are two Lockes in American liberalism: the egalitarian Locke of the Revolution and the contractarian Locke of civil society. Both may be found in *Two Treatises of Government* and both, although frequently at odds, have shaped the contours of the liberal tradition in America.[7] As Louis Hartz argued, although not entirely for the correct reasons, a long line of American political thinkers, regardless of their apparent ideological bias, owe a great debt to Lockean liberalism.[8] However, American liberalism has never been one-dimensional or free of internal contradictions. Contrary to Hartz, moreover, this so-called "natural liberalism" was and is more than an ethos or an inchoate predisposition nurtured by the conditions of American life. Like all ideologies, American liberalism constitutes a set of beliefs that must be expounded, perhaps revised, and transmitted by individuals in each generation.

American liberalism therefore began as a composite of native experience and inherited ideas. What Americans borrowed from the European experience they often bent to their own ends. While some ideas gained easy acceptance, others were resisted and never took hold. Shaped by religious doctrine and republican ideals, synthetic rather than monolithic, liberalism in America has developed on its own terms, a fact that has undoubtedly contributed to its pervasiveness and resilience over the last two centuries.

American ideological developments, therefore, must be understood within their specific socioeconomic context. This is especially relevant for assessing the ideological justification of corporate power. It is ironic, though not at all fortuitous, that Adam Smith's economic theory, which was outspokenly critical of the inefficiencies of corporate enterprise within the marketplace of individuals, eventually became a source of the corporation's greatest ideological strength. To accomplish this result, the long-held view of the business corporation as a tool of monopoly power would have to be jettisoned for a modern, anthropomorphic conception of the corporation suited to the individualistic premises of liberalism. The unique contribution of American constitutional law to this ideological trick of mirrors, what I shall term "the doctrine of corporate individualism," took hold in American jurisprudence in the early decades of the nineteenth century. Not only did it confer on the corporate entity the legal rights and capacities of the contracting individual during the dawn of American industrialization, but it also personified this legal fiction, thereby transforming a collectivity into an individual. In Britain, legislation that made incorporation a general privilege (as opposed to an exclusive right conferred by special charters) was not enacted until the mid-1800s, when the industrial revolution stood as a monument to the era of individual enterprise. In the United States during the same period, the proliferation of general incorporation acts, justified by the doctrine of corporate individualism, signaled the beginnings of an industrial revolution led by a corporate vanguard. With the rise of corporate power in the final decades of the nineteenth century, the doctrine of corporate individualism could be easily accommodated to the moral directives of laissez-faire, which either derived from classical political economy or found novel expression in the Spencerian strictures of social Darwinism and its American counterpart. In America, the age of individualism promoted the ascendancy of corporate power first by disguising it and then by denying its existence.

By the turn of the century, however, the laissez-faire premises of corporate individualism were under attack from numerous quarters. A growing and widespread social discontent over economic, social, and political problems associated with the rise of the large corporation heralded a dramatic change in American political and economic life. As the marketplace was radically transformed through merger and other means of corporate combination, laissez-faire ideology began to lose its moral appeal. In justifying economic and political reform, Progressive Movement leaders initiated a reevaluation and revision of the nineteenth-century liberal creed.

In the early decades of the twentieth century, political and corporate leaders, economists, legislators, judges, liberal reformers, and political thinkers formulated the premises and methods of corporate liberalism in an effort to adapt nineteenth-century liberal institutions and ideology to the exigencies of corporate capitalism—to effect, in other words, the corporate reconstruction of American society through the law, politics, and the market. As a central, if not primary, ideological aspect of this social movement, the liberal justification of corporate power found its most important expression in the law and in political thought that justified public regulation of corporate enterprise while preserving the constitutional separation of state and society.[9] This process of ideological revisionism, I shall argue, embodies the dominant intellectual tendencies of liberalism in the twentieth century, tendencies that not only have shaped legal and political thinking but permeate the social sciences as well.

My analysis of the liberal conception of corporate power consists of two interrelated aspects. One concerns the adaptation and revision of American liberalism to justify the rise and consolidation of corporate power. The other involves an examination of analytical approaches that have been conceived within the precepts of liberalism and applied to the concept of corporate power. Accordingly, I shall demonstrate that the liberal justification of corporate power in American law and political thought extends to other realms of social thought that share the same premises. This work, therefore, entails an investigation of the ideological process by which ideas that justify particular interests come to form general principles within the law and politics and thereby influence, if not mold, the intellectual presumptions and outlook of an era.

3. CORPORATE POWER AND THE LAW

In matters affecting social control, consensus, and change, ideologies constitute an integral aspect of social arrangements; they justify and mediate the various relationships that comprise the social order, including relationships of control. For a relationship of control to endure without the dominant party continually resorting to coercion, the relationship itself must be perceived as being legitimate. Power acquires legitimacy through ideological justification. Judicial bodies interpret (and apply) law or make new law in accordance with legal procedures and in light of ideological beliefs. However, in addition to instilling or communicating ideological doctrine that may justify power relationships, law may also mediate and structure these relationships. The interrelated functions of law, power, and ideology therefore raise analytical issues that pertain to the operation of law in effecting social control. For the purposes of this analysis, I shall examine the two most pervasive aspects of law as an instrument of social control in liberal society—namely, law as coercion and law as ideology.

As a coercive means of effecting social control, laws articulate rules that seek to regulate or control the behavior of individuals by threatening sanctions. This is perhaps the most apparent function of law in society. Less obvious, but no less significant for the preservation of order, is the role of law in establishing and maintaining power relationships. The exercise of power presupposes the existence of the condition for its exercise—specifically, a relationship of control, a condition of dominance and subordination. As a relationship of control acquires a general social character, it develops structural attributes or characteristics—patterns of behavior conducive to control by the dominant party, rules and sanctions, institutional support and linkages—designed to ensure its stability and persistence. Law helps to establish the condition for the exercise of power in the dual sense that it enables and enforces. Law confers powers and rights necessary for the exercise of control, and it protects these prerogatives with the threat of sanctions and various legal remedies. In this manner, the legal basis of control or dominance by an individual, group, or class may be instituted and then revised to accommodate changing social conditions.

This is not to say that law alone creates conditions for the exercise of power. Other factors that give rise to the inequality inherent in power relationships must exist or develop. Law, however, may create opportunities that are conducive to the development of a structure of control. By conferring the capacity to act in a certain way, legal rights and powers may endorse other behavior that is consistent with that capacity. For example, it is precisely because property rights ensure security that they encourage the accumulation of wealth and the invention of techniques to achieve that end. This behavior, in turn, may produce social conditions—including relationships of control based on the ownership of property—that require new laws to regulate or enforce these relationships. Thus, by defining the changing contours or limitations of power relationships, the law implements a structure of control, the legal foundation and justification of which rests on the right to possess and accumulate property.

The notion that law may structure or restructure relationships of control holds special significance for analyzing the development of corporate power in the United States. Corporate power may be conceived as consisting of two dimensions of control that derive from the organization and legal structure of the corporation itself—namely, the external and internal dimensions of corporate power. The former refers to the capacity of the corporation to exercise power in society at large, while the latter strictly concerns the relationships of control within the corporation. This conceptual division of power defines the object of control but says nothing about the nature of control. An analysis of the legislative and judge-made law that structures these relationships of control, however, yields significant insight into how this power may be exercised. In other words, what the law permits and prohibits will in some way inform our understanding of the nature of corporate power.

An analysis of the law that structures the internal and external dimensions of corporate power is especially important for explaining the rise and consolidation of corporate power in the late nineteenth and early twentieth centuries. The transition from competitive industrial capitalism to corporate capitalism at the turn of the century entailed a dramatic restructuring through the law of the two dimensions of corporate power. Statutory and judicial revisions of the law of corporations restructured the internal dimension to enable the transition from democratic to oligarchic rule within the large corporation. During the same period, the Supreme Court began to expound the basic rules of antitrust law that structure and regulate corporate power in the marketplace of corporate capitalism. An inquiry into these substantive areas of law sheds light on the most fundamental issues concerning the nature and organization of corporate power in the modern era, including the problem of corporate control (who rules the corporation) and the legal principles and rules governing the public regulation of corporate power.

As ideological justification of social control, law instills beliefs and doctrines that justify rules that seek to regulate or control behavior or that establish power relationships. A historical examination of the arguments and standards employed by the American judiciary in resolving legal disputes in constitutional law, for example, provides considerable evidence of the ideological function of law. Besides justifying decisions in light of precedent or rules of construction, courts often invoke moral or ideological doctrine to buttress their opinions. Yet, in many instances, ideological justification cannot be avoided and may even be considered a proper function of the judiciary, especially if the law itself embodies or is based on ideological precepts, as is frequently the case with constitutional law and with significant social legislation. When the ultimate power to determine the constitutionality of law lies within the judiciary, as it does with the Supreme Court of the United States, ideological interpretation becomes inevitable.

The ideological function of those who promulgate and interpret the law in liberal society stems in part from the central importance accorded belief in the rule of law by liberals. As guardians of the legal order, legislators and judges are charged with the task of devising and interpreting law in accordance with certain moral, legal, and political values of liberal ideology. A conception of justice based on the rule of law and on equal treatment before the law constitutes the highest standard or ideal by which the liberal legal community judges and ultimately justifies its own actions. Indeed, the rule-of-law ideal comprises the very core of the liberal belief in the autonomy (and hence political neutrality) of the legal order. Observance of this ideal, if only in principle, therefore serves an ideological purpose.[10]

Law may justify relationships of control in both a general and specific manner. If the legal order is perceived to be legitimate, in light of its own standards or ideals, then the laws comprising that order will acquire legitimacy, provided that they do not appear to violate those standards. In this fashion, the legal order furnishes ideological justification of power relationships sanctioned by law. Judges and legislators might also justify relationships of control with reference to certain tenets or beliefs of the prevailing ideology, or offer specific justifications for laws that affect relationships of control. Restructuring of relationships of control through the law might also entail ideological revision of legal doctrines. This has occurred, for example, in public law regulating corporate power, such as antitrust law, which has been interpreted and applied in light of the tenets of corporate liberalism. Furthermore, the precepts of limited government in liberal society may be invoked to impose specific ideological limitations on the use or scope of power. By defining boundaries to the exercise of power, the law serves to legitimize the power relationship itself.

The foregoing examination yields a central observation that can be stated in the form of a proposition: when law provides ideological justification of power relationships that are themselves sanctioned by law, one encounters the essential interrelationship between law, ideology, and power. In short, the coercive and ideological functions of law combine to enable and stabilize relationships of control. Law also mediates these relationships by establishing limits to the exercise of power. The effort to check or balance power in liberal society, however, can also serve an ideological purpose that may prove to have greater practical significance than the actual effect of the limitations imposed. Belief in a balance of power will endure while legislatures and courts define and redefine limits to suit the temperament of the times.

For centuries, the quest to understand the law, to explore its manifold nature, has led thinkers in numerous directions. One scholar accurately defined the scope of this endeavor when he observed, "Jurisprudence is the study of law in light of other disciplines than the law."[11] The examination of corporate power in American law and legal theory in Chapters 2 and 4 brings to the study of law the issues of power and ideology. My objective in these chapters is therefore to provide a detailed historical account of the vital role of law in structuring and justifying relationships of control engendered by the rise and consolidation of corporate power. Moreover, Chapters 2 and 4 provide, respectively, the historical context for the studies of corporate power in American political thought in Chapters 3 and 5. As conceived in this work, the critical analyses of corporate power in American law, legal theory, and political thought establish the foundation on which a political theory of the corporation will be constructed. In the next section, I shall examine the major analytical and empirical issues that such a theory must address and explain the method and theoretical objectives that inform this work in its entirety.

4. CORPORATE POWER AND POLITICAL THEORY

A political theory of the business corporation in the United States that aspires to explain the phenomenon of corporate power in all its complexity must necessarily draw on the knowledge and insights of several academic disciplines. Above all, it must be informed by a historical interpretation of the rise and consolidation of corporate power. At issue here is the impact of the corporate reconstruction of American capitalism on the development of corporate power.

The political study of the corporation gives rise to a number of basic analytical and empirical issues. What is the meaning of corporate power? Should it be conceived solely as a form of economic power, or does the political nature and behavior of the business corporation necessitate the use of a more inclusive frame of reference? Similarly, for the purposes of studying corporate power, should the business corporation be conceived as an interest group, an economic and political institution, or both, depending on what aspect of corporate power is being studied? Conceptual choices of this sort are especially important because they will define the scope of the inquiry. Such choices, however, are often influenced by ideological considerations that serve either to preclude certain options or to filter out types of empirical information that might open other avenues of investigation. To some extent, this screening process is inevitable. But one would hope that ideological bias would not be the determining factor in choosing a conceptual approach when the objective is to construct a theory that purports to explain the empirical reality. While this is easier said than done, there are fundamental issues that must be addressed, regardless of ideological predisposition, if one intends to study corporate power on its own terms.

To begin with, before one can accurately conceptualize corporate power it is essential to have an understanding of how the structure of the marketplace, including the rules that regulate it, might influence or shape the exercise of such power. Likewise, conceptualizing the scope of corporate power over society requires not only that one take into account the nature and impact of corporate decision-making affecting the marketplace, but also that one consider the capacity of corporate leaders to influence or shape governmental policy and legislation. And one cannot adequately conceptualize the internal dimension of corporate power without a knowledge of how decision-making is organized within the corporation and how influence might be brought to bear on decision-makers by stockholders or outside directors, such as financial institutions. On the basis of these inquiries, one must decide which, if any, mode of analysis (e.g., pluralist, institutionalist, class-analytic) best accounts for the empirical reality. It may be that a choice of one analytical approach over others will delimit the ability to explain fully both the internal and external dimensions of corporate power, in which case the analyst should seek an alternative that can remedy these limitations.

In constructing a political theory of the corporation, I shall be concerned primarily with addressing conceptual and empirical problems pertinent to the study of corporate power. This is not to diminish the importance of normative issues raised by this analysis, which include dangers posed by corporate power to democratic institutions and to individual liberty. To be sure, a political theory of the corporation might also entail an examination of issues that fall within the domain of traditional political philosophy, especially those related to problems of legitimacy, political community, and democracy. As I have conceived it, the present work is a necessary precursor to that sort of undertaking, which deserves a separate and thorough treatment of its own.

My effort to reconstruct the ideology of corporate liberalism through an analysis of legal theory and political thought, however, does serve a normative as well as an analytical purpose. This work offers a critical perspective of that ideology from the standpoint of the progressive democratic tradition in American political culture, a tradition that has been cognizant not only of tremendous economic benefits but also of social costs associated with the productivity and the power of the large corporation. Today, as in the past, debates concerning corporate power among social scientists are profoundly shaped by ideological considerations. While I do not expect this to change, I do believe that these debates can be broadened by questioning ideological presumptions that have obscured or masked the study of corporate power in the United States. My hope is that this work will contribute to that end.

For the purposes of indicating the direction of my argument and laying an empirical foundation for subsequent analysis, a preliminary examination of several conceptual and empirical issues raised above is in order. I shall proceed with an introductory analysis of the organization and structure of corporate power that provides the context for the discussion of theoretical problems and objectives that concludes this chapter. I caution, however, that the complexity and vastness of the subject matter make it necessary to delay more detailed exposition of much of the reasoning and evidence supporting the foregoing observations and claims until later chapters.

a. The Organization and Structure of Corporate Power

What is the nature of corporate power? In its most basic form, corporate power is the power wielded by individuals, often working in concert, who, by virtue of their dominant positions within the marketplace, make the critical decisions that largely determine the production, distribution, and consumption of goods, the development of technology, and the conditions and location of employment. Corporate power affects virtually every aspect of social existence—work, education, the arts, leisure, communication, transportation, entertainment. It can shape, if not determine, the economic condition and fate of communities, cities, regions, and even nations.

As an oligarchic social and political institution, the corporation's internal and external dimensions of control have been secured through legal doctrine that ensures the autonomy of the ruling group. The legally sanctioned "private" sphere of corporate decision-making justifies and protects the exercise of broad public powers. Corporate power also takes the form of a pervasive influence, if not often control, over governmental institutions and processes in the era of corporate capitalism. An inquiry into the nature of corporate power therefore entails an examination not only of who rules the corporation but also of the (internal and external) organization and methods of corporate control.

Corporate power cannot be understood apart from its historical development, and especially (for the United States) its formative period in the Progressive Era. Two interrelated aspects critical to the rise and consolidation of corporate power determine the essential nature of this power in its modern form—the restructuring of relationships of control through the law, and the reorganization of the market through combination and attendant methods of cooperation. These changes constituted a comprehensive reconstruction of the capitalist mode of production, including social relationships. The transformation from the competitive to the oligopolistic marketplace marked the eclipse of capitalism conceived as warfare by capitalism conceived as cooperation.

Corporate capitalism, in its prevalent oligopolistic form, constitutes a collective mode of production that requires regulation, prudent or "fair" competition between firms, and a considerable degree of cooperation, if not concerted action, albeit not necessarily collusive under the law. Corporate power in the marketplace is subject to its own constitutional rules and constraints, as they have been interpreted by the judiciary through the law of antitrust. This power, moreover, is centralized within the very largest corporations, which is reflected in the high levels of market and aggregate concentration in American industry and finance. In this sense, there exists a hierarchy of control within the corporate sector itself. The first step in examining the organization of corporate power, therefore, is to identify this dominant element within the marketplace of corporate capitalism.

A noted scholar of the American corporation, Adolph A. Berle, maintained throughout his numerous works that a few hundred giant industrial corporations dominated the corporate economy and controlled the development of economic resources and technology. This measure of corporate concentration, first offered by Berle and Gardener C. Means in 1932,[12] has since been widely accepted among students of the corporation and employed in a variety of studies. Periodic statistical reports compiled by the Bureau of the Census of the U.S. Department of Commerce, for example, reveal that aggregate concentration in manufacturing industries has remained at a high though stable level in the second half of the twentieth century. For 1987, concentration ratios (measured as the share of value added by manufacture)[13] were based on a survey of 200,000 manufacturing establishments. The largest 200, 150, 100, and 50 corporations, respectively, accounted for 43 percent, 39 percent, 33 percent, and 25 percent of the total value added for all corporations surveyed.[14] As significant as these figures are, they underestimate the true extent of aggregate concentration because they exclude the entire category of "mining" establishments, and hence all the major oil corporations. Other measurements (e.g., sales and assets) also point to the dominance of 200 or so major industrial corporations within American industry. In 1991, out of a total of $2.76 trillion in sales for all manufacturing and mining corporations in the United States, the top 500 accounted for $2.26 trillion (82 percent), the top 200 for $1.94 trillion (70 percent), and the top 100 for $1.62 trillion (59 percent). Assets of the same 500 largest industrials amounting to $2.46 trillion, comprised 91 percent of all industrial assets, while the top 200 and 100 held, respectively, 80 percent and 68 percent of the total. It is significant that the largest 500's share of total assets had increased by 14 percent since 1986.[15] Using the "Fortune 500 Largest U.S. Industrial Corporations" for 1993, we find that the 500 amassed a grand total of $2.37 trillion in sales. The overwhelming portion (89 percent), or $2.1 trillion, was accounted for by the top 200 corporations, but the concentration of sales becomes even greater as one ascends into the ranks of the giants. Sales for the top 100 were $1.78 trillion (75 percent), and for the top 50, $1.31 trillion (55 percent). The ten largest corporations, led by General Motors with $133.6 billion in sales, amassed $681 billion (29 percent) of the total sales of the Fortune 500. In that same year, the 500, which also employed 11.5 million workers in the

United States, realized $81.7 billion in profits, of which $32.5 billion (40 percent) was earned by the largest 50 corporations.[16]

Within the realm of finance, 50 banks occupy a dominant position similar to that of the 200 industrials. Of the $3.43 trillion in total financial assets for 11,926 insured commercial banks in 1991, $2.38 trillion (69 percent) were held by the largest 100 banks, and $1.95 trillion (57 percent) by the top 50. Deposits for the leading 100 banks ($1.73 trillion) accounted for 74 percent of all commercial bank deposits, and deposits for the top 50 banks ($1.43 trillion) comprised 43 percent of the total. The largest 10 banks held 29 percent of all assets and recorded 28 percent of all deposits, while the dominant leader of the group, Citicorp, set the pace with $217 billion in assets and $146 billion in deposits.[17]

Philip I. Blumberg's systematic analysis of the empirical dimensions of corporate power in the United States revealed that 200 "megacorporations" continue to hold sway within the marketplace of corporate capitalism. His conclusions concerning the relationship between market concentration and centralized control support the concept of a dominant stratum composed of the ruling oligarchies of the major industrial and financial corporations:

> The empirical review of the dimensions of corporate power has disclosed the serious concentration of economic power in the national economy. Aggregate concentration is high and increasing. Market concentration continues at a high level in about one-third of manufacturing industries and shows no signs of diminishing. Concern with economic concentration has been widened by the growing concentration of share ownership in the hands of financial institutions, which have emerged as a potential source of control over industry. A few hundred industrial megacorporations under the potential controls of an even smaller group of financial institutions today represent the central core of economic power. . . .
>
> The concentration of economic power in the megacorporations and of potential control in the leading financial institutions interconnected as a result of multiple or interlocking directorships presents serious questions for the nation. These questions are all the more important because of the far-ranging reach of corporate power.[18]

To be sure, the reach of corporate power cannot be adequately appreciated without the knowledge that the largest American corporations are among the leaders of the world economy. In 1993 the 100 largest U.S.-

based transnationals amassed a total of $703 billion in foreign sales. The foreign revenue of the top 10 industrial companies, calculated as a percentage of their total revenue, suggests the true extent of their global operations: Exxon (77 percent), General Motors (28 percent), Mobil (67 percent), IBM (59 percent), Ford Motor (30 percent), Texaco (53.5 percent), E. I. du Pont de Nemours (51.4 percent), Chevron (41 percent), Procter & Gamble (52 percent), and Philip Morris (30 percent). American financial institutions also have a tremendous stake in the world market. All but one of the largest 20 U.S. banks (ranked by assets) are transnationals. In terms of volume of foreign revenue, Citicorp ranked seventh among the 100 largest U.S.-based transnational corporations in 1993, while J. P. Morgan, Chase Manhattan, Bank of Boston, and Bankers Trust New York ranked in the top 35.[19]

In many cases these corporate empires span several continents employing hundreds of thousands of workers from dozens of countries. When individuals wield such power, their economic objectives, and the social responsibilities they entail, transcend national boundaries. The exigencies of empire necessitate a global perspective. Executives of transnational enterprise can no longer afford to be ethnocentric ruling cliques, if they ever could. Moreover, the chief executive officers of these mammoth organizations are not salaried technocrats. They are, in the main, highly paid, wealthy men, with substantial stockholdings in their own corporations. In terms of income, wealth, prestige, and power, they comprise a discrete group within American society and the world. They are the acknowledged vanguard of the corporate leaders of America, the denizens of the higher circles of power in industry, finance, and government.

From its very inception, the dominant firms of the corporate order have been linked by interlocking directorates. In recent years, studies have revealed numerous interlocks between industrial corporations and financial institutions, especially the largest commercial banks, which point to the strategic position of financial corporations within the web of interlocking relationships that connect the major industrial corporations. For example, Edward S. Herman's study of financial representation on the boards of the 200 largest nonfinancial corporations in 1975 (not including outside directors from financial institutions) revealed that a commercial bank officer sat on 65.5 percent of these boards and an investment banker was a director on 29 percent. For the largest 100 industrial corporations, these representations, respectively, were 76 percent and 42 percent. Total representation of financial institutions (commercial banks, investment banks, and insurance companies) was 162 (81 percent) for the 200 largest nonfinancials, and 98 (98 percent) for the

100 largest industrial corporations. The large commercial banks held a disproportionate number of these directorships and were also well represented on executive committees of the 200 corporations.[20]

The numerous directorships held by financial institutions may reflect the dependence of industrial corporations on banks for financial reasons (e.g., loans), in which case interlocks with banks would be desirable and necessary from a business standpoint, just as it may also in some instances reflect an increased influence of banks through stock ownership.[21] There does seem to be a definite correlation, however, between the frequency of interlocks, the size of the corporation, and market concentration.[22] This pattern suggests a centralization of the communication network within the very largest of the top 200 corporations (plus 15 or so major banks). Johannes M. Pennings's study of the largest 797 corporations taken from *Fortune*'s May 1970 listing confirms the correlation between size and interlocks. Pennings also concluded that "all measures of interlocking relate linearly to market structure: The frequency of interlocks—both horizontal and vertical—is highest in the most concentrated industries, those most nearly resembling a monopoly."[23] Moreover, out of 8,623 directors in the 797 corporations Pennings studied, only 1,572 held two or more directorships:

> The 1,572 individuals who hold two or more directorships are central to this study because they are among the agents of interorganizational co-ordination and communication. It is striking that they represent such a small proportion of all directors. It is also striking to note that the twenty individuals who are the strongest linkers, holding seven or more directorships, are .3 percent of all directors—but they reach 16 percent of the 797 organizations. . . . The prominence of banks and insurance firms in that 16 percent further accentuates the pronounced role that banking directors play in forming social linkages between organizations.[24]

Herman's study shows that, as one would expect, this select group of interlocking directors becomes even more discrete within the largest 250 corporations (200 nonfinancial and 50 financial companies). Out of the total of 2,959 directors on the boards of these 250 companies, only 596 (13.6 percent) held two or more directorships. Herman also found that the largest financial institutions interlock more frequently as a group (with the 250 corporations) than the largest nonfinancials do. Furthermore, only 15 of the 200 nonfinancials and only 1 of the 50 financials had no interlocks with the 250.[25]

Within the largest 200 industrial corporations and the major financial institutions in the United States, several hundred prestigious directors (the majority of them CEOs) comprise a centralized network of communication that facilitates joint control over markets (even in the absence of horizontal interlocks, since competitors meet on other boards) and that may in some cases be indicative of centralization effected through interest-group coalitions bound through common ownership and business dealings. The available evidence, however, does not support the theory of interest-group dominance (i.e., pervasive control by finance capital) that was current (and feasible to many observers) in the first four decades of the twentieth century, though one certainly cannot discount the significant influence, leadership, and organizational role of large financial institutions within the modern structure of corporate capitalism.[26]

In any event, it appears that interlocking directorates facilitate a community of interest among the elite of the corporate world that supplants the competitive and socially divisive ethos of an earlier stage of capitalism with an ethic of cooperation and a sense of shared values and goals. Michael Useem, in his studies of the social and political significance of interlocking directorates, has defined the discrete group of interlocking leaders that comprise the "inner circle," an elite that shares and promotes a "class-wide rationality" or corporate political consciousness that transcends individual corporations:

> The classwide principle asserts that top corporate managers are more influenced in their political thinking by their position in a set of interrelated networks transecting large corporations. Acquaintanceships circles, interlocking directorates, webs of interfirm ownership, and major business associations are among the central strands of these networks. Entry into the transcorporate networks is contingent on successfully reaching the executive suite of some large company, and it may be facilitated by old school ties and other trappings of old wealth. But both corporate credentials and upper class upbringing become subordinated to a new political logic of classwide organization. The central participants in this overarching network are prone to favor policies that coincide with the interests of the largest corporations.[27]

Interlocking directorates have been a subject of recurring interest to members of Congress since the Pujo Committee's report of 1913 exposed the organization and methods of the infamous "money trust," the handiwork of the captains of finance, most notably J. P. Morgan. More recently, in summarizing the economic, social, and political significance of the extensive interlocks that bind the largest 130 industrial and financial corporations in the United States, the U.S. Senate Governmental Affairs report, *Interlocking Directorates Among the Major U.S. Corporations*, has suggested the comprehensive scope of corporate power:

> Such interlocking directorates among the Nation's very largest corporations may provide mechanisms for stabilizing prices, controlling supply and restraining competition. They can have a profound effect on business attempts to influence Government policies. They can impact on corporate decisions as to the type and quality of products and services to be marketed in the United States and overseas. They can influence company policies with respect to employee rights, compensation and job conditions. They can bear on corporate policies with respect to environmental and social issues and possibly control the shape and direction of the Nation's economy.[28]

Further evidence of the organization of this ruling group of corporations can be found in the extensive network of organizational ties that link the elite of the corporate world. In addition to the massive system of interlocking directorates and the various industry and trade associations, there is a handful of highly influential business and political organizations, such as the Business Council and the Business Roundtable, where the representatives of the leading industrial and financial corporations may convene to discuss joint concerns and plan common strategies. Founded in 1933 (originally as an advisory group to the Department of Commerce, now a private organization), the Business Council meets with the President of the United States several times a year to present its views on a broad range of issues. Since the early 1970s, the Business Roundtable, composed of the chief executives of approximately 200 major U.S. corporations, has wielded considerable influence in both Congress and the White House. It functions both as a supracorporate lobby (organized into issue-oriented task forces) and as a forum for developing common corporate policies and goals. Prominent business executives, moreover, have played a central role in the organization, funding, and leadership of the so-called policy-planning groups, such as the Council on Foreign Relations and the Committee for Economic Development, which bring together leaders of industry, finance, government, labor, and selected members of the legal and academic professions. Corporate-funded think tanks abound, and corporate foundations finance research in all areas of academic scholarship.

The economic, social, and political linkages of the leaders of the corporate bourgeoisie are not fortuitous, nor are they conspiratorial in the pejorative (colloquial) sense in which that term is often used. There is considerable evidence that a highly organized class-conscious oligarchy exists in the dominant corporate sector of American society.[29] However, the significance of this organizational network for a theory of corporate power remains a controversial issue. Specifically, it must be demonstrated that social cohesiveness is related to the structure and exercise of corporate power in the marketplace and in government.

The reality of corporate capitalism—its organization of production, its market structure, its methods of competing, its common directorates, its multitude of organizational ties, its joint ventures and international cartels—suggests the need for a theory of corporate power that can account for the essentially cooperative and highly socialized structure within which large-scale enterprise operates. The basis of corporate power in the marketplace, domestic and global, entails a sphere of control that transcends individual corporations, that requires cooperation, planning, and noncollusive concerted action. Market power, based on control through administered prices, is shared and mutually protected, while the law works to stabilize the position of entrenched oligopolists. During periods of significant restructuring of markets stimulated by mergers, the market power of some corporations may become less stable or may be absorbed or consolidated through combination. Nevertheless, a restructuring of the market, although possibly fatal to some firms, will yield a new balance of power within the marketplace, which in turn will be regulated by antitrust rules of fair competition.

The tendency of corporate capitalism, from its inception to the present, is toward greater market concentration through merger or consolidation. This tendency constitutes a movement toward monopoly, which under antitrust law is regulated broadly to maintain oligopoly. The interpretation and application of antitrust law structures and regulates the exercise of corporate power in the marketplace. This fact highlights the need for a theory of corporate power that can account for the generality of the law. Indeed, the very construction of antitrust law recognizes the implications of individual decisions for general principles governing market behavior. It comprehends that corporate power extends beyond the activities or transgressions of individual firms.

Corporate power therefore constitutes a comprehensive form of economic and social control—namely, control over the means of production and consumption, including the development of industrial and military technology and the determination of the nature and location of employment. Moreover, when corporate power reaches into the realm of government it does not necessarily undergo a progressive atomization of the sort predicted by interest-group analyses of American politics. The political mobilization of business in recent decades, spearheaded by the Business Roundtable, has introduced a new style of business politics. Leading corporations in industry and finance have utilized their extensive trans-corporate networks to establish a highly organized and centralized lobby in Congress. On several occasions, coalitions of big-business and small-business organizations have joined forces to win on Capitol Hill. Bipartisan in approach, the Roundtable has often served as a mediator within the business community and among various other groups, just as it has demonstrated a capacity for leadership on broad policy issues. In various reports and working papers, the Roundtable has developed a domestic and international policy agenda that includes plans or recommendations concerning international competitiveness, international information flow, trade policy, regulatory reform, antitrust reform, industrial policy, health reform, and the restructuring of the nation's elementary and secondary educational systems. A new era of business leadership in national politics has dawned. In conjunction with this massive mobilization of political resources, the same corporate leaders have conducted an advertising campaign designed to shape public opinion on a variety of issues and to improve the image of the corporation.

The ways in which corporations exercise influence in government and attempt to shape public views through the media, and for what ends, require careful empirical investigation. These matters, however, must be addressed from the standpoint of theory as well. Specifically, the relationship between the power wielded by large corporations in the marketplace and in government or politics must be explained. This requires, among other things, that one examine the possible motivations underlying corporate political activity. If the goals of the dominant corporations in industry and finance appear to transcend narrow economic objectives, such political behavior must be explained on its own terms.

In one basic sense, corporate power is political by its nature because it is based on a reconstituted relationship between the public sphere and the private sphere. Regulation of economic activities through the law, government supports and subsidies for corporate business, state and federal administration of social services, and federal responsibilities over fiscal and monetary policies all constitute integral features of the corporate reconstruction of American society. The business of government is preponderantly corporate business. Moreover, it seems highly unlikely that large corporations have mobilized their political resources out of a sense of altruism or civic responsibility. Nor does it appear that they are simply protecting or advancing their individual economic interests. Indeed, corporate leaders have defined their interests to embrace national issues of the first importance. Increasingly, political factors, as well as economic factors, shape the exercise of corporate power.

The consolidation of corporate power in the twentieth century has been accomplished through the promulgation of statutory and judge-made law and a concomitant intermeshing of public and private spheres. However, the separation of state and society has been preserved by conferring on the corporation constitutional rights of property and by securing the autonomy of the corporate hierarchy through the law of corporations. Although the increasing interaction of public and private realms has not produced a form of statism, corporate power has been increasingly subjected to regulation in the public interest. Accordingly, in order to understand the developmental tendencies of corporate power over the past century, one must examine the mixture of corporate autonomy and public regulation in the internal and external dimensions of that power. Whether large corporations over the course of several decades have become more or less autonomous (and therefore more or less powerful vis-à-vis government), however, cannot be reduced to a single formula. The complex issue of the impact of government regulation of enterprise on corporate power must be addressed within specific historical contexts and in terms of the different forms, purposes, and effects of regulation. In examining this issue, an analysis of how the law structures and regulates relationships of control is essential.

It is of considerable importance to the empirical study of regulation that the regulatory reforms of the Progressive Era and the New Deal period be distinguished from many of the reforms of the late 1960s and early 1970s—specifically, the so-called "new social regulation" concerning environmental, health, safety, and various consumer issues. This new form of regulation, which affects numerous industries and is administered directly by agencies in the federal government, constitutes an important departure from the long-standing method of regulation by independent commission. The well-documented capture of independent commissions by the industries being regulated is not likely to be reproduced under these new regulatory methods. On the other hand, political influence in Congress and in the White House has dramatically affected the implementation and enforcement of these procedures. Indeed, there is no doubt that the new social regulation, combined with the ascendancy of the public-interest movement in the 1970s, greatly contributed to the resurgence of corporate political activity.[30] This development points to the need for political explanations of regulatory policies capable of distinguishing among different forms of regulation.[31] One cannot assume that corporate power will always bend regulatory policy to its own ends. Clearly, the political resurgence of business is testimony to the fact that corporate leaders have learned this lesson well.

Corporate political influence and leadership, however, is not a recent phenomenon. Organized, informed, and well-funded, corporate executives have taken the initiative in public affairs in the twentieth century. Beginning with the creation of the Interstate Commerce Commission in 1887, corporate leaders have often sought to shape the form and substance of regulatory legislation affecting their own industries. The organization and methods of the National Civic Federation, formed in 1900, ushered in the modern era of corporate political activism symbolized by the sophisticated leadership of the corporate statesman. As corporate power was consolidated and acquired increasing legitimacy, the corporate mogul's undisguised predilection for "owning" politicians gradually gave way to more subtle forms of accomplishing the same end and to more public methods of exercising control that did not depend on corruption. Throughout this century, executives on leave from the corporate sector have regularly occupied the command posts of the White House in both Democratic and Republican administrations.[32] Since the New Deal period, federally created business councils have proliferated in the thousands to advise and consult with government agencies on policy-making. Corporate access to the higher reaches of government, formal and informal, does indeed suggest that business leaders occupy an influential position in American political life, just as it points to the fact that corporate power constitutes a socially comprehensive form of influence or control.

Not since the critical periods of corporate reconstruction during the Progressive Era and the New Deal, however, has the influence of corporate power in all aspects of American politics been so pervasive. Considerable evidence suggests that the resurgence of corporate political activity constitutes one aspect of a more general corporate movement designed in large part to effect a transition to a changing global economy. An analysis of corporate power in the United States must therefore take into account the significance of the rise of transnational enterprise for the organization of corporate power in the marketplace and in politics. In short, a political theory of the corporation must be able to address the phenomenon of transnational corporate power from a historical perspective that can account for this most recent event in the development of corporate capitalism. It becomes increasingly apparent that corporate power cannot be meaningfully analyzed in exclusively national terms when the external dimension of that power is transnational. An investigation into the transnational dimension of corporate power, therefore, may also shed light on the resurgence of political activity by large corporations. Accordingly, in assessing the future of corporate power in the United States one must examine the global implications of the rise of transnational corporate power.

b. The Theoretical Task

It is one thing to describe the structure and organization of corporate power. It is quite another to construct a theory capable of explaining the empirical dimensions of such power. Pluralist, institutionalist, and conventional Marxist approaches have all failed to provide a satisfactory theoretical explanation of corporate power. Several factors have contributed to this state of affairs, the most important being ideological limitations, academic specialization and division of labor, and the paucity of new ideas. Even though the American antimonopoly tradition spans the entire history of the United States, the phenomenon of corporate power has only recently gained wide acceptance as a subject that warrants serious political analysis. Consequently, notwithstanding the growing number of studies on the corporation, the theoretical study of corporate power is still in its infancy.

The relative neglect of this subject by American political thinkers and social scientists cannot be attributed to its novelty. In this matter, as with other aspects of political analysis, the role of ideology should not be overlooked. In the United States, liberal ideology has not only inhibited political studies of the corporation but has also shaped the assumptions and scope of the vast majority of such studies. In American political thought and political science alike, most conceptions of corporate power are based on the traditional liberal distinction between the state or politics (the public realm) and the marketplace or society (the private realm). The liberal predisposition to separate the political and economic spheres of life for analytical purposes, however, cannot be understood apart from the belief that they should be separate, with the consequence that issues of power in the marketplace are not readily acknowledged, and therefore frequently ignored.

This method of analysis is exemplified by pluralist scholarship, which treats the problem of corporate power as one aspect of the study of interest-group political behavior. In pluralist studies, the influence of corporations on government is the primary focus of analysis, while the role of corporations in the economy (if it is recognized at all) has significance only insofar as it relates to the specific exercise of corporate power in politics. By design, issues concerning the organization and structure of corporate power in the marketplace lie outside the compass of the pluralist conceptual framework. Such studies often produce valuable information about the activities of corporations in American political life, but their findings address only one aspect of the external dimension of corporate power. Thus, the pluralist approach does not provide a theoretical explanation of the possible interrelationship between corporate economic and political power.

Institutionalist (or elite) studies fare somewhat better. Such analyses examine both economic and political aspects of corporate power, yet they do not yield a satisfactory theoretical explanation of the comprehensive character of corporate power for which they provide extensive documentation. By focusing narrowly on the institutional basis of corporate power, this approach cannot adequately explain the organization and scope of the external dimension of that power in the marketplace, society, and government. Moreover, by distinguishing between generic types of power wielded by governmental bodies and by corporations, institutional analyses tend to disguise the functional interrelationship— the integration of these two spheres of power—necessary to the very existence of corporate capitalism as we know it. The erection of a rigid division between the political and economic spheres distorts reality for the sake of alleged analytical precision.

An alternative, therefore, would seem to be a conceptual approach that unifies rather than divides the political and economic spheres. This type of approach is generally associated with class analysis of the Marxist variety. Indeed, Marxist class-analytic theory stands alone among the competing modes of analysis in social science as an approach that can in principle comprehend the empirical dimensions of corporate power. However true that may be, in attempting to accommodate orthodox Marxist theory to the world of corporate capitalism, Marxist theoreticians have had to devise new doctrines. In this effort, the "role of the state" has become the central theoretical issue, an attempt to reconcile the traditional Marxist conception of class rule with the avowed complexity of modern capitalism and the apparent autonomy of centralized governmental structures and bureaucracies. This preoccupation of Marxist theory, however, disguises a more fundamental problem, which is that it lacks an adequate conception of power itself.[33] To the extent that conventional Marxist theory addresses the subject of corporate power, it tends either to rely on a class analysis derived from the classical Marxist model of competitive industrial capitalism, or to veer toward a type of institutional analysis. In either case, the theoretical understanding of corporate power is not advanced.

For differing reasons and in varying degrees, pluralist, institutionalist, and Marxist approaches all fail in theory to explain the external dimension of corporate power. But this constitutes only part of the problem. A

political theory of the corporation must also address the internal dimension of corporate power and the issue of corporate control. The problem
of corporate control concerns the implications of the historic separation
of ownership and control within the large corporation for the actual
control of decision-making within the enterprise. The enduring debate
over who rules the corporation—managers, directors, owners, or some
combination thereof—has important theoretical implications for explaining the nature of corporate power. For example, the view that large
corporations are controlled by nonowner managers whose decisions are
not determined solely or even primarily by the profit motive has led
many managerial theorists to conclude that the corporation is not just an
economic institution but an oligarchic political institution as well. Accordingly, institutional objectives and imperatives shape the exercise of
corporate power. Thus, the behavior and motivations of managers may
be likened to that of technocrats rather than owner-capitalists.

In contrast, the orthodox Marxist view holds that, despite the apparent separation of ownership and control within the large corporation,
the reins of control are still held by a relatively small group of capitalists
(owners and/or directors). According to this view, managers ultimately
do the bidding of the ruling class, whether it be through owners exercising control within the enterprise or through subordination of the enterprise (via directors) to financial institutions that are controlled by the
dominant sector of the capitalist class. There are several variations on
this thesis that often involve complex empirical and conceptual analyses.

The contending claims of managerial and Marxist theories of corporate
power have created a theoretical impasse. Managerial theory correctly
identifies the political character of the modern corporation by recognizing
that corporate decision-making often entails important social and political
consequences. It acknowledges that nonpecuniary considerations frequently enter into or shape corporate decision-making. Managerial
theory, however, typically employs an institutional perspective that cannot adequately explain the external dimension of corporate power while it
rejects the relevance of class as an analytical construct. Marxist class-
analytic theory, on the other hand, offers an approach that can conceptualize the socially comprehensive nature of corporate power in the era of
corporate capitalism, but it proceeds on the basis of a nineteenth-century
conception of class domination. It argues, often in an attenuated fashion,
that the traditional capitalist class (or ruling class) governs through its
ownership of the means of production. There are Marxists who reject this
view, but they are confronted with the same alternatives. Thus, it is not
surprising that many Marxist accounts of class domination are in reality
institutional analyses. There is a parallel here with Marxist theories that

rely on structuralist explanations to salvage the idea of class domination. The belief that a traditional ruling class must rule in *some* fashion, or that capitalism necessarily reproduces an essential form of class domination, has produced arguments that have more to do with the logical require- ments of the theories being adumbrated than with the nature of class domination in the twentieth century.

In important ways, Marxist and managerial theories of corporate power each contain part of the solution to the theoretical problem, just as both are limited by their analytical and ideological premises. What is needed is a partial synthesis that combines the strengths of both theo- ries, in a revised and updated form, and that also eliminates the explana- tory weaknesses of these theories. But how does one accomplish such a union? I have argued that managerial theory, unlike conventional Marx- ist theory, provides a conception of corporate control that can account for the political nature of the corporation, whereas class analysis in Marxist theory, unlike institutional analysis in managerial theory, holds forth the promise of an analytical approach capable of comprehending the exter- nal dimension of corporate power. By wedding a conception of corporate control derived from managerial theory with a revised class analysis based on Marxist theory, a potent theoretical alternative emerges.

But this merely describes the end of the journey, not the road taken. The path of reasoning that leads to this solution begins with a historical analysis of judge-made and statutory law that enabled and regulated the rise and consolidation of corporate power in the late nineteenth and early twentieth centuries. An examination of legal changes associated with the transition from competitive industrial (or proprietary) capital- ism to corporate capitalism yields knowledge of the internal and external dimensions of corporate power crucial to the formulation of an alterna- tive theory. Specifically, I shall argue that in the era of corporate capital- ism the internal and external powers of the large corporation are not based exclusively on legal rights of property ownership, as they were during the previous era, but on relationships of control that have been refashioned through law to accommodate the changed character of cor- porate property, the oligopolistic structure of the marketplace, and the internal growth of the firm.

For nearly 200 years the law of corporations in the United States has defined and regulated relationships of control within the business corpo- ration. Throughout most of the nineteenth century, state incorporation laws imposed numerous constraints on corporate owners or managers, while courts generally deferred to these regulations in holding corporate officers to strict standards of accountability. In the 1890s, however, New Jersey and Delaware drastically revised their incorporation statutes to attract corporate business and thereby sparked an enduring competition among numerous states. This development, which aided the merger movement of 1898–1904 and therewith the transition from competitive to corporate capitalism, produced revolutionary changes in the law of corporations. During the first four decades of the twentieth century, legislatures and courts eliminated or rendered insignificant most traditional rights of shareholders, delegated powers of shareholders to corporate managers to achieve centralized control, and further expanded the prerogatives of management by allowing it to exercise novel "political" (nonpecuniary) powers. For the most part, state and federal courts now permit corporate officers considerable discretion in exercising their legal powers over internal (or "private") matters, thus sanctioning a broad ambit of corporate self-regulation. In presiding over and maintaining the reconstitution of power relationships within the business corporation, judges have based their holdings on reasoning that embodies what I shall term "the principle of political autonomy."

The principle of political autonomy justifies the wide discretion afforded corporate decision-makers within the legal framework that regulates the powers and duties of corporate officers and the rights of shareholders. Political autonomy supersedes the traditional principle of "managerial efficiency," which presumes that management's primary obligation to the shareholder is to ensure the profitability of the enterprise. The idea of political autonomy focuses our attention on the fact that, in addition to the profit-making function, the modern corporate hierarchy operates on the basis of political and social considerations that include, but may be more comprehensive than, short-term pecuniary goals. With increasing frequency in the twentieth century, statutory and judge-made law have sanctioned a variety of "political" decisions made by corporate managers—that is, decisions that cannot be justified in terms of any tangible financial benefit to shareholders. The concept of political autonomy conveys the nature of this legal transformation and thus elucidates a salient feature of corporate power in the era of corporate capitalism—that *power based on property relations has been superseded by power based on more inclusive relationships of control.* The implications of this development for a political theory of the corporation are far-reaching and necessitate a revision of the Marxist axiom that class relationships in capitalist society are based exclusively on the rights and prerogatives of property ownership.

By permitting the corporate hierarchy to exercise its (private) internal powers over public matters, the law of corporations both enables and accommodates the socially comprehensive character of corporate power. However, to understand fully how relationships of control have been reconstituted in the era of corporate capitalism, one must also analyze law that structures and regulates the external dimension. I shall argue that government regulation of the oligopolistic marketplace and of corporate political activity have not only preserved corporate autonomy (by allowing considerable self-regulation) but also imposed constraints on corporate power in the public interest. This method of corporate-liberal regulation does not (and is not intended to) affect the classwide organization of corporate power in the marketplace and in politics. Instead, it promulgates rules and procedures that are consistent both with an ethic of fair competition within the community of large corporations and with changing public standards of corporate social responsibility. To gauge the effect of complex regulatory procedures on the exercise of corporate power, one must analyze the mixture of corporate autonomy and public regulation in relevant areas of law in light of changing economic, social, and political circumstances.

A political theory of the corporation constructed along these lines endeavors to reconcile the heretofore contradictory observations that the modern business corporation is a political institution and that the socially comprehensive character of corporate power constitutes a form of class domination. If this seems to be an unlikely combination, it is perhaps because the theoretical alternatives have been defined too narrowly, in ways that exclude empirical evidence that cannot be explained or that reject explanations that might require a revision of conceptual frameworks. If one reasons from the premise that law structures and regulates relationships of control, much of the conceptual confusion attending the study of corporate power can be remedied with a basic understanding of the legal framework within which the power is exercised. By exposing the inability of both traditional Marxist and managerial theories to explain fully the dimensions of corporate power, a historical analysis of the legal foundations of corporate power offers a way out of the theoretical impasse.

I argue that corporate power constitutes the dominant form of power in the United States. This is not to deny the existence of independent realms of governmental power that may constrain as well as enhance corporate autonomy. Nor am I contending that corporate power necessarily entails the domination of democratic institutions. This is an empirical question, not a logical consequence of the structure of power in the marketplace. But I do maintain that corporate power in the marketplace and in government are aspects of the same organization of power, which is hierarchical in structure although by no means monolithic. The capacity for concerted action among leading corporations in industry and finance does exist and has been demonstrated on numerous occasions throughout the twentieth century. The exercise of corporate power in the marketplace, as it is currently structured and regulated through the law, however, does not require collusive behavior in the premanagerial sense of the term. Corporate power in government is more decisive when it presents a unified front, but this is not the only gauge of its effectiveness. When leaders of large corporations serve to mediate conflicting interests in Congress or to advise Presidents, they are acting from a position of strength to influence policy. Corporate political influence does not result exclusively from adversarial politics. Certainly, determining who wins and loses is significant, particularly on issues that large corporations have defined as crucial. However, qualitative as well as quantitative analyses of corporate influence in government are needed to assess accurately the impact of corporate power in American politics.

The pervasiveness of ideology must also be considered when assessing the dominant position of corporate power. Throughout this work, I endeavor to reconstruct the interrelationship between legal change, the growth of corporate power, and the ideological justification of that power within specific historical settings. I demonstrate through an analysis of case law, legal theory, and political thought how corporate liberalism developed in the early decades of the twentieth century as an alternative to the competing doctrines of laissez-faire liberalism and statist socialism. Highly critical of the dangers posed by corporate power for democratic politics, while recognizing the productive potential of the large corporation, the political activists who articulated the tenets of corporate liberalism formulated comprehensive schemes of reform designed to ensure the viability of liberal-democratic institutions and to fortify corporate autonomy against state command. Thereafter, corporate liberalism evolved from its reform-minded origins as political thinkers embraced a more sophisticated defense of the legitimacy of corporate power. In the writings of managerial theorists, the ideological precept of corporate autonomy assumed the status of an inviolable "natural" law of industrial society, whereas the legal doctrine of corporate individualism gave credence to the ideological construct of the corporate citizen. This tendency toward reification in political and legal discourse, which coincided with the consolidation of corporate power, has served to legitimize, but also to disguise, the power wielded by large corporations. Outside of academic and professional domains, the same ideological view is communicated daily to a wider audience through the artful use of mass media in various forms and forums, including political advertising, commercial advertising, and the incessant reproduction of popular culture.

The argument advanced herein derives from an attempt to explain power relationships as they exist in the era of corporate capitalism. It assumes that the phenomenon of corporate power must be studied on its own terms, not as an adjunct of structuralist or instrumentalist theories of the state and capital. An understanding of the role of law in structuring relationships of control provides insight into how the capacity to exercise power can be regulated as well as transformed by individuals in legislative bodies and courts. This perspective suggests that power is rarely exercised in an absolute fashion—that is, unmediated by constraints. Corporate power offers no exception to this rule; it is a complex phenomenon that resists equally the analytical straitjackets of monolithic and atomistic conceptions of power. Corporate power is also dynamic. It continues to grow and change within the global marketplace of corporate capitalism, thereby affecting dimensions of power in nation-states. Increasingly, transnational corporate power, not state power, constitutes the formative agent of change in world development.[34]

In ensuing chapters, I pursue the task of constructing the theoretical alternative outlined above. This requires considerable groundwork, and not only a systematic exposition of the argument sketched thus far, but also an in-depth analysis and critique of various approaches or theories. Chapters 2 and 4 examine the concept of corporate power in American law and legal theory and provide the historical background, respectively, for the analyses of corporate power in American political thought in Chapters 3 and 5. Chapter 6 outlines a theoretical alternative, based in part on a revised class analysis formulated by Richard L. Sklar,[35] that can both explain the empirical dimensions of corporate power and account for the restructuring of relationships of control through the law to effect the consolidation of such power. This approach is also employed in Chapter 7 to analyze ideological aspects of transnational corporate power. Toward that end, the first task of this work is to reconstruct the rise of corporate power by examining the role of law in structuring its internal and external dimensions.

Chapter 2

THE RISE OF THE LARGE CORPORATION: LAW AND LEGAL THEORY

> *I am of the opinion, on the whole, that the [American] manufacturing aristocracy which is growing up under our eyes, is one of the harshest which ever existed in the world; but at the same time it is one of the most confined and least dangerous. Nevertheless the friends of democracy should keep their eyes anxiously fixed in this direction; for if ever a permanent inequality of conditions and aristocracy again penetrate into the world, it may be predicted that this is the channel by which they will enter.*
>
> —*Alexis de Tocqueville, 1840*

1. INTRODUCTION

In Anglo-American jurisprudence, the law comprises more than a set of rules to be obeyed or rights to be enforced. It is also an evolving body of principles, ideals, and practical knowledge that shape the course of human events. When interpreting the law, jurists often remold ideas of the past to meet the exigencies of the present. In this way, the law comes to embody the dominant beliefs of an era while it also influences the content of those beliefs. Although legal reasoning and processes, on the whole, are inherently conservative, law may be employed to facilitate economic and social change, including the restructuring of relationships of control. The development of the public and private law of corporations in the nineteenth and twentieth centuries in the United States provides considerable evidence to support the conclusion that those in the legal profession—judges, legislators, and lawyers—have played a vital and innovative role in shaping the law both to enable and to regulate the growth of corporate power.[1]

This chapter traces the rise of corporate power through major stages in the development of American law and the concomitant growth of corporate enterprise from 1781 to 1916. My central objective is to demonstrate how legislatures and courts established conditions that are essential to the exercise of corporate power, and then regulated the growth of that power by restructuring its legal conditions and limitations. In addition, I show how ideological aspects of law that justified the rise of the large corporation were subsequently revised and superseded by legal doctrine that validated the corporate reconstruction of the marketplace. As indicated in the previous chapter, corporate power will be conceived as consisting of an external dimension and an internal dimension. The external dimension concerns the exercise of corporate power in society at large; the internal dimension refers to the relationships of control within the corporation itself. This same division of powers, moreover, develops within the law as corporate enterprise matures. As such, it provides critical insight into how law may be devised or interpreted to establish and restructure relationships of control.

A brief analysis of the colonial experience with the business corporation provides a context for assessing the novel interpretation and application of corporation law during the formative era (1781–1864), out of which developed the legal framework that enabled the rise of corporate power at the close of the century. I argue that when legislators and judges in early-nineteenth-century America proceeded to expound the principles of corporation law, they also established the legal foundation for the exercise of corporate power. Armed with little precedent, but gifted with considerable ingenuity, American jurists strongly aided the business corporation to adapt to the requirements of a market economy and breathed life into its soul by vesting it with rights and legal capacities that would ensure its survival within the American federal system.

Legal reasoning also provided ideological support for the corporation in the doctrine of corporate individualism. Originally a defense of the corporation's constitutional rights of property, as well as an imposition of responsibility and liability, corporate individualism gradually merged with the entrepreneurial ethos of competitive industrial capitalism to justify an expanding corporate autonomy. The legal doctrine of corporate individualism first acquired ideological significance outside the law in political argument that personified the corporation as an individual within the competitive marketplace. Beginning in the late 1830s, this ideological construct—the business corporation's entrepreneurial cloak—promoted the liberalization of state incorporation laws by undermining the widely held view of the corporation as an instrument of special privilege and monopoly. Indeed, by 1870, most states had passed statutes making incorporation a general right rather than a privilege granted by special legislative act. Moreover, corporate individualism acquired an enhanced legal status when the corporation became a "person" within the meaning of the Fourteenth Amendment in 1886, an event that would aid the ascendancy of corporate power in industry and finance at the close of the nineteenth century.

In the 1870s, corporate leaders resorted to various means of regulating prices or combining capital in an effort to supplant competitive methods of business with cooperative methods, and thereby remedy the instabilities of the marketplace. In the late 1880s, widespread public opposition to the "trusts" (large corporate combinations created through the trustee device) inspired Congress to pass the Sherman Antitrust Act in 1890 to regulate monopolistic practices and unreasonable restraints of trade. In the absence of significant antitrust enforcement in the mid-to-late 1890s, however, the combination movement gained momentum. Between 1898 and 1904, the first great merger wave of corporate capitalism—its act of self-creation—transformed the very structure of the American economy.

This development also coincided with far-reaching changes in the law of corporations. Following New Jersey's lead in 1896, wholesale revisions of state incorporation laws aided an expanding corporate autonomy in both the internal and external dimensions of power as numerous states relinquished traditional regulatory controls over their corporate creations. During the same period, legal theory began to incorporate the ideological conception of the corporate individual. In the era of corporate capitalism, the personified corporate individual gradually supplanted the "artificial" legal fiction to produce an autonomous corporate entity.

While acknowledging the unprecedented productive potential of corporate capitalism, most Progressive Era reformers believed that the power of the large corporation posed a threat to liberal-democratic institutions and to the American promise of unlimited opportunity. As laissez-faire individualism began to lose its moral authority in a society transformed by giant corporations, the "trust question"—the political and judicial debate over the regulation of corporate power—occupied center stage in national politics. The resolution of this debate in antitrust law, in 1911, signaled the triumph of corporate liberalism on the Bench. In adopting the rule of reason, the U.S. Supreme Court accommodated the law to the corporate reorganization of markets in the new era. Judicial interpretation of the law of antitrust, founded on a conception of fair competition (in administered markets) that embodied the contending values of equal opportunity to compete and freedom to contract, thereafter provided the judiciary with a means for both limiting and enabling the growth of corporate power.

The modern large corporation, hierarchical in structure and with billion-dollar assets and thousands of employees, bears little resemblance to its early-nineteenth-century predecessor. Its incredible growth and the scope of its power, however, have been secured and facilitated by legal doctrine expounded in an earlier era. In one respect, the business corporation carries on very much as it began—a collective form of enterprise endowed by law with the special privileges of incorporation and vested with legal rights and capacities to act as an individual. Yet it is the ingenious adaptation of this legal entity to the changing requirements of enterprise and to the demands of society that accounts for its viability. Therefore, it is only through a historical examination of this aspect of American jurisprudence that one can fully appreciate the essential interrelationship between legal change, the growth of corporate power, and the ideological justification of that power in American law and legal theory.

2. ENGLISH LAW AND THE COLONIAL HERITAGE

In expounding the law of the business corporation, American lawyers, legislators, and judges produced an original body of theory and doctrine tailored to American economic and political conditions. Colonial experience with corporations and English corporation law aided in this undertaking, though only in the most rudimentary fashion. Throughout the entire colonial period, governments granted merely a handful of corporate charters for business-related activities, the majority of these going to companies that performed a public service, such as the proprietorship of wharfs or the supply of water.[2] To be sure, colonists formed a variety of nonbusiness corporations—municipal, educational, philanthropic, and ecclesiastical—most of which were chartered by colonial governments. For numerous reasons, however, economic and political conditions stifled the growth of corporate enterprise during this period.[3]

The scope of the task confronting American legislatures and courts becomes clear in light of the fact that neither the colonies nor Britain had produced any quantity of law pertaining specifically to the business corporation that could serve as relevant precedent for the legal problems of corporate enterprise following the Revolution. Clearly, both the paucity of colonial business corporations and their public-service orientation explain why colonial law could be of only limited assistance to legislators and judges in the late eighteenth and early nineteenth centuries, when corporations flourished in banking, insurance, transportation, and a variety of industrial concerns. On the other hand, British experience with corporate enterprise, including joint-stock companies, had already spanned three centuries by 1800. Despite this wealth of practical experience, English law had little to say about the business corporation except that it was a type of civil corporation that fell under the broader classification of "lay," as opposed to "clerical."[4]

In England and America, incorporation was a privilege that could be granted only by an act of the sovereign, who also stipulated the terms of incorporation in the charter. English law declared certain legal capacities to be attributes of incorporation. A corporate association could create its own government insofar as its bylaws were not in conflict with the law of the land. In the eyes of the law, a corporation became a fictitious person with legal and property rights distinct from its membership. Moreover, as a legal entity, the corporation could exist in perpetuity.[5] In addition to these well-established characteristics, individual limited liability for corporate debts, though not an essential aspect of incorporation until the nineteenth century, may also be included in this list of legal attributes.[6]

The American legal community had inherited from English law only a juristic concept of the corporation that applied more or less equally to all types of incorporated bodies. Curiously, the nation that had colonized the New World and established a trading empire through the medium of the corporation had yet to develop a legal theory of corporate enterprise. A brief examination of the political and legal significance of the business corporation in Britain before 1781 helps explain this state of affairs and provides a historical perspective necessary for analyzing the early development of American corporate law.

The rule that corporations can be created only by an act of the sovereign took root in English law during the reign of the Tudors in the sixteenth century.[7] This development, which coincided with the appearance of the earliest business corporations, evidenced the increasing centralization of power in the national government and the corresponding decay of the decentralized manorial system of feudal England, a transition that had been under way for two centuries. Beginning in the Tudor period and continuing under the reign of the Stuart kings, English corporations (often organized as joint-stock companies) would serve as a means for establishing industrial and trading monopolies, expanding the frontiers of trade, and colonizing continents. Throughout the era of nation-building and the rise of British imperialism in the sixteenth and seventeenth centuries, English rulers granted royal charters under conditions that normally vested their control in agents of the Crown and ensured that the monarchy would receive a substantial portion of the profits.[8]

By the late seventeenth century, with British home rule stable and centralized, and the empire firmly established, the private character of the English business company began to eclipse its public function.[9] On the eve of the industrial revolution, competition and free trade supplanted the mercantilist policies of government regulation and monopoly. The privately controlled joint-stock company (the predecessor of the modern business corporation) flourished in the first two decades of the eighteenth century. Yet no sooner did this form of enterprise come into prominence than it incurred the wrath of the public. Whereas the industrial and trading monopolies of the previous two centuries often abused their monopoly powers, the private joint-stock company (both incorporated and unincorporated) established its own propensity for corruption in the form of extravagant speculation, fraud, and stock-jobbing. Companies rose and fell in dramatic fashion while unscrupulous entrepreneurs reaped huge profits at the expense of gullible investors.

With the passage of the Bubble Act of 1720, Parliament sought to put an end to these swindles by outlawing unincorporated joint-stock companies with transferable shares.[10] Although chartered companies were not legally affected by the act—indeed, they urged its passage—they too suffered from the public distrust that rampant stock speculation had engendered. It would be nearly 100 years before the joint-stock company would regain its favored status as a means of accumulating capital. With this legacy of fraud and monopolistic privilege embedded in a nation's consciousness, the English business corporation did not figure greatly in the formative decades of the industrial revolution. Out of necessity, inventive lawyers and receptive courts would discover other ways to combine capital. And while most industrial capitalists proclaimed the virtues of individual enterprise and railed against the defenders of the business corporation, British industry became increasingly concentrated, with or without the aid of the joint-stock company.[11]

Two factors loom as most significant for explaining the virtual absence of English law pertaining to the business corporation at the time of American independence. First, the industrial and trading monopolies of the fifteenth and sixteenth centuries were, for the most part, quasi-public corporations—in effect, private enterprises that served the government's objectives of regulating industry and trade. As a consequence, the opportunity to distinguish the business function of such corporations from their public function did not often arise. Second, as we have seen, the decline of monopolies and the proliferation of joint-stock companies soon fomented the passage of the Bubble Act and its aftermath—an enduring anti-corporate sentiment. While the Bubble Act did not outlaw corporations, it undoubtedly hampered their growth and turned attention to other forms of enterprise. Finally, even when eighteenth-century British lawyers and judges had the opportunity to contribute to a legal theory of the business corporation, they did not do so.[12]

English law therefore provided only a definition—the essential attributes of incorporation—from which the American law of business corporations would be constructed. The novel application of these venerable concepts to corporate enterprise and the invention of new doctrine suited to domestic needs and experience would be among the most challenging and significant tasks facing American lawyers, legislators, and judges in the nineteenth century.

3. THE FORMATIVE ERA

In antebellum America, an evolving body of law pertaining to the business corporation—state and federal, judge-made and statutory—both accommodated and aided social forces impelling the transition from an agrarian to an industrial economy. Responding to the diverse needs of capitalists, economic exigencies, and changing public perceptions of corporate enterprise, legislatures and courts devised the framework within which the internal and external dimensions of corporate power would develop. Initially through special charters and later through general incorporation laws, state governments and judiciaries regulated the internal affairs of corporate business by defining the size and structure of the enterprise, the powers of stockholders and management, and the conditions under which incorporation would be granted. During this same period, the metamorphosis of the corporation through the directives of the law, from an instrumentality of government to a constitutionally protected individual, vested the corporate entity with rights and legal capacities that would form the foundation of its external dimension of power.

Following American independence, corporate enterprise gradually supplanted other forms of business association as economic conditions and opportunity favored a device peculiarly suited to the accumulation of large sums of capital. Whereas governments granted only 33 corporate business charters from 1781 to 1790, the total number of new charters rose steadily to 328 by the year 1800.[13] During this period, and continuing for three decades into the nineteenth century, public-service companies, especially in the field of transportation, received the majority of corporate charters.[14] By 1830, however, the number of manufacturing and mining companies had increased significantly, signaling a trend that would accelerate dramatically with the boom in railway construction in the 1850s.[15] Indeed, the total number of business corporations in the United States increased nearly twofold from 1850 to 1860, a decade that also witnessed the marriage between railroad tycoons and finance capitalists, the precursors of the emergent corporate order.[16]

Until the universal adoption of incorporation by general statute in the second half of the nineteenth century, most states granted corporate charters for business only by a special legislative act.[17] In the early decades of the new republic, a charter so conferred, depending on the nature of the enterprise, might include special privileges such as the power to fix tolls, exemption from taxation, or the right to exercise the state's power of eminent domain. Virtually all charters, whether for public service or general business, contained provisions that, typically, defined the scope of the company's business and possibly its duration, limited its capitalization, determined the voting rights of stockholders, and provided a method for payment of dividends.[18]

Detailed special-action charters served the interests of the government entities that sought to promote and direct economic development and, arguably, the interests of stockholders who could better assess their risks before investing. The power to grant such charters rested on the long-standing precept of English law that the corporation, which may be created only by an act of the sovereign, exists at the behest of its creator. No doubt the principle seemed reasonable, if not incontestable, when applied to a corporation that had been formed for the purpose of performing a public function. But as corporate enterprise began to acquire a distinctively private orientation, the extent of the sovereign's power and, conversely, the nature of the corporation's legal rights became issues of vital concern to American entrepreneurs. In the course of defining the lawful boundaries between state regulation and the rights of business corporations—a task for which English law could offer no precedent—courts and legislatures in the first half of the nineteenth century constructed the legal foundation of corporate power.

a. The Legal Entity and Its Rights: The External Dimension of Corporate Power

While early state cases concerning the scope of legislative power over the property rights of corporations indicated a judicial predisposition to give such rights special protection,[19] for nearly two decades American law-makers and judges did not have at their disposal relevant constitutional precedent. Not until Justice Joseph Story delivered his opinion in *Terrett v. Taylor,* [20] in 1815, did the Supreme Court unveil its intent to establish a rationale by which the constitutional right of property might be ex-tended to the business corporation. In striking down a series of Virginia statutes authorizing the confiscation of lands owned by a corporation, the Protestant Episcopal Church of Alexandria, Story distinguished be-tween the legislature's power over public as opposed to private corpora-tions. The Court ruled that state legislatures may not encroach on or confiscate property by amending or repealing the charters of private corporations, whereas legislatures may exercise some control over the fortunes of corporations created solely for public purposes.[21] Story de-clared that the Court's ruling that private corporations enjoy the rights of property against their sovereign creators rests upon ". . . the principles of natural justice, upon the fundamental laws of every free government, upon the spirit and the letter of the constitution of the United States, and upon the decisions of most respectable judicial tribunals."[22] Justice Story, however, did not state the provision of the Constitution the Court had in mind.[23] Four years passed before Chief Justice John Marshall in *Dartmouth College v. Woodward,*[24] translated the higher law principles of *Terrett* into constitutional doctrine.

The *Dartmouth* case does not appear, on its face, to provide the appropriate context for deciding the constitutional status of the business corporation. In 1769, King George III granted to Dartmouth College a corporate charter that authorized a twelve-member board of trustees to govern the college and to appoint their own successors. Following an internal struggle for control of the board, the New Hampshire legisla-ture, in 1816, amended the charter to increase the number of trustees to twenty-one, to vest the power of appointment in the state's governor and council, and to establish a board of overseers to review the acts of the trustees. Dartmouth's original board of trustees brought suit claim-ing that the amendments of 1816 violated the contract clause of the U.S. Constitution. Chief Justice Richardson of the New Hampshire Court of Appeals ruled against the trustees of the college, stating that Dartmouth was a public, not private, corporation and that the act in question there-fore fell within the scope of the legislature's power. Richardson did not cite *Terrett v. Taylor,* but he clearly adopted the logic of that case, thus giving the U.S. Supreme Court, on appeal, the opportunity to expound on its earlier ruling.[25]

Writing in the assertive style that characterized his most creative inter-pretations of the Constitution, Chief Justice Marshall declared in *Dart-*

mouth: "It can require no argument to prove that the circumstances of this case constitute a contract." The property transactions attendant to the granting of a charter to Dartmouth College, he maintained, entailed "every ingredient of a complete and legitimate contract."[26] However, what the Court must determine, in the first instance, was whether the terms of incorporation created a public corporation—in effect, a government instrumentality—or a private eleemosynary corporation "endowed with a capacity to take property, for objects unconnected with government, whose funds are bestowed by individuals, on the faith of the charter."[27] Invoking Justice Story's distinction in *Terrett*, Marshall reaffirmed the doctrine that only a private corporation—in this case, an eleemosynary or charitable institution—may be afforded the constitutional protections of property.

In examining the terms of the charter, Marshall seized the opportunity to expound on the legal theory of the corporation and to ground constitutional doctrine in general principles of corporation law. He observed that in addition to the attributes expressly granted in its charter, a corporation possessed characteristics "incidental to its very existence." Of these, the most important included "immortality, and . . . individuality; properties by which a perpetual succession of many persons are considered as the same, and may act as a single individual."[28] Though it be a "mere creature of law," the corporation, the legal entity, "is no more a State instrument, than a natural person exercising the same powers would be."[29] And while its original donors and trustees may change, the corporate entity "is the assignee of their rights, stands in their place, and distributes their bounty, as they would themselves have distributed it had they been immortal."[30]

Having established that a corporate charter is a contract under the Constitution and that the corporate entity, endowed with perpetuity, enjoys the same legal standing as a "natural person," Marshall proceeded to find in favor of the plaintiffs: "it appears that Dartmouth College is an eleemosynary institution, incorporated for the purpose of perpetuating the application of that bounty of the donors to the specified objects of the bounty. . . ."[31] By altering the intent of the original donors, he argued, the acts of the New Hampshire legislature violated the constitutional prohibition against laws "impairing the obligation of contracts."[32]

While ascribing to the corporation the attributes of immortality and individuality, Marshall also described the corporation as "an artificial being, invisible, intangible, and existing only in contemplation of law."[33] The question therefore arose how an artificial being, a mere creature of law, could possess constitutional rights against its sovereign creator. Marshall attempted to sidestep theoretical confusion by taking notice of the interests of the individuals who form a corporation: "It is chiefly for the purpose of clothing bodies of men, in succession, with qualities and capacities, that corporations were invented, and are in use."[34] To argue that a legal fiction actually represented real persons, however, did not address the fact that by vesting the corporation with constitutional rights of property, endowing it with immortality, and charging it with the task of fulfilling the expectations of its donors, the Court necessarily attributed an existence or reality to the corporate entity apart from its membership. But this is precisely what Marshall intended, the broader objective of which was to secure for the corporation a status, as an individual, under the contract clause of the Constitution. A plausible explanation of the apparent conceptual confusion in his argument, therefore, may be found in his effort to justify the constitutional protection afforded the corporate entity by analogizing its rights and legal capacities with those of the mere mortals who comprise the going concern.[35]

Although *Dartmouth* concerned an eleemosynary corporation, the Court left no doubt that the holding applied with equal force to all private corporations. If Marshall's ingenious opinion delighted the business community, Justice Story's thoughtful concurrence gave them reason to pause in their celebration. While agreeing on the major points of Marshall's argument, Story added that a state may reserve the right to amend or repeal a charter by so stating in the charter itself.[36] The immediate practical impact of *Dartmouth*, therefore, might be easily overstated in retrospect, considering the fundamental importance of this decision in American corporate and constitutional law.[37] For several decades following the decision, states continued to regulate corporate enterprise by defining the terms of incorporation and by reserving the right to amend or repeal the charter according to Justice Story's suggestion.[38] More important, despite the security *Dartmouth* afforded the business corporation, it was not necessarily a boon to the entrepreneur during the nascent years of American industrialization. Indeed, by extending constitutional protection to the corporate charter, *Dartmouth* could be invoked as a bulwark against the forces of competition by corporations possessing special privileges.[39]

In *Dartmouth*, the Supreme Court began the task of constructing the legal foundation of corporate power by vesting the constitutional rights of property in the corporation. As the legal entity acquired rights, duties, and obligations as a person under state and federal law, the corporation realized an autonomy that was essential to the growth of corporate power. Marshall's opinion in *Dartmouth* also articulated the core of American law's contribution to the ideological justification of corporate power—the doctrine of corporate individualism. Initially a mere legal fiction, the corporate individual gradually acquired an ideological significance in legal and political debate. In fact, in the second half of the nineteenth century the identification of the corporation with the enterprising individual, the corporate personification of the American entrepreneur, would constitute the very basis of the ideology of a rising corporate bourgeoisie.

Even before the *Dartmouth* ruling, decisions by courts in the law of contract and torts had initiated the process of fleshing out the artificial being of English corporate law by putting the corporation on an agency basis similar to that of natural persons. To rigidly observe legal precedent that might undermine business efficiency by limiting the contractual powers of corporations or that might negate their liability for tortious acts did not suit the temperament of the times. By 1830, federal and state courts had adopted the rule, first stated in 1813,[40] that an agent of the corporation could make binding contracts without affixing to a document the corporate seal (the symbol that denoted an official act of the members of the corporate body), thereby relieving corporate representatives of the task of gaining approval for every contractual agreement. In addition, the contract could be verbal and its authorization reasonably presumed if warranted by the facts.[41] In the same manner that corporate contract law proceeded by naturalizing the artificial being symbolized by the common seal, corporate liability in tort was established by making the corporation responsible for the acts of its agents—which is to say, an act of an agent would be deemed an act of the corporation.[42] By expanding the legal capacities of the corporate individual, while retaining all of the essential attributes inherited from English law, American courts embarked on a course that would stimulate the growth of corporate enterprise in the formative years of industrialization.

Consistent with American jurists' efforts to adapt the corporate form to native conditions, Supreme Court decisions concerning the legal standing of the corporation in federal court initially were shaped more by practical considerations than by an overriding concern for theoretical clarity. As early as 1809, in *Bank of the United States v. Deveaux*, the Court struggled with this issue, which like other matters affecting the constitutional status of the corporation clearly had not been anticipated by the framers of the document.[43] Under Article III, Section 2, of the Constitution, and the interpretation of this provision in the 1789 Judiciary Act, a case could be heard in federal court either on appeal from the highest state court or on an original action between citizens of different states or between a state (or its citizens) and foreign states, citizens, or subjects. In order to be granted jurisdiction in federal court, therefore, a corporation would have to be considered a citizen under Article III, Section 2. The thorny constitutional question then presents itself: if a corporation were a citizen under Article III, would it also be a citizen as defined in the privileges and immunities clause in Article IV, Section 2? To grant "all Privileges and Immunities of Citizens in the several states" to corporations most likely would undermine, if not destroy, the system of state regulation of corporate business. On the other hand, without a solution to this constitutional dilemma, corporations (in this case, the Bank of the United States) would have no standing to sue in federal courts.

In *Deveaux*, Chief Justice Marshall managed to evade this problem by ruling that even though the corporation "is certainly not a citizen" its membership may be examined for purposes of determining jurisdiction.[44] Thus, if individuals who compose a corporation actually reside as citizens in a state other than the party being sued, then the corporation may avail itself of the federal forum—a solution that would become increasingly impractical when the activities and shareholders of numerous corporations began to assume a national character. Nor was this decision conceptually palatable. To dispense with the corporate fiction because of the wording of the Constitution seemed arbitrary and, in later years, inconsistent with courts' efforts to attribute the rights and legal capacities of the corporation solely to the entity, the corporate individual. In an important series of cases culminating with *Marshall v. Baltimore & Ohio R.R.*, decided in 1853, the Court eventually devised the rule that for the purposes of federal jurisdiction a corporation would be presumed to be a resident (but not a citizen) of the state in which it was domiciled.[45] In addition to giving corporations the alternative of suing in federal court, rather than in the courts of the defendant's own state, this ruling paved the way for the time when, following the passage of the Fourteenth Amendment, corporate litigants would employ the federal forum to battle state economic regulation and to expand their constitutional rights.

In *Bank of Augusta v. Earle* (1839), the applicability of the privileges and immunities clause to corporations came before the Court once again, but this time with regard to the rights of corporations to do business in other states.[46] On behalf of one of the plaintiffs, Daniel Webster argued that *Deveaux*'s holding that a corporation be viewed as a group of citizens for purposes of determining federal jurisdiction be applied to the privileges and immunities clause, thereby extending the rights of citizenship to corporations. Chief Justice Roger B. Taney rejected Webster's argument on practical grounds. To endow corporations with the privileges and immunities of citizenship, he cautioned, would "deprive every state of all control over the extent of corporate franchises proper to be granted in the state." Furthermore, if corporations were to be granted citizenship under the Constitution, the Chief Justice explained, individual shareholders would be liable for the debts of the corporation, since as a citizen a corporation could no more claim limited liability in its contractual obligations than could any other citizen involved in a business venture.[47] Taney, perhaps more avidly than Marshall before him, refused to extend to the corporation the constitutional status of citizenship at the expense of state mercantilism.[48] Instead, he devised a practical accommodation based on rules of comity observed by sovereign nations (now made applicable to states of the Union through Article IV, Section 1, of the Constitution) that would allow corporations chartered in one state to do business in another, provided that the corporation's charter and the laws of the state did not prohibit such activity.

While Webster's argument in *Bank of Augusta* anticipated the direction that corporate law would have to take as banking and industrial concerns increasingly conducted business across state lines, Taney's decision in that case nevertheless provided a solution to the immediate problem. Indeed, the ability to find solutions in the law, rather than to create new law, typified the Taney Court's approach to the business corporation throughout its tenure from 1836 to 1864. Though not predisposed to "expound" the Constitution, as Marshall would have it, Taney was keenly aware of the practical limitations of constitutional doctrine and its implications for the growth of corporate enterprise. Concerns such as these proved to be decisive in shaping the Chief Justice's opinion in *Charles River Bridge v. Warren Bridge Co.*, decided in 1837.[49]

In that case, the Court refused to recognize an implied right of exclusivity in the charter of the Charles River Bridge Company, noting that "any ambiguity in the terms of the contract must operate against the adventurers, and in favor of the public."[50] Justice Story, in dissent, argued that the Court's ruling would undermine the constitutional protection established in *Dartmouth*, thereby discouraging investment in corporate enterprise. For the majority of the Court, however, the contrary was true. Exclusive franchises that no longer served the public welfare stood in the way of economic and social progress. Hindsight suggests that Taney's opinion provided a judicious compromise that limited the reach of *Dartmouth* without altering its basic doctrine, and at the same time accommodated the law to changing social forces.[51] While Taney's application of the principle of strict construction in this case, coupled with the reserved powers of states to amend or repeal charters, seriously limited the prospects for judicial expansion of the contract clause,[52] it also encouraged the adoption of general incorporation acts by undercutting the security of the special-action franchise. This fact was especially significant for the growth of the railroads, whose advance was impeded by the exclusive right-of-ways of canals, turnpikes, and bridges.[53] Thus, by applying the law with an eye to changing economic conditions, the Court also facilitated the next stage of corporate development. Still fortified by its constitutional shield, the business corporation continued to proliferate as it gradually supplanted other forms of business enterprise in an industrializing America.

b. The Ascendancy of Corporate Individualism

For Taney's contemporaries, the *Charles River Bridge* case was replete with symbolism. It signaled the triumph of Jacksonian over Federalist (or Whig) policies on the Bench, and it also struck a blow for the rising entrepreneur against the monopoly interests.[54] Several times during the half-century following the adoption of the Constitution, antimonopoly and anticorporate sentiment became an important, if not decisive, factor in shaping state and national political debates. While Americans in the antebellum period had no experience with monopoly abuse comparable to that of the British, a deep-seated distrust of concentrated power and of the prerogatives of the wealthy seemed to motivate much of the early opposition to corporate enterprise, regardless of the issues of the specific case.[55] When combined with the predisposition to identify incorporation with monopoly privilege—though not without justification in the initial decades of the nineteenth century—the rhetorical attack on the business corporation could assume the proportions of a class war. This was indeed the case in the enduring struggle of Jeffersonian and Jacksonian forces against the Bank of the United States.[56]

Under the autocratic leadership of Nicholas Biddle since 1823, the Second Bank of the United States had acquired effective control over the nation's currency and system of credit by the time of Jackson's first election in 1828. Although the Bank was a federal instrumentality exempt from state taxation and possessing plenary powers sanctioned by the Constitution, it operated as a privately controlled corporation.[57] When President Jackson unveiled his plan to oppose the rechartering of the Bank, on his reelection in 1832, the issue of corporate power on the national level fueled the anticharter movement within state politics as well. Inevitably, arguments against the Bank, a corporation with unique and exclusive powers, became part of a less focused attack on corporate enterprise in general. Out of this often muddled debate would emerge the initial efforts of corporate ideologists to counter the claims of their critics with the free-enterprise doctrine of corporate individualism.[58]

Indeed, as Louis Hartz has demonstrated, the debate at the Pennsylvania Constitutional Convention of 1837, which concerned the Pennsylvania legislature's power to revoke its charter with the Second Bank, imme diately spilled over into broader issues encompassing the economic, social, and political significance of corporate enterprise. In their effort to expurgate the taint of monopoly, antirevocation proponents, now cast in the role of defenders of the business corporation, invoked Marshallian doctrine—what Hartz termed the Dartmouth College principle—to undermine the foundation of the anticharter and prorevocation position:

> When it identified the corporation and the state with two individuals in a relation of business contract, it served to clothe the corporation with a kind of personal individuality—a symbolic effect . . . which nullified the distinction between individual and corporate enterprise which was at the heart of the anticharter theory.[59]

In this fashion, the legal fiction acquired ideological significance. As the corporate individual became identified with the entrepreneur, the business corporation lost its negative association with the privileged few— the commercial and financial interests aligned with the Bank of the United States and the old guard of the Federalist Party.

Even though the holding in *Dartmouth*, prior to Taney's opinion in *Charles River Bridge*, was generally regarded as creating a bastion for special privilege, the ideological implications of corporate individualism in an industrial society were gradually coming to light in the decades following Marshall's opinion, as the number of corporate business charters granted by states continued to grow. Because eighteenth-century English law regarded corporate enterprise as an instrumentality of the state (and made no distinction between public and private corporations), the conception of property on which it was based contained wellestablished presumptions in favor of monopoly and immunity from competition. Once the distinction between public and private corporations had been clearly drawn in *Terrett* and *Dartmouth*, however, the English common-law doctrine establishing these presumptions became increasingly difficult to defend.[60] Consequently, early decisions of the Supreme Court securing constitutional protection for private corporations, while protecting the vested rights of property in a manner consistent with the mercantilist policies of the federal and state governments, also contributed to changes in the law that would encourage the growth of a competitive industrializing economy in the first half of the nineteenth century.[61]

In order to appreciate the magnitude of the transformation that occurred in American economic life in the five decades spanning the ratification of the Constitution and the decision in *Charles River Bridge*, one must bear in mind that, by 1837, antimonopoly sentiment had already merged with the demands for free enterprise and for the adoption of general incorporation acts.[62] Monopoly was now perceived as a barrier to industrial advance, not as an essential method of industry. With the demise of the Second Bank a few years hence and the subsequent collapse of the national anticharter movement, the primary locus of opposition to corporate enterprise would shift in the two decades preceding the Civil War as industrial workers in increasing numbers organized and demanded shorter hours and better working conditions.[63] During the same period, the association of the corporation with monopoly privilege became less persuasive as several states, beginning in 1837, adopted general incorporation acts, thereby making incorporation a right of the entrepreneur rather than a special prerogative of the chosen few. Moreover, this development in the law contributed to the growth of economic and social conditions in which laissez-faire corporate individualism could take root.[64]

c. Corporate Charters and Regulation: The Internal Dimension of Corporate Power

In the formative years of corporate enterprise, incorporation by special charter provided the means by which government entities regulated the internal as well as external activities of the business corporation. Prevailing legal theory held that a corporation's powers were strictly limited by the terms of its charter as granted by the sovereign. The mercantilist policy of granting corporate charters with special privileges on the grounds that they provided a public function or benefit entailed a fairly extensive regulation of corporate affairs. And even though general incorporation acts eliminated legislative review before a charter was granted, they still imposed numerous regulatory provisions.[65] In addition to stating the purpose of the enterprise, its capitalization, and special conditions or privileges, corporate charters contained detailed provisions, not unlike constitutions, that defined the internal organization and operations of the corporation.[66] While the private law of the business corporation might vary from state to state depending on the terms of charters, legislative policies, and the rulings of state courts, certain legal practices and principles were generally adopted.

In the early decades of the nineteenth century, American jurists lodged effective control of corporate enterprise in the shareholders, who as owners were deemed to be ultimately responsible for its conduct. This was accomplished by reserving solely to the stockholders—not to the delegated management—the power to change, by unanimous vote, the fundamental structure or operations of the enterprise.[67] Powers delegated to the directors or managers of the corporation derived from explicit authorization in the bylaws. And while some courts sanctioned discretionary powers of boards to appoint agents, corporate law did not generally recognize the existence of implied powers in boards of directors until after mid-century.[68] On the other hand, the right of stockholders to remove directors at will was recognized in common law and provided for in some statutes.[69] Still another indication of the extent of stockholder control in the formative era can be found in the doctrine of preemptive rights established in a Massachusetts case, *Gray v. Portland Bank*, in 1807.[70] In that case, the court held that shareholders have a preemptive right to subscribe to new offerings of stock in an amount that would retain the proportion of their stock to the total number of shares issued. This ruling, which was universally adopted, established the stockholder's right to preserve the value of the initial investment and its voting power as the corporation prospered.[71]

In an era in which the operations of the vast majority of corporations required only a very basic managerial structure and the number of shareholders was few enough for all of the owners to be present at meetings, the legal presumption in favor of stockholder control reflected the economic reality. State regulation of the size, structure, and operations of the corporation throughout the nineteenth century indicated an enduring distrust or fear of this institution, perhaps rooted in its early association with monopoly privilege, and stood as a constant reminder that the unique capacities of the business corporation were not to be abused or exploited at the public's expense. This concern notwithstanding, courts and legislatures gradually revised the legal framework of the internal dimension of corporate power in response to the needs of enterprise for greater managerial discretion and centralized control.[72] By the end of the century, incremental change would give way to wholesale revision of statutory law just as the captains of industry and finance ushered in the new order.

The formative era of corporate law stands as testimony to the role of American jurists in creating, interpreting, and revising law to enable the growth of corporate enterprise and fuel the progress of industry. From the English law of corporations, rooted in a medieval conception of the corporate entity, developed the modern corporate individual, an entity capable of entering into contractual relations in a market economy. In the first half of the nineteenth century, the essential legal attributes of the remodeled corporate entity—the foundation of the business corporation's external dimension of power—were firmly established in both state and federal law. While not a "citizen," the corporation, as an individual, possessed legal and property rights under the Constitution. By vesting it with the constitutional right of property and by granting it the legal standing to sue in federal court, the Supreme Court would guarantee the survival of the business corporation within the American federal system. Endowed with perpetuity, the corporate entity could persist indefinitely, insofar as it remained a going concern and its duration was not limited by law. Moreover, the practice of granting to shareholders limited liability for the corporation's debts would be adopted in most states, before mid-century, through statutes and judicial decisions.[73] In other areas of law—contracts and torts—courts proceeded to refashion the powers and obligations of the business corporation to accommodate its needs to transact business efficiently and to establish its accountability as an individual under the law.

Throughout this period, the power to define the nature and scope of business activity through the corporate charter rested primarily with state courts and legislatures. Corporate leaders might strongly influence legislative policy and their counsel might shape judicial opinion, but in important ways the corporation remained subject to the sovereign's will through the terms of its charter. It did not possess the autonomy or the size and structure characteristic of the modern corporation.[74] Weaknesses inherent in this system of corporate control, rooted in mercantilist policies of a preindustrial economy, however, began to appear by the end of the formative era. Steady westward expansion of the population, the development of a national railway system and, with it, incipient national markets, and the increasing competition between states and regions to attract capital, already were eroding the economic foundation on which the state system of corporate regulation was based. Legal changes in the late nineteenth century facilitating the rise of corporate power and the ensuing abdication by state legislatures of their traditional regulatory controls over corporate charters would complete the collapse of this system and at the same time provide corporate enterprise with the autonomy essential to the full exercise of its internal and external dimensions of power.

4. CONSTITUTIONAL LAW AND THE RISE OF CORPORATE POWER

Although American entrepreneurs in the antebellum period had begun to realize the benefits of incorporation as an efficient and secure means for doing business, most corporations had neither the need nor the opportunity—given the state of the economy, industrial methods, and transportation—to accumulate huge sums of capital. The major exception, the efforts of which played a critical role in industrializing America, was the railroad companies. With considerable aid from state and federal governments, including millions of acres in land grants, railroads literally paved the way for corporate expansion by creating a national network of transportation that opened new markets and spurred the growth of an interdependent national economy.[75] By any previous standard, the railroad corporations were huge. Capitalized in the millions of dollars through securities and bonds, railroads became a breeding ground for unscrupulous financiers and executives who would in effect use the investments of others to amass their personal fortunes.[76] Beginning in the 1870s, railroad leaders also devised various pooling agreements whereby the pool members agreed on a schedule of rates or prices and a division of markets. By embracing a strategy of cooperation in the face of cutthroat competition, the railroad magnates exemplified the corporate ethos of the new era.[77] They also led the way in organizational innovation by being the first corporations to develop a modern managerial structure with separate functional divisions and a hierarchical chain of command.[78] Both the heroes and the villains of their day, the railroad barons were the original architects of corporate power in the modern era.

In the wake of the tremendous surge in railroad building in the two decades following the Civil War—more than 100,000 miles between 1865 and 1885—corporate enterprise in old and new industries flourished. During the same period, however, Supreme Court decisions seemed to offer little promise for corporation attorneys who, like Daniel Webster before them, pleaded for greater constitutional protection for the business class. To be sure, the contract clause, the constitutional bedrock of corporate law, no longer served as a vehicle for augmenting corporate rights. Heeding Justice Story's advice in *Dartmouth*, most states had passed provisions reserving their right to amend or repeal corporate charters, and the rule of strict construction discouraged expansive interpretations of the clause.[79] At the same time, the majority of the Court was not yet of a mind to cultivate the rights of property in new areas of law, most notably the due process clause of the Fourteenth Amendment. While hindsight reveals that by 1890 the seeds had been carefully sown, nearly another decade passed before these labors came to fruition in the substantive due process doctrine of liberty of contract.

Passed by Congress in 1868 for the purpose of guaranteeing the rights of citizenship to blacks, the Fourteenth Amendment seemed an unlikely choice for advancing the cause of business. From the outset, however, its broad language and general application to "citizens" and "persons" tantalized the ablest minds in the legal profession.[80] In 1873, in the first case to come before the Court under the new amendment, the dispute at bar concerned not the civil liberties of the newly enfranchised but the constitutional status of a Louisiana act granting a monopoly to a slaughterhouse.[81] Former Supreme Court Justice John Archibald Campbell, now attorney for the aggrieved butchers of New Orleans, urged the Court to adopt his latitudinarian view of the rights bestowed by the recent additions to the Constitution. He claimed that the monopoly had deprived his clients of their natural right to pursue a calling and hence their right of property, thereby violating the privileges and immunities, due process, and equal protection clauses of the Fourteenth Amendment.[82] Although losing a 5 to 4 decision, Campbell set in motion a monumental debate on the Court. Spearheaded by the loud dissents of Justices Stephen J. Field and Joseph P. Bradley, the judicial crusade to expand the rights of property, the historic quest of the Marshall Court, had been rejoined in the era of the large corporation.

Throughout the 1870s and 1880s, pooling agreements and discriminatory rate practices of railroads spawned a variety of state measures, many in response to the demands of the Granger movement, to regulate the rates of the roads. When growing labor unrest during the depression of 1873–1878 exploded in the Great Railroad Strike of 1877 and continued with numerous strikes in the mid-1880s, battle lines were also being drawn on the industrial front. Often at the center of this political maelstrom, state and federal courts increasingly became the arbiters of social justice. In a controversial opinion that seemed to sanction the cause of social democracy, the Supreme Court, in *Munn v. Illinois*, decided in 1877, upheld a statute that set a maximum rate that grain elevator operators could charge for storage.[83] Rejecting the plaintiff's claim that the regulation deprived him of his property in contravention of the due process clause of the Fourteenth Amendment, Chief Justice Morrison R. Waite invoked the common-law doctrine stated by Lord Hale two centuries before, concerning private property "affected with a public interest." When "one devotes his property to a use in which the public has an interest," Waite declared, "he, in effect, grants to the public an interest in that use, and must submit to be controlled by the public for the common good, to the extent of the interest he has just created."[84] He admonished that the courts were not the proper forum for deciding the reasonableness of such regulations. For redress of legislative abuse, "the people must resort to the polls, not to the courts."[85] In an impassioned dissent, Justice Field criticized Waite's opinion as "subversive of the rights of private property,"[86] then proceeded to expound on the inextricable bond that joins the pursuit of life, liberty, and property. Still unable to convert a majority of his fellow justices to his substantive due process interpretation, Field could only await the company of like minds on the Bench.

The shift in policy by which the Supreme Court would claim new regulatory prerogatives over economic activity crystallized in a series of decisions handed down between 1886 and 1890. By the latter year, only Field and Bradley remained from the Court that decided the *Munn* case in 1877. Notable among the new entrants were Chief Justice Melville W. Fuller, a former corporation lawyer who replaced Waite in 1888, and Justice David Brewer, ideological kinsman and nephew of Field, appointed in 1889. In 1886, the Court declared its intention to strike down, under the commerce clause, all state regulations of railroad rates,[87] served notice that the contract clause would not be interpreted to achieve that same end,[88] and in the same case hinted that the Court was now inclined to apply the Fourteenth Amendment's due process clause to limit state economic regulations. In that same year, with little fanfare but with profound implications for the development of corporate power, the Court also accepted, without argument, the proposition that the term "person" in the equal protection clause of the Fourteenth Amendment included corporations.[89]

In *Chicago, Milwaukee & St. Paul R.R. Co. v. Minnesota*, decided in 1890, the intention of the Supreme Court to regulate property rights of private (nonstatist) enterprise became manifest as the slow evolution of substantive due process approached fulfillment.[90] After holding that a Minnesota regulation that did not provide for judicial review of rates constituted a deprivation of property under the due process clause, the Court apparently overruled its decision in *Munn* by declaring that henceforth it would determine the reasonableness of rates.[91] Seven years later, on the eve of Justice Field's retirement after nearly thirty-five years of service, the Court held, in *Allgeyer v. Louisiana*,[92] that petitioner's liberty, as guaranteed under the due process clause of the Fourteenth Amendment, had been violated.Thereafter, substantive due process (liberty of contract) provided the Court with a tool to redefine the permissible scope of state regulation of business. By 1897, however, when *Allgeyer* was decided, numerous state courts and some federal courts—notably, those in Justice Field's own Ninth Circuit—already had developed a body of decisions based on the natural liberty doctrine, as articulated in the opinions of Field and Bradley.[93] Indeed, for nearly a decade before *Allgeyer*, five or more justices had recognized the existence of property rights in the due process clause, albeit never in sufficient number in the same case to form a majority.

The doctrine of liberty of contract, however, constituted only one aspect of a complex body of regulatory law devised by courts in the last quarter of the nineteenth century to accommodate a rapidly growing industrial economy. Focusing on the rise of substantive due process to the exclusion of doctrinal developments affirming the regulatory powers of state governments invites distortion by examining only half the equation. What state governments could properly regulate under their police powers was a crucial ingredient in defining the boundaries between state and federal regulatory powers and in delimiting the scope of economic freedoms. Equally significant in this regard was an expanding body of law demarcating the regulatory spheres of national and state governments over commerce and transportation. Moreover, interrelated with and often based on doctrinal developments in constitutional law were decisions by state and federal courts in antitrust law and corporation law. Because Supreme Court rulings in one area of law often had implications for other areas, an adequate analysis of legal changes affecting the rise of corporate power requires some clarification of the interrelationships that comprised this network of judge-made law.

Clearly, in declaring the corporation to be a person under the Fourteenth Amendment, the Waite Court picked up where the Marshall Court had left off. This constitutes the most important development affecting the constitutional rights of the corporate entity—and hence the legal basis of the external dimension of corporate power—during the rise of the large corporation in the late nineteenth century. In an era of rapid industrial expansion and burgeoning national markets, corporations were tugging at the reins of a legal system that restricted their freedom to do business outside their state of incorporation. Corporate individualism had broken down the barriers of monopoly privilege, but the nationalizing forces of corporate capitalism were fettered by a legal structure that had been erected on the regulatory policies of state mercantilism and the constitutional limitations of federalism. The Court's application of the Fourteenth Amendment to corporations did not explicitly alter the states' powers to deny entry to a foreign (nonresident) corporation or to impose conditions on that entry. But once entry had been granted, the corporation could then challenge state regulations in federal court by invoking the protection of the due process and equal protection clauses. This development, in conjunction with the rise of substantive due process, encouraged out-of-state ventures of corporate enterprise, which in turn expanded the network of interstate business and limited the practical scope of state regulations.

The other essential objective of this policy of securing and enabling corporate expansion was to limit the constitutionally permissible domain of state regulations through a broad reading of the national commerce power. Supreme Court rulings accomplished this end by holding that a state could not deny entry to or unduly burden foreign corporations whose business involved interstate commerce.[94] While these developments remained consistent with the Anglo-American doctrine that the corporation is the creature of the state in which it is incorporated—the legal basis for denying national citizenship under both of the privileges and immunities clauses—they provided a constitutional means for overruling or circumventing state law that thwarted corporate expansion.[95] In this fashion, constitutional law played a key role in restructuring the national economy and encouraging the rise of corporate power.

These constitutional innovations, however, must be understood within the broader contours of a judicial policy that, while attempting to accommodate and aid the growth of industry and interstate business, sought to preserve the states' powers to regulate enterprise that was not engaged in interstate commerce. In attempting to promulgate new rules for a competitive marketplace, and comcomitantly for an expanding national sphere of economic freedom, the Waite and Fuller Courts confronted anew the difficult task of establishing the boundaries separating interstate commerce from intrastate commerce. States' control over their own corporate creations and over foreign corporations (subject to the rule of comity) had been well established in the antebellum period and reaffirmed thereafter.[96] The states' authority to regulate in these matters derived from their inherent police powers—which is to say, the powers that were not in conflict with the delegated powers of the national government and that were deemed necessary to the preservation of the health, safety, and morals of the community or otherwise deemed consonant with "public policy."

Consistent with the police powers doctrine, the Supreme Court developed the rule in the postbellum period that state governments could at their discretion regulate enterprise involved in manufacturing (or production), including mining and insurance companies, unless the activities of these businesses were directly related to, or imposed a burden on, interstate or foreign commerce (or traffic).[97] The manufacturing/commerce distinction sanctioned the states' traditional powers to regulate both corporations (through corporation law) and intrastate commerce, which by 1890 also included state laws that compelled the segregation of races in transportation.[98] Indeed, as one author has observed, the Court's definition of state regulatory powers over economic matters during this period "paralleled and anticipated its treatment of restrictions on blacks."[99] Rather than economic liberties gaining constitutional protection at the expense of the civil rights of blacks, such denial of rights was an integral component of the post-Reconstruction judicial policy that left to the states control over domestic matters (including race relations), intrastate business, and the structure and operations of corporations.[100] Thus, a ruling that went against established precedent regarding a state's power either to regulate intrastate commerce or to deny entry to or regulate foreign corporations not involved in interstate commerce could have far-reaching consequences for the division of state and federal regulatory responsibilities and corresponding public policies.[101] Faced with the prospect of having to reconcile conflicting policy objectives, the Court emphasized on numerous occasions that the line separating interstate and intrastate commerce was often difficult to draw with precision. When assessed within this broader context, cases that otherwise might appear inconsistent or based on expediency acquire a certain logic.

Between 1887 and 1892, nine states passed laws compelling segregation by race in common carriers. Many of these segregative acts coincided with or constituted a component of railway reform legislation instigated by agrarian protests.[102] During the same period, in response to capitalists' method of combining capital through the trustee device, numerous state governments as well as private parties brought successful suits in state courts leading to the dissolution of several of the more notorious trusts.[103] However, the combination movement was in large part an effort to substitute cooperative methods of business for competitive methods, in order to remedy the instabilities of the competitive market, notably its ruinous cycles of expansion and depression. Chronic business failures and social dislocations stemming from these cycles stimulated demands from railroad executives, farmers, and merchants for national railroad reform, resulting in the creation, in 1887, of the Interstate Commerce Commission.[104] Inspired by the proliferation of trusts, antimonopoly agitation in numerous states also led to the passage of the Sherman Antitrust Act in 1890. Thus, in the last two decades of the nineteenth century a rising tide of racism impelling the legalization of Jim Crow practices and the resurgence of widespread antimonopoly sentiment, coupled with demands for a solution to the instabilities of the competitive marketplace, generated new law and, therewith, legal disputes that presented the Fuller Court with unprecedented challenges.

Far from evincing an overzealous solicitude to the needs of big business, Supreme Court decisions between 1890 and 1897 demonstrated a considerable degree of restraint and a self-conscious attempt to preserve the regulatory domain of the states. At the same time that the Court was laying the basis for a substantive interpretation of due process and facilitating corporate expansion through a broad interpretation of congressional power under the commerce clause, it was also broadly defining the scope of the police powers doctrine (and intrastate commerce) and reaffirming principles supportive of state economic regulations.[105]

In *Plessy v. Ferguson*,[106] decided in 1896, the Court upheld the constitutionality of mandatory segregation in common carriers, thereby giving federal sanction to the doctrine of separate-but-equal. Although the outcome in this case would appear to have never been in doubt given previous holdings and the justices' personal inclination in these matters (with the lone exception of Justice Harlan), *Plessy* nevertheless represented the consummation of one aspect of the Court's federal-state regulatory scheme.[107] Less successful was the Court's policy of leaving to the states the exclusive responsibility of regulating enterprise engaged in manufacturing or production, which also entailed control over the structure and operations of corporations, including the discretion to initiate actions to dissolve corporate combinations. Despite earlier successes, state attorneys-general in the mid-to-late 1890s failed to bring suits that might have crippled the great merger movement of 1898–1904 at its inception. This failure, moreover, was greatly influenced by wholesale revisions of incorporation laws in New Jersey, which along with other changes favoring large-scale enterprise legalized mergers and consolidations.

Beginning with a series of acts, between 1888 and 1893, that authorized one corporation to hold stock in another, and followed in 1896 by a radical revision of its general incorporation statute, New Jersey ignited a revolution in corporation law that has yet to run its course. What had captured the heart of corporate America, and soon would become the model for a host of states competing in the charter business, was an incorporation act that completely eliminated restrictions on a variety of essential matters, including capitalization and assets, mergers and consolidations, the issuance of voting stock, the purpose(s) of incorporation, and the duration and locale of business. Now allowed to amend their own charters, corporate directors could exercise control over their internal affairs free from legislative scrutiny. When Delaware joined the bandwagon in 1899, with tax inducements, among other favors, the new course was firmly set.[108] Incorporation statutes became enabling acts that, for all practical purposes, liberated the internal and external dimensions of corporate power from state control.

Fearing a loss of business and the enmity of an ever increasing number of foreign corporations domiciled in New Jersey, most state governments, after 1895, chose not to initiate proceedings against *ultra vires* transactions involving mergers or consolidations, thereby shifting the burden of regulating combinations almost entirely to the federal government.[109] The Court's interpretation of the Sherman Act would therefore necessarily affect the incipient merger movement in some fashion. As the states grew lax in the regulation of their corporate creations or simply chose not to regulate certain types of business in order to preserve and encourage economic activity, the Fuller Court nevertheless remained steadfast in upholding doctrine that validated the states' traditional controls over domestic and foreign corporations.[110]

5. THE EARLY DEVELOPMENT OF ANTITRUST LAW: REGULATING CORPORATE POWER IN THE MARKETPLACE

By the turn of the century, with American industry and finance booming in the midst of its first great merger movement, the dominant trend of the previous two decades toward corporate consolidation and concentrated control of industry and finance by large firms had been realized.[111] In dramatic fashion, the much feared corporate takeover prophesied by democratic reformers and antimonopolists of earlier generations was under way. Indeed, to many observers, the scope and permanence of this transformation signaled the advance of a new order that threatened to undermine the aspirations of a people nurtured on the promise of unlimited opportunity. In attempting to fathom this strange new world, Progressive Era reformers glimpsed the future. The corporate financiers and industrialists had built their kingdoms and permanently altered the course of American life.

Leaders and propagandists of antimonopoly movements in the early nineteenth century developed the initial analyses and criticisms of corporate power in American society. Conceived within the premises of liberalism, the antimonopoly position evolved from an assault on the perceived political and economic evils of monopoly privilege and state-sponsored industrialization to a demand for general incorporation acts and equality of opportunity in the expanding marketplace of early industrial capitalism. This ideological transition within the antimonopoly movement, typified by the entrepreneurial ethos of Jacksonian democracy, marked the emergence of competitive capitalism and the gradual eclipse of state-centered mercantilism.

A resurgent antimonopoly sentiment in the last quarter of the nineteenth century redefined the issue of monopoly power from the standpoint of the farmer, the industrial worker, and the small proprietor. During this period of burgeoning industry, intense competition in many markets, and chronic cycles of expansion and depression, the foes of corporate power did not share their predecessors' view of this force as the product of an artificial legal privilege endowed by state or federal gov-

ernments. Rather, with the widespread adoption of general incorporation acts by mid-century, the subsequent proliferation of corporations in
the decades immediately following the Civil War, and the formation of
several large industrial corporations or trusts by the late 1880s, in addition to the highly capitalized railway companies already formed, the
public perception of monopoly power shifted from the idea of monopolization of industry or commerce through exclusive legal privilege to that
of dominance or disruption of markets through unfair practices. Thus,
for the antimonopoly movement of the late nineteenth century, the economic basis of the power of the trust or industrial combination was
understood as an established (though undesirable) attribute of capitalist
methods, which can be greatly aided by, but was no longer primarily
dependent on, the beneficence of political rulers.

What *was* anomalous to the antimonopoly reformer of the late nineteenth century (and, indeed, it had to be if democracy were to be a viable
ideal) was the extraordinary influence and control that corporate mo-
guls and their compatriots wielded over the institutions and processes of
American politics. Corporate power had created its own domain within
which it dispensed wealth in return for special privileges. It ruled politics just as it ruled the market. To tame corporate power, therefore, the
means of government would have to be reclaimed by "the people,"
which would require nothing less than dethroning the plutocracy.[112]

At the same time, however, the productive potential that corporate
enterprise promised to realize within a unified national economy, combined with astounding technological advances in the last quarter of the
century, mitigated against the wholesale opposition to corporate enterprise by most reformers. A noted scholar on the law of corporations,
William W. Cook, expressed this sentiment succinctly in *The Corporation
Problem*, published in 1891: "It is an established principle of economics
that the displacement of numberless small concerns by large ones is not
only a natural process but it is beneficial in its results." Noting at length
the array of cost-saving, organizational, and technological advantages of
corporate enterprise, he turned to the problem of trusts, referring to
them as "artificial" combinations—as distinguished from "natural" or
"legitimate" combinations, which developed from the competitive struggle of the marketplace. For Cook, the trust was a *"nefarious* mode of
forming a few great establishments" because its *"sole* object" was "to
establish a monopoly."[113] In effect, he articulated the idea embodied in
the common-law distinction between reasonable ("natural") and unreasonable ("artficial") restraints of trade.

This prevalent notion of "good" and "bad" trusts largely accounted for
the apparently contradictory conception of corporate power expressed in

American law and political thought in the late nineteenth and early twentieth centuries. For many reformers and social critics, combination was desirable so long as it was the product of a "natural process" or evolution of competitive, and therefore fair, business practices. From this reasoning evolved a guiding principle of the Progressive Movement—namely, that in order to restore and preserve these salubrious market forces, economic regulation would have to replace the Invisible Hand of the competitive marketplace.

By 1900, in the dawn of the era of corporate capitalism, the debates concerning corporate power that had been raging for two decades prior had crystallized around the "trust question." The issue of corporate power, in all of its manifestations, dominated the arena of politics and produced the major issues confronting American jurists. Literature, political writing, and social science all evinced a society's trepidations and hopes, if not its awe, in the presence of this enigmatic force that appeared to be at once an unprecedented instrument of progress and a juggernaut of tyranny. An entire nation—from the Populist outposts in the western states to the midwestern and eastern centers of industrialism—had come to realize that its future would depend fundamentally on the resolution of the economic, social, and political problems engendered by the rise of the large corporation.

Clearly, the public outcry against the trusts inspired the drafting of the Sherman Act in 1890. Congressional debate on Senator John Sherman's original bill revealed both a sense of urgency to pass an antitrust measure, perhaps motivated by a desire to pacify an angry electorate, and a genuine concern to outlaw the flagrant abuses of monopoly power. In his dramatic defense of his bill on the Senate floor, Senator Sherman proclaimed: "If we will not endure a king as a political power we should not endure a king over the production, transportation, and sale of any of the necessaries of life." But he assured his fellow members that the aim of the proposed legislation was to prohibit only "the unlawful combination" under common law, not to undo the economic and social advantages realized from "the lawful and useful combination."[114] After considerably rewriting its key provisions, which entirely eliminated the bill as presented by Senator Sherman, the authors of the final version of the bill concluded that its constitutional authority under the commerce clause and the English and American common-law doctrines on which it was based were sufficient for its purposes.[115]

There are two major types of violations that the Act envisions: unlawful restraints of trade and monopolization. Section 1 declares to be illegal "every contract, combination in the form of trust or otherwise, or conspiracy, in restraint of trade or commerce among the several States, or with foreign nations. . . ." Section 2 punishes "every person who shall monopolize, or attempt to monopolize, or combine or conspire with any other person or persons, to monopolize any part of the trade or commerce among the several States, or with foreign nations. . . ." Early interpretations of the Sherman Act by lower federal courts, however, produced significant differences of opinion as to the framers' intent and the precise meaning of its language.

On the eve of the merger wave, in 1897, following its decision in *Allgeyer*, the Supreme Court, in *United States v. Trans-Missouri Freight Association*, attempted for the first time to interpret in a comprehensive manner the provisions of the Sherman Antitrust Act.[116] The decision of the majority, under the leadership of Justices John M. Harlan and Rufus W. Peckham, to eschew the long-standing common-law doctrine that prohibited only unreasonable restraints of trade and to adopt the novel view that *all* restraints of trade, whether reasonable or unreasonable, were unlawful, involved a judicial arrogation of regulatory powers clearly not intended by the authors of the act.[117]

Justice Peckham's construction of the Sherman Act in *Trans-Missouri*, which would be the majority view from 1897 to 1911, therefore threatened to upset the separation or balance between public and private spheres and between federal and state powers, which the Court had labored to establish for over two decades. Indeed, the scope of the interstate commerce power underpinning the Sherman Act, as interpreted by the Harlan-Peckham majority, strongly limited the freedom to contract, as it had been established in common law with respect to restraint of trade and in constitutional law through the natural rights doctrine of liberty of contract.[118] Thus, the exercise of individual contractual liberty in the market—the sphere of private decision-making that, under common law, allowed for considerable self-regulation over markets by capitalists—henceforth would be subordinated to the regulatory prerogatives of the national government. In rejecting the common-law doctrine that freedom to contract was the rule and restraint the exception, the Court thwarted the adaptation of common-law and constitutional doctrines of contractual liberty to changing economic conditions.[119]

The contention of Harlan and Peckham that the Sherman Act superseded common law was sharply criticized by other members of the Court, notably Justices Edward D. White and Oliver W. Holmes, who maintained that the act should be interpreted in light of the common-law doctrine on restraints of trade. This split on the Court also evinced different ideological responses to the rise of the large corporation. In its effort to enforce competition and restore the competitive market of a precorporate capitalist economy, the Harlan-Peckham majority aligned itself with the anticorporate ideology of small proprietors and populists who sought a return to an earlier form of industrialism and its harmonic vision of an unfettered marketplace. Justices White and Holmes, on the other hand, argued forcefully that the common law was well suited for adapting the jurisprudential rules of the market to changing economic conditions. Contractual liberty, as embodied in common-law doctrine, preserved the regulatory role of capitalists over the market while also allowing for government regulation of the market in the public interest. This approach, flexible in its application and pro-corporate in its acceptance of large-scale enterprise and combinations (subject to public regulation), accepted the growth and proliferation of the business corporation, along with its substantial technological advances, as a "natural" or evolutionary product of an earlier stage of capitalist development.[120] These contending ideological views concerning the economic and social significance of the large corporation had their counterparts in the political struggles of the day. The debate on the Court was one aspect, albeit fundamental, of the larger debate concerning the rise of corporate power and the corporate transformation of the competitive market that engaged politicians, reformers, intellectuals, workers, farmers, proprietary capitalists, and corporate leaders throughout the Progressive Era.[121]

This debate attracted considerable national attention in the famous *Northern Securities* case of 1904,[122] in which Theodore Roosevelt, intent on making the trust issue a priority of national politics, turned an antitrust case into a cause. The size and economic significance of the Northern Securities holding company, which controlled the Northern Pacific, the Great Northern, and the Burlington railroads, combined with the notoriety of the principal defendants—railroad magnate James J. Hill and financier J. P. Morgan—certainly aided Roosevelt in his crusade to establish a legal and administrative regulatory framework.[123] In ruling that the holding company constituted a combination in direct restraint of commerce, Justice Harlan reiterated the ruling stated by Justice Peckham in *Trans-Missouri*. While lending support to Roosevelt's determination to break up the Northern Securities Company, the decision denied his contention that the legislation was intended to distinguish reasonable from unreasonable restraints of trade and permit the former while prohibiting the latter.[124]

Justice White's formulation of the rule of reason in these earlier cases, which became the majority position in the landmark *Standard Oil* case of 1911,[125] rejected the view that the Sherman Act made all restraints of trade unreasonable, thus compelling unrestricted competition while giving the national government the sole legal authority to regulate markets. The rule of reason decision therefore restored the Sherman Act to the same common-law principles that had informed its drafting more than two decades earlier. By allowing for regulation of markets by both government and private parties, the traditional common-law construction permitted the adaptation of public law to nonstatist administered markets.

White expounded the rule of reason in light of his analysis and application of the common-law doctrines of restraint of trade and monopoly to Sections 1 and 2 of the Sherman Act. Based on his review of precedent, he maintained that English common law forbade only unreasonable restraints of trade and that competition, "freedom to contract," had become "the rule in English law." In American common law, contracts deemed to have "a monopolistic tendency, especially those that were believed to unduly diminish competition and hence to enhance prices—in other words, to monopolize"—had come to be regarded, as in England, "as being in restraint of trade."[126] Accordingly, White reasoned that Sections 1 and 2 differ only in that the latter was intended to reach "the many new forms of contracts and combinations" that may bring about "an undue restraint of interstate or foreign commerce." Because the classes of illegal acts and contracts contemplated by the act are not enumerated in it, it followed that "the standard of reason which had been applied at the common law and in this country" must have been intended to be the measure for ascertaining whether the law had been violated in a particular case.[127]

With the rule of reason, the Court possessed an interpretative tool that allowed it to apply the law to specific factual situations and to accommodate legal doctrine to changing social and economic conditions, in a similar if not identical fashion to the method of interpretation that guides and shapes the development of constitutional law. Chief Justice Hughes's succinct observation in *Appalachian Coals v. United States*, is relevant in this context:

> The purpose of the Sherman Anti-Trust Act is to prevent undue restraints of interstate commerce, to maintain its appropriate freedom in the public interest, to afford protection from the subversive or coercive influences of monopolistic endeavor. As a charter of freedom, the act has a generality and adaptability comparable to that found to be desirable in constitutional provisions. It does not go into detailed definitions which might either work injury to legitimate enterprise or through particularization defeat its purposes by providing loopholes for escape. The restrictions the act imposes are not mechanical or artificial. Its general phrases, interpreted to attain its fundamental objectives, set up the essential standard of reasonableness.[128]

The analogy with constitutional law holds as well with regard to the problems of limiting judicial discretion and of devising manageable standards by which an evolving body of law may be construed. Both these concerns influenced White's application of the rule of reason to the facts in *Standard Oil*. In upholding the lower court's ruling that the Standard Oil Trust and its successor, Standard Oil of New Jersey, effectively destroyed the "potentiality of competition" that would have otherwise existed, the Court discovered in the methods and dealings of the companies a "prima facie presumption of intent and purpose to maintain the dominancy over the oil industry, not as a result of normal methods of industrial development, but by new means of combination."[129] Throughout his opinion, Justice White emphasized that the mere existence of a monopoly attained through "normal methods" did not offend the common law or the provisions of Section 2 of the act. Rather, the violation inhered in the "intent and purpose" to dominate and to restrict the field of competition. The sin is neither the size nor the market share of the enterprise, but willful domination and disregard of the rules of fair play—that is, the infringement of the right of others to compete on equal terms in the marketplace, a view at once paying tribute to the common-law right (as opposed to compulsion) to compete, and at the same time validating the modern, neoclassical affirmation of large-scale enterprise engaged in intercorporate or "potential" competition.[130]

Here we find at work the fundamental precept of American constitutionalism—the principle of limited government—and its concomitant conception of a balance of power. The conception of balance as a remedy for concentrated power permeates the fabric of American institutions and informs the distinctive development of American liberalism. The constitutional analogy is more than coincidental. Unchecked power in the marketplace represents a form of tyranny that the laws of the market themselves have failed to remedy or to prevent. When natural law falters, human artifice must intervene. Whether a competitive balance can be restored within the market in any meaningful sense, however, is less important than the fact that corporate power has been apparently checked in the public interest. In this way, "competition" comes to be associated with the legal and moral conception of fairness, and while still retaining its ideological identification with classical economic theory, justifies the "postclassical" transition from competitive to administered markets.[131]

Justice White's formulation of the rule of reason embodies the ideological assumption, consistent with the framers' intent, that antitrust law was designed to regulate corporate power without undermining the economic efficiency of the corporate order. Freedom to contract, White informs us, is the rule, but restraints of trade in practicing this freedom must be reasonable, as judged in light of the standard of fair competition. While certain types of restraints—namely, those that since have been classified as per se violations—will automatically fail this standard, other restraints will stand or fall under the test of reasonableness.[132] Economic analysis may be employed to determine whether a violation has occurred or whether a particular practice would deleteriously affect competition. But such an analysis must necessarily be restricted to the facts of a case as applied to the legal issue at bar. In applying the rule of reason, therefore, the Court, in principle, does not accept as part of its function the duty to propound economic theory in order to decide the specific issues before it, which would amount to imprinting its own economic philosophy on the operation of the law.[133] This formal abnegation of the role of economic legislator, moreover, is mirrored in the federal judiciary's historic reluctance to impose remedies that might seriously disrupt or destabilize existing markets.

The concept of fair competition and its implications rest on the presumption that there is an abiding public interest in a regulated marketplace that preserves the contending values of equal opportunity to compete (potential competition) and freedom to contract. That this was the Supreme Court's original intent can be deduced from its declaration that, in the absence of a finding of unreasonable restraint, the "normal methods of industrial development"—which is to say, the methods of lawful combination justified by the freedom to contract—will be presumed to operate in the interest of the public. The concept of fairness, as applied to the reasonableness of restraints of trade, therefore entails a judicial weighing of the values of equality of opportunity to compete and freedom to contract in the marketplace of corporate capitalism. To state the issue another way, the concept of fairness in antitrust jurisprudence justifies the attempt to devise a regulatory framework for an administered market system that, by permitting both government and corporate regulation of markets, avoids the alternatives of statist command and unlimited corporate power.

Application of the rule of reason by different Courts may reflect a predisposition to tip the judicial scales either in favor of government regulation of the market or corporate regulation, just as the test of reasonableness in other areas of law can be interpreted as requiring a high or low degree of proof, and thereby shift the burden. Thus an inherent flexibility, facilitating revision and adaptation in response to the needs of the corporation and to the prevailing public consensus as ascertained by the judiciary, ensures the law's viability. On this foundation, antitrust law developed as the primary legal framework—indeed, the constitutional law—governing the external dimension of corporate power, an evolving and often complex, body of rules and doctrine that, by defining limits to the exercise of power, confers legitimacy on the regime of the large corporation.

Standard Oil therefore not only established the interpretative framework of antitrust law but also represented a turning point in the Progressive Era debate over the methods and objectives of corporate regulation. The need for doctrinal consistency on the Court was matched by the demand of corporate capitalists for a measure of certainty and flexibility in the law by which to plan and to gauge the legal consequences of business decisions. This development achieved its modern form when the Court adopted the rule of reason and with the enactment, in 1914, of the Federal Trade Commission Act and the Clayton Antitrust Act.[134] Thus, in the early decades of the twentieth century, through the agency of public law and the judicial creation of a constitutional framework to define and regulate the external dimension of corporate power, federal judges and legislators, presidents and corporate statesmen, fashioned the tools with which the tenets of classical liberalism could be adapted to the structure and exigencies of corporate rule.

6. THE PROGRESSION TOWARD CORPORATE AUTONOMY

The corporate reconstruction of American society dates from the emergence of the large corporation in the late nineteenth century and the ascendancy to power of the first generation of corporate managers. In the modern era, corporate enterprise developed as a social and political force on a reconstructed economic foundation. Evidence of this transformation can be found in the oligopolistic and monopolistic control of industry and finance by large corporations, the renovation of old and the creation of new industries through technological advance and the development of mass markets, and the restructuring of control within the corporation itself.

By 1900, the rights, privileges, and capacities of the corporate entity that secure and enable the external dimension of corporate power had a solid constitutional foundation. Corporate power emerged when firms expanded their production capacity and market shares and then proceeded, through combination or by another means, to protect and expand their strong position. Over the course of the previous century, a familiar pattern of development had manifested itself: the growth of enterprise incited legal change, which in turn stimulated or facilitated the next stage of corporate development and the demand for new law. Legal changes thereby permitted and regulated the rise of corporate power, and the growth of corporate power created the need for further facilitative and regulative law.

This intertwining of cause and effect affecting the growth of enterprise contained a logic of its own that unfolded as a progression toward a mixture of corporate autonomy and public regulation in both the external and internal dimensions of power. As corporate enterprise matured, these two dimensions progressed unevenly. The expansion of corporate power in its external dimension induced economic and social change, which in turn created a demand for new law governing both the external and the internal dimensions in order to accommodate the changing structure and requirements of enterprise. Legal changes accommodating and facilitating the expansion of the external dimension of corporate power therefore also contributed to an enhanced autonomy in the internal dimension, which aided further expansion of corporate power in the market and society. In the nineteenth century, the dynamics of this evolving relationship between the external and internal dimensions of corporate power constituted an integral aspect of the transition from state-centered mercantilism, to early industrialization, and finally to the full-scale emergence of corporate capitalism within a unified national economy. Thus, the progression toward an enhanced autonomy in both dimensions entailed critical transformations of the American economy and federalism by legislators, judges, and capitalists at various stages in the development of enterprise.[135]

In the early nineteenth century, the corporation's acquisition of constitutional rights of property marked the first significant movement away from strong dependence on the state. While the constitutional protection afforded investors initially encouraged entrepreneurial activity, the prerogatives of exclusivity vested in many special-action charters increasingly posed barriers to competition. In this way, the exclusive franchise (perceived as a device of privilege and monopoly by a new generation of entrepreneurs) contributed to its own demise. As antimonopolist sentiment converged with laissez-faire ideology in the period of Jacksonian democracy, legislatures passed acts of general incorporation that made incorporation a right rather than a special privilege. By mid-century, legislative and judicial policies promoting competition in an industrializing economy had eclipsed earlier developmental strategies based on state-centered mercantilism. General incorporation acts thereafter reduced state control over the internal dimension of corporate power, aided the proliferation of corporate enterprise, and thereby facilitated the next stage in the process of an expanding autonomy.

Concomitant with the dramatic increase in railroad construction in the aftermath of the Civil War, corporations increasingly sought to enter into a variety of interstate business transactions. This demand for greater autonomy was partly satisfied in the late nineteenth century when the Supreme Court outfitted the corporation with new constitutional rights and broke down barriers in interstate commerce, both of which encouraged the spread of enterprise and accelerated competition among states for corporate patronage. Moreover, as centralized control supplanted stockholder democracy in larger corporations, hierarchy became the organizational paradigm of corporate power, just as autonomy became synonymous with centralized control. Increasingly, the internal and external dimensions became distinct spheres of power governed by the same executives or managers under a principle of limited oligarchy.

Yet in the latter decades of the nineteenth century, a condition of dependence still persisted through constraints imposed on corporate growth, collusive behavior, and internal operations, by now most apparent in statutes limiting capitalization, assets, and debt and prohibiting merger acquisitions and pooling agreements. At this point, the law of corporations once again became a fetter to the growth of corporate power in the marketplace, and the rulers of industry and finance increasingly operated on the fringe of the law or invented their own law. Through pools, trusts, and holding companies, capitalists of every size and stripe—in industry, railways, trade, and finance—initiated a restructuring of the economy that transcended the jurisdiction of individual states. With these developments, the stage was set, by the late 1880s, for another dramatic event in the progression of corporate autonomy—the abdication of traditional regulatory responsibilities by the states themselves.

The revolution in incorporation law certainly aided, if it did not spark, the merger movement of 1898–1904, which in turn thoroughly transformed the marketplace, largely shifting regulatory responsibility over corporate economic activity from the states to the federal government. Thereafter, judicial interpretation of corporation law redefined the legal relationships between stockholders and management to suit the organizational structure and power of the large corporation in a reconstructed economy.[136] Court decisions accelerated the trend toward centralized control within the corporation and hastened the day when its internal government would rival that of its creator. Thus, as the judiciary secured the autonomy of corporate management to govern its internal affairs, the private law of the corporation lost its public function, and the regulation of the external dimension of corporate power became the province of both corporate management and public law.

In adopting the rule of reason in 1911, the Supreme Court implemented a uniform regulation of the oligopolistic marketplace under the auspices of the federal government and the large corporation, thereby superseding the division of federal and state regulatory responsibilities established under Chief Justices Waite and Fuller. By the close of the Progressive Era, in 1916, statutory and judgemade law had effected a restructuring of the internal and external dimensions of corporate power in a manner that was consistent both with the enhanced autonomy of the modern large corporation and with public demands for regulation of corporate power.

a. The Birth of the Corporate Citizen

With the decline of the contract clause and the rise of substantive due process in the latter nineteenth century, corporate individualism acquired an ideological significance within the law. As a juridical person afforded the protections of the Fourteenth Amendment, the corporation achieved a new measure of autonomy and security consistent with the rights embodied in the doctrine of liberty of contract. By making the right to enter into a contract (that is, to pursue one's calling free from government interference), a form of property itself, the Supreme Court incorporated into the Constitution the idea that property includes intangible capacities and opportunities. Translated into the real world, this individualistic doctrine justified and secured the extraordinary accumulation of wealth, including invisible assets, that was the economic basis of corporate power. Accordingly, liberty of contract, by allowing for a redefinition of rights of property, aided the transition from a competitive economy to a corporate-capitalist economy.[137]

At the same time, however, in the name of individual liberty, the due process clause could be invoked by the Court to strike down legislation that established a minimum wage or maximum hours[138] or that gave workers the right to join unions,[139] under the rationale that such regulations deprived both the employer and the employee of their natural liberty to contract freely. In this judicial abstraction, the individual worker and the employer (proprietor or corporation) bargained on equal terms in the marketplace, each retaining the right to buy or to sell services free from government regulation. The merits of the Court's holdings aside, such reasoning stirred controversy and revealed the fragility of an older dogma when confronted with real-life inequalities. Corporate consolidations and oligopolistic markets had utterly transformed the competitive marketplace and the conditions of labor. To many Americans during the Progressive Era, nineteenth-century corporate individualism (embodied in the natural-rights doctrine of liberty of contract), seemed out of touch with reality, if not pernicious. In the world created by Gould, Rockefeller, Carnegie, and Morgan, the corporation had out-grown its laissez-faire garb. Transformed from a legal protection of vested rights and the exclusive franchise into an ideological justification of the competitive marketplace, corporate individualism would undergo still another transfiguration in the era of the large corporation.

As liberty of contract gradually lost its ideological sway, the Supreme Court created doctrine in antitrust law consistent with an emergent corporate liberalism. Legal reasoning in the law of antitrust recognized not only that corporate power posed dangers to individual liberty and equality of opportunity, but also that it produced social and technological benefits when regulated in the public interest. With the adoption of the rule of reason, antitrust law embodied the belief that the rules of the oligopolistic marketplace must be consistent with the principle of fair competition. Thereafter, Supreme Court decisions articulated a moral standard, a business ethic of fairness, that sought to preserve the faith in the natural laws of capitalism precisely by acknowledging the failure of the market to regulate itself and the need for government regulation. Moreover, the principle of fair competition implied that the corporate individual had a moral obligation to obey the law. Through these moral and legal aspects of fair competition, private enterprise ideology gradually merged with the idea of social responsibility. As corporate autonomy subject to government regulation in the external dimension became associated with a legal and moral standard of conduct, the idea of corporate social responsibility gave substance to the ideological concept of the corporate citizen. Having achieved realization at law and in the market, the corporate individual evolved from nineteenth-century laissez-faire entrepreneur to twentieth-century regulated citizen and business statesman.[140]

Corporate individualism could be invoked to justify the rise of corporate enterprise in a competitive economy. But, standing alone, it could not legitimize the power of the modern corporation. For this, another ideological construct was created—the doctrine of corporate social responsibility and its legal corollary, the public accountability of corporate power through law. Antitrust law therefore succeeded precisely where liberty of contract failed. But the ideological doctrine of corporate individualism survived, and indeed prospered, under the new ethic that justified corporate power. That this development still does not seem strange to most Americans testifies to its homespun qualities. An ingrained disposition to view all manner of business as private, an ardent individualism coupled with an enduring belief in the existence of equality of opportunity, and the tendency to accept modern corporate concentration as a necessary trade-off for its utility and productivity, all contribute to the process by which individuals may come to embrace as their own the legal theory that defines corporate power as legitimate, provided it is checked by public regulation and law. When one adds to this confluence of ideas the doctrine of corporate individualism, the improper exercise of corporate power may be explained as a discrete act, a violation of law by one or more autonomous individuals in the marketplace.

In the late nineteenth and early twentieth centuries, the restructuring of relationships of control through the law—in constitutional law, the law of corporations, and antitrust law—adapted and preserved the American liberal tradition of constitutionalism and its guiding principle of the separation of state and society. Moreover, with the decision to employ the rule of reason in antitrust law, the Supreme Court initiated the effort to accommodate the tenets of laissez-faire liberalism to the realities of corporate power within an administered market system. This stands as the most important contribution of the judiciary to the early development of corporate liberalism.

Ideological conceptions interwoven with legal doctrine constitute important aspects of the adaptation of liberalism to the corporate order, but they do not comprise the whole. In justifying power relationships, the law does not—indeed cannot—provide a systematic and comprehensive defense. This task necessarily falls to political thinkers, philosophers, and ideologists.

Chapter 3

THE RECONSTRUCTION OF AMERICAN LIBERALISM

The popular mind is agitated with problems that may disturb social order, and among them all none is more threatening than the inequality of condition, of wealth, and opportunity that has grown within a single generation out of the concentration of capital into vast combinations to control production and trade and to break down competition.

—Senator John Sherman, 1890

1. CORPORATE POWER AND THE PROGRESSIVE MOVEMENT

During the last quarter of the nineteenth century, laissez-faire liberalism in the United States both justified and promoted the tremendous proliferation of corporate enterprise. The rise of corporate power, however, ordained the demise of nineteenth-century individualism. Dedicated to economic concentration, corporate enterprise rapidly restructured the economic foundations of American capitalism, transforming social relationships and the conditions of political action. These were the halcyon days of wealthy entrepreneurs, the original captains of industry and finance, who built empires with their personal fortunes and projected their interests abroad.

Writing in 1902, in the midst of the first great merger wave, William

Graham Sumner proclaimed, "The concentration of wealth is but one feature of a grand step in societal evolution." In noting the implications of this development for the successful rise of the business corporation, Sumner emphasized the role of the corporate entrepreneurs in setting a new course of economic strategy and development:

> Some may admit that the concentration of wealth is indispensable, but may desire to distinguish between joint-stock aggregations on the one side and individual fortunes on the other. This distinction is a product of the current social prejudice and is not valid. The predominance of the individual and personal element in control is seen in the tendency of all joint-stock enterprises to come under the control of very few persons. Every age is befooled by the notions which are in fashion in it. Our age is befooled by "democracy"; we hear arguments about the industrial organization which are deductions from democratic dogmas or which appeal to prejudice by using analogies drawn from democracy to affect sentiment and industrial relations. Industry may be republican; it never can be democratic, so long as men differ in productive power and in industrial virtue. In our time joint-stock companies, which are in form republican, are drifting over into oligarchies or monarchies because one or a few get greater efficiency of control and greater vigor of administration. They direct the enterprise in a way which produces more, or more economically. This is the purpose for which the organization exists and success in it outweighs everything else.[1]

This tendency toward centralized control within the business corporation and other forms of enterprise, which coincided with an ever greater concentration of wealth in the hands of progressively fewer industrialists and financiers, initially had developed as a strategy of survival within the competitive marketplace and had in turn facilitated the accumulation of capital that served as a basis for the emergence of corporate capitalism in the first decade of the twentieth century. The "grand step in societal evolution" described by Sumner, however, was not accepted with equanimity by large segments of the American public. For two decades before the merger wave of 1898–1904, major social and political problems associated with the development of competitive industrial capitalism, including chronic social dislocations stemming from the competitive marketplace and its business cycle of expansion and depression, fueled the growth of a broad-based and heterogeneous movement of protest and reform. The radical and reformist elements of this social ferment included, among others, the Grange, the Greenbackers, the Knights of Labor, the Populist Party, militant craft and industrial unions, utopian societies, and socialist parties and organizations. Each of these groups, organizations, or movements must be understood on their own terms, in the light of economic and political events that shaped their growth and policies. In many respects, their different outlooks and goals may be more noteworthy than their similarities but there are important continuities that link them as expressions of protest or revolt against the economic disparities and social dislocations associated with the transition from competitive to corporate capitalism. In this sense, the farmer, the industrial worker, the craftsman and the proprietary capitalist could all find common ground, even though, in practice, their differing job-related needs, which were primarily influenced by the state of the economy, itself in flux, militated against the type of unity that many reformers aspired to.[2]

The state of social and economic upheaval, which preceded the corporate reconstruction of American capitalism, increasingly nurtured forces that opposed the emergent industrial order. In this fashion, the Granger revolts, antimonopoly agitation, labor wars, and the Populist uprising ushered in the groundswell of social dissent that would sustain the movement for reform in the Progressive Era. What may strike the modern reader as hyperbole in the service of a cause was to many Americans of the late nineteenth century a matter-of-fact description of the ruthlessness and rapaciousness of the captains of industry and finance, precursors of the rulers of the modern large corporation. The air was charged with dissent and apocalyptic forebodings. Some prophesied a final reckoning as the politics of class threatened to rip apart the consensual fabric of American society. As the frontier vanished, American radicals reconstructed their democratic heritage. In an effort to assail the ideological fortress of laissez-faire individualism, Populists invoked romantic images of Jefferson, Jackson, and Lincoln. Revolutionary socialists and anarchists prepared for the inevitable cataclysm. And utopian visionaries evoked the longing for simpler times.

The early decades of the twentieth century were the formative period of the corporate reconstruction of America, a period of social strife and change engendered by the dislocations of competitive industrial capitalism and the rise of corporate power. The major economic, social, and political issues of the period—the plight of the farmer, labor's struggle for recognition, the trust question, social inequality, political corruption, imperial expansion—all interwove with and to some degree stemmed from the dramatic development of corporate enterprise. As complex as the social forces that produced them, the ideological responses to the corporate reorganization of American society—populism, anarchism, feminism, socialism (Marxian, Fabian, Christian, and utopian)—each claimed devoted adherents. The proliferation of significant radical, populist, and progressive parties and organizations reflected both a growing class consciousness and a pervasive social discontent that frequently could not be accommodated by the policies of the Democratic and Republican parties.

Stimulated by this volatile political environment, a movement for liberal reform—typified by the coalition of leaders representing industry, finance, labor, politics, farming organizations, small business, and the professions, who formed the National Civic Federation in 1900—developed out of the perceived necessity to offer an alternative to the divisive politics of class confrontation. In broad agreement on the general principle that corporate power must be regulated in the public interest, this pro-corporate movement, in accordance with its cross-class composition, sought to frame realistic solutions that could accommodate a range of social interests. In this sense, it made a virtue of being nondoctrinaire—which is to say, it strived for compromise and amelioration rather than confrontation and conflict. To accomplish this, the ideological rigidities of the past would have to be jettisoned, and the views of the left and the right, of the captain of industry and the worker, of the money lords and the small producer, would have to seek common ground—a synthesis forged within the tenets of liberal-capitalist ideology and reflective of the class structure of the corporate order.

The agenda of this Progressive Movement, formulated by its leading intellectuals, required a fundamental revision of the goals and promises of American liberalism. In adapting the individualistic beliefs and doctrines of an earlier era to changing economic, social, and political conditions, the exponents of an emergent corporate liberalism anticipated the legitimation of corporate power, and hence the transformation of the large corporation into a socially responsible institution.[3]

Clearly, for those who sought to analyze critically these rapidly changing and often chaotic times, the issue of corporate power could not be avoided. In their efforts to understand the social reality of their day, Herbert Croly, Walter Weyl, and Thorstein Veblen developed through their writings a set of common observations. They agreed that the rulers of the large industrial and financial corporations, especially trusts and holding companies, were the most powerful group or class within American society. They also maintained that corporate power stemmed from economic dominance, that it exhibited a high degree of concentration that encouraged but did not necessarily produce collusion, that it entailed excessive influence if not actual control over government institutions, and that it enjoyed the support of a widespread ideological consensus. Furthermore, each of these thinkers argued that corporate hegemony constituted the central problem of modern society. That the era of small-scale competitive capitalism had been irradicably transformed was therefore apparent to each of them. Nor did they lament this fact. Rather, each maintained that economic concentration, though at present socially destructive, contained the potential for unparalleled economic efficiency. Yet, in coming to this conclusion, they insisted that substantial progress toward a more humane and efficient social order would not be achieved until the conventional mode of thinking about politics and society had changed. If the public's political beliefs, ideals, and expectations were to be brought in line with the socio-economic reality of the corporate order, the premises of the liberal faith, as embodied in the individualistic creed of laissez-faire, would have to be questioned and substantially revised.

The reconstruction of American liberalism, therefore, grew out of the attempt to devise solutions to the social and political problems posed by the power of the large corporation, including the restructuring of economic and social relationships. Among the most articulate exponents of this ideological revisionism in the Progressive Era were the liberal critics of corporate power. My designation of Croly, Weyl, and Veblen as liberal thinkers, although subject to qualification in the case of Veblen, refers to the fact that they shared a common ideological tradition and to their role as critics or revisionists within that tradition.[4] While Croly and Weyl, who together with Walter Lippmann founded the progressive journal *The New Republic* and along with Lippmann assumed the role of intellectual leaders of liberal reform, believed that reformist measures offered the only solution, Veblen was less sanguine about such prospects. In this and other respects, Veblen sharply distinguished himself from the new school of liberal thinkers. At one point he supported revolution, but was ultimately skeptical about its eventuality. Although more critical and iconoclastic than Croly or Weyl, Veblen's thought has much that warrants including him in the early group of liberal critics of corporate power. If nothing else, his preoccupation with efficiency and his anticipation of managerial thinking place him in the mainstream of modern liberal revisionism. In any event, Veblen would appear to defy ideological labeling. What remains important is that each of these thinkers has made a distinctive contribution to the political study of the corporation and to the reformulation of liberal ideology. Their impact on subsequent thinking and events must be judged in this light.

I shall make the case that the revision of American liberalism in the early twentieth century constituted both a criticism of and an accommodation to the new corporate order. Sweeping proposals for institutional reform were sustained by the belief that corporate power could be regulated in the interests of all social classes. Corporate liberalism, as articulated in liberal political thought in the Progressive Era, therefore emerged as a justification for a socially responsible corporate order. As such, it offered an alternative to the competing doctrines of laissez-faire liberalism and statist socialism. In many respects, the new liberalism developed out of a criticism and revision of the laissez-faire ethos in light of the socialist challenge and the democratic legacy of populism, including the anti-monopoly tradition and its concern with equality of opportunity in the marketplace of corporate capitalism. By adapting the individualistic prem-ise of classical liberalism to an increasingly specialized and interdepen-dent society and to a highly socialized mode of production, corporate liberalism provided a liberal defense for the corporate reconstruction of American society. But it accomplished this only by incorporating (albeit in a manner consistent with the class structure of corporate capitalism) ele-ments of socialist and democratic thinking that exposed the inequities of capitalist property relations and thereby compelled the recognition of the need for a comprehensive social solution.

In synthesizing beliefs that were both critical of and accommodating to corporate power, corporate liberals sought to overcome the conflict within liberalism between liberty and equality in order to justify compre-hensive reform. With the large corporation ascendant, no less of an ideological revision would suffice.

2. HERBERT CROLY: THE LIBERAL FAITH AND THE CORPORATE RECONSTRUCTION OF AMERICA

In his major work, *The Promise of American Life*, published in 1909, Her-bert Croly expounded the thesis that changes in the American economy from the close of the Civil War to the turn of the century had not only given rise to an extreme concentration of industrial and financial wealth, but also had dramatically transformed social and political relationships.[5] While the new form of industrial organization—the large corporation—held out the promise of unprecedented efficiency and serviceability, the social and political effects of the growth of corporate capitalism had been largely destructive. Widespread political corruption and glaring social inequalities constituted the most apparent ills fomented by the corporate takeover; yet, in Croly's estimation, these were symptomatic of a more fundamental malady seizing the body politic—the disintegration of society itself. The "social problem," as Croly conceived it, was how to prevent such a dissolution, stem the tide of class warfare, and restore social stability as well as a sense of national purpose and unity.

The task of social reconstruction, according to Croly, must also entail "a partial revision of some of the most important articles in the traditional American creed."[6] If the historic promise of American life—that is, increasing material prosperity, equality of opportunity, individual liberty, and free political institutions—were to be fulfilled, then the "optimistic fatalism" of past generations would have to be abandoned. Croly granted that under earlier economic and social conditions such an optimism may have been warranted, but the fact remained that the unbridled individualism sanctioned by the traditional faith had justified and encouraged the abuses of the present. In short, the American liberal tradition had produced its own contradiction in the form of an extreme concentration of wealth and its iniquitous social consequences. Because the fulfillment of the American promise could no longer be taken for granted, because the fatalism of the past no longer sufficed, Croly insisted that the traditional beliefs and goals of American democracy must be reformulated in light of a conscious social ideal.

To fully understand the ideological significance of this ideal and the reforms it entailed, however, we must first examine the author's conception of corporate power. Croly identified the emergence of corporate power as one aspect of the transformation of society and politics in the second half of the nineteenth century. During this period, the dramatic growth and increasing complexity of American society, which coincided with the development of a national economy, gave rise to specialization in the professions, business, and politics. The appearance of a new group of "unofficial leaders"—the business specialist, the political specialist or boss, the corporation lawyer, and the labor leader—must be viewed, according to the author, as a response to the need for specialized and efficient organization and methods in practical affairs.[7] Though he linked the general transformation of society to common causes, Croly argued that the development of each sphere must be understood on its own terms. In the case of the business specialist—the captains of industry and finance—specialization developed in an effort to establish a competitive advantage. The battle for profits not only fueled technological advancements and hence economic growth, but it also encouraged capitalists to seek out special privileges in order to control their markets. Whether through alliances with political bosses or arrangements with other corporate leaders, the business specialists eventually cemented their dominance over the American economy.[8]

Corporate power, in Croly's view, therefore developed out of the transformation from a competitive economy to an essentially noncompetitive
economy. Extreme concentration of industrial and financial wealth, centralized control of production and markets, and the often collusive organization of corporate business were the basis of this power. In many if
not most cases, the corporate oligarchs and their families were the principal owners of the enterprise. Even though the wielders of this power
constituted a discernible group or class, Croly preferred to conceptualize
their dominance as grounded in control of economic resources and institutions. Corporate or economic power can therefore be distinguished
from political or governmental power, which inhered in the control of
political resources and institutions.

As the corporate economy grew, Croly explained, these two forms of
power had become interrelated. Coincident with the emergence of the
business specialist and the political specialist, which were "the parallel
effects of the same conditions and ideas working in different fields," an
alliance between these "two independent and coordinate powers" was
formed.[9] Albeit mutually beneficial to the parties involved, this alliance
had led to inordinate corporate influence or control over state and local
politics. For the most part, the various political machines had been no
match for their allies in business whose superior organization provided
them with the capacity for concerted (though not necessarily conspiratorial) action.[10] In essence, the decentralized system of American government, dominated by party bosses and their machines, had been substantially taken over by a highly centralized and nationally organized group
of business specialists: the rulers of the large corporations. Corporate
political power or influence therefore constituted nothing less than a
perversion of the American democratic tradition.

On the basis of this analysis, Croly developed a general strategy for
social reconstruction. To regulate or control corporate power, he reasoned, government must be reformed. The abuses of corporate political
power could be abolished only when control of government had been
returned to the people and their elected representatives. To be effective,
however, the organization of political power, like its corporate counterpart, must achieve a considerable degree of centralization. Through the
same process of political reform, the excesses of corporate economic
power might also be curbed.

To summarize, the problem of corporate power, as Croly conceived it,
can be stated thus: How can the beneficial economic consequences of
corporate capitalism—namely, greater efficiency and centralization of
decision-making—be retained, and its detrimental social and political

consequences be eliminated? In other words, how can corporate power be directed to socially useful ends without fundamentally altering the basis of that power? Croly's solution contained two interrelated aspects: ideological revisionism which entailed a reformulation of the democratic ideal, and a plan for reform of political and economic institutions. While his analysis of corporate power dictated the direction of institutional reform, Croly's critique of American liberalism provided the justification and normative standards for its practical application. To adequately assess his proposals for reform, we must therefore first reconstruct his ideological argument.

Croly identified two major traditions within democratic theory and practice: the Republican or Jeffersonian, and the Federalist or Hamiltonian. By themselves, he argued, the guiding principles of these two traditions were inadequate, and a combination of them had never been realized in American politics. While both schools of thought were concerned with securing and establishing individual rights, especially those of an economic nature, they differed fundamentally on the political means for realizing this end. Hamilton had become the spokesman for the upper class and the nationalist principle of centralized control, whereas Jefferson had advanced the cause of democratic decentralization and the plight of the average person. In the early years of the Republic, Hamilton, whose antidemocratic pretensions prevailed in the Constitution, won an early victory. But the creed of Jefferson, the democratic ideal, would have the greatest impact on the American experience.[11]

The flaw of the Jeffersonian tradition, Croly maintained, inhered in the wedding of an extreme individualism with a naive faith in the goodness of human nature. Jefferson's attempt to gain essentially egalitarian results through individualist means was internally contradictory because it "implied a complete harmony both in logic and in effect between the idea of equality and the idea of liberty." Whereas the principle of equal rights required "an equal start in the race, while at the same time expecting an equal finish," it could not reconcile "the fact that under a legal system which holds private property sacred there may be equal rights, but there cannot possibly be any equal opportunities for exercising such rights."[12] Thus, in practice, the "optimistic fatalism" of the Jeffersonian tradition had encouraged a policy of national irresponsibility while sanctioning the excesses of economic individualism. Hamilton's legacy, on the other hand, though marred by its antidemocratic bias, was "one of energetic and intelligent assertion of the national good."[13] Constructive social reform, in the author's view, required that a synthesis of these two traditions be effected. As we shall see, Croly envisioned his ideological justification for reform—that is, his reformulation of the democratic ideal—to be a combination of a class-neutral Hamiltonian nationalism and a socially conscious Jeffersonian individualism.[14]

In its broadest reaches, Croly's democratic ideal would revise the classical liberal conception of the individual's relationship to the state. This would entail, first, a rejection of the liberal view of government as inimical to individual freedom, and the corresponding recognition and acceptance of the state's positive social function; and, second, a revision of the classical doctrine of economic individualism. Thus, while Croly's revisionism would appear to represent a significant departure from traditional American beliefs, it nevertheless aimed to restore the historical promise of American life.

The democratic ideal—or "national democracy," as Croly sometimes called it—contained three major components: the national principle, the national purpose, and the national democratic faith. He defined the national principle, or standard by which a democracy should be governed, as social balance—the amelioration of social conflict through national government policy.[15] Underlying and guiding the practical application of the idea of social balance, however, was the norm of efficiency.[16] Indeed, in the author's view, the task of establishing an efficient social balance no longer could be left to the mechanism of the marketplace. Henceforth, he argued, the state must actively assume the responsibility of creating and maintaining such a balance.

Croly defined the national democratic purpose as the attainment of "a higher type of individual and associated life." This purpose, moreover, presupposed a revision of the traditional notion of sovereignty: the people would "become Sovereign only insofar as they succeed[ed] in reaching and expressing a collective purpose." It could be argued, then, that the phrase "popular sovereignty" was equivalent to the phrase "national Sovereignty." The state thus would become the embodiment of the sovereign will. Yet a "morally authoritative Sovereign will" could not be easily attained. It could be achieved only when the people of a democracy were "united in spirit and purpose," and this could occur only when democratic and nationalist objectives were merged.[17] To effect this merger, the national purpose would require a national democratic faith.

Effective national organization and the preservation of civil and political rights could therefore not by themselves constitute sufficient conditions for attainment of the national purpose. National democratic development would require a faith in the national purpose, and consequently a staunch loyalty to the nation. Furthermore, it would necessitate faith not only in the policies of the state at a given time, but also in an ideal of progress towards "human brotherhood."[18] The practical means for realizing this ideal, however, would at all times have to remain flexible and experimental: pragmatism rather than absolutism would inspire the democratic faith.[19]

The popular realization of this secular faith, like the attainment of religious faith, would require an institution that could articulate and embody its precepts. This responsibility, according to Croly, must be assumed by the modern state, which alone could provide the type of association and community that were formally the province of religious associations. The state would become the secular church, and like the church, one of its primary objectives would be the education of the faithful: it would teach citizens "how they must feel, what they must think, and what they must do, in order that they may live together amicably and profitably." This "collective education" could be acquired only through a deeper understanding of the democratic ideal and by practical experience nurtured by "experimental collective action aimed at the realization of the collective purpose."[20] Ultimately, the success of such an education must be judged by its ability to instill a social conscience, an ethic of "collective responsibility," and a national spirit and unity in the pursuit of an ideal.

Croly's reformulation of the democratic ideal also entailed a critique and revision of the concept of individualism in the American liberal tradition. America's brand of economic individualism, he explained, had imposed severe limitations on the national character. It had exalted the pursuit of pecuniary gain into a social ethic that not only justified extensive inequalities but also demanded conformity rather than encouraging true diversity of personal expression.[21] It had become a hollow ethic that lacked a disinterested purpose or goal, and therefore the means for melding private interest with the common good. The democratic ideal, on the other hand, made possible true individual freedom and fulfillment by encouraging and recognizing individual excellence in all realms of human endeavor, and by judging individual work not by the conventional standard of pecuniary success but by the technical and artistic standards of proficiency. Thus Croly observed that "a condition favorable to genuine individuality would be one in which men are divided from one another by special purpose, and reunited in so far as these individual purposes were excellently and successfully achieved."[22] To be socially constructive, however, individual excellence must also be wedded to a broader social ideal. Individual distinction must be rewarded for its own sake and for its contribution to the public good. In this way, the interests of individual and society would be consciously tied to the pursuit of the democratic ideal.

To fully understand the practical implications of Croly's revision of

American liberalism, his program for social reform must be assessed in light of the precepts of the democratic ideal. For the purposes of this analysis, I shall be concerned primarily with the two major categories on the author's agenda for social change—political reform and economic reform—each of which was devised in accordance with the national principle of social balance and its underlying standard of efficiency.

Croly's proposals for reform of both state and federal political institutions aimed to bring about greater centralization of power and responsibility and thereby effect a more efficient administration of political affairs. In an effort to wipe out political corruption at the state and local levels, and, as a result, to destroy the alliance between the political machines and the large corporations, Croly would increase the power of the executive and severely cut that of the legislative branch. Wherever possible, he would centralize power in one office, which would in theory be directly responsible to the people.[23] Although presently corrupt, the organization created by the political boss nevertheless represented a more specialized and efficient form of administration.[24] Accordingly, a substantial part of the task of state and local political reform would involve the replacement of the machine boss by an elected boss.[25]

Even though Croly supported the extension of the franchise, his proposals were not intended to encourage or increase popular political activity, as evidenced by his plan to mediate the referendum and initiative by special commissions, his opposition to direct primaries, and his desire to limit the number of elections.[26] Rather, his reforms consistently sought to establish stronger and more efficient political leadership. State governments, Croly explained, were "not competent to deal effectively in the national interest and spirit with the grave problems created by the aggrandizement of corporate and individual wealth and the increasing classification of the American people." For this reason, the federal government must assume the burden of acting in the public interest as defined by the democratic ideal.[27] Indeed, the national government must function as the executor and mediator of the social balance. But in order to perform this duty, its powers must be centralized within the executive branch. Otherwise, government would remain impotent to meet the challenge of corporate power. Croly's scheme for national political reform, therefore, was largely a means for effecting economic reform.

Croly's major economic proposals, which concerned the regulation of corporate enterprise and the organization of labor, also embodied the imperatives of an efficient social balance.[28] Any effort to regulate the large corporation, he argued, would require that it be given legal standing.[29] Legal recognition, moreover, would amount to a discrimination in favor of the corporation because it entailed acceptance, and therefore legitimation, of the existing structure and size of corporate enterprise. In other words, regulation should not be confused with reconstitution. In fact, the contrary would be true since "the recognition of the large corporation is equivalent to the perpetuation of its existing advantages." Regulation would therefore offer a means of stimulating and perpetuating the tremendous efficiency of modern corporate enterprise that had largely resulted from the substitution of cooperative for competitive methods of economic activity.[30]

To transform or reorganize the structure of the corporate economy, therefore, would "constitute a step backward in the process of economic and social advance." Instead, this process of economic development "should be allowed to work itself out." This view of the economy implied not only that unsuccessful competitors "should be allowed to drown" but also that government regulation must not interfere with the management and efficient running of large corporations.[31] While the public's interest in economic efficiency necessitated that business activities be regulated, such regulation must not violate corporate autonomy: "The essential condition of efficiency is always concentration of responsibility."[32] When government meddled in the internal operations of corporations, decision-making became divided and efficiency suffered. By the same token, if the public interest should demand that a certain class of corporations be nationalized, then the concentration of responsibility must shift substantially from private to public hands.[33]

The increasing politicization of the labor movement and the accompanying growth of a class consciousness opposed to the existing social and political order, Croly warned, posed a grave threat to the ideals and objectives of American democracy.[34] Whatever the validity of labor's grievances, it had become clear that so long as organized labor remained outside the legal framework of society, class hatred and conflict would only increase. Unions, like large corporations, therefore required legal recognition and, as in the case of corporations, such recognition necessitated discrimination in their favor. Specifically, the law must favor union labor over nonunion labor. It could be justified, according to the author, because unions had demonstrated their effectiveness in bringing about "the economic and social amelioration of the laboring class." Besides legal recognition, labor should also be granted a minimum wage, a minimum day, and collective bargaining. These concessions, however, could be justified on grounds of efficiency as well as political expediency. An organized work force regulated by law would provide the necessary incentive for productivity and reduce the labor-management conflict that existed under nonunion conditions.[35]

In *Progressive Democracy*, Croly advanced this argument a step further and argued for the creation of "industrial democracy" within a system of "scientific management."[36] Industrial democracy would provide the worker an effective voice in matters concerning the workplace: "The wage-earner must have the same opportunity of being consulted about the nature and circumstances of his employment that the voter has about the organization and policy of the government."[37] If industrial democracy were to succeed, however, workers ultimately must transcend mere class consciousness and embrace the democratic ideal; they must make "a conscious attempt to convert internally remunerative work into a source of both individual and social fulfillment." As workers gained greater control and responsibility over their tasks, they would not only achieve a measure of independence and personal satisfaction, but also become aware of the interrelationship between their individual and cooperative efforts and the attainment of the social good.[38]

By contributing to a more efficient organization of labor and therefore to greater productivity, industrial democracy, according to Croly, would hold forth the promise of a steadily increasing standard of living for the wage earner. However, increased efficiency would depend upon "the more comprehensive and more successful application to industry of scientific research and of the results of essentially scientific research."[39] It followed that industrial democracy could achieve its purpose only with the aid of scientific management. In fact, the application of scientific techniques to the management of business paralleled the growth of administration by experts in the public sector. Both constituted a response to the burgeoning need for efficient management throughout society, and both remained essential for the realization of the democratic ideal. Furthermore, because scientific management required that workers "submit to an amount and a degree of regimentation not dissimilar to that required of an army," it could not function without the "self-governing workshop." But, the author cautioned, simply imposing such a discipline would violate the freedom of the workers. Consequently, they must be allowed to make their own choice: "The workers must have the sense that they are imposing the discipline on themselves for the good of the service."[40]

In Croly's analysis, scientific management and industrial democracy are linked by their common goals of efficiency and stability. The organization of labor, like the regulation of corporate enterprise and the reform of government institutions, must be guided by the national democratic principle of social balance. To be sure, Croly viewed his reforms in each of these areas to be interrelated: "An organic unity binds the three aspects of the system together." "A constructive tendency in one area," he observed, would "introduce constructive methods of organization into the other divisions of the economic, political, and social body."[41] Structured in accordance with the twin standards of efficiency and centralization of control, Croly's vision of the democratic state does indeed suggest an organic unity in its construction as well as in its purpose.

The author's analysis of corporate power, his theory of democracy, and his program for reform constitute a watershed in twentieth-century American political thought. Croly was the first American thinker in the era of corporate capitalism to put forth a systematic and comprehensive justification for corporate-liberal reform. His analysis, which rests on a distinction between realms of economic and political power, assumes that no necessary connection obtained between these two types of power. The increasing influence and, in some cases, dominance of corporate power in politics must therefore be explained as a consequence of institutional defects—namely, the social irresponsibility of corporations and the corruption of political life by machines. This aspect of Croly's argument is crucial, because it implied that political reform could solve the problem of corporate intrusion into politics, and also provide an institutional base for bending corporate power to socially useful ends. In essence, political reform would provide the lever for economic reform. Meaningful reform, as Croly conceived it, would have to accommodate the needs of large-scale enterprise for political stability, centralized control, and efficient management of resources and personnel. But it also would have to accommodate the needs of an expanding legion of organized workers and satisfy the claims of a progressive democratic movement. His political reforms therefore mirrored but also could reshape the structural economic changes fomented by the rise of corporate power.

In Croly's theory of democracy, efficiency—the underlying standard of the principle of social balance—constitutes the unifying norm of both the political realm and the economic realm. His conception of social balance represents a departure, in this regard, from the purely mechanical balance envisioned by the authors of the Constitution. For Croly, social balance did indeed entail an institutional separation of powers— but it also implied an organic unity, a conception of society as an interrelated and efficient whole. The idea of social integration or harmony served the purpose of defining institutional relationships as well as the relationship between individual and society. A conception of the individual within the social whole thereby supplanted the laissez-faire notion of individual and state as natural antagonists.[42]

Croly combined this harmonic conception of society with a hierarchical principle of organization. Within his scheme, the hierarchical structure of corporate power remained unchanged, just as his redefinition of democracy necessitated centralization of political power at all levels.

Moreover, his conceptions of industrial democracy and scientific management justified the integration of labor within the corporate power structure. Indeed, Croly's entire argument constituted an appeal to the "enlightened" political leaders and not to the average citizen: the nemesis of democracy, as he defined it, was decentralized control.[43] In a very fundamental sense, the author's conception of a national democracy in which citizens would be bound together through the democratic faith evokes a preliberal (Christian) corporate conception of society with a corresponding corporate ethic. Yet, within this social whole would exist a capitalist economy, liberal political and legal institutions, and protection for individual rights. Furthermore, the basis of Croly's secular religion, the democratic faith, is not absolutist in conception but pragmatic and evolutionary. To be sure, the democratic faith represents a revision of the traditional promise of American life. But the ideological message remains essentially the same. Depending on how one looks at it, Croly's political philosophy for the modern era may be viewed as a liberal justification of the corporate order or as an adaptation of classical liberalism to developments in the economy and politics—hierarchy, specialization of function, centralization of control—associated with the rise of the large corporation. In either case, his reforms clearly aspired to effect a consolidation of corporate power.

Croly's argument, however, should not be confused with the pro-corporate apologetics of his time. To the contrary, he exposed the central contradiction of American liberalism at the turn of the century—namely, the failure or inability of laissez-faire ideology to address the problem of corporate power realistically. He squarely posed the issue for national debate of how and in whose interest corporate power should be exercised. He asked, How can corporate power be made legitimate? His answer was clear and, in its fundamentals, uncompromising. To be legitimate, corporate power would have to conform to the basic tenets of the American liberal-democratic tradition and hence remain consistent with the American promise as revised and adapted to the corporate capitalist economy. Croly's scheme of reform, therefore, would ultimately depend on a significant change in the class content of political power as he conceived it. Leaders responsible to the electorate as a whole—to all classes and groups—would have to replace those beholden to the money lords and corporate chieftans. This revitalization of democratic control over political institutions would provide the lever for regulation of economic power in a manner consistent with the principles of efficiency and corporate autonomy. In short, he envisioned the melding of social democracy with an administered (nonstatist) market system.

Croly did not embrace violent revolution or state socialism as viable remedies for the social upheaval he chronicled. The course he charted, though strongly influenced by socialist thought, envisioned a liberal alternative, based on a separation of state and society, that would preserve the autonomy of corporate enterprise to ensure efficiency and profitability while allowing for national ownership of certain types of industry when justified by the public interest. Thus a mixed economy, though not a mixed enterprise, would remain consistent with the principle of social efficiency. The democratic ideal, which served to justify corporate power and at the same time to legitimate the corporation as a social institution, would also provide the moral standards by which American liberalism would be reconstructed. Croly's revisionism, moreover, clearly entailed a rejection of the socially destructive consequences of unbridled corporate power, just as his vision of the efficient and socially responsible corporation anticipated the consolidation of corporate rule in America. His theory of democratic reform, however, continues to provide critical standards by which we may assess the nature of this transformation.

Croly's analysis of corporate power and its regulation, his critique of economic individualism, his intense concern with social inequality, and his dream of "human brotherhood," establish him as a leading figure in an influential line of twentieth-century American liberal thinkers who have sought to advance the cause of democracy and to improve the human condition while retaining the economic and social benefits of large-scale enterprise in the era of corporate capitalism. Publicist, reformer, and, after his own fashion, political theorist, Croly offered a new (and enduring) vision of the American promise in the formative stages of the corporate reconstruction of American society.

3. WALTER WEYL: PLUTOCRATIC POWER AND THE POLITICS OF AFFLUENCE

Like Croly, Walter Weyl rose to prominence as a major advocate of liberal reform in the first decade of the twentieth century. A scholar and a journalist by profession, Weyl employed his research and literary skills during this period, most notably on behalf of the labor movement, to further the cause of progressive social change. With the publication of the *The New Democracy* in 1912, however, Weyl soon took his place alongside Croly as a leading theorist of the new liberalism.[44] Although strongly influenced by Croly's *Promise of American Life*, this work contains an analysis of corporate power that is more concrete and systematic than the former as well as a distinctive justification for political and economic reform. A pronounced democratic bent distinguishes Weyl's work from that of Croly in important ways, but both authors shared common assumptions and methods that aimed to revise and adapt American liberalism to a changing society.

Weyl, like Croly, attributed the growth of corporate power to the transformation of the American economy in the years following the Civil War.[45] This transformation, which was facilitated by the dominant individualistic ideology and its institutional corollary, the "weak state," led to the creation of trusts and monopolistic control of markets. As the individual pioneer gave way to the large corporation, so did westward expansion reach its dramatic climax with the closing of the frontier. In the course of this development, however, it was not the individual of American folklore who triumphed but a new class of corporate overlords, the plutocracy.

The costs exacted for this conquest were great, for the new oligarchy had ascended on a social foundation of extreme inequality and had secured its dominance through a corruption and perversion of the democratic process. But at the same time, the increased efficiency and productive potential of large-scale corporate enterprise heralded a new beginning. As the economic and social forces of corporate capitalism transfigured the physiognomy of American society, the imperfect features of a new democracy began to appear. In laying waste to the old structure, Weyl argued, the architects of the new order had prepared the way for a revolutionary social transformation. Out of the ruins of the early industrial society came the promise of a "socialized democracy," a reconstitution of economic and political institutions on democratic principles.

Control of the nation's wealth by the rulers of the large corporation constituted the basis of corporate or plutocratic power, according to Weyl. Factors contributing to corporate dominance included high market concentration with monopolistic or semimonopolistic conditions obtaining in most large industries, increasing integration of corporations through finance capital, and a highly centralized and systematic decision-making process.[46] Moreover, the increasing separation of ownership and control within the modern corporation had led to a "progressive amalgamation" of corporate capital and thus to a "narrow control of enlarging funds."[47] By this process, corporate power came to rest in the hands of a business oligarchy while the average investor remained powerless.

While it did not yet fully resemble a "class ruling by virtue of its wealth," and while its control over society at present remained "only partial, undefined, and unadmitted," the plutocracy nevertheless constituted the most powerful force in American society. Composed of "a more or less fluctuating group of very wealthy men," the plutocracy exerted "an enormous, if not preponderating, influence over industry, politics, and public opinion." Rooted in the control of industrial and financial wealth, plutocratic power had been erected on the institutional foundation of the large corporation and its most recent offspring, the trust. Indeed, Weyl argued that the financial lords, the trust builders, contributed most to the "plutocratic reorganization" of American society. In the process of designing and constructing the edifice of corporate power, the financial wizards transformed the very foundations of the economy. It was therefore possible "to speak of the plutocracy not only as a group of very wealthy men . . . but also as a system of industrial organization."[48]

Corporate or plutocratic power, as Weyl conceived it, was fundamentally economic in nature and could be distinguished for analytical purposes from the type of power whose exercise depended on the control of government organizations and institutions. The dominance of the plutocracy, he argued, stemmed in large part from its influence over politics and public opinion. In fact, without this political control and in the absence of a strong though often unwitting public support, the plutocracy would be merely an economic oligarchy and not the dominant social force that it had become. From Weyl's standpoint, a determination of the scope of corporate power therefore entailed an investigation into the nature and extent of its control and influence over politics and public opinion.

The structure of power in American politics, according to the author, had been built on the control of the political party by the professional politician, the party boss. Through the control of the electoral machinery and the political spoils, the bosses directed the "business" of politics. As normal business expanded in the second half of the nineteenth century, so did its political counterpart. Rather than giving rise to two autonomous centers of power, however, this parallel development resulted in their integration:

> As business became synthetic and integrated, as the railroads, coal mines, banks, trust companies, and insurance companies drew closer together, politics, which had grown from small to large, independent business, became in some parts of America, *a mere branch* in a still larger, integrated business. The state, which through the party formally sold favors to the large corporations,

became one of their departments. The biggest client bought out
the concern, as the railroad buys up the factory which once sold it
supplies.[49]

Thus an already corrupt political system was appropriated by its "biggest client." The political party remained in control of the state, and the
boss reigned over the party. The only difference was that now the trust
controlled the boss.

In order to adequately gauge the extent of the plutocratic takeover of
politics, Weyl argued, one must understand how the methods and organizational skills of corporate business had been applied to the field of
politics. Corruption of political parties, legislators, administrators, and
judges had become so widespread that it was "difficult to avoid exaggera-
tion both as to its volume and significance." "The organizing skill of the
business magnate in systematizing political corruption," he explained,
"has changed it from a local though chronic phenomenon to one which
is organic and nation-wide." From the municipality to the state to the
national government, the plutocracy had constructed an elaborate system of influence-peddling through its control of the political party. In the
beginning, there was no plan, no "thought-out, class-conscious campaign of a cohesive plutocratic group."[50] It developed piecemeal, on an
individual level, with each business purchasing the political favors it
needed. But economic conditions had drastically altered this primitive
method of political commerce:

> These individual spheres of political influence are now beginning
> to coalesce, just as big businesses themselves are coalescing.
> There is in process a political integration, similar to our industrial
> integration, and due to precisely the same causes. Corporations,
> financially interlinked, are brought together automatically on the
> political field. . . . There is a political as well as an industrial,
> "community of interest."[51]

Weyl likened this political integration to a financial merger in which
"political holdings" were consolidated "first for a single political 'operation,' and later for a whole political policy." Eventually, there emerged "a
secret, interstate, bi-partisan political machine." Party lines became
blurred as Republicans and Democrats fell under the sway of the
wealthy plutocracy. Ideological differences gave way to a higher loyalty,
and "a political trust came into being." Based on "the elimination of
surplus political machinery, the standardization of corruption, and the
organization of all legislative bodies on the approved model of the

dummy board of directors," the political trust ascended pyramid-like from the local to the national level. Although the "national boss, seated perhaps in the speaker's chair or in the Senate of the United States," as of the present was "non-existent," Weyl implied that this position would soon be filled.[52]

Money constituted "the mortar of this edifice," but the political trust, Weyl emphasized, could not be sustained by greed alone. It thrived in part because it was nurtured by the orthodox American ideology— "ancient political ideas which still cumber our modern brains."[53] Indeed, vast numbers of Americans opposed the plutocracy and the tremendous power it wielded, yet at the same time they remained loyal to the ideas that gave it life. These ideas were embodied in the Constitution and were interpreted by perhaps the most revered of American political institutions, the Supreme Court. Unlike other political institutions, the plutocracy did not own the Court. But the Court did not have to be purchased, presuming that it could be, because it already served plutocratic interests. The Constitution, Weyl noted, "was especially designed for a class which bore a similar relation to the America of 1787 that the plutocracy bears to the America of 1911."[54] It was designed to protect the interests of the propertied class, and the Court's interpretation of America's founding document had remained consistent with that objective. Judicially imposed limitations on state and national efforts for reform, the difficulty of the amending process, and perhaps most important, the Court's steadfast protection of property rights had made the Constitution "an obstacle to a true democracy, and a strong bulwark of the plutocracy." Through the power of judicial review, "the widest possible powers had been given to a growing and entrenched plutocracy," and, as a consequence, the large corporation had been afforded "an almost impregnable constitutional position."[55]

Despite its unabated growth, corporate power, Weyl maintained, did not stand unopposed. As the political trust became visible to the public, "the countervailing and curative forces of democracy [would] multiply astoundingly." Once exposed, the plutocracy would be forced to justify its actions in light of the values of democracy, to appeal to the moral authority of the sovereign people, and to enter the public debate and become engaged in "the struggle for public opinion." If the plutocracy were to thrive, it would have to join the struggle and shape the national mind, for an adverse public opinion posed the gravest threat to its hegemony. The plutocracy's means for waging this war, however, were considerable. Where it did not control the press outright, it exerted tremendous influence through its huge advertising revenue. "Year by year," Weyl observed, "the subservience of the editorial to the business policy of the newspaper becomes more apparent." Plutocratic influence over the press had grown along with the circulation and budgets of newspapers, magazines, and journals. In journalism, as in politics, the need for great sums of money opened the door to corruption. It also encouraged acquisitions: "The trend of plutocratic domination of the press has been from influence to control and from control to ownership." Just as the political system was bought out by its biggest client, it seems that the news business was being appropriated by its chief sponsor.[56]

While there could be no doubt that the plutocracy had gained the upper hand in the struggle for public opinion, Weyl insisted that its victory was by no means assured. For one thing, the plutocracy had to contend with an increasingly enlightened public, especially as its deeds were exposed and became a subject of popular debate. Eventually it would have to take the stand and answer to the public tribunal. When this occurred, the plutocracy would have to plead its case openly, on the facts, and allow the American people to be the judge.

Weyl argued that one would find the political solution to the problem of corporate power in the social conditions that it had engendered. In spite of the havoc they had wreaked in their pursuit of personal gain, the corporate oligarchs, albeit unintentionally, had created conditions that required a new conception of progress and efficiency, conditions that were inconsistent with the narrow individualism of a younger America. "The more rapidly our plutocracy, acting under the stimulus of profits, introduces the cooperative element into our businesses," Weyl observed, "the sooner will the democracy be able to adapt this cooperative element to the socialization of industry." The old theory of democracy based on an individualistic conception of wealth must make way for a new democracy that "does not believe that a nation is rich because the majority owes the minority money and labor."[57] The new democracy, like the old, would stand for prosperity and for the efficient utilization of natural resources, but it would impart a new meaning to the concept of utility:

> The democracy interprets utilization as such a production, distribution, and consumption of wealth as will give the highest excess of economic pleasure over economic pain to the largest number of people for the longest time. Upon this end all the industrial, political, social, and ethical ideals of the democracy converge.[58]

Before exploring the practical implications of Weyl's utilitarian premises, however, let us examine the ideological justification for the new democracy.

Weyl's theory of democracy constituted both a justification for a program of political, social, and industrial reform and an effort to make sense of the complex social forces of his time. In other words, he understood his conception of a "socialized democracy" to be a set of principles and practical objectives which were based on a more or less accurate reconstruction of the "spirit" of a broad-based anticorporate movement. We have seen that the ideals of Weyl's new democracy rest on a social-utilitarian foundation. But what are these ideals? "The inner soul of our new democracy," Weyl explained, "is not the unalienable rights negatively and individualistically interpreted, but those same rights, 'life, liberty, and the pursuit of happiness,' extended and given a social interpretation." A social interpretation of individual rights, moreover, "conceives of society as a whole and not as a more or less adventitious assemblage of myriads of individuals."[59] It is on this point that Weyl's ideological revisionism hinges, for once society is viewed as an interdependent whole or collectivity, the extreme individualism of classical liberalism is no longer tenable. Premised on an associational conception of society, the ideals or objectives of the socialized democracy necessarily would be social ideals, expressions of the collective good—that is, the greatest good for the greatest number.

Weyl described these ideals in terms of three interrelated "levels of democratic striving"—the economic, the political, and the moral or intellectual—which corresponded, respectively, to three programs of social reform: the socialization of industry, the democratization of government, and the civilization of the citizen.[60] The ideals of the socialized democracy, the levels of democratic striving, could not be achieved apart from one another, according to the author, for they were the interdependent objectives of a social revolution in progress. It was a revolution, "gradual, peaceful, and evolutionary," that would "effect a radical displacement of the center of gravity of society," a revolution that would substitute "a new for an old social equilibrium."[61]

Rejecting the Marxist conception of proletarian revolution as untenable from both an economic and a political standpoint, Weyl maintained that a democratic social revolution must be based on the theory of democratic change through "national adjustment" and of "progress through prosperity."[62] "The increasing wealth of America, not the growing poverty of any class," he argued, would provide the foundation for a true democracy. Specifically, it was "the social surplus, our clear gain in wealth after the year's business is over," that would constitute the material basis of a socialized democracy.[63]

A product of the tremendous growth of corporate enterprise, the social surplus, which represented social and not individual wealth, made the transition from a pain economy to a pleasure economy possible.[64] The ideals of the new democracy were therefore dependent on the social surplus:

> It is the social surplus which permits the economic advance of the people, which in turn facilitates their intellectual enfranchisement, which in turn tends strongly in the direction of political representation.[65]

Weyl reasoned that poverty and ignorance were the nemesis of democracy. The poor and illiterate were desperate and therefore easily misled. They evolved "religious, not political policies." They dreamed of "kingdoms in heaven, not materialized cooperative commonwealths." For this reason, they may be converted into "engines of tyranny and revolution." "A really effective discontent," he concluded, "accompanies a larger income, a greater leisure, a fuller education, and a vision of better things."[66] Democracy therefore would depend on the social surplus and the economic and educational advances it would make possible.

Increasing social wealth, however, constituted a necessary but not a sufficient condition for realizing a socialized democracy. Democratic change could be effected only by "the democratic masses, the impelling force of democracy."[67] The democratic mass, according to the author, consisted of a "residue of the population, after a majority of the very rich and of the abjectly poor have been drawn off."[68] Though somewhat disjointed in action and heterogeneous in composition, the social groups that composed the democratic mass were increasingly united by a common aim as consumers to attain a "share in the conquered continent, in the material and moral accumulations of a century."[69] Because of its size, composition, and commitment to gradual, peaceful change, the democratic mass must achieve its ideals slowly through piecemeal reforms rather than violent confrontation. Like Croly, Weyl envisioned a pragmatic resolution of the nation's ills. Furthermore, being composed of property owners, the democracy would not advocate confiscation of property in general, but would only attack monopoly and special privilege. In its quest to control the social surplus, it would distinguish "between property and privilege, between earned, and unearned, increment; between legitimate investment and promoters' profits."[70]

Weyl delineated the practical objectives of his conception of a socialized democracy in his discussion of the three programs of social reform: the socialization of industry, the democratization of government, and the civilization of the citizen. The socialization of industry, the economic goal of democracy, strived for "the attainment by the people of the largest possible industrial control and of the largest possible industrial dividend." The means the people would choose for achieving the industrial goal of democracy, however, might vary greatly depending on the industry in question. Socialization might require, for example, government monopoly, government ownership with private management, government competition with private firms, thoroughgoing regulation of prices, hours, wages, and labor conditions, subsidization of business by the state, or no regulation at all. In every instance, however, the means would be determined by the "animating ideal" of industrial socialization—"the greatest happiness and the highest development to the largest number of individuals, and to society as a whole."[71]

Socialization of industry, Weyl reassured, would not oppose profits per se: "The love of gain is a tough and wholesome human fiber. It is the crude motive power of industry." Profits and wages, rather, would be regarded as "contributions to a larger end"; they would be "balanced as such against other results of the industry." Individual industries must therefore be viewed as parts of a whole, an industrial unit within a larger social whole: "In emphasizing this oneness of business, socialization is doing on a large scale and from the point of view of society what the trust did on a smaller scale from the point of view of the profit-taker." Several factors, according to the author, would contribute to such a socialization of industry, including the perceived advantages of government, as opposed to private, monopolies, the increasing efficiency of civil service programs and regulatory agencies, and the growth of industrial democracy through unionization. The most important factor, however, would be the democratization of government. Not only was democratic control of government essential for implementing a program of industrial reform; it was also necessary for effecting the redistribution of wealth that must accompany a truly socialized democracy. The harnessing of corporate power for socially constructive ends must therefore await democratic control of the state.[72]

To attain "complete control over governmental machinery and processes" in an effort "to break the power of the politically entrenched plutocracy" would constitute the central political objective of the democratic mass. Because corporate political power, as Weyl conceived it, flowed from the plutocracy's control of the political party, the most important objective of the democratic mass was to democratize the parties and, hence, to destroy "the alliance between corrupt business and corrupt politics." Once the plutocracy had lost its hold on the political party, the pyramid of corruption would begin to crumble. When they no longer owed allegiance to the money power, he reasoned, elected representatives would have to answer to the people.[73]

Weyl insisted that if a socialized democracy were to come about, government at all levels must become more efficient. This would involve not only a simplification of political arrangements (complexity worked to the advantage of the well organized plutocracy), but also a proper delegation of powers between the state and federal governments.[74] The federal government, for instance, must assume the burden of controlling the corporations, conserving natural resources, and taxing income and inheritances. In Weyl's democratic society, an efficient political system would resemble a well-oiled machine, with each part contributing to the smooth functioning of the whole. Through an efficient political machinery, moreover, the democratic mass would gain control of the nation's wealth, and the ensuing socialization of industry would usher in a new era of prosperity for the majority of Americans. Weyl cautioned, however, that a political democracy could not ensure political wisdom. The intellectual and moral improvement of the people must accompany democratic advances so that "the gains made on the political and industrial fields may be increased, retained, and wisely utilized."[75]

For Weyl, like Croly, democracy included not only a form of government but also a way of life. A socialized democracy therefore embodied a moral ideal as well as a political ideal. If the social goal of the democracy—the civilization of the citizen—were to be achieved, the democratic mass would have to strive for the advancement and improvement of all people "through a democratization of the advantages and opportunities of life." "The basis of democratic strivings toward human life," Weyl observed, was "an ethical belief in the sanctity of human life, and a desire for an equality in this universal possession." The equalization of life chances would require that health be viewed as a social responsibility, not solely as an individual responsibility. Moreover, because a socialized democracy presupposed an intelligent citizenry and a high level of individual and national efficiency, equality of educational opportunity must be extended to all the people. Education was also essential to the socialization of consumption, according to the author. Only an educated public could halt the "anarchy of consumption" and the conspicuous use and waste of unhealthful products that it encouraged. A truly socialized consumption, furthermore, would depend on an increase in "common goods," in public commodities and services. By socializing and therefore controlling consumption, Weyl concluded, Americans would ultimately socialize production as well. When these along with other needed social reforms had been instituted, a socialized democracy, committed to the material, moral, and intellectual improvement of the individual, would begin to replace the socially irresponsible democracy of an earlier era.[76]

Weyl's analysis of corporate power paralleled that of Croly in several important respects. Both employed the same analytical distinction that separated the realms of economic and political power. They agreed as well that corporate power was based on the control of the nation's wealth by a small, close-knit group of industrialists and financiers. Furthermore, both viewed corporate political power primarily in terms of a corrupt alliance between business magnates and political bosses and maintained that effective social reform would not succeed until public opinion had been aroused and the alliance destroyed.

Their analyses of corporate power, however, also produced some significant contrasts. Whereas Croly's conception of corporate political power, for example, suggested a temporary aberration—in essence, the invasion of the political realm by the economic realm—Weyl's analysis of the scope of this power would seem to render the underlying analytical distinction virtually meaningless. He not only argued that America was well on its way to being ruled by a class-conscious oligarchy, but also detailed how this form of rule had been institutionalized through the political trust, the media, and the Supreme Court. In short, the author's analysis of the plutocratic reorganization of society ventured well beyond a temporary alliance between business leaders and political bosses. Thus, even though Weyl explicitly rejected the Marxist conception of a ruling class on theoretical grounds, he came very close to demonstrating a similar conception of class domination on empirical grounds.

Weyl also echoed Croly's conviction that a general revision of American ideology must precede meaningful efforts at political and economic reform. In attempting to construct an alternative to the beliefs and doctrines of laissez-faire liberalism and statist socialism, both thinkers envisioned a new social equilibrium, an efficient balance, within a society in which a cooperative ethic would supplant class antagonism. Moreover, each conceived democracy as a social ideal to be achieved through gradual, pragmatic means. They appear to have disagreed, however, on how the democratic polity should be organized. Weyl's advocacy of widespread participation and unmediated popular control wherever possible contrasts sharply with Croly's reliance on the exceptional leader and hierarchical control. These differences also stemmed from their views on how an efficient social balance could be achieved within the corporate-capitalist economy. For Weyl, the increasing material prosperity made possible by the social surplus heralded a new age of affluence for the majority of Americans. The utilitarian principle of the greatest good for the greatest number would serve as the standard for determining the efficient allocation of the social surplus. Decisions reached on this basis, however, could not be a product of a mere calculus, unless, of course, the social good referred exclusively to individual pecuniary gain. Rather,

Weyl's brand of utilitarianism rested on the hope that an enlightened and increasingly affluent majority would define the social good in a matter consistent with the material and moral advancement of society as a whole. In effect, he advocated a humanized and socialized version of the stake in society theory applied on a grand scale.

Weyl's advocacy of a consumer-oriented democracy revealed another side of his commitment to majoritarian rule. The author's plan for socializing industry and consumption by severely curtailing corporate political power, regulating corporate economic power, and establishing protections for consumers would ultimately depend on the mobilization of the democratic mass and the development of a consumer consciousness. Accordingly, the long-term task of making corporate power socially responsible would require the presence of an effective opposition, the countervailing power of the democratic mass. Yet, Weyl knew that an unorganized and internally contradictory group of consumers would not be a fair match for a well-organized and like-minded plutocracy. Indeed, he admitted that the latter had the advantage.[77] The terms of his argument, therefore, seem to require that a *cohesive* democratic organization must control government institutions in order to bring about needed reforms. In the absence of such a shift of control, reform could be legislated and imposed only from the top down. Weyl's democratic rhetoric obscured the extent to which his own proposals for national reform necessitated a greater centralization of power.

This is not to say that Weyl's commitment to democratic principles of organization and to equality of opportunity were not genuine. Quite the contrary. His willingness to counsel democratic reforms, and his belief that majoritarian rule would lead to a socialized democracy and not to state socialism or to some form of reactionary government, ultimately stemmed from his faith in the curative powers of the social surplus and the prospect of increasing material prosperity. In this respect, Weyl provided an influential reformulation of the traditional promise of American life. To be sure, the ideological appeal of associating widespread affluence with the concept of democracy has not been lost on his successors.[78]

Weyl's conception of America's future democracy, like that of Croly, envisioned an efficient management of the new corporate economy and a just distribution of its rewards, both of which entailed a solution for ameliorating the destructive social and political consequences of corporate power. For each thinker, the prospect of a renovated democracy presupposed the regulation or control of the political and economic activities of the large corporation. The success or failure of their proposed reforms would therefore depend on the validity of their analyses of corporate power.

We have seen that both authors continually emphasized the primacy of eliminating political corruption in the new social order. But Weyl took his analysis a step further and envisioned an institutionalization and consolidation of corporate power through the law, a democratic restructuring of society that would eliminate the opportunity for systematic political corruption and thereby alter the class content of political power. Had he fully pursued the practical and theoretical implications of his empirical analysis of corporate power, however, he may have been less sanguine about the viability of his scheme for a reformed democracy. In this respect, his analysis contains its own self-critique. The case he made for plutocratic dominance, which explained a good deal about the structure of corporate control in detailing its methods of corruption, is perhaps more compelling than his vision of a socialized democracy.[79] On the other hand, his conception of the socialization of industry clearly comprehended the form, although not necessarily the content, of the future regulation of corporate enterprise in the United States. Such regulation has taken into consideration the social responsibility of the large corporation by imposing limits on the exercise of its power, while it has consolidated the control of capitalists over corporate enterprise under the aegis of the law.

The theory and practice of the new liberalism, as articulated by Croly and Weyl, was therefore both an accommodation and a criticism, an innovative and ambitious agenda of reform, that sought to shape reality in light of ideals that could provide justification for a socially responsible corporate order. Together, Croly and Weyl charted a new course for American liberalism. Critical yet nondoctrinaire, visionary yet pragmatic, they rejected conventional categories of thought in their effort to redefine the goals of the American promise and to map a novel direction for political, social, and economic change. Their reformulation of the principles of constitutionalism and democracy, in response to the challenges posed by the rise of corporate power, constitutes a formidable contribution in the history of American political thought. The hallmark of this contribution will be found in their attempt to synthesize the individualistic precepts of classical liberalism with the egalitarian ideals of social democracy. In this quest, they proposed a solution to the central political problem of their time: the accommodation of corporate power to the demands of society and to the tenets of the American liberal-democratic tradition.[80] Indeed, the legacy of these two architects of corporate liberalism is made all the more enduring by its continuing relevance for the understanding of corporate power in the United States and throughout the world.

Not all the early analysts of corporate power, however, believed that a reformed democracy could cure the ills of society. As we shall see, Thorstein Veblen's social theory led him to very different conclusions concerning the political and ideological significance of the large corporation.

4. THORSTEIN VEBLEN: EXPLOIT VERSUS EFFICIENCY— CORPORATE RULE AND THE MODERN INDUSTRIAL SYSTEM

Of the three thinkers whose writings are the subject of this chapter, Thorstein Veblen alone produced a body of work that could be considered a social theory. From his first major work, *The Theory of the Leisure Class* (1899), to his last, *Absentee Ownership* (1923), his analysis of history, culture, politics, economics, and social change remained remarkably consistent.[81] For the most part, Veblen's social thought constituted an interrelated whole. His theory of human nature and social evolution shaped all his writings, from his cultural critique of the leisure class to his economic theory of business enterprise. Veblen's conception of corporate power, like every other aspect of his thought, must therefore be understood in the context of his broader social theory.

Unlike Croly and Weyl, Veblen rarely enlisted his considerable talents on behalf of a cause. Throughout his career, he preferred the role of scholar and social critic to that of journalist and political activist. No doubt this choice was due in part to the fatalistic assumptions of his theory of social evolution and to his thoroughly critical analysis of corporate enterprise. As the ensuing analysis reveals, the structure of his thought simply ruled out reform as a viable alternative. Nevertheless, his writings were widely read and had a considerable impact on the thinking of his generation. In terms of its originality, depth, and comprehensiveness, Veblen's social theory had no rivals among the works of his American contemporaries.

I argue that Veblen's analysis of corporate power rests on an analytical distinction between business and industry and that this distinction is founded on his theory of human nature and social change. Moreover, I demonstrate that this distinction serves both an analytical and a normative purpose within his theory, and as a result gives rise to a tension in his thought that complicates his conception of corporate power. In order to understand the basis of this distinction, we begin by reconstructing his theory of human nature and social evolution, including his account of the historical development of the corporation. Once this has been accomplished, I return to a detailed analysis of his conception of corporate power, with special emphasis on the role of the state, the political significance of ideology, and the economic basis of corporate rule. Finally, I assess the ideological significance of Veblen's conception of corporate power and his critique of American liberalism in light of the normative assumptions underlying his social theory.

Veblen maintained that, from its earliest beginnings, the social existence of human beings, like that of other species, had been a struggle for survival. In the course of this struggle, a process of natural selection had compelled the gradual adaptation of human nature and behavior to changing social conditions. However, human institutions and their corresponding modes of thought were not only a result of a "selective and adaptive process," but also were in themselves "efficient factors of selection."[82] Social change or evolution, according to Veblen, was therefore a product of a complex process in which human thought and behavior, by adapting to a changing social environment, transformed the institutional basis for later selection. The fact that selective adaptation would take different forms in societies, depending on the character of the people, further complicated this process. In other words, the dominance of certain innate characteristics in a nation or a people would either facilitate or hamper the process of adaptation. To grasp Veblen's theory of social change fully, therefore, we must examine the conception of human nature that informed it.

Human behavior, Veblen observed, was rooted in and conditioned by a complex of "instinctive proclivities and tropismatic attitudes."[83] Instinctive action was purposeful or teleological—that is, it involved "consciousness and adaptation to an end aimed at."[84] Unlike tropismatic behavior, which was purely psychological and could not be consciously altered or controlled, instinctive behavior was shaped by social norms, customs, and habits. Consequently, even though human instincts were innate, the way in which the instinctive ends of life were worked out would depend on a host of cultural factors.[85]

Veblen's analysis of instinctive behavior focused primarily on three major instincts—workmanship, the parental bent, and idle curiosity. Essential to the material well-being of a people, workmanship referred to the human propensity for effective work including the efficient use of resources and technological mastery.[86] The parental bent induced a concern for the community as a whole as well as for the welfare of one's offspring. Like the instinct of workmanship, the parental bent was also necessary to the survival of the species. Idle curiosity motivated the quest for knowledge for its own sake. Human curiosity was "idle," Veblen argued, because it had no utilitarian aim.[87] This did not imply, however, that knowledge produced by this instinctive disposition could have no practical application. Indeed, the development of science and technology provided ample evidence to the contrary.[88]

Instinctive action, according to Veblen, was always a product of an interplay and overlapping of the various instinctive dispositions. Because of the interdependence of human instincts, the modification or accentuation of one instinct due to environmental factors would result in a "mutual contamination" of other instincts and thereby bias the process of selective adaptation.[89] At any given point in the evolution of a society, human nature therefore consisted of a set of instinctive proclivities that had been selected for specific economic and social conditions. But once modified, instinctive dispositions would affect future selection by either facilitating or hampering adaptation. In the author's view, this fact clearly revealed the fallacy of the simplistic idea of progress often associated with human social evolution. In fact, Veblen characterized the notion that "the institutional outcome of men's native dispositions will be sound and salutary" as "an article of uncritical faith [taken] from the historic belief in a beneficent Order of Nature."[90] This is not to say that he rejected the idea of survival of the fittest, only that what was fit and unfit carried no normative connotation.[91]

While Veblen believed human beings to be purposeful creatures— agents "seeking in every act the accomplishment of some concrete, objective, impersonal end"—his analysis of the evolutionary process suggested that human behavior was largely constrained and determined by external forces. Societies evolved, he argued, when individuals were compelled to adapt their habits of thought and institutions to an "altered environment." Social change therefore occurred "in response to pressure from without," which was "of the nature of a response to a stimulus."[92] Whereas a variety of factors contributed to the evolution of societies, "the forces which made for readjustment of institutions, especially in the case of a modern industrial community," Veblen related, were "in the last analysis, almost exclusively of an economic nature."[93] Forces generated by existing economic institutions eventually outgrew their institutional mode:

> As population increases, and as mens' knowledge and skill in directing the forces of nature widen, the habitual methods of relations between the members of the group, and the habitual method of carrying on the life process of the group as a whole, no longer give the same result as before.[94]

Social evolution therefore was largely induced by changing economic forces that, in turn, were driven by advances in the industrial arts—that is, by technological improvements. Veblen's theory of social change clearly embodies a type of technological determinism, albeit qualified by his premise that the development and application of technology will be affected by the institutions and instinctive proclivities of a people. Furthermore, he argued that the impact of technological change on human behavior and thought might vary within a society depending on the degree to which different groups or classes had been exposed to the forces of change.[95] Prospects for change must also be weighed in light of the fact that power was usually exercised to conserve and not to transform social arrangements. Veblen also contended that, as creatures of habit, human beings generally resisted innovation.[96] Thus, when adaptation finally did occur, however haltingly, the adjusted institutions and habits of thought were once again on the verge of being outmoded by newly arisen economic forces.

Because this process of selective adaptation could "never catch up with the progressively changing situation in which the community finds itself at a given time," the dominant beliefs and institutions of a society would be conservative, though some more so than others.[97] This evolutionary process of adaptation resulted in a more-or-less persistent condition of cultural lag in which the knowledge, beliefs, and customs of a society (with the exception of scientific knowledge) were not in accord with the material advances made possible by technological change. This state of affairs, moreover, legitimated prevailing power relationships, because the dominant ideas of a society were those of its rulers.[98] Veblen's theory of social evolution therefore seems to imply that individuals can never completely control their own destinies, precisely because human thought and behavior always lag behind economic change.[99]

To understand the historical basis of corporate power in Veblen's analysis, we must first examine his account of the genesis and transformation of the institution of ownership. Although he rejected the notion that human social evolution proceeded according to immutable laws of development, Veblen maintained, on the basis of evidence, that certain broad generalizations were possible. Throughout his works, he identified four major eras or periods of social evolution, each of which corresponded to a different stage in the advance of technology and social organization: the era of primitive or peaceable savagery, the barbaric or predatory era, the era of the handicraft economy, and the modern era of machine technology. It was during the transition from the period of peaceable savagery, which was characterized by a crude technology and a subsistence economy, to the stage of barbarism, that the institution of ownership emerged.[100] Ownership was established when societies recognized an individual's "customary right of use and abuse over an object which was obviously not an organic part of his person."[101] Veblen argued that this practice first appeared in cultures in which goods and people, especially women, were seized and hence claimed as property[102] and that the ownership of property presupposed certain technological advances which made possible the accumulation of wealth, which in turn often encouraged aggression.[103] His concern, however, was merely to locate the beginnings of ownership, not to posit a causal relationship between that institution and a particular social practice. "Whether property provokes to predation or predation initiates ownership," he concluded, "the situation that results in the early phases of the pecuniary culture was much the same."[104]

Veblen's account of the historical development of ownership significantly influenced his general theory of social evolution as well as his analysis of corporate power. The institution of ownership in predatory societies, he argued, gave rise to a leisure class. This class developed from "an early discrimination between employments, according to which some employments are worthy and others unworthy." Those deemed worthy "may be classed as exploit," while the unworthy constituted "those necessary everyday employments into which no appreciable element of exploit enters." Veblen explained that the "invidious distinction" between exploit and industry flowed from the institution of ownership and its underlying motive of pecuniary emulation. The possession of wealth became a symbol of prowess and thereby conferred honor, just as the lack of wealth relegated one to an ordinary or ignoble social position. One will find, the author observed, that the material and psychological foundations of the leisure class—the institution of ownership and pecuniary emulation—had been substantially developed in predatory societies and, from that point on, remained basically unchanged, even though the class itself did not fully mature until a later stage of social evolution. Indeed, a "distinction is still habitually made between industrial and non-industrial occupations; and this modern distinction is a transmuted form of the barbarism distinction between exploit and drudgery."[105]

In his scathing cultural critique of modern society, *The Theory of the Leisure Class*, Veblen continually exposed the habits, norms, and tastes of the wealthy as an outgrowth of an earlier predatory culture. Combining healthy doses of satire with an incisive analysis of the ludicrousness of upper-class mores and social conventions, he argued that the leisure class had been and remained an unproductive and parasitic class that thrived on the toil of others. Nevertheless, because people admired and emulated the wealth of this class, its members continued to dominate the cultural life of society. The significance of Veblen's analysis of the institution of ownership, however, goes well beyond his observation concerning the cultural hegemony of the leisure class. His account of the rise of corporate power in the era of machine technology rests on a distinction between business and industry that directly parallels and complements his analysis of the origins of the leisure class. What Veblen described from a cultural standpoint as the leisure class would become, from an economic and political standpoint, the capitalist or business class of vested interests. To be more precise, the leisure class constituted a "kept class" that depended on the business class for its income. In spite of his awkward terminology, Veblen did not view these as distinct classes so much as different sectors or aspects of the same class. Class behavior, in both cases, could be traced to the instinctual dominance of exploit over industry—that is, of pecuniary emulation over workmanlike efficiency.[106]

In Veblen's evolutionary scheme, the handicraft era marked the transition from the predatory to the peaceable commercial phase of pecuniary culture. This stage roughly corresponds to what scholars generally label the transitional period from feudalism to capitalism. For Veblen, the era of handicraft constituted the preindustrial phase of capitalism, the stage in which the small-scale competitive economy developed around the activities of craftsmen and petty traders.[107] By combining technological mastery with the quest for profit, the craftsman joined the skills of industry and business. Both these skills "counted equally," for the handicraft system remained "a practicable plan of economic life only so long as the craftsman [could] combine both of these capacities in good force and only so long as the technological exigencies [would] admit the exercise of both in conjunction."[108]

As it became increasingly productive, the handicraft system planted the seeds of its own destruction. Technological advances in various crafts eventually made the cost of equipment prohibitive for most craftsmen. Soon crafts became organized within industrial plants that were owned by individuals with sufficient wealth to purchase the means of production. Improvements in methods of communication, transportation, and trade facilitated, directly and indirectly, the process of industrial advance. Eventually, the handicraft system broke down, or perhaps outgrew itself, and the rudiments of an industrial system began to take shape. In the process, however, a division of labor separated the two skills once embodied in the craftsman. Under the new system, pecuniary control was vested in a class of owners while the tasks of production were consigned to a propertyless class of workers.[109]

Although the industrial revolution in England definitively ushered in the era of machine technology, its formative principle—the dominance of business over industry—grew out of the handicraft economy. The progressive separation of these two realms of economic activity constituted the dominant trend of modern technological development. With the ascendancy of the business class, moreover, new relationships of power were established:

> The transition from the original predatory phase of the pecuniary culture to the succeeding commercial phase signifies the emergence of a middle class in such forces as presently to recast the working arrangements of the cultural scheme and make peaceable business (gainful traffic) the ruling interest of the community. . . . It is the conscious interest of this class to further the gainfulness of industry, and as this end is correlated with the productiveness of industry it is also, though less directly, correlated with improvements in technology.[110]

Society thus became organized in the interests of business or profit-making, and pecuniary principles or habits of thought soon acquired "supreme dominance . . . both as standards of efficiency and as canons of conduct." This "pecuniary system of social organization" further instituted "class divergence of material interests, class prerogative and differential hardship, and an accentuated class disparity in the consumption of goods."[111] Thus, the rise of the bourgeoisie in the era of modern industry initiated the final conquest of exploit over industry.

Veblen reminds us throughout his writings that the split between business and industry did not occur suddenly, but developed gradually with the growth of modern industry. This division initially became apparent with the phasing-out of the independent craftsman and the ascendancy of the first great class of business leaders, the so-called "captains of industry." The captains of industry were in actuality entrepreneurs who possessed, in varying degrees, considerable industrial expertise.[112] It was during the "era of free competition"—roughly the period that "lies between the industrial revolution of the eighteenth century and the rise of corporation finance in the nineteenth"—that the captain of industry emerged as a major economic, political, and social force.[113] For nearly a century, the captain of industry was "the dominant figure in civilized life, about whose deeds and interests law and custom have turned, the central and paramount personal agency in Occidental civilization." Yet, as technology became more complex and scientific in character, as the efficiency and output of industrial production increased, and as business transactions expanded, "the function of the entrepreneur, the captain of industry, gradually fell apart in a two-fold division of labor, between the business manager and the office work on the one side and the technician and the industrial work on the other side."[114] With this most recent split between business and industry, which amounted to a division between financial and industrial management with the former retaining ultimate control, the era of corporate dominance began.

The rise of the corporation in the late nineteenth century, Veblen argued, coincided with the failure of the competitive system to prevent excessive (i.e., unprofitable) production. In order to limit production and thereby prevent retrenchment of assets or earnings, the pecuniary captains increasingly resorted to the corporate form of business enterprise.[115] The corporation, he explained, "is a business concern, not an industrial unit"; moreover, it is a "business concern which has been created by a capitalization of funds, and which accordingly rests on credit." While corporations may have indirectly facilitated industrial expansion, their purpose has always been investment for profit. "Business enterprise may be said to have reached its majority," he asserted, "when the corporation came to take first place and became the master institution of civilized life."[116]

The proliferation of corporate enterprise in the last quarter of the nineteenth century marked the beginning of a new order of industry and business.[117] Scientific advances in chemistry and physics revolutionized industrial technology, and the operations of industry increasingly came under the supervision of scientifically trained experts or technicians. The "modern machine process," as Veblen called it, gave rise to greater specialization and division of labor within industry. It created industrial interdependence through standardization of processes, machinery, and labor requirements, and ultimately standardized and routinized all of social existence—work, consumption, leisure—as though it were merely an extension of the mechanical workings of industry. Built on the precepts of science and "matter-of-fact thinking," the modern machine process held forth the promise of industrial efficiency on a scale hitherto unimagined. This promise, however, was continually thwarted by the overlords of business. Unlike the scientifically oriented technicians and engineers who were concerned with the efficient operation of industry, the business magnates—the czars of finance and the rulers of the great industrial corporations—were driven solely by the quest for profits. Modern business enterprise and the credit economy on which it rested were designed to stabilize prices, and therefore profits, by regulating competition and limiting production. Because they provided for centralization of control, allowed for routinization of business transactions, and created a greater interdependence within the financial community, corporations constituted the institutional foundation of the new order of business. The rise of the corporation therefore represented the demise of the captain of industry and the triumph of the modern business leader, the "captain of finance."[118]

Veblen's historical account of the emergence of corporate power may be summarized as follows. From the handicraft era to the ascendancy of the captain of finance in the era of machine technology, the split between business and industry steadily widened as economic and technological imperatives produced an increasing division of labor. Once united in the person of the craftsman, the activities of workmanship and pecuniary exploit gradually separated and came to characterize the realms of industry and business respectively. This transformation also induced different instinctive dispositions and habits of thought. Whereas the day-to-day activities and objectives of the technician and engineer instilled a scientific mode of thinking, and a concern with efficiency, the affairs of the business leader emphasized pecuniary gain and individual aggrandizement to the detriment of efficiency. The separation between business and industry, rooted in the division of labor in modern capitalism, thus gave rise to two antagonistic classes within the corporate economy, each of which operated according to different principles and each of which held forth a different model of social organization. Accordingly, within this most recent phase of industrial capitalism, the historical division between industry and business—that is, between workmanlike efficiency and pecuniary exploit—achieved its logical culmination. Veblen's analysis of corporate power, as well as his projections for social change, were thoroughly shaped by his interpretation of this development.

The emergence of the large corporation in the closing decades of the nineteenth century signaled the complete separation of business and industry, an event that Veblen viewed as a necessary precondition for the consolidation of the power of the business class. In the author's analysis, corporate power constituted a form of class domination—rule by the business class of advanced capitalist societies. As business institutions, corporations comprised the institutional foundation of the modern credit economy; they were the primary means through which the business class controlled the economy and society at large. This modern ruling class—which he also referred to in various works as absentee owners, vested interests, captains of finance, and the One Big Union of Financial Interests—included the major owners and managers of the large industrial and financial corporations, including such financiers as those who built the trusts and the holding companies. For the most part, the leaders of the business class came from the "key industrial" corporations and the major banks, which comprised the dominant sectors of the economy. Whereas the former controlled the essential raw material industries and therefore the country's natural resources, the latter commanded the nation's finance through the dispensing of credit and control of the money supply.[119] Even though they were interrelated through corporate mergers, interlocking directorates, and business dealings, the banking and industrial sectors, Veblen insisted, were not co-equal. While the possibility for a true coalescence of the two sectors could not be discounted, he consistently held the view that the lords of finance retained ultimate power through their control of credit and capital.[120]

It remains to be explained in what sense Veblen's analysis of corporate power constitutes a class analysis and how it differs conceptually from the analyses of Croly and Weyl. To begin with, Veblen did not distinguish, for analytical purposes, between separate realms of economic and political power. Rather, he contended that in the era of machine technology economic dominance entailed control of the state or government institutions. Furthermore, he conceived power as a relationship of control that existed between groups or classes within society. Despite the similarities with classical Marxism, Veblen rejected the Marxist conception of class war between the proletariat and the bourgeoisie. Although the business class dominated the whole of society, the potentially decisive class confrontation, in his view, was between the leaders of business and the new class of technicians and trained engineers, the vanguard of modern industrial methods and thinking. Whether this small but cohesive group of technical workers would commit themselves to revolution or to a quiet surrender, the inherent contradiction between business and industry would in some way be affected.[121]

Unlike Croly and Weyl, Veblen did not maintain that government institutions had been recently captured by the capitalist class, so his analysis did not emphasize political corruption by business interests. Neither did he view corporate dominance as an anomaly or a defect of the democratic polity. He argued instead that modern democratic or constitutional government, since its inception, had consistently served the interests of the business class. With the ascendancy of the capitalist class, business ends replaced dynastic ends as the chief concern of the state. "A constitutional government," Veblen asserted, "is a business government."[122] The state in capitalist societies provided the means for exercising social control and for realizing the goals of business.[123] Moreover, personnel of government institutions consisted largely of individuals drawn from the business community. For Veblen, there was no great revelation in the fact that American government at all levels was "administered by a businesslike personnel, imbued with the habitual bias of business principles—the principles of ownership; that is to say, under current conditions, the rights, powers, and immunities of absentee ownership."[124]

Control of the government by the business class was facilitated by the fact that the major political parties constituted "rings or syndicates" of business interests. "The ring of business interests which secures the broadest approval from popular sentiment," he observed, "is, under constitutional methods, put in charge of the government establishment."[125] The hegemony of the business class also extended over "the clergy, the military, the courts, police, and legal profession," each of whose livelihood was "conditioned on their serving the purposes of those principal and self-directing vested interests whose tenure rests immediately on large holdings of invested wealth."[126] There was, then, no doubt in Veblen's mind that the business class constituted a ruling class:

> The effectual control of the economic situation, in business, industry, and civil life, rests on the control of credit. Therefore the effectual exercise of initiative, discretion and authority is perforce vested in those massive aggregations of absentee ownership that make up the Interests. Within certain wide limits of tolerance, therefore, the rest of the community, the industrial system and the underlying population, are at the disposal of the Interests, as ways and means of business. . . . The nation, both as a habit of thought and as a governmental going concern, comes into the case, in effect and in the main, as an auxiliary agency the function of which is to safeguard, extend and facilitate this work of surveillance and usufruct.[127]

Although the corporate business class controlled the political machinery, the state or nation, according to Veblen, was an institutional outgrowth of the dynastic period of early modern Europe in which "the rival princely or dynastic establishments . . . each sought its own advantage at the cost of any whom it may concern."[128] In modern times, "the divine right of the prince has passed over into the divine right of the Nation," but the predatory animus of the era of state-making remained in the imperialistic ambitions of the business interests.[129] With the advent of this latest stage of predatory culture, the ruling class ensured its dominance through control of the state. Yet, Veblen contended, control of government institutions was possible only because the vast majority of people supported the present regime. The scope and resiliency of corporate power ultimately depended on the habits of thought of a people, the ideological cement of the new order of business and industry.

Just as the ascendancy of the captain of finance established the supremacy of pecuniary exploit over workmanlike efficiency, so did the era of corporate dominance represent the highest development of pecuniary culture. In shaping the styles and tastes of the ruling class, and ultimately the underlying population, business principles and ideology also served to justify class rule. Because class governance in advanced capitalist societies depended on widespread ideological consensus, control over the production and dissemination of ideas was of vital importance to the perpetuation of existing power relationships. Indeed, the institutions of higher learning, according to the author, were dominated by individuals who were thoroughly imbued with pecuniary and nonscientific habits of thought, a fact that was clearly evidenced in the biased curriculum of these schools. While scientific thinking had made some inroads, the system of higher education continued to be administered on the basis of businesslike principles, to propagate the ideas of pecuniary culture, and to serve the needs of the business class.[130] Schools of business and law, and to a lesser extent other vocational schools, "serve the advantage of one class as against another" because they "increase the advantage of such men as already have some advantage over the common run."[131] Thus, even though Veblen did not employ the actual phrase, it is clear that he adhered to a conception of the ideological hegemony of liberalism in the era of corporate rule.

Interpreted within the logic of Veblen's social theory, ideological hegemony was as much a product of cultural lag as of overt control. Ideological justification of the new order of business and industry, he argued, consisted of principles of ownership derived from the era of the handicraft economy.[132] Both the legal and the moral foundation of the corporate order rested on the Lockean theory of property rights, which posited a unity of ownership and workmanship—that is, of business and industry. This theory, however, like all habits of thought or ideological beliefs, had long since ceased to depict the reality it justified. In fact, once the split between business and industry had become established in the competitive era, the unity of ownership and workmanship gave way to the institution of absentee ownership.[133] Even though absentee ownership separated the productive use of property from its ownership, its legal and moral justification stood squarely on Locke's defense of property rights.

Under modern conditions, the Lockean theory obscured the economic reality (for example, the doctrine of liberty of contract could not be said to apply to the hired worker in the same sense that it did to the craftsman) while it justified private profits by falsely assuming that the individual who acquired wealth was also the producer of that wealth. "By force of this sophistication," Veblen observed, "the acquisition of property by any person is held to be, not only expedient for the owner, but meritorious as an act serving the common good."[134] When applied to the business corporation, which constituted "an incorporation of absentee ownership, wholly and obviously,"[135] this rationale became even more ludicrous. The joint-stock company, he asserted, "is a conspiracy of owners, and as such it transgresses that principle of individual self-help that underlies the system of Natural Rights."[136]

Veblen maintained, as did Croly and Weyl, that the individualistic ethos of American liberalism reigned supreme largely because of its widespread acceptance: "America is the native habitat of the self-made man, and the self-made man is a pecuniary organism."[137] Venerable beliefs instilled the notion that "the people of the republic are made up of ungraded masterless men who enjoy all the rights and immunities of self-direction, self-help, free bargaining, and equal opportunity," whereas, in reality, the present order had produced gross inequality and a new division of masters and serfs.[138] While the rule of the business class derived its ideological sustenance, in the main, from the traditional theory of property rights, it also found justification in the sentiment of nationalism. Originally a means for ensuring loyalty to feudal overlords, nationalism or patriotism in its modern form served as a guise to mask the imperialist ambitions of the business class.[139] Through an evolutionary process of adaptation and rationalization in response to changing social circumstances, the institutions of ownership and nationalism continued to justify the predatory aims of society's rulers. Until material conditions necessitated a rejection of these habits of thought and their attendant customs, Veblen concluded, they would stand as a bulwark against an equitable and rational society.[140]

It remains to be demonstrated why Veblen ascribed ultimate power to the banking sector of the economy. To fathom this, his conception of class domination must be viewed in light of his theory of business enterprise, including his analysis of the separation of ownership and control.

Veblen's theory of business enterprise focused primarily on three interrelated aspects of the economy: the use of credit, the nature of corporate capital, and the dynamics of business crises or depressions.[141] Veblen maintained that during the era of competitive capitalism and before the ascendancy of corporate finance, the extensive use of loan credit gave rise to periods of speculative expansion, rising prices, and business prosperity. Eventually, such periods of prosperity waned and prices dropped, with the result that many businesses had difficulty meeting their financial obligations to creditors. Because loans had been secured on the basis of an inflated earning capacity, a steady drop in prices revealed the extent to which businesses had overextended themselves.[142] The discrepancy between the putative and actual collateral basis of capitalization became apparent to the creditors, and a period of liquidation and business depression ensued. Liquidation resulted in a redistribution of ownership of collateral property among creditors, a period of adjustment and re-capitalization, and eventually another speculative movement. Veblen maintained that before the 1870s the discrepancy between capitalization and actual earning capacity was never too great to prevent a renewed speculative advance. As a consequence, depressions during this period tended to be short-lived and rarely disabled the economy as a whole.[143]

Under modern conditions, however, technological advances reduced costs at such a great rate that there was a chronic discrepancy between capitalization and earning capacity. As technological improvements persistently outstripped the readjustment of capitalization, a steady decline in profits resulted, thereby preventing a renewed speculative expansion of the type that had occurred in the earlier decades of the nineteenth century. Furthermore, depressions in the era of modern machine technology took on a systematic character due to the interdependence of the industrial system. The technological factor not only complicated the problem of credit inflation, but basically altered the nature of depressions as well. So long as business was conducted on a competitive footing, Veblen observed, chronic depression, was "normal to the industrial situation."[144]

Veblen concluded that competitive business practices were not compatible with the increased efficiency and productivity of modern industry. Accordingly, the dominant business interests in the latter decades of the nineteenth century had sought to eliminate competition by controlling prices and limiting production, mainly through combination and monopoly.[145] In this fashion, the first lords of high finance proceeded to reorganize the economy through mergers and trust-building. Thus, high finance—the buying and selling of enterprises, the financing of mergers, and the control of credit—came to dominate business enterprise. The investment banker reigned supreme as the master of high finance, and what the trust builders had initiated in their quest for profits, within a few decades, acquired an institutional basis in the major banks and the Federal Reserve System.[146]

By the turn of century, Veblen explained, control of corporate finance, and thus effectual control over the economy as a whole, came to rest in the hands of the large business interests.[147] The reorganization of the economy, however, also entailed a transformation in the structure of control. Corporate consolidation, in the form of a trust or a holding company, had centralized financial control within a group of "ultimate owners." This restructuring of control within the business class, moreover, was built on a separation of ownership and control within the large corporation.

Veblen argued that the separation of ownership from control, which involved a separation of the ownership and control of the capital goods or industrial equipment, resulted from the basic method by which corporations were capitalized: the issuance of stocks.[148] The stockholders delegated powers to the managers, who, more often than not, were owners themselves. This did not produce a complete separation of ownership and control, but instead vested power in the hands of a small group of owner-managers. When corporations merged within a holding company or trust, however, the link between ownership and control became further attenuated. When this occurred, there was indeed a more pronounced separation of ownership from control, because those who exercised the ultimate discretion in business affairs were the "owners of intangible forms of property," not necessarily owners of the industrial capital, and had "only a remote interest in the efficient working" of industry. For Veblen, the separation of ownership and control therefore implied a further divergence of the industrial interest in workmanlike efficiency from the business interest in pecuniary exploit.[149]

Veblen's analysis of this development within large-scale enterprise, which in effect involved a separation of property and power, did not lead him to conclude that the rulers of the corporate economy no longer held a tangible pecuniary interest in the affairs under their control. For one thing, he never seriously entertained the possibility of a complete separation of ownership and control. But more important, in his view, was the fact that this separation involved a *shift of control* to the financial sector of the business class, whose pecuniary interest was dictated by the imperatives of the credit economy. In short, the separation of ownership and control did *not* imply rule by a class of propertyless managers who were in principle accountable to stockholders, but rather suggested that a new hierarchy, accomplished through a restructuring of control by the captains of finance, had emerged. Owing to the strategic position of the financial sector of the business class, the leaders of finance now wielded ultimate control over the economy—and it was not necessary that they actually own the industrial capital, for the nature of their power entailed "an effectual usufruct of these resources."[150]

This highly centralized network of business interests, whose "work of initiative, discretion, foresight, and control . . . has habitually taken effect by way of collusion or concerted action," not only oversaw the affairs of the business class but also held final responsibility for the material welfare of the nation.[151] The structure of corporate power—which is to say, the organization of power within the ruling business class—could therefore be conceived as a hierarchy in which the large financial interests dominated, followed by the business managers of the key industrial corporations and, below them, the managers of the remaining industrial and manufacturing concerns whose livelihood depended largely on the strategic decisions of the ruling business interests.[152] According to Veblen's theory of modern industrial society, the pecuniary interests of the business class as a whole (which included the leisure class) stood opposed to the community's interest in efficiency and serviceability. Increasingly, this conflict took the form of a confrontation between the interests of the "One Big Union of Financial Interests" and their agents in government, on the one hand, and the vanguard of modern technology, the new class of technicians and engineers, on the other hand. The contradiction between business and industry therefore boiled down to a conflict between an exploitative class interest in profit-making and a general social interest in full production and efficient use of technology and resources.[153]

Veblen's hope and vision, which he argued with more commitment in some works than in others, was that the industrial experts would seize control of the industrial apparatus and subsequently organize and run the country's great industries according to the principle of efficiency. He envisioned a revolutionary change in the structure of power in American society in which a technocratic vanguard would dethrone the ruling business interests. In place of workers' councils, Veblen would have a "soviet of technicians," an elite who understood the logic of the machine process and the requirements of efficiency.[154] When left to their own devices, he insisted, the technicians and engineers would realize the full potential of the modern industrial system.

Veblen's social theory stands as a justification of technocracy and as an indictment of business enterprise from the standpoint of efficiency. Like Croly and Weyl, he approved of the tremendous technological advances and the unprecedented productive potential of modern industry. In explaining the scope of this development and the promise it held for a humane and rational system of production, he documented the increasing interdependence, routinization, and standardization of industry and society as a whole due to technological change. Thus, his overriding concern with efficiency, his mechanical conception of industrial society, and his technocratic vision of the future linked Veblen's thought in important ways both to the liberal revisionists and to socialists. Like Croly and Marxist-Leninists, Veblen advocated rule by experts, and like Weyl and the majority of socialists, he envisioned the future industrial society as an efficient, smoothly operating machine. By separating workmanship from exploit, however, Veblen divorced efficiency from business appropriation of surplus profit-making. By divorcing industry from business, he separated production from finance. On the basis of this logic, it was possible to conceive technological change as an autonomous force, an evolutionary development rooted in human instinct, with corresponding social interests that had cultivated their own distinctive habits of thought and an incipient vision of a technocratic order. This aspect of his analysis is therefore also the source of the enduring ideological impact of his thought.

Veblen's social theory has lent itself to diverse interpretations that to some degree stem from the problematic character of the distinction between business and industry. Unless this distinction is assessed in light of its normative purpose, his analysis of corporate power cannot be adequately comprehended. On the one hand, the business-industry distinction provided him with a critical standard—a technocratic vision—by which to judge society, past and present. On the other hand, Veblen's empirical analysis demonstrated how the separation of business and industry (from an ideological *and* practical standpoint) was disappearing in his own time, especially how technology was increasingly coming under the control of business interests. In this respect, the distinction would appear to be artificial in light of his own analysis. There is, then, a certain tension created within his theory by these conflicting currents. It would appear that the separation between business (pecuniary exploit) and industry (workmanship) increasingly served primarily a normative purpose in his theory that was at odds with his empirical findings. More the social scientist than the hopeful revolutionary, Veblen coldly documented the impending triumph of pecuniary exploit, which in his view continued to pervert the salutary instinct of workmanship. Clearly Veblen was not a millenarian. There was nothing inevitable to his way of thinking about the technocratic revolution. Nevertheless, it would appear that he could not jettison the business-industry distinction without also abandoning his critical perspective. Indeed, the instinct of workmanship was the very core of Veblen's humanism.[155]

Veblen remained to the end a bitter, if not often shrill, critic of capitalist enterprise. In his view, the American economic system was wasteful, exploitive, irrational, and unjust. But as he was condemning the business class, the more farsighted corporate and political leaders were acting to change this image in the public mind. Liberals, among them Croly and Weyl, and their cohorts and champions in government and industry, were constructing a revised justification that would undercut the anticapitalist analysis of radical critics, such as Veblen, while absorbing the aspects of the radical critique that might, from another perspective, lend support to the new regime.

What Veblen documented more lucidly and with greater depth than any of his contemporaries, however, was the manner in which the rise of the large corporation had fomented a reorganization of the structure of power in American society. While he differed with Croly and Weyl on how to remedy the ills of the corporate ascendancy, he was in essential agreement with them on what was at stake—namely, by whom and in whose interests the corporate order should be governed. In addressing this fundamental question, Croly, Weyl, and Veblen revised the ideological beliefs of an earlier era and, in doing so, anticipated the modern conception of the corporation as a social institution. As a group, they defined the parameters of the early-twentieth-century debate over corporate social responsibility and thereby forged a new direction for American political thought.

5. THE RECONSTRUCTION OF AMERICAN LIBERALISM

Croly, Weyl, and Veblen all stressed the fundamental political importance of widespread ideological consensus in American society. A product of the era of competitive capitalism, the dominant ideology, in their view, served to justify the power of a newly arisen corporate oligarchy. Their critiques therefore aimed to expose the discrepancies between the claims of classical liberalism and the reality of the corporate order. Whereas the reformist objectives of Croly and Weyl dictated a revision of American liberalism, Veblen envisioned an alternative in the scientific habits of thought associated with modern industry. Each author's criticism of the dominant ideology, however, contributed to its revision merely by exposing the inadequacies of the traditional justification. Thus, as a group, the early analysts of corporate power mounted an effective assault on the premises and claims of laissez-faire liberalism.

The revision of American liberalism during the early decades of the twentieth century anticipated the legitimation of corporate power, and hence the acceptance of the large corporation as a socially responsible institution. While a full account of this ideological transformation must await further analysis, I shall outline here its basic features as articulated by Croly, Weyl, and Veblen.

In adapting American liberalism to changing economic, social, and political conditions, the exponents of corporate liberalism attempted to redefine and reconstitute the individualistic beliefs and doctrines of an earlier era. This ideological revisionism contained several interrelated aspects—the critique of economic individualism, the revision of the concepts of social balance and limited government, the redefinition of the relationship between individual and society, and the reformulation of the ideals of democracy and of history as material progress.

The critique of economic individualism entailed a rejection of the marketplace mentality of classical liberalism—the view that the unregulated pursuit of individual gain would yield socially beneficial results. In place of the automatic balance of the marketplace, a conscious social balance would have to be imposed. This balance, in effect, constituted a response to the extreme inequalities produced by an unbridled individualism. It also recognized the inherent contradiction in liberalism between the prerogatives of property and the assumption of equality of opportunity; and it attempted to regulate this conflict through the balancing of social interests. Although still the bedrock of the social order, the rights of property would therefore have to relinquish their absolutist claims. Economic freedom, however, would be preserved by maintaining a separation of the political and economic realms, and thus preserving "free enterprise" or, what is the same, corporate autonomy.

The conscious social balance therefore entailed a revision of the concept of limited government to the extent that the logic of laissez-faire must now be preserved through regulatory means that would in effect assume the role of the Invisible Hand. In practice, the revised balance would require a stronger central government and regulatory legislation, to meet the needs of a transformed economy. From an ideological and practical standpoint, however, the idea of limited government, retained in the rule of law and in the separation of political and economic spheres, would preserve the continuity of the liberal tradition. Finally, the revision of economic individualism—which is to say, laissez-faire corporate individualism—would pave the way for a reevaluation of the individual's relationship to society. In place of the atomistic view of individuals in society portrayed by classical liberalism, a conception of society as an interrelated whole would be adopted. In the thought of Croly, this reevaluation took an ideological turn toward a corporate ethic, whereas in Weyl's writings it assumed the trappings of social democratic philosophy.

The revision of American liberalism in the early decades of the twentieth century also gave rise to a redefinition of democracy. Democracy, literally, describes a method of social control in which the *demos*, or people, rule. In the traditional sense of the term, therefore, it embodies the belief that sovereignty resides in the people. For Croly and Weyl, however, democracy connoted much more than a formal method of governance. It embraced a conception of history and a vision of progress.

Indeed, it became synonymous with the promise of American life. But once democracy had become associated with a way of life, the organizational principles on which it depended—that is, the actual mechanisms of democratic control—became instrumental to the realization of a higher ideal. Whereas Croly's democratic ideal called for hierarchy and centralization of power at the national level, Weyl's socialized democracy required democratic control by the new majority, the democratic mass. In both instances, the organization and methods of democracy aimed to achieve the goal of an efficient social balance. That Croly's proposals anticipated the actual course of reform in later years deserves special notice. His identification of efficiency with centralized control and rule by experts or exceptional leaders represents the major trend of democratic revisionism in the twentieth century. Increasingly, democracy became dissociated from its original meaning and served to justify hierarchy couched in terms of social balance. It should be noted as well that Veblen's advocacy of technocracy also contributed to this development.

The redefinition of democracy also occasioned a revision of the American liberal conception of progress. With the closing of the frontier and the failure of the automatic balance of the marketplace, the liberal faith in the Invisible Hand and its corollary, the weak state, was replaced by a faith in technological advance and gradual social improvement through pragmatic problem-solving and an expanding governmental role. In this fashion, the traditional American promise of material progress and individual opportunity evolved a new rationale to accommodate a changing society. Weyl's notion of progress through prosperity, Veblen's technological determinism, and Croly's democratic faith exemplify this ideological transformation. Thus, while the revised doctrine of progress recognized the need for a conscious social design, it retained the element of faith and the vision of increasing affluence.

Binding these versions of the new American promise is a fundamental belief that modern production and technology, when harnessed in the interests of society, will unleash its curative powers. Each of these thinkers, in his own way, viewed (socially irresponsible) corporate power as a fetter on the salutary development of economic forces. In the arguments of Croly and Weyl, this presumption favored the view of corporate capitalism as a "natural" and progressive evolution from earlier forms of business enterprise; in Veblen's social theory, technological advance served a similar ideological purpose.

The economic and social upheaval associated with the rise of corporate power in the late nineteenth and early twentieth centuries produced a volatile political environment within which revisionist political thinking flourished. Sharply critical of the new order, the corporate-liberal vision offered an alternative to the competing doctrines of laissez-faire liberalism and statist socialism, an alternative that envisioned a society reconstituted (and to a certain extent reinvented) to effect an accommodation between the tremendous growth of enterprise and the traditional liberal-democratic ideals. This process of ideological revisionism, however, did not end with the close of the Progressive Era. In ensuing years, liberal analysts of corporate power continued to examine the political significance of the corporation and to refine and expand the new liberalism in response to a changing environment. These later developments, which evinced an abiding concern with the issue of corporate social responsibility and the legitimation of corporate power, paralleled changes in American law and legal theory that both implemented and justified the consolidation of corporate power.

Chapter 4

THE CONSOLIDATION OF CORPORATE POWER: LAW AND LEGAL THEORY

The modern corporation may be regarded not simply as one form of social organization but potentially (if not yet actually) as the dominant institution of the modern world. In every age, the major concentration of power has been based upon the dominant interest of that age.
—Adolph A. Berle and Gardiner C. Means, 1932

1. THE CONSOLIDATION OF CORPORATE POWER

The growth of corporate enterprise in the late nineteenth and early twentieth centuries inspired ideological shifts that justified sweeping economic, social, and political transformations. To a large extent, these changes had become fully visible by the end of World War I. Still, it must be kept in mind that the events of the Progressive Era initiated a process of corporate reconstruction that did not run its course until the era of social reform that followed the Great Depression. After World War II, a new structure of control emerged to guide an economy dominated by large corporations in close association with government agencies. To stabilize and regulate the corporate economy, power was increasingly centralized within the executive branch of the federal government. As

Croly foresaw, consolidation of corporate power had indeed occasioned the rise of big government.

The consolidation of corporate power must also be explained in light of the rise of the United States as a world power. In the years immediately following World War II, the position of the United States as the dominant partner among capitalist nations became firmly established. Conventional belief holds that the war and its consequences—the devastation of Europe, the development of the atomic bomb, and the breakdown of Soviet-American relations—thrust the responsibilities of world power on American policy-makers. There is substantial truth in this view, yet it remains only a half-truth when it fails to take into account the economic foundation on which American global hegemony was built. I refer not only to the various international agreements that established the United States as the leader of the non–Communist world economy, but also to the increasing dominance of American-based corporations within that economy. Viewed from this standpoint, the ascendancy of the United States as a global power must be explained in light of the growth of U.S. direct foreign investment in the decades before and after World War II. The expansion of U.S.-based corporations during the interwar period not only hastened the collapse of British dominance in international markets but also paved the way for a new structure of international control. The structure of the postwar economy was carefully designed to accommodate the internationalization of American corporate enterprise.

Throughout the twentieth century, the transformation of the internal relationships of control within the modern corporation proceeded apace with the consolidation of corporate power in its external dimension. A thorough revision of corporation law (which entailed a substantial transfer of power from shareholders to management) secured the autonomy of corporate executives. This restructuring of relationships of control within the corporation effected a transition from an internal structure founded on the primacy of shareholder rights (the principle of managerial efficiency) to one based on broad managerial powers held in trust (the principle of political autonomy). In transforming this legal edifice, corporation law delegated to the corporate hierarchy powers that fortified and expanded its sphere of decision-making, while at the same time it eliminated or eroded most of the traditional rights of shareholders. To accomplish this end, judges devised legal reasoning and doctrine— consistent with the principle of political autonomy—that would permit corporate executives to exercise powers that exceeded the scope of traditional managerial justifications of profit-making. In this way, the principle of political autonomy validated the transfer of power from shareholders to management and thereby contributed to the development of the corporation as a political institution. Moreover, as managerial control over the private, internal dimension of corporate power became increasingly insulated from public regulation, the issue of corporate social responsibility acquired a broader significance in public law regulating the relationship between corporations and society.

In the twentieth century, the unfolding distinction between the private or internal dimension of control (the law of corporations) and the public or external dimension of corporate power (public law) reflected ideological as well as practical decisions of legislators and judges to adapt the law to the organizational structure and power relationships of the large corporation. This development in the law was anticipated by Croly's demarcation between the inviolable sphere of corporate autonomy, on the one hand, and public regulation of enterprise in a nonstatist administered market system, on the other. But in arguing strongly for corporate autonomy, Croly could not have foreseen the full extent to which corporation law would vest the modern corporation with public powers. The internal-external distinction had an additional parallel in Progressive Era political analyses of the relationship between management and labor— namely, the idea, championed by both Croly and Weyl, that unions should be legalized and regulated under public law; in effect, a recommendation that this internal power relationship, which had developed into an external (or social) relationship of conflict, should be mediated and regulated by public law.[1]

The consolidation of the external dimension of corporate power under the aegis of public law facilitated the corporate reconstruction of American capitalism while securing reconstituted relationships of power within society. This development entailed a thorough restructuring and reorganization of economy and society accomplished through a growing interaction of public and private spheres. Analyses that adhere to a rigid distinction between political (governmental) and economic (corporate) spheres tend to explain this process as an intrusion of the public into the private sphere, or as a co-optation of public functions by private entities—hence the preoccupation of these studies with the dangers of big government or big corporations. Both conclusions mistake symptoms for cause. The intersecting of public and private functions constitutes the dominant tendency of corporate capitalism in the twentieth century, a tendency toward a mixed economy in which corporate autonomy has been preserved and enhanced. Economic responsibilities of the federal government notwithstanding, the pattern of development in the United States is consistent with a more pervasive and comprehensive form of corporate domination that has been secured in large part through governmental support and regulation, not with statism or state capitalism.[2]

This developmental process has by no means been a one-sided affair unmediated by opposing forces or movements, as witnessed by the economic and political crises of the Progressive Era and the Great Depression and by the activism and reforms of the 1960s and 1970s. Corporate capitalism in the United States has shown remarkable resiliency and adaptability, just as corporate liberalism has endured precisely because it has incorporated aspects of socialist, republican, and populist ideologies without abandoning the central tenets of liberalism. When analyzed from this perspective, the social engineering that emanated from Progressive Era and New Deal reforms can be viewed for what it accomplished: the intermeshing through public law of public and private sectors to effect the corporate reconstruction of American society. This process of reconstruction has been implemented through numerous areas of law and regulatory bodies—most notably, labor law, antitrust law, administrative law, the various commissions and quasi-legal agencies created to regulate industry, finance, and labor, the Federal Reserve Board, and acts of Congress that have expanded presidential power and responsibilities in making national economic policy.[3] One need not rely on conspiracy theory to explain corporate representation in the White House and Congress or to fathom government subsidies, bailouts, and tax incentives for large corporations. On all fronts—economic, social, political— corporate power has advanced and consolidated its position through the agency of public law and the concomitant integration of public and private spheres.

The foregoing analysis does not deny that a public policy may be devised or legislated with the intent of affecting the nominally private interests or activities of corporations. Indeed, this is an essential aspect of the interaction of public and private realms, though it is often portrayed, in ideological terms, as government intrusion. Rather, the central issues for investigation concern how public policy is defined and how it is applied, which in turn depend on how we understand the broader social context of policy formation. These issues raise the further question of whether, on a given issue, a clear public interest actually can be identified and distinguished from the avowed or tacit interests of corporations. Under these circumstances, it may be that the corporate interest and the public interest have been defined or interpreted to be one and the same. Yet, there is also evidence in the twentieth century of significant regulatory legislation that clearly pitted the public's interest in environmental and consumer reform against corporations' concern for the bottom line. Corporate power has not always prevailed in such confrontations, but it does eventually respond to changing public sentiment. When the legitimacy of corporate power has been seriously questioned, corporate leaders have demonstrated considerable flexibility and political acumen. On the whole, corporate leadership in America has been more farsighted and capable of adaptation than the critics of corporate power often realize or care to admit.

The sections of this chapter examine the role of law in structuring and regulating the dimensions of corporate power in the era of corporate capitalism. Section 2 surveys trends in corporation law to demonstrate how the principle of political autonomy has shaped the restructuring of power relationships within the enterprise and thereby influenced the development of the corporation as a political institution. I argue that in addition to expanding the prerogatives of directors and officers by revising or eliminating duties owed to shareholders, the law of corporations has delegated new public (or nonpecuniary) powers to the corporate hierarchy. This aspect of my analysis lays the legal foundation for the theoretical analysis of corporate power in Chapter 6.

Sections 3 and 4 examine the regulation of corporate power in the economy, society, and politics. My overriding purpose is to demonstrate that, by design, the corporate-liberal method of regulating enterprise usually preserves, if it does not fortify, corporate autonomy. This, among other factors, helps to explain why numerous regulations affecting corporations do not necessarily produce a diminution of the power they exercise. These sections analyze the significance of the "new social regulation" of the 1960s and 1970s, the mobilization of corporate political activity in response to this form of regulation, and Supreme Court decisions concerning corporate political speech. I shall make the case that in the early 1970s, the CEOs of America's major corporations organized for direct political action and, through unprecedented lobbying efforts combined with new methods of funding campaigns, succeeded in "institutionalizing" corporate influence in electoral and congressional politics. This political mobilization of business, which has become a staple feature of national politics, is best conceived as the work of a "capitalist movement,"[4] the leaders of which have developed an agenda for both domestic and international reform.

Corporate political activity, moreover, has acquired a measure of legitimacy through Supreme Court decisions that have conferred political rights of speech on corporations. I shall argue that the evolving constitutional doctrine of "corporate free speech" must be assessed within an analytical framework that can account for judicial regulation of corporate power in both the marketplace and politics. Recent Supreme Court opinions concerning corporate political speech (similar to the method and reasoning of antitrust law) have applied the idea of fair competition to the marketplace of political ideas in order to regulate corporate political activity in candidate elections, and in doing so have acknowledged the power of large corporations to distort political debate. This development in constitutional law is part of an ongoing dispute on the Court concerning the appropriate scope of the political rights of corporations, a dispute that harkens back to the ideological division on the Bench before it adopted the rule of reason in antitrust law, in 1911.

Section 5 examines developments in antitrust law, especially as they affect mergers, and on the basis of this analysis suggests how merger regulation might shape the restructuring of the global marketplace. The Justice Department's current approach to regulating corporate power in the marketplace strongly indicates that it has revised its antitrust policy to accommodate the rise of transnational corporate enterprise. This approach is quite consistent with the policy advocated by the leaders of the new capitalist movement, who have influenced presidential decisions affecting antitrust policy since the Carter administration.

Finally, in sections 4 and 6, I further develop and summarize themes relevant to ideological aspects of law introduced in Chapter 2—most notably, the evolution of corporate individualism and the ideological ascendancy of the corporate citizen. I attempt to demonstrate the enduring importance of these ideas in providing legitimacy for law and in sustaining widespread acceptance of corporate power.

2. THE LEGAL FOUNDATION OF CORPORATE OLIGARCHY

The growth of corporate enterprise in the late nineteenth and early twentieth centuries coincided with a dramatic increase in the number of individuals holding stock in corporations. Large corporations with numerous stockholders generally were governed by boards of directors, themselves usually major stockholders in the company, who selected and supervised the executive officers of the corporation. The greater the number of stockholders, the greater the dilution of ownership, and hence the greater the likelihood that most stockholders would not be involved in most of the decision-making affecting the business of the corporation. During this same period—due largely to technological innovations, the integration within firms of methods of mass production and mass distribution, and the growth of corporations through mergers (vertical and horizontal)—the internal operations of major industrial corporations became more complex, requiring a sophisticated division of labor and a managerial structure capable of overseeing multidivisional production. To accommodate these changes affecting the distribution of stockholdings and internal growth, the large-scale corporation, like many other modern organizations of considerable size or membership, evolved the organizing principles of hierarchy and centralization of control.[5]

The combination movement, which preceded the merger wave of 1898–1904, gave impetus to the growth of large firms, and the radical revision of state incorporation laws further hastened their ascendancy. New Jersey accommodated the combination movement and legalized the holding company. But the inadequacy of state law to control the forces of corporate capital cannot be attributed solely to New Jersey's opportunism.[6] Among various logical alternatives, some Progressive Era political, business, and intellectual leaders proposed a federal incorporation statute that would have brought both the external and internal dimensions of corporate power under a unified legal authority. Instead, antitrust law settled on regulation of the external dimension of corporate power, while state law (statutory and judge-made) systematically restructured the internal government of the corporation.[7] Two developments in corporation law, mutual in their effect, enabled consolidation of the internal dimension of corporate power: the steady elimination of shareholder rights, and the delegation of powers to directors and officers to achieve centralized control.[8]

This transition from majoritarian stockholder control to oligarchic rule shapes the modern debate concerning the political significance of the internal governance of the large corporation. In order to justify the coexistence in American society of massive oligarchic structures with democratic traditions and institutions, pro-corporate writers have on occasion sought to revive romantic notions of shareholder democracy. Numerous other attempts have been made to explain the private government of the corporation within a theory of American politics. One enduring aspect of this debate, initiated in the exchange between Adolph A. Berle and Edwin Merrick Dodd in 1932, concerns the broader political and social implications of this development within corporation law itself.[9] The premise on which both Berle and Dodd based their arguments is that the expansive powers delegated to directors and management are held in trust on behalf of the corporate entity. They differed, however, as to whom the law recognized or could recognize as the beneficiaries of this trusteeship. Berle maintained that, despite the increasing separation of ownership from control within the large corporation, the consequent seizure of power by "self-perpetuating oligarchies," and the emergence of corporations as political institutions, the law continued to recognize only the disenfranchised shareholder as the sole beneficiary while it ignored the claims of society. Writing in the throes of the Great Depression, Berle argued for legislative change and expressed his skepticism about the prospect of an evolving doctrine of social responsibility taking root in the law. Dodd, on the other hand, cited legal precedent in corporation law, developments within constitutional law affecting the rights of property, and changing attitudes of enlightened corporate executives, to make the case that the law was capable of expanding from within to accommodate the perceived public responsibilities of the corporation. While it is noteworthy that Berle conceded the issue several years later, one might still question whether the matter has been settled or whether a different explanation is in order. An analysis of developments in corporation law in the twentieth century and their ideological significance provides the context for addressing this issue.

While the powers delegated to directors and the rights reserved to shareholders will vary in some respects under state incorporation laws, there is sufficient uniformity in the construction of these statutes and in their interpretation by courts to warrant generalization. The extent of the shift within the law from democratic to oligarchic control over the fortunes of the enterprise can be measured by the fact that the vast majority of shareholders in large corporations do not exercise any appreciable influence over the selection of corporate leadership or its policies. However, where ownership is widely dispersed, "control" may (theoretically) be wielded by an individual, group, or institution that owns enough stock to elect or remove a member of the board, thereby affecting corporate policy. Whether control is exercised through this means or another device or by Berle's self-perpetuating oligarchies, the fate of the enterprise, under the law of corporations, rests in the hands of the few who govern.[10]

In defining the powers and duties of the officers and directors of the corporation and the rights of its stockholders, courts in the twentieth century have in large part based their holdings on reasoning that embodies the principles of managerial efficiency and political autonomy. Managerial efficiency is a strictly economic concept that justifies the profit-making function of the corporation. It stresses the private character of enterprise and manifests a judicial predisposition to preserve and enable the apparatus of private control in the interests of traditional rights of ownership. In principle, it justifies decision-making that may be deemed to promote the pecuniary interests of the corporation as a whole. Berle and Dodd both argued, however, that this rationale did not adequately account for the nature and scope of the powers wielded by the modern corporate hierarchy. Political autonomy, on the other hand, generally includes these traditional purposes, but also encompasses policy-making and administrative decisions that extend beyond the profit-making function or what normally would be termed economic decisions. It also justifies the powers and duties of directors and officers in terms of the interests of, or benefit to, the corporate entity. But it does not ground this justification solely in the rights of ownership. I have chosen the term "political autonomy" not to indicate a discrete line of cases but to account for the expansion of the traditional rationale of managerial efficiency to embrace a variety of new matters and to suggest the breadth of the discretionary powers of directors and management. The dominant ideological trend within the law of corporations in the twentieth century may be characterized as the absorption, though not the elimination, of managerial efficiency by political autonomy. An analysis of this development will determine what significance can properly be assigned to the concept of social responsibility within the current law.

In response to the dramatic internal growth of corporations in the late nineteenth century, courts began to whittle away at the venerable doctrine of *ultra vires*, a means by which powers delegated to directors and officers had been held to strict judicial standards of accountability. At that time, an *ultra vires* violation referred to an act deemed to be outside the express purpose of the corporate charter or the powers granted therein.[11] Even before states allowed promoters to define the purpose(s) of incorporation in their charters broadly, courts had employed the concept of "implied powers" to achieve the same end, albeit in an incremental fashion. In 1896, this doctrine, which authorized acts or transactions held to be "reasonably incidental" to the express powers of the corporation, was applied by the U.S. Supreme Court to allow a Florida railroad company to lease and operate a resort hotel along one of its lines.[12] In recent years, it has been invoked to justify charitable contributions of corporations (a practice that most state laws now explicitly sanction), under the theory that a reasonable donation would satisfy social needs, thereby ultimately benefiting the corporation and hence the shareholders.[13] Of course, a more direct benefit, as courts have also noted, can be found in the federal tax deduction for such contributions, the standard employed by one court for determining the reasonableness of the amount donated. In that same case, the Court of Chancery of Delaware observed that "contemporary courts recognize that unless corporations carry an increasing share of the burden of supporting charitable and educational causes that the business advantages now reposed in corporations by law may well prove to be unacceptable to the representatives of an aroused public." To cement this point, the court declared that in virtually all state laws there exists a "recognized obligation of corporations toward philanthropic, educational and artistic causes." Whether the motivation be pecuniary or otherwise enlightened (i.e., a moral obligation with tax incentives), the legal justification recognizes the autonomy of corporate management in exercising reasonable—which is to say, broad—discretion in conducting the affairs of the enterprise.[14]

The judicial eradication, between 1880 and 1910, of the *ultra vires* doctrine forbidding directors to contract with their own corporation further enhanced the autonomy of corporate management by providing a legal basis for sanctioning the business ventures of the corporation's trustees. In the place of this once firmly entrenched principle of *ultra vires*, courts applied the fiduciary standard of loyalty which requires that a director act in good faith and not sacrifice the welfare of the corporation for personal aggrandizement. If a majority of the disinterested directors have approved the contract, courts will be inclined to find the transaction fair, provided that it is not fraudulent or blatantly wasteful of corporate assets. This presumption of disinterestedness on the part of other board members, however, is precisely what earlier case law had rejected as lacking credibility.[15] Nevertheless, courts have never offered a reasoned justification for the new policy.[16]

It would be a mistake, though, to attribute this dramatic reversal in the law simply to the amenability of judges to enlarge the personal fortunes of corporate directors. When understood within the context of the combination movement, and in light of the modern rule that also upholds contracts formed through interlocking directorships, its practical purpose becomes clear. In an 1895 decision, the New York Supreme Court succinctly explained the dilemma:

> Indeed, it would be difficult to conduct the affairs of the multifarious corporations of the country, many of which, although apparently sustaining the relations of rivals in business, are nevertheless practically controlled by the same directors, if the element of good faith, instead of individual interests, were not established as the basis of intercorporate action.[17]

By accommodating the internal dimension of corporate governance to the growth of power in the external dimension, courts and legislatures enabled and validated oligarchic rule in the large corporation. It would seem to be a reasonable conclusion, moreover, that the unstated rationale that justified this legal acquiescence was the principle of political autonomy.

As trustees of the corporation, directors and officers must observe the fiduciary duty of care as well as loyalty. Judges generally have interpreted the standard of care in light of the broad and flexible test of reasonableness. Thus, if a rational basis for an act exists, however unwise or unprofitable the outcome, a director will be absolved of negligence. Courts have devised a special doctrine for such cases—the business judgment rule—which may be invoked to insulate the responsible parties within the corporation from legal scrutiny. If an act may be deemed to fall within the bounds of "sound business judgment," subject to the test of reasonableness, the court declares it to be a matter of internal management outside the reach of the law.[18] The application of this rule in modern cases provides substantial evidence of increasing judicial deference to the principle of political autonomy. It applies, for example, to corporate refusal to sue, the pricing and issuance of stock, executive compensation, the valuation of property exchanged for stock, the declaration of dividends, *ultra vires* contracts, preventative strategies to ward off hostile takeover attempts, and the purchase of stock to retain control in the face of a takeover bid.

With marked frequency, the business judgment rule has been employed to dismiss derivative suits—that is, suits initiated by shareholders on behalf of the corporate entity when directors refuse to pursue a cause of action, for example, refusal to sue a fellow director for alleged breach of duties.[19] In *Gall v. Exxon Corporation*, decided in 1976, District Court Judge Robert L. Carter considered the reasonableness of Exxon's stated policy of not instigating suits against present or former directors or officers of its subsidiary, Esso Italiana, who were involved in making secret payments and other contributions totaling $59 million, between 1963 and 1972, to Italian political parties. Judge Carter's approach to the problem typifies the judiciary's application of the business judgment rule:

> In recent months, the legality and morality of foreign political contributions, bribes and other payments by American corporations has been widely debated. The issue before me for decision, however, is not whether the payments made by Esso Italiana to Italian political parties and other unauthorized payments were proper or improper. Were the court to frame the issue in this way, it would necessarily involve itself in the business decisions of every corporation, and be required to mediate between the judgment of the directors and the judgment of the shareholders with regard to particular corporate actions. . . . Rather, the issue is whether the Special Committee, acting as Exxon's Board of Directors and in the sound exercise of their business judgment, may determine that a suit against any present or former director or officer would be contrary to the best interests of the corporation.[20]

Clearly, the court's concern in *Gall*, not unlike cases involving corporate contracts with directors, stems from the judiciary's long-standing trepidation about unraveling the veil of privacy that shrouds corporate affairs and from its presumed incompetence to judge matters of internal policy—a familiar refrain in the law of corporations. Furthermore, the business judgment rule has been invoked to justify corporate policies on grounds that expand (but still embody) the traditional rationale of managerial efficiency, similar to arguments upholding charitable donations. For example, in dismissing a derivative suit against the Chicago Cubs board of directors alleging negligence for failure to install lights for night games, the Appellate Court of Illinois surmised that the best interests of the corporation and its stockholders might be served by a decision that incorporated concerns for preserving, not disturbing, the surrounding neighborhood.[21] Thus, the long view of corporate welfare, which would appear to include the interests of stockholders and the public, supplants profitability in the short term.

In such instances, motives may prove to be elusive. Whether social considerations outweigh pecuniary objectives at board meetings, however, is of less import than the fact that courts are willing to allow, though not to impose, a corporate ethic that, in principle, preserves the interests of ownership while demonstrating a concern for public issues.[22] To view this as evidence of a movement within the law (of the sort championed by Dodd) to redefine the beneficiaries of the corporate powers held in trust would be misleading. Rather, it is better understood as a movement toward corporate hegemony over society, an ideological expression that is consistent with the structure and power of the modern corporation and informed by the principle of political autonomy. From this standpoint, the Berle-Dodd debate is resolved and transcended as the claims of ownership lose their primacy and meld with the exigencies of expanding power. The legal foundation of shareholder rights continues to be eroded in the interests of broadening the reach of corporate powers. But no new constraints on management's prerogatives appear in their place. In the name of the social good, of enlightened corporate citizenship, the discretion of the corporate hierarchy grows, while the checks on its power dwindle or become impotent. Increasingly, under the modern rules of law governing the internal dimension of corporate power, the beneficiaries of the trust are, quite simply, those whom the corporate policy-makers choose to benefit.

In addition to granting broad discretionary powers, the business judgment rule seems to establish a general presumption of judicial noninterference in internal corporate affairs. This judicial deference to the political autonomy of the corporation has rendered traditional means of holding corporate directors and officers accountable for their actions ineffective. It has greatly contributed to the historic eradication of legal doctrines once deemed essential to protect the interests of shareholders. Although this trend has not been fully realized,[23] its success can be gauged by the systematic expansion of broad powers vested in the board of directors and by the corresponding diminution of shareholder rights evidenced by the steady dismissal of derivative suits, the qualification and elimination of preemptive rights by statute and corporate powers to issue stock, and the control of the proxy machinery by the dominant few.[24] Struggles for control have of course increased with the recent merger battles. But this is the trench warfare of the modern combination movement, not a resurgence of stockholder democracy.[25]

Corporation law, therefore, has accommodated managerial control of corporate enterprise through doctrines that justify the private nature of corporate decision-making. The effect of this method of judicial reasoning is clear. The internal organization and exercise of corporate power, however public in its consequences, may be relegated to the private sphere, where oligarchy will presumably be tolerated. In this sense, private enterprise is private government. To judge one is to judge the other. Under the ideological cloak of privacy, corporate policies—political and economic— may be shielded from judicial scrutiny and public view. But in an oligopolistic economy where combination and cooperation render traditional notions of competition meaningless, the "private" decisions of the marketplace do not hold the same theoretical significance for "competition." If traditional justifications do not apply, if classical theory must be constantly buoyed up to preserve its ideological purpose, then one may conclude that the private realm created by corporation law, the legal bastion of free enterprise, legitimizes oligarchic rule in addition to the profit-making function of the corporation. This, rather than the emergence of a legal presumption favoring corporate social responsibility, would seem to be the lesson of the past century. While the public law of antitrust broadly regulates the external dimension of corporate power, under the theory that concentrated power poses dangers to individual liberty and to equality of opportunity, the law of corporations shields and fortifies the private structure of this power under the theory that, barring fraud or illegal acts, the internal decision-making process of the corporation should be governed by the discretionary principle of sound business judgment. Thus, as the public law of the corporation assumes new jurisdictions over the marketplace, the private law of the corporation delegates public powers to the corporate hierarchy.

In the twentieth century, the transformation of corporation law initiated by New Jersey in 1888 evolved as statutory and judge-made law redefined relationships of control within the enterprise. By vesting new powers in corporate officers and eliminating shareholders' rights, the common law of corporations augmented the prerogatives of majority ownership of the previous era while rendering inutile its principle of majoritarian control. Courts validated this restructuring of power relations with decisions that emphasized the paramountcy of political rule, not the rights of property ownership, as the determinative principle of control within the corporation. Accordingly, as the judicial precept of political autonomy superseded that of managerial efficiency, power based on managerial control superseded power based on property relations. Thus, by enabling and regulating the public (or nonpecuniary) aspects of corporate decision-making, the law helped to shape the political nature of the modern corporation.

3. CORPORATE SOCIAL RESPONSIBILITY, THE LAW, AND POLITICS

a. Corporate Liberalism and Regulation

The Progressive Era and New Deal reforms established the legal framework within which the federal government regulates the marketplace, financial dealings, labor relations, and agricultural production. Although legislation has been amended, rules and procedures judicially revised or augmented, and some regulatory bodies eliminated, the basic structure and methods of economic regulation remain in effect. These two critical episodes in the corporate reconstruction of American capitalism were followed by a third period of regulatory reform, which began in the late 1960s and ended about a decade later. Between 1969 and 1975, more than thirty major regulatory acts were passed. The most important innovations occurred in areas of the so-called "new social regulation," such as consumer protection, enivironmental protection, and health and safety.

Regulation provides a means whereby the public interest, as defined or interpreted by legislative bodies, commissions, agencies, and courts, can be invoked to subject corporate decision-makers to standards of social responsibility. Typically, regulation consists in establishing rules and procedures that prohibit certain forms of behavior. Most types of economic and social regulation rely on the threat of penalties to encourage compliance. While prohibiting specific forms of behavior, however, regulation implicitly sanctions other behavior. Regulation is therefore not simply a coercive tool; it is also a method of achieving a desired result by defining the boundaries of self-regulation.

Traditionally, the agencies and commissions responsible for economic regulation have proved to be sensitive to the needs of the large corporation. Flexibility in the law and discretion accorded the rule-making bodies have more often than not been conducive to producing a sympathetic regulatory environment, although several other factors may be crucial in determining the relationship between the regulators and the regulated parties over time.[26] The new form of social regulation, on the other hand, while subject to judicial review, is most likely to be ameliorated through legislative action, and to some extent through policy changes in the executive departments responsible for administering the relevant law. Because of this, efforts of corporations to influence regulatory policy concerning environmental, consumer protection, and health and safety issues have been highly politicized since the early 1970s.

The corporate-liberal method of regulation, whether by government agency, commission, or the judiciary, has preserved corporate autonomy while establishing limitations on the exercise of corporate power. Corporate autonomy refers to the capacity of the corporate hierarchy to exercise power. This capacity arises from the conditions that establish and structure relationships of control. Autonomy is thus a function of how power is structured and regulated. Regulation often imposes limitations on the exercise of corporate power and can therefore affect corporate autonomy, in the sense that autonomy can be enhanced or diminished by the presence or absence of constraints. This means that a corporation can be more or less autonomous with regard to making certain decisions.

Autonomy, therefore, becomes problematical only when the condition necessary for the exercise of power is altered—that is, when the basic relationships of control no longer exist. Theoretically, autonomy could be regulated out of existence, but this would in effect entail the arrogation of corporate decision-making by the state, and elimination of various rights that secure the conditions for the exercise of corporate power in both the internal and the external dimensions. Therefore, regulation should not be confused with state command or control of enterprise. The foregoing analysis, moreover, does not preclude the possibility that government may on occasion issue directives that diminish or eliminate autonomy with regard to specific matters affecting the public interest.

Because regulation imposes constraints on the exercise of power, one might reason that as the total number of regulations increase, corporate autonomy diminishes. One could conclude that the complex and extensive regulatory apparatus of state and federal governments in the United

States seriously intrudes on corporate decision-making.[27] However, the relationship between regulation and corporate power must be analyzed in light of several factors that militate against such a conclusion.

To begin with, constraints on the exercise of corporate power in the marketplace generally serve to stabilize power relationships. For example, by prohibiting a variety of anticompetitive practices, antitrust law generally preserves oligopoly and prohibits monopoly. The autonomy of individual firms to make decisions is reduced, but their market power acquires a degree of stability and legitimacy that might enhance autonomy in other respects, precisely because the power of all corporations in the marketplace is likewise limited. This type of regulation endeavors to divide market power (and thereby preserve oligopolistic or potential competition), rather than permitting firms to engage in destructive competition leading to monopolistic control of the market. Thus, regulation is not necessarily antithetical to the interests of those being regulated. Corporate power in unregulated competitive markets is far less stable than it is in regulated markets. Indeed, this was the lesson that inspired many corporate leaders in the last quarter of the nineteenth century to seek regulatory relief in the first instance.

In assessing the relative increase or decrease of corporate autonomy, one must also take into account how effective regulations are in compelling a change in behavior. Numerous variables come into play, including the amount of resources committed to enforcement, the likelihood of enforcement, and the relative costs or benefits to corporations for complying with the regulations. The existence of regulations does not preclude the possibility of working around constraints or simply ignoring them. Other strategies might be adopted depending on the nature of the regulation. For example, decisions of regulatory bodies or courts can be appealed, and various delaying tactics can be employed, to keep cases in litigation for years. Of course, large corporations might quickly comply with regulations that they have previously opposed, or might decide not to appeal a decision of a court or agency, not out of narrow economic interest but out of broader political considerations. A short-term loss may be preferable to a serious drop in public confidence that could influence the corporation's effectiveness in influencing policy in other areas.

Regulation does not always involve enforcement. Behavior can be regulated by interpreting rules more liberally to enhance corporate autonomy and to allow for greater self-regulation. This is an essential aspect of regulatory policies that structure the marketplace. For example, in an effort to aid American firms in global competition, the Department of Justice under the Reagan and Bush administrations loosened restrictions on mergers, thus accelerating a restructuring of markets through combination. Moreover, the history of regulation in the United States strongly suggests that the adversarial nature of the relationship between regulators and the corporations being regulated is subject to significant fluctuation over time. Personnel changes on federal courts, commissions, and administrative agencies can have a profound impact on regulatory policies, as evidenced by the appointments President Reagan made to the federal judiciary, the Federal Trade Commission, the Environmental Protection Agency, the National Labor Relations Board, the Occupational Safety and Health Administration, and numerous other agencies or commissions.[28]

Even as regulations of corporate power increase, corporate autonomy can be enhanced by other legal changes affecting the structure of corporate power. Indeed, there seems to be almost an inverse relationship between regulation of the internal and external dimensions of corporate power. As corporate power over society has been subject to increasing regulation through public law, the powers of the corporate hierarchy have been increasingly fortified through the law of corporations. But the external dimension of corporate power has been strengthened as well. Just as the wave of new social regulation reached its peak in the late 1970s, the Supreme Court conferred First Amendment political rights on corporations. On balance, this development in constitutional law might have done more to enhance corporate autonomy than all the new social regulations might have done to decrease it.

The rise of transnational enterprise adds yet another dimension to the analysis of corporate autonomy. Most corporations that dominate industry and finance in the United States are transnational; they do business in a global marketplace. Accordingly, the CEOs of these corporations make decisions from a global perspective. Constraints imposed on corporate autonomy in one nation must be examined in terms of how they affect the corporation's operations in other nations. CEOs of transnational firms make strategic economic and political decisions in light of numerous variables and constraints. They adapt to their environments. If the long-term benefits for the corporation as a whole outweigh the projected costs, regulatory inconviences can be endured. Whether or not managerial autonomy within a transnational firm is enhanced or diminished significantly by regulations within a particular country will depend on a variety of factors, including what is being regulated, the cost of complying, the possible effects of regulation on other decisions, the options available if regulation becomes too burdensome, and the prospects of changing regulatory policy. Increasingly, it becomes misleading to analyze corporate power in strictly national terms when the external dimension of that power is transnational.

Consequently, what may seem plausible at first glance—that an increase in the number of regulations results in a diminished corporate autonomy—is not necessarily true. At the very least, it is misleading in its simplicity. The intersecting of public and private spheres in the era of corporate capitalism in the United States has produced a mixed economy in which corporations, not the state, command the marketplace. The internal dimension of corporate power, as it has been reconstituted and regulated through the law of corporations, guarantees the autonomy of the corporate hierarchy and generally shields the private realm of corporate decision-making from public scrutiny. While it is true that regulations affecting the external dimension of corporate power can impose constraints that complicate decision-making and thereby diminish corporate autonomy, such regulations might also stabilize (external) relationships of control and confer legitimacy on corporations by subjecting them to a standard of social responsibility.

While scholars continue to debate whether the regulatory reforms of the 1960s and 1970s have made corporations more socially responsible, they do not dispute the fact that these reforms encouraged large corporations to develop new means of influencing electoral outcomes and congressional politics. Corporations also have access to the hearts and minds of Americans through mass media, especially television commercials that aim to shape public opinion on issues of corporate social responsibility. A systematic public-relations campaign waged by leading corporations since the early 1970s has gone a long way toward transforming a negative public image of the large corporation. Indeed, the renewed public acceptance of the corporate statesman is evidenced in the celebrity status of business executives and the willingness of Americans to look to these individuals for political leadership.

Corporate political activity complicates the analysis of corporate social responsibility because corporations are not only subjects of regulation but also usually active participants in the political process that promulgates the regulatory policies that affect them. Thus it would appear that corporate political activity introduces a variable into our analysis that may prove to be decisive in assessing the relationship between corporate power and regulation.

b. The New Politics of Business

Croly, Weyl, and other Progressive Era thinkers argued that corporate domination stemmed from the ability of corporations to control or influence political leaders. A revived democracy was essential to their programs of reform. In addition to state enactments providing for the referendum, initiative, and recall (designed to make politicians more accountable and to enhance direct democracy), numerous states and the federal government in the early twentieth century also passed corrupt-practices acts that aimed, in part, to prohibit corporations from influencing the political process through campaign contributions. Large corporations nevertheless devised various ways of getting around these constraints.[29] Regardless of the law, the chief executives of America's leading industrial and financial corporations retained considerable influence in Congress and the White House through numerous informal as well as formal contacts. Except in times of crisis, corporate leaders did not resort to a community-wide mobilization of its resources to influence congressional policy.

In the aftermath of the Great Depression and World War II, the American economy thrived while corporate executives enjoyed unprecedented prestige. The warlike confrontations between business and labor in the 1930s had given way to collective bargaining. Strikes had become an integral aspect of negotiating wages and benefits, rather than a potential lever for radical change.[30] During this period, the AFL-CIO's influence in Congress and in electoral politics expanded as a result of its alliance with the Democratic Party. However, big business and big labor managed to coexist. Cold war ideology helped them forge a common bond that precluded a revival of revolutionary unionism, and labor did not pose a threat on the industrial front so long as the economy prospered. Corporate power had never been more secure.

In the late 1960s, however, the public image of the large corporation gradually began to change. The apparent intransigence and arrogance of certain corporations in refusing to acknowledge or remedy numerous problems associated with public health and safety had nurtured a growing public suspicion that corporations were not socially responsible.[31] This perception was reinforced by an outpouring of books and well-publicized accounts of Congressional hearings on corporate negligence in matters affecting the environment, health, safety, and consumer protection. Anticorporate sentiment among youth and political activists ran high, undoubtedly fueled by a more general dissatisfaction with the war in Vietnam, racial injustice, and the many revelations of Watergate, especially the illegal corporate funding of campaigns. Yet discontent with corporate leadership was not limited to activists and the counterculture. Public concern with pollution, the energy crisis, and a host of consumer issues was genuine and widespread. For a brief period, a burgeoning public-interest movement thrived in a political environment that had become increasingly hostile to large corporations. In the decade of the 1970s, corporate power in America once again faced a crisis of legitimacy.

From 1969 to 1972, Congress established the Environmental Protection

Agency and passed the Coal Mine Safety Act, the Clean Air Act Amendments (1970), the Consumer Product Safety Act, the Occupational Safety and Health Act, the Poison Prevention Packaging Act, the Federal Water Pollution Control Act, and the Federal Environmental Pesticide Control Act. Of these, the Clean Air Act Amendments, which imposed strict deadlines on states and industry for compliance with national air-quality standards, constituted a resounding defeat for the giants of the auto industry. The legislative outcome of the other acts was not as decisive. Because the prospect of defeating these acts was unlikely, corporate lobbies adopted the strategy of compromising on key points or not opposing the legislation. But clearly the new wave of regulatory reform signaled a decline in corporate influence in Congress and the White House. Business leaders had been caught off guard. As a group, large corporations were unprepared to battle the lobbying efforts of well-organized public-interest lobbies that enjoyed broad public support. A confluence of events, some quite unexpected, had made Congress increasingly susceptible to the influence of the public-interest movement.

Between 1968 and 1970, some 253 new Democratic members were elected to the House of Representatives. By 1975, an additional 150 freshmen members had entered. The liberal tendencies of the House from the late 1960s through the mid-1970s reflected this dramatic turnover. Beginning in 1971, the Democratic majority in the House radically revised the rules governing the committee system. Under the old rules, power was lodged in committee chairmanships, a position acquired solely on the basis of seniority (years of consecutive service), and subcommittee chairmen were deprived of autonomy. A new majority of Democrats found itself powerless under these rules and soon remedied the situation. By empowering subcommittee chairmen and limiting the number of committee chairmanships that could be held by senior members, the new rules of the 1970s democratized, but also fragmented, power in Congress. Unwittingly, the Democratic reformers made the legislative process more vulnerable to a variety of special interests.

In 1968, insurgents in the Democratic Party eliminated the winner-take-all rule in primaries, caucuses, and party conventions, thus ensuring proportional delegate representation in the nominating convention. Moreover, delegates were required to commit to a candidate before being elected to the convention. Between 1968 and 1976, the number of states holding primaries nearly doubled. By the latter date, approximately three-fourths of convention delegates (Democrats and Republicans) were selected by this method. These events severely diminished the ability of party leaders to influence the selection of presidential candidates, thereby further weakening party leadership in an already fragmented Congress. Although unintended, the Federal Election Campaign Act's limitations on individual contributions to candidates only enhanced these tendencies by encouraging the proliferation of political action committees (PACs). Rapidly, PACs became the preferred means whereby special interests sought to influence members of Congress through funding their campaigns. In such an environment, corporations could no longer rely on the traditional power brokers—party leaders and committee chairs—to defend corporate interests, especially when large segments of the public supported regulatory reform.

In the early 1970s, many of America's most powerful corporate executives organized to meet a perceived attack on the business community as a whole. Combining their formidable resources, they launched a new-style political activism on several fronts and set out not only to reclaim some of the ground they had lost, but also to curb the influence of the public-interest movement as well as that of organized labor. Less than a decade later, all these objectives had been accomplished. However, big business did not win in Congress only as a result of its financial capability. Funding campaigns through PACs constituted but one aspect of a three-pronged strategy; a new style of lobbying and a massive campaign to shape public opinion accounted for the other two.

The Business Roundtable was formed in 1972–73 from the merger of three business groups: the Labor Study Group, the Construction Users Anti-Inflation Roundtable, and the March Group. Composed exclusively of the CEOs of America's leading 200 industrial, financial, and service corporations, the Roundtable's membership represents corporations whose combined sales account for approximately half the gross national product of the United States and who employ more than 10 million people. The Roundtable's organization and methods constitute a sharp break with corporate tradition. In the past, CEOs of major corporations had rarely taken time to lobby one-on-one with members of Congress. Even more important, these efforts had never been systematically coordinated among different industries and sectors of the economy. By pooling the combined resources and talent of its membership, centralizing leadership in the small Executive Committee that makes recommendations to the Policy Committee, then dividing responsibilities among issue-oriented task forces (thereby efficiently using its reservoir of influence and expertise), the Roundtable has applied modern managerial techniques to cope with the fragmented power structure of Congress. This strategy is aided by contracting out. On several occasions, the Roundtable has retained the services of influential legal and lobbying firms in Washington, D.C., to help fight its battles. In addition, Roundtable members have personally lobbied, consulted with, and advised Presidents on a regular basis since the Ford administration.[32]

But the Business Roundtable is not alone. It has often forged alliances with other business lobbies, such as the Committee for Effective Capital Recovery, the American Business Conference, and numerous trade associations. Some of the Roundtable's most dramatic successes in national politics have been the result of joint efforts with the small-business lobby led by the United States Chamber of Commerce, the National Association of Manufacturers, and the National Federation of Independent Business. Generating massive grass-roots support was also crucial to the new lobbying strategy. A revived Chamber of Commerce, nurtured by the Roundtable, achieved considerable success in orchestrating grass-roots campaigns on important legislation. And the proliferation of corporate PACs, from 89 in 1974 to 1,467 in 1982, helped many CEOs realize the objective of involving corporate employees in political activities.[33]

Another aspect of the new style of corporate politics is evidenced by the method employed to channel PAC monies to candidates. In 1974, corporate PACs contributed only $4.4 million to congressional candidates, whereas corporate contributions had grown to $27.4 million in the 1982 congressional election. While the Federal Election Commission (FEC) ruled in the *Sun-Pac* advisory opinion of 1975 that corporations may form as many PACs as desired, the law permits each PAC to contribute a maximum of $5,000 to a candidate per election. Thus with the huge proliferation of corporate and trade association PACs in the 1970s, the prospect of wielding influence through campaign contributions became increasingly problematic. A means of channeling these contributions was necessary. In meeting this need, the Business Industry Political Action Committee (BIPAC) and the U.S. Chamber of Commerce PAC have served as information clearinghouses for business PAC contributions. Both publish newsletters that provide up-to-date information on electoral contests, recommend candidates, and analyze the possible impact of contributions on the outcome of races and congressional policy.[34] Incumbents and conservative Republicans have been the greatest beneficiaries of this strategy, which had some immediate success in transforming the voting patterns of a once-liberal majority in Congress.[35]

Signs of a renewed business influence in Congress and the White House were apparent by 1975, but the most dramatic shifts in congressional policy occurred during the Carter presidency. The victories in which the Business Roundtable played a key role were all the more impressive because they were achieved in the same Democratic Congress that had boldly confronted corporate power on the most controversial issues of social regulation. The highlights include the defeat of the proposed Consumer Protection Agency, the defeat of common situs picketing, the defeat of the Labor Law Reform Bill (which sought to repeal the right-to-work provision of the Taft-Hartley Act), the passing of the 1978 Revenue Act (which decreased both corporate income tax and capital-gains tax), the revision and elimination of deadlines in the Clean Air Act Amendments (accomplished with the support of the United Automobile Workers), and the passing of legislation that restricted the rule-making powers of the FTC. The Roundtable was also instrumental in persuading President Jimmy Carter to institute voluntary rather than mandatory wage-price controls in 1978 and to scuttle his plans for a more vigorous antitrust policy.[36]

By 1980, the Roundtable had acquired a unique reputation as both a powerful business lobby capable of building broad-based coalitions and a bipartisan political organization skilled in the art of negotitation and compromise. Indeed, the Roundtable's positions sometimes baffled and angered segments of the business community who believed that the Roundtable was sacrificing the interests of business out of political expediency. The fact that the CEOs of America's leading corporations were taking positions that were inconsistent with the bottom-line expectations of many business groups might have caused some critics to mistake corporate statesmanship for mere opportunism.[37]

The Roundtable's leadership role in Congress during the early 1980s was also significant. For example, the business community displayed remarkable unity in its successful lobbying efforts to revise federal tax policy in 1981. Meeting over breakfast at the Carlton Hotel, the so-called "Carlton Group," composed of leaders of the Roundtable, the Chamber of Commerce, the Council for Capital Formation, the National Federation of Independent Business, the Committee for Effective Capital Recovery, and the American Business Conference devised a joint strategy that they successfully implemented through unprecedented lobbying efforts.[38] On the whole, however, unified business action was not as pronounced throughout the 1980s as it had been in the late 1970s, largely because it was not necessary and partly because the failures of Reaganomics had affected sectors of the business community differently. This became apparent in the inability of business groups to reach a consensus on the complex and divisive issue of tax reform in 1986.[39] The Roundtable also failed to persuade Congress to pass legislation regulating hostile takeovers and was unsuccessful in its attempt to make notification of plant closings voluntary rather than mandatory.

The issues that helped to forge a unification of big and small business in the late 1970s were not present throughout most of the 1980s. To be sure, the major opponents of big business had been defeated or held in check. Labor's power in Congress continued to diminish, while the influence of the consumer and environmental movements had been greatly reduced, as had the effectiveness of the federal agencies once aligned with these movements. Through budget and staff reductions, poor or nonexistent enforcement of the law, and incompetent management, the policing activities of the EPA and OSHA—the symbols of the new social regulation much despised within large segments of the business community—had been severely diminished.[40]

It would be misleading to measure the Roundtable's significance in national politics by a tally sheet alone. Its presence represents more than a temporary resurgence of corporate political activity to meet a crisis. Corporate America has become politicized and has shown no signs of returning to business as usual.[41] The Roundtable's approach provides an insight into this development. By addressing broad issues that affect the corporate community as a whole, devising a common strategy, working with small-business organizations and other groups to that end, developing strong grass-roots support among employees, and promoting a cooperative relationship with government officials, the Roundtable has redefined the nature of corporate political activity in Congress. The Business Roundtable simply does not fit the traditional definition of an economic interest-group.

One might consider, for example, the Roundtable's plan to overhaul the American educational system by the year 2000 (detailed in *The Business Roundtable Education Initiative*, in 1989). The premise of the Roundtable's initiative is that elementary and secondary schools in the United States must be restructured to adapt to the realities of a dynamic global marketplace.[42] In 1989, the Roundtable established a CEO Education Task Force, which assigned 150 CEOs to discuss the initiative with the governors of states where their firms do business. Several other major business organizations—the National Alliance of Business, the United States Chamber of Commerce, the Committee for Economic Development, and the National Association of Manufacturers—are also involved in promoting educational reform consistent with the Roundtable's proposals for a corporate reconstruction of American education.[43]

While matters affecting trade and global competition remain at the top of its political agenda, the Roundtable has also ventured into areas of national policy that defy the narrow logic of interest-group politics. In 1991, it took upon itself the task of negotiating a compromise on the Jobs-Rights Bill, which was vehemently opposed by the Bush administration. After intense pressure from small business and the White House, the Roundtable negotiators backed off, having been told in effect that they had overstepped their bounds. The supporters of the bill disagreed. Apparently, the Roundtable was very close to reaching a satisfactory solution that would ensure passage. In any event, this debacle made it clear that the most powerful corporations in the United States were willing to support a measure that would have reversed all or portions of six 1989 Supreme Court decisions limiting rights of workers to challenge discrimination in the workplace.[44]

During the first two years of the Clinton administration, the Business Roundtable again proved that it is a force to be reckoned with. Indeed, the Roundtable's decision to support a version of Representative Jim Cooper's health-care plan, while rejecting President Clinton's proposal altogether, spelled final defeat for the administration's efforts to pass its bill in 1994. Roundtable Chairman John D. Ong, CEO of B. F. Goodrich Company, explained that most of the membership feared that the Clinton plan would give the federal government too much control over health care and at the same time create an uncontrollable entitlement program. Moreover, Ong denied the charge that Roundtable representatives from insurance, drug, and other industries involved with health care had unduly influenced fellow members to vote against Clinton's plan. In any event, the Roundtable's decision, which was endorsed by the National Association of Manufacturers and the Chamber of Commerce, was generally consistent with the views of the three major insurance lobbies—the Health Insurance Association of America (small and medium companies), the Group Health Association of America (health maintenance organizations), and the Alliance for Managed Competition (large companies). Through these organizations, the insurance industry spent more than $45 million on a media campaign that quickly put the Clinton administration on the defensive. Despite the administration's efforts to counter this attack with its own media blitz, a steady barrage of television and radio commercials opposing the bill proved to be widely influential and were an important factor in convincing many members of Congress not to support the Clinton plan. Although differing on certain aspects of health-care reform, the leaders of big and small business had found common ground and joined forces once again to win an impressive victory in Congress.[45]

There is yet another aspect of corporate political activity that indicates the broad objectives of corporate power. Beginning in the early 1970s, numerous corporations initiated a variety of advertising and public-relations campaigns designed to shape public opinion. As part of this effort, an estimated $1 billion are spent annually by firms to sell an image of the responsible corporation or to advocate a position on an issue.[46] Image advertising, whether on radio, television, or in print, usually takes the form of an unobtrusive self-endorsement presented as a public relations announcement. Advocacy advertising—selling a point of view—appears most frequently in print media. Not surprisingly, the most conspicuous users of image and advocacy advertising have been the major oil and chemical companies, which have often been targets of consumer and environmental groups; however, the practice of corporate self-promotion is quite widespread and growing. Positive corporate images can also be conveyed effectively on television through product endorsements. Smiling faces, high production values, and a corporate logo can also shape attitudes, especially those of a new generation.

While the impact of these campaigns on public opinion is difficult to measure, there is no question that the frequency and intensity of public outcries about the lack of corporate social responsibility have diminished considerably since the early 1970s.[47] Numerous other factors, such as concern with the worsening state of the economy, can help account for this change. But it is clear that a revived commitment to traditional business values combined with an antigovernment (anti-"liberal") backlash coincided with massive and sustained efforts of corporations to shape the public mind in the late 1970s and early 1980s. During this same period, the budgets of several conservative, corporate-funded think tanks grew dramatically. Dedicated to influencing academic debate and providing policy proposals for all levels of government, such newly formed organizations as the American Enterprise Institute (1970), the Heritage Foundation (1973), the American Council for Capital Formation (1973), the Center for the Study of American Business (1975), and the long-established Hoover Institution on War, Revolution, and Peace (1919) and National Bureau of Economic Research (1920), played an important role in the resurrection of free-market ideology and the ascendance of the conservative wing within the Republican Party.[48]

Pro-business values perhaps received their greatest boost from President Ronald Reagan, who was the undisputed choice of the business community in the 1980 election. Although ideologically more at home with the laissez-faire homilies of small business, Reagan, by constantly reciting the moral virtues of capitalism, paved the way for a kinder image of capitalism, if not of the large corporation. In practice, however, Reagan proved to be a right-leaning corporate liberal in the tradition of Harding and Coolidge, not a genuine throwback to the age of laissez-faire. Deregulation, by no means a strictly Republican issue, did radically alter the structure of the airlines industry and entailed significant restructuring in the trucking, railroad, savings and loan, natural gas, and telecommunications industries. While these changes have had mixed results for consumers, they did not constitute a significant dismantling of the regulatory process. But the much-vaunted reform of the bureaucracy failed, and indeed was abandoned fairly early in Reagan's administration. On the other hand, tax cuts and incentives for corporations and a revised antitrust policy helped to fuel a merger movement and, as a consequence, a restructuring within enterprise and the market.

c. Corporate Power and Political Reform

As an issue in American politics, corporate social responsibility is closely linked with the legitimacy of corporate power. During three periods of regulatory reform in the twentieth century, when corporate social responsibility became an issue of widespread concern in American society, the accountability of corporate power came under close scrutiny. Regulatory innovation and reform have served to quell public opposition to corporate power and to provide it with a measure of legitimacy. During periods of relative calm, when corporate power has not been subjected to similar scrutiny, Americans have been more likely to favor greater self-regulation by corporations and to show more trust in the corporate conscience.

Through this process of recurrent regulatory reform, corporate leaders have on the whole become more socially conscious and responsible, but they have also become more politically astute. They have learned that Americans possess an ingrained distrust of concentrated power and that the acceptable standards of corporate social responsibility will depend largely on the public's perception of that power at a given time. They have also learned that it would be foolhardy to assume that there will not be another period of upheaval in American politics that brings with it new demands for regulation of corporations. But corporate statesmen are now better prepared for political adversity. They know that, to shape the future, one must have the means to influence the present. To this end, the leading industrial and financial corporations in the United States (and in many cases throughout the world) have established a formidable presence in Congress and continue to conduct a sophisticated public-relations campaign through the media.

Corporate political activity in the late twentieth century constitutes one aspect of a concerted effort by leading corporations to mold public opinion and influence national policy on numerous issues, domestic and international. This effort is best conceived as a capitalist movement in the reformist tradition of corporate liberalism. However, it is a movement that represents an important departure from the corporate-liberal coalitions that emerged from the social turmoil of the Progressive Era and the Great Depression. Conspicuous in its lack of cross-class leadership, it is truly a business-dominated movement consisting of thousands of active supporters across the country. Managers, corporate employees, shareholders, and members of trade associations and small-business organizations have become involved in the new politics of business. Supporters will also be found in government, in academic institutions, in think tanks, and in the media. This movement strongly overlaps with traditionally Republican groups and has contributed to and taken advantage of the revitalization of the Republican Party, but its corporate leadership has remained bipartisan. Because of this, there have been and will continue to be significant divisions within the movement on particular matters of policy.

To describe the political mobilization of business as one aspect of a capitalist movement, therefore, does not imply that business is of one mind or acts monolithically. The business community's ability to present a unified front will depend on a number of factors.[49] But the idea of a capitalist movement does describe a degree of organization, planning, communication, and concerted activity that cannot be explained simply as the product of a fortuitous convergence of interests. This is as true for grass-roots organizing as it is for strategizing and planning at the higher levels.[50] It is in the nature of social movements to rise and dissipate. Although this may prove to be the case insofar as a lasting alliance between big business and small business is concerned, such a schism would not prevent the corporate leadership of this movement from pursuing its broader goals in Congress or the White House. Because the balance of power within the business community is strongly tilted in favor of the large corporation, a more likely scenario is that small business will find ways to compromise to retain its effectiveness. And there is no reason to believe that the new politics of business will be pursued with less vigor. Political participation has become an essential component of modern corporate culture.

The political mobilization of business is therefore not a passing fad. Leaders of the Business Roundtable, in league with other business groups, have successfully forged a new direction in American politics by institutionalizing corporate influence in the electoral process and in Congress.[51] Acting alone or together, corporate lobbies will still pursue particular economic or institutional interests. In many respects, however, the activities of the Business Roundtable represent a departure from the normal routine of interest-group politics. The institutionalization of corporate influence in Congress involves a type of cooperation and planning that resembles the organizational role of political parties more than it does the behavior of traditional interest-groups. Many corporate PACs figure prominently in this organizational network by providing a means of mobilizing grass-roots support, disseminating information, and coordinating electoral strategies among corporations. Moreover, PACs (corporate and other) have supplanted the national parties as the primary means of fund-raising for campaigns. Corporate and trade-association PACs now account for more than two-thirds of all PAC contributions in congressional campaigns. Thus, simply to focus on wins and losses by studying legislative outcomes could understate the full importance of the new politics of business by overlooking the extent to which business organizations now perform tasks that were formerly the exclusive province of the political parties.

Furthermore, business leaders have adapted well to changes affecting the politics of Congress. During the late 1970s, the Business Roundtable and other business lobbies learned how to operate effectively within the decentralized congressional power structure, following the example of the public-interest/organized labor coalition a decade earlier. It is significant that, when party leadership became more of a factor in congressional politics in the 1980s, the *bipartisan* leadership role of the Business Roundtable seemed to increase rather than decrease. The organizational structure of the Business Roundtable, which may have been designed to compensate for (or to exploit) the fragmentation of power within Congress that existed in the 1970s, is also well suited for a congressional power structure in which party leaders have greater influence over policy-making. While the Roundtable has its own version of a committee system in the form of task forces, it has avoided the inefficiencies that are typical of the congressional committee system by centralizing power in its Executive and Policy Committees and by establishing a clear chain of command between them. The Roundtable is a superlobby that also functions like a legislative body insofar as it assigns responsibilities on the basis of expertise, researches numerous legislative proposals, informs its constituent members and legislators, makes recommendations on bills, drafts its own proposals, and supports or opposes legislation based on a vote of a diverse membership. With an affiliation that humbles heads of state, an efficient organizational structure, and strong attachments to members of both parties, it has established itself as perhaps the most formidable lobby on Capitol Hill. However, by taking the long view on numerous issues and showing a willingness to compromise, the Business Roundtable has also demonstrated a capacity for bipartisan leadership that, more often than not, has been enhanced by a cooperative relationship with the White House.

Having achieved their initial goals against considerable odds, the leaders of this capitalist movement will continue to pursue policies consistent with the attainment of their long-term objectives of social and economic reconstruction. Corporate executives of Fortune 500 companies now consider political activity to be an integral aspect of their managerial responsibilities. They have emerged from shadow politics to participate vigorously in the political arena. They have demonstrated a desire to take the lead in shaping national priorities. In the bipartisan tradition of corporate liberalism, the inner circle of the corporate elite has drawn up an agenda of reform.[52] But in the age of the global marketplace, corporate statesmen do not contemplate domestic reform in a strictly national context. Corporate liberalism in the late twentieth century has acquired a transnational orientation. It is not a coincidence that the political resurgence of the large corporation parallels the rise of transnational enterprise. Indeed, corporate political activity since the 1970s appears to mark the ascendancy of the corporate statesman in the era of the transnational corporation.[53]

4. REGULATING THE CORPORATE CITIZEN: WEALTH, POWER, AND THE POLITICAL MARKETPLACE IN FIRST AMENDMENT JURISPRUDENCE

a. The Political Rights of the Corporate Individual

Supreme Court decisions have accommodated and encouraged the dramatic surge in political activity by corporations in recent decades. This development in constitutional law also coincides with changes in antitrust policy that have permitted significant increases in the size of corporate mergers. Corporate autonomy has been expanded in both the economic and the political domain with implications for domestic and transnational power of corporations. These two developments, moreover, tend to be mutually reinforcing. Just as enhanced power in government ensures that large corporations will have greater influence over regulatory policies affecting the marketplace, big mergers tend to further consolidate and extend corporate power in the marketplace, domestic and global, thereby enhancing the political leverage of these corporations. This is only a tendency, but it is consistent with the fact that the CEOs of the dominant corporations in industry and finance continue to be the most influential members of the business community in Congress and the White House.

Regulation of the two most prominent aspects of the external dimension of corporate power—the marketplace (antitrust) and politics (constitutional law)—parallel one another in important ways. They share similar methods of reasoning. Both involve analysis of a marketplace and of rules of fairness. The regulation of corporate political activity, however, is in its infancy. Indeed, the Supreme Court is still defining the constitutional parameters of such regulation. It remains a very controversial issue. On the Court, a debate continues to build over the proper scope of this form of regulation—a debate of some importance for the political rights, and hence the power, of the large corporation.

For many in the academic profession, this division of opinion on the Supreme Court will bring to mind aspects of the ideological battle between pluralists and their various opponents that began in the 1950s and reached its peak in the 1970s. What I shall label the "self-regulating political marketplace" position on the Court, which tends to be formalistic in method, maintains that the unfettered expression of ideas in "the marketplace of political ideas," regardless of the source of the ideas, is essential to liberty in a democratic society. For lack of a better term, the "market power" position, which tends to embrace a realist type of argument, contends that the source of political ideas does indeed matter when the marketplace consists of corporate individuals with resources not available to corporeal citizens. An unregulated market may lead to a monopoly of political ideas or to a distortion of the political processes. A conception of fairness therefore must be entered into the equation if the marketplace is to function in a truly competitive and democratic fashion. The very nature of the debate, however, indicates the extent to which corporate political activity has been legitimized. The issue is not whether corporations should have political rights (they do), but under what conditions and to what extent they should be restricted.[54] A review of the relevant case law will set the stage for a more thorough examination of this debate and its implications for corporate power.

The regulation of corporate political activity derives from two sources: the Federal Election Campaign Act of 1971 (as amended in 1974 and interpreted by the Supreme Court in 1976, in *Buckley v. Valeo*[55]) and the First Amendment rights conferred on corporations in *First National Bank v. Bellotti*,[56] decided in 1978. The 1971 act also established the Federal Election Commission to implement the new law and to supervise elections. As an enforcement agency, the FEC is empowered to monitor the mandatory public disclosure of campaign contributions, levy fines, initiate civil lawsuits, conduct audits of members of Congress, write regulations, and issue advisory opinions.

In *Buckley v. Valeo*, the Court expanded the First Amendment's freedom-of-speech protections to include financial contributions to candidates or parties and independent expenditures made on behalf of candidates, parties, or ballot issues. Subsequently, in *Bellotti*, the Court extended to the corporation itself constitutional guarantees of political speech under the First Amendment. Because *Bellotti* concerned a referendum, not a candidate election, the decision did not fully address the scope of the corporation's constitutional rights of speech in electoral politics. Nevertheless, *Bellotti* reversed the Court's long-standing policy of denying such rights to nonmedia business corporations. It is somewhat ironic that the reform of campaign financing in the aftermath of Watergate loosed the great financial resources of the modern corporation in the service of political participation and competition in the marketplace of ideas. These developments have had a dramatic impact on the conduct of electoral politics (through the proliferation of corporate PACs and corporate financing of "independent" campaign organizations) and have aided the growth and influence of corporate lobbies in national policy-making.

The First Amendment doctrine of commercial speech, first articulated in a *Virginia State Board of Pharmacy v. Virginia Citizens Consumer Council*,[57] in 1976, might also be viewed as part of this new regulatory policy.[58] The commercial speech doctrine actually anticipated corporate free speech by focusing attention on the marketplace as the arbiter of competing ideas, thereby emphasizing the rights of the listener—the so-called "hearer-centered approach"—which can be juxtaposed to the "speaker-centered approach," which identifies the rights of the speaker as primary. A wide range of commercial speech or advertising now receives constitutional protection, which can be invoked against many government regulations designed ostensibly to protect consumers or to otherwise regulate advertising. The doctrine of commercial speech, however, tends to blur the line between advertising and traditional political speech. Commercial advertising that is not explicitly political and that might otherwise be subject to regulation is now afforded constitutional protection under the commercial-speech doctrine.[59] In any event, the doctrines of corporate political speech and commercial speech stand as testimony to the fact that corporate capitalists in the late twentieth century are transforming the marketplace of ideas just as their predecessors reconstructed the economic marketplace in the early twentieth century.

By legalizing political action committees, the Federal Election Campaign Act of 1971 provided corporations with a new method of soliciting campaign contributions and participating in electoral politics. Three years later in the aftermath of Watergate, Congress passed amendments to the act that established strict limits on contributions and expenditures in candidate elections. In deciding the constitutionality of the amended act, the Supreme Court, in *Buckley*, introduced the constitutional theory that the use of money for the purposes of expressing political views constitutes a form of speech protected under the First Amendment: "A restriction on the amount of money a person or group can spend on political communication during a campaign necessarily reduces the quantity of expression by restricting the number of issues discussed, the depth of their exploration, and the size of the audience reached."[60] Limiting the use of money for that end, therefore, could not be permitted unless the government could demonstrate a compelling reason or interest for such an infringement of First Amendment rights. In short, because a fundamental right is at stake, the state bears a heavy burden of justification.

Reasoning from the premise that the purpose of the Federal Election Campaign Act was to prohibit *"quid pro quo* corruption," the Court upheld the act's limitations on contributions to candidates and political parties but struck down the provisions limiting total expenditures. Contributions, the Court argued, were more likely to produce corruption or the appearance of corruption than were expenditures. Accordingly, a compelling state interest did not exist for restricting expenditures: "The absence of prearrangement and coordination of an expenditure with the candidate or his agent not only undermines the value of the expenditure to the candidate but also alleviates the danger that expenditures will be given as a *quid pro quo* for improper commitments from the candidate." The Court emphasized, however, that in upholding the limitations on contributions, it was not sanctioning the concept, "wholly foreign to the First Amendment," that "government may restrict the speech of some elements of our society in order to enhance the relative voice of others."[61]

Two years later, Justice Lewis F. Powell, writing for the majority in *Bellotti*, declared that corporate expenditures to influence the outcome of a referendum "is the type of speech indispensable to decision-making in a democracy, and this is no less true because the speech comes from a corporation rather than an individual."[62] Addressing the contention that corporate wealth may constitute an unfair advantage in the contest to win votes, Powell rejected the notion that the First Amendment embodies a standard of equality that can be imposed to guarantee the free exchange of ideas. Instead, he asserted that new constraints or mechanisms to safeguard the pursuit of truth are not needed, because "the people in our democracy are entrusted with the responsibility for judging and evaluating the relative merits of conflicting arguments."[63] Dissenting, Justice Byron R. White, joined by Justices William H. Brennan and Thurgood Marshall, disagreed with the logic of the majority and opined on the magnitude of its error:

> Corporations are artificial entities created by law for the purpose of furthering certain economic goals. In order to facilitate achievement of such ends, special rules relating to such matters as limited liability, perpetual life, and the accumulation, distribution, and taxation of assets are normally applied to them. . . . It has long been recognized, however, that the special status of corporations has placed them in a position to control vast amounts of economic power which may, if not regulated, dominate not only the economy but also the very heart of our democracy, the electoral process. . . . The State need not permit its own creation to consume it. . . . Such expenditures may be viewed as seriously threatening the role of the First Amendment as a guarantor of a free marketplace of ideas.[64]

Justice William H. Rehnquist, in a separate dissent, added the caution that "the blessings of potentially perpetual life and limited liability . . . , so beneficial in the economic sphere, pose special dangers in the political sphere."[65]

The debate was joined again eight years later in *Pacific Gas & Electric Co. v. Public Utilities Commission*,[66] where the Court, per Justice Powell, overturned a PUC ruling requiring PG&E to allow a consumer advocacy group to use extra space in a billing envelope. The plurality reasoned that PG&E might feel compelled to reply to critical editorials, thus unconstitutionally infringing on PG&E's freedom of speech and freedom of mind: "For corporations as for individuals, the choice to speak includes within it the choice of what not to say. And we have held that speech does not lose its protection because of the corporate identity of the speaker."[67] In effect, the Court held that the PUC regulation favored one speaker over another by coercing PG&E to reply or by discouraging PG&E to speak on issues out of fear of having to reply to future criticisms. By preventing the free flow of ideas, the PUC regulation entailed an unconstitutional tampering with the marketplace of political ideas. But by implying that the corporate entity possessed a mind, *PG&E* would also appear to have supplemented the hearer-centered rationale of *Bellotti* with a speaker-centered rationale for matters involving political advocacy not related to the electoral process.

In a dissenting opinion, Justice Rehnquist, joined by Justices White and Stevens, sharply attacked the Court's expansive reading of *Bellotti*:

> To ascribe to such artificial entities an "intellect" or "mind" for freedom of conscience purposes is to confuse metaphor with reality. Corporations generally have not played the historic role of

newspapers as conveyors of individual ideas and opinion. In extending positive free speech rights to corporations, this Court drew a distinction between the First Amendment rights of corporations and those of natural persons. It recognized that corporate free speech rights do not arise because corporations, like individuals, have any interest in self-expression. It held instead that such rights are recognized as an instrumental means of furthering the First Amendment purpose of fostering a broad forum of information to facilitate self-government.[68]

The plurality's extension of individual rights of self-expression to corporations, as Justice Rehnquist's criticism implies, appears to have placed corporate speakers on an equal footing with natural persons with regard to political advocacy outside of electoral politics. But this is not the only implication of the decision. Although political advocacy was at issue in *PG&E*, the speech in question was also commercial because it involved an effort to advance the commercial interests of the utility. Consequently, this case appears to support the idea that commercial speech, when combined with political advocacy in the same publication, will be protected on a par with corporate political speech.[69]

Bellotti did not address the controversial issue of corporate speech in candidate elections. In the first case to do so, *Federal Election Commission v. National Right to Work Committee*[70], a unanimous Court upheld a provision of the Federal Election Campaign Act[71] that prohibited corporations from soliciting contributions for use in a segregated campaign fund from persons other than stockholders and their families and executive or administrative personnel and their families. The Court's deference to congressional judgment in this matter was based on a review of the history of congressional efforts to regulate campaign finance and the potential danger of quid pro quo corruption posed by corporate wealth. The holding in this case was limited to the issue of solicitation of funds, because the National Right to Work Committee had conceded the constitutionality of the FECA provision[72] that prohibited corporations and unions from directly making contributions or expenditures to federal elections but allowed them to establish separate funds (e.g., PACs) for such purposes. In *Federal Election Committee v. Massachusetts Citizens for Life Inc.*,[73] decided in 1986, the Court upheld this provision while establishing a test for distinguishing, in the application of the provision, between such corporations as MCFL, which are devoted entirely to political advocacy, and profit-making corporations. Noting the Court's concern in *FEC v. National Right to Work Committee* over "the corrosive influence of concentrated corporate wealth" on "the marketplace of political ideas," Justice Brennan articulated the central rationale of the majority opinion:

> Direct corporate spending on political activity raises the prospect that resources amassed in the economic marketplace may be used to provide an unfair advantage in the political marketplace. Political "free trade" does not necessarily require that all who participate in the political marketplace do so with exactly equal resources. . . . Relative availability of funds is after all a rough barometer of public support. The resources in the treasury of a business corporation, however, are not an indication of popular support for the corporation's political ideas. They reflect instead the economically motivated decisions of investors and customers. The availability of these resources may make a corporation a formidable political presence, even though the power of the corporation may be no reflection of the power of its ideas.[74]

Four years later, in *Austin v. Michigan State Chamber of Commerce*,[75] the Supreme Court for the first time upheld limitations on corporate spending in candidate elections for state governments. The restrictions in the Michigan law were essentially the same as the federal provisions at issue in *FEC v. MCFL*. The statute, like the FECA provision, also entitled corporations to solicit campaign monies for use in a segregated fund. Applying the *MCFL* test, Justice Marshall, writing for the Court, concluded that the Michigan Chamber of Commerce was not an ideological nonprofit corporation in the sense intended in *MCFL*, and was therefore not exempt from the Michigan statute's prohibition against the expenditure of corporate treasury funds in candidate elections. Justice Marshall held that the Michigan Chamber of Commerce's First Amendment rights of speech could be infringed because the state in this instance had demonstrated a compelling interest—namely, the need to prevent "the corrosive and distorting effects of immense aggregations of wealth that are accumulated with the help of the corporate form and that have little or no correlation to the public's support for the corporation's political ideas."[76]

In separate dissents, Justice Antonin Scalia and Justice Anthony Kennedy (joined by Justices Sandra Day O'Connor and Scalia) roundly attacked both the logic of Marshall's opinion and a concurring opinion by Justice Brennan. Scalia asserted that the Court's decision constituted an "Orwellian announcement" that endorsed "the principle that too much speech is an evil that the democratic majority can proscribe." He totally rejected the contention that the special advantages of the business corporation justified the "forfeiture of First Amendment rights" as a price that could be exacted by the state for granting those advantages. And he was not persuaded that massive aggregations of wealth would cause an imbalance in the marketplace of political ideas; the evil to be regulated was not the quantity of speech but, as the Court held in *Buckley*, the potential for quid pro quo corruption.[77] In a similar vein, Justice Kennedy argued that the Court's ruling constituted a departure from previous decisions and that the Michigan act discriminated on the basis of the speaker's identity: "By using distinctions based upon both the speech and the speaker, the Act engages in the rawest form of censorship: the State censors what a particular segment of the political community might say with regard to candidates who stand for election."[78]

Austin constitutes a watershed in the debate over the permissible regulation of corporate political speech and activity under the First Amendment. On the surface, the disagreement in *Austin* concerns the nature of the corporation's political rights and the extent to which they can be regulated in the public interest. At a deeper level, however, the dispute concerns the power of the business corporation and its capacity for influencing or distorting the electoral process. *Austin* stands for the proposition that the political marketplace is not self-regulating and can be regulated in the public interest when free trade in ideas is threatened by massive aggregations of corporate wealth. To that extent, it establishes a corporate speech exception (in candidate elections) to the rule of free trade of ideas established in earlier cases. Yet the Court's justification for upholding the Michigan statute appears to provide a rationale for a more general regulatory approach that contradicts the approach in *Buckley* and *Bellotti*.

Austin holds that direct contributions and expenditures from a corporation's treasury in candidate elections can be regulated because of "the unique state-conferred corporate structure that facilitates the amassing of large treasuries." In reaching this conclusion, the Court invoked the traditional "artificial entity" (or "concession") theory of the corporation to justify regulation. Implicit in this formulation is the notion that the corporation is a creature of the state. Because its ability to amass large treasuries is made possible by the state (or by law), the business corporation can be held accountable in the expenditure of its funds in candidate elections to ensure that the "expenditures reflect actual public support for the political ideas espoused by corporations." According to Marshall, the act does not attempt to equalize the relative influence of speakers on elections. The fact that corporations might accumulate large sums of wealth is not a justification for the statute. Wealth per se is not the issue, since a billionaire could use wealth to distort an election; rather, the issue is that advantages in accumulating wealth under the corporate form are unfair in the context of a political campaign. This approach, therefore, is based on a new theory of corporate accountability derived in part from corporation law, a theory that asserts that corporate officers are accountable to the public as well as to its shareholders when expending funds in a candidate election.

The rationale in *Austin* is potentially expansive and appears to conflict with an important line of argument based on the expenditure/contribution distinction of *Buckley*. Whereas *Buckley* upheld limitations on contributions (but not on expenditures) on the basis of the quid pro quo corruption standard, *Austin* justifies a ban on the use of corporate treasury funds for both expenditures and contributions in candidate elections under the public-accountability standard for business corporations. *Austin*'s gloss on *Buckley*'s corruption rationale is a major step toward a realistic constitutional theory of corporate power in American electoral politics—namely, that unfair competition can be caused by massive aggregations of wealth, and not solely by quid pro quo corruption.

The decision, however, is limited in its reach. *Austin* holds that business corporations may not use their treasury funds to spend independently on behalf of a candidate in a campaign, but it allows business corporations to establish segregated funds to achieve the same end. And the holding does not prevent corporations from using treasury funds to spend directly on ballot issues involving referenda (and presumably other noncandidate ballot issues), thus distinguishing and preserving *Bellotti*. Nevertheless, the reasoning in *Austin* appears to compel a reevaluation of *Bellotti* and its theory of the political marketplace as applied to corporate speech in elections. The rationale in *Austin* also has implications for other types of corporate political advocacy based on the *Bellotti* approach. Justice Marshall, however, stopped short of offering a convincing explanation of the difference between the election of candidates and other aspects of electoral politics (referenda) and political activity. If and when the Court confronts this issue, the contradictory premises of the *Bellotti* and *Austin* approaches will have to be reconciled in some fashion.

b. The Political Economy of Corporate Free Speech

Bellotti and *PG&E* employ a theory of the political marketplace of ideas derived from the logic of classical political economy. Competition in ideas, as it were, is subject to the laws of supply and demand. When left to its own devices, the political marketplace will yield the truth, or at the very least truth will not become the casualty of government censorship. Thus, whereas efficiency separates winners from losers in the economic marketplace, reason serves as the arbiter of truth and falsehood in the political marketplace. The analogy has certain strengths insofar as one is speaking of individuals who rely on their own resources and initiative in a truly competitive marketplace, but it breaks down when the parties competing have vastly different means to express their points of view.

One ideological solution to this problem, embraced by the Court in *Bellotti* and in *PG&E*, is to treat corporations as natural persons. This approach has the added consequence of disguising, by ignoring, the power of the large corporation. Indeed, from this perspective, the threat to the political marketplace of ideas is not corporate power (it does not exist) but quid pro quo corruption. Corporations, like other individuals, must adhere to the rules of fair play, but they should not be prevented from playing simply because they possess greater wealth. Indeed, that would be tantamount to expelling wealthy citizens from the town meeting. Thus, with regard to political advocacy outside of electoral politics, the corporation enjoys the same protections as the natural person and assumes no special responsibility to the public that would justify a different form of government regulation.

The justification for equating the expenditure of money with speech is based on the idea that free speech is essential to the free flow of ideas and competition in a political campaign, and that a person should have the right to express views on candidates and political issues as a *participant* in the political process. Speech should not be suppressed because of the identity of the speaker or the content of the speech. The rights of political speech and participation are essential attributes of citizenship in a democratic society. By extending First Amendment rights to the corporation in *Bellotti* and then imputing a freedom of mind to the corporation in *PG&E*, the Court has conferred these attributes of citizenship on the corporation.[79] The ideological concept of the corporate citizen thereby finds constitutional sanction in the modern First Amendment doctrine of corporate individualism. Although *Bellotti* and *PG&E* never squarely addressed the issue of the moral agency of the corporation, they nevertheless upheld rights that assume such an agency. Moreover, the dissenters in *Austin* employed language that confirms this reading of *Bellotti* and *PG&E*.

The alternative theory, first outlined in dissenting opinions in *Bellotti* and *PG&E*, introduced in *MCFL*, and fully argued in *Austin*, rejects the model of classical political economy for a theory of market power. It does not thereby jettison altogether the idea of a political marketplace of ideas. Rather, it contends that the political marketplace is not self-regulating when certain parties have an unfair advantage, not because of their wealth but because of their favored treatment by the state. In coming to this conclusion, this approach acknowledges the existence of corporate power in the political marketplace of ideas. It requires that the political ideas expressed by the corporation "reflect actual public support" for such ideas. In short, this approach applies a standard of social responsibility to corporate speech in candidate elections. Because "the unique state-conferred corporate structure" makes possible "the amassing of large treasuries," the source of the business corporation's speech (i.e., the source of the funding that produces this speech) must conform to a standard of public accountability.

Following *MCFL*, one would presume that the relevant public in *Austin* consists of shareholders and customers whose investments or purchases do not necessarily reflect their support for the corporation's political ideas. Justice Marshall's argument, however, appears to have a broader application that embraces the public at large. Perhaps his purpose was to free this issue from any possible entanglements with state corporation law. To be sure, managerial accountability to shareholders is not an especially strong argument, given the steady elimination of shareholder rights in the twentieth century and the concomitant insulation of managerial power through broad interpretations of the business judgment rule. Indeed, derivative suits concerning the political activities of corporate executives have not faired well.[80] Moreover, it could be argued that shareholders and consumers can sell their stock or boycott if they disagree with a corporation's policies or political activities. "Actual public support" for the political ideas espoused by a corporation would therefore appear to establish a political, not a pecuniary, standard of accountability consistent with the notion that the corporation derives its "unique advantages" from the state, which is to say the public. Accordingly, in candidate elections, the political rights of the business corporation may be subjected to a different standard of regulation than natural persons.

In many respects, the approach in *Austin* mirrors the dominant trend of corporate-liberal economic regulation, which secures corporate autonomy while allowing for regulation of the external dimension of corporate power in the public interest. The effort in *Austin* to regulate competition by imposing a standard of fairness parallels the Court's balancing of freedom to contract and equality of opportunity in antitrust law. Just as antitrust law subjects the corporate individual to rules of fair play, *Austin* retains the ideological conception of the corporate citizen in a modified (nonreified) form that allows for a realistic assessment of corporate political activity. As individuals in the political marketplace, corporations may be regulated to prevent them from monopolizing ideas, to guard against "the corrosive and distorting effects of immense aggregations of wealth." Whereas restraints of trade must be prohibited to ensure fair competition, free trade in ideas nevertheless permits considerable self-regulation.

Austin recognizes that the political marketplace, like the economic marketplace, has been transformed by corporate power. Furthermore, it takes note of the threat that economic dominance poses to political processes. Business corporations are not excluded from participating in the political realm; however, for elections involving candidates, they must compete fairly, on terms that preserve the mechanisms of competition. This approach would appear to be essential for establishing the legitimacy of the corporation as a political actor. The sometimes odd logic of the opinion is a consequence of an attempt to regulate the constitutional rights of the corporation without undermining the *Buckley* doctrine that money is an expression of speech and that the First Amendment does not permit the quantity of speech to be restricted in order to equalize voices in the marketplace of ideas. For example, the use of concession theory to justify a standard of public accountability, while not consistent with modern theories of corporate personality, provides a method for circumventing the *Buckley* speech doctrine by focusing on the state-conferred advantages as opposed to the wealth of the corporation as such. Justice Powell's majority opinion in *Bellotti*, and the dissenting opinions of Justices Scalia and Kennedy in *Austin*, squarely posed the problem: If the political rights of the billion-dollar corporation are no different from those of the billionaire, how can a regulation of corporate expenditures in elections be justified without a showing of quid pro quo corruption? To answer this argument, Justice Marshall apparently resorted to an older theory that depersonalizes the corporate entity in order to justify its regulation in the public interest.

Austin's broad justification for regulating corporate treasury funds in candidate elections (but not in referenda), therefore, would appear to supplant *Buckley*'s distinction between contributions and expenditures based on the idea of quid pro quo corruption. When applied to corporations, the corruption rationale of *Buckley* yields an empirically outmoded theory of corporate power. It assumes that the political power of corporations is solely a consequence of their ability to control politicians through influence-peddling. *Austin* states unequivocally that this is no longer the issue. In a time when corporate power has become institutionalized in Congress and in the electoral process, the threat or appearance of corruption constitutes an insufficient basis for regulating highly organized and politically sophisticated corporations.

Under the Court's current policy, free trade in ideas is still the rule, and restraint the exception. Whether *Austin* becomes the basis of an expanding regulatory policy for corporate speech or remains an exception to the rule of unfettered expression of political ideas, the corporation's political rights appear to be secure. Although the business corporation cannot vote as an entity or run for office, its executives, employees, and shareholders can. Moreover, the corporation can participate in the political process as any individual would, with the sole limitation that it cannot use its treasury funds in candidate elections. It may, however, draw on a segregated fund established for that purpose. Thus far, PACs have served quite well as a means of funding campaigns. *Austin* distinguishes and preserves *Bellotti*. There are no limitations on the source or amount of money a corporation may spend in other electoral contests or on political advocacy in general. Corporate lobbies and PACs participate freely in the political process and are not burdened by special regulations. On balance, the limitations imposed on corporate autonomy are minimal, compared with the behavior that has been sanctioned.

Viewed from one perspective, the constitutional issues in the corporate-speech cases concern the rights of individuals insofar as the Court's rulings in some cases affect all political rights. But the debate becomes far more meaningful when analyzed in terms of the regulation of corporate power or influence in American politics. This is not to say that some Justices are being disingenuous when they equate corporate political rights with the rights of actual individuals, but rather to suggest that the peculiar language of the debate is largely a product of the law and its ideological moorings. If the Court wants to extend the rights (and hence the power) of the corporation in electoral politics, it will depict the corporate individual as an actor competing within the marketplace of political ideas. If the Court wants to circumscribe the rights of the corporation in electoral politics (and hence limit its power without undermining the rights of all individuals), it must devise a new doctrine or draw on precedents that can achieve this end with a minimum of confusion. Judicial policy-making of this sort is not unusual when divisions on the Court yield antithetical approaches.

Consequently, to perceive the debate as being about the extent to which individual liberty in the political marketplace of ideas may be curtailed to ensure democratic participation, *is* to mistake metaphor for reality. Likewise, the philosophical and ideological differences separating the two sides must be analyzed in terms of their jurisprudential and practical implications. Precedent imposes constraints that often encourage the creation of new or conflicting interpretations. The equal protection clause enters *Austin* through the back door, as it were, in order to preserve the political marketplace of ideas for real individuals, not to impose on them a doctrine of equal participation. Thus, by employing alternative rationales designed either to promote free competition of ideas or to ensure fairness in the political marketplace, the Court seems to have formulated for corporate political activity a crude facsimile of the rule of reason.

This is not to say that what is reasonable for the economic marketplace will be reasonable for the political marketplace, but only that some balance between the freedom to speak and equality of opportunity to speak (and be heard) will be sought. The analogy of the two marketplaces, however, is suggestive. Just as the Court's formulation of the rule of reason embodied the contending ideas of "good" (natural) and "bad" (artificial) trusts, so *Austin* seems to embody opposing ideas of "good" (representative) and "bad" (nonrepresentative) corporate speech. Following this line of reasoning, a reappraisal of *Bellotti*'s holding seems to be in order. Indeed, the likelihood that corporate wealth may distort the political marketplace in noncandidate elections may be even greater than in candidate elections. To require business corporations to use PACs in all elections, therefore, is not unreasonable, especially when the corporate citizen is free to speak its mind on all other matters of political importance.

In the tradition of the Progressive Era debate over the trust question, *Austin* reminds us that unchecked power in the marketplace represents a form of tyranny that the laws of the market themselves have failed to remedy or to prevent. Monopolization of ideas, no less than unreasonable restraints of trade, threatens both liberty and equality of opportunity. Regardless of the nature of the market activity, the solution is the same: a competitive balance must be engineered. Whether such a balance can be restored within the market in a meaningful way, however, is perhaps less important than the fact that corporate power has apparently been checked in the public interest. Thus, "competition" in the political marketplace of corporate capitalism comes to be associated with a legal and moral conception of fairness while still retaining its ideological identification with the ideal of the self-regulating marketplace of an earlier era. In this way, the corporate citizen acquires legitimacy under the auspices of public law while an expanding corporate autonomy is accommodated and regulated in the interest of democratic participation.

Public law structures and regulates the external dimension of corporate power in politics and in the marketplace. As the corporation has acquired new constitutional rights that have further consolidated its power, so too it has acquired an enhanced autonomy in the marketplace consistent with the growth of the transnational dimension of that power. While corporate lobbies and PACs transformed the face of American politics in the 1970s and 1980s, the greatest merger movement in the history of corporate capitalism, enabled by a revised antitrust policy, fueled the corporate reconstruction of the global marketplace. It is to this subject that we now turn.

5. RESTRUCTURING CORPORATE POWER FOR THE GLOBAL MARKETPLACE

a. The Constitutional Law of the Marketplace

Since the passage of the Sherman Act, in 1890, political analysts, legal scholars, and economists have often disagreed about the purpose of antitrust law, how it should be applied, and whether it should be enforced with greater vigor. Virtually all commentators do agree, however, that for better or for worse, antitrust law continues to be of vital ideological significance in American society.[81] To interpret its ideological import, one must first understand the law on its own terms, in light of specific rulings and their justifications, as expounded by the judiciary. To be sure, an act of interpretation often manifests the analyst's own ideological objectives. In recent decades, significant criticisms have been leveled by scholars at the failure of antitrust law to constructively bring about or, from a different perspective, to not impede, effective competition.[82] In arguing what antitrust should be, however, one could fail to appreciate what it has become: not a formula for competitive capitalism, not an empty vessel for changing economic policies, but a body of legal principles and rules that define legitimate power in the marketplace. The rules of antitrust law constitute legal commands with a political content, not unlike the rules that comprise the Constitution. Courts interpret the laws of antitrust, in light of ideological doctrine, in order to define legal boundaries of permissible behavior in the marketplace of corporate capitalism. In assessing its ideological content, therefore, one must take into account the economic activities and structures that the law legitimizes and sanctions, either explicitly or implicitly, as well as those that it prohibits.

The substantive areas of antitrust law that have had the greatest impact on the economic basis and the concerted exercise of corporate power—agreements among competitors in restraint of trade, monopolization, and mergers—illustrate well the enduring political character of this body of law. By "political," I mean that it is an evolving product of political and social forces, shaped from the outset by ideological interpretations of the appropriate relationship between government and the market, and that its subject matter, the regulation of corporate power, is primarily a political matter in the constitutional sense, insofar as the proper scope of that power becomes a subject of litigation. The fact that some decisions may have significant economic consequences follows directly from the nature of the power being regulated. Policy-making becomes unavoidable in antitrust decisions, as it does when the Court interprets and applies the substantive provisions of the Constitution. Similar issues concerning the judicial function apply in both areas, not the least of which is the necessity for constructing a principled basis for applying the law to divergent factual situations. It is likely, therefore, that the Court's sensitivity, or lack thereof, to its own limitations as a policy-maker often will prove to be decisive in shaping its approach to a particular area of antitrust law. That this eventuality can be interpreted simply as bad economics or plain incompetence only betrays a failure to appreciate the nature of these limitations and the inevitable political character of the Court's policy-making function.

Corporate power in the external dimension acquired ideological justification through the antitrust principle of fair competition, which embodies the contending values of equal opportunity to compete (potential competition) and of freedom to contract.[83] Antitrust law incorporated these antagonistic ideological strains within an evolving corpus of rules that is peculiarly American in conception and application. It is at once a political critique of corporate power and a justification of its social worth. The internal contradictions of antitrust law, furthermore, reflect the essential opposition within liberalism between the promise of equal opportunity to compete and the inequality fomented by the pursuit of liberty and property.

In practice, antitrust law generally prohibits monopolization while sustaining the methods and structure of entrenched oligopolistic markets, albeit in accordance with the rules of fair competition. The legal principle of reasonable restraints of trade may be invoked to justify corporate concentration, consolidation, merger, and noncollusive oligopolistic practices, which fall under the rubric of shared monopoly. It would be a mistake, therefore, to view antitrust law as consisting solely of a compendium of prohibitions; it is equally significant for what it sanctions because of what it does not or cannot regulate, under its own methods of reasoning. Most pertinent in this regard are a variety of oligopolistic practices that do not clearly fall within the evidentiary requirements of the doctrine of conspiracy. In the absence of an express agreement or sufficient evidence to infer such an agreement, courts have refused to expand the concept of conspiracy to embrace the practice of price leadership that requires the leading firm in an oligopolistic market to take the initiative in announcing prices, thereby ostensibly allowing fellow oligopolists prudently to avoid price competition.[84] Nor does the law deem adequate the mere existence of "conscious parallel action" as a basis for inferring an agreement or conspiracy.[85] If it did, oligopolistic behavior or shared monopoly might then come within the monopolization strictures of Section 2, thus allowing the inference of a "conspiracy to monopolize" on the basis of noncollusive behavior.[86] This is not to say that collusion in restraint of trade cannot be inferred from circumstantial evidence, but only that in matters with such potentially profound consequences for the structure and operation of existing markets, courts have decided it is best not to interfere.[87]

The law of antitrust articulates the constitutional principles and rules that govern the external dimension of corporate power in the marketplace. At its foundation one finds the idea of constitutional government, which embodies the liberal ideal of the rule of law. By imposing limits on the exercise of corporate power and on its economic substratum, antitrust law defines the legitimate scope of that power. From its inception, the judicial task of interpreting the broad commands of antitrust statutes has been shaped fundamentally by ideological assumptions that, on the one hand, accept the modern corporation as a "natural" product of the evolution of business enterprise (and as such, highly preferred for its productivity and efficiency) and, on the other, embody the concern or fear that corporate power, lest it be checked or regulated, will be exercised to the detriment of individual liberty and equality of opportunity. These dual presumptions create within the law a tension that has manifested itself in the divergent interpretations of the rule of reason under the Sherman Act and in the disparate treatment of economic concentration under the Clayton Act.[88]

The ideological strength of antitrust law ultimately derives from the authority that only the law can confer and from reasoned justification that provides both the continuity and the flexibility that are characteristic of constitutional doctrine. By the very act of defining boundaries of acceptable behavior, the law of antitrust legitimizes corporate power. In this way, the legal and moral principle of fair competition comes to embody the concept of corporate social responsibility. Perhaps of greatest importance is that antitrust law recognizes the rule of law as the central legal principle guiding the regulation of corporate power, a principle that, one scholar notes, "is even recognized by business interests as a protection against the government of men which might otherwise descend on them in such forms as price controls, state regulation and ultimately public ownership."[89]

I shall argue that antitrust decisions of the Supreme Court under Chief

Justices Warren Burger and William Rehnquist, and the enforcement policies of the Department of Justice under Presidents Ronald Reagan and George Bush, significantly revised antitrust law and policy to enable firms to compete more effectively in the global marketplace. Perhaps because it never became a major political issue, the implications of the modern merger movement for corporate power, particularly since 1980, have not been widely discussed or appreciated in political studies of the corporation. Yet the scope and scale of this movement has been truly remarkable by any previous measure. It has not only fomented an internal restructuring of firms, but also aided a significant corporate restructuring of the marketplace accomplished through various forms of corporate combination.

Since the mid-1970s, antitrust law and enforcement policy have evolved in a direction that strongly favors the presumption of freedom to contract. This development constitutes a significant departure from the three decades immediately following World War II. Judge Learned Hand's 1946 decision in the *Alcoa* case, and Warren Court antitrust jurisprudence in the 1960s, established a general presumption within the law to view internal growth and market concentration in terms of their possible political consequences, as well as their economic consequences.[90] While earlier opinions had emphasized the predatory acts of individual corporations, the Hand-Warren approach, in expanding the practical reach of the potential competition doctrine, explicitly identified the economic basis of corporate power, whether it be monopoly or market concentration, as the source of the evil to be remedied. This period of antitrust activism redefined the doctrinal framework, against which subsequent majorities, by modifying or narrowly interpreting past opinions, have sought to reinstate the presumption of freedom to contract to the exclusion of legal theory that recognizes corporate power as a social and political force, not simply as a phenomenon of the marketplace.

The most recent shift in antitrust policy, as evidenced in the regulation of mergers, entails a redefinition of the potential competition doctrine to accommodate the realities of global competition. Yet the new policy appears to represent much more than a cyclical phase similar to those of the past. A reversion to the Hand-Warren doctrine in merger law seems highly improbable and perhaps unworkable in the restructured global marketplace of corporate capitalism. Rather than regard the current policy as an episode that will eventually give way to demands for a return to tighter regulation of market concentration, it may be more accurate to view the Reagan-Bush policy as marking a more-or-less permanent transition in antitrust philosophy designed to accommodate the global integration of those markets.

b. Oligopoly versus Monopoly

Judicial interpretation of the Sherman Act's prohibitions against monopolization, from the *Standard Oil* and *American Tobacco* decisions of 1911 through World War II, generally followed the method established in those opinions of defining the intent to monopolize in terms of predatory practices while discounting the mere existence of monopoly power as an indication of this intent or purpose. Justice Joseph McKenna's majority opinion in *United States Steel* (1920) exemplifies this approach. In observing that "the corporation is undoubtedly of impressive size," having consolidated 180 separate firms upon its creation in 1901, McKenna cautioned: "The law does not make mere size . . . or the existence of unexerted power an offense."[91] Although the Court found that monopoly power had not been exerted—indeed, did not exist—it nevertheless felt compelled to explain that U.S. Steel had "resorted to none of the brutalities or tyrannies that the cases illustrate of other combinations."[92] In other words, if monopoly power had been established by the Court, the steel company would have passed the test of reasonableness, the presumption being that it had acquired this power through "normal methods of industrial development."

Judge Learned Hand's opinion in the *Alcoa* case of 1946 (Court of Appeals, Second Circuit) marked an important transition from previous monopolization cases both in method and ideological emphasis, evidenced by his application of the rule of reason to the facts and the priority accorded to a competitive market over the putative benefits of lawful combination. It is significant that this doctrinal shift coincided with the introduction of modern techniques of economic analysis into antitrust law, notable in the court's attempt in *Alcoa* to define the relevant product and its market in order to ascertain monopoly power. Having established, on the basis of this analysis, that Alcoa's market share constituted monopoly power, Judge Hand proceeded to argue that Section 2 does not require a finding of "specific" intent, "for no monopolist monopolizes unconscious of what he is doing."[93] Alcoa's success in maintaining its monopoly was proof enough of its intent. But, at this point, Hand's argument tipped the scales of reason in the opposite direction of the *U.S. Steel* case. After explaining that a monopolist "may be the survivor out of a group of competitors, merely by virtue of his superior skill, foresight and industry," the judge determined that Alcoa's predatory or monopolizing conduct consisted precisely in its relentless expansion, in "doubling and redoubling its capacity before others entered the field," which had the effect of maintaining monopoly and excluding competitors.[94]

In defense of his analysis of Alcoa's monopolizing conduct, Judge Hand suggested what might have motivated Congress in passing the Sherman Act: "It is possible, because of its indirect social or moral effect, to prefer a system of small producers, each dependent for his success upon his own skill and character, to one in which the great mass of those engaged must accept the direction of the few." Furthermore, the prohibition against monopoly was "based upon the belief that great industrial consolidations are inherently undesirable, regardless of their economic results." In fact, Hand observed, "Senator Sherman himself showed that among the purposes of Congress in 1890 was a desire to put an end to great aggregations of capital because of the helplessness of the individual before them." Indeed, from the outset one objective of the act has been "to perpetuate and preserve, for its own sake and in spite of possible cost, an organization of industry in small units which can effectively compete with each other."[95]

Although based on a questionable interpretation of the framers' intent, and seemingly at odds with the rationale in previous rule of reason decisions, Judge Hand's statements in *Alcoa* may be viewed as consistent with earlier applications of the rule of reason if understood (within the context of the entire opinion) as a defense of the principle of potential competition and not as a vindication of the competitive market of a former era. Despite the apparent affinity that his historical interpretation of the Sherman Act shared with that of Justices John Harlan and Rufus Peckham, Hand did not give credence to the notion that the act compelled unrestricted competition.[96] Rather, the holding in *Alcoa* upheld oligopoly (and potential competition) against monopoly by ruling against excess-capacity investment as predatory per se. From a strictly legal perspective, however, it seems that Judge Hand left little room for a defense of monopoly on the basis of "normal methods of industrial development." But that is precisely the point of the opinion. Monopolies cannot be both good and bad, especially if they are bad for political reasons. While monopolies might justify their existence by "superior skill, foresight and industry," they will not be allowed to persist if they do so by actions that seek to exclude competitors or prevent others from seeking to compete or being able to compete. Such a determination, however, will depend on what a court perceives to be monopolizing conduct in light of the facts of a case. In essence, Hand's opinion was that the Sherman Act forbids monopolistic behavior. Still, the decision leaves room for a balancing of proofs, albeit presumptively weighted against the monopoly defendant.

While subsequent cases did not uniformly follow *Alcoa's* lead, they have nevertheless been shaped by its logic and its interpretation of what constitutes fair competition.[97] The broader significance of *Alcoa*, quite apart from the legal doctrine it announces, stems from its clarity of purpose and its ideological impact on modern antitrust thinking. This focus in the law of antitrust involving a greater emphasis on the principle of potential competition in oligopolistic markets, which reached its high point during the tenure of the Warren Court, also evinced a recurring public concern with the growth and entrenchment of corporate power in this century, as evidenced by periodic efforts to reform antitrust laws. Judge Hand's attempt to establish an affirmative defense of oligopoly against monopoly, absent a finding of specific intent, presaged later courts' treatment of mergers under the revised Clayton Act, which, as we shall see, reflected a similar concern with the increasing concentration of market power and its implications for American society. The Hand-Warren approach to potential competition, however, was devised solely with domestic markets in mind. If its effort to preserve oligopolistic competition seemed extreme in the 1940s and 1950s (and it did to many commentators), it appeared even more so with the dramatic rise of transnational enterprise in the 1960s and 1970s.

c. The Corporate Restructuring of the Marketplace

In the 1970s, the disposition of federal antitrust policy once again became an important issue for political leaders, judges, and corporate capitalists. This matter was not high on the agenda of the public-interest movement, and the general public showed little interest in it. Between 1969 and 1975, Presidents Richard M. Nixon and Gerald R. Ford appointed five Justices to the Supreme Court. By 1974, an ideological shift had occurred on the Court, and that made possible a change in its antitrust policy. In a series of opinions delivered in the mid-to-late 1970s, the Burger Court initiated a quiet revolution in antitrust law that President Carter chose to nurture (on the advice of the Business Roundtable) and that Presidents Reagan and Bush later carried to completion. This transformation, which has profound implications for the structure of corporate power in the marketplace, was accomplished mainly through the revision of Justice Department guidelines regulating mergers. An overview of merger law in the twentieth century provides the context for assessing the significance of this change in policy.

Mergers—a general term describing the combining of firms under the formal control of one managerial group—have served a variety of purposes since the late nineteenth century, including the monopolization of industries, the control of markets through vertical integration, economic survival for failing firms, speculation, expansion through diversification, and centralization of control over related industries and markets. Mergers, therefore, have provided the primary means by which corporate capitalists have restructured the marketplace to achieve greater economies of scale and to enhance market power both as an offensive and as a defensive strategy. Three market relationships describe the types of mergers: horizontal (competitors), vertical (buyer-seller), and conglomerate (all others). Each of the three great merger waves in the twentieth century have involved at least two of these forms: 1898–1904 (horizontal and vertical), 1924–1930 (horizontal and vertical), and 1955–present (all three).[98] Moreover, each successive wave has increased the trend toward greater industrial and financial concentration, although in the case of conglomerate mergers it appears that this trend takes the form of aggregate, as opposed to traditional market, concentration.[99] At the risk of some simplification, one might also ascribe an overriding purpose or strategy to each of these waves. In the first period, horizontal and vertical acquisitions accomplished the restructuring of markets into their modern forms of oligopoly and monopoly; during the second wave, vertical integration served to stabilize and consolidate control of these markets, which for some industries were international in scope; and the ascendancy of the new conglomerate merger in the decades since World War II marks a new era of corporate expansion and increasing centralization of control effected through diversified acquisitions, both domestic and global, on a scale that dwarfs its precursors.[100]

In debating the provisions of the Sherman bill, its authors certainly had in mind as its primary target the great trusts that had achieved their dominance by absorbing competitors. At about the same time, the industrial trust (and other collusive practices) had been threatened with extinction by *ultra vires* suits brought by state governments, but New Jersey and Delaware revised their corporation laws to legalize mergers through acquisition. What effect, if any, the Sherman Act would have on this development was not immediately apparent, although it is likely that the merger movement at the turn of the century drew its stimulus in part from the selective and infrequent enforcement of the act by the executive branch of the federal government under Presidents Grover Cleveland and William McKinley, and the more frequent but selective enforcement under Theodore Roosevelt.[101] Thus, the first great merger wave, essential in the construction of the modern corporate economy, proceeded without significant interference. Although few cases were brought, the only successful case involving a merger in the first twenty years of the Sherman Act was *Northern Securities* in 1904, which, however, because of the uncertainty it created in the law, did have the effect of slowing merger activity. The *Standard Oil* and *American Tobacco* decisions of 1911, both of which involved mergers, ended this period of uncertainty with the adoption of the rule of reason and were followed by wholesale prosecutions under the Sherman Act by President William Taft.[102]

Passed by Congress in 1914, the Clayton Act aimed to restrict the use of the holding company device by forbidding the acquisition of stock by one firm in competing firms if the effect of the acquisition "may be to substantially lessen competition . . . or tend to create a monopoly."[103] But the Clayton Act did not prohibit the purchase of one corporation's assets by another, or even the stock, if it could be shown that it did not substantially lessen competition or tend to create a monopoly. The qualifying clause in the act, together with the "assets loophole," spelled the demise of the Clayton Act as an effective means for regulating mergers. When the largest holding company of all was given a clean bill of health under the Sherman Act, in the *U.S. Steel* case (1920), the great merger wave of the ensuing decade followed the now predictable path of its predecessor. However, after the Supreme Court upheld the union of U.S. Steel and Consolidated Steel in 1948,[104] the regulation of merger activity once again became an issue of national importance. That decision inspired Congress to amend the Clayton Act in 1950 with the Celler-Kefauver Act.

Having plugged the loophole by bringing the acquisition of assets within strictures and revised language of the Clayton Act, so that all types of mergers or consolidations (not just those between competitors) would be subject to the provisions of the act, Congress was confident that it had provided the FTC and federal judiciary with an effective regulatory tool.[105] The Supreme Court, under Chief Justice Earl Warren, agreed. In its 1962 opinion in *Brown Shoe Co. v. United States*,[106] the Court expounded on the intent of the 1950 amendment and established the principles and basic tests for judging the legality of both vertical and horizontal mergers. Reviewing the legislative history of the Celler-Kefauver Act, the Chief Justice observed that the "dominant theme pervading congressional consideration . . . was considered to be a rising tide of economic concentration in the American economy." This development, Warren explained, evoked concern for the viability of locally controlled industries and small business. Moreover, "Congress' fear not only of accelerated concentration of economic power on economic grounds, but also of the threat to other values," shaped the drafting of the legislation.[107] As in *Alcoa*, the Court, in interpreting Congress's intent, defined the malady that the statute sought to remedy in terms of the undesirable social effects of increasing economic concentration and the attendant power wielded by the large corporation. Because the objective of Congress, Warren argued, was to quash anticompetitive practices in their infancy before they were swept up in the "rising tide of economic concentration," the phrase "may be substantially to lessen competition" necessarily refers to "probabilities, not certainties."[108]

For both vertical and horizontal mergers, the preliminary analysis remained the same. The "area of effective competition" must first be determined by defining the product market (and its possible submarkets) and the geographical market. This accomplished, the "probable effects" of the merger on competition may be assessed. In *Brown Shoe*, the Court identified two probable effects as having the greatest bearing on determining the legality of the merger between Brown and Kinney Shoes: (1) the size of the market share that is "foreclosed" vertically or "controlled" horizontally, and (2) the historical tendency toward concentration within these two markets.[109] By these standards, even though the merger would give Brown only 5.5 percent of total shoe production in the United States and move the company up from fourth to third largest producer of shoes, the Court found that its probable effect ran afoul of the law. With *Brown Shoe*, and several cases that followed, merger law not only erected formidable barriers to incipient oligopoly, not to mention monopoly, but also effectively eliminated the prospect of a horizontal merger when one party was a dominant firm within an oligopolistic market. Thus it seems to have accomplished for oligopoly what *Alcoa* achieved for monopoly— namely, to limit concentration by defining the test in terms of the size of the market share. By adopting the interpretation that "substantially to lessen competition" refers to "probabilities not, certainties," the Court expanded the concept of potential competition to comprehend the regulation of mergers whose probable effects would substantially limit or foreclose competition in markets, regardless of whether the markets possessed a relatively low or high degree of concentration.[110]

Perhaps more important for the state of the economy and polity, by the mid-1970s, was the issue of regulating conglomerate mergers. In several decisions in the 1960s, the Court, under Chief Justice Warren, had developed various and complicated economic rationales to explain the probable effect of conglomerate mergers on competition. The most evolved of these, the "perceived potential entrant theory," seems to stretch the judicial function to its limits through its difficult logic and complex analysis of economic variables.[111] Two other tests of anticompetitive effects— the "market entrenchment theory" and the "reciprocity threat theory"— were applied by the Supreme Court only once.[112] The Warren Court's rulings on conglomerate mergers, however, were tempered by the new "antitrust majority" that emerged in 1974 on the Burger Court and subsequently by the enforcement policy of the Department of Justice.

Conglomerate mergers pose especially difficult problems of fact and theory that do not arise in other merger cases. To begin with, a conglomerate merger may be one of three types as determined by the product markets of the merging firms—market extension (same products in different geographical markets), product extension (related products), or diversification (different products)—each of which involves special considerations in determining the probable effect of the merger on the relevant market. Because the markets of the merging corporations are distinct, the effect of the merger on competition cannot be assessed by the increase in market concentration. However, there have been arguments (thus far rejected by the courts) that invoke concentration in some form as a standard for finding anticompetitive effects. In the *ITT* case of 1970, concerning the merger between ITT and Grinnell, the District Court repudiated the government's claim that "anticompetitive consequences will appear in numerous though undesignated lines of commerce." Chief Judge Timbers pointed out that the Clayton Act proscribes only mergers that substantially lessen competition in specific markets, not all mergers that could conceivably increase economic concentration.[113]

Similarly, on two occasions the Burger Court found unconvincing the argument that a merger of banks in the same state, albeit in distinct geographical markets, "would tend to produce a statewide linkage of oligopolies."[114] However, neither of the anticompetitive consequences alleged in these cases appear to have had anything to do with market concentration. Instead, these arguments reflect concern about the tremendous concentration of assets in one corporation and the implications of that for the exercise of corporate power, and about the capability of the conglomerate to centralize its control over numerous firms that, in the bank cases, operate in the same product market. For these reasons, the principle of potential competition has not been applied with the same degree of effectiveness to conglomerate mergers as it has to horizontal and vertical mergers.

It may be that the difficulty the Warren and Burger Courts had in agreeing on criteria for assessing the legality of this relatively new form of merger only reflects the state of economic opinion on the matter. It is clear as well that the antimonopoly logic of Judge Hand and Chief Justice Warren does not readily apply to conglomerate mergers that do not foment increasing market concentration in the same manner as horizontal and vertical mergers do. It may turn out to be the case, therefore, that the strongest argument for regulating conglomerate mergers rests primarily on political rather than economic grounds, precisely because the motivation, in addition to profit-making or achieving maximum returns, appears to be a quest for dominance within the corporate order.

By centralizing control over large firms that themselves dominate their respective markets, the great conglomerates already are becoming the holding companies of the future, but with one important difference from their turn-of-the-century predecessors. While both the old and the new forms are erected on the organizational principles of centralized control and hierarchy, the developmental logic of the conglomerate leads to the control of numerous (often related) industries, not just one industry. We know, based on a century of evidence, that the dominant trend of horizontal and vertical mergers, when left unregulated, is the ascendance of one or a few firms per industry, monopoly, or oligopoly. Based on the evidence at hand, we can surmise that the dominant trend of the conglomerate merger, when left to its own devices, is the ascendance of an elite group of mega-firms in all of industry and finance, an industrial-financial oligarchy controlling the entrenched oligopolies. This prospect becomes more compelling when viewed in light of the current strategy of large firms to acquire companies doing business in related markets and product lines.[115] It also gives a new meaning to horizontal mergers (in effect, mergers of conglomerates controlling competing and related industries), which now become a method for attaining conglomerate control over several industries, rather than solely a means for dominating a specific market. And with the rise of transnational corporate enterprise, this "oligarchy of oligopolists" increasingly assumes a global character.[116]

In light of the complexity of the Supreme Court's opinions and the fact that the number of mergers in 1968 had soared to an all-time high, the Department of Justice, beginning in that same year, assumed the responsibility of publishing guidelines, based in part on court decisions, that detailed the conditions under which it would challenge a merger.[117] In 1982, the Justice Department revised the 1968 guidelines and significantly relaxed the standards for vertical and conglomerate mergers.[118] A major justification offered for this revision was that it would improve the competitive position of American corporations in domestic and international markets, and specifically with respect to Japanese companies. Six months before the issuance of the new guidelines, Attorney General William French Smith, in announcing the Reagan administration's antitrust policy, declared: "Federal antitrust law forms the constitution of our economic liberties." Having made this gesture, he then added that he would "spare no effort in also eliminating anti-competitive governmental practices."[119] On the same occasion, William F. Baxter, head of the Antitrust Division, clarified the Justice Department's policy when he flatly rejected the notion that large corporations "by virtue of their size have something called economic power."[120]

By establishing a policy of enforcement that selectively incorporates legal precedent, that relies heavily on sophisticated economic analyses not employed in Supreme Court or FTC decisions, and that allows for "discretionary factors" to enter the analysis, the Department of Justice has been able to imprint its own interpretation on judge-made law to effect a new direction in antitrust policy. Under this policy, antitrust enforcement affecting mergers has swung sharply in favor of the presumption of freedom to contract by redefining or loosening restrictions on corporate combinations.

The Hand-Warren approach justified an expanded government regulation of markets in its application of the principle of potential competition. In allowing a greater freedom for corporate regulation of markets, the Burger and Rehnquist Courts and the Justice Department under Presidents Reagan and Bush in effect took steps to redefine, by enlarging, the sphere of potential competition to include transnational markets. By devising guidelines that permit mergers that would have failed the tests under the Warren Court antitrust decisions, the revised antitrust policy accommodated and facilitated the restructuring of world markets by transnational firms. Antitrust policy that is facilitative of the rise of an oligarchy of oligopolists in the United States, is therefore consistent with the redefinition of the concept of potential competition to embrace the global spread of corporate capitalism. In short, the proliferation of transnational enterprise and the subsequent restructuring of the world economy apparently have provided both the need and the justification for incorporating into antitrust law a transnational conception of oligopolistic competition.[121]

6. THE EVOLUTION OF CORPORATE INDIVIDUALISM

In erecting the legal edifice of corporate power over the last two centuries, American jurists have facilitated the growth of that power in its external and internal dimensions and secured corporations against state command. It is difficult to measure fully the contribution of the law to the rise and consolidation of corporate power, because it is impossible to separate this form of power from its legal attributes and limitations. The interplay between law and economy further complicates the task of analysis. Law can accommodate and facilitate economic change as well as shape the course of future economic strategy. This becomes especially apparent when legislation replaces the "natural laws" of the marketplace and seeks to regulate economic behavior once presumed to yield, by its own logic, beneficent social consequences.

Under the due process, equal protection, and commerce clauses, the Supreme Court in the late nineteenth and early twentieth centuries both restructured American federalism to aid the rise of corporate enterprise and expanded the rights of property to encompass the complex structure of ownership under corporate capitalism. The revolution in state corporation law substantially freed both the external and the internal dimensions of corporate power from state regulation and imposed on the federal government (through default) the primary responsibility of regulating the external dimension. This development heralded the realization of an expanding corporate autonomy within both the internal and the external dimensions. With the adoption of the rule of reason in the law of antitrust, in 1911, the Supreme Court devised the principle of fair competition, which defined legitimate power within the corporate-capitalist marketplace. Henceforth, antitrust law became the constitutional law of the external dimension of corporate power. The putative "private" domain of corporate enterprise, founded on the constitutional property rights of the corporate individual, was thereby maintained ideologically through the concept of oligopolistic (or potential) competition in antitrust law, while it was cemented in the law of corporations through rulings that guaranteed the political and managerial autonomy of the corporate oligarchy. The root of this historical progression, which was also the foundation of the external dimension of corporate power, was the legal fiction of the constitutional corporate individual, the essential concept that links the public and private laws of the corporation. From this fiction also flows the most enduring aspect of corporate legal ideology: the doctrine of corporate individualism.

Corporate power in its internal dimension was never dressed for public view. Legal doctrine therein betrays a revolution in search of an ideology. As the corporate oligarchy presided over the withering away of shareholder democracy, however, courts gradually infused the law with principles—consistent with the political autonomy of corporate rule and the ideological concept of private enterprise—which secured the hierarchical structure of corporate power. As corporate social responsibility continued to acquire significance within a corporate ethic that justified broad powers, the internal and external dimensions approached ideological convergence through the doctrine of corporate citizenship.

We return, then, to the legal fiction, the central concept of corporate ideology that makes possible the transformation, through reification, of massive collectivities into individual Americans who compete in the marketplace or the political arena or, for that matter, contribute to the local charity. Writing in 1937, Thurman Arnold expounded on the significance of this phenomenon for American beliefs and institutions:

> One of the essential and central notions which give our industrial feudalism logical symmetry is the personification of great industrial enterprise. The ideal that a corporation is endowed with the rights and prerogatives of a free individual is as essential to the acceptance of corporate rule in temporal affairs as was the ideal of the divine right of kings in an earlier day. Its exemplification, as in the case of all vital ideals, has been accomplished by ceremony. Since it has been a central ideal in our industrial government, our judicial institutions have been particularly concerned with its celebration. Courts, under the mantle of the Constitution, have made a living thing out of this fiction. Men have come to believe that their own future liberties and dignity are tied up in the freedom of great industrial organizations from restraint, in much the same way that they thought their salvation in the future was dependent on their reverence and support of great ecclesiastical organizations in the Middle Ages.[122]

Arnold's observations apply with even greater force today. The corporate individual—the entrepreneur, the statesman, the citizen—represents the ideological triumph of the fusion of liberalism with the principles of corporate rule. It is more than an ideological mask that shields the realities of corporate power. It is a way of thinking, profoundly ingrained in the law and in the consciousness of a people. Without this concept, the use of liberal ideas to justify the structure of corporate power would lack credibility, or perhaps appear to be manifestly contradictory. It accounts for the naturalization of the corporate entity, for the attribution of constitutitonal rights to the corporation, for the ideological viability of antitrust law, and for the enduring presumption that corporate enterprise is a private affair.[123]

Corporate individualism continues to be the most important ideological weapon in the arsenal of corporate power. Through modern methods of advertising—especially television commercials—the corporate persona regularly advises, entertains, and indoctrinates a captive audience. Recent Supreme Court rulings concerning corporate political and commercial speech have provided constitutional protection for this practice. This is not to say that corporations are necessarily irresponsible, only that they spend huge sums of money and countless hours year-round trying to convince the public that they are good citizens.

The corporate individual simply has no rival in the world of appearance, in the corporate-created universe of high-tech sounds and images, of glitter and fads, of mass conformity hawked as the latest style. A bottomless pit of assimilation, corporate advertising reproduces over and again the same mass culture that teaches us the obsessive habits of conspicuous consumption, instills in us the fear of being different, then extols the heroic virtues of individuality—which is to say, the touted social advantages of appearing to be a stylish individual. As styles change, the message remains the same. Corporate power over consumption reverses the traditional logic of the competitive marketplace by first creating needs (usually through fear, invidious comparisons, or inducements to emulate the fashionable) in order to sell products that are waiting for buyers. To sustain this economy, we are instructed on every mundane detail of daily existence. We are lectured endlessly on personal habits, hygiene, and appearance. We are indoctrinated in the principles of pecuniary culture and tantalized with the trappings of material success. Accordingly, we worship at the altar of things. Then we purchase our salvation.

A pattern of behavior deeply instilled in millions of Americans becomes an even more potent means of indoctrination when these masters of illusion, however subtly, blend political and ideological messages with the latest sales pitch. The selling of corporate America takes many forms in which commercial and political advertising often become indistinguishable. Increasingly, the sales pitch fades into the background in what appear to be public-service announcements or self-congratulatory "commercials" lauding corporate good deeds and praising the American way. Selling soap and America has always been good for business, but in the era of corporate capitalism there is more at stake for the large corporation than making a buck. Public responsibility becomes increasingly important as corporate power transforms social relationships. To succeed in the long term, corporate leaders must take into account social and political realities.

Corporate citizenship, although never granted to the corporation under the privileges and immunities clauses, had found an ideological domain long before receiving constitutional sanction under the First Amendment. It has thrived for decades. Born with the *Santa Clara* case in 1886, and bred with the creation of the National Civic Federation in 1900, it grew to maturity with the New Deal. Its virtues have since been extolled countless times in self-promotion on television, over radio, in speeches, and in public-relations publications. The triumph of corporate citizenship is all the more significant in the era of transnational enterprise, for it lends credibility to the vision of the corporate statesman. A movement is afoot. Ideological and legal doctrines coalesce in the service of corporate expansion. Liberal ideals, refashioned to serve the global objectives of the modern corporation, find expression in an antitrust policy predicated on the elimination of "anticompetitive governmental practices," in the constitutional protections of corporate speech in the marketplace of politics and ideas, and in the Free Trade doctrine of transnational corporate ideologists. It is the stuff of power wrapped in the garb of liberty and efficiency. It is indeed a capitalist movement of global proportions that marks the present stage in the historic ascendance of the corporate bourgeoisie.[124]

Both the public and private law of the modern corporation stand as testimony to its autonomy, and to the essential role of corporate-liberal ideology in justifying the consolidation of corporate power. However, ideological aspects of legal doctrine constitute only one component of an evolving corporate liberalism in the twentieth century. In addition to doctrinal changes in the law, the consolidation of corporate power inspired a reassessment of corporate social responsibility in political thought, and therewith an effort to construct a political theory of the corporation.

Chapter 5

THE MANAGERIAL THEORY OF CORPORATE POWER

*Organizations which exercise governing powers of a perma-
nent character do not maintain their power by force. Force is
entirely too exhausting. They do it by identifying themselves with the faiths and loyalties of the people.*
—Thurman Arnold, 1937

1. THE MANAGERIAL THESIS

With the exception of the later works of Veblen, the Progressive Era
studies of corporate power were undertaken at a time when most large
corporations were still controlled by the majority stockholder, whether it
be an individual, family, or financial group. During that period, the
dominance of the captains of finance and industry clearly rested on the
prerogatives of ownership and great personal wealth. Both Croly and
Weyl based their conceptions of corporate power and proposals for reform on this fact. Of the three, Veblen alone attempted to explain the
political implications of the separation of ownership and control, which
in his view resulted from the basic organization of the joint-stock company. As we have seen, Veblen concluded that the separation of corporate ownership from control produced a shift of power from nonmajority

stockholders to a group of "ultimate owners" who controlled the means of access to credit and finance. Veblen's distinctive conception of corporate power, like those of Croly and Weyl, assumed a direct relationship between the control of wealth and the exercise of power in society.

With the publication of Adolf A. Berle and Gardiner C. Means's *The Modern Corporation and Private Property*, in 1932, this assumption was boldly challenged. In assessing what they claimed to be a widespread trend toward separation of ownership and control, the authors argued that control within most large corporations had been assumed by a substantially propertyless group of managers. A host of related problems accompanied the Berle-Means hypothesis. For instance, once property and power had been dissociated, could it be assumed that the profit motive would take precedence over nonpecuniary motives, such as the desire for power? Moreover, with the control and ownership of property divided, what became of the traditional legal theory of property, which assumed a unity of these functions? Must all profits still accrue to the owners? If this was not feasible, given the imperatives of corporate enterprise, on what basis could managerial control of profits be justified? Could it be argued that, apart from providing reasonable dividends for stockholders, the modern corporation performed a social function and must therefore be held accountable to society as a whole? If this was a valid argument, as Berle and Means implied, then the traditional logic of property and profits would have to be amended accordingly.

The issue of corporate social responsibility added an uncharted dimension to the Berle-Means analysis. In their view, the concentration of power associated with the tremendous size of corporate enterprise warranted the novel conception of the corporation as a social and political, as well as an economic, institution.[1] With this observation, the liberal justification of corporate power entered the realm of traditional political theory. Henceforth, the defense of corporate social responsibility would have to include a conception of the legitimacy of corporate power.

Although the writings of Croly, Weyl, and Veblen had anticipated the idea of the corporation as a political institution, the effort to construct a normative and empirical political theory of corporate enterprise actually began with the seminal work of Berle and Means. Their study, published in the early stages of the Great Depression, provides a useful benchmark for the evolving conception of corporate power in American political thought.

In the tradition of the Progressive Era reformers, *The Modern Corporation and Private Property* strongly hinted at the possibility (and desirability) of greater public regulation of corporate enterprise, but unlike the works of Croly and Weyl, it did not offer an actual plan for how this should be achieved. Berle, who gave the book its energetic style, was at his radical best without committing to a specific cause. In all fairness, however, it is the book's argument, and not its political tone, that has endured. No other work on corporate power, with the possible exception of Croly's *Promise of American Life*, has had such a lasting impact on American political and economic thought in the twentieth century.

The fact that Berle and Means recognized the need for a political theory of the corporation reflected the extent to which the corporate reconstruction of economy and polity had already succeeded. Yet, if Croly's and Weyl's proposals might be used as a measure, there were still some basic tasks of reform to be completed in 1932. Federal law had not yet recognized the right of workers to organize in unions or to bargain collectively; the national government had not instituted sufficient measures, let alone a comprehensive program, to meet social welfare needs; and the federal government had yet to devise a coherent industrial policy, including a plan for coping with chronic unemployment. All these problems, among others, were addressed through legislation and presidential action during the first two terms of Franklin Delano Roosevelt's presidency. When the United States entered World War II, the corporate reconstruction was nearing completion. The war effort strengthened old and created new ties between the federal government and corporations, introduced an unprecedented degree of economic planning, ushered in an era of prosperity based on new technologies, and secured the ascendance of the United States among capitalist nations.

During the war years and thereafter, managerial theorists abandoned the reformist zeal of the Progressive Era and the New Deal period in their efforts to explain the political significance of the corporation and to justify its power in terms of the precepts of liberalism. While their analyses differed in important ways from those of the Progressive Era thinkers, the managerial theorists also retained an analytical and ideological continuity with their reform-minded predecessors. Most important of all, the analysis of corporate power and the revision of American liberalism remained intimately linked. As the former achieved greater sophistication, the latter acquired a scholarly refinement and reputability. And as the radicalism of the corporate-liberal reformers became the accepted doctrine of the new order, the adaptation of American liberalism to corporate capitalism approached fulfillment.

In this chapter, I critically examine the quest for a political theory of the corporation by analyzing the writings of Peter F. Drucker, Adolph A. Berle, and John Kenneth Galbraith. Each of these authors, like their Progressive Era counterparts, has made a distinctive and influential contribution to the study of corporate power and to the interpretation of American liberalism. It has often been the case that important thinkers acquire great influence because, in shaping the direction of social thought, they anticipate or sum up the intellectual tendencies of the period. I believe that this is true, in varying degrees, of each of these individuals. This observation gains greater force when we realize that the writings of Berle, Drucker, and Galbraith that are the subject of this analysis span approximately four decades. To understand better the contributions of these men to recent American political thought, however, we must place their analyses of corporate power in historical context.

Perhaps best known as a leading theorist of business management, Drucker first achieved prominence in the United States as a political theorist of the corporation. Born in Vienna, Drucker had attended the universities of Hamburg and Frankfurt, worked for four years as an editor of the *Frankfurter General Anzeiger*, and served as an economist for an international banking house in London before coming to New York in 1937.[2] A philosopher and economist by training, Drucker published extensively in German before publishing his first major work in English, *The End of Economic Man*, in 1939.[3] Although primarily a study of the historical and philosophical roots of fascism, this work laid the foundation for the author's critique of liberalism, which inspired his political study of the corporation. In his next three works, *The Future of Industrial Man*, *Concept of the Corporation*, and *The New Society*, published between 1942 and 1949, Drucker developed his social and political theory of corporate enterprise.[4] The influential vision of a modern "corporate society" that was articulated in these works had its roots in the ideological struggles of World War II, but also in his study of managerial science. In fact, *Concept of the Corporation* was the product of a managerial study of General Motors Corporation that the company had funded.

Something of a prodigy, Berle entered Harvard as an undergraduate at the age of fourteen and graduated from Harvard Law at the age of twenty-one. In 1927, he accepted a position to teach law at Columbia University. His publications on corporation law as of 1932, which included numerous articles and a case book, had already earned him a reputation as a leader in his field. *The Modern Corporation and Private Property* not only enhanced this reputation but also helped to launch Berle's long involvement in politics. An influential member of President Franklin D. Roosevelt's "brain trust" during the 1930s, Berle served as an Assistant Secretary of State and as Ambassador to Brazil in the 1940s, advised President Kennedy on Latin America, and was actively involved in New York City politics for more than three decades. After resigning as ambassador to Brazil in 1946, Berle resumed his academic career at Columbia and, in the mid-1950s, began in earnest to develop further his political theory of the corporation.

A strong supporter of the New Deal, Berle was a liberal Democrat but also staunchly anticommunist. Arguably, his antipathy toward the Soviet Union, shaped by a distrust of Soviet leaders he had acquired when serving under Roosevelt, could have contributed to his determination to construct an ideological defense for corporate power. But the phenomenon of power itself had long been a source of fascination to him, and, as he conceived it, the philosophical justification of corporate power was but another aspect of this phenomenon. If he had shed his youthful radicalism during his years of government service, he had not, in doing so, compromised his intellectual seriousness and integrity.[5]

An economist and political thinker in the tradition of Thorstein Veblen, Galbraith achieved great distinction in his academic endeavors, served as Ambassador to India under President Kennedy, and acted as an advisor to several Presidents of the United States. His thinking on the corporation, however, offers a study in contrast to that of Berle and Drucker. Galbraith's views on the power of the large corporation and its implications for liberal-democratic institutions became increasingly critical during the period in which he wrote his major works. His skeptical assessment of the future of industrial society evolved in three books he published during the 1950s and 1960s: *American Capitalism: The Concept of Countervailing Power* (1952), *The Affluent Society* (1958), and *The New Industrial State* (1967).[6] In the last of these works, Galbraith's analysis of the "technostructure" (the modern structure of domination produced from the merging of corporations and the state) coincided with and influenced a growing dissent among liberal intellectuals and political activists in the late 1960s and the early 1970s. Within the context of Cold War ideological struggles in academic institutions, his political analysis of the corporation was destined to spark controversy. Galbraith also breathed new life into Veblen's critique of pecuniary culture and offered his own version of rule by technocrats.

In addressing the central social and political issues posed by the consolidation of corporate power, the theories of Drucker, Berle, and Galbraith shaped the contemporary debate about corporate social responsibility. These issues included, among others, the significance of labor unions (both within the enterprise and in politics) as a means of balancing managerial power, the social responsibilities of the corporation, the dangers posed to democracy by corporate power, the legitimizing principles of that power, the regulatory responsibilities of government, and the meaning of individuality in the workplace and in a society reconstructed in the image of the corporation. Although the theories of these authors contained significant differences on some issues, their studies of corporate enterprise shared several basic assumptions. Each viewed the corporation as an autonomous or self-sufficient entity capable of generating its own capital and therefore no longer dependent on the capital markets. A product of modern technology, the structure and organization of the corporation, they emphasized, had been built on a highly specialized division of labor. They also maintained that as a consequence of the separation of ownership from control and the need for expert decision-making, power within the corporation was exercised by professional managers or experts whose position of leadership was not a function of their pecuniary interest in the enterprise.

The authors' analyses of the internal and external dimensions of corporate power also paralleled important developments in the public and private laws of the corporation. Consistent with the legal principle of political autonomy, which insulated corporate decision-making from public scrutiny,[7] the managerial theorists argued that corporate autonomy was an essential condition, if not an inviolable "law," of modern industrial society. They also contended that the corporation was a species of political institution that exercised power in the course of performing its economic function and, accordingly, must be held accountable to the dominant beliefs and ideals of society. Thus, the political theory of the corporation had its counterpart in legal theory: as the private realm of corporate governance evolved into a limited oligarchy that exercised public powers, the external (or public) dimension of corporate power achieved legitimacy through the ideological doctrine of corporate social responsibility.

It is also significant, and perhaps not at all coincidental, that the works of each of these thinkers parallels in important ways the thought of one of the early analysts of corporate power. Drucker, like Croly, advocated rule by experts and identified efficiency as the measure of corporate social responsibiity; Berle shared Weyl's faith in the panacea of countervailing power; and Galbraith believed in the autonomy of technological development, as did Veblen in his day. Although several other parallels may be drawn, these are perhaps sufficient to indicate that the liberal managerial theories of corporate power have remained within fairly constant analytical and ideological contours.

It should be emphasized as well that the normative aspects of managerial theory also reveal how corporate liberalism has evolved with the consolidation of corporate power. The idea of corporate autonomy, which justified the private nature of corporate decision-making on pragmatic and policy-making grounds (thereby ensuring the separation of state and society), achieved the status of historical necessity, thus becoming a "natural law" of enterprise. The redefinition of democracy became further associated with hierarchy and rule by experts, while the idea of social balance gradually lost its reformist connotations and served to justify disparities in power based on class divisions. And although individualism was still celebrated, its meaning became increasingly problematical. In the era of the "organization man," the "individual" became a team player or perhaps an unwitting conformist, while the nonconformist became a social pariah. But even as this occurred, the older belief in material progress reigned supreme, albeit with a diminishing role for human agency. Indeed, the reified "laws" of corporate liberalism would appear to counsel ideological acquiescence. Under such conditions, corporate power would be more readily accepted, just as ideological dissent could be more easily assimilated.

While the liberal managerial theorists wrestled with the normative and empirical issues inherited from their predecessors, they also confronted new challenges. In the aftermath of the Progressive Era, the consolidation of corporate power, facilitated by the corporate reconstruction of American law, squarely posed the need for a political theory of the corporation.

2. PETER F. DRUCKER: POLITICAL THEORIST OF THE CORPORATE SOCIETY

In redefining the terms of the debate about corporate social responsibility and arguing for a distinctively political conception of the corporation, Berle and Means not only transformed the way we think about corporate power but also identified the tasks involved in constructing a political theory of corporate enterprise. Peter F. Drucker's major works on the social and political significance of the corporation constituted the first effort to formulate, in a systematic way, the principles of such a theory.

Drucker's political study of the corporation was shaped by his conviction that the beliefs of classical liberalism must be adapted to the exigencies of the corporate order—what he called "industrial society." He constructed his theory of corporate enterprise with reference to the great issues of modern society as he understood them. These issues included the conditions necessary for attaining freedom in industrial society, the quest for individual meaning and purpose, the problem of legitimacy within the corporation, and the values and beliefs on which corporate enterprise and society as a whole should be based. Because the corporation constituted the "representative social institution" of industrial society, he argued that "pre-industrial" beliefs should be revised to reflect this change. For Drucker, the tasks of explanation and prescription went hand in hand. His normative recommendations flowed from the very organization of industrial society as he conceived it. I shall argue that Drucker's effort to combine a theory of managerial control with a corporatist conception of society and a corporate ethic produced a distinctive philosophical justification for the consolidation of corporate power.

Drucker argued that industrial society had been built on revolutionary changes in technology made possible by the principle of mass production. Originally a method of organizing the productive process, mass production was also a principle of social organization. As such, it entailed a specialization of functions and an integration of these functions into a pattern.[8] "For the individual as well as society," Drucker observed, "the really productive element in modern society is a concept, . . . the view of the whole, the vision of a pattern." Because it is an interdependent whole, industrial society "will not be able to function or even to survive . . . unless the members see the relationship between their own work and purpose and the purpose and pattern of their society."[9] As the basic productive unit, the corporation provided an organizational model for society. Indeed, it embodied not only the principle of mass production but also the political and philosophical challenges of the modern era. The fate of industrial society, therefore, would hinge on the ability of the corporation to successfully meet these challenges.

Drucker argued that as a result of the separation of ownership from control within the large corporation, a new group of rulers (although not a ruling class) now governed the economic sphere of society.[10] The fact that the power of corporate managers was no longer based on the rights of ownership constituted the "central institutional challenge of our times." This development proved instrumental in transforming the corporation into an "autonomous social entity which exercises power by its own authority." However, the autonomy of enterprise characterized industry in both capitalist and socialist countries and therefore could not be attributed solely to the divorce of ownership from control.[11] As an "autonomous institution," the enterprise did not "derive its power and function from the motives, purposes, or rights of the owners," nor did it "derive its structure, aims and purpose from the political or legal organization of society." Rather, it possessed "a 'nature' of its own" and followed "the laws of its own being."

Drucker insisted that corporate enterprise "cannot and must not be operated in the interests of any one group . . . but in the interest of society"—which is to say "in the interest of economic performance."[12]

But he also maintained that the first law of any institution was survival.[13] Thus, his definition of the problem appears to require that the survival interests of enterprise and society's interest in economic performance be compatible, if not identical.

As an autonomous institution, the corporation possessed a "triple personality." It was "at one and the same time an economic, a governmental and a social institution." Because the survival of the enterprise depended on "the efficient performance of its economic responsibility" of turning out goods or services, the economic function necessarily took precedence over the governmental and social functions.[14] The logic of Drucker's argument, however, necessitated a compatibility between the survival interest of the corporation and the interest of society in economic performance. He provided a solution to this problem with his conception of the "laws of the enterprise"—namely, the "law of avoiding loss" and the "law of higher output."[15] Because efficient economic performance (given the corporation's size and capital investment) required that enterprise be able to plan for the future, avoiding loss was essential for the long-term survival of the corporation. The second law, Drucker explained, constituted "both the purpose of an industrial economy and its imperative need." Expansion not only prevented economic dislocation but also increased productivity and released productive resources (i.e., technological innovation) that fueled further expansion. Both of these laws, which together determined the survival interest of the corporation, expressed the social interest in economic performance as well. As such, they were laws of survival as well as "social duties" of the enterprise.[16]

But how, Drucker asked, would the members of society know whether these duties were being met—that is, how could one measure the efficient economic performance of the corporation? The only means for assessing this, he argued, was the standard of profitability, which "measures both the size and adequacy of the provisions against future costs and increased productivity." Profitability therefore had nothing to do with the profit motive or any other motive. It originated in the "objective necessity and purpose of industrial production and industrial economy." In fact, "the rationale, behavior, policies and decisions of the enterprise are the same regardless of the legal or political structure of industrial society." The actual distribution of profits therefore had no bearing on the behavior of corporate management. As an autonomous institution— a universal phenomenon of industrial societies—the enterprise obeyed its own imperatives.[17]

Unlike the economic function of the corporation, which was determined by the objective laws of survival, the governmental and social functions could not be dissociated from the beliefs and ideals of a society.

In Drucker's view, these functions gave rise to the major social issues of modernity. Because their fulfillment would depend on the political, legal, and ideological makeup of a given society, the governmental and social functions of corporate enterprise must be understood within their specific cultural context.

The governmental function stemmed from the basic political character of the corporation: the fact that it exercised power. Corporate power was rooted in the control of "access to the productive organization," which amounted to a control of "access to the citizen's livelihood." Moreover, access to the productive organization of society determined "the citizen's social effectiveness, if not indeed his very citizenship." Thus, the scope of the power exercised by the managers of industrial society was extensive. Not only did managerial decisions and policies "affect the lives and livelihoods of a large number of citizens," but they also "determine[d] very largely the character of our society."[18] The corporation was therefore an economic institution that performed a political function entirely separate from the political functions of the state. However, the successful functioning of the enterprise required that the state respect corporate autonomy. In this fashion, the traditional liberal separation of the economic and governmental spheres could be preserved, even though the private (economic) realm now exercised public powers.

Corporate power, if exercised in the interest of survival, would satisfy the needs of enterprise and the demands of society for efficient economic performance. In this sense, there were implicit checks on the power of management. However, the governmental function of the corporation included another responsibility, which could not be fulfilled by adhering to the imperatives of survival. "The organization of industrial production," Drucker observed, required "an internal order based on authority and subordination, that is, on power relationships."[19] This internal governmental function gave rise to a basic political conflict or tension between management and unions. Because this conflict amounted to a struggle for allegiance, the legitimacy of corporate power became an issue. But this constituted only part of the problem. To be a legitimate government, the corporation must exercise power in the interests of the governed, yet its first responsibility was to perform its economic function efficiently in the interest of society. Thus, the interests of the worker and of society as a whole would appear to be fundamentally at odds.[20] In order to assess Drucker's solution to this problem, we must first examine the social functions of the corporation.

Because the enterprise was the "representative social institution" of industrial society, and the plant community was the "distinctive representative social unit," the corporation necessarily assumed certain responsibilities to society. In its capacity as representative social institution, the enterprise determined "the individual's view of his society." It constituted "the true symbol of our social order" because its "internal order and its internal problems" were "the distinctive and the pressing problems of an industrial society." Accordingly, the solutions for its problems would determine "the structure and the solutions of industrial society altogether."[21] In performing its social function, the corporation must "fulfill the beliefs and promises of its society by giving social status and function in the plant community."[22] The corporation's social function, therefore, concerned the relationship between an individual's freedom and the responsibility owed to society. Drucker's analysis of this relationship and his solution to the problem of legitimacy were linked through the "unifying political principle of industrial society," the concept of harmony.

Drucker maintained that the successful functioning of the enterprise required not only that each of its functions be fulfilled but also that this be accomplished without fulfilling one at the expense of another. The functions of the enterprise must therefore be viewed as interdependent components of a whole; furthermore, they must be in harmony with the basic promises and beliefs of society and with the successful functioning of the social order. "The concept of harmony," he explained, "thus emerges as a basic concept of political action."[23] It followed that the corporation

> should be so organized as to fulfill automatically its social obligations in the very act of seeking its own best self-interest. An industrial society based on the corporation can only function if the corporation contributes to social stability and to the achievement of social aims independent of good will or the social consciousness of individual corporation managements.[24]

Drucker claimed that the concept of harmony was the great "rediscovery" of nineteenth-century laissez-faire, but failed because it assumed an automatic harmony rather than one produced by statesmanship. Harmony implied an accommodation, a balance between the needs and aims of society and those of the corporation. While the state reserved the right to limit the exercise of corporate power, it must not encroach on the autonomy of enterprise and thereby threaten its survival. But this did not imply a strictly mechanical conception of balance. Rather, a social balance based on the principles of harmony rested on a "philosophy of society which . . . sees the one and the many, the whole and its parts, as complementing each other."[25] The same philosophy informed the author's solutions to the problems of legitimacy and individual freedom in industrial society.

Because the governmental function of the enterprise must always be subordinated to its economic function, the corporation could never be a truly legitimate government—a government that ruled "in the interests of its subjects." Moreover, this was true regardless of the economic and political organization of society, because management must perform "an objective function, grounded in the necessity of the enterprise." Consequently, there was an unavoidable conflict built into the corporation, a conflict between "the worker's interest as a member of the enterprise and as subject to its governmental authority" and "society's interest in the economic performance of the enterprise." Since this "political duality" could not be avoided, it must be institutionalized; it must be "built into the very structure of the government of the enterprise." Under these conditions, the government of the corporation could be made legitimate only "through a counter-power which represented the members against their government while, at the same time, forming part of this government."[26]

The labor union thus developed as "the institutional expression of the basic political tension of the enterprise." This division within the internal government of the corporation also gave rise to a "split allegiance" for the members of the union, and therein laid the challenge of legitimacy. If the enterprise were to be a legitimate government and fulfill its governmental function without undermining its primary economic function, the split allegiance must become a "twin allegiance." In short, the union must become a "loyal opposition."[27]

The best means for realizing a twin allegiance was through a plant government based on the union contract. While such a government would necessarily be subordinated to the economic function of the enterprise, it would be autonomous within its own sphere. Drucker reasoned that the plant government would serve as a means for establishing a common ground between management and union and thus would provide a "foundation of harmony" underlying the inherent conflict within the enterprise. Although the plant government would be concerned primarily with matters pertaining to the social life of the plant, it would also work with management on a variety of problems that concerned the economic performance of the corporation. By allowing for cooperation and opposition within the enterprise, the plant government cultivated a twin allegiance and hence promised to resolve the problem of legitimacy.[28] The self-governing plant community also held the solution to the social problem of the enterprise.

As the representative social institution, the corporation must strive to fulfill the promises and ideals of American society—namely, those of status and function. Status, which "defines man's existence as related in mutual necessity to the organized group," embodied the promise of equal opportunity. The demand for status was the demand for an equal opportunity to become unequal, the demand of the individual in a liberal society. Function, on the other hand, referred to the integration of the individual within the social whole; it "ties his work, his aspirations, his ambitions to the power and purpose of the organized group in a bind that satisfies both individual and society." Function, as Drucker conceived it, provided the context within which individual endeavor acquired meaning in terms of the goals and beliefs of society. This synthesis of individual and social aims, however, required that function be organized "according to the belief in the Dignity of Man as it is expressed in the responsible participation of the citizen."[29] This conception of citizenship, moreover, was rooted in the Christian conception of human nature: the view of human beings as imperfect yet morally responsible for their own actions. Indeed, the essence of freedom in this tradition was that individuals must assume responsibility for the social good as well as for their individual actions.[30]

To the extent that the individual's demand for status and function were satisfied in accordance with the principle of responsible citizenship and the Christian conception of freedom, the demands of the individual and society would be in harmony. But the economic and social functions of the enterprise must also be in harmony. To achieve this, management must demand a "managerial attitude" on the part of the worker. The managerial attitude, according to the author, "makes the individual see his job, his work and his product the way the manager sees them, that is, in relation to the work of the group and the product of the whole." Because of the interdependence created by modern industry, such an attitude was necessary in order to achieve efficient economic performance. Furthermore, the managerial attitude was entirely consistent with society's demand for responsible participation by the citizen, that individuals assume responsibility for the social good. Drucker therefore concluded that "the demands of the enterprise on the plant community and the demands of society and of individual" were in harmony.[31]

Drucker cautioned that the managerial attitude could not simply be imposed on the members of the plant community. To take hold, it would have to be developed through the internal structure of the enterprise, the government of the plant community. By participating in self-government, the workers would not only gain individual recognition while practicing responsible citizenship; they would also acquire a sense of responsibility for and allegiance to the enterprise as a whole. In this fashion, the individual's demand for status and function, society's demand for responsible citizenship, the enterprise's demand for the managerial attitude, and the problem of legitimacy were all capable of resolution through the self-governing plant community. Moreover, the successful fulfillment of these ends would ultimately contribute to the primary economic function of the enterprise: the efficient and profitable production of goods and services.[32]

Drucker's theory of corporate enterprise and industrial society, including his proposals for industrial reform, constitute an important contribution to the political study of the corporation. The conception of the corporation as an autonomous entity governed by a managerial elite and subject to the "laws of industrial society" marked a significant transition from the Progressive Era view of corporate power as an anomaly of the marketplace. Henceforth, the issue of corporate social responsibility was no longer tied exclusively to the problem of corporate influence or to control over government institutions. With an increasing separation of ownership and control within the large corporation, and a growing recognition and acceptance of the corporation as a political institution, the analysis of corporate social responsibility focused on the question of legitimate rule by the new class of managers. Drucker thus posed the question, as Berle and Means had before him, To what extent must corporate managers be held accountable to the demands of society? His unique solution to this problem warrants a close scrutiny.

On the basis of his definition of corporate enterprise and his functionalist assumptions, Drucker reformulated the issue of corporate social responsibility as a functional problem. Management's first responsibility was to ensure the survival of the enterprise. The successful functioning of the corporation, however, depended on observance of the "laws of industrial society," which by definition were harmonious with the interests of society. Insofar as enterprise efficiently performed its economic function as measured by the objective standard of profitability, it had automatically fulfilled its primary social responsibility. By this same logic, the author delimited the problem of legitimacy to the internal governmental function of the enterprise, even though corporate power, in his view, extended over society as a whole. Accordingly, the question of the legitimacy of corporate power outside the corporation was not an issue, and it could not become one insofar as the external dimension of corporate power was governed by objective laws.

On the other hand, the governmental and social functions of the corporation could not be assumed to be consistent with the goals of society. Rather, this harmony must be consciously constructed within the enterprise. In this case as well, though, the interests of society—legitimate rule, responsible citizenship—were, in principle, harmonious with the economic interests of the corporation. Indeed, Drucker defined the harmony between enterprise, society, and the members of the plant community in terms of the needs of the corporation—profitability and stability. Just as society's demand for efficient economic performance coincided with the imperatives of profitability, so did society's demand for responsible citizenship harmonize with the managerial attitude. However one unravels the logical skein, the result is the same: the interests, needs, and demands of society cannot be separated from the interests, needs, and demands of corporate enterprise. By positing a functional harmony between an objective social interest and the interests of the corporation, Drucker largely eliminated the problematic character of corporate social responsibility.

Despite this apparent convergence of interests, if the policies of the state and the needs of corporate enterprise actually conflicted, the harmony between corporate and social interests surely could be undermined. Drucker reasoned that this harmonious relationship could not be realized unless corporate power remained autonomous within its sphere. Above all else, this meant that the state must not interfere with the actual functions of management. Corporate autonomy, moreover, was essential both to the needs of enterprise and to the conditions of freedom in industrial society. If the government assumed control of the corporation and the plant community, Drucker warned, "a free society is impossible."[33]

Drucker argued that governmental domination of industry, which he associated with socialism, would lead to the "suppression of unionism" and to "complete governmental control over the private citizen."[34] Another, more fundamental, reason for equating corporate autonomy with freedom was to argue that true liberty and individuality were possible only within a "free enterprise system." Such a system must be in the hands of individuals "who are neither appointed by the political authorities nor responsible to any political agency other than the courts of law."[35] The separation of the economic and political realms was therefore essential for the preservation of freedom within the industrial sphere and hence, within society as a whole. Within Drucker's theory, the "laws of avoiding loss and of higher output" and the objective necessity of profitability served much the same purpose as did the Invisible Hand of the marketplace in Adam Smith's classical theory of competitive capitalism. In both cases, freedom and social harmony were the product of the efficient working of an autonomous economic realm. And in both theories, the greatest threat to a free society came from the disruption of "natural" economic laws through government interference. That Smith urged the liberalization of government policies on behalf of the individual entrepreneur, whereas Drucker defended the large corporation against the prospect of statist command, therefore, does not alter the ideological point.

Drucker's formulation of the problem involved an adaptation of the free-market ideology of classical political economy to the exigencies of corporate capitalism in the same fashion that the law of corporations had been accommodated to the tenets of liberalism. Corporation law preserved the autonomy of the internal (private) sphere of corporate power while it conferred public powers on the corporate oligarchy, thereby avoiding statist command of enterprise. Drucker's theory mirrored and justified this development within the law by insisting that the internal governmental functions of the corporation, albeit subject to regulation under the law, remain free from state control.

Drucker's conception of the corporation as a political and social institution necessitated a rejection of the narrow individualism of nineteenth-century American liberalism. His theory, like those of Croly and Weyl, urged a revision of the beliefs of classical liberalism in order to accommodate the economic, social, and political realities of corporate capitalism. The ideological principles of the new order, as Drucker conceived them, were based on a corporate conception of society and on a conception of the corporation as an autonomous entity. Whereas mass production provided the organizational principle for industrial society, the successful functioning of this order was determined by economic imperatives—that is, by objective laws that expressed the social interest. As the institutional core of the new regime, the corporation embodied the organization, beliefs, and ideals of society as a whole.

In this new order, hierarchy constituted the political principle, efficiency or profitability the economic principle, and harmony the unifying ethical principle.[36] The desire for status within the corporate whole was preserved by promoting both equality of opportunity and means for attaining individual recognition. Yet, individual achievement was necessarily interrelated with one's function in society. Individual purpose and meaning, therefore, must be sought within the whole, through an understanding of one's place in the scheme of things, combined with an allegiance to authority. Responsible citizenship and the managerial attitude symbolized the new corporate philosophy of industrial society—in effect, the Christian corporate ethic in liberal guise. In place of devotion to religious dogma, however, Drucker substituted the needs and objective laws of industrial society. Ultimately, his theory attempted to justify corporate enterprise as a "natural" and universal phenomenon that transcended both capitalism and socialism.

Drucker's political theory of the corporation was representative of the neo-conservative thinking among academics, during and after World War

II, that developed in response to the rise of fascism in Europe and that was later employed to do battle with Soviet communism. But his theory might also be viewed as a distinctive formulation within corporate-liberal political thought—an argument shaped by world crises and therefore conceived within a global context, yet intended as a justification of corporate power in the United States, the new world leader of capitalist nations. To be sure, his conception of the corporation as the representative social institution—in effect, the institutional microcosm of society—was itself a reflection of the corporate reorganization of American society. Yet, in all fairness, Drucker's idea of the corporation as an "autonomous institution," which is neither capitalist or socialist, offered a progressive vision that was far in advance of its day.

Other aspects of Drucker's analysis of the corporation place it squarely within the tradition of corporate-liberal political thought. Like Croly and Weyl, Drucker separated the economic and political realms for both analytical and normative purposes, conceived society as an interdependent whole, emphasized the importance of social balance (conceived as harmony), and offered a defense for liberal principles in a corporate society. He also agreed with Veblen that modern industrial society was a product of technological—which is to say, organizational—change. It was the innovator, not the timid capitalist, Drucker argued, who had inspired the new order.[37]

Clearly, Drucker's argument shared numerous affinities with that of Croly. His managerial attitude and conception of social harmony paralleled Croly's democratic faith and idea of an organic unity. Each author advocated rule by experts, defined corporate social responsibility in terms of the standard of efficiency, and urged the integration of labor within the corporate structure. Whereas Croly counseled restraint and pragmatic gradualism in achieving the democratic ideal, Drucker drew on the philosophy of Edmund Burke to defend a similar conception of social change.[38] Furthermore, both thinkers exhibited corporatist tendencies, although Drucker's theory was far more evolved in this respect and contained none of Croly's commitment to democratic reform.

In adopting a functionalist view of society, Drucker spoke of society's interests, needs, and demands as if it existed independently of the individuals, groups, and classes that composed it. This conception also shaped his analysis of corporate enterprise. Drucker's idea of the corporation as an autonomous entity transformed the ideological defense of corporate autonomy in Croly's thought into an iron law. More than any other, this development symbolized the consolidation of corporate power. It paralleled the growing political autonomy of management under the law of corporations and anticipated the evolution of the corporate citizen in constitutional law. In Drucker's words, the corporation, by attaining autonomy, had become "socially and politically a priori."[39] In the course of obeying its own laws and fulfilling its economic and social functions, corporate enterprise must remain beyond the reach of misguided reformers.

Although Drucker's theory of industrial society evinced important similarities with Progressive Era political thought, his conception of the corporation as an institution with a "triple personality"—economic, political, and social—represented a significant evolution in the political study of the corporation. Moreover, his contention that the corporation performed political and social functions, in addition to its economic function, reflected a general shift in thinking that identified corporate power with managerial control, as opposed to personal wealth. Also noteworthy was his conception of the dual nature of corporate power, as control over the means of production and as control within the enterprise. Yet, in this matter, as with the issue of legitimacy, the author's functionalist assumptions appear to have served an ideological purpose.

From an analytical standpoint, Drucker's distinction between the internal and external aspects of corporate power is quite clear. Furthermore, to conceive the internal aspect of corporate power in terms of a governmental function based on relationships of control makes a good deal of sense. He did not explain, however, why the external dimension of corporate power did not also give rise to relationships of control and hence to the potential for conflict. One answer appears to lie in the fact that, in his analysis, corporate power exercised over society as a whole was subject to the laws of the enterprise. In other words, the external aspect of corporate power was by definition essential to the successful functioning of industrial society. To conceive this form of power in terms of relationships of control, therefore, would contradict his functionalist assumptions. There simply is no room for the concept of control within an interdependent functioning system. Drucker's formulation of the problem could not change the fact that, regardless of the definition of power one chooses—whether it involves the general capacity to exercise one's will over another, or the ability to compel compliance or otherwise produce a desired result—the idea of control remains fundamental. As an aspect or component of an interdependent functioning system, therefore, power can have little meaning, let alone analytical significance. To view power exercised outside the enterprise as functional effectively eliminates the need to study its conditions and its consequences.

According to Drucker, his revision of classical liberal beliefs entailed a substantial ideological debt to Burkean conservatism. To be sure, this influence is apparent in Drucker's conception of society as an entity or organism that obeys its own laws, but his theory also embraced the premises of corporate liberalism and articulated a distinctive version of the "natural" evolution of corporate enterprise that was undoubtedly influenced by Burke's political theory but that also evinced the Comtean blend of religious purpose and technological progress that shaped Croly's political thought. Most important of all, in defending the inviolability of corporate autonomy, Drucker employed the liberal's precept of the separation of state and society. That Drucker's classical conservative assumptions could accommodate a defense of the modern free-enterprise system, albeit one in which the autonomous corporation had become "socially and politically a priori," illustrates well the corporatist tendencies of managerial theory, which aims to justify the consolidation of corporate power on the basis of the needs, organization, and philosophy of the large corporation.

3. ADOLF A. BERLE: CORPORATE POWER, PLURALISM, AND "THE CITY OF GOD"

As noted in the introduction to this chapter, Berle and Means's influential work, *The Modern Corporation and Private Property*, constituted a watershed for the contemporary liberal analysis of corporate power. The major analytical and normative issues raised by the separation of ownership and control within the large corporation—the nature of corporate control, the problem of corporate social responsibility, the status of the corporation as a social and political institution—were all posed by this path-breaking study. While Berle's expertise in law and economics was most in evidence in his collaborative effort with Means, his legacy as a theorist of corporate power actually began with this work. Once it was recognized that the large corporation constituted a political institution in its own right, the need for a new theory of the corporation became apparent. For Berle, such a theory must account for the political character of the corporation. In short, it must be a theory of corporate power.

Few individuals have contributed as much to the political study of the corporation as has Adolf A. Berle. Furthermore, his passion for the study of power sets him apart from other students of the corporation. Berle's quest for a theory of power was from the beginning wed to a concern with problems of political philosophy. In addition to his analysis of corporate power, he also constructed a justification for the legitimacy of corporate rule. Like many innovative thinkers, his writings defy rigid disciplinary boundaries. But perhaps this is what one should expect from a lawyer, businessman, political adviser, statesman, and scholar whose intellectual life was largely devoted to the political study of the corporation.[40]

Berle maintained that the rise of the large corporation as the dominant form of business enterprise occasioned a revolutionary transformation of economy, polity, and society. Initially a means for accumulating capital and concentrating huge sums of wealth, the modern corporation eventually revolutionized methods of production and distribution, transformed the institution of property, changed the locus of economic power, and altered the relationship between the political and economic realms. A creature of the law, in its origins strictly a business device, the corporation emerged as a "social institution in the context of a revolutionary century."[41] Specifically, it was a "non-statist" social and political institution that "may be regarded not simply as one form of social organization but potentially (if not yet actually) as the dominant institution of the modern world."[42]

One consequence of the concentration of wealth within the large corporation, according to Berle, was an increasing dispersion of stock ownership that gave rise to a separation of ownership and control. The author described the evolution of this separation in four stages.[43] In the first stage, majority control of the voting rights of the stock was held by an individual or group, thereby allowing for stockholder control of the corporation. "Control" referred to the ability to choose the board of directors. Acting directors often had considerable latitude as decision-makers and did not always follow the dictates of the majority owners— in which case, of course, they could be replaced.

As stock ownership became sufficiently dispersed to preclude majority control, effective control could still be wielded by an individual or group holding a significant minority share.[44] During this second phase, the holder of a significant minority interest achieved a "working control" through close ties with, or influence over, the corporate management. In the third stage, however, stockholding had become so widely dispersed that no individual or group could effectively challenge or influence the control of management. At this point, the power of management, for all practical purposes, became absolute. Because it could rely on the vast majority of shareholders to follow its lead so long as dividends remained reasonable, management unilaterally determined who would control the corporation. In Berle's apt phrase, the board of directors became a "self-perpetuating oligarchy." Furthermore, the separation of property and power altered the nature of corporate rule. In the place of the capitalist entrepreneur now sat the modern managers of industry and finance, who bore more of a resemblance to a "professional civil service" than to a wealthy stratum of owner-capitalists.[45]

Once the third stage was reached, a more-or-less complete division between property and power had occurred. This development necessitated a reevaluation of the traditional legal and economic justifications of property and profits. Before examining the analytical and normative issues raised by the separation of ownership and control, however, let us turn briefly to the fourth stage described by the author.

Although this most recent phase in the evolution of control within the large corporation constituted a trend rather than an accomplished fact, Berle argued that it heralded a shift of power within the corporate structure. He observed that institutional ownership of stock by pension trusts, insurance companies, and mutual funds, which purchased shares on behalf of their members or policyholders, had initiated a return to majority control by stockholders. But unlike the earlier phase of majority control, the actual owners were virtually powerless because the legal title to the stock, and therefore voting rights, was held by the trustees of the investing institutions. Should this trend continue, Berle explained, control would shift from corporate management to the administrators and trustees of the institutional stockholders, individuals who are "more or less representative of the banking and industrial world." At present, institutional investors had chosen not to exercise their power, a decision that "freezes absolute power in the corporate managements."[46] In any event, many of the problems raised by the separation of ownership and control were basically the same in the third and fourth stages, because in either case the owners of stock have in effect ceded their power to a ruling group of managers or trustees, although in the fourth stage the separation of property and power became even more pronounced.

Berle observed that, under law, the rights of property in business enterprise assumed that the ownership and control of property attached to the same individual or group. It followed that powers delegated by stockholders to management were "powers in trust."[47] In theory, therefore, individuals managed a corporation (i.e., maximized profits) in the interest of a specific group within the corporation. The separation of ownership and control, however, thoroughly undermined the traditional logic of property. With the division of property and power, the stockholder became a "passive" recipient of wealth, whereas management assumed the "active" or creative role of determining the use and distribution of wealth.[48] The question thus arose whether "an owner who has surrendered control of his wealth should likewise be protected to the full?"[49] In other words, in whose interest should the corporation be managed? It is this situation, according to Berle, that gave rise to the issue of corporate social responsibility. However, to fully understand the nature of this problem, we must ascertain how the separation of ownership and control affected the assumptions of classical economic theory.

"A long line of economists," Berle explained, have held that by "protecting property rights in the instruments of production, the acquisitive interests of man could thus be more effectively harnessed to the benefit of the community." This proposition assumed that profits served to motivate the individual, as an inducement both to risk wealth and to manage enterprise efficiently. The current problem stemmed from the fact that, in the modern corporation, contrary to the predictions of classical theory, these two functions were performed by different groups. In keeping with the traditional logic of property, all profits must accrue to the owners, and not to the propertyless managers. But if this occurred, the pecuniary motivation for efficient control would disappear. On the other hand, if profits were distributed between the owners and managers, the rights of property would appear to be abridged. In either case, the traditional justifications for property and profits came into conflict.[50]

In Berle's view, the classical concepts of property and profits were clearly inadequate when applied to the modern corporation: "New concepts must be forged and a new picture of economic relationships created." Because it involved "a concentration of power in the economic field comparable to the concentration of religious power in the mediaeval church or of political power in the national state," and because it involved "the interrelation of a wide diversity of economic interests," the modern corporation must be conceived "not in terms of business enterprise but in terms of social organization."[51] The characteristics of the corporation brought to the fore the issue of corporate power, its nature, and its justification. Not only must the corporation be studied as a political and social institution, but the legitimacy of corporate power must also be examined. The problem of corporate social responsibility therefore became a problem of legitimate rule. Whether one believed that the corporation should be managed in the interests of ownership, of control, or of society as a whole would depend on one's analysis and justification of corporate power. It is to these issues that we now turn.

Berle defined power as a "universal experience" rooted in human nature and subject to the same "natural laws" regardless of the form it assumed.[52] He identified five natural laws that constituted his general theory of power. The first law expressed the proposition that power "invariably fills any vacuum in human organization." "As between chaos and power, the latter will always prevail." This was a consequence of two factors: the "social necessity" for peace, and the human "instinct for power." That power was "an attribute of man" and therefore "invariably personal" constituted the second natural law. Rooted in human nature, power may be conceived as the capacity of an individual to gain the compliance of others in accordance with one's wishes.[53]

Though it might take a variety of forms in society, power "is invariably based on a system of ideas or philosophy" and "is exercised through and depends on, institutions." These two imperatives, which comprised the third and fourth laws, defined the conditions for the effective and continuous exercise of power. Institutions required idea systems just as power could only be "generated, used, or expanded" through institutions. Moreover, the philosophy underlying an institution served to limit the exercise of power by providing a standard by which it could be judged. The fifth law held that power "is invariably confronted with, and acts in the presence of, a field of responsibility." This law expressed the fact that power holders must take into account the opinions and desires of those subject to their rule. Whether organized or unorganized, open or furtive, a dialogue of some sort between rulers and ruled could not be avoided.[54]

Economic power, Berle argued, "arises with capacity to cause or to refuse production, purchase, sale, or delivery of goods, or cause or prevent the rendering of service (including labor)." Corporate power, which constituted a type or form of economic power, developed out of the capitalist revolution of the twentieth century. We have seen that Berle attributed the corporate managers' rise to power to the increasing concentration of wealth within the large corporation. The managerial ascendancy was also facilitated by another major development made possible by corporate concentration: the ability of corporations to accumulate and control their own capital.[55] The shift of control over capital accumulation from capitalist entrepreneurs and investment bankers to corporate managers not only altered the structure of power within the capitalist economy but also laid the foundation for the extensive powers of the large corporation. With the capacity to generate its own capital, corporate enterprise freed itself from dependence on the capital markets and achieved self-sufficiency. As a result of this development, the modern corporation "acquired a separate entity, dependent on its ideology and organization from top to bottom, just as an army or government department acquires such being."[56]

Berle, like Drucker, conceived corporate power as having an internal and an external dimension.[57] The internal dimension, which concerned the exercise of power in relation to individuals within the corporation, encompassed the power to grant or deny employment, to determine conditions of employment, and generally to devise and administer policies that affected the internal operations of the enterprise.[58] A corporation's external dimension of power referred to the impact of corporate decisions and policies on society as a whole.[59] This dimension included the power to set and administer prices and thereby control markets, the capacity to accumulate and apply capital and thus determine the present and future economic development of a country, and the ability to develop and control new technology and hence shape the forces of production. To these formidable powers must also be added the more limited capacities to form public opinion and to induce consumption through advertising. When combined in a few hundred large corporations, these powers fundamentally altered the nature of the capitalist economy. "Mid-twentieth-century capitalism," Berle concluded, "has been given the power and the means of a more or less planned economy, in which decisions are or at least can be taken in the light of their probable effect on the whole community."[60]

But economic power in advanced capitalist societies did not inhere solely in the corporation. In many respects, it was shared with the state. Just as the large corporation had transformed the structure and operations of the capitalist economy, so had it altered the economic responsibilities of government. State intervention in the economy had been induced by the needs of the new system and by the need to remedy the deleterious results of laissez-faire. With the rise of corporate capitalism, an "economic republic" emerged, an order based on a novel organization of economic and political power.[61]

The economic functions of the state, in Berle's view, had become essential to the stability and profitability of the corporate economy. Through its antitrust policies, for example, the state maintained an artificial competition within oligopolistic markets and thus prevented monopoly.[62] Numerous government agencies were also created to regulate or control the economic activities of various industries.[63] The fiscal and monetary policies of the state, moreover, served to maintain economic stability and growth. Berle observed that the Federal Reserve Board was "rapidly reaching unwritten constitutional status as a coordinate power, like the Supreme Court."[64] In addition to its planning functions, the government provided numerous services and supports—for example, public education, social welfare programs, construction and maintenance of highways, funding for scientific research—without which the economic republic could not operate.[65]

Although the federal government in the twentieth century had increasingly become involved in what amounted to economic planning, the "American system has in wide degree separated its means and methods of political action from its means and methods of economic operation."[66]

Political and economic power always interacted, Berle observed, but rarely did they merge in the same institution or individual. When a merger did occur, the two forces tended to divide, precisely because of the "differing imperatives of the two forms of power."[67] Political and economic power in the United States therefore remained functionally distinct.

Despite the expanding role of the state in the economy, the corporation retained the primary power of "initiative and action."[68] Within its sphere, corporate power had steadily grown as a result of economic concentration. Yet this increasing centralization of power did not pose a threat to the power of the state.[69] If anything, "an erosion of the relative power of the great corporations and financial institutions" had occurred in recent decades as the economic responsibilities of the government had increased. In addition to the check of the political power of the state, corporate power was limited by the "pluralist" organization of the American polity and economy. Berle maintained that, "within and without the government," power remained sufficiently decentralized to prevent the emergence of a unified "establishment."[70] Corporate power, though highly centralized, could be exercised only within certain limits determined by the economic functions of the enterprise. Because "no single organization has been permitted to grasp more than a limited number of functions, or even, as a rule, to achieve monopoly in any one function," the general result had been "an equipoise of strong organizations." Pluralism not only divided power; it divided "functions as well, reducing power burdens to sustainable limits."[71]

Berle's account of American pluralism must also be understood in light of his conception of balance. The development of "absolute power in any form of organization," he observed, "is commonly accompanied by the emergence of countervailing power elsewhere in the same organization usually in quite different form." These "two nuclei of power coexist in opposition to form a balance . . . which preserves the continuity of the power itself."[72] If power goes unchecked, it becomes "anarchic" and "eventually destroys both its surroundings and itself." "Wise statesmanship from earliest times," Berle contended, had "recognized and accepted this fact."[73] But why did absolute power generally give rise to countervailing power? The answer must be sought in the human disposition to demand that power be accountable—that is, be made legitimate.[74] The issue of social balance (or countervailing power), therefore, was directly connected to the problems of legitimacy and corporate social responsibility. Indeed, Berle's claims that power is always based on and checked by "a system of ideas or philosophy," and that power "is invariably confronted with, and acts in the presence of, a field of responsibility," would appear to give lawlike status to the phenomena of balance and legitimacy.[75]

For Berle, it was the *political* character of the modern corporation—the nature and scope of power exercised by this nonstatist political institution—that raised the issue of legitimacy. Once control had separated from ownership, corporate economic power could not be justified on the basis of the traditional logic of property and profits. The need for a new justification became apparent. Berle defined legitimacy as a "rightful possession of power." For power to be legitimate, it must accord with a criterion that specified the acceptable conditions for the possession and use of that power. Such a standard, moreover, must be based on the prevailing ideas and beliefs that comprised the "public consensus" of a community at a given point in time. Unlike public opinion, which may vary from issue to issue, the public consensus was based on those "unstated but very real premises" that shaped the ideas and tenets of a people.[76]

The legitimacy of corporate power, like the two general relationships of that power, had both an internal and an external dimension. Whereas the former concerned the legitimate exercise of power within the enterprise, the latter referred to "the legitimacy of the existence and use of the power itself." Legitimate rule within the corporation presupposed that the individuals exercising power "got it by a method which the community recognizes; through prescribed or accepted process or ritual." Albeit not an exercise in democracy, the stockholders' election of the board of directors constituted such a ritual. Berle likened this process to a ritual coronation of a king inasmuch as both established the right of an individual or group to hold power under specified conditions. Even though the modern corporation's methods of "locating power and choosing its holders" had become "obsolete by rational standards," because management in effect elected its own officers, the methods nevertheless worked "remarkably well." Because stockholders generally lacked the technical and managerial expertise to competently select the most capable leaders, the ritual satisfied the requirements of legitimacy without hindering the efficient management of the enterprise.[77]

Berle suggested that the legitimacy of corporate power could be tested by the standard of "whether the power is appropriate to the function of the organization." Even though the economic function of a corporation frequently expanded or changed in response to changing conditions, there was "a clear and recognizable distinction between economic power used to carry out or reasonably extend a function, and economic power used for entirely other reasons." In addition to the performance of a specific economic task, legitimacy assumed the necessity of profit-making and growth. However, such functional criteria did not address the social aspects of corporate power. The perceived legitimacy of corporate power ultimately depended on the changing character of the public consensus—"the final arbiter of legitimacy."[78] As the consensus gradually changed, so did the standards of legitimacy. Furthermore, the public consensus would appear to provide the link between legitimacy and countervailing power in Berle's analysis, for such power necessarily developed in accordance with a system of ideas or philosophy. In other words, countervailing power, like the standards of legitimacy, received its philosophical justification from the evolving public consensus. But who defined or revised the public consensus, and how exactly were corporations to be held answerable to it?

Berle explained that in the common-law tradition, countervailing power developed from the belief that absolute power must be held accountable to a higher law. Originally expressed by an appeal to the "conscience of the king," this belief, which became part of the public consensus, was later institutionalized in law and served to check monarchial absolutism.[79] Gradually, this early precept of limited government found expression through the writings and pronouncements of essayists, scholars, theologians, judges, and political leaders. Then, as now, the task of giving form to the public consensus necessarily fell to those who constituted the intellectual and spiritual elite of a society.[80] Berle's argument was itself an appeal to the corporate leaders as well as to the intellectual elite. He cautioned them not to lose sight of the fact that the right to appeal to the king's conscience had been granted by the king for both practical and moral reasons. Thus, if corporate power were to become legitimate, and thereby achieve a measure of stability, the soulless corporation would have to cultivate a conscience so that it might acknowledge similar appeals.

Incipient signs of the reappearance of this common-law tradition already could be observed: "a counter force which checks, and remotely acts on, and in time may modify in certain areas the absolute power of business discretion, is beginning to appear in the form of law."[81] Berle noted that recognition of the right of appeal had been established within the internal operations of various corporations.[82] Although still in "the field of inchoate law," such checks represented the first stages of a familiar evolution: "the rules of political organization have exhibited a degree of uniformity throughout the history of the western world." Why, he asked, "is it far-fetched to predict that the rules . . . will reappear in modified dress when power centralizes itself around a politico-economic instead of a governmental institution?"[83] One could find evidence of such a development outside the corporation as well. In the field of constitutional law, for instance, the doctrinal groundwork was being laid for subjecting corporations to the prohibitions of the Fourteenth Amendment. For Berle, such a prospect represented far more than a legal trend. He contended that if individual rights and liberties were to be preserved, corporate power, like governmental power, must be limited by the strictures of the Constitution. The corporate conscience, like the conscience of the king, "must be built into institutions so that it can be invoked as a right by the individuals subject to the corporate power." When this occurred, the assimilation of corporate power within the American liberal tradition would be complete.[84]

Yet all this must await the future. The present reality of corporate power raised more immediate problems. Whether it was fully acknowledged or not, twentieth-century capitalism necessitated planning by both statist and nonstatist institutions. The power to plan, Berle explained, was "perhaps the highest trust granted to statesmen." It therefore entailed considerable social responsibility. While most of them did not relish it and many ignored it, the managers of the large corporations had "reached a position for the first time in their history in which they must consciously take account of philosophical considerations." Corporate leaders, like their counterparts in government, could not avoid the moral responsibilities of rulership. Each must exercise their power in accordance with a vision of what society should be, a conception of the "good life."[85]

The central dilemma of corporate social responsibility thus became apparent. Corporate power must be exercised in accordance with a philosophy, but no such philosophy existed. "As yet the community has not created any acknowledged referent of responsibility." Nor was there a "recognized body of doctrine" by which corporate leaders might judge their decisions. Vested in "tiny self-perpetuating oligarchies," corporate power could therefore be exercised only in light of the "the real, though undefined and tacit, philosophy of the men who compose them." Hence, "the corporation, almost against its will, has been compelled to assume in appreciable part the role of conscience-carrier of twentieth-century American society."[86]

This fact, Berle explained, should not cause undue alarm. Even though the imperatives of corporate organization stressed conformity and teamwork, the individuals who composed these organizations were capable of acting according to their consciences. "Once the business community has learned to honor difference and deviation as well as agreement and conformity," a corporate conscience "need be neither impractical nor dangerous." Still, the "greater hope" lay in the fact that the individuals within the corporation were "invariably influenced by certain great philosophical premises."[87] These ideas did not come from within the corporation; they came from the intellectual, philosophical, and spiritual leaders of a society. It was Berle's hope, if not his expectation, that such individuals would come forth in the near future to answer the call for philosophical direction.

It seems, then, that we have returned to our starting point, for Berle's conception of corporate social responsibility would appear to presuppose (or require) the development of countervailing power, expressed through an evolving public consensus. To illustrate his conviction that corporations would in time be forced to work within a philosophical framework imposed by the community, he drew on the political thought of Saint Augustine. Berle explained that, in his major work of political theory, *The City of God*, Augustine put forth the hypothesis that underlying and controlling every organization of human affairs was "a moral and philosophical organization which . . . ultimately directed power."[88] This philosophical organization, which "alone gave permanence to institutions," Augustine named "The City of God." Augustine's idea constituted perhaps the first significant expression of "the theory of dichotomy of power."[89] With the growth of the corporation as a political institution in the twentieth century, the stage had been set for the formulation of a modern, albeit secular, version of "The City of God." Berle concluded that this eventuality, which already could be discerned in an emerging public consensus, would determine the future development of corporate power in the United States.

Of the liberal analysts of corporate power discussed thus far, Berle stands alone in his effort to formulate a general theory of power. For the most part, the analytical and ideological aspects of his conception of corporate power are rooted in the various "laws" of power that are part of that theory. In order to assess his conception of corporate power, we therefore must first examine the methodological and analytical assumptions underlying these laws.

Berle argued that even though power was exercised through institutions it was "invariably personal." Moreover, he insisted that the economic and political realms of power were quite separate in practice and must remain that way. Clearly, both these arguments served a normative as well as an explanatory purpose within his theory. Berle maintained that power within American society was distributed among numerous individuals whose capacity to obtain and exercise it varied in accordance with their ability to gain the compliance of others. To a large extent, the methodological assumptions of this argument determined its conclusions. If power is conceived solely as a personal attribute that is distributed within numerous institutions, then it is only logical that it will appear to be dispersed throughout society. Accordingly, corporate power, although highly concentrated within individual industries or sectors, appears decentralized when viewed as an aggregate. Far from monolithic, corporate power consisted of numerous power pyramids, each of which was autonomous within its sphere and not one of which was capable of exercising inordinate control. An actual centralization of corporate power, therefore, could come about only through massive conspiracy or effective control of industry by literally a handful corporations.

Berle's pluralist conception of American politics also stemmed from the analytical separation of economic and political power. He argued that while statist economic power had become essential to the profitable and efficient operation of the corporate economy, it had remained functionally distinct from the economic power of corporations. For the most part, the state had assumed a supportive and regulatory role, albeit on a considerable scale, and the corporation had retained the initiative and primary control in economic matters. The functions of statist and nonstatist economic power therefore had not merged. Indeed, for this to occur, economic and political power would have to be combined in the same group of individuals.

Berle employed the same analytical approach to examine the two types of power exercised by the state. Indeed, he contended that the political power of the state generally remained separate from its economic power. Moreover, individual liberty required that neither governmental nor corporate economic power should be allowed to control (or to be controlled by) any other form of power. But this issue may well be the Achilles' heel of his theory. The question arises whether the political and economic powers of government can be realistically separated in practice. Berle noted, for example, that the principle of functional separation of powers applied to government regulatory agencies such as the ICC and the SEC, both of which exercised economic power.[90] Such agencies, however, have never operated in a political vacuum, nor have they been entirely free from the influence of the corporations whose activities they regulate.

But assuming, for the sake of argument, that Berle's example is sound, it still represents only one aspect of governmental economic power. For instance, it appears to be an incontrovertible fact that the fiscal policies of the state are thoroughly shaped by political considerations. One might also add to this list the discretion exercised by every administration over antitrust policy, international trade and tariff policies, and myriad other economic matters. But there is another and perhaps even greater weakness in Berle's analysis: his failure to examine the considerable and long-standing influence of corporate interests over electoral, congressional, and presidential politics. Berle skirted this issue by arguing that nonstatist holders of economic power had not seized control of governmental decision-making and had not posed such a threat since the first decade of the twentieth century.[91] But this ignored the fact that influence could be wielded by numerous methods short of outright control. While Berle observed that "frequently an uneasy struggle for balance between the two forms of power seems to characterize the internal structure of most twentieth-century states," he did not explain how this struggle might affect the alleged functional division of powers.[92]

Berle's rigid functional separation of types of power prevented him from acknowledging the essential interrelationship of governmental and corporate power. To be sure, these powers (defined institutionally) rarely merge in the same individual or group of individuals, but on the basis of his own evidence of "state intervention" into the economy, there would appear to be between these two realms of power a significant interaction that cannot be explained by his analytical approach.

Berle argued that because it is a nonstatist political institution, the corporation must establish the legitimacy of its power. It must be held accountable to the public consensus. By efficiently performing its economic function and by observing the functional separation of powers in society, the corporation contributed to that end. The phenomenon of balance or countervailing power, however, also constituted an essential ingredient in establishing legitimacy. For Berle, countervailing power was a historical imperative; it was itself one of the laws of power. When balance was not achieved, he reasoned, power became self-destructive. Yet balance or equilibrium was also a precept of liberalism in his analysis—an idea, closely associated with social efficiency and limited government, that justified a separation of state and society. When transformed into a lawlike force or thing, this liberal doctrine of balance took on an aspect of faith. Indeed, Berle's interpretation of Augustine's *City of God* embodied this faith. It represented an attempt to establish corporate social responsibility, and thereby justify corporate power, by universalizing certain principles of liberal ideology.

Because corporate power was "actually controlled . . . by the operation of the public consensus which can engender public opinion leading to political intervention," it remained consistent with the goals of "the American democratic State."[93] Thus Berle's theory of pluralism, his economic standard of legitimacy, and his idea of balance coalesced in the notion of "economic democracy" to provide a liberal justification for corporate power. Insofar as corporate executives efficiently managed their economic activities, observed the functional separation of powers, and responded to a changing public consensus, they fully satisfied the requirements of democracy, while at the same time they protected and ensured their autonomy over economic decisions. While awaiting the second coming of "The City of God," the collective corporate conscience must perforce be constrained by the institutional safeguards of pluralism and the dictates of an emerging public sentiment.[94]

Although the political theories of Berle and Drucker yield some significant contrasts, the similarities in their arguments underscore important continuities in the liberal analysis of corporate power. Both authors conceived corporate power as a form of economic power that was functionally distinct from the power exercised by government. They also described the corporation as an autonomous, or self-sufficient, entity ruled by experts and dependent on long-term profitability for its successful operation. And both maintained that the functional separation of political and economic power was essential to individual freedom and to democracy. Although modified in light of the growth of corporate power and the separation of ownership and control, many of these ideas will also be found in the works of the early-twentieth-century analysts of corporate power.

But Berle and Drucker necessarily viewed the issue of corporate social responsibility somewhat differently than their predecessors did during the Progressive Era. Once corporate enterprise had been defined as a political institution, the legitimacy of corporate power became an issue of first importance. With the increasing separation of ownership and control, the decline of the capitalist entrepreneur, and the demise of the traditional justification of property and profits, the door had been opened for far-reaching claims against corporate enterprise on behalf of society. To meet this challenge, Berle and Drucker each constructed an elaborate defense of corporate power within the institutional setting of American society. With this development, corporate liberalism matured. The compatibility of corporate power and democracy no longer depended on the success of economic reform or regulation, but rather on a much broader convergence of corporate and social interests.

While the theoretical tasks that confronted Drucker and Berle differed from those that challenged Croly and Weyl, the ideas and methods employed by these four thinkers were similar in many respects. Indeed, the parallel between Croly and Drucker, on the one hand, and Weyl and Berle, on the other, is striking. Whereas the first two thinkers expounded a corporatist conception of society premised on a harmony of corporate and social interests (albeit with a strong commitment to democractic accountability in the case of Croly), the latter two articulated a theory of countervailing power based on a conception of mechanical balance. But it is the underlying similarities in the works of all four of these authors that contained the greatest ideological significance.

In each of their analyses, the idea of social balance—which presupposed a functional separation of political and economic power and therewith, the preservation of corporate autonomy—became synonymous with democracy. Indeed, democracy had become an idea, much like James Madison's concept of republicanism, that described a systemic balance of forces. And like Madison's notion of republicanism, the corporate-liberal concept of democracy emphasized leadership rather than participation, while claiming that sovereignty resided ultimately in the people. An important difference is that Madison did not confuse republicanism with democracy. In fact, he was very much concerned to distinguish these two concepts. In "Federalist 10," he employed the idea of balance as a justification for either inhibiting majoritarian control or preventing the majority from abusing its power. By contrast, many modern theorists of democracy use a similar conception of balance as a surrogate for democratic control. For Madison, democracy was a radical doctrine. In the era of corporate capitalism, the tendency is to regard democracy as a euphemism for political and economic stability.[95]

We must also keep in mind that the idea of balance (conceived as equilibrium) within liberal thought can be employed to justify reform. And in some instances—Weyl's recommendations provide an example—it might imply greater popular participation and control, although this appears to be the exception to the rule. As corporate power matured and consolidated its position in American society, the liberal analysts of the corporation argued that democratic control of corporate enterprise was no longer practicable, let alone desirable. And as the idea of corporate autonomy supplanted the self-regulating market of classical liberalism, it reproduced the ideological separation of public and private spheres. Accordingly, the "laws of industrial society" defended corporate autonomy in much the same manner that the "natural laws of the marketplace" justified entrepreneurial freedom in the era of competitive capitalism.

Even for critics of corporate power, such as John Kenneth Galbraith, whose conception of balance shared Weyl's reformist implications and whose analysis of industrial society, in other ways, took issue with the presumptions of managerialism, the doctrine of corporate autonomy acquired the status of an inviolable law. However, Galbraith's vision of industrial society also constitutes a distinctive contribution to the liberal managerial theory of corporate power. Moreover, his theory, like that of Veblen, broadens the spectrum of ideas in light of which one might better understand the evolution of corporate-liberalism.

4. JOHN KENNETH GALBRAITH: TECHNOLOGY UNBOUND—CORPORATE POWER AND THE DEMIURGE OF MODERN SOCIETY

Galbraith's theory of industrial society stands squarely within the critical tradition of Progressive Era political thought. Like Croly and Weyl, he urged liberal reform and upheld the values of equality and individualism. While not sharing Veblen's unrelieved pessimism, Galbraith's works demonstrate a similar affinity for unmasking the contradictions of capitalism. Also, in much the same manner as Veblen, Galbraith gained recognition among his contemporaries as an original, if not iconoclastic, thinker whose ideas greatly influenced the social and political thought of the day. And although the ideological aspects of his thought proved to be significant, Galbraith, like Veblen, generally preferred the role of social critic to that of ideologist.

Galbraith's analysis of corporate power must be understood within the context of his theory of industrial society. He expounded this theory in *The New Industrial State*, which, by the author's own admission, constituted a refinement and synthesis of previous works.[96] My reconstruction and analysis of his theory of industrial society therefore will be based almost entirely on that work. I first elaborate the major features of this theory, then turn to a more detailed examination of his conception of corporate power. I also show how his critique of liberalism shaped his theoretical approach and practical recommendations. Finally, I assess the ideological aspects of Galbraith's theory in light of his analysis of corporate power, his suggestions for reform, and his conception of social change.

Of the numerous economic changes that had occurred since the turn of the century, the "most visible," Galbraith observed, had been "the application of increasingly intricate and sophisticated technology to the production of things." The consequences that flowed from the use of modern technology were far-reaching. Because technology involved "the systematic application of scientific or other organized knowledge to practical tasks," it compelled "the division and subdivision of any such task into its component parts." Technology therefore gave rise to specialization, which in turn required organization. "More even than machinery," Galbraith explained, "massive and complex business organizations are the tangible manifestations of advanced technology."[97]

While technology possessed "an initiative of its own," it was also a response to change. It was, therefore, both a cause and a consequence of specialization and organization. The more sophisticated technology became, Galbraith argued, the more it necessitated capital-intensive investment and complex organizational skills. To supply the needed capital and mobilize the requisite skills, the large corporation, which alone could satisfy these needs, assumed the task of planning. This development determined the technological and organizational imperatives of the modern planned economy, an economy dominated by the large corporation and supported by the state. The fact that the structure and needs of the American economy bore fundamental similarities to those of other modern industrial societies indicated a "broad convergence between industrial systems." This convergence can be further explained by the fact that "the modern large corporation and the modern apparatus of socialist planning are variant accommodations to the same need."[98]

Because modern technology dramatically increased the commitment of time and capital needed in production, and thereby reduced the reliability of the market, control of prices became necessary for effective planning.[99] Under modern economic conditions, planning consisted in "minimizing or getting rid of market influences."[100] But if prices were controlled, so too must demand be controlled, because the traditional market mechanisms no longer applied. In fact, the control or management of demand embraced "a vast and rapidly growing industry" that included "a huge network of communications, a great array of merchandising and selling organizations, nearly the entire advertising industry, . . . and much more."[101]

In addition to the control of specific demand, aggregate demand must also be managed. Galbraith observed that although planning made possible a high level of savings, there was no planning method to ensure that savings would be offset by investment and hence stabilize aggregate demand.[102] This situation had provided the occasion for the state to assume a major role in stabilizing the corporate economy. Through the powers of taxing and spending, the state thus supplied "the missing element in the planning of savings."[103] Indeed, Galbraith argued that both the requirements of planning and the imperatives of advanced technology had necessitated an increasing integration of the activities of the large corporation and the modern state.

New technology and the requisites of planning also produced a shift in the basis of economic power. In explaining this transformation, Galbraith offered an economic rationale for the historical development of power in capitalist societies. He explained that power "goes to the factor which is hardest to attain or hardest to replace."[104] With the transition from a feudal economy to a capitalist economy, the basis of power shifted from land to capital. Marx's prediction that the internal dissolution of capitalism would then transfer power from capital to labor (the third factor of production), however, did not occur. In fact, since the second or third decade of this century, a shift of power wholly different from the long-awaited proletarian revolution had been taking place.[105]

Symptoms of this change can be found in the increasing separation of ownership and control within the large corporation, the diminishing importance of the financier or banker, and the new prestige of educators. The cause of these symptoms must be explained with reference to the fact that modern technology and planning had created a tremendous need for specialized talent that, unlike the supply of capital, could not be internally generated by the corporation—nor, for that matter, did an adequate supply of capital ensure that such talent could be acquired. The most recent shift in power within capitalist enterprise, therefore, had been from capital to "organized intelligence." This "new factor of production" consisted of "the association of men of diverse technical knowledge, experience or other talent which modern industrial technology and planning require," and extended "from the leadership of the modern industrial enterprise down to just short of the labor force." Galbraith christened this complex organization of specialized intelligence "the technostructure."[106]

The emergence of the technostructure marked not only a shift in the basis of power in capitalist society, but also a change in the organization of that power. Technological developments had created a need for group decision-making within corporate enterprise. This occurred because specialized knowledge made the exercise of power dependent on expertise, thereby necessitating a system of decentralized decision-making that reflected the division of intellectual labor. Furthermore, unless reviewed by a group or committee with a similar type of expertise, group policy-making within the technostructure "tend[ed] to be absolute." In this way, corporate power was reorganized within the technostructure and, as a consequence, no longer rested primarily in the hands of the chief executive officers and directors of the board, who stood atop a pyramid of control. Indeed, the conventional idea of an authoritative chain of command had become virtually obsolete in the day-to-day world of corporate decision-making.[107]

When assessed in light of the actual organization of power within the technostructure, Galbraith argued, conventional views about the requirements and goals of corporate enterprise would no longer stand. New explanations were in order. It was apparent, for example, that the tremendous size of modern enterprise was directly related to the needs of the technostructure: "Size is the general servant of technology, not the special servant of profits."[108] Size allowed for specialized organization and an internal supply of capital, both of which served the technostructure's need for autonomy, thereby protecting its decision-making process from interference from stockholders, financial institutions, and the state. This need for autonomy actually originated with the growth of modern technology and the increasing size and complexity of corporate enterprise. Once decision-making was based on expert knowledge, only those who had the relevant expertise were capable of making an informed decision. This was equally true for enterprise in both modern-day capitalist and non-capitalist societies.[109]

In Galbraith's theory of modern industrial society, the emergence of the technostructure coincided with the transition from a market economy to a planned economy. This development, he argued, required a reassessment of the traditional economic motivation of profit maximization. Galbraith analyzed several factors that pointed to the need for such a reevaluation. To begin with, as the market's mechanisms broke down, so did its traditional function of reinforcing profit maximization. Furthermore, decentralization of power within the technostructure "dissolves entirely" the view of corporate managers as maximizing their return by maximizing that of the stockholders. Finally, since the technostructure "does not supply capital but specialized talent and organization," one could not assume that it would seek a maximum return on its capital. A more plausible outcome would be that it "maximize its success as an organization."[110] A revision of the traditional theory of motivation, therefore, was necessary to account for these changes.

Galbraith identified four types of motivation that can be said to influence behavior within corporate enterprise: compulsion, pecuniary gain, identification, and adaptation. Whereas the first two were commonplace in human affairs, the latter two had special relevance for large-scale organization. Identification referred to the process whereby one accepted the goals of the organization as one's own. When an individual adapted or accommodated the goals of the organization to personal goals, adaptation became the operative motivation. The collective influence of all four types of motivation within an organization can be termed the "motivating system." An "effective organization" can be said to exist when the motivating system was "internally reinforcing"—that is, when individual goals were consistent with organizational goals.[111]

Whereas compulsion was the primary motivation in an economy based on the control of land, and pecuniary inducements characterized the reign of capital, identification and adaptation, Galbraith argued, constituted the "operative motivations" of the technostructure.[112] While granting that the motivational system within the modern corporation would be mixed and that different tasks might encourage a different set or priority of motivations, he nevertheless maintained that identification and adaptation would become "increasingly plausible motivations" as one moved "toward the center of the technostructure."[113]

Citing historical example, Galbraith observed that the goals of individuals, as well as those of the organizations they served, were generally consistent with the broader goals of society.[114] "Consistency in the identification of individuals and organizations with social goals is possible," he explained, "because running as a parallel thread from individual through organization to social attitudes, is the presence of adaptation as a motivating force." Accordingly, "much of what is believed to be socially important is, in fact, the adaptation of social attitudes to the goal system of the technostructure." By this same process, the members of the enterprise were able to identify with the corporation "on the assumption that it is serving social goals when, in fact, it is serving their own." This was not an "analytical or cerebral" process, according to the author, but "a triumph of unexamined but constantly reiterated assumption over exact thought."[115]

On the basis of his general theory of motivation, Galbraith described the goals of the industrial system as rationalized to accommodate the needs of the technostructure. Because the survival of the technostructure required preservation of "the autonomy on which its decision-making power depends," a primary goal of the corporation was to secure a minimal level of earnings and thereby avoid loss. In other words, the technostructure's primary self-interest was organizational autonomy, not profit maximization or high revenues, neither of which served its immediate needs. For the present, corporate autonomy found its ideological justification in the traditional distinction between private enterprise and government, which assumed that the market determined economic behavior. Even though this rationale was "palpably bogus," it nevertheless served a real need. That adaptation "can win social attitudes favorable to the autonomy of the technostructure that have such negligible relation to reality," he concluded, is a testimony to its power.[116]

Once a minimum level of earnings was realized, a major goal of the technostructure was "to achieve the greatest possible rate of corporate growth as measured in sales." Economic growth, unlike profit maximization, served the immediate interests of the members of the technostructure because it led to more jobs, promotions, and advancements and prevented contraction of the technostructure.[117] Furthermore, the members of the technostructure easily identified with the corporate goal of economic growth because they viewed it as being consistent with the broader social goal of economic growth. A minimum level of earnings and maximum economic growth therefore constituted the primary goals of the technostructure. When these were achieved, the secondary goals of technological advance and a rising dividend rate, along with numerous lesser goals, such as educational improvement, health care, and political activity, might also be adopted by the corporation.[118]

For Galbraith, the growth of the technostructure in the twentieth century occasioned a shift in the basis of power within industrial society as well as a transformation of the needs and goals of enterprise in accordance with the imperatives of modern technology. These developments also coincided with a change in the relationship between the state and the corporation, which resulted from the needs of a planned economy. Not only was the industrial system "inextricably associated with the state," through a variety of activities, but "the line between public and private authority in the industrial system was indistinct and in large measure imaginary."[119] Whereas the relationship between the entrepreneurial corporation and the state was primarily pecuniary—that is, corporate rulers purchased favors and political advantage with their great wealth—the mature corporation depended on the state to perform functions that were vital to its survival and therefore had less of a need for partisan political activity.[120] In addition to regulating aggregate demand, the state supplied educated workers, sponsored scientific and technological innovation, provided technology, and regulated wages and prices.[121] Unlike the entrepreneurial corporation, the political significance of modern enterprise, in the author's view, stemmed not so much from its political activity as from its ability to influence government as "an extension of the arm of the bureaucracy."[122] In any event, the decentralized decision-making process of the technostructure was less suited for "direct political action" than the hierarchical structure of the entrepreneurial corporation.[123]

Galbraith contended that the increasing integration of the state and industrial system, which threatened a convergence into one large complex, contained profound social and political implications. As this convergence proceeded, government policy would be increasingly influenced by the needs and objectives of the corporation. To the extent that the primary goals of society were economic, moreover, the technostructure would have a major role in shaping and defining those goals, and hence in influencing social beliefs. These prospects, Galbraith warned, posed a grave threat to the freedom of individuals in a liberal society. "The danger to liberty," he cautioned, "lies in the subordination of belief to the needs of the industrial system."[124] This threat would become all the more real when it was realized that the unions in industrial society no longer functioned as an effective opposition to the power of the corporation. In fact, far from representing a basic conflict within the industrial system, they had become an essential component of the planning apparatus of the technostructure and had otherwise aided the stability of industrial relations.[125] This state of affairs raised the question of "whether the industrial system, in absorbing economic conflict, ends all examination of social goals."[126] To this issue we now turn.

I have attempted to demonstrate that in Galbraith's theory, the imperatives of technology (and, derivatively, the organizational requirements of enterprise) determined the direction of economic and social change. Ideology served to justify existing arrangements, to legitimize the power of the technostructure and its economic goals. In much the same fashion as Veblen, Galbraith maintained that ideological beliefs lagged behind technological and economic developments. Beliefs were not consciously revised to justify change so much as they were unconsciously adapted or accommodated to a changed reality. Thus, in arguing for the classical liberal separation of the economic and political realms, modern advocates of free enterprise were in reality defending the autonomy of the technostructure. Similarly, the conception of the individual in classical economic theory as "the ultimate source of power in the economic system" had come to justify a reality in which the market no longer determined economic behavior. In this way, "a doctrine that celebrates individuality provides the cloak for organization." This same doctrine, moreover, provided the members of the corporation with the rationale that corporate goals extended the freedom of the individual consumer.[127]

Through the process of adaptation, the goals and ideological beliefs of society could be accommodated to the needs of the technostructure. Once adapted to changed social and economic conditions, the principles of classical liberalism served as a guise for corporate power.[128] The "genius of the industrial system," Galbraith related, was that it made the goals that reflected its needs "coordinate with social virtue and human enlightenment."[129] Social priorities were redefined, as it were, behind people's backs. As industrial society and the state continued to fuse, and as economic goals became the dominant goals, a new form of despotism emerged. Galbraith envisioned a future society in which individuality had become so circumscribed as to be meaningless, a society in which cultural, aesthetic, and political values that served no function within the technostructure would be deemed socially worthless—a society, in essence, in which the "organization man" had come to be the standard-bearer of civilization.

What then, if any, are the prospects that the present trend may be reversed? To begin with, Galbraith did not put forth a comprehensive plan for social reform. In his view, there were definite limits to the types of change that were possible, limits imposed by the imperatives of technology and organization that shaped modern industrial society. "The technical complexity and planning and associated scale of operations, that took power from the capitalist entrepreneur and lodged it with the technostructure," he explained, "removed it also from the reach of social control."[130]

Reform that aimed to reorganize power within the industrial system, therefore, would be ill-fated. What Galbraith proposed, in much the same manner as the corporate liberals of the Progressive Era, was to restore some semblance of social balance and, in doing so, to salvage the promise of American society—namely, a pluralism of beliefs and social thought, a realm for true individuality and, hence, criticism of the established order, and therewith the prospect for a reversal of the hegemonic tendencies of modern industrial society. If this could be achieved, the complete dominance of the state by the industrial system might be prevented, and the industrial system would "fall into place as a detached and autonomous arm of the state, but responsive to the larger purpose of society."[131] The principal responsibility for bringing about this change, according to Galbraith, rested with the educational and scientific estate, the new source of power created by the needs of modern industry.[132] Just as the banks and financial institutions provided the entrepreneurial corporation with capital, so did educational institutions supply the mature corporation with the new factor of production, "qualified talent." The influence of the educational and scientific estate stemmed from its newfound prestige, its increasing size "with consequent political implication," its "privileged access to scientific innovation," and its "nearly unique role in social innovation."[133]

Because of their strategic position within the industrial system, the academies of higher education could either enhance the monolithic tendencies of the system by uncritically supporting its beliefs and serving its needs, or aid the cause of individual freedom. To achieve the latter, the beliefs of the industrial system must be critically questioned and challenged, but there must also develop a "political pluralism which voices the ideas and goals of those who, intellectually speaking, choose to contract out of the industrial system." Neither of these objectives would be realized, however, unless the educational and scientific estate retained complete control over the educational process and subordinated the needs of the industrial system "to the cultivation of general understanding and perception."[134] In essence, Galbraith appealed to the intellectuals to take "the political lead" so that they might use their power to check the "monolithic character" of the industrial system. It is an argument for a balance of powers—a new social balance—that would preserve the realm of individual freedom, of critical social thought, and of alternative values by which to live.[135]

Galbraith's theory of modern industrial society and his conception of the technostructure are important contributions to the contemporary analysis of corporate power. His analysis of decision-making by expert committees and the corresponding disappearance of an authoritative chain of command within the corporation strongly paralleled Veblen's vision of the ascendancy of a technocratic elite that would govern on the basis of technical or scientific, rather than pecuniary, considerations.

The political thought of Galbraith and Veblen have often been compared, and for good reason. Both employed similar assumptions concerning the role of technology in socioeconomic development, and similar conceptions of ideology. Each demonstrated a flair for insightful social criticism, a disdain for orthodoxy, and a penchant for revealing the ideological character of reigning economic theory. Moreover, in their analyses of power, Veblen and Galbraith rejected the conventional liberal approach that separated economic and political realms, described a trend toward increasing corporate dominance, and identified a rising class or group that alone could reverse or mitigate this trend. Each of these similarities, along with others that could be cited, however, must be understood in light of one basic difference, which is that Galbraith's theory of modern industrial society, albeit in a perverse way, constituted a fulfillment of Veblen's vision of technocracy. This observation will provide a useful point of reference for assessing the analytical and ideological significance of Galbraith's conception of corporate power.

Each of the major tenets of Galbraith's theory of modern industrial society—the nature of planning within the large corporation, the historic shift of power from the capitalist to the technostructure, the merger of the economic and political realms, and the convergence of industrial systems—can all be traced to his conception of technology as the motive force of social change. That is to say, technology is itself an agent of change, a force that has a life of its own, which determines the structure of society and defines the limits of human control. Accordingly, in identifying the factors that contributed most to the transformation of the entrepreneurial corporation during the late nineteenth and early twentieth centuries, Galbraith did not include the competitive struggles of the marketplace, or the increasing concentration of wealth and power produced by the combination movement, or even the tendency for ownership and control to divide within the large corporation. Rather, in his view, technological development and its concomitants—increasing specialization and division of labor, and complex organization—preceded and superseded all other factors in accounting for the growth of the modern corporation.

"What the entrepreneur created," he asserted, "only a group of men sharing specialized information could ultimately operate."[136]

It followed that both the nature and the organization of power within corporate enterprise were thoroughly shaped by technological imperatives. To be sure, Galbraith maintained that "power goes to the factor which is hardest to obtain or hardest to replace." But this is just a more interesting way of stating what had already been determined by the assumptions of his theory, which was that technical and organizational concerns had achieved primacy over pecuniary objectives within the corporation. In other words, the shift of power from finance capital to the technostructure was a result of a new factor of production—organized intelligence—which, in turn, was a product of technological and organizational innovation. Although industry-wide power was highly centralized in relatively few corporations that controlled the forces of production, power within the enterprise was widely decentralized. In the former case, technological change had necessitated planning by large corporations, whereas in the latter, decision-making was a function of expert knowledge and specialization. Corporate power constituted a form of technocratic control—governance on the basis of technical expertise. What Galbraith constructed, therefore, was not so much a theory of corporate power in industrial society as a new organizational theory of management, a pluralistic version of technocracy. According to this theory, power within individual corporations was distributed among numerous groups or committees, each of which enjoyed a high degree of autonomy grounded in a particular expertise and not one of which was capable (insofar as autonomy was respected) of exercising inordinate control.

Galbraith maintained that, out of practical necessity, the functions of the state and corporate enterprise had been conjoined. Political and economic power, although distinct types of power, had become interrelated and interdependent. But this did not imply the inevitability of a complete merger, which in Galbraith's view probably would result in corporate domination of the state and of society as a whole. Indeed, it was at this point that he suggested a strategy that might preserve the realm of human freedom from further encroachments due to technological change. His proposal to reverse the trend toward a more thorough form of corporate domination depended on the prospect that intellectuals (the educational and scientific estate) would organize for political action and seek to influence the future course of industrial society.

But even this hopeful remedy was dictated by Galbraith's technological determinism. The requirements of modern technology had ruled out institutional economic reform, let alone public control of the industrial system. What remained was a battle for the hearts and minds of the citizenry, an ideological warfare whose outcome would decide whether economic goals would reign supreme or whether a pluralism of beliefs and ideals would thrive. One must wonder, though, whether the decision to place the burden of leadership on the intellectuals was at all practical—if not much less so than Weyl's vision of a consumer democracy. Intellectuals, like the groups that comprised Weyl's democratic legion, are a heterogeneous and normally contentious lot. Furthermore, Galbraith would be the first to point out that the organization of higher education had been transformed to serve the needs of the industrial system. He contended, nevertheless, that because they were less used to functioning as a part of an organization, intellectuals were better suited for direct political action than groups within the technostructure.[137] This too was a dubious proposition, for to have any effect at all, intellectuals would have to organize and act through committees, as the technostructure did. In any event, Galbraith seemed to have overlooked the fact that organization by committees did not preclude effective individual action on behalf of those committees.[138] His appeal to the intellectuals therefore constituted an attempt to salvage what remained of the liberal tradition in America. More than anything else, it was a plea for intellectual freedom and individualism in the faceless world of mammoth organization and impervious technology. It was also the author's solution to the problem of corporate social responsibility.

Drucker's and Berle's conceptions of the corporation as an autonomous institution, and Galbraith's requirement of autonomy for the technostructure, justified the insulation of corporate decision-making from statist command. However, each thinker offered a somewhat different solution to the problem of corporate social responsibility. For Drucker, the task of making the corporation socially responsible came down to the problem of harmonizing social and corporate interests. He maintained that this harmony must be built into the very organization of industrial society, rather than be contingent on the conscience and discretion of individual managers. Berle, on the other hand, believed that, pending developments in the law, corporate social responsibility depended on the conscience of corporate managers, their responsiveness to the public consensus, and the maintenance of a functional separation of powers. While Galbraith argued that corporate and social goals would be consistent, he did not agree with Drucker that consistency resolved the problem of corporate social responsibility. In fact, he maintained that consistency, aided by the process of adaptation, served the interests of the technostructure and facilitated the dominance of economic goals throughout society.

For Galbraith, the task of holding corporations socially accountable could not be accomplished by achieving a state of harmony, or entrusted to the members of the technostructure whose personal goals were unwittingly adapted to the needs of the enterprise. The responsibility for such a task must be lodged instead in an independent force that had the requisite power to counter the hegemonic tendencies of the industrial system. Indeed, the truly pressing issue was not whether the technostructure could be justified within the precepts of liberalism (it had already accomplished this in its own way), but whether liberalism could be saved from the insidious dominance of the technostructure.

Although Galbraith rejected, as ideological, the view of corporate power that assumes a rigid separation of political and economic spheres, he did not jettison the ideological conception of social balance. In appealing to the educational and scientific estate, he articulated a plan for a new social balance, a conception consistent with the American liberal tradition of checking power with power. Thus, Galbraith's influential concept of countervailing power (formulated in *American Capitalism: The Concept of Countervailing Power*[139]) reappeared in *The New Industrial State*, albeit not as an impersonal law or phenomenon but as a justification for reform. But unlike Drucker and Berle, Galbraith (in the tradition of Weyl and Croly) employed the idea of balance as a call to action in order to remedy an imbalance of power, rather than as a defense of the status quo. These two applications of the concept of balance therefore reflected differing political concerns with regard to the proper scope and exercise of government and corporate powers deemed necessary to maintain a separation of state and society, and hence to preserve liberty and democratic accountability. In this sense, the idea of balance might be invoked either to justify more extensive public regulation of enterprise or to justify greater protection for corporate autonomy. But in both cases, the balance to be struck assumes that a separation between state and society is essential to the preservation of liberty.

I have demonstrated that Galbraith's theory of industrial society must be assessed in light of the role he attributed to technology in social development. However, his technological determinism also informed the ideological aspects of his analysis of corporate power. For Galbraith, technology was the demiurge of modern society, an autonomous force that transformed economic and political relationships in accordance with its own needs. Individuals adapted their behavior and motivations to principles they were only dimly aware of. Decisions were made and power was exercised, perhaps unwittingly, to preserve the system. Domination thus became depersonalized. The monolithic character of the industrial system stood as testimony to the rule of technology over the course of human events. Within this austere world where humanity was enslaved by its own creations, corporate power could not be altered in any meaningful sense precisely because it served the interests of the industrial system. To be sure, corporate domination might be checked or constrained, but only in a very limited fashion, and only then by not interfering with the autonomy of the technostructure.

However critical of the social order it may be, Galbraith's argument, in its ideological aspects, justified corporate hegemony. His unique variation on the managerial thesis—the concept of the technostructure—did not justify corporate autonomy and rule by experts on the basis of a free-enterprise rationale, as did the theories of Drucker and Berle, but the practical implications of each theorist's concept of corporate autonomy are much the same. In basing the operations of the technostructure on the imperatives of technology, Galbraith identified the economic interests of society with those of the corporation. The identity of social and corporate interests, moreover, became problematical only with regard to the total dominance of industrial goals. In contrast to Drucker's theory, this coincidence of interests did not constitute a harmonious union, but rather a fait accompli. Thus, it appears that Galbraith's technological determinism, rooted in a profound fatalism, justified the very tendencies he abhorred.

After the fashion of Veblen, Galbraith offered a technocratic justification for corporate power. As a critic of the present order who wanted to restore a balance between corporate and statist power, however, he stood squarely within the liberal reform tradition of Croly and Weyl. But unlike the proposals of his predecessors, Galbraith's plan for achieving social balance did not entail institutional economic reform. In his view, the objectives of such reform had almost always been "identical with the goals of the industrial system."[140] The solution to the problem of corporate power must be sought elsewhere, outside of the industrial system. For Galbraith, like the early liberal analysts of corporate power, corporate domination constituted the central issue of politics and society. His account of the consolidation of corporate power, however, drastically narrowed the range of solutions. In place of the hopeful optimism of the Progressive Era, one senses in his analysis of modern industrial society an impending doom in a world remade in the image of the corporation.

5. CORPORATE LIBERALISM AND MANAGERIAL THEORY

In their efforts to construct a political theory of the corporation, liberal managerial theorists refined, and to some extent revised, the precepts of corporate liberalism articulated in Progressive Era political thought. For Drucker and Berle, the quest to establish the legitimacy of the corporation as a social and political institution largely determined how each would accommodate liberal beliefs to the new order. Galbraith's critical analysis of corporate power also entailed an interpretation and revision of liberal ideology. As it unfolded, this development in political thought lent a certain cogency and theoretical sophistication to the corporate-liberal justification of corporate power.

Corporate power could not be justified by a revised laissez-faire liberalism without a concept of balance that retained the classical separation of the political and economic realms. Croly, Weyl, Drucker, and Berle all argued that economic efficiency, political stability, and democracy required that a conscious social balance be imposed in place of the automatic balance of the marketplace envisioned by classical political economy. Yet, once the legitimation of corporate power became the central issue, as opposed to the reform of the abuses of that power, the idea of balance lost its activist connotations and served primarily to justify existing arrangements. Accordingly, in managerial theory the emphasis shifted from the objective of regulating enterprise in order to preserve democratic institutions, to that of limiting the regulatory powers of government in deference to the value of corporate autonomy. As this occurred, the managerial theorists of corporate power attempted to ground their conceptions of balance in impersonal laws or forces in a manner reminiscent of the classical theorists of political economy.

While Drucker and Berle maintained that a conscious social balance—in effect, a functional separation of powers—must be established in order to limit government power and thereby preserve the free-enterprise system, meaning administered markets, they also invoked the laws of balance or harmony to legitimate corporate power in its external and internal dimensions. Thus, once the corporation was conceived as an autonomous institution, the legitimation of its power no longer depended on the success of economic and political reform. Balance, defined either as equilibrium or as harmonious interdependence, henceforth became a justification of the status quo. This ideological development also took root in the social sciences, primarily through functionalist theory in sociology and pluralism as well as through systems theory in political science. Even Galbraith contributed to the ascendancy of the academic theory of balance in his influential *American Capitalism: The Concept of Countervailing Power*. Although he relinquished the concept of countervailing power in *The New Industrial State*, Galbraith's technocratic vision in that work revealed the extent to which corporate autonomy had replaced the self-regulating market as the "natural" law of the economic realm.

Balance—in American law, political thought, and political science—is an ideological concept derived from the constitutional conception of checks and balances and from classical political economy. However, its influence on political thought is long-standing and can be traced to the works of Plato and Aristotle. The Platonic conception of balance emphasizes interdependence or harmony; by contrast, the Aristotelian idea defines balance in terms of equilibrium or countervailing power. As a hypothesis about the empirical consequences of contending forces or impersonal laws that operate within the twentieth-century American political economy, including the domain of corporate power, the ideas of balance as social harmony and equilibrium have proven to be either unverifiable or patently false. Rather, in the era of corporate capitalism, the concept of balance has served mainly to delineate the proper separation of political and economic realms and to determine the proper internal ordering of these two areas of control. The idea of social balance, whether conceived as equilibrium or as interdependence, evolved as a conception of the whole (inclusive of economic and political balance) that sought to assign the appropriate relationship between classes in accordance with a revised conception of American democracy. In contemporary political thought, the significance of balance (conceived as equilibrium) derives from the effort to devise an ideological justification of oligarchic power that would be consistent with the American democratic ethos—that is, to reconcile de facto oligarchy with the precepts of republican government and the antimonopoly tradition. Balance (conceived as harmony) serves the same end but favors a corporatist conception of society and therefore lacks the ideological appeal of equilibrium, although the harmonic conception of balance may be more consonant with the actual ideology of those who govern corporate enterprise—what Drucker would term the "managerial attitude."

The managerial interpretation of corporate autonomy was influenced in part by the revision of the classical justifications of property and profits. In view of the separation of ownership and control within the modern corporation, Berle and Means argued that the traditional legal justification for property rights and the economic rationale for profits appear to be in conflict. If the profits of enterprise no longer accrued exclusively to the owners of property, but instead were administered by a largely propertyless group of managers, they reasoned, the motives underlying economic behavior were brought into question. For the liberal managerial theorists, the profit motive could not by itself account for corporate decision-making in modern industrial society. Yet, as the profit motive lost its explanatory significance, the *profitability* of enterprise assumed the status of an institutional necessity. Thus, while profits were no longer associated with personal greed, the capitalist imperative of profit-making had become identical with the objective needs of the corporation and the economic interests of society. Because it was essential to the successful functioning of the enterprise and therefore to society as a whole, profitability, like corporate decision-making, must be protected by the doctrine of corporate autonomy. In this fashion, the individualist creed of classical liberalism was revised to accommodate the requirements of corporate power in "industrial society."

This critique of the economic individualism of laissez-faire liberalism also entailed a revision of the relationship between individual and society. Croly and Drucker argued that individual meaning or purpose could be realized only within the corporate whole. Individuality, as they conceived it, must be defined in terms of a corporate ethic or philosophy consistent with the liberal conception of individual rights. Veblen's scathing critique of the dominance of pecuniary exploit under the reign of business enterprise served the ideological objective of justifying the instinct of workmanship, which, in his view, represented the salutory tradition of American individualism. Weyl sought to remedy the destructive consequences of laissez-faire individualism through a reconstructed democracy and enlightened social consciousness. Berle and Galbraith also perceived threats to individuality from the large corporation. While Berle placed his faith in the liberal tradition to preserve the integrity of the individual, Galbraith believed that intellectual independence could be retained only by creating a counterpower to the corporation. All six of these thinkers recognized that the individualist doctrine of the past had lost much of its meaning in the era of corporate capitalism, and argued to varying degrees that the disparity between traditional beliefs and social reality had exposed the moral bankruptcy of laissez-faire and therewith given rise to a crisis of belief.

Only Croly and Drucker, however, offered philosophical justifications to restore the tenets of the liberal faith. This aspect of the adaptation of liberal belief to the corporate order defended the integrity of the individual and upheld individual rights and freedoms. But it also embodied a corporate social ethic, an ideological justification that, as it developed in managerial theory, reflected the needs, organization, and philosophy of the large corporation.

From its inception, the corporate ethic in modern American liberal thought served as a means to resolve the inherent conflict between individual liberty and equality of opportunity, a conflict that appears to be incapable of resolution within the traditional precepts of the liberal faith. Fully cognizant of the formidable limitations to equality of opportunity in a highly stratified and specialized society, the corporate social

ethic sought to accommodate the liberal premise of individual freedom
to the logic of the corporate whole. In rejecting the atomistic conception
of the individual under competitive capitalism, the new ethic redefined
individualism within a social system that aimed to remedy the destructive consequences of inequality and hence of liberty. It is significant that
this liberal adaptation of socialist philosophy to capitalist social structure
also contained the ideological solution to revolutionary unionism. In this
regard, the corporate social ethic, while not a liberal idea, has been fused
with liberal and democratic principles to justify corporate power in the
workplace. In the era of corporate capitalism, cooperation in the oligopolistic market has its corollary in the industrial plant. And in both cases,
hierarchy has emerged as the operative principle of organization.

As in the political thought of Croly and Weyl, the concept of democracy
in the works of Drucker and Berle came to be associated with a way of life
and certain moral and material ideals, in addition to a specific organization of government. With increasing frequency in this century, political
analysts and philosophers have revised the concept of democracy in order
to justify hierarchical organization and rule by experts in government and
corporate institutions. The belief that if power is to be deemed legitimate it
must be held accountable to the members of society has found ideological
expression in the ideas of balance and the functional separation of economic and political power. Once the legitimacy of corporate power was
established in managerial theory, the ideological accommodation of democracy to the new order was complete. Democracy transmuted into an
all-purpose ideological prop, an idea that justified the preservation of
existing relationships of power and embodied a belief in material progress
and technological advance—similar, in the latter respect, to the evolutionary fulfillment of the promise of American life envisioned by Herbert
Croly. In the aftermath of the Progressive Era, however, it became a faith
without a cause. With consolidation of corporate power now a reality, the
reformist zeal of Croly's "national democracy" and of Weyl's "socialized
democracy" gave way to Berle's hopeful anticipation of "The City of God"
or to Galbraith's plea for a reconstituted balance of power. It would seem,
therefore, that the present crisis of liberal democracy is directly related to
the fact that Americans are still individualists and democrats in a world
that has become increasingly hostile to both. Thus, while Berle's solution
would restore a sense of purpose and direction, if not moral authority, to
the liberal tradition, Galbraith's reforms would revitalize the libertarian
creed of individualism.

The nineteenth-century American conception of history as material
progress has acquired an even greater importance in modern liberalism
through managerial ideology. But in the world of the large corporation,

the individual's role in this historical development has become increasingly uncertain. As technology replaced the frontier at the shrine of the liberal faith, prosperity depended not so much on individual initiative as it did on impersonal forces. In the reified universe of corporate liberalism, "objective laws" became the motive force of history. Whether they be Drucker's laws of enterprise, Berle's laws of balance, or Galbraith's relentless technology, these forces dictated the course of human events and defined the realm of human agency. Berle summed up this pervasive sentiment when he stated: "Machines develop economic forces of their own whose impact is perhaps beyond control of inventor, capitalist, or corporate manager."[141] It is ironic, though perhaps oddly intelligible to the modern mind, that at a stage in the development of capitalism when human beings have forged and mastered technology on an unprecedented scale, humanity's creations, as it were, would rise up and become the masters of its fate.

This sense of historical inevitability, depending on the tenor of the times, may be expressed on a continuum ranging from overwhelming optimism to guarded pessimism. In conjunction with the doctrine of corporate individualism, the so-called "laws of industrial society" constitute the great mystification of the era of corporate capitalism. Each idea in its own way disguises the reality, if not the existence, of corporate power. One idea accomplishes this by personifying the corporation, the other by denying that corporate capitalism was and is the creation of people. While the corporate individual bonds with the masses, the "laws of industrial society" teach us that we are all passengers on the same train speeding ahead to its appointed destiny. And although we may, on occasion, change engineers or invent a better engine or a fancier dining car, we are constrained, within the realm of our meager powers, from ever altering our ultimate destination. Thus, unwittingly, we remain children of the Progressive Era, believers in the "natural" evolution of corporate enterprise yet lacking the critical perspective that only a period of tremendous social upheaval can provide.

Corporate power was the great issue of the Progressive Era. Today, it is seldom recognized as an issue. Discrete instances of the exercise of corporate power often attract considerable public notice, but the issue of corporate power itself is rarely discussed. Indeed, the ideological conquest of the corporation has been so thorough that scores of influential academicians have accepted the romantic view of the corporation as an apolitical economic institution that enters politics only to protect its pecuniary domain. In every epoch, human beings produce illusions that serve to rationalize the existing order while fulfilling psychological wants. So long as we devise explanations of the past to satisfy the needs of the present, a realistic understanding of corporate power will continue to elude us.

In the twentieth century, the liberal analysts of corporate power initiated and developed the political study of the corporation. As a group, they have paved the way for the contemporary analysis of corporate power, which in recent years has given rise to increasing scholarly interest. Half a century after Berle and Means proclaimed the need for a political theory of the corporation, the search continues. The pioneering studies of corporate power surveyed in this work have greatly advanced our knowledge of the phenomenon and have yielded insights as well about the implications of corporate capitalism for the human condition, including the moral and philosophical dilemmas of modern liberalism. Following the method of traditional political theory, the premises of the corporate-liberal analysts of corporate enterprise found expression in the form of ideological recommendations. The same assumptions, however, shaped these theorists' conceptions of corporate power. One can easily spot the determinative influence of ideology in arguments that urge reform or explicitly justify a course of action. While this ideological suasion becomes less apparent in analyses that claim to be empirically valid, it is nonetheless determinative when it frames the central concepts and structures the analytical approaches of such studies.

We must ask the social scientist whether one can adequately understand a subject within a conceptual framework that seeks to provide moral justification for that object of study, or that in other ways encourages the analyst to ignore empirical reality and to employ concepts that preserve and perpetuate the illusions of the past. What one sees but cannot explain or accept without relinquishing or revising ideological beliefs becomes, through a familiar method of rationalization, what one wants to see, and therefore believes, despite the incongruity between this vision and the world we experience. It is this psychological process that sustains ideological belief, in all of its variety, in the face of events that demand a new explanation. Between the desire for knowledge and the need to believe, the latter tends to prevail. And there appears to be no solution to the crisis of belief in the era of corporate capitalism:

> And so the modern world is haunted by a realization, which it becomes constantly less easy to ignore, that it is impossible to reconstruct an enduring orthodoxy, and impossible to live well without the satisfactions which an orthodoxy would provide.[142]

Chapter 6

TOWARD A POLITICAL THEORY OF THE CORPORATION

What has happened, I believe, is the reorganization of the propertied class, along with those of higher salary, into a new corporate world of privilege and prerogative. What is significant about this managerial reorganization of the propertied class is that by means of it the narrow industrial and profit interests of specific firms and industries and families have been translated into the broader economic and political interests of a more genuinely class type. Now the corporate seats of the rich contain all the powers and privileges inherent in the institutions of private property.

—C. Wright Mills, 1956

1. INTRODUCTION

In Chapter 1, I argued that a political theory of the corporation must be able to reconcile two seemingly contradictory observations: that the business corporation is a political institution, and that the socially comprehensive character of corporate power constitutes a form of class domination. The first proposition has long since been established by managerial theorists and is widely accepted, although the implications of this idea for the exercise of corporate power have not been fully developed. In this chapter, I argue that, largely by default, the managerial theory of corporate power continues to define the theoretical state of the art. While it has not discovered a mode of analysis that can adequately explain the external dimension of corporate power, managerial theory does acknowledge the political nature of the corporation. On the other hand, conventional Marxist theory has not contributed significantly to the political study of the corporation. The reasons for this remain to be demonstrated, but the gist of my argument can be easily summarized: orthodox Marxism assumes either that corporate power is a manifestation of class domination based exclusively on the ownership of the means of production, or, what amounts to the same, that economic interests always or ultimately determine the exercise of this power. Explanations that rely on economic motivation necessarily loom large in any account of corporate power, but they do not fully explain the nature or scope of that power in the era of corporate capitalism. While the burden of proof for this contention must rest primarily with the legal and empirical analyses of corporate power presented in Chapters 2 and 4, I shall here expand on and clarify the theoretical significance of this argument.

Having already examined the rise and consolidation of corporate power in the United States through an analysis of American law and political thought, I now take up the theoretical task outlined in Chapter 1. To begin, I analyze the problem of "corporate control" and assess the significance of this issue for theories of corporate power. I shall argue that the empirical issues raised by the separation of ownership and control must be analyzed in light of the fact that corporation law (i.e., both statutory and judge-made law, which embody the principle of political autonomy) permits the exercise of broad powers by the corporate hierarchy, powers that derive from relationships of control that are not based exclusively on the ownership of property. This analysis is followed by a critical review of theoretical explanations of corporate power in American political thought, political science, sociology, and Marxist theory. With these critiques in mind, I then offer an alternative approach that is based upon a synthesis of Richard L. Sklar's revision of Marxist class analysis and my own analysis of the internal and external dimensions of corporate power. I demonstrate that this approach can explain the dimensions of corporate power as they have been restructured and regulated through the law in accordance with the tenets of corporate-liberal ideology. As such, it is intended to offer a solution to the present theoretical dilemma posed by managerial and Marxist conceptions of corporate power and to provide an alternative view of the structure of power in American society.

2. WHO RULES THE CORPORATION?

The issue of who actually rules the corporation is a disputed matter. It is a question of class, ownership, and control that holds implications for the theoretical study of corporate power. The trend toward the separation of ownership and control within the large corporation was analyzed in some detail by Veblen in *The Theory of Business Enterprise*, in 1904.[1] In this and later works, Veblen made the argument that this increasing separation further centralized control within the ruling oligarchy of finance capitalists, who became the "ultimate owners." Walter Weyl reached a similar conclusion in 1912, in *The New Democracy*, noting that the separation of ownership from control was producing a "progressive amalgamation" of business interests.[2] But it was Walter Lippmann, in *Drift and Mastery*, published in 1914, whose formulation of the problem anticipated the familiar thesis of modern managerial theory:

> The real news about business, it seems to me, is that it is being administered by men who are not profiteers. The managers are on salary, divorced from ownership and from bargaining. They represent the revolution in business incentives at its very heart. For they conduct gigantic enterprises and they stand outside the higgling of the market, outside the shrewdness and strategy of competition. The motive of profit is not their personal motive.[3]

Observing that the trust was "sucking the life out of private property" and that traditional principles that assumed a unity of ownership and control of property no longer applied, he concluded: "The trusts have concentrated control and management, but ownership they have diffused and diluted till it means very little more than a claim to residual profits." The future course of industry, therefore, most likely would be shaped by nonpecuniary incentives that motivated the corporate executive. In Veblenesque fashion, Lippmann claimed that "the trusts have created a demand for a new type of business man—for a man whose motives resemble those of the applied scientist and whose responsibility is that of a public servant." Following Veblen again, he concluded that "with the diminishing importance of ownership, the control has passed for the time being into the hands of investment experts, banking interests."[4]

One can see, then, how the managerial thesis developed. With the perceived decline in control by finance capital, which corresponded to the growing capability of corporations to generate their own capital, the self-sufficient and autonomous corporation emerged on the basis of an institutional separation of ownership and control. Employing essentially the same logic as Lippmann, Berle and Means addressed the implications of the divorce of ownership from traditional profit incentives for the conduct of corporate management, while restructuring the debate to focus on the issue of control within the corporation. Capital self-sufficiency, therefore, is the foundation of the managerial thesis. The validity of the concept of corporate autonomy with its various explanations of rule by technocratic managers, will at any given time stand or fall on the claim that industrial firms have achieved independence from the control of financial corporations. Unless one is willing to argue that corporate autonomy is impervious to environmental conditions, the managerial thesis must be regarded as an empirical proposition pertaining to a certain stage of corporate development, rather than as an expression of the inviolable laws of "industrial society."[5] Indeed, in the present era of giant mergers financed by multi-billion-dollar loans, one cannot totally discount the possibility that financial institutions might choose to influence policies of their corporate clients. Neither can one eliminate the possibility that with the tremendous growth of stock ownership by institutional investors (i.e., commercial banks, insurance companies, and investment companies) control could be exercised by these institutions or by financial groups with common stockholdings. While most observers believe that this power has not yet been exercised, at least not in a manner that can be ascertained through empirical investigation, there have been indications that some institutional investors intend to change this state of affairs.[6] In any event, the reason for considering such matters is not to revive Veblen's argument in modern form, but rather to advance the empirical study of corporate power by cutting through the layers of ideological doctrine that inform the accepted wisdom.

No tenet of the managerial thesis, however, has been accepted so widely and so uncritically as the claim of the increasing separation of ownership from control. Berle and Means's evidence for this phenomenon was far from conclusive, and indeed has been disputed in other studies that examined the same evidence. Nevertheless, if there is an iron law of managerial theory, this is it.

There are several aspects of this issue that need sorting out, one of which is the problem of control, which belongs to a complex of issues that have significant implications for the exercise of corporate power. In the modern corporation in which stockholdings are widely dispersed, control through stock ownership refers to the capacity to determine the composition of the board of directors, and hence management. This theoretical power is based on changing estimates of the percentage of stock held by an individual, group, or institution that is necessary to successfully influence corporate policy. From the original estimate of 20 percent by Berle and Means, the percentage required for control has decreased in proportion to the increase in general stock ownership, down to a current estimate of 5 or 10 percent.

This concept of control, it must be stressed, is a working hypothesis, not a lawlike empirical generalization. In any given instance, the amount of stock necessary to have control will vary depending on a variety of circumstances affecting the exercise of power within a corporation. One cannot simply claim, for example, that an individual who owns 5 percent of a corporation's stock has control. Proof of control would require further information about the individual's relationships (personal and business) with the management and directors, perhaps some inside knowledge of the corporation's internal power structure, including the influence of the board of directors on decision-making, and the individual stockholder's capacity and resolve to contest management in a proxy fight—which is the ultimate test of control. But in the normal course of corporate business proxy contests occur rarely—the notable exception being the proxy battle following a hostile takeover. Struggles to retain control pursuant to a tender offer for shares or external acquisition of significant minority stock-holdings, however, do not necessarily test the hypothesis, because under these circumstances, the percentage to retain or assume control will most likely be greater than in the case where there is no outside threat.

We must therefore begin with the observation that the pioneering work of Berle and Means, along with other studies that have employed their methodology, does not adequately distinguish between types of struggles to maintain or assume control. Adopting a single percentage to designate the threshold of control is therefore not an empirically sound procedure.[7]

But let us assume that the basic standard of control (5 or 10 percent), as it applies to the retention of control in the absence of threats from with-out, is a reasonable criterion. We are still confronted with a host of other problems. First, as Maurice Zeitlin has capably demonstrated, there are serious questions that can be raised concerning the methodology Berle and Means used for determining the number of corporations that can be said to be controlled by minority stockholders and those designated as management-controlled. In brief, the authors of *The Modern Corporation and Private Property* made presumptions, in the absence of evidence, that significantly skewed their conclusions and that have influenced subsequent studies.[8] Second, Berle and Means's findings concerning the number of large corporations controlled by management, as opposed to those controlled by stockholders, were contested by other studies of the same period that examined the identical corporations. In recent decades, this debate has been rejoined.[9] Third, the concept of control as percentage of stockholding does not speak to the ways in which control may be effected through alliances or noncollusive concerted action.[10] Finally, much of the evidence needed to confirm hypotheses of control has not been accessible to the public and does not seem to be forthcoming.[11]

Thus, what appears to many to be an obvious result of increasing dispersal of stock ownership is, on closer scrutiny, a complex subject fraught with analytical and empirical problems. Berle's fascination with laws of balance and laws of power, themselves empirical propositions transformed into natural forces, could have also shaped his and Means's analysis of the separation of ownership and control. One must therefore assess the social and political significance attributed to the division of ownership and control in light of the broader ideological claims of managerial theory.[12]

But let us again assume, for the sake of argument, that the trend projected by Berle and Means, and further developed by Berle in later works, is essentially accurate. Let us also assume that the large corporation, as Berle argued, is controlled by a "self-perpetuating oligarchy." If this is true, then the shift from family ownership to propertyless managers must have occurred at a definite period in the development of corporate capitalism. In other words, for most corporations there must have been a transition period during which the captains of industry and finance who controlled the board and management stepped down and the new rulers took the reins of power. We may surmise that this change of the guard transpired mainly during the first three decades of the twentieth century. In this short span of time, we must further assume that the imperatives of enterprise, as the managerial thesis proclaims, divorced traditional capitalist control from the day-to-day operations of management. All this, however, presumes that the oligarchy that was destined to become self-perpetuating, at some point, became the heir to the entrepreneur. Moreover, it would be reasonable to assume that this original oligarchy was appointed by the majority owners of the enterprise and that this ruling body would be chosen on the basis of its compatibility with the views of the owners. Talent, experience, shared ideology, class origin, and perhaps even the flexibility to adapt to changing social conditions, would all be important factors of selection. But one would not suspect that the original oligarchy would lack a commitment to the goal of profit-making. If indeed this oligarchy is self-perpetuating, then it would most likely appoint successors—directors and executive officers—that also shared its commitment to the pecuniary success of the enterprise.

To maintain that the rise of the so-called "propertyless managers" signals the imminent decline of the profit motive therefore assumes (but does not demonstrate) a remarkable transformation in the thinking and objectives of corporate executives in the course of a few decades. In short, the managerial thesis, as an explanation of the development of corporate capitalism, infers "facts" from the perceived nature of the enterprise, from the "laws of industrial society," not from an actual analysis and documentation of the changing character of corporate rule. Therefore, Berle and Means's analysis of the "traditional logic of property and profits" is an ideological argument, not a historical inevitability. To say that traditional incentives of profit-making depend on the unity of ownership and control overlooks the fact that the modern corporation, at least since the turn of the century, has provided substantial pecuniary incentives to its chief executives in the form of salary and stockholdings.[13] Most important, the logic of the "traditional logic of property and profits" was not based on a study of individual corporations' market performance or on evidence of changing levels of profitability. It was simply inferred from the internal structure of the large corporation and the emergence of science-based industry. Profitability henceforth became an "objective law" of enterprise, just as the profit motive—which is to say, old-fashioned capitalism—became a thing of the past.[14]

In the midst of all the presumptions of managerial theory lurks an essential truth, conveyed by Berle's most important contribution to political science: the concept of the corporation as a "non-statist political institution." Shorn of the ideological trappings of managerialism, this idea emphasizes the political character of the modern corporation. It suggests that corporate governance can be guided by political as well as pecuniary motives, that political rule, in addition to profit-making, has become a factor in the realm of corporate decision-making. Ultimately, it compels the conclusion, to which Berle's writings of four decades are a testimony, that one cannot begin to fathom the transformation of American society and politics in the twentieth century without a concept or theory of corporate power.

One more point will help to put this entire discussion into proper perspective. Once the issue of control is recognized as an empirical problem that entails a variety of considerations in addition to the distribution of stockholdings, the need for a sophisticated theory of corporate control and decision-making becomes apparent. Even if the matter of control as defined by Berle and Means—percentage of stockholdings—could be decided conclusively in every case, it would still identify only a controlling group (owners or self-perpetuating oligarchy) that could determine or influence the composition of the ruling body. The capacity to choose the board and management constitutes a type of control that can cement the power of an entrenched oligarchy, function (not unlike a veto power) as a constraint on the ruling group, or provide a power base for influencing corporate policy in various ways. Without a method of analysis that takes into account the locus of power in a particular corporation, the relationship of the stockholding individual(s) or group to manage-

board, the dollar amount of the stockholdings, and the
ᵊnce of outside directors and financial institutions over
te policy, the concept of corporate control will remain fro-
f lifeless statistics. By itself, a percentage of stockholding
ᵴsarily mean that an individual or group wields significant
power nor does it tell us how (under what circumstances and constraints) this theoretical power might be significant.

In the normal course of business, however, the task of managing the
enterprise on a daily basis, including the myriad decisions and responsibilities that this entails, remains under the control and supervision of the
corporate officers, subject to broad review by the board of directors at
periodic meetings. While management might be "controlled" by minority interests (or might be part of the controlling group), the structure of
power in the modern corporation nevertheless differs in important ways
from the majority-owned enterprise in the era of competitive capitalism.
Conceptions of who (ultimately) governs the corporation too often do
not adequately address the issue of decision-making within the internal
political structure of the corporation. In *Corporate Control, Corporate
Power*, Edward S. Herman states the case for the political rule of management in the large corporation:

> The strategic position and power of the management (the top full-
> time officers of the organization, some of whom are usually on the
> board of directors) stem in large part from its authority and domi-
> nance over day-to-day operations, the disposition of company re-
> sources, and the planning and long-term decisions of the company.
> The top officers and their employee subordinates devote full time
> to doing the business of the company, assessing its problems and
> prospects, and making and implementing plans for its improve-
> ment. By virtue of this concentrated effort and presence, they have
> special command over the technical details essential to an intelli-
> gent consideration of company problems. They also must of neces-
> sity make a great many immediate decisions that require experi-
> ence, knowledge, and on-the-spot presence. Most of the specific
> decisions involved in day-to-day operations are made by middle
> managers, but those at the top call the tune, set the parameters
> within which choices are made, and make some of the important
> specific decisions (including the compensation, promotion, and
> ouster of those below them in the managerial hierarchy). These are
> the built-in advantages of top management that give it a structure
> of dependencies both within the organization and outside (custom-

ers and suppliers), and thus give it power. This power extends to the board selection process and board decisionmaking.[15]

The power of the ruling oligarchy within the corporation has been secured through doctrinal developments in the law of corporations that evince the declining importance of property ownership as the legal principle that structures internal relationships of control. In both statutory and judge-made law, the political autonomy of management has been greatly expanded through the delegation of broad corporate powers, the relaxation of the fiduciary standards of care and loyalty, and the steady diminution of shareholder rights. The business judgment rule has been invoked to justify decisions that cannot be easily reconciled with the traditional doctrine of managerial efficiency, which presumes that management's primary obligation to the shareholder is to ensure the profitability of the enterprise. Erosion of shareholders' rights, especially denial of derivative suits, further cements oligarchic control by undermining the traditional claims of ownership. Thus, quite apart from who might actually control the electoral machinery, the law of corporations ensures the hegemony of the ruling group (subject to judicial review of alleged violations of fiduciary duties) on the basis of decisions that emphasize the paramountcy of political rule, not the rights of property ownership, as the determinative principle of control within the corporation. Political autonomy subsumes managerial efficiency. It preserves and expands the prerogatives of majority ownership of the previous era by vesting broad powers in the ruling oligarchy. In this fashion, power based on relationships of control supersedes power based on property relations.[16]

The foregoing conclusion does not in any way vindicate the broader claims of managerial theory; neither does it deny the empirical significance of identifying controlling groups. Rather, it directs our attention to the central theoretical problem of corporate power: the fact that the internal and external powers of the large corporation are in most cases no longer determined exclusively by the legal rights of property ownership, as they were in the era of proprietary capitalism, but by relationships of control that have been restructured through law to accommodate the internal growth of the firm and the oligopolistic structure of the marketplace. Much of the confusion that attends the study of corporate power stems from a failure to grasp the essential interrelationship between legal change and the growth of corporate power. The political theory of the corporation in the United States, therefore, must begin with the study of the formative role of the law in shaping the internal and external dimensions of corporate power.

Managerial theory, as represented in the writings of Berle, Drucker, Galbraith, and others, makes critical assumptions based on perceived trends or "objective" necessities, not on empirical analysis and documentation of the caliber normally required in the social sciences. Herman's study demonstrates that the so-called "fact" of the separation of ownership from control, when examined within an analytical framework capable of comprehending numerous and complex variables, does not yield conclusions that are consistent with the ideology of managerialism. Corporate power must be studied carefully as an empirical phenomenon. Furthermore, there is no body of evidence to confirm the alleged decline of the profit motive in the ruling hierarchy of the large corporation. Quite the contrary. Capitalism is thriving and expanding around the globe. Based on the evidence at hand, it seems that one cannot proclaim the rise of a neutral technocracy, or in many instances discount the possibility of broad control or influence over corporate policy through stock ownership.[17] Should the issue of control ever be ascertained to the satisfaction of all, however, there would still be a need for a theory of corporate power, because neither managerialism nor various contending analyses of corporate power that resist the concept of managerial control have adequately met the theoretical challenge.

In the remainder of this chapter, therefore, I make the case for an approach to the study of corporate power that can better account for the facts as we know them, or even as we do not know them. To this end, I shall offer a critical review of the theories surveyed in Chapters 3 and 5, and then assess the ability of various other theories or arguments to explain the internal and external dimensions of corporate power. On the basis of these conceptual critiques, I outline a theoretical approach that can account both for the political nature of the business corporation and for the socially comprehensive scope of corporate power.

3. THE STATE OF THE ART: THEORIES OF CORPORATE POWER

a. American Political Thought

The analyses of corporate power in the works of Croly and Weyl emphasized the overriding significance of corporate wealth as a means of effecting a systematic corruption of American politics and thereby securing economic dominance. For Veblen, this state of affairs represented business as usual. He too, however, identified an anomalous aspect of corporate rule in the reign of pecuniary exploit over the instinct of workmanship—which is to say, the dominance of business enterprise over industry. Progressive Era political thinkers characteristically defined corporate power in terms of abuse, as an anomaly that could be regulated and thereby legitimized or simply eradicated.[18] Even though Veblen ultimately believed neither of these alternatives to be possible, he did not relinquish his view of corporate power as a perversion of social organization rooted in the evolution of pecuniary culture in the United States.

Despite their general agreement on the nature and scope of corporate power, Croly, Weyl, and Veblen did not all conceptualize the problem in the same manner. The analyses of Croly and Weyl assumed a separation between the realms of economic power and political power. In their view, corporate power was a form of economic power that could be exercised to influence the political realm. Because both these thinkers attributed corporate dominance largely to the invasion and corruption of government by wealthy industrialists and financiers, they reasoned that as this influence, or indirect control, expanded or contracted, so would the scope of corporate power in both the political and the economic realms. This conclusion followed from the authors' assumption that corporate influence in government stemmed from a desire to acquire or consolidate economic advantage. The degree of political power wielded by corporate rulers would therefore have a direct bearing on the economic basis of corporate power.

Croly and Weyl distinguished between economic and political power for analytical purposes, but they also believed that these two realms should be separate and divided in practice as well. As a consequence, it is often difficult to determine the extent to which their ideological presuppositions influenced their analyses of corporate power. Yet, despite their overriding concern to retain, by revising, the classical liberal conception of balance, Croly and Weyl—especially the latter—marshaled empirical evidence that suggested a convergence of political and economic realms with implications that extended well beyond the putative causes of corruption. Weyl's conceptions of the plutocracy and the political trust, for instance, depicted an organization of power in which economic and political control had been merged. Croly's analysis envisioned a very similar state of affairs. Yet neither author abandoned the image of separate realms of economic and political power, largely because each viewed corporate hegemony as an abnormality, a condition produced by the extensive corruption of government.

This view, of course, informed their proposals for reform, which aimed to restore a putative balance between the economic and political realms. From an ideological standpoint, the idea of separate spheres for economic and political power was vital both to Croly's democratic ideal and to Weyl's socialized democracy. Even so, their plans for reform implicitly recognized the increasing integration of government and economy under the aegis of corporate capitalism. In fact, they sought to accommodate and legitimate this development by establishing government controls over the economy. The difference between the reality they described and the reality they envisioned, therefore, seems to hinge on the issue of corruption. If corruption could be eliminated and democratic control were restored, corporate power could then be regulated in the interests of society. Political corruption, as both authors conceived it, had become the focal point of the struggle or contest for control over the government and hence over the economy. Within the context of their arguments, the issue of corruption could therefore not be analyzed apart from the issue of who would govern. On the other hand, if corruption was not the source of the problem, if corporate dominance stemmed from the imperatives of the corporate reconstruction of American capitalism, the distinction between economic and political power would appear to have greater ideological, as opposed to analytical, significance.

Weyl's empirical analysis compared favorably with that of Veblen, who did not separate economic and political realms of power for analytical purposes in his numerous studies of the corporation. Veblen's conception of class dominance in the reign of business enterprise was perhaps no more comprehensive in its scope than Weyl's analysis of plutocratic domination, but it could better comprehend the nature of this power from a theoretical vantage point, albeit subject to the difficulties that Veblen's distinction between business and industry introduced into his analysis. Veblen's explanation of the rise of the ruling business class was inseparable from his moral critique of that class from the standpoint of efficiency. The distinction between business (finance) and industry (production)— respectively, the evolutionary social products of instinctual dispositions toward pecuniary exploit, on the one hand, and workmanship, on the other—served a dual purpose within Veblen's theory, the significance of which became problematical with the increasing dominance of the business class. The author's examination of corporate power, however, is appropriately viewed as a class analysis that focused on the role of finance capital in determining the structure of power and the ruling principles (and customs) of the new order.

Veblen argued that the business class dominated society by virtue of its strategic control of the economy. Because he maintained that economic control entailed control of the government, he did not distinguish, for analytical purposes, between the power generated in these two spheres. With the ascendancy of the business class in capitalist societies, he observed, the state became an "auxiliary agency" of this class, a means for protecting and extending class interests and prerogatives. Indeed, the coercive resources of the national government were regularly exercised in the defense of business at home and abroad. He maintained, moreover, that business interests determined government policy through control of the major political parties and that government was managed by a businesslike personnel, individuals imbued with the dominant ideology. Thus, from Veblen's standpoint, corruption became less of an issue when a shared ideology ensured an identity of interests.

The pathbreaking work of Berle and Means, *The Modern Corporation and Private Property*, initiated the search for a political theory of the corporation. No longer conceived as a perversion or anomaly of the marketplace or politics,[19] corporate power became a subject of theoretical import that, as it developed, evinced the need for a comprehensive conception or theory of power in American society. Berle's conception of the corporation as a "non-statist political institution" defined the magnitude of the theoretical challenge. While neither Drucker nor Galbraith shared Berle's passion for the study of power, they both contributed significantly to the managerial theory of corporate rule.

In the writings of the managerial theorists, the distinction between the internal and external dimensions of corporate power served as an important analytical tool. It accounted for the facts that the corporation was a political and social institution with an internal organization of control, and that those who held positions of power also made decisions that affected individuals outside of the organizational structure. These characteristics might also be applied to many bureaucratic institutions. However, what made the corporation a distinctive case was that its external dimension of control appeared to defy the narrow logic of institutional analysis. This issue laid bare the basic theoretical problem: Which conceptual approach, if any, could explain the external dimension of corporate power? Drucker, Galbraith, and Berle each formulated a distinctive approach to this problem.

For Drucker, the corporation was a social and political institution, an "autonomous social entity which exercises power by its own authority." Corporate power, which can be distinguished from governmental power, was rooted in the control of the productive organization of society, the means of production. Corporate managers therefore exercised broad powers that fundamentally affected the condition and quality of life for vast numbers of individuals and "determine[d] very largely the character of our society." Rather than develop a theory of power consistent with this conception, however, Drucker subsumed the external dimension of control within the "objective laws of the enterprise" while identifying corporate autonomy with social harmony, democracy, and progress. Accordingly, the promise of a theory of corporate power disappeared in the metaphysical mists of functionalism.

In arguing that oligarchic rule within the corporation was obsolete, Galbraith made the case for a theory of managerial control in which power was distributed among numerous groups or committees, each of which possessed a special talent or expertise. His technocratic pluralism mirrored the technological and organizational imperatives of corporate enterprise as he conceived them. Galbraith's conception of the scope of corporate power, however, indicated an extensive, if not socially comprehensive, realm of control. He based this assessment on the increasing integration of governmental and corporate functions, which in modern industrial society subordinated public goals to the needs of enterprise, and specifically to the needs of the technostructure. Indeed, he envisioned corporate dominance through merger with the state.

This conception, which jettisoned the idea of functionally distinct economic and political realms, did not achieve theoretical clarity in his thought. Instead, it embodied a notion of dominance through absorption and encroachment—induced by the imperatives of technology, the needs of the technostructure—not through an analysis of relationships of control. In this regard, the power wielded by the technostructure resembles the monolithic conception of corporate rule that is fashionable in theories of the corporate state, the primary difference being that the technostructure lacks an analytical concept of domination. While he formulated an incisive critique of the conventional liberal analysis of corporate power, Galbraith's own analysis fell short of providing an adequate conception of the external dimension of that power. The analytical value of the technostructure with regard to power exercised outside of the corporation is dubious. Indeed, in the absence of a theory or conception of power that can explain the convergence of the economic and political realms, Galbraith must fall back on the inexorable laws of technological advance.

Of the three managerial thinkers, only Berle squarely addressed the theoretical challenge posed by the external dimension of corporate power. He too documented the broad reach of this power, which included the capacity to control markets, to determine the economic development of society, to develop and control technology and forces of production, to induce consumption through advertising, and to shape public opinion. Berle's analysis of corporate power was based on a distinction between economic and political power, which he maintained must be conceptualized in terms of institutional control. The type of power exercised by the rulers of an institution (economic or political) would be determined by the nature of its activities. This logic led Berle to the conclusion that government bodies might exercise either type of power, and that within their institutional domains economic and political power remained functionally distinct from one another. It is significant that this functional separation of powers was not so much the result of a conscious effort as it was a consequence of the "differing imperatives" of these two forms of power, which compelled a division when there was a tendency toward merger. In other words, the intrinsic characteristics of economic and political power ensured their separation—an idea analogous perhaps to the repelling qualities of protons and electrons.

Berle's institutional analysis of power, when combined with his laws of balance and his notion of the pluralist organization of American society, effectively compartmentalized corporate and political power and then further divided up these realms of control into discrete institutional spheres that could be subdivided further into economic and political functions within government. He then completed this progressive atomization by defining power relationships strictly in terms of the capacity of one individual to gain the compliance of another. Berle accomplished this, however, only by infusing the concept of balance with the certainty of natural law, by attributing physical properties to types of power, and by imposing artificial analytical distinctions on a reality that, in terms of his own empirical analysis, illustrated the essential integration of political and economic spheres in the era of corporate capitalism.

Berle's elaborate balancing act and his multiple divisions within divisions, etc., of power appear to be the product of an analytical approach that increased in degrees of complexity as it attempted to comprehend a reality that did not fit neatly into the conceptual categories of a previous era. Although his analysis shared a superficial affinity with the pluralist approach favored by American political scientists in the 1950s, it represented a major departure from that school of thought in its effort to examine corporate power as a form of economic power. In effect, Berle offered an alternative to the exclusively political conception of power employed by the pluralistic group theorists, and by doing so took pluralist methods well beyond the logic of interest-group politics. His approach might be appropriately described as an institutional analysis of corporate power that incorporated ideological aspects of pluralism.

Despite their significant contributions to the study of the modern corporation, Drucker, Berle, and Galbraith did not succeed in constructing theories that could adequately account for the nature and scope of corporate power as it was empirically documented within their own studies or in light of other evidence pertinent to their analyses. It might be expected that works such as these, with avowedly normative purposes, would produce ideological interpretations. By the same token, one could also expect that social scientists who do empirical studies of corporate power would monitor their normative biases and avoid ideological presuppositions that seriously limit their ability to explain empirical phenomena. It is somewhat suprising, then, that the same ideological assumptions and distinctions that have shaped American political thought in the twentieth century have also influenced the social sciences—in particular, American political science.

b. Political Science

In one respect, a large segment of political science today has not yet developed an understanding of corporate power comparable to that articulated by the social critics and political thinkers of the Progressive Era. Although Croly, Weyl, Veblen, and numerous others recognized the need to analyze the power of the large corporation, modern political science has largely rejected or avoided this challenge pursuant to the reasoning that the political or governmental realm, as opposed to the economic or corporate realm, is the sole and proper object of political study. Political scientists in America have not only retained the classical laissez-faire separation of the economic and political realms, but they have also made it a cardinal rule of scholarship in the field. In recent years, this narrow conception of politics has been expanded by a few thinkers to include the revised laissez-faire distinction between economic and political power employed by Croly, Weyl, Drucker, and Berle. But there is more to this tale of power—which, to be told properly, requires an examination of various approaches and arguments.[20]

Systems theory, a reigning orthodoxy of the 1970s, does not lend itself to the study of corporate power, partly because it conceives the "political system" to be a discrete entity that for analytical purposes can be distinguished from the "economic system," and partly because power analysis is an incidental aspect of this approach. The logic of systems theory emphasizes the interdependence of the body politic, or "political system," with other subsystems of the social universe.[21] The ideological significance of this approach as an expression of a corporate ethic is clearly demonstrated in Drucker's analysis of industrial society. As a metaphor for interpreting politics, systems theory rules out serious treatment of social conflict and change, political domination, class relationships conceived as relationships of control, and hence, the politics of power. In any event, systems theory in political science is not a theory that explains events—which is to say, reality. Rather, it is best conceived as a taxonomic device for ordering political phenomena within the classificatory schema of the "system." This method then can be used to analyze and compare various political "systems." In this respect, the approach bears a strong resemblance to the task of comprehending the ideal Forms in Plato's *Republic*. Unlike the Good, however, politics belongs on earth, not in the clouds. Thus the constant temptation to transform the "system" into the system leads invariably to the transgression of reification.

No longer regnant but still influential, the pluralist approach in American politics resurrects classical political economy in the service of the modern political marketplace. Essays, enough to fill tomes, have criticized the ideological content of this method. Its normative implications aside, the pluralist approach to the study of interest-group politics does explain the dynamics of certain aspects of corporate political behavior. But it stops short of providing an adequate theoretical explanation of this behavior because it defines corporate power solely in terms of corporate political activity—that is, in terms of one aspect of the external dimension of corporate power. The methodological assumptions of this approach, moreover, preclude conceptualizing corporations as political institutions that have interests and objectives that transcend narrow economic or institutional concerns. In measuring power by who wins or loses in the political arena, pluralist theory does not acknowledge that there is a structure of control within the marketplace that has profound implications for the exercise of corporate power in politics.[22]

The pluralist definition of politics as a contest among individuals and interest groups to influence political decision-making derives from the atomistic assumptions of its conception of power. Class-conscious political action among corporations can be discerned by this approach only when corporate interests appear to converge on key political issues. It tends to view corporate political behavior in all-or-nothing terms, in terms of wins or losses, rather than to analyze this behavior in light of broader economic, social, and political objectives that might shape corporate political strategies. In the absence of unified action, pluralists reason that class consciousness dissipates as corporate political activity reverts back to its normal atomistic state. Accordingly, pluralism fails to account for the fact that large corporations may be politically influential when they do not behave as economic interest-groups. This conceptual weakness is evidenced by the fact that pluralists simply do not examine the relationship between the organization of corporate power in the marketplace and in politics, other than to identify economic motivations for political action.[23]

The failings of pluralist analyses of corporate power might also be gauged by the fact that two of the leading exponents of pluralism during its formative period, Robert Dahl and Charles E. Lindblom, have criticized the approach as ill-equipped to address empirical and normative problems that the large corporation poses for political science and democratic theory.[24] Lindblom defected from the camp of equilibrium pluralism, and he has written one of the few theoretical works on corporate power in political science, *Politics and Markets*. He employs an institutional analysis that recognizes distinct spheres of political and economic authority and power. Lindblom does not, however, join Berle in applying the logic of pluralism—balance or countervailing power—to the external dimension of corporate power. Furthermore, Lindblom's inquiry into the scope of corporate power in liberal-capitalist societies challenges the pluralist orthodoxy that corporations, as economic interest-groups, compete on equal terms in the arena of American politics.

Lindblom conceives of politics as a "struggle for authority," universal and unending, that occurs within the world's "politico-economic systems." In liberal capitalist societies ("market-oriented polyarchies," in the author's terminology), this struggle takes place both in the market and in the realm of public authority or the polyarchy. Although it involves economic matters, corporate decision-making in the market is nonetheless public in its nature and consequences. In his analysis, the struggle for authority often entails a rivalry for power, just as the outcome of this struggle could establish the capacity to exercise power legitimately. Corporate power or authority, therefore, is that which business leaders in market-oriented polyarchies exercise or hold as non-elected public officials. In a private-enterprise system, corporate executives will "decide a nation's industrial technology, the pattern of work organization, location of industry, market structure, resource allocation, and, of course, executive compensation and status."[25]

Business leaders, however, also hold public positions in government and occupy a "privileged position" within the polyarchy. Privileges, which are regularly bestowed, formally and informally, to induce businessmen to perform the tasks of the market system, include "income and wealth, deference, prestige, influence, power, and authority, among others." The author characterizes the relationship between business and government leaders as one of rivalry on "secondary issues," but not on "the fundamentals of their symbiotic relationship—private enterprise itself, private property in productive assets, and a large measure of enterprise autonomy." In this rivalry, there is no doubt about who holds all the trumps: "Businessmen do not get everything they want. But they get a great deal. And when they do not get enough, recession or stagnation is a consequence." But one should not underestimate the capacity of corporate statesmen to get everything they want when so motivated. Corporate political activity cannot be matched by any group within the polyarchy. Businessmen "enjoy a triple advantage: extraordinary sources of funds, organizations at the ready, and special access to government." Corporate executives regularly exploit their privileged status and connections even while they marshal their tremendous resources. They out-organize, they out-spend, they out-lobby, and they out-maneuver their opposition. They provide the overwhelming majority of contributions in electoral politics (despite officially reported expenditures), just as they finance both major political parties. Add to this the dominating influence of mass media and the use of advertising (commercial and political) in pacifying, by indoctrinating, American citizens, and the process is complete.[26] Business, in effect, keeps a low profile, shapes public opinion, and avoids the grand issues, all the while extolling traditional American values and selling beer to boot. Bread and circuses on a scale that even the Roman emperors could not imagine.

If the fundamental relationship between the market and the polyarchy is indeed symbiotic, and if the alleged "rivalry" is usually a case of government leaders complaining before they capitulate, then one must question the utility of the analytical distinction that separates public authority in the market and in the polyarchy. Of course, the distinction reminds us that the polyarchy has rules and procedures that govern the conduct of its elected and appointed leaders, rules that do not apply in the same fashion to the public (corporate) decisions in the market or to the privileged position of business leaders in the polyarchy. Even though it is not a power approach, Lindblom's analysis points to the need for a unified conception of power (economic and political spheres) to explain the comprehensive scope of corporate decision-making and influence.

Lindblom's work has stimulated research pertinent to his claims concerning the privileged position of business and has also invited some strong criticism, particularly from defenders of pluralist conceptions of corporate power.[27] Unfortunately, neither of these developments has greatly advanced the theoretical discussion of corporate power. The increase in studies of the corporation by political scientists following the publication of *Politics and Markets*, however, indicates a growing acceptance of the subject matter.

Recent interest in the political study of transnational corporations has highlighted the need for a theory of corporate power that can account for both the domestic and the global dimensions of control. Noting the "intimate and necessary connection between growth and concentration" in large corporations, Richard J. Barnet and Ronald E. Müller concluded:

> In a world dominated by oligopolistic competition, the quest for one leads inevitably to the other. The result is that managerial control of the technology, the finance capital, and the instruments for developing and disseminating ideology vest in a few hundred individuals. The principal decision makers in the top 200 industrial corporations and the 20 largest banks, which control such a huge proportion of the nation's wealth and its capacity to produce wealth, number fewer than a thousand persons. These individuals are the planners of our society.[28]

While Barnet and Müller's description of the corporate rulers of America (and the world), as a group, is straightforward enough, their conception of corporate power does not possess the same virtue of clarity. This becomes apparent when one examines their analysis of corporate rule under the "World Managers," who, they assert, "are the embodiment of the new meritocracy which Thorstein Veblen predicted more than fifty years ago would end up running this country." Neither wealth nor class origin, but "the development of certain skills" accounts for the rise to power of these individuals. Unlike their entrepreneurial predecessors at the turn of the century, the "World Managers," for the most part, "have been empire managers rather than empire builders."[29]

Thus, it appears that the authors of *Global Reach* have turned Veblen's "soviet of technicians" into modern corporate executives, many of whom, they point out, are millionaires with substantial stockholdings in their own corporations.[30] If Veblen were alive today, however, it is doubtful that he would conclude that the reign of pecuniary exploit in America and throughout the world had been supplanted by his vision of scientific management and industrial efficiency. Indeed, Barnet and Müller's dubious interpretation of Veblen is compounded by the fact that they list "the control of finance capital" as the second major element of global corporate power following "the control of technology"—which, they claim, is the basis of oligopoly.[31] The reign of finance capital, as we have seen, is the core of Veblen's thesis of class rule and, in his view, posed the major obstacle to the rise of the engineers (meritocracy)—that is, to the triumph of workmanship over pecuniary exploit. Barnet and Müller's analysis of corporate power constitutes a variation on Galbraith's theme of technocratic rule, which Veblen perhaps inspired but did not believe possible short of revolutionary change and the transformation of capitalism (and pecuniary culture) as it exists in the United States. And Veblen did not ever argue that a relative decline of the hegemony of finance capital would by itself usher in the age of technocracy. Barnet and Müller have confused the issue by combining aspects of Veblen's analysis of corporate power with his ideological argument, the social order that he championed and hoped for but ultimately did not believe to be imminent.

The explanatory strength of the authors' concept of corporate power, however, does not depend on the accuracy of their account of Veblen's social theory. Consistent with Galbraith's interpretation of modern industrial society, they argue that the merger of economy and polity is near completion: "To a significant degree, Big Business and Big Government represent identical interests." This "government-business interlock," like the technostructure, works to the advantage of the corporations, not the people. Corporate domination is also secured through influence or control of the political parties and Congress, the ownership of mass media, "the industry-government shuttle in the regulatory agencies," and widespread ideological indoctrination. What does all of this portend? Mainly that the federal government of the United States, and for that matter the governments of the world, are not able to "protect their people" from the giant (global American) corporations. Because of this, "the United States is looking more and more like an underdeveloped country."[32]

Despite its many insights, *Global Reach* does not contain a concept of corporate power that advances theoretical inquiry beyond the familiar conceptual confines of managerial theory. It is in essence an institutional analysis of corporate hegemony, domestic and global, that in attempting to portray the socially comprehensive character of corporate domination, resorts to a technocratic explanation. The basic flaw in Barnet and Müller's analysis lies in the conviction that the control of technology—for example, through the control of patents, research and development, and technology transfers—constitutes the foundation of corporate power in the market, instead of being viewed as one aspect of control over the means of production and consumption. The latter would be a more comprehensive idea that entails an explanation of corporate capitalist development and market structure in terms of relationships of power, not the control of a particular resource. Technocratic explanations of corporate domination cannot stand on their own because they claim too much and explain too little. They require either impelling forces (e.g., technological determinism) or additional concepts of domination (e.g., finance capital) in order to comprehend, on a theoretical level, the complexity of corporate power.

What Barnet and Müller have devised is an eclectic theory of corporate power that does not account for the rise of technocratic "World Managers" other than to posit that managers (organization men) have replaced entrepreneurs in a world in which the control of technology is "the key to economic power." At the same time, they consistently claim that the motive force of global capitalism is "worldwide profit maximization."[33] And they do not explain how the rise of technocracy can coexist with the global influence of banks, which, they argue, is exercised through the dominant banks' control of finance capital, through their stock ownership of (and interlocks with) major industrial companies, and through their tightly knit economic interest-groups, such as the Rockefeller-Morgan group of banks.[34] This unwieldy synthesis of technocratic managers and finance capitalists constitutes a unique formulation in the study of corporate power. It refutes, without argument or documentation, the central claim of managerial theory that the technostructure or neutral technocracy—the rulers of the autonomous enterprise—ascend to power as the reign of finance capital comes to an end.

Perhaps more to the point, Barnet and Müller seem to have turned Veblen's analysis of corporate power on its head by exalting the control of technology (industry) above the control of finance (business). But in doing so they argue that the changed nature of corporate rule—the rise of the technocratic "World Managers"—constitutes a realization of Veblen's hopeful predictions. On what basis? Clearly not economic change rooted in the transformation of instinctual proclivities. Veblen's scientific managers aspired to the workmanlike ethic of efficiency and serviceability, not to pecuniary exploit—that is, global profit-maximization through the hoarding of technology. Understood within the full context of his social theory, Veblen's analysis of business and industry, of finance capital and scientific management, undermines rather than lends support to the technocratic idea of "World Managers."[35] Thus, on scrutiny, the concept of corporate power in *Global Reach* yields logical dilemmas that seem to arise from eclectic theorizing. Technocracy and the rule of finance capital derive from two very different and largely contradictory explanations of the nature and organization of corporate power. Although Barnet and Müller provide extensive documentation of the empirical reality of transnational corporate domination, they do not adequately explain this evidence from a theoretical vantage point.

c. Sociology

Beginning with sociologist C. Wright Mills's influential work, *The Power Elite*, published in 1956, analyses of institutional elites in the social sciences have made strides in advancing the empirical, but not the theoretical, study of corporate power. Mills documented the rise to power in America of three ruling elites: the corporate chieftans, the political directorate, and the warlords. He criticized the pluralist conception of political balance as an ideological device for disguising the reality of domination and offered an alternative explanation that emphasized oligarchic rule and convergence between institutional elites at the highest levels of power. The peculiar contribution of *The Power Elite*, however, inheres not in its theory of corporate power but in its claim that America, in the Cold War period, was witnessing the ascendance of the military elite along-side the corporate rulers and the concomitant descent of the political directorate to a position of secondary importance within the ruling troika.

This thesis must be understood in light of Mills's conception of the "permanent-war economy," which in his view signaled the institutional-ization of the priority of military-industrial aggrandizement over social needs. Even so, his actual analysis of the relative power of the ruling groups in the *The Power Elite* did not support a theory of military-corporate dominance so much as it demonstrated the preponderant control of the corporate elite. On a theoretical plane, Mills failed to explain what he described so convincingly on the empirical level. His documen-tation of the power of the corporate chieftans and the rise of the corpo-rate rich—the corporate capitalist class—did not fit well within the con-straints of an institutional conception of power. In attempting to remedy this problem, he devised a convergence theory of elites (relative powers) that only highlighted the inadequacy of his institutional analysis of cor-porate power.[36]

Following Mills's methods in *The Power Elite*, there has been amassed a good deal of evidence that points to the common social characteristics of elites—sociological indices of class, shared ideology—and to the move-ment of elites (corporate, political, military, and professional) between their respective institutional bases of power. Such studies have provided substantial documentation to confirm the correlation between class posi-tion (including class origin) and the control of institutions. But try as it might, elite theory cannot infer class domination strictly on the basis of sociological evidence. For this, it needs a concept of power that tran-scends institutional control. On the other hand, those who favor an institutional analysis of power will have to be content with theories that cannot adequately account for the external dimension of corporate power or for the functional interrelationship between political and eco-nomic spheres that the study of elites substantially confirms.

In the tradition of C. Wright Mills, G. William Domhoff's studies of the American upper class (as a ruling class) have provided pertinent evidence of the social and political behavior of the corporate elite that demonstrate, in varying degrees, the cohesiveness and class conscious-ness of the rulers of the large corporations.[37] His work is especially infor-mative with regard to the organizational (social and political) ties that instill and reinforce these bonds and that establish linkages between the corporate sector and political rule. Domhoff's studies of the American ruling class, however, conceive of class domination (which he tends to equate with corporate hegemony) as upper-class control of economic, social, and political institutions. Hence, the relationship between class origin and institutional control becomes the critical focus of his methodology. But these works are not (and are not intended to be) a class analysis of power relationships. However accurate his conception of the upper-class social milieu of ruling elites may be, his theory of class rule lacks an adequate analytical conception of corporate power.

Along with the work of Mills and Domhoff, the writings of Maurice Zeitlin in the 1970s inspired a number of studies that explored the issue of corporate control as well as economic, social, and organizational aspects of the internal dimension of corporate power.[38] Extensive research on the organizational and social implications of interlocking directorates initially yielded competing analytical models that tended to support either managerial or Marxist theories of corporate control. Beginning in the late 1970s, however, a somewhat different direction emerged in power structure research that pointed toward a synthesis of the earlier models and a more sophisticated empirical analysis of corporate power. Noteworthy in this regard are the works of sociologists Michael Useem and Mark S. Mizruchi and economist Edward S. Herman, all of whom have bridged gaps in the theoretical debate between Marxist and managerial explanations of corporate power. Useem's analysis of the "inner circle," Mizruchi's "interorganizational model of class cohesion," and Herman's concept of "strategic control" (as applied to corporate control) have all contributed to a theoretical understanding of the large corporation that acknowledges a political (or organizational) as well as a pecuniary basis of corporate power, while also providing empirical evidence of the classwide structure and linkages of this power.[39] These theoretical insights are consistent with the restructuring of relationships of control through the law in the era of corporate capitalism. They point to the fact that the structure of control within the enterprise requires a political explanation of corporate autonomy that is also consistent with the classwide organization of corporate power in the marketplace and politics.

This convergence of managerial and Marxist theories implies the acceptance (and synthesis) of two seemingly contradictory ideas. First, one must accept the idea that the corporation is a political and social institution in its own right and not exclusively an instrument of corporate-capitalist control over the means of production. Second, one must also accept the notion that the organization of corporate power constitutes a form of class domination. Although a synthesis of these two ideas would be consistent with the empirical evidence on corporate power, it has not been effected. Managerial and other institutional theorists have decided the issue either by denying the relevance of class analysis or by arguing that political unification of the corporate elite must be demonstrated to prove class cohesion. Marxist thinkers, for the most part, have also failed to analyze the relationship between corporate power and class formation in the era of corporate capitalism. If class analysis is to become a credible alternative, it must explain how corporate power developed from the reconstituted relationships of control that accompanied the corporate reorganization of American society. But it cannot accomplish this without a conception of corporate power. In the absence of such a conception, leading Marxist theorists have devised various meta-theoretical explanations to sustain the idea of class domination.

d. Marxist Theories of the State

In a debate that engaged two leading Marxist theorists, Ralph Miliband and Nicos Poulantzas, each author devised a similar logic, conceived from a panoramic view of the social structure, that might salvage the idea of class hegemony. For Poulantzas, class relationships (and hence power relationships) were "determined in the last instance by economic power." The "state" in capitalist society—a product of political, not economic, power—while ultimately ("in the last instance") serving the interests of the dominant class, nevertheless retained a position of "relative autonomy" in relation to that class.[40] While differing with Poulantzas on other theoretical issues, Miliband also adopted the notion of the "relative autonomy of the state." Neither author, however, constructed a theory of power that is capable of comprehending class relations apart from the frail logic of economic determinism. In this fashion, the "relative autonomy of the state" became a theoretical prop that masked the failure of traditional Marxist theory to explain the reality of corporate power in both industrialized and industrializing societies. While Poulantzas theorized in the abstract realm of "instances" of the capitalist mode of production—all of which may be reduced, in the end, to "the last instance"—Miliband's theoretical (and empirical) problems with the concept of relative autonomy led him away from class analysis toward a theory of the state in capitalist society that embraced the premises of elite analysis.

The essential similarity of Miliband's analysis to that of C. Wright Mills in *The Power Elite* is apparent and intended. Indeed, it was Mills who made the point that "the phrase 'ruling class,' in its common political connotations, does not allow enough autonomy to the political order and its agents, and it says nothing about the military as such."[41]

Miliband's concept of the "class state" bears a remarkable likeness to the convergence theory of institutional elites in Mills's study. Miliband distinguished state power from class power (i.e., "the general and pervasive power" of the dominant class), which might or might not be exercised through state institutions and agencies. He maintained, however, that "while the state does act, in Marxist terms, on behalf of the 'ruling class', it does not for the most part act at its behest." As a "class state," it is the state of the ruling class: "But it enjoys a high degree of autonomy and independence in the manner of its operation as a class state, and indeed must have that high degree of autonomy and independence if it is to act as a class state."[42] What Miliband appears to have argued is that the state will be dominated more or less by class interests (or protect these interests), depending on what is at stake and who wields power within the state—an empirical matter not unlike that which Mills analyzed from a historical perspective in terms of the relative strength of the three ruling groups that comprised the power elite.[43] Substitute the corporate elite for the ruling class (class power), and the political and military elite for state functionaries (state power), add the element of shared ideology, and the "relative autonomy of the class state" in relation to the ruling class looks more and more like the power elite. To say that state institutions in capitalist society generally aid the cause of the capitalist class (act on its behalf)—an observation that many non-Marxists would totally agree with—does not suffice as an explanation of class domination.

Miliband and Mills also shared the same theoretical problem, although they arrived at this point from different directions. Mills's rejection of Marxist class analysis left him with the task of explaining, from an institutional standpoint, the apparent integration and convergence of elites—a phenomenon he analyzed in terms of "structural trends" rather than class dominance. Miliband's effort to salvage the Marxist conception of the ruling class led him to embrace an institutional conception of power—state power and class power—as an explanation of the relative autonomy of the state. Both authors rejected simplistic Marxist explanations of the ruling class, just as both were in need of a theory that could better explain the structure of power in the era of corporate capitalism, though Mills was very clear about his analytical options. Miliband's analysis, on the other hand, foments confusion. In holding on to an attenuated logic of class domination, he relinquished the method of class analysis. Indeed, his *State in Capitalist Society*[44] reads much like an institutional study of elites with a Marxist gloss. In this sense, Miliband's theory confuses, by relativizing, two different modes of analysis. Relative autonomy is the linchpin of a theory that is only relatively correct.

Poulantzas's conception of the relative autonomy of the state derived from his assumption that corporate leaders were incapable of achieving political unity on their own. In other words, he adopted the managerial argument that corporate decision-makers, being constrained by institutional imperatives or objectives, were incapable of acting on behalf of classwide interests. Hence the state (political power) served as a mechanism or mediating instrument through which the interests of the dominant class (economic power) were represented. In this fashion, the state became essential (albeit "objectively" or without human volition) for the preservation of class domination. To perform its mediating role, however, the state required a degree of autonomy vis-à-vis the self-interested fractions of the capitalist class. It should be noted that this crucial assumption, axiomatic to the structuralist thesis, was based on an unsupported assertion, not on an evaluation of the available evidence. Poulantzas's conception of the relative autonomy of the state derived from an abstract logical argument (informed by a creative exegesis of Marxist texts) that bore only a remote relationship to the real world he claimed to describe. Indeed, his method, in the tradition of Louis Althusser, exhibited a certain disdain for empirical inquiry, a point that became quite clear in his aforementioned debate with Miliband.[45]

By employing the analytical distinction between economic and political realms to expound the thesis of the relative autonomy of the state, both Miliband and Poulantzas unwittingly adopted an institutionalist conception of corporate power. In doing so, they abandoned the Marxist conception of class analysis, which assumes a unity of economic and political spheres for the purposes of analyzing class domination. The same criticism may be leveled at all proponents of the "relative autonomy of the state" thesis and its various permutations, which includes many, if not most, Marxist analyses that attempt to address the relationship between corporate power and class domination. Moreover, by making the state its central analytical and theoretical focus, the Miliband-Poulantzas debate paralleled the introduction into contemporary Marxist theory of (non-Marxist) organicist conceptions of the state. The "capitalist state," like the "the political system" in functional analysis, became a thing unto itself, with needs and autonomous objectives. Hence, discussions of the role of the state in preserving class hegemony have been extended to the analysis of how "it" functions to sustain the capitalist economy. This too is sign of the inability of traditional Marxist class analysis to explain the nature of class domination within the twentieth-century domain of corporate power. Economic analyses of monopoly capitalism attribute domination to systemic forces in much the same way that managerial ideology explains capitalist development as the inexorable progress of the "laws of industrial society." Systemic logic takes the place of real-life domination, of the analysis of power relationships in society.

The Miliband-Poulantzas debate inspired a formidable literature that shaped the direction of Marxist theorizing for over a decade.[46] Rather than advance class-analytic theory, however, this engagement sparked an intensified study of the state by Marxist and non-Marxist scholars alike,[47] a development that became self-defeating for Marxist structuralist theory, which now appears to have been consumed by its own creation. But the issue was wrongly conceived from the beginning. Both Miliband and Poulantzas had set out to prove (empirically and/or logically) that the state served the interests of the bourgeoisie. In this fashion, class domination could be inferred or deduced, thereby vindicating orthodox Marxist theory. Yet, the very terms of the debate revealed the vulnerability of the general theory, which apparently was to be saved at all costs. Instead of contributing to the analysis of class relationships in the era of corporate capitalism, Marxist theoreticians produced a new scholasticism that further inhibited the study of corporate power.

In the aftermath of this academic revival of Marxist theory, numerous alternative approaches or theories have gained prominence. Dedicated to reconceptualizing forms of domination and explaining the structure of power in modern society, various schools of thought—"post-Marxist," "post-liberal," "post-modern"—have rejected the method of class analysis. But this is not surprising. Traditional Marxist theory does not adequately explain the nature of class domination under corporate capitalism. Rather than revise the fundamentals of the theory, most Marxists chose instead to define and circumscribe their investigations in accordance with ideological imperatives that necessitated a rejection of empirical evidence or argument that could not be accommodated within the conceptual framework of the orthodox theory. In this way, the progressive impulse associated with the quest for knowledge was transformed into an ideological impulse, a critical posture that masqueraded as seeker of truth while it defended the citadel against the intrusion of new ideas. When a theory dearly held can no longer explain the social reality, its adherents perfect the methods of ideological warfare. They gird for battle by constantly honing their critiques, fortifying their positions, weeding out the heretics. Internecine debate and sectarianism inhibit empirical research as social theorizing slowly ossifies and succumbs to scholasticism. Ultimately, scholasticism breeds contempt and, therewith, a vigorous anti-intellectualism.

The abandonment of Marxist class-analytic theory, therefore, was encouraged by its practicioners. Disillusioned by the theoretical dead-ends of structuralism, some Marxists have turned to rational choice methodology, while others have embraced "post-Marxist" explanations, rejecting state-centered theory altogether. Lacking a conception of corporate power, Marxist theories of the state contributed to the resurgence of neoclassical political economy and to the pluralist theory of the political marketplace. Thus, while nineteenth-century theories of political economy do battle over the corpse of laissez-faire capitalism, managerialism remains largely unchallenged as the political theory of the corporation. But this could still change. There is an approach—a revised class analysis within the nondoctrinaire tradition of Marxism—that holds forth the promise of fully comprehending the nature and scope of corporate power in its internal and external dimensions. Unlike its kindred analyses, it is not weighted down with the ideological baggage of a previous century. Most important, it moves the concept of power from the wings of class analysis to center stage.

4. A CLASS ANALYSIS OF CORPORATE POWER

a. The Corporate Bourgeoisie

In his critical review of the concept of power in political economy, Richard L. Sklar argues that traditional Marxist political theory is based on "two prime postulates": "the economic basis of class determination" and "the class basis of political power." The former "teaches that feudal, capitalist, and certain other forms of society are divided, as a consequence of their respective modes of economic production, into dominant and subordinate classes"; the latter holds that "political power is a consequence of class domination." A theory built on these postulates, however, is "difficult to reconcile with developments in the various types of modern societal organization." For example, the economic basis of class determination cannot explain the fact that in authoritarian capitalist states "the political structure of society, more than any other factor, has determined the pattern of social conflict and solidarity." Moreover, in liberal-democratic states, "political forces often operate on bases that are non-economic in nature." The problems for traditional Marxist theory, however, are compounded by its inability to explain bureaucratic power in socialist, nonindustrial, and industrial capitalist countries. This observation applies to the business corporation in which "bureaucratic power and property ownership are closely related" but in which "the bureaucratic form of control does not arise from property ownership."[48]

Thus, Sklar explains, the propensity of Marxist theory to define class domination primarily in terms of economic causes, has created the need for a "compensatory doctrine," the notion of "the relative autonomy of the state"—a development, among others, that has "resulted in a radical disjunction between class and power in Marxist political analysis." An alternative to the current efforts to sustain traditional conceptions, he suggests, would be to "broaden the basis of class determination from its narrow foundation in the relations of production to a more comprehensive and fundamental idea":

> That idea could be the concept of power itself, in which event, the class basis of power would have been superseded by the power basis of class. Marxism would then yield to a perfection of its own ideal: a unified social science based upon a unifying concept of social relations.[49]

What are the implications of this approach for a theory of corporate power? In superseding the "class basis of power," the "power basis of class" makes the concept of *control* the determinant element of class relationships. This allows for an analysis of the corporate bourgeoisie as a class that exercises power by virtue of its *common control* over (not, exclusively, ownership of) the means of production and consumption. Accordingly, class analysis lends itself to the empirical investigation of power—which is to say, relationships of control that can be analyzed in terms of class relationships. The "power basis of class," therefore, can account for the essential political character of corporate rule—rooted in the restructuring of relationships of control through the law—which, as I have argued, cannot be explained fully by traditional rationales of property ownership and control. As the principle of political autonomy supersedes, by transcending, that of managerial efficiency, thereby establishing the political nature of corporate rule, so does corporate power based on relationships of control supersede power based on property ownership.[50] With this approach, one can leave behind conspiratorial theories of a ruling class along with the doctrine of "relative autonomy of the state" and enter the twentieth-century domain of corporate power.

But we need not jettison the concept of class domination. Frequently, the idea of class domination in America is treated as an anachronism— an anomaly of an era dominated by ruthless empire-builders and money lords—an archaic (premanagerial) phenomenon that evokes stereotypical images of dimly lit rooms, of conspiratorial caucuses, of fat capitalists smoking even fatter cigars. To be sure, such images are anachronistic. In the present era of corporate capitalism, concerted action does not require conspiracy, thinness is a sign of success, and smoking in high places has lost its chic. Fashions have changed, and so has the structure of power in American society. By analyzing power in terms of relationships of control (which subsumes but does not eliminate the empirical study of ownership as a means of control), one can define the dominant class in terms of the structure of corporate capitalism. While the bourgeoisie or dominant class in the era of corporate capitalism comprises a large number of individuals from the ranks of the corporate and professional domains, a hierarchy of control is evident in the organization of power in the marketplace, in political activity, and in various social organizations. This dominant sector of the modern or corporate bourgeoisie consists of the corporate executives and board members that control the leading industrial and financial corporations of the United States.[51]

To state the problem another way—employing the terminology of Berle—the modern corporation, as a nonstatist political institution, is the most powerful institution of modern society. Its power may be gauged by the fact that the leaders of approximately 200 industrial and 50 financial corporations exercise control over the means of production and consumption, over the development of industrial and military technology, and over the nature and location of employment. Viewed from the standpoint of class analysis, the top executives of these institutions compose the hierarchy of the dominant class. They are not now, nor have they ever been, the technostructure, the managerial class, the World Managers, or the neutral technocracy of "industrial society."[52]

Class analysis focuses attention on the fact that relationships of control exist because of some basic social differentiation or condition of inequality that gives rise to a relationship of dominance and subordination. Marx did not invent this idea. John Adams employed class analysis to defend the Constitution. He translated checks and balances into the balancing of social forces and the containment of class conflict. William Graham Sumner, one of the founders of American sociology, was a class analyst of liberal persuasion and the nemesis of all socialists. And Thorstein Veblen, the preeminent American social theorist of his time (and avowedly not a Marxist), analyzed corporate power in terms of class relationships. To say that America is not Europe, or that Marxist theories of revolution do not apply to current social conditions in the United States, or that American political institutions tend to mediate class confrontations, is to say nothing about the pertinence of class analysis as a tool for explaining power relationships.

Where the conception of a dominant class is concerned, confusion often arises from the failure to clearly distinguish the analytical conception of class from its sociological conception. Marx's conception of class domination is analytical. It describes a relationship of control based on the owner-ship of the means of production. To be sure, "bourgeoisie" and "proletar-iat" refer to social classes that can be defined in terms of occupation, income, wealth, education, and other factors. But Marx's concern was to explain the unequal condition of capitalist and worker in terms of a con-cept of class domination or power that derived from the ownership of property, from a system of social control. This raises a methodological issue of prime importance. If one wants to analyze class relationships as relationships of power, one must employ an analytical conception of class. To infer class dominance by amassing evidence of the social charac-teristics of elites—their upper-class origins or connections—will produce knowledge of the profound differences and disparities between social classes that persist in capitalist societies, not of class domination. Indeed, in this regard, the sociological characteristics of the corporate bourgeoisie have been well documented.

One will find that the upper class is well represented in the corporate bourgeoisie, and that upper-class families or individuals can wield sig-nificant control (through ownership) in certain financial and industrial corporations. One will also find that numerous leaders of the corporate bourgeoisie were not born into the upper class. In the twentieth century, family control of corporate enterprise has steadily declined with the enormous growth of the large corporation and the consequent dispersal of stock ownership. The evolution of corporate capitalism from its entre-preneurial beginnings has given rise to methods of intraclass communi-cation and organization that do not depend on concerted action among a small group of ruling families. Although family dynasties still reign within various industrial and financial corporations, they do not wield the broad, classwide control that is sometimes attributed to them. There is, then, a certain confusion underlying the attempt to identify the corpo-rate bourgeoisie with the social upper-class in order to derive the exer-cise of corporate power, as a system of social control, from family wealth. Indeed, this theory of class rule, which lacks an adequate concep-tion of corporate power, does not advance beyond the unreconstructed Marxist view of class hegemony. The sociological analysis of the upper class may provide significant information about the social behavior, the shared culture, and the mores of many rulers of the corporate domain, but it does not by itself allow us to comprehend the complex reality of corporate power and class domination.

As an analytical construct, the concept of a dominant class does not in any way depend on sociological descriptions of an upper class to explain the *structure* of class domination. The extent of individual and family control of enterprise through stockholdings, and the growth of stock ownership in financial institutions, remain important empirical issues. But neither of these forms of control is necessary to the demonstration of contemporary class dominance. The task is not to locate (deduce or infer) ultimate control in the upper-class heirs of nineteenth-century entrepreneurs or in the super-rich of the twentieth century, but to examine power relationships as they exist, as they have been adapted to the exigencies and methods of corporate capitalism in this century.[53]

To fully comprehend how the corporate bourgeoisie differs from the bourgeoisie of the laissez-faire era, we must examine the political determinants of class formation in these two stages of capitalist development. The Marxist conception of a ruling class under competitive capitalism does not refer to the aggregate of capitalists who compete in the marketplace, but rather explains the transformation of this aggregate into a cohesive and class-conscious political force. It is an idea about domination born of class conflict. In the classical Marxist model, capitalists are individualists who find a certain pleasure in competing with one another, if not engaging in economic warfare. They realize common interests only when their collective individual interests are threatened. And only when this occurs does the bourgeoisie, in the Marxist class-analytic conception, become a ruling class and organize politically. Therefore, common social origins, shared beliefs, and consciousness as a social stratum may contribute to, but are not synonymous with, class consciousness in the political sense, which is the only sense in which it pertains to class rule. Class origin and shared ideology do not automatically translate into class-conscious political action.

Unlike its predecessor, corporate capitalism constitutes a highly socialized mode of production. It differs from competitive capitalism in market structure, organization of production, and methods of control, and accordingly alters the political determinants of class formation. Under corporate capitalism, class consciousness *begins* in a reconstructed marketplace that requires cooperation and the practice of "fair competition," regulated under the law. This type of class consciousness—celebrated in managerial ideology, institutionalized through a labyrinthine network of interlocking directorates, and reinforced through numerous social, organizational, and political contacts—therefore does not depend on class confrontation for its formation, though certainly, as events in recent decades have demonstrated, it may be greatly enhanced by perceived social and political threats. Increasing solidarity in the ranks of business has led some observers to conclude that a new form of class consciousness emerged in response to the rebellions of the 1960s and early 1970s, which engendered a growing public perception of corporations as greedy, corrupt, and socially irresponsible. What is new to this generation, however, was commonplace to earlier generations of Americans, especially during the Great Depression and the Progressive Era. Corporate class consciousness becomes more apparent, because it is more politicized, during periods of social strife or dramatic change, but it is not a recurring phenomenon dependent on external forces for its formation. Rather, a class-conscious bourgeoisie is essential to the very existence of corporate capitalism. It is an aspect of the revised liberalism that assumes the form of a corporate community of interest and a classwide view of political rule in which short-term pecuniary gain may be subordinated to long-term pecuniary and political goals consistent with the broad objectives of the enterprise or industry.[54]

This corporate ethos does not depend on, or rule out, the existence of traditional class warfare in the form of confrontations between the proletariat and the bourgeoisie. But as power based on relationships of control superseded power based on property ownership, thereby enabling the development of the corporation as a political institution, class confrontation acquired a broader social and political significance. The socially comprehensive scope of corporate power broadens the potential basis of class confrontation; henceforth, the fronts on which class conflict might appear expand concomitantly with the reach of that power. Corporate executives know better than anyone the diversity of social forces that are affected by their policies. They openly recognize the political nature of their rule. They actively seek to shape public opinion. They work assiduously to influence the substance of government policies, both legislative and executive, state and federal. There is no mystery involved. The class-conscious leadership of the corporate bourgeoisie has gone public. It organizes and agitates. It counsels and cajoles. And it remunerates for services rendered. For those willing to investigate, it has defined itself through interlocking directorates, business associations, and political organizations. There is no better expression of this than in the Business Roundtable, a political machine composed of the elite 200 CEOs of the corporate world, an exclusive club that one may join by invitation only.[55]

Moreover, corporate class consciousness, in principle, is not inconsistent with intraclass warfare in the form of merger battles. Indeed, the constitutional rules of antitrust law that govern that activity and that define legitimate power in the marketplace establish both the "rule of law" and the ethic of "fair competition" within the corporate community. Recent appeals to abide by these standards have been voiced by corporate leaders who believe that the merger mania of the 1980s has wreaked enough havoc in the pursuit of profit.[56] Corporate raiders, on the other hand, see themselves as classic entrepreneurs who, in the tradition of J. P.

Morgan and associates, revitalize competition through the "restructur-ing" of inefficient corporations and by instilling a healthy fear in the hearts of managers whose companies are ripe for the picking.[57] In any event, with or without the aid of merger waves, the expansionist tendencies of capitalist enterprise, since the turn of the century, have found an outlet in international as well as domestic markets. Capitalism is still capitalism. The nature, organization, and methods of capitalist rule, however, have been altered, expanded, and refined to a point that renders inutile concep-tions of the ruling class of competitive industrial capitalism.

The network of business, organizational, and social ties that unifies the corporate bourgeoisie, while suggesting the potential for concerted class action, does not by itself imply that this entity acts with one mind or with a single purpose, or that it is not sometimes wracked by intraclass divisions. Rivalries between corporations can be especially venomous in the heat of merger battles. Transnational and national segments of the corporate bourgeoisie can pursue different political strategies to preserve their eco-nomic interests. The degree of class cohesiveness also will vary consider-ably between times of social stability and turmoil, particularly periods of class confrontation. And the concept of a dominant class does not carry the implication that individuals who exercise power do so in an absolute fashion, unmitigated by other social forces or unmediated by the law. Rather, class relationships, conceived as relationships of control, are struc-tured, regulated, and sanctioned by the law. They are inconceivable in advanced capitalist societies apart from the law. The structural condition of class dominance and subordination is *part of the law.*

b. The Proletariat: Old and New

Power relationships, therefore, involve domination and cooperation, not just domination, repression, or the threat of sanctions. The essential inter-relationship between ideology, power, and the law in liberal-capitalist societies necessitates a transdisciplinary conception of relationships of control—in other words, class relationships. Both intraclass cooperation and interclass collaboration are central components of corporate capital-ism reflected in the ideology of corporate liberalism. Thus the solution to the problem of revolutionary unionism was the Wagner Act of 1935, which marked the consolidation of corporate power within the work-place, not through statist control but through an agreement regulated by law. The terms of the agreement did not completely eliminate class con-flict, but legitimated and contained it by recognizing the right to strike and by establishing collective bargaining. This solution entailed a restructur-ing of relationships of control through the law consistent with preserving the dominant position of the corporate bourgeoisie. It can be conceived as a social compact that can be legally amended or dissolved by means of revolution or withdrawal. By its own terms, the compact can work only through cooperation, compromise, and ultimately class collaboration.[58]

The analogy, however, breaks down when transnational enterprise subordinates the compact to its global needs and planning, in which case the terms of the original agreement begin to lose their meaning, and the prospect of successfully renegotiating these terms, barring the rise of international unionism, becomes increasingly unlikely. Under these circumstances, the ethic of industrial cooperation begins to give way to a widespread perception of exploitation and domination reminiscent of the political labor movement of earlier days. For this sentiment to find an organized expression beyond nationalist reactionism, the entrenched oligarchic structure of American labor, strongly nationalistic and dedicated to the principle of class collaboration, would have to yield to demands of a militant labor force or be deposed. While this does not appear to be a likely prospect in the immediately foreseeable future, one should not discount the political resolve and current organizational efforts of the international labor movement.

For traditional Marxists, class analysis necessarily involves class conflict—the historical struggle between workers and capitalists perceived, by the orthodox, as the final stage in the dialectical progression of humanity to socialism. The fact that Marx's ideas about proletarian revolution have not come to pass—indeed, have proven to be apochryphal for the societies he had in mind—does undermine the orthodox version of the Marxist dialectic but does not necessarily imply that class analysis should be jettisoned. The more logical implication is that class analysis should be extricated from interpretations of capitalist development in its competitive-industrial phase, which were conceived before the advent of corporate capitalism.[59]

It may be queried whether the "power basis of class," by transcending the "class basis of power," does not in its own way undermine class analysis by expanding our focus beyond the basic power relationship between labor and capital. Not at all. In fact, it allows us to assess this relationship as it exists, not as we would like it to exist or as it may have existed in the nineteenth century. With a declining membership and political influence, and with an oligarchic structure of control that has proven vulnerable to corruption, organized labor in the United States, as we know it, does not lend itself to romantic interpretations of class struggle. If there is indeed a dialectic of change that may be discerned in the present social ferment, it must be demonstrated empirically.

The analysis of class conflict, however, need not be limited to confrontations between labor and capital. As the basis of corporate power expands beyond economic forms to include social and political forms of control, so does the object of that control incorporate a broader social terrain. Indeed, the capacity of numerous groups to organize effectively in opposition to corporate power, as evidenced in the ascendancy of the public-interest movement of the 1970s, can produce a form of class-conscious political behavior. To be sure, coalition-building among interest groups is unexceptional in the normal give-and-take of politics. But when members of such groups or coalitions see their immediate political objectives as linked to a broader goal—namely, the regulation of corporate power in the public interest—they have defined themselves in terms of a social relationship that transcends interest-group politics. Increasingly, the oppositional role that was once the preserve of the politically active segment of organized labor has been adopted by a variety of social and political groups. As social democratic objectives are redefined to encompass the interests of broad sectors of society, the opportunities for expressing this form of class-conscious politics will grow.

If relationships of control are conceived as class relationships, the empirical dimension of class analysis might be extended to include the political behavior of all classes or class segments that are subordinate to corporate power. In other words, the socially comprehensive nature of corporate power requires that we be prepared to expand on traditional conceptions of class action in a manner consistent with the structure of power in modern society. One might prefer to speak of an anti-corporate or political sentiment expressed in the form of an environmental, health, or consumer consciousness, but to the extent that large numbers of individuals identify themselves as opponents of corporate power through their actions and stated objectives, they have adopted a way of thinking and acting that suggests a form of class consciousness. It could be objected that this formulation makes the concept of class struggle contingent on the development of consciousness rather than on objective conditions or structural conflict. This is true to the extent that I am not positing objective class interests based on a reified structural model of class conflict. I am, however, arguing that relationships of control under corporate capitalism in the United States can no longer be conceived exclusively or even primarily in terms of corporate capitalists, on the one hand, and industrial workers, on the other. This formulation does not jettison the concept of objective conditions that structure class relationships but instead broadens that idea to incorporate the empirical reality of corporate domination.

What I am suggesting might be demonstrated in a more conventional way. During the 1980s and into the 1990s, it became popular among politicians to speak of the declining American "middle class"—the great majority of the population, including organized labor, who do not comprise the corporate and professional hierarchy or exist in poverty. While derived from a conception of stratification based primarily on income and wealth, this so-called middle class is also a euphemism for people who do not control the major institutions of society. Increasingly, the distinction between a middle class and a working class seems to be disappearing from popular political discourse. This reflects both the changing composition of the work force and the fact that the income of a large segment of unionized workers places them well within the parameters of this vast middle. To state it another way, the socioeconomic middle class has been sinking relative to the upper-middle class and the upper class for some time. It is also the case that while the rich have gotten richer, the number of unemployed and unorganized working poor have increased significantly.[60]

Appealing to the woes of a nebulous middle class while making promises of prosperity is a time-honored strategy for garnering votes. Nevertheless, there is an underlying reality to this political posturing to the extent that middle-class Americans believe that their interests are not well represented in the councils of government. For the most part, this feeling of powerlessness is attributed to the failings of political leadership and only indirectly, if at all, associated with corporate power, which tends to be lumped together with a myriad of special interests. Politicians regularly exploit and channel this disenchantment for their own purposes, while generally avoiding issues or positions that would pit them against the dominant corporations.

On the other hand, in the 1970s and 1980s there have been a few significant episodes of widespread public opposition to corporate power that have produced a divisive "us against them" consciousness. Indeed, the regulatory reform movement of the 1970s embodied this sentiment, just as the political mobilization of business during that period seems to have been greatly stimulated by it. Thus, occasionally, out of this general sense of powerlessness or antiestablishment thinking that serves as grist for all politicians, emerges a consciousness that defines specific social or political problems in terms of power relationships that transcend politics as usual. Various factors will motivate individuals to pursue collective action, but it is the cause itself that supplants feelings of impotence, frustration, or alienation with a sense of empowerment. This is not to say that this class consciousness is necessarily radical or revolutionary, only that it is grounded in a shared acknowledgment of subordination to nonelected wielders of power. What distinguishes class consciousness from other forms of political consciousness is the manner in which individuals in groups define their collective efforts in relationship to other groups or classes.

In the aftermath of the civil rights and antiwar movements, a predominantly youthful and college-educated segment of the middle class formed the core of the public-interest movement.[61] One influential (non-Marxist) analysis of this phenomenon explains it in terms of the emergence of a "new class" of well-educated professionals, scientists, and public-sector administrators that sought to establish their own power base through a radical transformation of the regulatory process.[62] As such, the reform movement can be understood as a struggle between a power-seeking "new class" (actually a stratum of the socioeconomic middle class) and large corporations. The proponents of this analysis describe the new social regulation of the period as the means by which the "new class" sought to advance its own quest for power.

It might be more precise to state that when analyzing relationships of control there is no "middle" class as such. A middle class, in this sense, describes a socioeconomic position or ranking, but individuals within this social tier do not occupy a middle ground with respect to relationships of control. There is a hierarchy of control within the dominant class, and the exercise of power may have a disparate impact on subordinant classes, but there is no comparable hierarchy of subordination. Instead, there is the corporate bourgeoisie, which includes the members of the corporate and professional hierarchies that command the major institutions of society, and various other elites closely tied to the dominant social class, and, as Veblen would say, the "underlying population" or subordinant classes whose interests may diverge for numerous reasons having to do with socioeconomic and job-related circumstances. Thus, an alternative approach would be to analyze the reform movement of the 1970s in terms of these relationships of control. Understood from this perspective, the effort to regulate corporate power in the public interest may be viewed both as an expression of dissent rooted in the class structure of corporate capitalism and as a social movement in the antimonopoly tradition of American politics. This explanation will undoubtedly fall short for those who seek an exclusively economic basis for class-conscious political behavior; however, corporate power has long since superseded its original foundation in property ownership. Our conception of class conflict must be expanded accordingly.

David Vogel has identified the American tradition of civic activism as a motivating force behind the public-interest movement.[63] I concur, and add only that this tradition has found its most potent voice when it has arrayed itself against corporate power or class privilege. Whether they be Jacksonian Democrats, Progressive Era reformers, New Dealers, or public-interest activists, American reformers have been most effective when they have appealed to an evolving democratic ethos to achieve liberal-democratic ends. The fact that the leaders of the public-interest movement appealed to the "public interest," not to narrow class interests, suggests that it viewed itself as acting on behalf of all subordinate classes. This vanguard mentality constitutes a form of class consciousness that reflects the socially comprehensive nature of corporate power.[64] Both the scope of the public-interest movement's agenda (environmental, consumer, health, safety) and its method of regulation that allowed citizens to participate actively through the courts and regulatory proceedings, posed a threat to corporate power. However one chooses to characterize the class content of the public-interest movement, it is clear that its efforts to make corporate power accountable by reforming the regulatory process led to a decisive confrontation with a unified corporate bourgeoisie. Indeed, big business, in league with small business, roundly defeated the public-interest coalition and organized labor in a series of confrontations in the late 1970s.[65]

Efforts by neo-Marxist and Marxist theorists in the 1960s and early 1970s, either to identify the emergence of a "new working class" of technical and scientific workers or to reconceptualize the proletariat to include clerical and service workers, revealed the complex stratification that exists under corporate capitalism, as well as the lack of consensus on how to explain it.[66] The confusion and disagreement generated by this debate also revealed the fragility of a class-analytic theory that defines power relationships exclusively in terms of ownership of the means of production. Attempts to locate objective class interests in corporate capitalism by remaining faithful to Marx's labor theory of value paralleled other theoretical innovations, such as the concept of the relative autonomy of the state, designed to sustain orthodox convictions and prognostications. Uncomfortable with such intellectual gymnastics, other theorists distinguished the interests of the new working class from those of the old working class with reference to technological developments that had altered the mode of production. Still others appear to have combined aspects of both these approaches. All of these theories, however, defined class relationships primarily in terms of economic factors. Class domination necessarily presupposed exploitation and/or control of the worker based on the ownership of property.[67]

If the traditional bipolar explanation of class conflict was overly simplistic when applied to the realities of corporate capitalism, the "new working class" theories were overwhelmed by their own complexity. In a society with an old (primarily industrial) working class, a new working class (or stratum) of technical and scientific laborers, a newly organizing working class (or stratum) in the public sector, and an unorganized working class (or stratum) of clerical and service employees, each of which appeared to have different (or conflicting) objective interests, the prospects for a class-conscious working-class movement seemed remote at best. Instead of providing a guide to revolutionary action, these revisionist theoretical efforts produced discord and disillusionment. Of course, one could always fall back on the "false consciousness" of the American worker, or prophesy the impending collapse of capitalism once its internal contradictions had been fully disclosed, or, as most eventually did, turn to alternative state-centered explanations of how class conflict was contained or managed by government functionaries. Thus, the great assault against "instrumentalism" inspired by Poulantzas might in reality have been less of an attack on Miliband and company than an admission of the failure of conventional Marxist theory to explain the nature of class domination in the era of corporate capitalism.

While the industrial proletariat in the United States has been steadily shrinking rather than growing, the so-called "middle class" has become increasingly subject to corporate power, albeit not in the form of an industrial work force but as mental and technical workers, consumers, and citizens. Corporate control over the production and consumption of goods, the development of technology, and the conditions and location of employment will continue to have a disparate impact on various segments of the population. But the notion that the traditional working class is conspicuous by the degree to which it is directly subject to corporate power no longer appears tenable. Theories of a "new class" and of a "new working class" both are in part a reflection of this changed reality. Corporate power is a socially comprehensive phenomenon, and as it has grown, so has the object of its control. Corporate power is more visible in the workplace because that is where we look for it. Yet it influences or structures virtually every aspect of daily existence—consumption, transportation, communication, work, health, education, entertainment, the arts, leisure, popular culture, and political debate. Corporate decisions concerning production, marketing, investment, employment, research and development, acquisitions and divestitures, and exploitation of global resources profoundly affect the lives of millions in the United States and shape the future of the nation. In this broad sense, a "proletarianization" of the "middle class" does seem to be occurring. Corporate power permeates our lives, yet it is widely accepted as a "natural" state of affairs, and therefore is largely invisible. The forest cannot be seen for the trees, but sometimes even the trees escape our notice.

Class relationships are not disappearing, they are evolving. Long-

standing conceptions of class domination and class conflict must be reex-
amined in light of this transformation. By defining class relationships
and class conflict solely in terms of the ownership of the means of
production, Marxist theorists have neglected other possible sources of
class consciousness. Narrow economic and job-related interests tend to
inhibit unified class action in a highly stratified and complex society.
However, major social and political issues (e.g., health, environmental,
and consumer issues, and unemployment and education) affecting all
subordinate classes or strata thereof often cut across these intraclass
divisions. Thus, in monitoring signs of potential class conflict in the
modern era, one should look not only to the growing discontent of the
industrial proletariat, but also to protestations concerning the quality of
life (including economic well-being) expressed by other workers and
persons who are subject to corporate power.

A disclaimer is in order at this point. I do not in any way mean to
understate the complexity of power relationships that exist in modern
society, including those based on gender and race that might intersect
with or be integral to corporate power in its present form. The tendency I
have described merely suggests that as the external dimension of corporate power expands in domestic and international settings, it produces
relationships of control that could give rise to new forms of class-
conscious political activity. Numerous factors militate against a frequent
recurrence of this scenario in the United States, not the least of which
would be ideological resistance or plain indifference to such movements.
Moreover, the ideological predisposition to view corporate power as
diffused and atomized, ironically, only seems to be enhanced by its
pervasiveness. This problem is not merely a function of ideological indoctrination; it has an existential foundation. Corporate power is experi-
enced by individuals in myriad, seemingly unconnected, ways. While
the social meaning of these experiences can change dramatically if they
are perceived as interconnected and acknowledged as being widely
shared, the individualistic and competitive structure of work and social
existence strongly discourages such a reevaluation.

Nearly one hundred years ago, in reflecting on the persistence of
ideological beliefs that exalted exploitation and predation, Thorstein Veblen wryly observed: "America is the native habitat of the self-made man,
and the self-made man is a pecuniary organism." Today the ideological
concept of the "self-made man" has a certain nostalgic appeal, but America indeed remains the land of the "pecuniary organism." More than
ever, invidious distinctions based on "pecuniary emulation" determine
social status and inform habits of consumption. With the emergence of
mass culture, however, pecuniary canons of taste and fashion are for the

great majority of people no longer defined primarily in terms of the habits and preferences of the upper class. Rather, these standards are manufactured and promoted largely by the corporate overlords of popular culture, who understand better than anyone the enduring truth of Veblen's observation.

If recent experience provides a clue to future events, class-conscious movements in the United States will occur episodically and be short-lived, although not necessarily inconsequential. In the normal course of business, corporate social responsibility will not probably become a salient political issue save for discrete instances of corporate gross negligence or blatant disregard for the public welfare. Perhaps more important is that, through the use of media and various means of political influence, the capitalist movement that emerged in the 1970s has taken the lead in redefining the parameters of corporate social responsibility. For the foreseeable future, it appears that the institutionalization of corporate influence in Congress and the White House will serve to check, if not reconstitute, efforts to regulate corporate power in the public interest. Consumer, health, safety, environmental, labor, civil rights, social welfare, and educational initiatives or reforms increasingly will be shaped by corporate-liberal coalitions. In the absence of a broad-based democratic movement, class collaboration rather than class confrontation will be the order of the day.

Class analysis is an empirical tool for studying power relationships that includes analysis of the diverse forces that comprise American politics; it incorporates the study of electoral, presidential, and interest-group politics within a framework that can comprehend the broad dimensions of power within the American political economy. By focusing on the structure of domination, class analysis cuts through the ideological mystique that masks the reality of control. As an empirical method, therefore, class analysis does take a critical view of prevailing social relationships. It is necessarily critical because it questions the ideological presumptions that sustain the organization of power in society. In portraying the nature of domination in liberal-democratic societies, therefore, class analysis could pose moral dilemmas for both liberals and democrats. However, its theoretical viability depends not on moral suasion but on its capacity to explain the reality of corporate power.

By freeing class analysis from the imperatives of historicism, one can study class formation and class conflict—not as we imagine it to be but as it exists in the advanced industrial, socialist, and less industrialized societies throughout the world. Practical recommendations must be informed by political realities, by pertinent theoretical and empirical knowledge of a complicated and changing world, not by hopeful visions rooted in nostalgic yearnings. The existence of class conflict and the interpretation of class struggle, therefore, is a matter for empirical examination, not a foreordained structural condition of capitalism rooted in "objective" class interests. To claim otherwise, to invoke historical inevitabilities, however subtly, in the face of contrary evidence, is to exalt belief or faith above the quest for knowledge, theoretical and practical. It is identical in method to the attempt to explain the development of corporate capitalism as the product of "objective laws of industrial society."

c. Corporate Power and the State

While the concept of class domination, as defined herein, does not deny the existence of other seats of power, it does take issue with the idea of the "state" as a monolithic entity. The "state," understood as the complex of governmental and quasi-governmental bodies or institutions responsible for administering a vast range of social services, regulating economic activities, legislating, adjudicating, enforcing the law, conducting foreign policy, and prosecuting wars, is not a thing, an entity unto itself. One cannot simply reduce the manifold complexity of American federalism to a reified concept and claim to have grasped its essence. Controlling the state is not the issue, because "it" does not exist in the American scheme of government. Controlling or influencing policies or the promulgation of law or regulatory procedures or foreign policy initiatives or public opinion or the production of armaments, however, is the issue. The politics of class domination entails the empirical study of all facets of government, the political parties, and the electoral process. American politics and government, must therefore be analyzed on their own terms, not in light of abstract logical categories, themselves hypostatizations of nineteenth-century capitalist social relations.

I am suggesting, therefore, that the relationship between the corporate bourgeoisie and liberal-democratic institutions must be understood within the political tradition of American liberalism. Constitutional government in the United States, from its inception to the present, has been conceived both as a means to protect the rights of liberty and property (enterprise) and as instrumental to the advancement of these ends. Democratic ideas have had an impact on the development of American political institutions and practices, but they have never been implemented to the detriment of the core beliefs of liberalism, the ideology of capitalism. Oligarchic rule in state and federal governments in this century has largely displaced democratic control, but it too has preserved the principles of liberalism. The issue of the "state" derives in part from an inadequate understanding of American history (and liberalism) and particularly, in this regard, from the failure to comprehend the fact that the corporate reconstruction during the Progressive Era and later, while greatly expanding the responsibilities of government to meet the needs of corporate capitalism, did not initiate a trend toward statist command of the economy and society. Corporate liberalism justifies corporate power by revising and accommodating laissez-faire liberalism to the corporate reconstruction of American society. It does not alter the principle of constitutional government. Indeed, this principle was applied to the reconstructed marketplace through the rule of reason in the law of antitrust, and to the "private" sphere of corporate decision-making through the law of corporations. The corporate reconstruction of the law thereby preserved the instrumental relationship between capitalism and American political institutions in the American liberal tradition, while it facilitated the delegation of public powers to the corporate hierarchy.[68] Accordingly, if there is a dominant trend in the twentieth century it is not toward statism but toward a more comprehensive form of corporate domination.

Corporate power constitutes a form of class domination justified (and disguised) by the revised precepts of liberalism. The growth of corporate power, therefore, does not entail an abandonment of the principles of constitutional government, but arises on these very same principles, which have been employed to secure and extend the dominance of the corporate bourgeoisie. The structure of power in the United States in the era of corporate capitalism does not evince a slow and inexorable movement toward an authoritarian capitalist regime—a corporate state—but an accelerating movement toward a systematic and pervasive form of class domination consistent with the displacement of democratic by oligarchic rule throughout society, a development that increasingly takes on an international character with the rise of transnational enterprise. A corporate order structured in accordance with the principles of liberalism should not be confused with a corporate state, just as the declining significance of democracy as a form of political rule should not be confused with the viability of liberalism as the ruling ideology of corporate capitalism.

The intersecting of public (governmental) and private (economic) functions within the framework of constitutional government facilitates corporate domination, not statism. This applies, moreover, to instances in which the integration has become institutionalized within an existing bureaucracy, as is the case with the defense industries and the Department of Defense. In *Pentagon Capitalism*, Seymour Melman described this arrangement as a form of state capitalism in which the Secretary of Defense, as the CEO of the "state-management," manages the largest corporation in America (the syndicate of companies that comprise the defense industries), which is capitalized annually at the taxpayers' expense. Rather than ensuring civilian control, Melman argued, the state-management principle has effected a convergence between political, economic, and military elites within the Defense Department.[69] Although Melman emphasized that the final authority to grant contracts lies with political officials, it is clear that the noncompetitive structure of the defense industry, combined with the fact that the corporations determine the state of military technology, normally tilts the bargaining process decisively in favor of the companies. Hence, the case can be made that corporate power is the determinative element in this military-industrial merger. Pentagon capitalism has often fueled the growth of wasteful military expenditures, invited corruption, enhanced the national debt beyond manageable proportions, exalted military priorities over social needs, and posed a clear threat to civilian control of national defense. But it has not nurtured the rise of a corporate state. It makes corporate executives out of former generals, not warlords out of corporate chieftans.

Pentagon capitalism is a species of a long-standing tradition in American government of granting monopoly power, special privileges, subsidies, and legal immunities to corporations that perform a public function deemed to be indispensable to the national welfare or interest. Such favored treatment has repeatedly been attacked throughout American history as being inconsistent with democratic values. While Pentagon capitalism does not accord with the republican principle of civilian control of the military, or with the concept of constitutional checks and balances, it is consistent with the privileged position of business in American society, including corporate influence or control over government institutions, which is also part of the political tradition of the United States. To question the legitimacy of corporate power in the Pentagon, therefore, is also to question the legitimacy of all manifestations of corporate rule in government.

Once freed from the imperious logic of economic determinism, class analysis can examine power relationships on their own terms. In the decades to come, one can expect that corporate power, as a socially comprehensive force, will be exercised with broad social objectives in mind, objectives that have traditionally been associated with the political governance of nations and empires, objectives that transcend mere economic interest. Indeed, the resolve of the business community to rule in an open, if not aggressive, fashion has grown in recent years. Corporate power in the twentieth century brought with it an outlook shaped by a period of prolonged social strife and economic crisis. To achieve stability, corporate power aspired to a cooperative ethic in the marketplace, in the workplace, and in politics. The decline of the captains of industry and finance, and the rise of the corporate statesman, signaled the consolidation of a new order in which, increasingly, the responsibilities of power replaced the unconstrained (socially destructive) pursuit of self-interest. This was both an ethical and ideological choice, and a practical accommodation to the reconstructed marketplace. It was not the only choice, though perhaps it was the most consistent with the American creed of individualism, which in retaining its ideological preeminence necessitated a reformulation of the concept of equality of opportunity. This is not to discount the significance of greed in human behavior, or the primacy of profit-making for capitalist enterprise, but power, if it is to endure, cannot long avoid the issue of legitimacy.

Today's corporate leaders are better organized for direct political action than their predecessors. They fully comprehend the challenge of legitimacy and more. They have responded in force to the clarion call sounded by Lewis F. Powell Jr. (shortly before becoming Justice Powell) in his 1971 "Memorandum" to the Chamber of Commerce. Describing the "massive assault upon its philosophy, upon its right to continue to manage its own affairs," he concluded that "business and the enterprise system are in deep trouble and the hour is late." If the hour were to be saved, business leaders would have to join the battle, in politics and in the courts. "Political power," he advised, "must be assiduously cultivated and, when necessary, it must be used aggressively and with determination."[70] With the aid of Supreme Court rulings shortly thereafter, in accordance with Justice Powell's majority opinions, the corporate citizen and statesman have been afforded new rights and prerogatives. To understand the power wielded by the rulers of the modern corporation, as Berle clearly foresaw, one must delve into the history of political thought. But in the present era of corporate political activity, we must supplement our reading list. In the years to come, we will need a working knowledge of Machiavelli's *The Prince* as well as Saint Augustine's *City of God*.

5. CONCLUSION

The analytical framework I have outlined conceptualizes the internal and external dimensions of corporate power in terms of relationships of control rooted in the law. It compels a rethinking of the traditional notion that economic and political power are distinct phenomena that occupy separate realms of social existence. Indeed, it rejects this formulation for a unified conception of power: "the power basis of class." The idea that class relationships constitute relationships of control provides us with an analytical construct that can explain the organization and scope of corporate power in a manner that is consistent with the historical development of corporate capitalism and with the reality of domination in the modern era. Moreover, a class analysis that can comprehend corporate power satisfies the need for a transdisciplinary approach, and hence for the requisites of a political theory of the corporation.

The plodding of political thought toward a theory of corporate power in this century has been a Sisyphean task. Theoretical insights stimulate a brief advance in empirical research, only to fall back on old assumptions, to return to the same starting point, to embrace, in Walter Weyl's felicitous phrase, those "ancient political ideas which still cumber our modern brains." The failure of most social scientists to break new theoretical ground becomes an issue perhaps only when one steps outside the current orthodoxies and disciplinary boundaries. From this vantage point, the need for transdisciplinary approaches becomes apparent. The yawning gap between the empirically documented reality and the conventional theories that attempt to explain it suggests the imperative need for a reintegration of knowledge of society and, with this, the elimination of analytical distinctions and logical categories born of ideological doctrine and artificial (academic) divisions of social existence.

These problems become all the more apparent in the realm of international affairs. Because the challenges posed by the study of corporate power extend beyond national boundaries, a political theory of the corporation must also be able to comprehend transnational corporate power. Both Marxist and institutional approaches employ a deficient conception of power that cannot fully explain either the essential political nature and organization of corporate rule or the role of law in structuring relationships of control. Institutional approaches divide up reality for the sake of alleged analytical clarity. In doing so, they divide up the domain of corporate power. It is as though one attempted to decipher the mechanical principles of an automobile by removing its wheels and lifting its engine, and then inventing a theory of wheels and a theory of engines. One could undoubtedly make many valid observations about the properties of wheels and of engines, but by themselves these findings would not be sufficient to explain the principles of locomotion.

Traditional Marxist class-analytic theory, on the other hand, has reached a point of crisis. It is ironic that this fact has become painfully clear by the inability of Marxist theoreticians to explain (without undermining the integrity of the postulates of class determination) the empirical reality of corporate power documented in studies of non-Marxist scholars, especially the evidence amassed by the liberal managerial theorists and students of elite analysis. It is a crisis of pandemic proportions. Theories of modern imperialism, like their counterparts that flounder on the issue of the state, resort to logical (structuralist or systemic) explanations of domination that fail to account for the empirical reality of class formations and corporate power in industrializing nations.[71] So it is that in the reconstructed world of corporate capitalism the mysteries of corporate power continue to defy the intellectual presumptions of an earlier era.

The study of transnational corporate power leads unavoidably beyond the present and into the realm of prediction. In looking into the future of corporate capitalism, however, we must first understand its past. And we cannot begin to fathom the past without a theory that explains the interrelationship between liberalism, class, and corporate power. A class analysis that can comprehend corporate power in America will provide us with the analytical tool for beginning our journey into the global universe of the transnational corporation.

Chapter 7

LOOKING BACKWARD TO THE FUTURE OF TRANSNATIONAL CORPORATE POWER

Now I have described to you as truthfully as I could the structure of this commonwealth, which I think the best, and indeed the only one which can rightfully be called by that name. In other places where they speak of the common good, every man is looking out for his own good. But in Utopia where there is no private property and where they zealously pursue the public business, there the name commonwealth is doubly deserved. Elsewhere, even though the state is prosperous, most men know that they may die of hunger if they do not look out for themselves, and so they are forced to take care of themselves rather than other people. In Utopia where everything belongs to everybody, they know that if the public warehouses and granaries are full, no one will lack anything for his personal use.

—Sir Thomas More, 1516

1. TRANSNATIONAL ENTERPRISE IN THE ERA OF POSTIMPERIALISM

Contemplating the future of nations in 1917, Walter Weyl theorized about the international development of corporate capitalism. Noting the increasing internationalization of corporate capital and the continuing trend toward market domination by large corporations domestically and (by extrapolation) internationally, Weyl envisioned the organization of transnational enterprise:

> We may seek to understand this eventual international evolution of business by visualizing a world organization of the steel industry. Either one corporation might be formed or a common control

might be established among national steel companies through an interchange of stock. . . . Such a world corporation would be a financial aggregation immensely greater than any in the past. . . . In each country a board of directors would hold control over constituent companies, and at London, Paris or New York a high Federal Council would settle controversies and make arrangements for the business of the world. Each company would have two elements of protection against unfair treatment: a community of interest secured through an interchange of stock and a representative on the Federal Council.[1]

While such an eventuality was "in advance of the psychological preparation of the world," Weyl maintained that it was entirely consistent with the direction of international capitalism. Indeed, he observed that "the machinery for an international combination of capital is already present" and that "further progress waits only upon the removal of barriers, in part traditional." These barriers, which had been erected by nations to protect their economic interests, were the root causes of international tensions and war, according to the author. Once removed, however, economic cooperation would eventually create a situation in which "the interest of each nation in the welfare of its neighbors would become so great as to make international war as unthinkable as war of Pennsylvania against New York."[2]

Although somewhat visionary for his times, Weyl's predictions might easily be mistaken today for the matter-of-fact pronouncements of corporate executives or heads of state on the future of the world economy. The internationalization of capital has proceeded as Weyl expected, and while monopoly power has for the most part been constrained, oligopolistic control of domestic and international markets typifies business as usual. Thus, in place of a single "world corporation" for each industry—in effect, a global holding company—there are a handful of transnational giants within most major industries and the realm of finance. All that separates the present reality from Weyl's prognostications—and indeed this still strikes many as somewhat utopian—is the international regulation of corporate enterprise along the lines of a world government. It is perhaps not at all fortuitous that Weyl, one of the architects of the modern liberal justification of corporate power, would envision such a possibility. Writing with the conviction of one who has glimpsed the future in the unfolding logic of the present, he argued that the model for the development of international capitalism may be found in the ascendancy of corporate capitalism in the United States. Walter Weyl was the first student of corporate power to grasp the implications of the corporate-liberal solution of the Progressive Era for international relations in an interdependent world economy.

Transnational or multinational business corporations have existed since before the turn of the century,[3] yet only recently have they become a subject of intensive study and wide-ranging debate. The events that have given substance to Weyl's predictions, therefore, require some elaboration.

Direct foreign investment provides a useful standard for measuring the growth of transnational corporate enterprise in the twentieth century. The book value of direct foreign investment of American firms stood at $2.65 billion in 1914 and rose steadily to $11.8 billion by 1950. Between 1950 and 1971, however, it increased dramatically to $86 billion, and in 1974 it had reached $119 billion. From 1974 to 1984, the yearly average of direct foreign investment amounted to more than $11 billion, reaching a high of $25 billion in 1979.[4] The growth of direct foreign investment, though, does not fully convey the magnitude of the recent proliferation of transnational corporate enterprise within the world economy. To offer one example, the annual sales of the largest transnational corporations exceeds the gross national product of many countries. Using company sales and gross national product to rank the 100 largest entities in the world, a Library of Congress study compiled a list for the year 1970 in which companies (51) outnumbered countries (49). The largest corporation in the 100 entities, General Motors, ranked twenty-fourth. A similar study published by the Conference Board in 1978 revealed that GM had moved up a notch to twenty-third.[5] With 1993 sales of $133 billion, assets of $188 billion, and a global work force of 711,000 operating in 122 U.S. cities and 42 foreign countries, General Motors—producer of automobiles, jet and diesel engines, gas turbines, aerospace computers, telecommunications satellites, tanks, and missiles—is indeed a power to be reckoned with throughout the world. But it is not alone. GM is merely one of several extremely powerful companies that dominate global markets.

Foreign sales provide still another indication of the global economic significance of U.S. transnational enterprise. In 1993, the foreign revenue (as a percentage of total revenue) of the largest 50 U.S.-based transnationals (ranked according to volume of foreign sales) averaged 44.8 percent, while the foreign assets of these same companies averaged 36.5 percent of their total assets. In just six years, from 1987 to 1993, these percentages increased, respectively, by 11.8 percent and 6.5 percent. It is significant that 31 of the largest 100 U.S.-based multinationals in 1993 (compared with 14 in 1987), acquired more than 48 percent of their total revenues in foreign lands. These top 100 "American" transnationals, which constitute a "Who's Who" of the giants of industry and finance in the United States, are in reality global companies.[6]

But this is no longer an American phenomenon. Japanese and European transnational corporations have grown significantly in number and size in recent decades. Moreover, international mergers and joint ventures have contributed substantially to the integration of worldwide economic activities.[7] In order to prosper, if not survive, transnational corporations must gain access to expanding global markets. Because of this, the CEOs of these companies adapt to political realities. They aspire to be good corporate citizens in all the nations in which they operate, but in truth they have no country.

Yet, out of habit or convenience, or for lack of alternatives, we still identify multinational corporations by their legal domicile—a method of classification that has become increasingly arbitrary. Does it make sense, for example, to say that Exxon, Citicorp, Gillette, and Coca Cola, each of which conducts more than 60 percent of its business outside the United States, are more "American" than Toyota, Shell, Nestle, and Sony, each of which owns subsidiaries in the United States and has achieved a strong position in U.S. markets? Conventional perceptions of corporate enterprise still lag behind the reality of global capitalism, but this is not unusual in a period of rapid economic change. The growth of transnational corporations due to mergers and acquisitions, and the restructuring of markets that this entails, continue at a breathtaking pace. There is no doubt that we are witnessing a worldwide economic transformation that has profound social and political implications. That is widely acknowledged, but there is considerable disagreement about what this development portends for the future of nation-states.

To be sure, much of the controversy attending the proliferation of transnational enterprise concerns its long-term economic, social, and political consequences, some of which have become manifest and some of which remain speculative. The belief that global corporations pose a grave threat to the sovereignty of nation-states constitutes the basis of the nationalist reaction. This widespread trepidation has been articulated from a variety of standpoints. Labor union leaders in advanced capitalist countries such as the United States and Great Britain, for example, have expressed concern about the impact the transfer of production sites has on employment and collective bargaining. Protectionist reactions have also come from domestic producers in numerous countries. But in nations as diverse as Saudi Arabia and Canada, where transnational enterprise accounts for a substantial portion of domestic production, protectionism has less significance as a strategy. In such instances, governments have often sought to regulate the activities of foreign corporations with the hope of retaining some control over their own economies. However, for some leaders of developing countries and several radical critics, national integrity is only part of the issue. The belief that the growth of transnational enterprise represents the newest stage in the development of capitalist imperialism underlies their claim of economic, and therefore political, dominance by the capitalist powers. More important, regardless of official ideology, rulers of all industrializing nations must weigh the perceived social and political consequences of direct foreign investment against the uncertain promise that multinational corporations hold for economic advance and well-being. In such nations, the quest for autonomy is inextricably bound up with the problems of poverty, social inequality, and political strife.

In an effort to respond to these criticisms and volatile social issues, the defenders of the multinational corporation have constructed an ideological justification. This global vision, which can be culled from the writings of several individuals, contains a distinctive rationale for the spread of transnational corporate enterprise as well as a prophecy concerning its economic and political consequences. The tenets of this ideological position, formulated in the 1960s and 1970s, appear to have greatly influenced many of the objectives of recent free trade policies, initiatives, and agreements affecting the United States, Canada, the European Community, Mexico, and numerous other countries. I shall first reconstruct this justification and then assess its significance for liberal ideology and its practical import for the growth of corporate power.[8]

I argue that modern Free Trade ideology serves to justify the rise of transnational corporate power and endeavors to secure the consolidation of that power through corporate-liberal methods. My analysis supports the postimperialist theory of international class formation set forth by Richard L. Sklar: that the internationalization of corporate capital through direct foreign investment, combined with the steady proliferation of transnational enterprise in recent decades, heralds the rise of a transnational bourgeoisie. In stating the case for transnational class formation engendered by the emergence of a corporate international bourgeoisie, Sklar concludes: "Corporate internationalism is a social movement and a rising class interest." Moreover, as transnational corporations continue to multiply, "power in world affairs comes to be organized in accordance with class rather than national interests and values." This development, he argues, signals the eclipse of the era of capitalist imperialism by the new stage of corporate international capitalism in the era of postimperialism.[9] Viewed in light of Sklar's analysis, the affinities that modern Free Trade ideology shares with corporate liberalism and with classical laissez-faire doctrine can be understood in their proper contexts. A considerable portion of my analysis will therefore be devoted to examining the ideological significance of corporate internationalism both as a social movement and as a rising class interest.

My broader thesis is that the corporate reconstruction of the world political economy in the late twentieth century, including the restructuring of markets through corporate combination and government regulation, appear to be modeled on the corporate transformation of North American society in the early-to-mid-twentieth century. This observation has significance for assessing the interrelationship between corporate power, ideology, and the law in national and transnational settings. To fully understand the ideological justification of transnational enterprise and its political implications, a historically based theory of corporate power in the United States becomes essential.

2. THE MODERN DOCTRINE OF FREE TRADE

Although the corporate ideologists and their allies in academia have cited numerous reasons for the recent growth of transnational enterprise, they all share certain fundamental assumptions. To begin with, they maintain that the proliferation of global corporations represents a response to the needs of an emergent world economy. Although transnational corporations have clearly facilitated the growth of this market, they are viewed more as a conduit than as an agent of change. David Rockefeller, formerly Chairman of Chase Manhattan Bank and more recently Chairman on the bank's International Advisory Committee, has written that "economic growth must follow its own laws," which require "the greatest degree of freedom for individuals and institutions." "It is this very freedom to move and grow," he observed, "that has fed the mushrooming of multinational enterprise."[10] In a similar fashion, George Ball, former Chairman of Lehman Brothers International, who served as an Under Secretary of State and U.S. Ambassador to the United Nations, argued that global economic survival requires that the world's resources be employed in "the most efficient manner," and that this can be accomplished "only when all the factors necessary for the production of goods . . . are freely mobilized and deployed according to the most efficient pattern." Multinational corporations have responded to this need, he explained, by "moving to recast their plans and design their activities according to the vision of a total world economy."[11] Peter Drucker, discussing the transformation from an international to a truly global economy, came to a similar conclusion. He viewed the growth of transnational business as increasingly a response to "the need to plan, organize, and manage on a scale appropriate to the magnitude of technical and managerial resources required for modern technology, economical operations, low-cost production, and mass distribution."[12]

A second assumption shared by the liberal defenders of transnational enterprise concerns the impact of technological advances in communications and transportation on the development of a world market. Liberal managerial theory holds that modern technology has shaped the very organization and operations of the large corporation. Moreover, the concept of the corporation as an autonomous institution subject to impersonal forces or laws rests in large part on this belief. A similar logic has been applied to the transnational corporation as the institutional unit of an interdependent world economy. According to this argument, both the daily operations of transnational enterprise and the global structure of the corporation depend on new technologies in communications and transportation. In Drucker's view, for example, these technological advances have created a "global shopping center" that in turn has established a new global community.[13] Because the operations of the multinationals are global in scope, the perspective of their managers must be global too. Drucker's view typifies the managerial justification of transnational enterprise in the sense that he emphasizes technological imperatives, as opposed to the quest for profit, in accounting for the growth of a world market. Profitability remains the underlying standard for efficiency, the objective arbiter of global economic behavior. But in keeping with liberal managerial theory, the economic factor deemed most responsible for the growth of the world economy is technological advance, rather than the expansionist tendencies of capitalist enterprise.[14]

Writing in 1954, in the early stages of the recent proliferation of global corporations, Adolph Berle observed:

> The twentieth-century revolution is steadily, ineluctably, breaking up the classic organization of international relations. It is imposing a new organization of affairs whose nature and outlines we can only dimly apprehend. . . . The economic life of the civilized world, and the standard of living demanded by peoples of twentieth-century nation states is not being maintained, and apparently cannot be maintained, within the sovereign-state framework.[15]

The facts that the "political framework of foreign affairs is nationalist" and that the "economic base is not" suggested to Berle that the "classic nation-state is no longer capable by itself alone, either to feed and clothe its people, or to defend its borders."[16] With this observation, Berle articulated a fundamental premise of the liberal justification of the corporation in world affairs—that the emergence of transnational enterprise heralds the development of a true world economy, and with it the demise of the nation-state as an autonomous economic unit.

More recently, George Ball has stated the case for the "withering away" of the nation-state in view of the steady growth of the world economy. While the nation-state, according to Ball, is "rooted in archaic concepts unsympathetic to the needs of our complex world," the multinational corporation "is a modern concept designed to meet the requirements of a modern age."[17] This "lack of phasing between . . . archaic political and modern business structures," he maintained, constitutes the central challenge to global enterprise in its quest to build a genuine world economy.[18] If allowed to flourish, multinational corporations "will have a long-term effect in bringing about the gradual erosion of the nation-state as an economic unit."[19] Yet the promise of transnational enterprise, in his view, holds forth much more than the transcendence of the "narrow and constrictive" boundaries of nation-states. For Ball, as well as for others, the transnational corporation promises a new era of global cooperation, greater individual freedom, and increasing prosperity and opportunity for all peoples of the world. In order to understand the ideological basis of the new globalism and all that it portends for the future, however, we must first delve backward into the lore of capitalism and consult the logic of laissez-faire liberalism.

The classical doctrine of laissez-faire holds that market forces, if allowed free rein, not only determine economic behavior but produce social and political harmony as well. Competition in the marketplace creates bonds of self-interest. A common interest in pecuniary gain induces social and political cooperation within, and ultimately between, nations. The belief that the logic of the market contains the solution to international peace and prosperity inspired the early advocates of the Free Trade movement in nineteenth-century Britain. Richard Cobden, a founder of the Anti–Corn Law League and passionate advocate of the internationalist ideal, wrote in 1844 that "Free Trade by perfecting the intercourse and securing the dependence of countries one upon another must inevitably snatch the power from the governments to plunge their peoples into wars."[20] However, Cobden did not view Free Trade as a justification for British imperialism—quite the contrary. Unlike those who would later invoke this doctrine to justify empire, Cobden counseled nonintervention in foreign affairs.[21] As one author observed, Richard Cobden believed that "the interests of the individual, the interests of the nation, and the interests of all nations are identical," and that all these interests are "in entire and necessary concordance with the highest interests of morality."[22]

The liberal defense of transnational corporate enterprise clearly borrows the logic of the nineteenth-century doctrine of Free Trade. Economist Neil Jacoby, for example, argued that the multinational corporation is "fundamentally an instrument of peace" whose "interest is to emphasize the common goals of peoples, to reconcile or remove differences between them."[23] In a similar vein, A. W. Clausen, CEO of the Bank of America and former President of the World Bank, observed that the emergence of the global corporation offers "perhaps the last real chance to build a world that is less coercive than that offered by the nation-state."[24] To Drucker, a world economy based on multinational enterprise provides "a great opportunity . . . for creating a focus of unity in a fragmented and strife-torn world."[25] George Ball similarly claimed that the spread of global corporations "brings about . . . a cross fertilization of ideas and cultures that can be an important element in reconciling the diverse peoples of the world."[26] Courtney C. Brown, former dean of the Columbia School of Business and a director on the boards of numerous corporations, joined the chorus: "The role of business in promoting world peace is properly connected with the idea of trade. In expanding his markets, the trader necessarily forges ties of mutual respect, understanding and support."[27] For these Corporate Cobdenites, then, the growth of corporate enterprise within an interdependent world economy holds forth the promise of global peace. For a world divided by nationalist, class, religious, and racial animosities, they offer the panacea of enlightened self-interest.

The ideologists of transnational enterprise have argued that a true world economy promises to close the gap between rich and poor nations by unleashing the productive potential of all peoples. To accomplish this, less-developed countries must be fully integrated into the emergent global economy. Indeed, this is "the one real hope for most of the developing countries," according to Drucker.[28] Far from creating a condition of economic and therefore political dependence—a new form of capitalist imperialism—transnational corporations bring with them the forces of economic liberation. Courtney C. Brown concluded that multinational enterprise promises to become "a major vehicle to carry the have-nots toward 'take-off' and the haves into frontier fields." In serving this end, global enterprise becomes "an unmatched force for peace."[29] David Rockefeller observed that multinational corporations "have broadened the scope of opportunity, both for individuals and for nations, through the transfer of technology and through training in management skills."

Multinationals, therefore, should be viewed as agents of freedom rather than as instruments of tyranny. In fact, it is the opponents of the global corporation, Rockefeller argued, who "are arraying themselves in opposition to freedom."[30]

In the tradition of corporate-liberal reform, the Corporate Cobdenites have proposed various measures to strengthen transnational enterprise and to hasten the growth of an interdependent world economy. The modern advocates of Free Trade, much like their ideological parents, believe that domestic economic regulations and protectionist policies pose the most formidable threat to international economic cooperation. Accordingly, they have strongly urged reforms that would either unify the economic policies of nations or at least allow transnational enterprise greater freedom. Neil Jacoby, for example, has called for international cooperation on policies affecting corporate taxation, competition, and international trade. He has suggested that a "World Corporation Authority" be established by the United Nations to provide uniform charters and regulation for transnational corporations.[31] A. W. Clausen argued, in a similar vein, that the ultimate solution to the economic conflicts between companies and countries lies in "the development of the supranational corporation which will not owe its charter to any state."[32] Thus it would seem that one way to hasten the demise of the nation-state is to transcend it.

Clearly, it is the concept of supranational regulation which seems to have most captured the imaginations of the liberal defenders of transnational enterprise. Ball, for example, has written that the remedy to the present dilemma must be sought in "denationalizing the parent," rather than in "nationalizing local subsidiaries." To accomplish this, he urged the adoption of an "international companies law," which would be established by treaty and administered by a supranational body. This body, he explained, would have a multinational membership and "would not only exercise normal domiciliary supervision but would also enforce antimonopoly laws and administer guarantees with regard to uncompensated expropriation." He suggested that an international companies law might also limit the types of restrictions nation-states could impose on transnational corporations. The "operative standard" for determining these limitations, moreover, "might be the quantity of freedom needed to preserve the central principle of assuring the most economical and efficient use of world resources."[33] Because Ball measured efficiency by profitability, one can deduce that the operative standard would be principally concerned with the level of corporate profits.

Thus, the liberal ideologists envision a world of increasing prosperity and freedom, a world in which common economic concerns foster cooperation and ultimately peace among nations. And it is a world that has been remade through the magic of the market. "Today," Rockefeller observed, "broad human interests are being served best in economic terms where free market forces are able to transcend national boundaries."[34] Jacoby went so far as to assert that the multinational corporation was "leading Europe toward a more egalitarian, homogeneous, and democratic kind of society."[35] The visionaries of global peace, furthermore, stand as one in their prediction that as the forces of economic change spread, the ownership and control of corporate enterprise will become truly multinational. In a world without borders, corporate management will take on an international character.

These, then, constitute the principal claims of the modern Free Trade ideology—the liberal justification of transnational corporate power. Whether one regards this doctrine with skepticism or believes in the coming millennium, the historical significance of liberalism as the ideology of capitalism suggests that the visions of the Corporate Cobdenites must be assessed in light of the issue of power. It is to this matter that we now turn.

3. THE CORPORATE RECONSTRUCTION OF THE GLOBAL POLITICAL ECONOMY

On its face, the ideological justification of transnational corporate power appears to involve a rather straightforward adaptation of the nineteenth-century Free Trade doctrine to modern world conditions. As we have seen, the corporate internationalists owe a considerable ideological debt to Cobden and the early proponents of Free Trade—and for that matter to the political economy of Adam Smith and other liberals, such as Herbert Spencer, who saw in the increasing division of labor a panacea for nationalism and war. To view transnational corporate ideology as a simple reversion to the principles of classical laissez-faire, however, may well miss the point. After all, the practical implications of this justification lie in the tradition of progressive liberal reform, not to be confused with the modern doctrinaire laissez-faire associated with a certain brand of so-called conservatism. I shall argue that, laissez-faire homilies aside, the ideological justification of transnational corporate power represents an adaptation of corporate-liberal concepts and methods to the developing world economy. On the other hand, the striking similarities between the old and the new laissez-faire are not without significance. A comparison of these doctrines in light of their specific historical contexts will also provide insight into the social and political implications of Free Trade ideology in the era of postimperialism.

Liberal justifications of corporate power in the twentieth century all share the premise that the corporate transformation of the American capitalist economy constitutes a progressive, if not revolutionary, development. From a strictly economic standpoint, the large corporation is viewed as an agent of unparalleled prosperity. For the liberal managerial theorists, moreover, the corporation, as an autonomous entity, constitutes the institutional foundation of modern "industrial society," a social order that is neither capitalist nor socialist in the traditional sense and that is international in its scope. As conceived by these thinkers, it is a society in which objective laws and modern technology determine the very organization and operations of corporate enterprise. The liberal justification of corporate power also contains a conception of society as an interrelated whole within which social balance or harmony is maintained through a functional separation of the governmental and economic realms. In applying these same concepts to the international sphere, the Corporate Cobdenites have adapted the basic tenets of the liberal justification of corporate power to the global regime of transnational enterprise.

Through the ideological spectacles of the corporate internationalists, one can behold a future world order that mirrors the organization and needs of the global corporation. It is, quite literally, a corporatist world view, a vision of an interdependent global corporate society organized in accordance with the imperatives of modern technology and global planning. Yet, the corporate visionaries caution, this vision will not become a reality unless the autonomy of transnational enterprise can be ensured. Corporate autonomy in the international sphere therefore necessitates the development of a supranational corporation and hence, independence of corporate decision-making from individual nation-states (a process that may be likened to the realization of corporate autonomy within the American federal system, which occurred without the aid of national incorporation). By attaining global autonomy, the transnational corporation reproduces the ideological distinction between state and society on an international scale. In the best tradition of Adam Smith, nation-states represent the sphere of coercive power, whereas the laws of the market promise prosperity, freedom, and global harmony. According to this logic, moreover, there appears to be no such thing as transnational corporate power.

The question therefore arises whether the exponents of corporate internationalism have constructed an ideological double standard for national and transnational corporate power. To a certain extent this would appear to be the case.[36] A close reading of the claims and proposals of the ideologists of the multinational corporation, however, reveals that the apparent double standard may be less of a difference in kind than a matter of degree or emphasis. George Ball, for example, has argued that conflicts between multinationals and foreign governments give rise to "the central question of legitimacy of power."[37] The problem of transnational corporate power, as he conceived it, stems from the conflicting claims made against corporations by parent and foreign countries. In fact, the various proposals for establishment of an agency or law to regulate transnational enterprise aim to resolve power struggles not only between nations but also between corporations and countries. Furthermore, while the Corporate Cobdenites preach the virtues of Free Trade, they also advise that multinational corporations should behave like "good citizens" while domiciled in a foreign country—a suggestion that implicitly recognizes the importance of corporate social responsibility. Richard L. Sklar has analyzed this aspect of transnational corporate ideology in terms of the "doctrine of domicile," which refers to the practice whereby "individual subsidiaries of an international business group may operate in accordance with the requirements of divergent and conflicting policies pursued by the governments of their respective host states," with the ultimate objective of promoting "the interests of the enterprise as a whole." Thus the doctrine of domicile, the ideological practice of corporate citizenship, "justifies transnational corporate expansion while it also legitimizes large-scale foreign investments in the eyes of the host country."[38]

Despite the laissez-faire rhetoric, the methods and objectives of the modern Free Trade ideology—centralization of government power to effect reform, uniform economic regulation, efficiency (defined in terms of profitability) as the guiding standard of reform, and recognition of corporate social responsibility—are consistent with the methods and goals of corporate liberalism as it developed in the Progressive Era and later. Understood in this light, Walter Weyl's predictions do not seem utopian at all. Several other thinkers have since drawn parallels between the American experience and the future development of the world economy, but few have fully grasped the political implications of this development. By applying the logic of the corporate reconstruction of American capitalism to the international arena, Weyl envisioned the consolidation of transnational corporate power.

On the other hand, it would be a mistake to dismiss the Free Trade doctrine as mere ideological window-dressing. We must keep in mind that in addition to justifying interests, ideology also provides an index of social change. It is significant for the present analysis that laissez-faire liberalism developed as a justification for a rising capitalist class. Within their historical context, the tenets of classical liberalism constituted an assault on the economic, social, and political institutions of feudal society. At its inception, liberalism contained a vision of a new order as well as a practical justification. In the United States, the strictures of laissez-faire justified the rise of the corporate bourgeoisie just as it facilitated the demise of state-centered mercantilism. Although revised in this century to accommodate the exigencies of corporate capitalism, the original vision remained at the core of the corporate-liberal world view. It is a vision, a promise, of progress and social harmony through prosperity, of individual freedom and equality of opportunity for all members of society. It is also an ideological doctrine, developed under specific historical circumstances and fashioned to promote particular class interests and objectives, that seeks to universalize its claims by appealing to all classes.

Certain conclusions can be drawn from the preceding analysis. Liberalism has always justified class interests, and consequently, relationships of power. Moreover, the universal claims of liberal ideology, combined with its historical aversion to the idea of power in the marketplace, have effectively obscured its political significance as a dominant ideology. In the modern era, this justification finds its most potent expression in the doctrine of corporate individualism and the "objective laws of industrial society." When the ideological justification of transnational enterprise is viewed in light of these factors, the affinities that it shares with corporate liberalism and classical laissez-faire doctrine may be placed in proper perspective. Just as the rising corporate bourgeoisie in the United States invoked the strictures of classical political economy to justify the growth of enterprise and to defeat or alter government policies that interfered with corporate expansion, so do the Corporate Cobdenites recite the blessings of the market for international peace and prosperity in their battle with the forces of autarky and nationalism. And just as the corporate bourgeoisie, in conjunction with other social forces, justified the economic, legal, and political reconstruction of American society within the precepts of corporate liberalism, so does the corporate international bourgeoisie seek to alter the policies of, and transform the relationships between, nation-states in accordance with corporate-liberal methods of reform and good citizenship, as practiced under the doctrine of domicile. In the liberal tradition, the rising bourgeoisie must define the market as the realm of freedom, apart from the coercive realm of government or the state, so that it might accomplish its objective of restructuring relationships of control through the transformation of the law and the reconstitution of political rule. Thus, behind the idealism and utopian visions of the corporate internationalists lies the reality of control. And, as in the past, class interests are expressed in universal appeals while ideological doctrine accommodates social and political exigencies.

Historical parallels are often interesting but more often misleading. In the present case, however, something can be learned from a comparison between the growth of corporate power in the era of corporate capitalism, and the emergence of transnational corporate power in the dawning of international capitalism. Contrary to the ideological doctrine of the managerial theorists, corporate capitalism, which is to say "industrial society," did not evolve "naturally" or inevitably from autonomous and inexorable laws of technology or organization. To the contrary, corporate capitalism in America was constructed by human beings. It was the product of policy-making, politicking, legislating, adjudicating, infighting, and just fighting. In some cases it involved repression, but ultimately it involved compromise through transformation of the law, engendered by the struggles and accommodations of social forces. In order to demystify the origins of corporate capitalism, we must, as Martin J. Sklar has argued, conceive it as a "social movement": "Both capitalist industrialism and its corporate reorganization . . . are better understood not simply as an 'external force' or an 'objective' economic or organizational phenomenon but as a social movement, no less than populism, trade unionism, feminism, Afro-American equalitarianism, or socialism."[39] Indeed, it is in this precise sense that corporate internationalism as "a social movement and a rising class interest" must also be conceptualized.

Courtney C. Brown has stated the call to arms of this capitalist movement eloquently:

> There is now an urgent need for a vast creative effort in the affairs of mankind. To the surprise of many, and the satisfaction of some, political efforts by themselves have proved insufficiently creative, and in many instances misdirected. Mankind's insistence on action and its impatience with conventional political nostrums combine to provide the setting in which business organizations and their farflung activities have been brought to the center of interest on the global stage. In the afternoon of the 20th century, the people of the world are awakening to the realization that they must look to the day-to-day, no-nonsense activities of practical men of affairs to help achieve release from grinding drudgery.[40]

One need not look far for evidence that this call has been heeded. The Supreme Court has invoked the doctrine of corporate individualism to expand the political rights of corporations, to open the doors wide (or wider) to corporate political activity and influence in electoral and congressional politics. Corporate leaders have been quick to take advantage of their newfound freedoms. They have drawn up an agenda of reform that has shaped government policy on the issues of free trade and the revision of international agreements to spur the global integration of markets.[41] In newspaper editorials and advertisements, over radio, and on television, a concerted effort to shape public opinion consistent with these objectives has been building for more than two decades. While the corporate citizen argues its case and participates actively in the political arena, it thrives in the market. The merger movement continues apace with the blessings of the Department of Justice.[42] The resurgence of corporate individualism harks back as it looks forward. Indeed, it makes for a nice ideological fit with the laissez-faire premises of the Corporate Cobdenites. In the highest councils of government, in the halls of justice, and on the floors of Congress, the signs of a pervasive corporate influence have become apparent.

Looking backward, one can also draw a parallel between the merger movement of today and that at the turn of the century. Just as the first great merger wave involved a restructuring of markets that ushered in the era of corporate capitalism, so does the present wave appear to entail a restructuring of markets, albeit by a different method and on a global scale. The current trend in the merger movement suggests the emergence of an industrial-financial oligarchy controlling the entrenched oligopolies—that is, an oligarchy of oligopolists, a structure consistent with a transnational reorganization of markets on the model of corporate capitalism.[43] Whatever the impact of the merger movement for the structure of world markets, the internationalization of corporate capital already has secured the dominance of large firms within the global economy. Samuel Huntington's observation is to the point:

> Today's issues, arguments, and slogans neatly replicate those of a century ago between the "trusts" and the state governments. The feelings of powerlessness which the state legislatures in Illinois and Minnesota felt in their dealings with the New York Central and Great Northern railroads are duplicated today in the unease which national government leaders in Latin America, Asia, and even Europe feel in their dealings with IBM, Ford, or Unilever.[44]

With the rise of transnational corporate power, the doctrine of corporate individualism takes on a global significance. The entrepreneur, resurrected in classical fashion, joins the citizen and statesman in the quest for world markets and international peace. Corporate internationalism combines the personas of the corporate individual to justify the rise of transnational corporate power through the doctrine of Free Trade and to secure the consolidation of that power through corporate-liberal methods. As in the closing decades of the nineteenth century, the corporate reconstruction of markets establishes a condition in which the law lags behind the forces of capitalist development. Just as the states' regulation of enterprise through the corporate charter fettered the growth of corporate power in the United States before the state incorporation laws were transformed, now national regulation of the corporation constrains the global consolidation of corporate power. In the tradition of corporate-liberal reform, the Corporate Cobdenites apply the logic of the corporate reconstruction of American society to international relations and the world market. Adoption of an international companies act or of a supranational corporate charter, or establishment of a World Corporation Authority, would secure global regulation of, and hence an expanding autonomy within, the external and internal dimensions of corporate power by substantially freeing transnational enterprise from national regulation. It would be nothing less than a restructuring of relationships of control through the law on an international scale, thereby legitimating the dominant position of the international corporate bourgeoisie.

Indeed, a significant step in this direction has already been taken with the approval by the European Community (EC) of a "one-stop" merger control regulation, ostensibly an effort to establish global antitrust coordination.[45] Another measure proposed by the EC Commission—the European Company Statute—would create special structures independent of national legal systems for companies that incorporate under EC laws.[46] Consistent with achieving a similar uniformity of regulation while encouraging foreign direct investment, the North American Free Trade Agreement (NAFTA) between the United States, Canada, and Mexico eliminates a variety of protectionist measures, the most significant being the phasing-out of all tariffs over a fifteen-year period.[47]

If the corporate internationalists succeed in their mission and the economic and political integration of the capitalist world proceeds as planned, corporate power indeed will have achieved its apogee. Although perhaps in advance of the current world order, there is nothing illogical about the prospect of a federation of nations linked by common economic interests, bound by international laws, and subject to the power of a transnational bourgeoisie—an international oligarchy commanding the major industrial and financial global corporations. At present, the liberal justification of corporate internationalism serves the very real and immediate purpose of defending the dominance of the ascendant transnational class within global markets. If we can consult the past to predict the future, we can expect this ideological defense to become increasingly sophisticated as it gains a wider audience. Assuming the continued prosperity and growth of multinational corporations, we may also anticipate that liberal managerial theory will be adapted to the international arena in order to justify the transnational consolidation of corporate power.

4. LOOKING BACKWARD TO THE FUTURE

In 1888, Edward Bellamy wrote a novel titled *Looking Backward*. Few books have so stirred the imaginations of Americans before or since. Along with *Ben Hur* and *Uncle Tom's Cabin*, Bellamy's work was the most widely read of its time. Soon "Bellamy Clubs" were formed throughout the United States as the insurgent Populist movement of the 1890s gained momentum. But why the excitement? *Looking Backward* was really about looking forward as told from the perspective of a man mysteriously transported from 1887 to the year 2000. It defined the essence of utopian thinking—a society conjured up from the hopes of the present and the values of a romantic past, an innocence lost, and transplanted in the future, in a world of peace, prosperity, happiness, and equality. Progressive in its spirit, *Looking Backward* nonetheless shares with all utopian thought the ideological quality of being backward-looking. Bellamy's vision foretold the natural evolution of corporate capitalism into state socialism, "The Great Trust," which, by the year 2000, and without the aid of a proletarian revolution or capitalist repression, had forged a life of peace and plenty out of the strife and hunger that racked America in the dawn of this new era. Universal equality had supplanted class society, while the liberty to choose one's own calling in accordance with one's aptitude had become a basic principle of social organization.

Under the regime of socialism, as we have known it in various countries, Edward Bellamy's utopian vision has succumbed to the harsh realities of power. Only in a perverse way, in an ideological form that sanctions domination, does his vision live on. But there are still visionaries among us, albeit of a different faith. Now, with the year 2000 quickly approaching, we bear witness to the emergence of the "Great Trust," but not, alas, in the form that Bellamy had envisioned. For Bellamy, it would be a cruel irony indeed to learn that the present-day successors of the corporate rulers with whom he took issue would be the heralds of Utopia—not for one country, but for the world.

In the era of transnational enterprise, Utopia has taken the capitalist road. The "Great Trust" of the future is in our midst, but it does not aspire to a communal ethic. Although its caretakers do not promise the egalitarian Eden of utopian socialism, they do paint a glimmering picture of peace through prosperity. After the fashion of Adam Smith, Richard Cobden, and Herbert Spencer, the new utopians extol the social virtues of capitalism. In the tradition of corporate-liberal reform, they promote the spread of transnational class domination. But there is nothing inevitable about the outcome of this international social movement. In a world racked by nationalism, racism, zealotry, war, and poverty—that is, the real world in which utopia exists only in our imaginations—people, not impersonal forces, will decide the fate of humanity. Clearly, this fact has not been lost on the corporate vanguard of the twentieth-century capitalist revolution. As the Corporate Cobdenites invoke the magic of the market to disguise the reality of control, the corporate reconstruction of the world political economy forges ahead. Transnational enterprise continues to produce economic, social, and political transformations that shape the dimensions of power in modern societies. To be sure, signs of a new era of Free Trade have become manifest as the expansionist tendencies of corporate capitalism accelerate the integration of global markets.

For the present, it remains a matter of some debate whether the revised doctrine of Free Trade, like the original, will become an apologia for empire. But this much is certain. Should it come to pass, the modern Free Trade empire will be based on corporate control of the means of world production, not exclusively on trade or commerce. And this transnational order will not be ushered in on the heels of vanquishing armies. Its farsighted rulers conquer new domains through the power of the purse, not the might of the sword. In sum, we can safely predict that the global empire in the postimperialist age of the "Great Trust," constructed in the image of the corporation, will be unlike anything the world has known. The foundation is already laid. The new-age colossus swiftly rises. Its hour of unveiling draws near.

Notes

Chapter 1

1. Numerous distinguished thinkers have contributed to the development of classical liberalism. A list of the most notable would include Thomas Hobbes, James Harrington, John Locke, Baron de Montesquieu, Adam Smith, Jeremy Bentham, Herbert Spencer, and John Stuart Mill.

2. On origins of the idea of balance in political theory and the evolution of the doctrine of separation of powers, see Francis D. Wormuth, *The Origins of Modern Constitutionalism* (New York: Harper, 1949).

3. Adam Smith, *An Inquiry into the Nature and Causes of the Wealth of Nations*, 1776. Throughout this essay, reference will be made to laissez-faire liberalism. The beliefs and ideas associated with the ideological doctrine of laissez-faire, though they derive from the works of Smith and others, are not, however, necessarily representative of the depth and subtlety of the social thought of these thinkers. Ideologies must be analyzed as beliefs that justify particular interests or arrangements. Thus, for the purposes of analyzing ideological beliefs, it matters less what Adam Smith fully intended than what people think he said or what his ideas may represent in a given historical context. Ideology does not concern itself with empirical canons of truth, but with justification and moral persuasion.

On the derivation of the concept of laissez-faire (a term that Smith never employed), see John Maynard Keynes, "The End of Laissez-Faire" (1926), in *The Collected Writings of John Maynard Keynes*, vol. 9: *Essays in Persuasion* (New York: St. Martin's Press; London: Macmillan, 1972), pp. 272–94. Concerning Adam Smith's social theory, consult Leonard Billet, "Political Order and Economic Development: Reflections on Adam Smith's *Wealth of Nations*," *Political Studies* 23 (December 1975): 430–41; Billet, "The Just Economy: The Moral Basis of the Wealth of Nations," *Review of Social Economy* 34 (December 1976): 295–315; Jacob Viner, "Adam Smith and Laissez-Faire," in Joseph J. Spengler and William R. Allen, eds., *Essays in Economic Thought: Aristotle to Marshall* (Chicago: Rand McNally, 1960), pp. 305–29; David A. Reisman, *Adam Smith's Sociological Economics* (London: Croom Helm, 1976); Erich Roll, *A History of Economic Thought* (New York: Prentice-Hall, 1939), pp. 140–75; Donald Winch, *Adam Smith's Politics: An Essay in Historiographic Revision* (Cambridge: Cambridge University Press, 1978).

4. Harold J. Laski, *The Rise of Liberalism: The Philosophy of Business Civilization* (New York: Harper & Brothers, 1936).

5. Perry Miller, *The New England Mind: From Colony to Province* (Cambridge, Mass.: Harvard University Press, 1953); Miller, *The New England Mind: The Seventeenth Century* (Cambridge, Mass.: Harvard University Press, 1954); Alan Heimert, *Religion and the American Mind: From the Great Awakening to the Revolution* (Cambridge, Mass.: Harvard University Press, 1966); Edmund S. Morgan, "The Puritan Ethic and the American Revolution," *William and Mary Quarterly*, 3rd ser., 24 (January 1967): 3–43; Sacvan Bercovitch, *The Puritan Origins of the American Self* (New Haven: Yale University Press, 1975); Nathan O. Hatch, *The Sacred Cause of Liberty: Republican Thought on the Millennium in Revolutionary New England*

(New Haven: Yale University Press, 1977); Patricia U. Bonomi, *Under the Cope of Heaven: Religion, Society, and Politics in Colonial America* (Oxford: Oxford University Press, 1987).

6. Gary B. Nash, *The Urban Crucible: Social Change, Political Consciousness, and the Origins of the American Revolution* (Cambridge, Mass.: Harvard University Press, 1979); Dirk Hoerder, *Crowd Action in Revolutionary Massachusetts, 1765–1780* (New York: Academic Press, 1977); Eric Foner, *Tom Paine and Revolutionary America* (New York: Oxford University Press, 1976); Joyce Appleby, "Liberalism and the American Revolution," *New England Quarterly* 49 (March 1976): 3–26; Appleby, "The Social Origins of American Revolutionary Ideology," *Journal of American History* 64 (March 1978): 935–58; Alfred F. Young, ed., *The American Revolution: Explorations in the History of American Radicalism* (DeKalb: Northern Illinois University Press, 1976).

7. On the problem of equality and liberty in Locke's political theory, see Richard Ashcraft, *Revolutionary Politics and Locke's Two Treatises of Government* (Princeton: Princeton University Press, 1986). Once taken as an article of faith in American historiography, the influence of Locke on American Revolutionary ideology has been critically questioned by scholars seeking to revise or in some cases displace the (pre-1970s) consensus view with an interpretation that stresses the primacy of classical republican ideals in the formulation of American Revolutionary beliefs. In many respects, the debates sparked by the proponents of the republican thesis have come full circle, the republican revisionists now being perceived (and revised) as consensus historians. These debates, however, have produced a substantial understanding of the interrelationship between republican and liberal beliefs, not to mention the peculiarities of American liberalism, in the Revolutionary and early post-Revolutionary periods. Cf. Bernard Bailyn, *The Ideological Origins of the American Revolution* (Cambridge, Mass.: Harvard University Press, 1967); Gordon S. Wood, *The Creation of the American Republic, 1776–1787* (New York: W. W. Norton & Co., 1972); J. G. A. Pocock, *Machiavellian Moment: Florentine Political Thought and the Atlantic Republican Tradition* (Princeton: Princeton University Press, 1975); Pocock, "Between Gog and Magog: The Republican Thesis and *Ideologia Americana*," *Journal of the History of Ideas* 48 (April/June 1987): 325–46; Lance Banning, *The Jeffersonian Persuasion: Evolution of a Party Ideology* (Ithaca: Cornell University Press, 1978); Banning, "Jeffersonian Ideology Revisited: Liberal and Classical Ideas in the New American Republic," *William and Mary Quarterly*, 3rd ser., 43 (January 1986): 3–19; Joyce Appleby, "What Is Still American in the Political Philosophy of Thomas Jefferson?" *William and Mary Quarterly*, 3rd ser., 39 (April 1982): 287–309; Appleby, *Capitalism and a New Social Order: The Republican Vision of the 1790s* (New York: New York University Press, 1984); Appleby, "Republicanism in Old and New Contexts," *William and Mary Quarterly*, 3rd ser., 43 (January 1986): 20–34; John P. Diggins, *The Lost Soul of American Politics: Virtue, Self-Interest, and the Foundation of Liberalism* (New York: Basic Books, 1984); Robert E. Shalhope, "Toward a Republican Synthesis: The Emergence of an Understanding of Republicanism in American Historiography," *William and Mary Quarterly*, 3rd ser., 29 (January 1972): 49–80; Shalhope, "Republicanism and Early American Historiography," *William and Mary Quarterly*, 3rd ser., 39 (April 1982): 335–56; Isaac Kramnick, "Republican Revisionism Revisited," *American Historical Review* 87 (June 1982): 629–64; Thomas L. Pangle, *The Spirit of Modern Republicanism: The Moral Vision of the American Founders and the Philosophy of Locke* (Chicago: University of Chicago Press, 1988); Steven M. Dworetz, *The Unvarnished Doctrine: Locke, Liberalism, and the American Revolution* (Durham, N.C.: Duke University Press, 1990).

8. Louis Hartz, *The Liberal Tradition in America: An Interpretation of American Political Thought Since the Revolution* (New York: Harcourt, Brace & World, 1955).

9. Economic theorists, corporate leaders, politicians, the new group of scientifically trained engineers, and the federal judiciary, primarily through the interpretation of antitrust law, also contributed significantly to the revision of liberal ideology. In other words,

the corporate reconstruction of American society—economic, legal, political—was justified by the ideas that constitute the ideology of corporate liberalism as they were applied in practice to shape the new order:

"As it emerged in the Progressive Era, corporate liberalism was the prevalent ideology of the general movement seeking to transact the corporate reconstruction of the political-economic order on the basis of the mutual adaptation of corporate capitalism and the American liberal tradition. It sought, that is, to affirm administered markets and the growth of regulatory government without embracing a totalistic statism—or a corporate state. For this purpose, the distinction between positive government and statist command became crucial.

"Given the diversity within classes and strata and the strong tendencies toward, or the necessity of, accommodation and alignments among them, corporate liberalism expressed the cross-class character of the movement for corporate capitalism. Accordingly, corporate liberalism emerged not as the ideology of any one class, but rather as a cross-class ideology expressing the interrelations of corporate capitalists, political leaders, intellectuals, proprietary capitalists, professionals and reformers, workers and trade-union leaders, populists and socialists—all those who could, to a greater or lesser extent, identify their outlook, or their interest in administered markets and government regulation, with the rise, legitimation, and institutionalization of the corporate-capitalist order, and hence with the dominant position in the market of the corporate sector of the capitalist class." See Martin J. Sklar, *The Corporate Reconstruction of American Capitalism, 1890–1916: The Market, the Law, and Politics* (Cambridge: Cambridge University Press, 1988), pp. 34–35.

The concept of corporate liberalism was first employed by Martin J. Sklar in "Woodrow Wilson and the Political Economy of Modern United States Liberalism," *Studies on the Left* 1 (Fall 1960): 17–47. Subsequently, various interpretations of the political and ideological significance of corporate liberalism were advanced. Cf. James Weinstein, *The Corporate Ideal in the Liberal State, 1900–1918* (Boston: Beacon Press, 1968); David Eakins, "Policy-Planning for the Establishment," in Ronald Radosh and Murray N. Rothbard, eds., *A New History of Leviathan* (New York: E. P. Dutton, 1972), pp. 188–205; Ronald Radosh, "The Corporate Ideology of American Labor Leaders from Gompers to Hillman," *Studies on the Left* 6 (November–December 1966): 66–87; David F. Noble, *America by Design: Science, Technology, and the Rise of Corporate Capitalism* (New York: Alfred A. Knopf, 1977); Ellis W. Hawley, "The Study and Discovery of a 'Corporate Liberalism,' " *Business History Review* 52 (Autumn 1978): 309–20; R. Jeffrey Lustig, *Corporate Liberalism: The Origins of Modern American Political Theory, 1890–1920* (Berkeley and Los Angeles: University of California Press, 1982); Clyde W. Barrow, *Universities and the Capitalist State: Corporate Liberalism and the Reconstruction of American Higher Education, 1894–1928* (Madison: University of Wisconsin Press, 1990).

The interpretation of corporate liberalism in this work is in essential agreement with Sklar's definition (quoted above) and emphasizes that while justifying an expansion of government power (the positive state), corporate liberalism nevertheless preserves the basic elements of a liberal constitutional order founded on the separation of state and society. Accordingly, corporate liberalism should not be confused with ideologies of corporatism or corporativism conceived as justifications for a corporate state.

10. On the ideological significance of the rule-of-law ideal in liberal society, cf. Roberto Mangabeira Unger, *Law in Modern Society: Toward a Criticism of Social Theory* (New York: The Free Press, 1976), pp. 54–57, 170–81; Judith N. Shklar, *Legalism* (Cambridge, Mass.: Harvard University Press, 1964), pp. 1–28, 111–224; Lon Fuller, *The Morality of Law* (New Haven: Yale University Press, 1969), pp. 33–95; John Rawls, *A Theory of Justice* (Cambridge, Mass.: Harvard University Press, Belknap Press, 1971), pp. 235–51; Hans Kelsen, *The Pure Theory of Law* (Berkeley and Los Angeles: University of California Press, 1967), pp. 286–90.

Also, Harold J. Berman has provided an insightful analysis of theoretical issues pertinent to the study of law, power, and ideology in *Law and Revolution: The Formation of the Western Legal Tradition* (Cambridge, Mass.: Harvard University Press, 1983), pp. 520–58.

11. Julius Stone, *The Province and Function of Law: Law as Logic, Justice, and Social Control* (London: Stevens & Sons, 1961), p. 25.

12. Adolph A. Berle and Gardiner C. Means, *The Modern Corporation and Private Property* (1932), rev. ed. (New York: Harcourt, Brace & World, 1967), pp. 309, 313.

13. "Value added by manufacture—This measure of manufacturing activity is derived by subtracting the cost of materials, supplies, containers, fuel, purchased electricity, and contract work from the value of shipments (products manufactured plus receipts for services rendered). The result of this calculation is adjusted by the addition of value added by merchandising operations (i.e., the difference between the sales value and the cost of merchandise sold without further manufacture, processing, or assembly) plus the net charge in finished goods and work-in-process between the beginning and end-of-the-year inventories. . . . 'Value added' avoids the duplication in the figure for value of shipments that results from the use of products of some establishments as materials by others. Value added is considered to be the best value measure available for comparing the relative economic importance of manufacturing among industries and geographic areas." U.S. Department of Commerce, Bureau of the Census, *1987 Census of Manufactures: Concentration Ratios in Manufacturing* (Washington, D.C.: Government Printing Office, 1992), p. A-2, app. A.

14. Ibid., p. 6-3, table 1. This report provides a comprehensive listing of market concentration in all "manufacturing" industries. For analyses of aggregate and market concentration, see Philip I. Blumberg, *The Megacorporation in American Society: The Scope of Corporate Power* (Englewood Cliffs, N.J.: Prentice-Hall, 1975), pp. 16–83; Samuel Richardson Reid, *The New Industrial State: Concentration, Regulation, and Public Policy* (New York: McGraw-Hill, 1976), pp. 26–60; John M. Blair, *Economic Concentration* (New York: Harcourt Brace Jovanovich, 1972).

15. U.S. Department of Commerce, Bureau of the Census, *Statistical Abstracts of the United States, 1993* (Washington, D.C.: Government Printing Office, 1993), pp. 550–51, tables 883 and 884; p. 553, table 891 (the last year for which the 1993 report provides data on total sales and assets of industrial corporations is 1991). For percentage increase, compare with U.S. Department of Commerce, Bureau of the Census, *Statistical Abstracts of the United States, 1987* (Washington, D.C.: Government Printing Office, 1987), p. 513, tables 858 and 859; p. 516, table 865.

16. "The Fortune 500 Largest U.S. Industrial Corporations," *Fortune*, April 18, 1994, pp. 210–38.

17. These calculations are based on *Statistical Abstracts of the United States, 1993*, p. 509, table 797; "Bank Scoreboard," *Business Week*, April 27, 1992, pp. 94–101; and Federal Deposit Insurance Corporation, *Data Book: Operating Banks and Branches*, book 6 (June 30, 1993). (The last year for which *Statistical Abstracts 1993* provides complete data on total bank assets and deposits is 1991.)

18. Blumberg, *Megacorporation*, pp. 174, 177.

19. "The 100 Largest U.S. Multinationals," *Forbes*, July 18, 1994, pp. 276–79; "The Fortune 500 Largest U.S. Industrial Corporations" (note 16 above).

20. Edward S. Herman, *Corporate Control, Corporate Power* (Cambridge: Cambridge University Press, 1981), pp. 130–33.

21. The issue of a financial institution's influence or control within a nonfinancial corporation, however, is a subject for empirical investigation, not speculation or reductionist generalizations based solely on statistical compilations. Herman, for example, contests the

"naive theory" that the mere presence of significant numbers of banking representatives on boards of directors and executive committees of nonfinancial corporations gives bankers a position of control (ibid., pp. 129–37). He states: "The impact of financial enterprises on the large nonfinancial corporations of the 1970s has novel features, as compared with the past. Direct and decisive control has declined in importance and is rare, but shared power in the sense of important minority and/or constraining influence on decision making is applicable in perhaps as many as a fifth of the large companies" (ibid., p. 161). Cf. David M. Kotz, *Bank Control of Large Corporations in the United States* (Berkeley and Los Angeles: University of California Press, 1978).

22. Consider, for example, some of the findings of the 1978 (1,000-page) report of the Senate Governmental Affairs Committee on interlocking directorates: (1) 530 direct interlocks among the nation's 130 largest financial and industrial corporations, which account for $1 trillion in assets or 25 percent of all corporate wealth; (2) 12,193 indirect interlocks (i.e., corporations meeting on a common board) among these 130 corporations; (3) 123 of the 130 corporations connect on average with half of the 130 companies; and (4) each of the 13 largest corporations, which control about $400 billion in assets, reached an average of 70 percent of the 117 other firms through a total of 240 direct and 5,547 indirect interlocks, a "conservative statistic since the data base did not include the direct interlocks of the top 13 firms' 486 subsidiaries." U.S. Senate, Committee on Governmental Affairs, Subcommittee on Reports, Accounting, and Management, *Interlocking Directorates Among the Major U.S. Corporations* (Washington, D.C.: Government Printing Office, 1978), p. 280.

Based on this evidence, an argument could be made that interlocks appear to increase in number and scope with the increase in assets, which implies that the need or desire for centralized communication and control increases with the growth of the firm. The report states: "Indeed, the boardrooms of four of the largest banking companies (Citicorp, Chase Manhattan, Manufacturers Hanover, and J. P. Morgan), two of the largest insurance companies (Prudential and Metropolitan Life), and three of the largest nonfinancial companies (AT&T, Exxon, and General Motors) looked like virtual summits for American business" (ibid.).

23. *Interlocking Directorates: Origins and Consequences of Connections Among Organizations' Boards of Directors* (San Francisco: Jossey-Bass, 1980), pp. 68–73, 188–89.

24. Ibid., p. 67.

25. Herman, *Corporate Control*, pp. 200–201.

26. For a current analysis of the declining significance (or dissolution) of the eight interest groups identified by Paul Sweezy in his appendix 13, "Interest Groupings in the American Economy," in Natural Resources Committee, *The Structure of the American Economy, Part 1: Basic Characteristics* (Washington, D.C.: Government Printing Office, 1939), pp. 306–17, see Herman, *Corporate Control*, pp. 217–30. See also Blumberg, *Megacorporation*, pp. 166–73. One need not rely on unreconstructed theories pertinent to an earlier phase in the development of corporate capitalism to appreciate and explain the influential position of the major banks in the present constellation of supracorporate linkages. The prevalent theories of bank control either attribute to bankers a motivation that links their interest in profit-making with the desire or need to control major industrial corporations, and/or claim that the structure of American capitalism necessarily lodges power in the dominant financial institutions. Influence or constraint, however, is a more accurate description than control, except in cases where banks might be able to wield control through stockholdings, which are few in number. But this form of outright control is usually avoided, and probably undesirable and unnecessary barring instances of serious financial difficulty. Contrary to the belief of some analysts, bankers are in the business of managing and making money, not managing industrial enterprise. Their interests in the affairs of nonfinancial corpora-

tions are determined largely by their pecuniary stake in those companies. The prevalent idea that financial institutions hold the reins of power because they control the distribution of capital, more often than not, presumes that the major banks act in concert as the leaders of interest groups (linked through common stockholdings and interlocks) that are in turn ultimately controlled by an inner circle of tight-knit vested interests (the ruling families), the real power base of American capitalism. This argument, however, relies on a series of inferences that are no longer well supported by empirical evidence. There is a tendency in the finance-capital thesis, moreover, to erroneously equate or confuse continental European (and Japanese) practices with a very different tradition in the United States, Britain, and Canada. On this point, see Herman, *Corporate Control*, p. 154, and pp. 114–61, on financial control in general. For a work that documents the political causes of the fragmentation of the banking sector in the United States, dating back to the defeat of the U.S. Bank under President Andrew Jackson, see Mark J. Roe, *Strong Managers, Weak Owners* (Princeton: Princeton University Press, 1994), pp. 1–101. Roe argues that managers of the large U.S. corporation would not have acquired their present control over the fortunes of enterprise without successful efforts in state and national politics to prevent the consolidation of financial interests and to block or inhibit the ability of financial institutions to gain effective control of industrial corporations. And on the very different structure of corporate ownership in Japanese and German corporations, see ibid., pp. 169–86.

27. Michael Useem, "The Inner Circle and the Political Voice of Business," in Michael Schwartz, ed., *The Structure of Power in America: The Corporate Elite as a Ruling Class* (New York: Holmes & Meier, 1987), p. 144. See also Useem, "The Inner Group of the American Capitalist Class," *Social Problems* 25 (February 1978): 225–40; Useem, "Class-wide Rationality in the Politics of Managers and Directors of Large Corporations in the United States and Great Britain," *Administrative Science Quarterly* 27 (June 1982): 199–226; Useem, *The Inner Circle: Large Corporations and the Rise of Business Political Activity in the U.S. and U.K.* (New York: Oxford University Press, 1984). On the social and political aspects of interlocks, see Mark S. Mizruchi, *The Structure of Corporate Political Action: Interfirm Relations and Their Consequences* (Cambridge, Mass.: Harvard University Press, 1992); Mizruchi, "Similarity of Political Behavior Among Large Corporations," *American Journal of Sociology* 95 (September 1989): 401–21; Mizruchi, *The American Corporate Network, 1904–1974* (Beverly Hills, Calif.: Sage Publications, 1982); Thomas Koenig, Robert Gogel, and John Sonquist, "Models of the Significance of Interlocking Corporate Directorates," *American Journal of Economics and Sociology* 38 (1979): 173–86; W. Lloyd Warner and D. B. Unwalla, "The System of Interlocking Directorates," in W. Lloyd Warner, D. B. Unwalla, and J. H. Trimm, eds., *The Emergent American Society: Large Scale Organizations* (New Haven, Conn.: Yale University Press, 1967); Peter C. Dooley, "The Interlocking Directorate," *American Economic Review* 59 (June 1969): 314–23.

Herman (*Corporate Control*, 194–241) described three primary "channels through which supracorporate linkages can influence corporate behavior": (1) . . . "command" (e.g., common family ownership interest in several companies sufficient to dominate all of the companies), (2) . . . "communication" (formal and informal methods of communication between autonomous corporations—ranging from telephone conversations to social affairs to interlocking directorates—that facilitate common control or regulation of markets and that serve as a means for resolving disputes, etc.), and (3) . . . "community of interest" ("the feeling among corporate leadership of a mutuality of interdependence of business needs and obligations and a sense of shared goals," which is strengthened by personal contacts and business, social, and organizational ties).

28. U.S. Senate Committee, *Interlocking Directorates Among the Major U.S. Corporations*, pp. 280–81. Several other significant government studies of interlocking directorates have provided considerable data on the issues discussed above. The following reports are

among the most frequently cited: Federal Trade Commission, *Report on Interlocking Director-ates* (Washington, D.C.: Government Printing Office, 1951); House Committee on the Judiciary, Antitrust Subcommittee, *Interlocks in Corporate Management* (Washington, D.C.: Government Printing Office, 1965); House Committee on Banking and Currency, Subcommittee on Domestic Finance, *Commercial Banks and Their Trust Activities: Emerging Influence on the American Economy* (Patman Staff Report) (Washington, D.C.: Government Printing Office, 1968).

29. A considerable literature now exists on the social and political organizations that bind the leaders of large corporations and that provide them access to government forums. Recently, a number of scholars have focused on the political activity of business, and especially the highly significant role of the Business Roundtable. Evidence of a self-defined stratum of leaders within the corporate bourgeoisie is plentiful and often compelling. Indeed, several books and articles have specifically addressed the issue of corporate class-consciousness and cohesion. On these and related issues, see Useem, *The Inner Circle*; G. William Domhoff, *Who Rules America?* (Englewood Cliffs, N.J.: Prentice-Hall, 1967); Domhoff, *The Higher Circle: The Governing Class in America* (New York: Random House, 1970); Domhoff, *The Bohemian Grove and Other Retreats: A Study in Ruling Class Cohesiveness* (New York: Harper & Row, 1974); Domhoff, "Social Clubs, Political Groups, and Corporations: A Network Study of Ruling Class Cohesiveness," *Insurgent Sociologist* 5 (Spring 1975): 173–84; Domhoff, *The Powers That Be: Process of Ruling Class Domination in America* (New York: Random House, 1979); Schwartz, ed., *The Structure of Power in America*. Cf. Leonard Silk and David Vogel, *Ethics and Profits: The Crisis of Confidence in American Business* (New York: Simon & Schuster, 1976); David Vogel, "The Persistence of the American Business Creed," in Lee E. Preston, ed., *Research in Corporate Social Performance and Policy*, vol. 2 (Greenwich, Conn.: JAI Press, 1980), pp. 77–102. For sources on the Business Roundtable and the resurgence of business political activity, see below, Chapter 4, note 32.

30. David Vogel, *Fluctuating Fortunes: The Political Power of Business in America* (New York: Basic Books, 1989), pp. 59–92.

31. See, e.g., James Q. Wilson, "The Politics of Regulation," in James Q. Wilson, ed., *The Politics of Regulation* (New York: Basic Books, 1980), pp. 357–94.

32. Beth Mintz, "The President's Cabinet, 1897–1972," *Insurgent Sociologist* 5 (Spring 1975): 131–48; Philip H. Burch Jr., *Elites in American History* (New York: Holmes & Meier, 1980), vols. 2 and 3. For summaries, see ibid., vol. 2, table 13, pp. 320–21, and vol. 3, table 14, pp. 374–75; Peter Freitag, "The Cabinet and Big Business: A Study of Interlocks," *Social Problems* 23 (1975): 137–52.

33. Richard L. Sklar, "On the Concept of Power in Political Economy," in Dalmas H. Nelson and Richard L. Sklar, eds., *Toward a Humanistic Science of Politics: Essays in Honor of Francis Dunham Wormuth* (Lanham, Md.: University Press of America, 1983), pp. 179–206.

34. Richard L. Sklar, "Postimperialism: A Class Analysis of Multinational Corporate Expansion," *Comparative Politics* 9 (October 1976): 75–92; reprinted in David G. Becker, Jeff Freiden, Sayre P. Schatz, and Richard L. Sklar, *Postimperialism: International Capitalism and Development in the Late Twentieth Century* (Boulder, Colo.: Lynne Rienner Publishers, 1987), pp. 19–40.

35. Sklar, "On the Concept of Power" (note 33 above).

Chapter 2

1. On the role of law in effecting economic and social change in the nineteenth and twentieth centuries, cf. John R. Commons, *Legal Foundations of Capitalism* (New York: Macmillan, 1924); Lawrence M. Friedman, *A History of American Law* (New York: Simon &

Schuster, 1973); Morton J. Horwitz, *The Transformation of American Law, 1780–1860* (Cambridge, Mass.: Harvard University Press, 1977); James Willard Hurst, *The Legitimacy of the Business Corporation in the Law of the United States, 1780-1970* (Charlottesville: University Press of Virginia, 1970); Roscoe Pound, *The Formative Era of American Law* (Boston: Little, Brown , 1938); Martin J. Sklar, *The Corporate Reconstruction of American Capitalism, 1890–1916: The Market, the Law, and Politics* (Cambridge: Cambridge University Press, 1988).

2. Depending on the classification employed by scholars, the number of colonial business corporations will vary slightly. For example, Simeon Baldwin identifies six, Joseph Davis identifies seven, and between them they list a total of eight such corporations. Both authors include the Free Society of Traders, which although chartered in England by William Penn in 1682, was intended to be an American corporation. The Free Society of Traders appears to be the first American colonial business corporation, if one excludes the English trading companies that founded many of the colonies. (Baldwin lists the New York Fishing Company [1675] as the first, but Davis points out that this company was not incorporated.) See Simeon E. Baldwin, "American Business Corporations Before 1789," *Annual Report of the American Historical Association* 1 (December 1902): 257–73; Joseph Stancliffe Davis, *Essays in the Earlier History of Corporations*, 2 vols. (Cambridge, Mass.: Harvard University Press, 1917), 1:41–45, 87–96; 2:22–26, 345. On the history of American colonial corporations in general, see ibid., 1:3–107, 2:3–33.

3. Corporate enterprise in seventeenth- and eighteenth-century England typically lent itself to the development of industrial or commercial ventures that required significant capitalization, to opportunities for stock speculation, or to both. Neither of these alternatives was feasible in colonial America until perhaps the eve of the Revolution. Lack of communication and transportation, political and religious differences, local economies, and British rule all contributed to this state of affairs. On this, see Davis, *Essays*, 1:178–79, 2:5–8.

4. Ibid., 1:49, 2:3–4. See also Samuel Williston, "History of the Law of Business Corporations Before 1800," *Harvard Law Review* 2 (October 15, 1888): 105–6, 113; Edwin Merrick Dodd, *American Business Corporations Until 1860* (Cambridge, Mass.: Harvard University Press, 1954), pp. 13–14, 17–19, 195–96; Hurst, *Legitimacy*, pp. 8–9.

5. All the foregoing characteristics were identified as essential corporate attributes by the most prominent English jurists of the seventeenth and eighteenth centuries. For example, see Sir Edward Coke's opinion in *Sutton's Hospital Case*, 10 Coke's Rep. 1 (1612); William Blackstone, "Of Corporations," *Commentaries on the Laws of England*, 17th Ed. (London: Thomas Tegg, 1830), vol. 1, chap. 18; Stewart Kyd, *A Treatise on the Law of Corporations* (London: for J. Butterworth, Fleet-Street, 1793–94). For an analysis of these authorities, cf. Williston, "History," pp.113–17; Davis, 1:5–7; B. C. Hunt, *The Development of the Business Corporation in England, 1800–1867* (New York: Russell & Russell, 1936), pp. 3–5.

The essential characteristics of the corporation identified by Coke et al., originated in Roman law, if not before, and later shaped medieval Christian doctrine on corporate bodies. See Williston, "History," pp. 106–7, 121; Hurst, *Legitimacy*, pp. 1–2; Adolf A. Berle, *Studies in the Law of Corporation Finance* (Chicago: Callaghan & Co., 1928), pp. 3–8; Sir Henry Maine, *Ancient Law* (London: John Murray, 1906; reprint ed., 1930), pp. 207–9; Scott Buchanan, "The Corporation and the Republic," in *The Corporation Take-Over*, ed. Andrew Hacker (Garden City, N.Y.: Anchor Books, 1965), pp. 19–20. Whether papal doctrine and, through it, Roman law significantly influenced the secular development of English corporation law, however, is a matter of debate. Compare Hurst (*Legitimacy* p. 2), Berle (*Studies*, p. 6), and Williston ("History," p. 107).

6. On the significance of limited liability in English law before the nineteenth century, see Armand Dubois, *The English Business Company After the Bubble Act, 1720–1800* (New

York: Commonwealth Fund, 1938), pp. 93–96; Dodd, pp. 84–85; Oscar Handlin and Mary F. Handlin, "Origins of the American Business Corporation," *Journal of Economic History* 5 (May 1945): 11–13.

Although undoubtedly an essential attribute of the modern business corporation of the nineteenth and twentieth centuries, limited liability was granted in some but not all eighteenth-century English corporate charters. See Handlin and Handlin, "Origins," p. 9. Dubois reports that the concept of limited liability originated with the medieval joint-stock companies on the Continent, that it held little importance in seventeenth-century England, and that it first received "comprehensive recognition . . . as a factor in incorporation . . . in the proceedings of the Warmly Company in 1768." See Dubois, *English Business Company*, pp. 93–95. The evidence suggests that limited liability became a necessary aspect of incorporation—in effect, an inducement to investors—when the modern joint-stock company became the predominant means of accumulating capital.

7. Hurst, *Legitimacy*, pp. 22–24; Berle, *Studies*, pp. 8–9. Although the earliest English corporations—municipalities and trade guilds—antedated the practice, royal charters were occasionally granted to fourteenth- and fifteenth-century guilds that sought special privileges or protection. See Williston, "History," pp. 108–9. English law later would accommodate the fact that many corporations had been in existence before the exclusive power of the sovereign to create corporations had been established. Coke accomplished this in *Sutton's Hospital* by including "by prescription" as a means by which the "Lawful authority of incorporation" may be granted. See Williston, "History," p. 113; Davis, *Essays*, 1:6.

8. Christopher Hill, *The Century of Revolution: 1603–1714* (New York: W. W. Norton & Co., 1961), pp. 28–42, 145–61; Williston, "History," pp. 110–11; Berle, *Studies*, pp. 9–11. Parliament abolished industrial monopolies in 1640, but monopolistic trading companies thrived until the last decade of the century. See Hill, *Century*, pp. 146, 154–55, 262.

9. Hurst, *Legitimacy*, p. 4; Williston, "History," p. 111. Changes in the law aided this development. For example, judges ruled that monopolies of trade applied only with regard to other chartered companies and not to unincorporated companies, thus encouraging competition. See Hurst, *Legitimacy*, p. 4. In any event, after the Revolution of 1688, grants of monopoly had to be sanctioned by Parliament, a fact that signaled the demise of the trading companies. See Hill, *Century*, p. 262.

10. For an analysis of the events leading up to the Bubble Act and of its impact on the development of corporate enterprise in Britain, see Dubois, *English Business Company*, pp. 1–135; Hunt, *Development*, pp. 6–13; William R. Scott, *The Constitution and Finance of English, Scottish, and Irish Joint-Stock Companies to 1720*, 3 vols. (Cambridge: Cambridge University Press, 1910–12), vol.1, chaps. 17–21.

11. Following the passage of the Bubble Act, courts of equity, in the eighteenth and nineteenth centuries, allowed for pooling of assets by deeds of settlement. Such assets (shares) were to be transferable and to be managed by trustees of the business. In this way, an effective alternative to the joint-stock method of accumulating large sums of capital was devised. See Dubois, *English Business Company*, pp. 216-22; Hurst, *Legitimacy*, p. 6. The partnership, in various forms, eclipsed the joint-stock company as the predominant form of business organization in eighteenth-century England. Despite the Bubble Act (which was rarely enforced), unincorporated joint-stock companies again flourished in the early nineteenth century. After nearly five decades of ideological debate that eventually centered on the issue of limited liability, the benefits of incorporation to industrial growth were finally acknowledged in the English Companies Acts of 1844 and 1855, which made incorporation generally available. See Hunt, *Development*, pp. 14–144; Dubois, *English Business Company*, pp. 36–38; H. A. Shannon, "The Coming of General Limited Liability," *Economic History* 2 (January 1931): 267–91.

12. Dubois, *English Business Company*, p. 86. Dubois observes that eighteenth-century English law, as it pertained to the business corporation, was "remarkably fallow"—a result that may be due in part to "the stultifying effect which the Bubble Act had on theoretical speculation" (ibid.). It should be noted that Parliament extended the Bubble Act to the American colonies in 1741 in reaction to the floating of the Land Bank or Manufacturing Scheme, domiciled in Massachusetts. The act, which was never enforced, did not seriously limit the growth of colonial joint-stock business companies which in any event were few in number. See Davis, *Essays*, 1:25–27; Hurst, *Legitimacy*, p. 8; Dodd, *American Business Corporations*, pp. 366–67.

13. Out of 328 there were 18 ancillary, additional, or joint charters. Hence, 310 new corporations had been formed, 2 of which were chartered by the national government—the Bank of North America (1781, by the Confederation Congress) and the First Bank of the United States (1791). Some 219 charters were issued for the purpose of improving and constructing inland transportation on waterways and roads, 67 for banking and insurance, 36 for water supply and docks, and 8 for manufacturing. See Davis, *Essays*, 2:22–28, 36, 51.

14. From approximately 1781 to 1830, the granting of charters to companies that performed a public function roughly paralleled the sixteenth-century English practice of conferring corporate status with special privileges for the purpose of promoting economic development. States often granted monopoly powers either by establishing an exclusive right in the charter or by granting only one charter in an area of commerce, transportation, or other field of public service. See Hurst, *Legitimacy*, pp. 34–35.

15. By 1830, the New England states had granted 1900 corporate charters, 600 of which went to manufacturing and mining companies. From 1831 to 1862 the same states granted more than 2,600 new charters (out of an approximate total of 5,000) to manufacturing and mining concerns. See Dodd, *American Business Corporations*, pp. 11, 123. A similar pattern of incorporation developed in New Jersey, where charters for manufacturing and mining accounted for 32.8 percent of a total of 403 issued between 1782 and 1844. See John W. Cadman Jr., *The Corporation in New Jersey* (Cambridge, Mass.: Harvard University Press, 1949), pp. 443–44. In Maryland, of a total 625 corporate charters granted between 1783 and 1852, some 137 went to manufacturing companies, 120 of which were issued after 1820. See Joseph G. Blandi, *Maryland Business Corporations, 1783–1852* (Baltimore: Johns Hopkins University Press, 1934), p. 14. New York granted 512 charters for manufacturing companies from 1811 to 1848, and more than 4,700 from 1848 to 1866 following the enactment of several general incorporation statutes. See Ronald E. Seavoy, *The Origins of the American Business Corporation, 1784–1855: Broadening the Concept of Public Service During Industrialization* (Westport, Conn.: Greenwood Press, 1982), pp. 67, 195.

16. Thomas C. Cochran and William Miller, *The Age of Enterprise: A Social History of Industrial America*, rev. ed. (New York: Harper & Row, 1961), pp. 67–70. See also Edward Chase Kirkland, *Industry Comes of Age: Business, Labor, and Public Policy, 1860–1897* (Chicago: Quadrangle Books, 1961), pp. 52–55.

17. Even after several states passed general incorporation laws, they still provided the option of incorporation by special charter, presumably to avoid restrictions in the general acts—for example, limits on capitalization. See Hurst, *Legitimacy*, p. 29. In New Jersey, special acts also served as an enticement to lure entrepreneurs who might initially incorporate under a general act and then apply for a special charter once the business was under way. This method, however, eventually absorbed too much of the legislature's time. Special acts were dispensed with in 1875, when New Jersey liberalized its general incorporation statute. See Cadman, *Corporation in New Jersey*, pp. 152–88.

18. Dodd, *American Business Corporations*, pp. 201–71; Davis, *Essays*, 2:316–29; Hurst,

Legitimacy, pp. 20–21; Adolf A. Berle and Gardiner C. Means, *The Modern Corporation and Private Property* (New York: Macmillan, 1936), pp. 131–33.

19. *Trustees of the University v. Foy,* 5 N.C. (1 Murph.) 58 (1805); *Wales v. Stetson,* 22 Mass. 143 (1806). For an analysis of these and other early cases that anticipate later judicial theory of the business corporation, see Dodd, *American Business Corporations,* pp. 19–23; Horwitz, *Transformation, 1780–1860,* pp. 111–14.

20. *Terrett v. Taylor,* 9 Cranch 43 (1815).

21. Ibid., pp. 50–52. Justice Story's definition of private corporations includes corporations in which the property of the corporation was purchased by its donors or parishioners and excludes *"public* corporations which exist only for public purposes" (ibid., pp. 49, 52). See also note 27 below for Story's subsequent elaboration of this distinction.

22. 9 Cranch 43, 52 (1815).

23. In *Fletcher v. Peck,* 6 Cranch 87 (1810), and *New Jersey v. Wilson,* 7 Cranch 164 (1812), the Supreme Court, per Justice John Marshall, interpreted the contract clause of the Constitution to embrace legislative acts (grants), which could be construed as contracts. In so doing, the Court relied heavily on natural-law justifications of property rights, similar to the argument of Justice Story in *Terrett v. Taylor.* Given the Court's predisposition to impose constitutional restraints on states when property interests were at stake, an astute lawyer of the day might have anticipated what lay ahead. For an analysis of these cases, with particular emphasis on how the Marshall Court's political bias shaped the holdings, see Benjamin Fletcher Wright Jr., *The Contract Clause of the Constitution* (Cambridge, Mass.: Harvard University Press, 1938), pp. 29–39; see also G. Edward White, *The Marshall Court and Cultural Change, 1815–1835,* vols. 3 & 4 of *The Oliver Wendell Holmes Devise History of the Supreme Court of the United States* (New York: Macmillan, 1988), vols. 3–4, pp. 602–14. Cf. Sylvia Snowiss, *Judicial Review and the Law of the Constitution* (New Haven: Yale University Press, 1990), pp. 126–61, for an illuminating analysis of the Marshall Court's contract clause opinions in light of Marshall's evolving jurisprudence.

24. 4 Wheaton 518 (1819).

25. *Trustees of Dartmouth College v. Woodward,* 65 N.H. 473, 628–39 (1817). See also Dodd, *American Business Corporations,* pp. 26–27; Wright, *Contract Clause,* p. 41; White, *Marshall Court,* p. 614. In one of his more notable appearances before the Supreme Court, Daniel Webster maintained that Dartmouth was a private eleemosynary corporation, not a public corporation. As such, he argued, the charter of the college fell under the protection of the Constitution. Webster's forensic ability, not to mention his propensity for histrionics, made a deep impression on the Court. For a description of Webster's performance based on contemporary reports, see Charles Warren, *The Supreme Court in United States History,* 3 vols. (Boston: Little, Brown, 1922), 1:476–82; cf. White, *Marshall Court,* pp. 614–18. When arguments concluded in March 1818, it became clear that the Court's decision, still forthcoming, would turn on whether it classified Dartmouth as a public or private corporation. After overcoming serious differences of opinion, the Supreme Court delivered its ruling at the first session of the 1819 term.

26. 4 Wheaton 518, 627 (1819).

27. Ibid., p. 630 In a separate opinion, Justice Story discussed at length the distinction between public and private corporations. Using a bank as an example, he defined a private corporation as one "whose stock is owned by private persons . . . although it is erected by the government, and its objects and operations partake of a public nature" (ibid., p. 669). Story argued that the distinction between public and private corporations was well established in common law (pp. 668–77). More precisely, his citations support a common-law distinction between the public and private foundations of eleemosynary corporations and

attendant rights, especially with regard to the powers of visitation over such corporations. Story's classification (in *Terrett* and *Dartmouth*) of *types* of corporations as public and private based on the public or private source of the funding, however, constituted a doctrinal innovation. Marshall's opinion in *Dartmouth* contained only two citations (both to Blackstone), both of which supported the classification of eleemosynary corporations as private corporations—that is, corporations that were founded by the private donations of individuals. See 4 Wheaton 518, 633–34 (1819); Blackstone, *Commentaries*, 1:471, 481.

28. 4 Wheaton 518, 636 (1819).

29. Ibid.

30. Ibid., p. 642.

31. Ibid., p. 640.

32. Ibid., pp. 650–52. Article I, Section 10: "No State shall . . . pass any . . . Law impairing the Obligation of Contracts. . . ."

33. 4 Wheaton 518, 636 (1819). Marshall's definition of the corporate entity appears to paraphrase, in part, that of Sir Edward Coke in *Sutton's Hospital Case*, 10 Coke's Rep. 32 (1612), where Coke observed: "For a corporation aggregate of many is invisible, immortal, and rests only in intendment and consideration of law. They cannot commit treason, nor be outlawed, nor excommunicate, for they have no souls, nor can they appear in person but by attorney. A corporation aggregate . . . is not subject to imbecilities or death of the natural body and diverse other cases." Blackstone, who published his *Commentaries* between 1765 and 1769, followed Coke in using the term "invisible" to describe the legal existence of the corporate entity, but employed "perpetual succession" in place of "immortal." See Blackstone, *Commentaries*, 1:475, 476.

In 1793, Stewart Kyd defined a corporation as "a collection of many individuals, united into one body, under a *special denomination*, having perpetual succession under an *artificial form*, and vested, by the policy of the law, with the capacity of acting, in several respects, as an *individual*, particularly of taking and granting property, of contracting obligations, and of suing and being sued, of enjoying privileges and immunities in *common*, and of exercising a variety of political rights, more or less extensive, according to the design of its institution, or the powers conferred upon it, either at the time of its creation, or at any subsequent period of its existence" (emphasis in original). See Kyd, *Treatise*, p.13. Kyd argued that Coke's terms "invisible" and "immortal" were misleading and imprecise (ibid., pp. 15–18).

34. 4 Wheaton 518, 636 (1819).

35. The corporation enjoyed a favored status under the Constitution, compared with other forms of business enterprise, by virtue of its capacity to be treated, for the purposes of the contract clause, as an individual and as an entity that could exist indefinitely. Furthermore, *Dartmouth* established that the contract clause protects the charter itself (the contract) and its provisions, including any special privileges that may have been granted therein.

36. 4 Wheaton 518, 675.

37. See Warren, *Supreme Court*, 1: 487–93, on the lack of attention that *Dartmouth* received in the press. Warren argues that while the implications of the case were fully appreciated by Marshall, Story, and Webster, there was no immediate public awareness of the importance of this holding. See Albert J. Beveridge, *The Life of John Marshall*, 4 vols. (Boston: Houghton Mifflin, 1929), 4: 276–81.

38. Wright, *Contract Clause*, pp. 168–78; Dodd, *American Business Corporations*, pp. 141–50. See Stanley I. Kutler, *Privilege and Creative Destruction: The Charles River Bridge Case* (Philadelphia: J. B. Lippincott Co., 1971), pp. 61–63. The states' reservation powers over corporate charters, as stipulated in statutes and constitutions, greatly contributed to the

eventual decline of the contract clause as a bastion of corporate rights (see also note 79 below). Following the passage of the Fourteenth Amendment, corporate attorneys discovered a more secure constitutional domain for their clients just as the contract clause appeared to have outlived its utility. On this, see section 4 below.

39. For an analysis of the volatile nature of law concerning monopolies during this period, including disparate court rulings that denied and upheld a presumption of implied exclusivity in corporate charters, see Horwitz, pp. 116–26. The doctrine of implied exclusivity was eventually rejected by the Supreme Court in *Charles River Bridge v. Warren Bridge*, 11 Peters 420 (1837), discussed below, section 3b.

40. *Bank of Columbia v. Patterson's Administrator*, 7 Cranch 299 (1813). This and related cases are discussed in Dodd, pp. 93–99.

41. In *Bank of the United States v. Dandridge*, 12 Wheaton 64, 70 (1827), Justice Story stated, "the acts of artificial persons affords the same presumptions as the acts of natural persons." Dodd observed that, by 1830, in "a radical departure from English precedents," American courts had placed corporations "very much in the same position as individual entrepreneurs" with respect to their method of contracting. See Dodd, *American Business Corporations*, p. 99.

42. *Chestnut Hill & S. H. Turnpike Co. v. Rutter*, 4 S.&R. 6 (Pa. 1818). See Dodd, *American Business Corporations*, p. 112.

43. 5 Cranch 61 (1809).

44. Ibid., p. 86.

45. 16 Howard 314 (1853). Most notable in establishing federal jurisdiction for corporations before the *Marshall* case were *Osborn v. Bank of the United States*, 9 Wheaton 738 (1824), where the Court based the right of the Second Bank of the United States to sue and be sued in federal court on a provision in the bank's charter; and *Louisville, Cincinnati & Charleston Ry. Co. v. Letson*, 2 Howard 497, 588 (1844), where the Court stated that "a corporation created by and doing business in a particular state, is to be deemed to all intents and purposes as a person . . . capable of being treated as a citizen of that state, as much as a natural person." *Marshall v. Baltimore* overruled this holding, emphasizing that the corporation's right to sue in federal court was based on residency, not citizenship, thereby remaining consistent with its earlier ruling in *Bank of Augusta v. Earle*, 13 Peters 519 (1839), discussed below in the present section. Concerning the problem of federal jurisdiction for corporations during the antebellum period, see Carl B. Swisher, *The Taney Period, 1836–1964, The Oliver Wendell Holmes Devise History of the Supreme Court of the United States* (New York: Macmillan, 1974), 5:458–70.

46. 13 Peters 519 (1839).

47. Ibid., pp. 586–87.

48. Chief Justice Marshall's commitment to vested rights, national mercantilism, and federal supremacy usually did not prevent him from erecting barriers to state "interference" in these areas. Still, as *Deveaux* indicates, he did perceive certain limits to his quest. Related to this, see note 52 below concerning Marshall's construction of the contract clause in *Providence Bank v. Billings*.

49. 11 Peters 420 (1837).

50. Quoted from *Stourbridge Canal v. Wheely*, 2 Barn. & Adol. 793 (1837) at ibid., p. 546. In 1785, the Massachusetts legislature granted to the Charles River Bridge Company a charter authorizing the company to build a bridge on the Charles River and to collect tolls. The charter also stipulated that the company pay a yearly sum to Harvard College as compensation for the exclusive ferry rights the college had acquired in 1650. When the state legislature incorporated the Warren Bridge Company, in 1828, for the purpose of building a second bridge across the river, the Charles River Bridge Company brought suit,

arguing that the 1828 act impaired its charter, which contained an implied right of exclusivity, thereby violating the contract clause of the Constitution. On the history of the case, see
Kutler, *Privilege*, pp. 1–84; Swisher, *Taney Period*, pp. 71–98.

51. Kutler, *Privilege*, pp. 129–32, 155–62; Horwitz, *Transformation, 1780–1860*, pp. 130–
39; Hurst, *Legitimacy*, pp. 38–39; Wright, *Contract Clause*, pp. 63–65; R. Kent Newmyer,
"Justice Joseph Story, the Charles River Bridge Case, and the Crisis of Republicanism,"
American Journal of Legal History 17 (July 1973): 232–45.

Pragmatism, coupled with a deference to legislative judgment in matters affecting state
and regional economies, also characterized the Taney Court's approach to the commerce
clause. Arguably, the Marshall Court's broad interpretation of the power delegated to
Congress in Article I, Section 8, "To regulate Commerce . . . among the several states,"
could have been applied by the Taney Court to embrace the affairs of the business corporation. On one occasion, *Bank of Augusta v. Earle* (1839), the Court bypassed such an opportunity when counsel for one of the plaintiffs, a Mr. Ogden, argued that the right of corporations to do business in other states was implied by the commerce clause. The Court,
however, did not even consider Ogden's suggestion which like Webster's privileges and
immunities argument was somewhat ahead of its time. On this, see Dodd, *American
Business Corporations*, pp. 152, 156.

The holding in *Bank of Augusta*, however, must also be explained in light of the Taney
Court's sensitivity to the South's fear that a broad interpretation of citizenship for corpora-
tions might be extended in commerce cases to regulate interstate slave trade. On this, see
Seavoy, *Origins*, pp. 249–52.

52. The doctrine of strict construction, although normally associated with Taney's opinion in *Charles River Bridge*, was clearly stated by Marshall in *Dartmouth*: "Being the mere
creature of law, it possesses only those properties which the charter of its creation confers
upon it, either expressly, or as incidental to its very existence. These are such as are
supposed best calculated to effect the object for which it was created. . . . There can be no
reason for implying in a charter, given for a valuable consideration, a power which is not
only not expressed, but is in direct contradiction to its express stipulations" (4 Wheaton
518, 636, 638 [1819]). Also, in *Providence Bank v. Billings*, 4 Peters 514 (1830), Marshall strictly
construed the bank's charter so as to deny an implied tax exemption, thereby affirming the
state's power to tax in the absence of an express stipulation in the charter to the contrary. It
is significant that, in deciding *Charles River Bridge*, Taney relied on Marshall's construction
of the corporate charter in *Providence Bank*. On this, see Kutler, *Privilege*, pp. 64–69, 89–91.

The Court's ruling in *Ogden v. Saunders*, 12 Wheaton 213 (1827), also contributed to the
eventual decline of the contract clause. Here the Court held that the contract clause applies
only to retrospective legislation—which is to say, it cannot be invoked to strike down acts
in existence at the time the contract was consummated. In his first dissenting opinion in
twenty-six years on the Court, Marshall, with Justices Story and Duvall concurring, maintained that the right to contract is inalienable and that under no conditions can it be
abridged (retrospectively or prospectively) by government. For an analysis of *Ogden* in
light of the Court's effort to reconcile competing claims of property rights in a developing
market economy, see White, *Marshall Court*, pp. 648–57.

53. Horwitz, *Transformation, 1780–1860*, pp. 136–39; Kutler, *Privilege*, pp. 133–42.

54. On national reaction to *Charles River Bridge* and the "judicial revolution" of 1837, see
Kutler, *Privilege*, pp. 117–32.

55. For example, the following excerpt from a letter printed in the Philadelphia *General
Advertiser* on January 23, 1792, is typical of the early political critique of American business
corporations. Written in opposition to the recent New Jersey act establishing the "Society
for establishing useful Manufactures," a corporation aided and promoted by then Secre-

tary of the Treasury Alexander Hamilton, the author, identified only as "Anti-Monopolist," expounded on the social and political evils of corporate enterprise: "Wealthy speculators of all denominations are incorporated and vested with exclusive privileges, partial laws are made in their favor, the benefit of which others do not enjoy; and they are exempted from the common burthens imposed on the rest of society. This propensity for corporations is very dangerous to the liberties of a people; it raises up various bodies of men of the most influential description in the community, and separates them from the mass of the people; at the same time by distinguishing them with peculiar marks of favor, it attaches them to the ruling powers by the common ties of gratitude and self-interest, and therefore gives an additional or artificial weight to government which our Constitution does not warrant. But the subject becomes still more alarming, if we recollect that these corporations are looked on by those who frame them as sacred and irrevocable; for in the course of time if this notion continues, and new corporations succeed each other, as they have lately done, we shall inevitably have all our wealthy citizens, whether they be engaged as merchants, manufacturers, or speculators, formed into corporate bodies, to aggrandize themselves, and increase the influence of government." See Davis, *Essays*, 1:431. See also ibid., pp. 427–53; 2:84–87, 303–9; Frederick B. Tolles, *George Logan of Philadelphia* (New York: Oxford University Press, 1953), pp. 117–28.

56. The First Bank of the United States operated from 1791 to 1811, when its charter was allowed to expire. In 1816, a Second Bank, formed on the model of its predecessor, was created by Congress.

57. The constitutionality of the Bank, and its exemption from state taxation, were established by the Supreme Court in *McCulloch v. Maryland*, 4 Wheaton 316 (1819), a case in which Chief Justice Marshall also reiterated the supremacy of the national government and articulated the doctrine of the "implied powers" of Congress to pass laws deemed "necessary and proper" for accomplishing the ends of its enumerated powers.

58. On the conceptual confusion propagated by the anticharter movement, see Hurst, *Legitimacy*, pp. 30–35; Louis Hartz, *Economic Policy and Democratic Thought: Pennsylvania, 1776–1860* (Chicago: Quadrangle Books, 1948), pp. 69–79, 243–53.

59. Hartz, *Economic Policy*, p. 250. See also ibid., pp. 251–53 and 309–20, for an analysis of the emergent corporate ideology, and Seavoy, *Origins*, pp. 158–75, 179–82, 266–74.

60. In an effort to salvage what he could of the common-law doctrine, Story based his defense of the implied right of exclusivity in *Charles River Bridge* on a distinction between the public and private purposes of business corporations. He argued that immunity from injurious competition could not be invoked by private corporations unless they performed a public function. Private corporations that involved "public duties and public matters for the benefit of the people" were "affected with a juris publicum"; those that were "for mere private gain, involving no such consideration," were "always deemed privati juris." Only the former included an implied right of exclusivity under common law: "The tolls are deemed an equivalent for the burden, and are deemed exclusive, because they might not otherwise afford any just indemnity." See 11 Peters 420, 639 (1837).

61. On the relationship between corporate law, property law, and the emergence of the legal principle of competition in early nineteenth-century America, see Horwitz, *Transformation, 1780–1860*, pp. 109–26. See also G. Edward White, *The American Judicial Tradition: Profiles of Leading American Judges* (New York: Oxford University Press, 1988), pp. 47–63.

62. Arthur M. Schlesinger Jr., *The Age of Jackson* (Boston: Little, Brown, 1945), pp. 336–39; Richard Hofstadter, *The American Political Tradition* (New York: Vintage Books, 1948), pp. 64–65; Hofstadter, "William Leggett, Spokesman of Jacksonian Democracy," *Political Science Quarterly* 58 (December 1943): 588–90; Joseph Dorfman, *The Economic Mind in American Civilization* (New York: Viking Press, 1946), 2:621–22. On general incorporation acts,

see Seavoy, *Origins*, pp. 65–71, 177–223, 268–74; Cadman, *Corporation in New Jersey*, pp. 84–201; Berle & Means, *Modern Corporation*, pp. 135–37; Hurst, *Legitimacy*, pp. 21–22, 27–29, 56–57; Dodd, *American Business Corporations*, pp. 402–7, 410–11, 418–19; Hartz, *Economic Policy*, pp. 39–42; George Heberton Evans Jr., *Business Incorporations in the United States, 1800–1943* (New York: National Bureau of Economic Research, 1948), pp. 10–35.

General incorporation laws, which exemplified the emerging legal principle of competition, served as a catalyst in many states for the tremendous proliferation of corporate enterprise that occurred between 1837 and 1866. The movement away from special acts to general acts entailed widespread state constitutional reform: "During and after the decade of the eighteen forties, there was a distinct tendency in various states to restrict the power of state legislators to treat the problem of incorporation for business purposes in any manner they might see fit. Owing principally to a great increase in the number of business corporations and the use of the corporate form of organization by an ever-increasing variety of business enterprises, constitutional restraints on the freedom of legislators to incorporate business units became much more numerous in the years after 1844 than they had been previously." See Cadman, *Corporation in New Jersey*, pp. 183–84.

Thus decisions by state legislatures to adopt general incorporation acts or to liberalize existing incorporation statutes, or to do both, entailed a dramatic shift in public policy: "General incorporation statutes for banks and railroads were the ultimate expression of a laissez faire economic policy because banks and railroads were the two classes of business corporations that had an immediate and pervasive impact on public welfare. A laissez faire incorporation policy for both banks and railroads, as well as for other classes of business corporations, coming as it did on the verge of take-off into self-sustained industrial growth, was an extremely useful incentive to encourage industrialization. It had been recognized as early as 1837 that the large number and variety of business corporations were making a disproportionate contribution to the rapid industrial expansion of the United States." See Seavoy, *Origins*, p. 272.

63. Norman Ware, *The Industrial Worker, 1840–1860* (New York: Quadrangle / New York Times Book Co., 1964).

64. Antimonopoly, in its various forms, however, was not the only argument that could be marshaled effectively to attack the business corporation. As exclusive franchises and special privileges gave way to demands for general incorporation acts, thereby undercutting the egalitarian antimonoply argument, another anticorporate and laissez-faire argument was at hand in Adam Smith's criticism of the business corporation in *The Wealth of Nations*. Smith's attack on corporate enterprise derived from what he believed to be its critical flaw in a free market economy—namely, that the directors or management of a corporation would not exhibit the same initiative and pecuniary drive as the entrepreneur or sole proprietor. He therefore recommended that joint-stock companies be employed only in businesses in which operations followed a predictable "routine," in which the capital needs were great, and in which the risk of failure was considerable. In his view, only four types of business met these standards: banking, insurance, canal companies, and water supply companies. Smith also opposed monopolistic privilege as anathema to free enterprise, unless it served the temporary function of opening up a new branch of trade, as in the case of trading companies in foreign lands. See Adam Smith, *An Inquiry into the Nature and Causes of the Wealth of Nations*, ed., Edwin Cannan (New Rochelle, N.Y.: Arlington House, 1966), 2:325, 345–64.

While Smith's strictures against corporations might appear to have had a much greater impact on the debates in Britain than those in the United States, his argument did raise the significant question of whether the business corporation was truly suited to the competitive demands of early industrial capitalism. The steady proliferation of American business corporations in the initial decades of the nineteenth century suggests that doctrinaire opposition to corporate enterprise along the lines of Smith consistently gave way to native practical experience with the apparent efficiency of the corporate device, contrary to the author's claims. In any event, by the time the corporate bourgeoisie wholly embraced Smithian economics as its own in the second half of the century, corporate individualism already had stood Smith's anticorporate argument on its head. On the importance of Smith in antebellum debates, see Hartz, *Economic Policy,* pp. 60, 69–70, 79–80; Hurst, *Legitimacy,* p. 48; and Schlesinger, *Age of Jackson,* pp. 314–17; and on Smith in Britain in the first half of the nineteenth century, see Hunt, *Development,* pp. 22–23, 57, 71, 86, 116–18, 131–32. On the British debate, cf. John R. McCulloch, *Considerations on Partnership with Limited Liability* (London: Longman, Brown, Green & Longmans, 1856); Woodforde Ffooks, *The Law of Partnership an Obstacle to Social Progress* (London: W. G. Benning & Co., 1854).

65. By 1880, most states had enacted general incorporation legislation, but many of the regulatory provisions of these statutes were of "dubious effect." See Hurst, *Legitimacy,* p. 57.

66. The internal affairs of the special charter corporation were necessarily a matter of public record and scrutiny, given the fact that such corporations were created by special legislation. With the advent of general incorporation statutes, however, standardized administrative procedures allowing incorporators to create their own terms displaced public debate over the terms of incorporation. See Berle and Means, *Modern Corporation,* pp. 135–36.

67. Ibid., pp. 132, 140; Dodd, *American Business Corporations,* pp. 192–93.

68. Hurst, *Legitimacy,* pp. 25–26; Dodd, *American Business Corporations,* pp. 193–94.

69. Berle and Means, *Modern Corporation,* p. 139.

70. 3 Mass. 364 (1807).

71. Dodd, *American Business Corporations,* pp. 71–74; Hurst, *Legitimacy,* pp. 49–51; Berle and Means, *Modern Corporation,* pp. 144–46.

72. The practice of voting by proxy—an essential component of centralized control in the modern corporation—was already in widespread use during the antebellum period. Although created for convenience of the shareholder, it had received criticism even at this early date as a method of centralizing the internal control of the business corporation. See Hartz, *Economic Policy,* pp. 255–56.

73. Hurst, *Legitimacy,* p. 27; Dodd, *American Business Corporations,* pp. 364–437.

74. These legislative limitations on corporate power could be avoided or ignored, but it remains that the legislature's powers to regulate corporate business through the charter and to revoke charters were recognized as legitimate controls throughout the formative era. With regard to the issue of corporate autonomy, one important exception might be the highly capitalized early railroad companies. Although not treated under the law as private corporations, railroads were in effect privately controlled corporations that received special privileges and considerations because of their "public" character or function. Even so, the greater autonomy that the larger railway companies enjoyed must be assessed in light of the fact that the law granted special dispensations because railroads performed a public function; and by the same reasoning, railroads were subject to regulation in the public interest. See Leonard W. Levy, "Chief Justice Shaw and the Formative Period of American Railroad Law," *Columbia Law Review* 51 (1951): 327–48, 852–65.

75. By the end of the Civil War 35,000 miles of track had already been laid. That mileage would more than double within the next decade, by which time the first transcontinental railroad linking the East and West Coasts would be completed, and then steadily increase

to more than 180,000 miles at the close of the century. See Alfred D. Chandler Jr., *The Railroads: The Nation's First Big Business* (New York: Harcourt, Brace & World, 1965), pp. 13–14, tables 1 and 2.

76. Chandler, *Railroads*, pp. 48–88; Kirkland, *Industry Comes of Age* (note 16 above), pp. 52–55. See also Cochran and Miller, *Age of Enterprise* (note 16 above), pp. 131–35.

77. Although elusive to achieve, the goal of "reasonable" rates—which is to say, stable and profitable rates—had been sought by railroad leaders for nearly two decades before Congress created the Interstate Commerce Commission in 1887. During these years the great majority of pooling agreements had failed. For a history of rate regulation in the railroads, with special focus on the role of railroad leaders in shaping federal policies, see Gabriel Kolko, *Railroads and Regulation, 1877–1916* (Princeton: Princeton University Press, 1965).

78. Alfred D. Chandler Jr., *The Visible Hand: The Managerial Revolution in American Business* (Cambridge, Mass.: Harvard University Press, Belknap Press, 1977), pp. 94–109; Chandler, *Railroads*, pp. 97–125; Olivier Zunz, *Making America Corporate, 1870–1920* (Chicago: University of Chicago Press, 1990), pp. 38–66.

79. The constitutional protection afforded vested interests by the contract clause was also eroded through doctrinal developments that established the inalienability of the states' taxing powers and police powers. On this, see Charles W. McCurdy, "Justice Field and the Jurisprudence of Government-Business Relations: Some Parameters of Laissez-Faire Constitutionalism, 1863–1897," *The Journal of American History* 61 (1975): 987–95. See *Morgan v. Louisiana*, 93 U.S. 217 (1876); *Railroad Co. v. Maine*, 96 U.S. 499 (1877); *Boyd v. Alabama*, 94 U.S. 645 (1877); *Stone v. Mississippi*, 101 U.S. 814 (1880); *Butchers' Union Slaughter-House Co. v. Crescent City Slaughter-House Co.*, 111 U.S. 746 (1884).

80. Amendment XIV, Section 1: "All persons born or naturalized in the United States and subject to the jurisdiction thereof are citizens of the United States and the State wherein they reside. No State shall make or enforce any law which shall abridge the privileges and immunities of citizens of the United States; nor shall any State deprive any person of life, liberty, or property, without due process of law; nor deny to any person within its jurisdiction the equal protection of the laws."

81. *Slaughter-House Cases*, 16 Wall. 36 (1873).

82. Campbell also argued that the monopoly violated the Thirteenth Amendment's prohibition against involuntary servitude, a claim that the Court quickly disposed of. Justice Miller's opinion focused mainly on the privileges and immunities clause, which he rendered redundant and hence virtually meaningless by arguing that it did not create any new rights that citizens could invoke against state governments. However, by denying the due process claim only on the ground that it is unlike any construction "we have ever seen, or any that we deem admissible," Miller left the issue open for interpretation. It should be noted that even a favorable interpretation of the privileges and immunities clause for the rights of property would not necessarily have aided the cause of corporate enterprise, because only four years earlier, in *Paul v. Virginia* 8 Wall. 168, the Court again had rejected the application of the word "citizen" (in the Article IV version of this clause) to the corporation, in keeping with Roger Taney's opinion in *Bank of Augusta v. Earle*.

83. 94 U.S. 113.

84. Ibid., p. 126.

85. Ibid., p. 134.

86. Ibid., p. 139. For an analysis of Justice Field's dissent examined within the broader context of his jurisprudence, see McCurdy, "Justice Field," pp. 996–1005. McCurdy effectively demonstrates that Field's abiding concern with property rights must be understood

in light of his overriding objective of establishing "inviolable" rules separating the public and private spheres.

87. *Wabash, St. Louis & Pacific Railway Co. v. Illinois*, 118 U.S. 557 (1886). Congress created the Interstate Commerce Commission a year later to regulate railroad rates, making this decision inconsequential until the Supreme Court eviscerated the ICC's rate-setting powers in 1896. *Wabash*, however, signaled the increasing willingness of the Court to strike down state regulations of foreign corporations doing business in interstate commerce. The disposition of the Supreme Court in these matters was of considerable importance, since it determined whether a business operated in intrastate or interstate commerce, and hence when and to what extent the states or the federal government could properly regulate. Justice Miller held for the majority that "this species of regulation" was "of a general and national character" and therefore did not fall within the province of the states to regulate. Dissenting, Bradley argued that, in the absence of congressional legislation, Illinois could regulate commerce within the state even though it might indirectly affect interstate commerce. The Court employed each of these rationales to achieve different policy objectives throughout the ensuing decade. On the Waite and Fuller Courts' interpretation of the commerce power, see below, notes 94, 97, 105, 107, and below, in the present section.

88. *Stone v. Farmers' Loan & Trust Co.*, 116 U.S. 307 (1886). Whereas earlier cases upheld the states' reserved power, as set forth in the charters, to regulate rates, this case went a step further in upholding a state act that amended a charter provision giving the railroad the power to set rates. A year later in *Mugler v. Kansas*, 123 U.S. 623, Justice John Harlan, writing for the majority, issued another warning (or hint) to the effect that the Court was prepared to strike down state acts that constituted "a palpable invasion of rights secured by the fundamental law."

89. *Santa Clara Co. v. Southern Pacific R.R.*, 118 U.S. 394 (1886). Corporations were considered persons for purposes of the due process clause of the Fourteenth Amendment in *Minneapolis & S.L.R. Co. v. Beckwith*, 129 U.S. 26 (1889). In *Santa Clara*, the Court required no argument because it had accepted the theory expounded before it four years earlier by Roscoe Conkling, former U.S. Senator and member of the congressional committee that drafted the Fourteenth Amendment, that the framers of the amendment specifically used the word "person" (as opposed to "citizen") to include corporations within the equal protection and due process clauses. Conkling's famous conspiracy theory, based on a selective and entirely misleading use of evidence from the drafting sessions, has been thoroughly discredited by scholars in this century. See Howard Jay Graham, "The Conspiracy Theory of the Fourteenth Amendment," *Yale Law Journal* 47 (January 1938): 371–403; Louis Boudin, "Truth and Fiction About the Fourteenth Amendment," *New York University Law Quarterly Review* 16 (November 1938): 19–82; Joseph B. James, *The Framing of the Fourteenth Amendment* (Urbana: University of Illinois Press, 1965), pp. 194–98. In 1886, however, the Court, in accepting Conkling's argument on its face, was not inclined to question the integrity of a man who was a leader in his profession and who had twice refused appointments to the Supreme Court.

90. 134 U.S. 418.

91. While the Court did not determine the reasonableness of rates in this case, it claimed the power to do so: "The question of the reasonableness of a rate of charge . . . is eminently a question for judicial investigation, requiring due process of law for its determination." The Court also held that the equal protection clause had been violated. Justice Joseph Bradley, in dissent, argued that the ruling practically overruled *Munn* and other rate cases decided at the same time as *Munn*. However, in *Budd v. New York*, 148 U.S. 517, 538–548 (1892), the Court reaffirmed its holding in *Munn*, which it distinguished from *Chicago,*

Milwaukee & St. Paul R.R. Co. in terms of the nature of the regulation. Justice Blatchford explained that the Minnesota legislature had established a commission to set rates (which were subject to judicial review of reasonableness), whereas in *Munn* and in the present case, legislatures *directly* prescribed rates, the reasonableness of which the Court would not question absent a finding of an unconstitutional deprivation of property or violation of equal protection of the laws. Justice Brewer, joined by Justices Field and Brown, wrote a sharply worded dissent criticizing the reaffirmation of *Munn*. Deriding the "paternal theory of government" espoused in the majority opinion, Brewer warned that the Court's logic made *Looking Backward* "nearer than a dream."

92. 165 U.S. 578.

93. Roscoe Pound, "Liberty of Contract," *Yale Law Journal* 18 (May 1909): 454–78. Howard Jay Graham, "Justice Field and the Fourteenth Amendment," *Yale Law Journal* 52 (September 1943): 851–89. Many state courts relied heavily on the dissents of Justices Field and Bradley in *Slaughter-House Cases* and on Bradley's and Field's separate concurring opinions in *Butchers' Union Slaughter-House Co. v. Crescent City Slaughter-House Co.*, 111 U.S. 746, 755–66 (1884). See also Field's dissent in *Powell v. Pennsylvania*, 127 U.S. 678, 688 (1888), for an analysis of numerous state cases that invoked liberty of contract or similar doctrine to strike down economic regulations. Leading state cases on liberty of contract decided before *Allgeyer* include *Jones v. People*, 110 Ill. 590 (1884); *In Re Jacobs*, 98 N.Y. 98 (1885); *People v. Marx*, 99 N.Y. 377 (1886); *Godcharles v. Wigeman*, 113 Pa. St. 427 (1886); *Millet v. People*, 117 Ill. 294 (1886); *State v. Goodwill*, 33 W.Va. 179 (1889); *Ex Parte Kuback*, 85 Cal. 274 (1890); *State v. Julow*, 129 Mo. 163 (1895); *Ritchie v. People*, 155 Ill. 99 (1895).

On the rise of substantive due process, cf. Charles G. Haines, "Judicial Review of Legislation in the United States and the Doctrine of Vested Rights and of Implied Limitations on Legislatures," *Texas Law Review* 3 (December 1924): 1–43; Walton H. Hamilton, "The Path of Due Process of Law," in Leonard W. Levy, ed., *American Constitutional Law: Historical Essays* (New York: Harper & Row, 1966), pp. 129–54; John P. Roche, "Entrepreneurial Liberty," in Richard M. Abrams and Lawrence W. Levine, eds., *The Shaping of Twentieth-Century America* (Boston: Little, Brown, 1965), pp. 128–53; Benjamin R. Twiss, *Lawyers and the Constitution* (Princeton: Princeton University Press, 1942); Arnold Paul, *Conservative Crisis and the Rule of Law: Attitudes of Bar and Bench, 1887–1895* (Ithaca: Cornell University Press, 1960), pp. 1–81; Howard Gillman, *The Constitution Beseiged: The Rise and Demise of Lochner Era Police Powers Jurisprudence* (Durham, N.C.: Duke University Press, 1993).

94. *Philadelphia & Reading R.R. v. Pennsylvania*, 15 Wall. 232 (1873); *Welton v. Missouri*, 91 U.S. 275 (1876); *Hannibal & Saint Joseph Railroad Co. v. Husen*, 95 U.S. 465 (1877); *Pensacola Telegraph Co. v. Western Union Telegraph*, 96 U.S. 1 (1878); *Pickard v. Pullman Southern Car Co.*, 117 U.S. 34 (1886); *Wabash, St. Louis & Pacific Railway Co. v. Illinois*, 118 U.S. 557 (1886); *Robbins v. Shelby County Taxing District*, 120 U.S. 489 (1887); *Leloup v. Port of Mobile*, 127 U.S. 640 (1888); *Asher v. Texas*, 128 U.S. 129 (1888); *McCall v. California*, 136 U.S. 104 (1890); *Norfolk & Western Railroad Co. v. Pennsylvania*, 136 U.S. 114 (1890); *Brimmer v. Rebman*, 138 U.S. 78 (1891); *Crutcher v. Kentucky*, 141 U.S. 47 (1891); *Western Union Telegraph Co. v. Kansas*, 216 U.S. 1 (1910); *Pullman Co. v. Kansas*, 216 U.S. 56 (1910); *Ludwig v. Western Union Telegraph Co.*, 216 U.S. 146 (1910); *International Textbook Co. v. Pigg*, 217 U.S. 91 (1910). Cf. Gerard Carl Henderson, *The Position of Foreign Corporations in American Constitutional Law* (Cambridge, Mass.: Harvard University Press, 1918), pp. 112–31; Tony A. Freyer, "The Federal Courts, Localism, and the National Economy, 1865–1900," *Business History Review* 53 (Autumn 1979): 343–63; Charles W. McCurdy, "American Law and the Marketing Structure of the Large Corporation, 1875–1890," *Journal of Economic History* 38 (September 1978): 631–49.

95. The fact that the corporation was not afforded citizenship has proven to be largely inconsequential in light of the Court's narrow interpretation of the privileges and immuni-

ties clauses and the rights and capacities bestowed on the corporation through other clauses of the Constitution.

96. *Bank of Augusta v. Earle*, 13 Peters 519 (1839); *Paul v. Virginia*, 8 Wall. 168 (1869); *Crutcher v. Kentucky*, 141 U.S. 47, 50 (1891); *Hooper v. California*, 155 U.S. 648, 653–56 (1895).

97. *Paul v. Virginia*; *Cooper Manufacturing Co. v. Ferguson*, 113 U.S. 727 (1885); *Coe v. Errol*, 116 U.S. 517 (1886); *Kidd v. Pearson*, 128 U.S. 1 (1888); *Crutcher v. Kentucky*; *United States v. E. C. Knight*, 156 U.S. 1 (1895); *Hooper v. California*. On the significance of the manufacturing-commerce distinction for corporation law and the early development of antitrust law, see Charles W. McCurdy, "The *Knight* Sugar Decision of 1895 and the Modernization of American Corporation Law, 1869–1903," *Business History Review* 53 (Autumn 1979): 304–42; Sklar, *Corporate Reconstruction*, pp. 113, 123–27, 136–38, 159–61.

98. *Louisville, New Orleans & Texas Railway Co. v. Mississippi*, 133 U.S. 587 (1890). See also note 105 below.

99. Charles A. Lofgren, *The Plessy Case: A Legal-Historical Interpretation* (New York: Oxford University Press, 1987), p. 80.

100. The Supreme Court's narrow interpretation of the liberties afforded by the Fourteenth Amendment, including the scope of Congress's power under Section 5 to remedy discrimination and violations of civil rights, was also consistent with its refusal to recognize new rights of property in that amendment and its concomitant affirmation of the police powers doctrine. Cf. *Slaughter-House Cases*, 16 Wall. 36 (1873); *United States v. Cruikshank*, 92 U.S. 542 (1876); *Civil Rights Cases*, 109 U.S. 3 (1883); *United States v. Harris*, 106 U.S. 629 (1883). Throughout the decade or so that preceded *Allgeyer* (1897), during which time the views of Justices Field and Bradley steadily gained a foothold in the Court's rulings on due process, only Justice John Harlan maintained that the Fourteenth Amendment guaranteed both the civil rights of blacks (and empowered Congress to legislate accordingly) and the rights of property, as embodied in the doctrine of liberty of contract.

101. Similarly, rulings under the due process and equal protection clauses concerning the scope of the states' powers to enact economic and social regulations had a direct bearing on the constitutionality of mandated segregation inasmuch as these rulings involved an interpretation of rights guaranteed by the Fourteenth Amendment as weighed against the police powers of the states. For an informative analysis along these lines, see Lofgren, *Plessy Case*, pp. 61–92.

102. Ibid., pp. 21–24.

103. Plaintiffs in these suits employed both the common-law doctrine on restraints of trade and the *ultra vires* doctrine in corporation law that prohibited corporations from exceeding the powers conferred in the provisions of their charters—in this instance, provisions restricting methods of capitalization or prohibiting mergers and consolidations. See Sklar, Corporate Reconstruction, pp. 98–99; McCurdy, "*Knight* Sugar Decision," pp. 321–23; Hans B. Thorelli, *The Federal Antitrust Policy: Origination of an American Tradition* (Baltimore: The Johns Hopkins University Press, 1955), pp. 50, 80, 161.

The use of the trust as a means to effect consolidations developed out of the failures of the pooling agreements of the 1870s to control or eliminate competition. First implemented by Standard Oil, on the advice of attorney S. C. T. Dodd, the industrial trust served as a legal device through which competing corporations would transfer their stocks and assets to a board of trustees in exchange for trust certificates that represented a proportionate interest in the total value of the trust. Certificates, in effect, constituted stock that yielded dividends, determined voting interests, and could be transferred or sold. Typically, an elected board of trustees exercised complete control over the trust's operations, including the purchase of new companies.

Industrial trusts were specifically designed to circumvent the limitations of corporation law on capitalization and acquisition of stock in other corporations, and the common law prohibitions against restraint of trade and monopoly. Whether these trusts would be afforded special legal status by the courts, however, was less important than the fact that they were private agreements made outside the terms of the corporate charter and not intended for public scrutiny. Following the success of the Standard Oil trusts of 1879 and 1882, through which John D. Rockefeller secured his dominance in the petroleum industry, numerous imitators soon acquired monopolistic control in other industries. Among the most successful and notorious were the Sugar Trust, the Lead Trust, the Whiskey Trust, the Salt Trust, the Copper Trust, the Tobacco Trust, and the Cottonseed Oil Trust.

104. Cf. Kolko, *Railroads and Regulation;* Chandler, *The Visible Hand,* pp.145–87; Stephen Skowronek, *Building a New American State: The Expansion of National Administrative Capacities, 1877–1920* (New York: Cambridge University Press, 1982), pp. 121–62; Lee Benson, *Merchants, Farmers, and Railroads: Railroad Regulation and New York Politics, 1850–1887* (Cambridge, Mass.: Harvard University Press, 1955).

105. On several occasions, the Court felt obliged to reiterate the scope of its holdings concerning the constitutionality of state economic regulations. Cf. *Crutcher v. Kentucky* (1890); *Budd v. New York* (1892); *Lawton v. Steele,* 152 U.S. 133 (1894); *Brass v. North Dakota,* 153 U.S. 391 (1894); *Plumley v. Massachusetts,* 155 U.S. 462 (1894); *Hooper v. California* (1895); *United States v. E. C. Knight* (1895); *Louisville & Nashville R.R. Co. v. Kentucky,* 161 U.S. 677 (1896). A broad reading of the states' powers over intrastate commerce lent support to the Court's holding in *Louisville, New Orleans & Texas Railway Co. v. Mississippi,* 133 U.S. 587 (1890), that a Mississippi statute requiring separate cars for white and black passengers on all railroads in the state did not constitute a regulation of interstate commerce. Justice Brewer explained that "the supreme court of Mississippi held that the statute applied solely to commerce within the state," a construction, he asserted, which "must be accepted as conclusive here." Dissenting, Justice Harlan exposed the central contradiction of the majority opinion, pointing out that whereas in *Hall v. DeCuir,* 95 U.S. 485 (1878), the Court had ruled that a Louisiana statute prohibiting discrimination on common carriers constituted a direct burden on interstate commerce (arguing that confusion would result if each state were allowed to adopt its own rules affecting seating on an interstate journey), the Court in the present case refused to apply the same reasoning to a statute mandating separate accommodations on railroads involved in interstate commerce. In affirming Mississippi's ruling, Justice Brewer quoted from *Wabash,* 118 U.S. 557, 565 (1886), where Justice Miller remarked that if the statute in that case had "applied exclusively to contracts for a carriage which begins and ends within the state, disconnected from a continuous transportation through or into other states," it would have been upheld as a valid regulation of intrastate commerce. This line of reasoning, however, would appear only to confuse the issue inasmuch as the Court in *Wabash* (at pp. 570–74) relied directly on *Hall v. DeCuir* in finding that the Illinois statute imposed a burden on interstate commerce. Citing Miller's dictum only strengthened Harlan's point that *Hall v. DeCuir* and *Louisville* both involved interstate transportation.

Brewer also cited (though he did not quote from) *Stone v. Farmers' Loan & Trust,* 116 U.S. 307 (1886), which would appear to be the more relevant precedent. In noting that a railroad could be incorporated in all the states through which it operates, Chief Justice Waite observed in *Stone* (pp. 333–35) that the "corporation created by each state is, for all the purposes of local government, a domestic corporation" and that as such the state "may govern this corporation, as it does all domestic coporations, in respect to every act and everything within the state which is the lawful subject of the state government." Thus the state "may make all needful regulations of a police character for the government of the company while operating its road in that jurisdiction." Moreover, the fact that railroads were instrumentalities of interstate commerce did not prevent the state from acting: "Legislation of this kind, to be unconstitutional, must be such as will necessarily amount to or operate as a regulation of business without the state as well as within." Cf. *Coe v. Errol*; *Kidd v. Pearson*; *United States v. E. C. Knight*. In ruling only that the statute did not constitute a regulation of interstate commerce, however, *Louisville* did not decide the constitutional issue of the states' power to compel segregation on common carriers. For an analysis of the origins and development of American law as it pertained to segregation on common carriers, especially with regard to the effect of *Hall v. DeCuir* in federalizing the common-law reasonableness doctrine of separate-but-equal, see Lofgren, *Plessy Case*, pp. 7–27, 116–47.

106. 163 U.S. 537 (1896).

107. Employing a broad interpretation of the police powers doctrine, Justice Brown, in *Plessy*, held that the separate-but-equal law of Louisiana constituted a reasonable regulation and therefore did not violate the equal protection, due process, and privileges and immunities clauses of the Fourteenth Amendment. Lofgren observes that Justice Brown's "case citations, while not all relevant, pointed toward reasonableness not as a restrictive concept but rather as a doctrine of *empowerment*, or at least as a vehicle for importing broad public sentiment and existing legislative and judicial inclination into definitions of constitutional limitations" (p. 190). Because of earlier decisions under the commerce clause (note 105 above), *Plessy* in effect constituted the last resort for testing the constitutionality of Jim Crow legislation in common carriers. Between 1898 and 1907, five additional states passed mandatory separate-but-equal laws. See Lofgren, *Plessy Case*, p. 22. See also ibid., pp. 28–60, 148–208, for a detailed examination of the history, legal significance, and social impact of *Plessy*.

Sklar (*Corporate Reconstruction*, p. 161, n. 180) suggests that *Plessy* may have facilitated the Court's broad construction of the commerce power under the Sherman Antitrust Act in *United States v. Trans-Missouri Freight Association*, 166 U.S. 290 (1897): "by validating the states' control of race relations even where they might touch interstate commerce, [*Plessy*] in effect cleared the way for the Court's majority, including Fuller, to recede from the strict distinction between the police power (or "production") and interstate commerce in *Knight* (following *Coe v. Errol* and *Kidd v. Pearson*), without jeopardizing the legal structure of racial segregation then being installed in the southern states."

108. Pursuant to the changes in New Jersey corporation law eliminating restrictions on the issuance of stock and the purchase of the stock of one corporation by another, Standard Oil of New Jersey, in 1889, increased its capital stock from $10 million to $110 million, then used this stock to acquire the stock and properties held by the Standard Oil Trust, thereby transforming the trust into a holding company, entirely legal under New Jersey law. By 1904, New Jersey was the home for the seven largest holding companies in the nation, accounting for more than $2.5 billion in aggregate assets, including the biggest of them all, the United States Steel Corporation, which alone comprised nearly $1.5 billion of the total.

Delaware eventually took over the leadership in the charter competition. Delaware's 1899 act anticipated this development with a provision that effectively transferred traditional legislative functions to the corporation itself: "The certification of incorporation may also contain any provision which the incorporators may choose to insert for the management of the business and for the conduct of the affairs of the corporation, and any provision creating, defining, limiting, and regulating the powers of the corporation, the directors and stockholders; provided, such provisions are not contrary to the laws of this State."

Delaware's "model" act was passed in 1915, and by 1932 the state had chartered more than 40,000 corporations, including one-third of the industrials on the New York Stock Exchange. By 1988, some 179,000 firms, among them 56 percent of the Fortune 500, had chosen Delaware as their legal domicile. Delaware revised its incorporation statutes in 1967 in an effort to retain its leading position in the charter business. Thus, competition between states for corporate charters continues to be a factor in the development of corporation law.

109. For an analysis of the difficult choices confronting state policy-makers during this period, see McCurdy, "*Knight* Sugar Decision," pp. 336–40.

110. Cf. *Ashley v. Ryan*, 153 U.S. 436 (1894); *Hooper v. California; United States v. E. C. Knight; Pearsall v. Railway Co.*, 161 U.S. 601 (1896); *Louisville & Nashville R.R. Co. v. Kentucky*, 161 U.S. 677 (1896); *St. Louis & San Francisco Railway Co. v. Mathews*, 165 U.S. 1 (1897); *Oriental Insurance Co. v. Daggs*, 172 U.S. 557 (1899); *St. Louis, Iron Mountain & Southern Railway Co. v. Paul*, 173 U.S. 404 (1899). At the same time, however, in keeping with its rulings in *Santa Clara Co. v. Southern Pacific R.R.* (1886) and *Allgeyer* (1897), the Court reaffirmed the constitutional status of the corporation as a person entitled to protection of the rights of property guaranteed by the Fourteenth Amendment. See *Gulf, Colorado & Santa Fe Railway Co. v. Ellis*, 165 U.S. 150 (1897); *Smyth v. Ames*, 169 U.S. 466 (1898). Depending on the issues at bar and the nature of the regulation, the Court could either uphold state regulations under the corporate charter or statutory law, or regulate property rights (e.g., in rate regulation and liberty of contract cases) consistent with its nationalization of these rights through the due process clause of the Fourteenth Amendment.

111. Between 1898 and 1902, there were 2,653 reported mergers at a total capitalization of $6.2 billion, producing, by 1903, some 318 significant industrial combinations with more than 5,200 plants capitalized at $7.2 billion. Samuel Richardson Reid, *Mergers, Managers, and the Economy* (New York: McGraw-Hill, 1968), pp. 38–39. The total capitalization of all American corporations individually valued at $1 million or more came to $170 million in 1897, to $5 billion in 1900, and to $20 billion in 1905. Charles Forcey, *The Crossroads of Liberalism: Croly, Weyl, Lippmann, and the Progressive Era, 1900–1925* (New York: Oxford University Press, 1961), p. xviii, introduction. Between 1895 and 1904, some 75 percent of mergers resulted in consolidations of five or more enterprises. Naomi Lamoreaux found that of the 93 consolidations she studied for these years, 72 controlled at least 40 percent of their industries and, of these, 42 controlled at least 70 percent of their industries. See Naomi R. Lamoreaux, *The Great Merger Movement in American Business, 1895–1904* (Cambridge: Cambridge University Press, 1985), pp. 1–2, and generally, pp. 1–13, 87–158. See also, Sklar, *Corporate Reconstruction*, pp. 44–47; John Moody, *The Truth About the Trusts: A Description and Analysis of the American Trust Movement* (1904; reprint, New York: Greenwood Press, 1968), pp. 485–502; Chandler, *Visible Hand*, pp. 315–79; Ralph L. Nelson, *Merger Movements in American Industry, 1895–1956* (Princeton: Princeton University Press, 1959).

112. On the eve of the 1896 presidential election, General James B. Weaver, a national leader of the Populist Movement, urged fellow citizens to take to the polls to defeat the money lords:

"As in the day of the struggle with the slave power, the enemy has forced the issue, and, compared with the uprising which is just ahead of us, 1860 was but a skirmish. The great parent, law-enacted, man-eating crime of this age is the enthronement of capital above labor in the structure of government. The impious assertion by every department and by every commissioned satrap that property is more sacred than man, life or family. We have, by law, in this pretended republic closed the door of opportunity to the great body of the people, disinherited them by statute, compelled them to make bricks without straw and then in mockery counseled them to be law abiding, contented and prosperous. Have we not reduced man to the necessity of begging, in vain, for the opportunity to eat his crumb of poverty in the sweat of his face?" See James B. Weaver, "To the Ballot, O Men and Women," *American X-Rays*, October 1896 (Private collection of Sherman Silver Smith).

The demise of the Populist Party following the election of President William McKinley in 1896, however, did not silence the critics of corporate power or dissuade a growing legion of Americans from agitating for either comprehensive reform or a socialist alternative. On changing public perceptions of the large corporation during the Progressive Era, see Louis Galambos, *The Public Image of Big Business in America, 1880–1940* (Baltimore: Johns Hopkins University Press, 1975), pp. 70–156.

113. William W. Cook, *The Corporation Problem* (New York: Knickerbocker Press, 1893), pp. 226, 227–28, 233. For a similar argument by another Progressive Era legal scholar, see John Bates Clark, *The Problem of Monopoly: A Study of a Grave Danger and of the Natural Mode of Averting It* (New York: Macmillan, 1904).

114. From the Senate debate of March 21, 1890, quoted in Thorelli, *Federal Antitrust Policy,* pp. 180, 184. Sherman's reference to the American Revolution was consistent with the widespread sentiment that large corporations threatened the very foundations of liberty established barely a century earlier. In *The American Commonwealth* (1888), James Bryce made a similar observation:

"The power of groups of men organized by incorporation as joint-stock companies, or of small knots of rich men acting in combination, has developed with unexpected strength in unexpected ways, overshadowing individuals and even communities, and showing that the very freedom which men sought to secure by law when they were threatened with the violence of potentates may, under the shelter of the law, ripen into a new form of tyranny."

115. Sklar, *Corporate Reconstruction,* pp. 105–17; Thorelli, *Federal Antitrust Policy,* pp. 177–210; William Letwin, *Law and Economic Policy in America: The Evolution of the Sherman Antitrust Act* (Edinburgh: University Press, 1966), pp. 85–99. Sherman's original bill was amended extensively then referred to the Judiciary Committee, where it was rewritten. The substantive drafting of the final version was undertaken principally by Senator George Edmunds (R-Vt.), with contributions by other members of the Judiciary Committee, including Senator James George (D-Miss.), Senator George Hoar (Rep-Mass.), and Senator William Evarts (R-N.Y.). Sherman voted for its passage. His name remained on the act largely as a courtesy. Senators Edmunds and Hoar, however, shared Sherman's conviction that the act was intended to distinguish between lawful and unlawful restraints of trade, and they urged its passage on that basis. Sklar, *Corporate Reconstruction,* pp. 114–17; Letwin, *Law and Economic Policy,* p. 97.

Offenses under the Sherman Act are crimes punishable by fines and imprisonment. The act charges the U.S. Department of Justice with the responsibility of enforcement and with the duty to institute civil proceedings to enjoin violations of the law. The essential political character of the administration of antitrust law, therefore, stems from the fact that Presidents and their attorneys-general have considerable discretion in deciding whether to seek out and enforce possible violations. Section 7 of the act provides for civil suits to be brought in federal court by injured parties and authorizes an award for treble damages. Section 8 states that the word "person" includes corporations and associations.

116. 166 U.S. 290 (1897). Chief Justice Fuller's earlier ruling, in *United States v. E. C. Knight Co.* (1895), that the Sherman Act could not reach the monopolistic activities of the Sugar Trust (American Sugar Refining Company) under the commerce clause because it operated in "manufacturing" and therefore "only incidentally and indirectly" affected "commerce" (i.e., trade), while preserving the states' powers to regulate intrastate commerce, left unresolved broader issues of interpretation. This doctrine was specifically overruled, for the purposes of antitrust law, in the *Standard Oil* case of 1911. On the legal significance of *E. C. Knight,* see McCurdy, "*Knight* Sugar Decision"; and on the distinction between commerce and manufacturing in antitrust law, see Sklar, *Corporate Reconstruction,* pp. 113, 123–27, 136–38, 159–61.

117. "The Court's construction of the Sherman Act as having superseded the common law meant that either American business in interstate or foreign commerce must remain entirely and compulsively competitive, or it must be regulated, if at all, by the federal government to the exclusion of both the states and private parties. The alternatives, in short, were unrestricted competition or statist command." See Sklar, *Corporate Reconstruction*, p. 169.

118. Ibid., pp. 100–102, 127 n. 92, 132–34, 138–39, 147–48, 168–70. Cf. *United States v. Joint Traffic Association*, 171 U.S. 505, 571–73 (1898); *United States v. Addyston Pipe & Steel Co.*, 175 U.S. 211, 228–31 (1899). The following is part of Justice Harlan's majority opinion in *Northern Securities Co. v. United States*, 193 U.S. 197, 351 (1904): "It is the history of monopolies in this country and in England that predictions of ruin are habitually made by them when it is attempted, by legislation, to restrain their operations and protect the public against their exactions. In this, as in former cases, they seek shelter behind the reserved rights of the states and even behind the constitutional guarantee of liberty of contract. But this court has heretofore adjudged that the act of Congress did not touch the rights of the states, and that liberty of contract did not involve a right to deprive the public of the advantages of free competition in trade and commerce. Liberty of contract does not imply liberty in a corporation or individuals to defy the national will, when legally expressed. Nor does the enforcement of a legal enactment of Congress infringe, in any proper sense, the general inherent right of every one to acquire and hold property. That right, like all other rights, must be exercised in subordination to the law."

119. Justice Peckham's majority opinion in *Allgeyer*, no less than Justice Field's dissenting opinion in *Slaughter-House Cases*, expounded a view of liberty that comprehended both the freedom to contract and the right to compete. Although not necesarily at odds, these two rights posed the possibility, which became more likely as the combination movement gained momentum in the mid-1890s, that contractual liberty (to buy and sell enterprise, for example) would come into conflict with the right to compete. It was precisely in resolving such conflicts, however, that the common law had evolved the doctrine that only *unreasonable* restraints of trade were unlawful. On this see Sklar, *Corporate Reconstruction*, pp. 100–102.

120. For an analysis of this ideological division and debate on the Court, see ibid., pp. 138–45, 166–70. Cf. Justice White's dissents in *Trans-Missouri*, 166 U.S. 290, at 344–74, and in *Northern Securities*, 193 U.S. 197, at 364–400. See also Holmes's dissent in ibid., pp. 400–411.

121. From 1897 to 1911, the Harlan-Peckham majority remained intransigent despite sometimes avid and continuing protests from dissenting members of the Court, federal judges, intellectuals, political leaders, corporate capitalists, and labor leaders, all of whom urged that the Court adopt a common-law construction of the Sherman Act capable of adapting the law to the exigencies of corporate capitalism. Sklar, *Corporate Reconstruction*, pp. 139–46, 166–73. Justice Peckham's comments in *Joint Traffic Association*, pp. 573–75 (1898), are indicative of the rigid position adopted by the majority in the wake of sharp criticism:

"Finally, we are asked to reconsider the question decided in the Trans-Missouri case, and to retrace the steps taken therein, because of the plain error contained in that decision and the widespread alarm with which it was received and the serious consequences which have resulted, or may soon result, from the law as interpreted in that case. . . .

"This court, with care and deliberation, and also with a full appreciation of their importance, again considered the questions involved in the former decision.

"A majority of the court once more arrived at the conclusion it had first announced, and accordingly it denied the application. And now for the third time the same arguments are employed, and the court is again asked to recant its former opinion, and to decide the same question in direct opposition to the conclusion arrived at in the Trans-Missouri case. . . .

While an erroneous decision might be in some cases properly reconsidered and overruled, yet it is clear that the first necessity is to convince the court that the decision was erroneous. It is scarcely to be assumed that such a result could be secured by the presentation for a third time of the same arguments which had twice before been unsuccessfully urged upon the attention of the court."

122. 193 U.S. 197 (1904).

123. In 1903, at Roosevelt's initiative and leadership, Congress created the Bureau of Corporations, as an agency in the new Department of Commerce and Labor, that was charged with investigating corporations and providing the President with information he could then publish if he chose to. Roosevelt's aim from the beginning, in which he apparently succeeded, was to use the bureau to aid his own policy of establishing a legal and administrative framework for regulating combinations, and then employ the bureau's investigative powers to aid the prosecution of antitrust cases. Roosevelt's effort to centralize economic policy-making within the executive branch of the federal government, including executive regulation of corporate enterprise, was outlined in the Hepburn Bill of 1908, a measure originally drafted by the National Civic Federation and effectively rewritten by Roosevelt to try to achieve his purposes, but which was not passed by Congress.

On the problems and politics of the early interpretation and enforcement of the Sherman Act, including an incisive analysis of doctrinal developments within antitrust law and the central importance of the antitrust debates for the corporate reconstruction of American capitalism, see Sklar, *Corporate Reconstruction*, pp. 86–175, 179–332. See also ibid., pp. 203–85, for an illuminating analysis of the drafting of the Hepburn Bill (in its original and revised states) and a detailed examination of the role of Roosevelt related above. Cf. Thorelli, *Federal Antitrust Policy*, pp. 369–411; Letwin, *Law and Economic Policy*, pp.100–181, 238–50; Robert H. Wiebe, *Business and Reform: A Study of the Progressive Movement* (Cambridge, Mass.: Harvard University Press, 1962), pp. 79–85; Wiebe, "The House of Morgan and the Executive, 1905–1913," in Richard M. Abrams and Lawrence W. Levine, eds., *The Shaping of Twentieth Century America* (Boston: Little, Brown, 1965), pp. 254–68; Tony Freyer, *Regulating Big Business: Antitrust in Great Britain and America, 1880–1990* (New York: Cambridge University Press, 1992), pp. 11–158; Lamoreaux, *Great Merger Movement*, pp. 159–94.

124. The Harlan-Peckham interpretation of the Sherman Act provided a formidable means to break up corporate consolidations and mergers as well as pooling agreements and cartels. Thus, it seems to be an incontrovertible fact that it was the general failure of antitrust enforcement under the Sherman Act (not the manner in which it was interpreted from 1897 to 1911) that greatly facilitated the corporate ascendancy. The unwillingness, from the outset, of attorneys-general to enforce the Sherman Act produced only forty cases in federal courts under the administrations of Presidents Harrison, Cleveland, and McKinley, and only a handful of those cases found their way to the Supreme Court. As of 1903, the Justice Department had initiated only six of the twenty-three cases brought by the federal government, four of which concerned the activities of labor unions. In the second decade following its passage, corporate consolidations and mergers increased dramatically in the wake of the first great merger wave in American history, giving rise to the criticism that the Sherman Act was poorly conceived, although its proponents, notably Senator Edmunds, maintained all along that it had not been properly enforced.

On the relationship between early antitrust rulings, politics, and the merger wave, see Sklar, *Corporate Reconstruction*, pp. 154–66. Sklar observes: "It was not the law as judicially construed that facilitated or encouraged corporate consolidation; it was, rather, business and political policy—the decisions of capitalists and their lawyers in the private sector, and the decisions of the executive branch of the federal government under McKinley and Roosevelt, and up to a point under Taft, not to prosecute or to prosecute selectively" (ibid., pp. 162–63).

125. *Standard Oil Co. v. United States*, 221 U.S. 1 (1911). The case was decided 8 to 1, with Justice Harlan dissenting in part. In light of the obvious significance of the case as a statement of the principles of antitrust law, the near unanimous opinion sent a clear signal that the Court, in adopting the rule of reason as its standard, had overcome the major interpretative differences evident in the leading cases of the previous two decades.

126. 221 U.S. 1, 56 (1911).

127. Ibid., pp. 59–60.

128. 288 U.S. 344 (1933).

129. Ibid., p. 67. Rockefeller achieved his dominance over the petroleum industry through the control of oil refineries, of which he owned an estimated 90 percent by 1882, and by acquiring a virtual monopoly over pipelines. The litany of abuses alleged by the government, as reported in the opinion, included:

"Rebates, preferences, and other discriminatory practices in favor of the combination by railroad companies; restraint and monopolization by control of pipe lines, and unfair practices against competing pipe lines; contracts with competitors in restraint of trade; unfair methods of competition, such as local price cutting at the points where necessary to suppress competition; espionage of the business of competitors, the operation of bogus independent companies, and payments of rebates on oil, with the like intent; the division of the United States into districts and the limiting of the operations of the various subsidiary corporations as to such districts so that competition in the sale of petroleum products between such corporations had been entirely eliminated and destroyed" (ibid., pp. 42–43).

130. *United States v. American Tobacco*, 221 U.S. 106 (1911), handed down the same day as *Standard Oil*, complements and in many ways clarifies the Court's discussion of the rule of reason in that case. Justice White's explanation, in *American Tobacco*, of the Court's rationale for finding a violation is instructive:

"Indeed, the history of the combination is so replete with the doing of acts which it was the obvious purpose of the statute to forbid, so demonstrative of the existence from the beginning of a purpose to acquire dominion and control of the tobacco trade, not by the mere exertion of the ordinary right to contract and to trade, but by methods devised in order to monopolize the trade by driving competitors out of business, which were ruthlessly carried out upon the assumption that to work upon the fears or play upon the cupidity of competitors would make success possible. We say these conclusions are inevitable, not because of the vast amount of property aggregated by the combination, not because alone of the many corporations which the proof shows were united by resort to one device or another. Again, not alone because of the dominion and control over the tobacco trade which actually exists, but because we think the conclusion of wrongful purpose and illegal combination is overwhelmingly established" (221 U.S. 106, 181–82).

131. President William Howard Taft's interpretation of the Sherman Act is particularly relevant for understanding the ideological import of a common-law construction of the act. As a federal judge, Taft favored such a construction and decided *Addyston Pipe* on appeal by applying the common-law distinction between direct and ancillary restraints of trade, which was affirmed by the Supreme Court, and as President, he strongly supported Justice White's rule-of-reason decisions as an alternative to statist regulation of markets. With regard to Taft's interpretation of the act, as it shaped his administration's antitrust policy, see Sklar, *Corporate Reconstruction*, pp. 364–82, and pp. 378–81, on the use of the idea of potential competition in justifying oligopolistic markets as opposed to the alternative of statist command of monopolistic markets.

132. In *American Tobacco*, Justice White described the types of violations (i.e., unreasonable restraints) that the rule of reason prohibits:

"The words 'restraint of trade' at common law and in the law of this country at the time of the adoption of the Anti-Trust Act only embraced acts or contracts or agreements or combinations which operated to the prejudice of the public interests by unduly restricting competition or unduly obstructing the due course of trade or which, either because of their *inherent nature or effect* or because of the evident purpose of the acts, etc., injuriously restrained trade." (221 U.S. 106, 179; emphasis added).

Beginning with *United States v. Socony-Vacuum Oil Co.*, 310 U.S. 150 (1940), the Court has declared four types of restrictive agreements to be illegal *"per se"* under Section 1 of the Sherman Act: price-fixing, market division, group boycotts, and tying agreements. Although formally stated in *Socony-Vacuum*, the *"per se* concept" was clearly anticipated in *Addyston Pipe*, the *Standard Oil* and *American Tobacco* cases of 1911 (e.g., "inherent nature or effect"), and in *United States v. Trenton Potteries Co.*, 273 U.S. 392 (1927). The *"per se* rules" assert that certain acts, because of their illegal intent or effect, constitute an unreasonable restraint of trade and as such conflict with the public's interest in realizing the benefits of a regulated market—not because the economic consequences of the restraint are apparent or even discernible, but because the rule that purports to regulate in the public interest has been violated. In other words, when a fundamental principle of fair competition has been transgressed, it must be duly enforced to ensure the integrity of the law. While *"per se* rules" serve the administrative function of allowing the judiciary to summarily dispose of clear violations, they also represent the Supreme Court's effort to infuse the law with a degree of certainty and at the same time limit judicial discretion by establishing incontestable rules of corporate constitutional interpretation.

133. But the obvious fact that it is difficult to interpret competitive effects without the aid of a theory, or at least an understanding of the complexity of market forces, seems inevitably to impel the courts to incorporate aspects of economic theory, some would say speculation, into its decisions. This development underlies the wedding of law and economics in contemporary antitrust, which has exposed the judiciary to considerable criticism from an economic standpoint. When legal reasoning turns on economic analysis, it is argued, bad economics will make for bad law. This is precisely the sort of criticism that has been leveled against the Warren Court's opinions on mergers under Section 7 of the Clayton Act (as amended by the Celler-Kefauver Act of 1950), to be discussed in Chapter 4, section 5. But even though the role of economic analysis looms large in current law, it is the constitutional structure of antitrust that ensures its continuity, not its economic content. Despite the infusion into the law of economic concepts, cases are ultimately decided on the basis of legal principles as interpreted and applied in light of legislative intent and ideological objectives.

134. The substantive provisions of the Clayton Act, like the rule of reason under the Sherman Act, leave considerable room for judicial discretion. In attempting to regulate price discrimination, exclusive-dealing and tying contracts, acquisitions of competing companies, and interlocking directorates, the act was intended to complement the Sherman Act by providing a means for arresting the development of "incipient monopolies." The naming of specific offenses in the act, coupled with a broad rule of interpretation, is the product of a legislative compromise over the appropriate method to achieve its purpose. On the drafting of the Clayton Act, see Arthur S. Link, *Wilson: The New Freedom* (Princeton: Princeton University Press, 1956), pp. 427–36; Sklar, *Corporate Reconstruction*, pp. 330–31, 381, 420.

There are no criminal offenses under the Clayton Act. The Justice Department and the Federal Trade Commission are empowered to enforce its provisions, and the FTC can issue cease-and-desist orders upon finding a violation, subject to judicial review. The provisions concerning price discrimination (Section 2) and mergers (Section 7) have been revised, respectively, by the Robinson-Patman Act (1936) and the Celler-Kefauver Act (1950). The Robinson-Patman Act was passed by Congress primarily to prevent large retail store chains from using their superior buying power to obtain lower prices from manufacturers and wholesalers thus causing discriminatory pricing against independent retailers. The pertinent aspects of the Celler-Kefauver Act affecting mergers are discussed below in Chapter 4, section 5.

The Federal Trade Commission Act establishes the FTC and describes its powers and responsibilities. As an administrative agency with quasi-judicial powers, the FTC has jurisdiction over violations of the Clayton Act and over the FTC Act's one substantive provision prohibiting "unfair methods of competition in commerce." This prohibition, like those enumerated in the Clayton Act, was intended to serve only as a general rule, leaving the task of interpretation to the FTC on a case-by-case basis. Like the Clayton Act, it does not impose a criminal penalty, but the FTC Act charges the FTC with the responsibility of helping to enforce the Sherman Act (and its criminal penalties) and all other antitrust laws specified in the FTC Act. The Wheeler-Lea Act of 1938 amended the provision prohibiting "unfair methods of competition in commerce" to include also "unfair or deceptive acts or practices in commerce."

135. In describing this historical progression, I do not mean to imply that this particular development or evolution of corporate enterprise was in some sense inevitable or dictated by forces beyond human agency. During each stage of development, jurists, political leaders, and capitalists made critical decisions that either encouraged or discouraged certain forms of economic activity and regulation. On the other hand, there is an element of necessity in the developmental process in the sense that judicial and legislative decisions to accommodate or encourage the growth of enterprise helped produce economic and social conditions that would eventually require new laws either to accommodate these changes or to repudiate them. At critical junctures, these issues or choices were hotly debated and became the focus of social movements and groups seeking to shape state and national policies. What I am attempting to describe, then, is a general pattern of development that would probably not have occurred in the same way, if at all, in a society lacking a federal structure of government and a widespread commitment to the tenets of liberal-capitalist ideology. But even this does not do justice to the complexity of the American case. Americans have a long-standing love-hate relationship with the business corporation that has been fueled on both sides by liberal and republican beliefs. Certainly, throughout the nineteenth century, there was nothing particularly odd or contradictory in identifying one's politics as being both procapitalist and anticorporate. The antimonopoly tradition in the United States has by and large been a liberal (procapitalist) one, albeit not necessarily progressive in spirit. Consequently, the ideological triumph of the business corporation cannot be taken for granted. It must be critically examined and explained, especially with regard to the contribution of jurists in shaping legal and political conceptions of the corporate individual.

136. The transformation of corporation law is discussed below in Chapter 4, section 2.

137. Commons, *Legal Foundations of Capitalism* (note 1 above), pp. 11–18; Sklar, *Corporate Reconstruction*, pp. 49–51.

138. *Lochner v. New York*, 198 U.S. 45 (1905); *Adkins v. Children's Hospital*, 261 U.S. 525 (1923); *Wolff Packing v. Court of Industrial Relations*, 262 U.S. 522 (1923).

139. *Adair v. United States*, 208 U.S. 161 (1908); *Coppage v. Kansas*, 236 U.S. 1 (1915).

140. To clarify, I have argued that the legal doctrine of corporate individualism articulated in *Dartmouth* first acquired ideological significance outside the law in political think-

ing and discourse that justified the liberalization of state incorporation laws. The ideological expression of corporate individualism personified the corporation as an individual within the competitive marketplace, an idea that subverted the long-held view of the business corporation as an instrument of special privilege and state-sponsored monopoly. In the late nineteenth and early twentieth centuries, legal theory incorporated this ideological conception through the substantive due process doctrine of liberty of contract. During the same period, moreover, American jurists began to formulate the modern legal conception of the corporate entity as "real" or "natural"—the personified legal fiction that both reflected and justified a growing corporate autonomy. Before then, jurists generally viewed the corporate entity as "artificial," thus strongly indicating that the corporation was a creature of the sovereign. The transformation from "nineteenth-century laissez-faire entrepreneur to twentieth-century regulated citizen and business statesman" constituted one aspect of the ideological revisionism associated with the demise of laissez-faire liberalism and the emergence of corporate liberalism. This ideological transformation in the law and legal theory, therefore, coincided with the juristic reconceptualization of the corporate entity. On the development of modern entity theory, see John Dewey, "The Historic Background of Corporate Legal Personality," *Yale Law Journal* 35 (April 1926): 655–73; Morton J. Horwitz, "*Santa Clara* Revisited: The Development of Corporate Theory," *West Virginia Law Review* 88 (1985): 173–224; Gregory A. Mark, "The Personification of the Business Corporation in American Law," *University of Chicago Law Review* 54 (1987): 1441–83.

While extolling the virtues of the competitive marketplace, the individualistic doctrine of substantive due process aided the rise of corporate power in two important ways: (1) it provided corporations with constitutional rights that could be invoked against state regulations; and (2) it facilitated the transition from competitive to corporate capitalism precisely because it extended to corporations the same expanded rights of property (as legal persons) it extended to real individuals in the marketplace, albeit with very different consequences. In this fashion, laissez-faire corporate individualism justified legal innovations that contributed to the corporate reconstruction of the competitive marketplace.

In the twentieth century, the ideological doctrine of corporate individualism exists both within and outside the law and is typified by the idea of the corporate citizen. As a person under the Fourteenth Amendment, the corporation has First Amendment political rights that allow it to participate, in varying degrees, in state and federal political processes. As organizations that exercise power within national and international settings, large business corporations have often cultivated an image of acting as responsible citizens or have been held to public standards of social responsibility consistent with the ideological conception of citizenship. On the legal and ideological significance of corporate citizenhip, see below, Chapter 4, sections 4 and 6.

Chapter 3

1. William Graham Sumner, "The Concentration of Wealth: Its Economic Justification," in *Selected Essays of William Graham Sumner: Social Darwinism* (Englewood Cliffs, N.J.: Prentice-Hall, 1963), pp. 151–52; reprinted from *The Independent*, April–June, 1902.

2. On the condition of the American worker, the fight for industrial unionism, the politics of labor, labor law, and the repression of the labor movement during the late nineteenth and early twentieth centuries, consult Karen Orren, *Belated Feudalism: Labor, the Law, and Liberal Development in the United States* (Cambridge: Cambridge University Press, 1991); David Montgomery, *Workers Control in America* (Cambridge: Cambridge University Press, 1979); Melvyn Dubofsky, *Industrialism and the American Worker, 1865–1920* (New York: Thomas Y. Crowell Co., 1975); Dubofsky, "The Origins of Western Working-Class Radical-

ism, 1890–1905," *Labor History* 7 (Spring 1966): 131–55; Herbert G. Gutman, "The Worker's Search for Power: Labor in the Gilded Age," in H. Wayne Morgan, ed., *The Gilded Age* (Syracuse, N.Y.: Syracuse University Press, 1963), pp. 38–68; Philip Foner, *The History of the Labor Movement in the United States*, 4 vols. (New York: International Publishers, 1975), vol.2; Philip Taft, *The AF of L in the Time of Gompers* (New York: Octagon Books, 1970).

Concerning the Left, its internal conflicts, and its relationship to the labor movement, immigrants, and blacks, see John H. M. Laslett, *Labor and the Left: A Study of Socialist and Radical Influences Within the Labor Movement, 1881–1924* (New York: Basic Books, 1970); Melvyn Dubofsky, *We Shall Be All* (Chicago: Quadrangle Books, 1969); Foner, *History*, vols. 3 and 4; Ira Kipnis, *The American Socialist Movement* (New York: Greenwood Press, 1968); Charles Leinenweber, "The Socialist Party and the New Immigrants," *Science and Society* 32 (Winter 1968): 1–25; Sally Miller, "The Socialist Party and the Negro, 1901–1920," *Journal of Negro History* 56 (July 1971): 220–29; David A. Shannon, *The Socialist Party of America* (Chicago: Quadrangle Books, 1955); James Weinstein, *The Decline of Socialism in America, 1912–1925* (New York: Monthly Review Press, 1967).

3. Martin J. Sklar, *The Corporate Reconstruction of American Capitalism, 1890–1916: The Market, the Law, and Politics* (Cambridge: Cambridge University Press, 1988); Sklar, "Woodrow Wilson and the Political Economy of Modern United States Liberalism," *Studies on the Left* 1 (Fall 1960): 17–47. See also above, Chapter 1, note 9.

4. For intellectual biographies of Croly and Weyl, see Charles Forcey, *The Crossroads of Liberalism: Croly, Weyl, Lippmann, and the Progressive Era, 1900–1925* (New York: Oxford University Press, 1961). An excellent biography of Croly and a thorough analysis of his writings is in David W. Levy, *Herbert Croly of "The New Republic": The Life and Thought of an American Progressive* (Princeton: Princeton University Press, 1985). See also Eric F. Goldman, *Rendezvous with Destiny* (New York: Vintage Books, 1955), pp. 146–219. Joseph Dorfman has written the most comprehensive biography of Veblen: *Thorstein Veblen and His America* (New York: Viking Press, 1934).

5. Herbert Croly, *The Promise of American Life* (New Brunswick, N.J.: Transaction Publishers, 1993). Croly's other text on liberal reform, *Progressive Democracy* (New York: Macmillan, 1915), contains a stronger emphasis on the reform of state politics, but on the whole may be read as a sequel to the first work. So swift was the impact of *The Promise of American Life* on leaders of the Progressive Movement that by the time of its second printing, nine months later, Croly already had acquired a reputation for having penned one of the more thoughtful and original political treatises of his generation. A close friend of Croly's, Judge Learned Hand, was so impressed by the book that he sent a copy to Theodore Roosevelt, who was busy visiting European heads of state following an extended safari in Africa. Roosevelt, as it turned out, was also quite impressed. Roosevelt's opinion of the book mattered a great deal to Croly for both political and professional reasons. Indeed, Croly had written *The Promise of American Life* with Roosevelt in mind. Roosevelt's widely reported praise of *The Promise of American Life* greatly contributed to Croly's growing stature as the philosopher of a movement. Croly was even hailed as the architect of Roosevelt's "New Nationalism," an arguable claim even though Roosevelt lifted the phrase from the pages of Croly's book. Croly's reputation as the philosopher behind the politican no doubt was further enhanced by his close association with the former president between 1910 and 1914 and by the fact that Croly served as a campaign adviser for Roosevelt in his unsuccessful third-party bid for the presidency in 1912. Roosevelt abruptly ended his association with Croly, Weyl, and Lippmann in 1915, when an editorial in *The New Republic* criticized Roosevelt's seemingly intemperate attacks on President Wilson's policy toward Mexico.

6. Croly, *Promise*, p. 22.

7. Ibid., pp. 100–137.

8. Ibid., pp. 105–17.

9. Ibid., pp. 118, 123.

10. Ibid., pp. 113–14.

11. Ibid., pp. 28–33.

12. Ibid., pp. 43–44, 181.

13. Ibid., p. 45.

14. Croly described this synthesis in ibid., pp. 152–54.

15. "The national principle becomes a principle of reform and reconstruction, precisely because national consistency is constantly demanding the solution of contradictory economic and political tendencies, brought out by alterations in the conditions of economic and political efficiency. Its function is not only to preserve a balance among these diverse tendencies, but to make the balance more than ever expressive of a consistent and constructive democratic ideal" (ibid., p. 270).

16. Ibid., pp. 173, 202–4, 274, 358–59, 362, 368.

17. Ibid., pp. 280–81.

18. Ibid., p. 282. Croly's advocacy of a secular religion—the national democratic faith—was apparently influenced by his early exposure, through his parents, to the Positivism of Auguste Comte. The ideal or religion of "human brotherhood" clearly shared the essential humanism of Comte's "Religion of Humanity": "Before any great stride can be made towards a condition of better democracy, the constructive democratic movement must obtain more effective support both from scientific discipline and religious faith." See Croly, *Promise*, p. 282. One could also acknowledge the influence of one of Croly's teachers at Harvard, Josiah Royce, whose idealism, particularly his nonsectarian belief in Christianity, greatly affected Croly's own personal struggle with religious belief and seems to have also influenced Croly's secular ideal of "human brotherhood." In addition, Royce's works on the idea of loyalty clearly seem to have contributed to Croly's conception of political community and the need for a secular religion.

The influence of Comte's Positivism on the central themes of *The Promise of American Life* has been a matter of dispute among scholars. In large part, the disagreement concerns the nature and extent of Herbert Croly's rejection of Comte's teachings after having been exposed to other philosophical schools while a student at Harvard. Although it is clear that sometime before his father died in 1889, Herbert was no longer a practicing member of the Religion of Humanity, one should not deduce from this that he left behind his Comtean beliefs altogether. In any event, it is not solely Croly's religious beliefs that are at issue here, but perhaps more precisely the broad influence of Comte's Positivism on Croly's political thought. David W. Levy has shed new light on this debate by demonstrating quite effectively how David Croly's Comtean analysis of American society directly shaped the underlying assumptions and arguments in *The Promise of American Life*. Many of Herbert Croly's basic analytical constructs, his historical approach to the study of institutional change, and his position on the regulation of corporations, according to Levy, derive almost verbatim from his father's writings and tutelage. See Levy, *Croly*, pp. 36–42, 117–25. Cf. Forcey, *Crossroads*, pp. 11–21; Goldman, *Rendezvous*, pp. 148–50; Arthur Schlesinger Jr., "Introduction," in *The Promise of American Life* (Cambridge, Mass.: Harvard University Press, Belknap Press, 1965), pp. vi–vii; David W. Noble, *The Paradox of Progressive Thought* (Minneapolis: University of Minnesota Press, 1958), pp. 55–77; R. Jeffrey Lustig, *Corporate Liberalism: The Origins of Modern American Political Theory, 1890–1920* (Berkeley and Los Angeles: University of California Press, 1982), pp. 120–36.

19. Croly, *Promise*, pp. 282–83, 288, 315, 346–47, 405, 406–7; Croly, *Progressive Democracy*, pp. 177–183. Croly's conversion to pragmatism most likely was due to the influence of William James, one of Croly's professors at Harvard. See Forcey, *Crossroads*, pp. 15–21.

Like many of his Progressive Era counterparts, Croly drew on diverse and sometimes conflicting intellectual currents in constructing his political philosophy. While his political thought cannot be reduced to a particular doctrine or dominant influence, a strong case can be made that the theoretical distinctiveness of *The Promise of American Life* can be found in its fusion of ideas derived from Positivism (and, more broadly, evolutionary theory) with the epistemological assumptions of pragmatism. Although shorn of Comtean metaphysics, Croly's analysis of American history retained an evolutionary perspective of development and a conception of progress. Croly's faith in progress, however, was mediated by his pragmatism and his emphasis on joining theory with practice in the pursuit of a conscious social ideal. In this regard, his political thought bears some striking similarities to that of John Dewey.

Dewey, a fellow progressive, contributed frequently to *The New Republic* and, like Croly, greatly influenced the direction of political thinking in the first half of the twentieth century. Dewey's critique of laissez-faire individualism and advocacy of pragmatism (experimentalism) as a philosophy of reform in various works were similar in many respects to Croly's argument in *The Promise of American Life*. Dewey's commitment to an ideal of freedom (moral autonomy) based on participatory democracy within groups or associations, however, caused him to distrust statist solutions and to reject oligarchy as a form of political rule. Moreover, his often critical view of capitalism, especially in its cultural aspects, was clearly indebted to the writings of Veblen, with whom he served as an editor on *The Dial* in 1918. See John Dewey, *Democracy and Education: An Introduction to the Philosophy of Education* (New York: Macmillan, 1919); *The Public and Its Problems* (Denver: Alan Swallow, 1927); *Individualism Old and New* (New York: Minton, Balch & Co., 1930); *Liberalism and Social Action* (New York: G. P. Putnam's Sons, 1935); *Freedom and Culture* (New York: G. P. Putnam's Sons, 1939).

20. Croly, *Promise*, pp. 283–84, 406–7.

21. Ibid., pp. 409–12.

22. Ibid., p. 411.

23. Ibid., pp. 272–79, 324–31, 338–40. See also Croly, *Progressive Democracy*, pp. 294–348.

24. Croly, *Promise*, pp. 124–25.

25. Ibid., p. 339.

26. Ibid., pp. 328–31, 342–43.

27. Ibid., p. 275. In *Progressive Democracy*, pp. 220–66, Croly liberalized his position on direct popular government (e.g., initiative, referendum, recall) but held fast to the principle of national leadership, arguing that state governments should be conceived as subordinate parts of a national system rather than as independent centers of authority.

28. Croly put forth a plan for tax reform that aimed to effect a more efficient distribution of wealth. He proposed subjecting "excessive" corporate profits to a graduated tax, and individual wealth to a graduated inheritance tax. See *Promise*, pp. 369–71, 381–82. In the first instance, the object was to create a disincentive for seeking profits beyond a certain point. With regard to individual wealth, he reasoned that an income tax would discourage individual initiative while an inheritance tax would mitigate the creation of permanent inequalities and uphold the belief that individual distinction was socially productive only when it was earned. The objective of both his proposals, then, was to discourage excessive accumulation of wealth and thereby encourage a more efficient use and equitable distribution of the national wealth without undermining individual initiative. Croly's argument in this matter as well as others was timely. Congress passed the first corporate profits tax in 1909 with President Taft's support.

29. Croly suggested that such legal standing might take the form of a federal incorpora-

tion act (a measure Theodore Roosevelt sought to legislate), although Croly was doubtful about its constitutionality. In any event, Croly argued strongly for a frank recognition and acceptance of the large corporation under federal law. The Sherman Antitrust Act (as of 1909) had not accomplished this, he argued, because it constituted "an attempt to save the life of the small competitor" (ibid., pp. 359–60). With the Supreme Court's adoption of the rule of reason in *Standard Oil Co. v. United States*, 221 U.S. 1 (1911), and the passage of the Federal Trade Commission and Clayton Antitrust Acts in 1914, the lengthy national debate over the trust question was resolved—albeit not in precisely the fashion Croly had desired (he opposed regulation by commission), but in a manner consistent with his premise that large corporations must be allowed a degree of self-regulation consistent with their tendency toward consolidation (and hence greater efficiency) yet subject to federal regulation in the public interest. For Croly's contribution to Roosevelt's position on the trust issue in the 1912 election, see Levy, *Croly*, pp. 155–58.

30. Croly, *Promise*, pp. 357–59.

31. Ibid., p. 359.

32. Ibid., p. 362. Croly's conception of corporate autonomy is entirely consistent with the guiding principle of judicial construction in the law of corporations in the twentieth century. See Chapter 4, section 2, below.

33. Croly, *Promise*, pp. 372–79. Croly advocated a system of public ownership and private operation in cases in which a "natural monopoly" had developed, as with many municipal and public service corporations and the railroad companies. In other words, where competition was not feasible, the public's interest in efficiency should prevail.

34. Ibid., pp. 126–31.

35. Ibid., pp. 387, 389–91, 392–93.

36. Croly, *Progressive Democracy*, pp. 378–405.

37. Ibid., pp. 384–85.

38. Ibid., p. 392. "As soon as the business becomes in certain respects the business of all the participating workers, the latter will undergo a change of attitude towards their work. The dignity and serviceability of their calling and of their occupation will be recognized in the economic organization. . . . Thus the wage-earners will have won a kind of independence, in which devotion to work will individualize their lives without dividing them from their fellow workers" (ibid., pp. 395–96).

39. Ibid., p. 397.

40. Ibid., pp. 399–400, 402.

41. Croly, *Promise*, p. 397.

42. "Society is not merely the result of the harmony or the conflict of individual interests or wills. It is an end in itself, as is the individual, and correlative with the individual." See Croly, *Progressive Democracy*, p. 199.

43. Concerning the prospects of a democratic movement, Croly wrote: "If such a movement ever arrives, it will be partly the creation of some democratic evangelist— some imitator of Jesus who will reveal to men the path whereby they enter into spiritual possession of their individual and social advancements, and immeasurably increase them by virtue of personal regeneration." See Croly, *Promise*, pp. 453–54. Here Croly might have had in mind the leadership qualities of Abraham Lincoln and the promise of such qualities in Theodore Roosevelt, both political heroes of the author. It is not coincidental that Roosevelt's political philosophy of "The New Nationalism," as he expounded it in 1910–12, was strongly influenced by his interpretation of the egalitarian tradition of republicanism, which he associated with Lincoln. See Sklar, *Corporate Reconstruction*, pp. 352–64. The type of political savior Croly had in mind, therefore, was not a demagogue or would-be tyrant, but an unusually gifted and public spirited leader—"half saint and

half hero," as he put it—dedicated to the principles of liberty, equality, democracy, and social justice.

44. Walter E. Weyl, *The New Democracy: An Essay on Certain Political and Economic Tendencies in the United States* (New York: Macmillan, 1912). Croly, Weyl, and Lippmann had become acquainted while working on behalf of Theodore Roosevelt's third-party candidacy in 1912. In late 1913, Croly recruited Weyl and Lippmann to serve as editors of *The New Republic*, which began publication in 1914.

45. The reconstruction of his argument that follows is based upon Weyl, *New Democracy*, pp. 7–77.

46. Ibid., pp. 81–92.

47. Ibid., p. 92; also see pp. 87–91.

48. Ibid., pp. 75, 78, 84.

49. Ibid., pp. 62–63.

50. Ibid., pp. 96, 99, 106.

51. Ibid., p. 106.

52. Ibid., pp. 106–7.

53. Ibid., pp. 107–8.

54. Ibid., p. 108.

55. Ibid., pp. 108–9, 114–15. In this regard, Weyl's analysis of the Constitution anticipated Charles A. Beard's influential *Economic Interpretation of the Constitution of the United States*, published in 1913.

56. Weyl, *New Democracy*, p. 118, 120, 124, 125.

57. Ibid., pp. 149–50.

58. Ibid., p. 150.

59. Ibid., p. 161–62.

60. Ibid., pp. 207, 274.

61. Ibid., p. 166.

62. Ibid., p. 191. Weyl credited his teacher at the University of Pennsylvania, Simon N. Patten, with "the original statement of the transition from a pain economy to a pleasure economy" in Patten's *The Theory of Social Forces*, published in 1896. Weyl, *New Democracy*, p. 191 n. 1. Weyl argued that Marx's analysis of the increasing impoverishment of the working class had lost its validity under modern economic conditions and that therefore the belief in class war had no basis in economic reality. See ibid., pp. 170–78. Moreover, he rejected the contention that capitalism would self-destruct: "'Capitalism' develops elasticity. Instead of dying of its own excesses, it shows wonderful recuperative and self-reforming power" (p. 187).

63. Ibid., p. 191.

64. Ibid., pp. 191–95.

65. Ibid., p. 207.

66. Ibid., pp. 179–80.

67. Ibid., p. 237.

68. Ibid. Weyl included a broad range of occupational groups in the democratic mass—for example, farmers, skilled workers, all of the professions, clerical workers, and most merchants (pp. 238–39).

69. Ibid., p. 249.

70. Ibid., p. 264.

71. Ibid., pp. 276, 279–80. Weyl's proposal for economic reform is thoroughly pragmatic. He largely assumed that his utilitarian standard would provide an adequate basis for determining the proper course of action in each case. But this aspect of his analysis was somewhat vague.

72. Ibid., pp. 280, 281, 283–93, 294–97.

73. Ibid., pp. 298, 300. Weyl also advocated a variety of other democratic reforms, including direct primaries, the recall, the initiative, the referendum, constitutional reform, and proportional representation within the state legislatures (pp. 307–8, 316, 318).

74. Ibid., pp. 311–14.

75. Ibid., p. 319.

76. Ibid., pp. 320, 321, 324, 328–29, 330–32. Weyl also urged the eradication of slums, penal reform for children and adults, crime prevention, child labor laws, elimination of unsafe and unhealthful working conditions, and equal rights and opportunities for blacks (pp. 321–26, 334–46).

77. Ibid., p. 242.

78. On the cultural, ideological, political, and economic significance of increasing social wealth in twentieth-century America, cf. Warren Susman, *Culture as History: The Transformation of American Society in the Twentieth Century* (New York: Pantheon Books, 1973); Loren Baritz, *The Good Life: The Meaning of Success for the American Middle Class* (New York: Knopf, 1988); David Potter, *People of Plenty: Economic Abundance and the American Character* (Chicago: University of Chicago Press, 1954); Paul Baran, *The Political Economy of Growth* (New York: Monthly Review Press, 1957); John Kenneth Galbraith, *The Affluent Society* (Boston: Houghton Mifflin, 1958).

79. Weyl's nondoctrinaire conception of socialism or progressivism, however, remains an important formulation: "For the majority of avowed Socialists, however, to whom the general ideals, rather than the abstract philosophy or ultimate program of their party, appeal, a progressive *rapprochement* with other democratic elements of the population seems decreed by the logic of our development. What will be the name, badge, or token of the party, parties, or allied fragments of parties, which will result from such a union or absorption, is insignificant. The essential tendency, however, seems to be a progress of Socialist parties towards coalescence with other democratic movements, the socialists losing many of their separatist views, while infusing the democracy as a whole with broader concepts of industrial polity." See Weyl, *New Democracy*, p. 187.

80. Weyl characterized the momentous nature of this ideological accommodation in terms of the changing political climate of his day: "The old laissez-faire liberal philosophy is done for, and the old absolute socialism is dying in the embrace of its dead adversary. . . . The socialist, who is beginning to lose his faith in the class war and the rigorous nationalization of the means of production, is adopting a theory of a democratic socialization of industry and of life; the old individualist, losing his faith in economic harmonies that do not harmonize, and in the beneficence of a competition which has gone lame, is approaching in a more tentative manner a similar theory of democratic socialization of industry and of life. The men who were sharply sundered in interests and ideals by the conditions of an earlier machine production have been brought into partial accord by the conditions of a later machine era. The trust builder, the monopolizer, the new Titan of industry, has not only merged his factories, but united his opponents" (ibid., pp. 188–89).

81. Thorstein Veblen, *The Theory of the Leisure Class: An Economic Study of Institutions* (1899; reprint, New York: Mentor Books, 1953); Veblen, *Absentee Ownership and Business Enterprise in Recent Times* (New York: B. W. Huebsch, 1923).

82. Veblen, *Leisure Class*, p. 131.

83. Thorstein Veblen, *The Instinct of Workmanship and the State of the Industrial Arts* (New York: B. W. Huebsch, 1918), p. 1.

84. Ibid., p. 4; see also pp. 30–31. See also *Leisure Class*, p. 29.

85. *Instinct of Workmanship*, pp. 6–8; see also *Leisure Class*, p. 146.

86. Ibid., p. 29.; *Instinct of Workmanship*, pp. 25–26, 31–37.

87. Ibid., pp. 26–27, 88.

88. Ibid., pp. 84–89; Veblen, *The Place of Science in Modern Civilization* (New York: B. W. Huebsch, 1919), pp. 6–19.

89. *Instinct of Workmanship*, pp. 11, 40–41.

90. Ibid., p. 50 n. 1.

91. This aspect of Veblen's analysis is entirely consistent with Charles Darwin's theory of evolution by natural selection. At least one reviewer of *The Leisure Class* recognized that Veblen's use of evolutionary theory was scrupulously scientific (following Darwin) and not, as some had argued, merely a pretext for justifying the author's moral predilections or for satirizing the wealthy. See Lester Frank Ward, "The Theory of the Leisure Class," in Joseph Dorfman, ed., *Thorstein Veblen: Essays, Reviews, and Reports* (Clifton, N.J.: Augustus M. Kelley Publishers, 1973), pp. 619–30; reprinted from *American Sociological Review*, May 1900.

Widely current in the writings of American social scientists and political thinkers in the late nineteenth century, evolutionary theory assumed a variety of forms. Within this context, Veblen's theory may be juxtaposed to the apologetic tone of the ideology of social Darwinism. Veblen's rejection of social Darwinism, however, was by no means exceptional among thinkers, such as Lester Frank Ward, who believed that evolutionary theory could be applied scientifically to the study of societies. In any event, social Darwinism as an ideological doctrine was capable of expansive interpretation. Because social Darwinism (arguably derived from the works of Herbert Spencer, although Spencer did not expound the doctrine as such) assumed that the process of natural selection in society (effected through competition) determined the fittest—who, of course, passed on their genes—the argument could be made that class domination was rooted in inherent capacities of superiority. From this it was but a minor logical leap to make the claim that such superiority was an inherent characteristic of certain races. Weeding out the "weak" in the marketplace could then be analogized to the conquest (or paternalistic protection) of the "weaker" peoples or nations. This logic meshed well with the doctrine of Manifest Destiny which, like Calvinism, invoked God in the service of capitalism, albeit for imperial expansion. See Richard Hofstadter, *Social Darwinism in American Thought* (New York: George Braziller, 1955), pp. 170–200.

Moreover, the individualistic premises of Spencer's social theory did not justify war or imperialism as policies. Spencer, who identified evolutionary development with a historical progression to a more humane society (greater freedom and cooperation and hence less coercion), believed that militarism characterized a lower stage of social and economic evolution. An influential (albeit iconoclastic) exponent of social Darwinism in America, William Graham Sumner, argued consistently that the rationale of laissez-faire led inexorably to the conclusion that the mechanisms of the marketplace could not function properly when the state served special interests and abdicated its role as a neutral arbiter between classes. Sumner took the unpopular stance of opposing the Spanish-American War and viewed war as an unfortunate result of "the competition of life," a destructive but inevitable aspect of human existence. Neither author, therefore, championed the cause of imperialism, though certainly in other respects their arguments were not adverse to economic expansion.

92. *Leisure Class*, pp. 29, 133–34.

93. Ibid. see also Veblen's *Absentee Ownership*, pp. 16–17, 206.

94. *Leisure Class*, p. 134.

95. Ibid. See also Veblen's *Instinct of Workmanship*, p. 40; and Veblen, *The Theory of Business Enterprise* (1940; reprint, New York: Mentor Books, 1958), pp. 146–48.

96. *Absentee Ownership*, p. 17.

97. *Leisure Class*, p. 133. See also *Absentee Ownership*, pp. 18, 43; Veblen, *The Vested Interests and the Common Man* (New York: Viking Press, 1933), pp. 4–11.

98. See *Leisure Class*, pp. 138–42, for a general statement of Veblen's view that the dominant ideas and customs of a society reflect the interests and tastes of its rulers.

99. There appears to be an unresolvable tension in Veblen's thought between his fatalistic view of social change and his belief that human beings are rational, purposeful creatures capable of intelligent action. The difficulty here could be in his conception of instinct, which at once assumes that instinctive action is teleological and thoroughly shaped by habit and impersonal forces. In this respect, Veblen's theory of social development shares an affinity with that of Marx. Moreover, in Marx's thought a similar tension exists between his humanism, rooted in the concept of species-being, and his analysis of broader economic forces impelling social change.

100. Thorstein Veblen, "The Beginnings of Ownership," in *Essays in Our Changing Order*, ed. Leon Ardzrooni (New York: Viking Press, 1934), pp. 42–49; *Instinct of Workmanship*, pp. 146–60.

101. "Beginnings of Ownership," p. 47.

102. Ibid., pp. 44–49; *Leisure Class*, pp. 33–34.

103. *Instinct of Workmanship*, pp. 149–61.

104. Ibid., p. 160.

105. *Leisure Class*, pp. 25, 26, 35, 43.

106. It should be noted that pecuniary exploit is not technically an instinct in Veblen's theory, but rather a "self-regarding sentiment" or "motive" rooted in pecuniary emulation. Veblen argued that pecuniary exploit, which is essential to the institution of ownership, had come to thoroughly dominate the behavior and thought of the business (and leisure) class as well as large segments of the rest of society. In short, pecuniary exploit had imposed its own bias on the instinctive proclivities of individuals living in pecuniary culture. As a consequence, pecuniary exploit and the institution of ownership affected the way the instinct of workmanship was expressed. Veblen argued that, with the emergence of pecuniary culture, the system of "free workmanship" (i.e., cooperation, common use of resources and technology, social equality) gave way to pecuniary control of industry (i.e., self-interest, ownership, class distinctions). On this, see *Instinct of Workmanship*, pp. 142–51.

The fact that Veblen did not classify pecuniary exploit (or pecuniary emulation) as an instinct does not seem to be important to his analysis inasmuch as he often referred to pecuniary exploit and/or pecuniary emulation as though it were an instinct. His decision in this matter, however, appears to serve an ideological purpose, since, according to Veblen's theory, instincts were essential to the survival of the species.

107. For Veblen's analysis of the handicraft era, see ibid., pp. 209–98; *Absentee Ownership*, pp. 40–49.

108. *Instinct of Workmanship*, p. 211.

109. Ibid., pp. 210–14, 228–29, 233–34, 277–82.

110. Ibid., pp. 184–85.

111. Ibid., pp. 216, 187.

112. Veblen's most systematic analyses of the captains of industry is found in *Absentee Ownership*, pp. 101–18; and in Veblen, *The Engineers and the Price System* (New York: Viking Press, 1932), pp. 27–51.

113. *Absentee Ownership*, p. 102. See also ibid., pp. 70–71. To avoid terminological confusion, it should be noted that the era of machine technology in Veblen's analysis actually comprises two periods or eras: free competition and corporate finance.

114. Ibid., pp. 101, 106.

115. Ibid., pp. 78–79, 110–11, 331–53; *Business Enterprise*, pp. 115–16, 123–27; *Engineers*, pp. 36–38. Veblen's economic theory of business enterprise will be discussed in detail later in this chapter.

116. *Absentee Ownership*, pp. 82, 86.

117. Veblen discussed the financial and industrial characteristics of this new order at length in several works. See, generally, ibid., pp. 205–397; *Business Enterprise*, pp. 7–127; *Instinct of Workmanship*, pp. 299–355; *Engineers*, pp. 38–82; *Vested Interests*, pp. 35–113.

118. I discuss Veblen's analysis of the dominance of corporate finance below when I examine his conception of the economic basis of corporate power.

119. *Absentee Ownership*, pp. 231–39, 331–40.

120. Ibid., pp. 226–28, 231–32, 338–40, 398–99; *Engineers*, pp. 47–49; *Vested Interests*, pp. 89–92.

121. Veblen outlined his theory of revolution in a series of essays written in 1919, subsequently compiled in *The Engineers and the Price System*. While discounting a (Marxist) proletarian revolution as such, he emphasized that the prospect of revolution did indeed depend on an alliance between the vanguard class and industrial workers. After 1919, Veblen continued to believe that the engineers and technicians could shape the direction of social change, but he never again expressed this view with the same enthusiasm. Indeed, in his last and perhaps most comprehensive and mature work, *Absentee Ownership*, he did not even mention the prospect of such a revolution, but rather seemed resigned to the continued dominance of the business class. For a discussion of the different forms this dominance might take, see *Absentee Ownership*, pp. 226–28.

122. *Business Enterprise*, p. 135.

123. "The business community has an urgent need of an efficient national establishment both at home and abroad. A settled government, duly equipped with national pretensions, and with legal and military power to maintain the sacredness of contracts at home and to enforce the claims of its businessmen abroad." See *Vested Interests*, p. 155.

124. *Absentee Ownership*, p. 404.

125. *Business Enterprise*, p. 139.

126. *Vested Interests*, p. 163.

127. *Absentee Ownership*, pp. 398–99.

128. Ibid., p. 22. See also *Vested Interests*, pp. 123–31 and *Business Enterprise*, p. 135.

129. *Absentee Ownership*, p. 25. See also ibid., pp. 31–39, and *Business Enterprise*, pp. 139–40.

130. Thorstein Veblen, *The Higher Learning in America: A Memorandum on the Conduct of Universities by Businessmen* (New York: B. W. Huebsch, 1913), esp. pp. 1–134, 148–69, 191–218; *Leisure Class*, pp. 235–58.

131. *Higher Learning*, p. 212.

132. My reconstruction of Veblen's ideological critique is based on the following works: *Absentee Ownership*, pp. 12–68, 205–10, 398–445; *Business Enterprise*, pp. 37–48, 128–76; *Leisure Class*, pp. 131–64; *Vested Interests*, pp. 1–34, 114–37, 174–76; *Instinct of Workmanship*, pp. 340–55.

133. "It is only when and in so far as such useful things are worked by the help of others than their owners, or so far as they are held out of productive use by their owners, that they are rightly to be classed under absentee ownership; only in so far as their productive use is disjoined from their usufruct, so that workmanship and ownership part company." See *Absentee Ownership*, pp. 51–52.

134. *Business Enterprise*, p. 138; see also 42–43.

135. *Absentee Ownership*, p. 82.

136. Ibid., p. 409. See *Vested Interests*, pp. 29–30.

137. *Business Enterprise*, p. 131.

138. *Vested Interests*, pp. 174–75.

139. *Absentee Ownership*, pp. 35–36, 47.

140. "The great distinguishing mark of the common man is that he is helpless within the rules of the game as it is played in the twentieth century under the enlightened principles of the eighteenth century." *Vested Interests*, p. 163.

141. For Veblen's theory of business enterprise, see *Business Enterprise*, pp. 49–127; *Absentee Ownership*, pp. 82–100, 326–97.

142. Veblen argued that the extensive use of loan credit, especially in the form of "notes, stock shares, interest-bearing securities, deposits, call loans, etc.," had become normal practice in modern business. In effect, credit of this sort allowed for a greater rate of turnover of capital and served "much the same purpose, as regards the rate of earnings," as did "time-saving improvement in the processes of industry." See *Business Enterprise*, pp. 49–50. Because resort to loan credit provided a competitive advantage, however slight at first, loan credit soon became necessary in order to achieve a "reasonable" return on investment. See ibid., pp. 51–52; *Absentee Ownership*, pp. 356–58. The use of credit, however, also had the effect of enlarging business capital. Recapitalization on the basis of credit extension inflated the money value of an enterprise that at this point diverged from the actual value of the industrial capital on which the credit was based. This inflated value, plus the intangible asset of "good-will," provided the basis for a further extension of loans, and so on, with the result that the capitalized value of an enterprise came to rest in large part on credit that had no collateral basis. See *Business Enterprise*, pp. 52–58; *Absentee Ownership*, pp. 345–48, 218–20. These inflated values therefore created a discrepancy between capitalization or putative earning capacity and actual earning capacity.

143. *Business Enterprise*, pp. 94–100, 117–20.

144. Ibid., pp. 109, 120–21.

145. Ibid., pp. 115–16, 123–27.

146. *Absentee Ownership*, pp. 331–53; *Engineers*, pp. 47–49. On the role of the Federal Reserve system in consolidating the rule of corporate finance, see ibid., pp. 50–51, and *Absentee Ownership*, pp. 223–24, 352 n. 13.

147. Veblen discussed the nature of this control at length in *Absentee Ownership*, pp. 353–97.

148. *Business Enterprise*, pp. 73–74.

149. Ibid., p. 86. See also ibid., pp. 127, 202 n. 12; *Absentee Ownership*, pp. 331–33. Veblen argued that the interest of the community, which is a consumer interest, "demands industrial efficiency and serviceability of the product." Opposed to this interest stands "the business interest of the concern as such"—the pecuniary interest of the stockholders—which "demands vendibility of the product." With the ascendancy of corporate finance, however, a third interest emerged—that of the business managers and financiers who control the corporations—which "demands vendibility of the corporate capital." Veblen therefore concluded that "the interest of the men who hold discretion in industrial affairs is removed by one degree from that of the concerns under their management, and by two degrees from the interest of the community at large." See *Business Enterprise*, pp. 78–79.

150. *Absentee Ownership*, p. 265.

151. Ibid., pp. 340, 341.

152. Ibid., pp. 229–50.

153. Although Veblen believed that the new class of engineers and technicians constituted the vanguard of social change, he conceived the basic division within society to be between the business (and leisure) class and the "underlying population"—that is, workers, farmers, small business people. See ibid., p. 399; *Vested Interests*, p. 175.

154. *Engineers*, pp. 138–69.

155. We have seen that according to Veblen's social theory it is the nature of ideology to be out of step with social change. His theory, however, provides a basis for arguing that once society is governed by the principles of scientific thinking, this condition will no longer exist, because it is characteristic of scientific thinking continually to adapt in accordance with changing circumstances. The triumph of science, arguably, would also entail or necessitate the eventual dominance of the instinct of workmanship in society which under the modern regime of business enterprise could come about only through revolutionary, as opposed to normal evolutionary, change. The resolution of the contradiction between business and industry, between pecuniary exploit and workmanship, in Veblen's social theory, parallels Marx's analysis of the contradictions of competitive capitalism, class conflict, and socialist revolution as a restoration of alienated humanity. The split between business and industry, which involved a separation between ownership and workmanship, may be likened to Marx's conception of alienated labor, which involved a similar separation of the worker's ownership or control over the product of his or her labor. Veblen's technocratic vision, therefore, stands squarely in the humanist tradition of socialism. In this sense, although his theory in many respects anticipated the managerial theory of corporate power (see Chapter 5, below), it continues to provide critical standards by which one can assess or compare theories that would justify the dominance of pecuniary exploit over other values of modern industrial society.

Chapter 4

1. On this, see note 30 below.

2. This is not to say that the growth of government power associated with the rise of the "administrative state" (see Stephen Skowronek, *Building a New American State: The Expansion of National Administrative Capacities, 1877–1920* [New York: Cambridge University Press, 1982]) is not significant in its own right, only that my interpretation of this developmental process is based on a somewhat different view of the factors that shaped it from the outset and that continue to influence or guide it.

3. I do not mean to suggest that the New Deal reforms were simply a logical outgrowth of the Progressive Era reforms. Clearly, the Great Depression presented an economic and social crisis of unprecedented proportions that entailed considerable debate over, and experimentation with, different forms of government regulation. I do maintain, however, that the parameters of the debates in both the early and late New Deal periods were shaped by corporate-liberal ideology and that the solutions proposed or attempted were consistent (in varying degrees) with the legal structure and regulatory methods established as a result of Progressive Era reforms and related changes in law. If one conceives corporate liberalism as a cross-class, pro-corporate ideology that incorporates aspects of differing ideological perspectives (and not exclusively as the narrow ideology of corporate capitalists or a segment thereof), then it becomes possible to assess various ideological divisions that emerged during the New Deal in terms of a left-to-right spectrum based on the shared premises of corporate liberalism. See Martin J. Sklar's analysis of Progressive Era reform along these lines, *The Corporate Reconstruction of American Capitalism, 1890–1916: The Market, the Law, and Politics* (Cambridge: Cambridge University Press, 1988). See also Martin Sklar, *The United States as a Developing Country: Studies in U.S. History in the Progressive Era and the 1920s* (Cambridge: Cambridge University Press, 1992).

To state the problem another way, the debates of the New Deal were largely about the appropriate extent of government supervision and regulation of labor relations, production, consumption, and social welfare issues within the structure of the economy as it had been reconstituted under corporate capitalism. Corporate liberalism, then and now, could justify considerable experimentation and flexibility with regard to methods for achieving economic and social reform. Such methods often entailed an increasing cooperation between government and industry and the intermixing or sharing of various private and public functions while preserving corporate autonomy. The ideological spectrum of corporate liberalism can therefore be defined in terms of the alternatives that ultimately were rejected in the course of devising the major reforms of the Progressive Era and the New Deal period—namely, statist socialism (on the left) and so-called laissez-faire capitalism or unregulated corporate power (on the right). This is not to say that all political leaders, jurists, capitalists, and labor leaders embraced corporate liberalism in the spirit of compromise, or that significant political disagreements among corporate liberals did not exist. On the other hand, the economic, social, and political transformations associated with the corporate reconstruction of American capitalism in the first half of the twentieth century could not have been achieved or sustained without widespread acceptance of the basic (albeit flexible) tenets of corporate liberalism.

4. On the concept of a capitalist movement, see Sklar, *Corporate Reconstruction*, pp. 2–3, 11–14, 20–33. "Both capitalist industrialism and its corporate reorganization, in sum, are better understood not simply as an 'external force' or an 'objective' economic or organizational phenomenon but as a social movement, no less than populism, trade unionism, feminism, Afro-American equalitarianism, or socialism" (ibid., p. 13).

5. Alfred D. Chandler, *The Visible Hand: The Managerial Revolution in American Business* (Cambridge, Mass.: Harvard University Press, Belknap Press, 1977); Robert Michels, *Political Parties: A Sociological Study of the Oligarchical Tendencies of Modern Democracy* (New York: The Free Press, 1962); Grant McConnell, *Private Power and American Democracy* (New York: Knopf, 1967).

6. In his dissenting opinion in *Louis K. Liggett Co. v. Lee*, 288 U.S. 517, 548 (1933), Justice Brandeis, in analyzing the recent transformation of state incorporation laws, emphasized that the freedom of foreign (nonresident) corporations to do business in interstate commerce was a decisive factor in shaping state policies:

"The removal by the leading industrial states of the limitations upon the size and powers of business corporations appears to have been due, not to their conviction that maintenance of the restrictions was undesirable in itself, but to the conviction that it was futile to insist upon them; because local restriction would be circumvented by foreign incorporation. Indeed, local restriction seemed worse than futile. Lesser states, eager for the revenue derived from the traffic in charters, had removed safeguards from their own incorporation laws. Companies were eagerly formed to provide charters for corporations in states where the cost was lowest and the laws least restrictive. The states joined in advertising their wares. The race was one not of diligence but of laxity. Incorporation under such laws was possible; and the great industrial states yielded in order not to lose wholly the prospect of the revenue and the control incident to domestic incorporation."

7. Referring to the rise of the large corporation in the late nineteenth and early twentieth centuries, Charles W. McCurdy explains: "The *ultra vires* doctrine and the rule permitting the states to harass foreign corporations were subjected to increasing criticism by legal scholars; and beginning in 1906 both juridical principles were all but dismantled through a cooperative effort involving appellate courts, the National Conference of Commissioners on Uniform State Laws, and state legislatures. Over the course of a single generation, in short, the public law of corporations was reformed from top to botttom." See "The *Knight* Sugar Decision of 1895 and the Modernization of American Corporation Law, 1869–1903," *Business History Review* 53 (Autumn 1979): 306–7. See also note 11 below.

8. The legal powers of corporate management have evolved from the traditional organi-

zation of the corporate charter wherein shareholders elected a board of directors (who, in turn, appointed officers) to oversee the affairs of the enterprise:

"The de jure management of the modern corporation is vested almost entirely in the board of directors. The board of directors may and normally does delegate wide powers to the principal executive officers. These officers are, however, usually members of the board of directors, and even when they are not, the directors' duties include the duty of supervision over their acts. The directors' duties are in the main duties owed to the corporate entity as such rather than to the shareholders or creditors individually, but they are in many, perhaps in most cases, enforced on behalf of the corporation in suits instituted by individual shareholders." See William L. Cary, *Cases and Materials on Corporations*, 4th ed. (Mineola: Foundation Press, 1969), p. 513.

9. Edwin Merrick Dodd, "For Whom Are Corporate Managers Trustees?" *Harvard Law Review* 45 (May 1932): 1145–63; Adolph A. Berle, "For Whom Corporate Managers *Are* Trustees: A Note," *Harvard Law Review* 45 (June 1932): 1365–72. Dodd sparked the debate by responding to Berle's argument in "Corporate Powers as Powers in Trust," *Harvard Law Review* 44 (1932): 1049–79. Berle and Means's influential study, *The Modern Corporation and Private Property*, on which Berle relies in these papers, was in the process of publication.

10. The issue of "control" is critical to determining who rules the corporation. Most analysts now agree that ownership of 5 to 10 percent of a corporation's stock is sufficient to wield control—that is, the ability to elect or remove directors, depending on a variety of mitigating factors. This drop from 20 percent originally established by Berle and Means reflects increasing dispersal of stock ownership and therefore a decrease in the stock needed to influence corporate policies. To a large extent, however, control is a hypothetical power that is difficult to test in the absence of a proxy fight or evidence of the internal decision-making process of the corporation. In assessing the significance of control, one encounters important empirical and analytical issues that pertain to the social origins, organization, and motivation of those who wield it and to the types and degree of control that may be exercised under various circumstances. Determining the location of control is critical to the theory, or a variation thereof, that envisions the emergence of a managerial class that rules but does not own the enterprise, as well as to theories that emphasize the class content of corporate power. These issues are discussed in more detail in Chapters 5 and 6. For the purposes of the present analysis, suffice it to say that the location of control, whether it be in a minority stockholder or the directors, or some combination of the two, does not alter either the legal conception of corporate powers held in trust or the fact of oligarchic rule.

11. *Ultra vires* "has a broad application and includes not only acts prohibited by the charter, but acts which are in excess of powers granted and not prohibited, and generally applied either when a corporation has no power whatever to do an act, or when the corporation has the power but exercises it irregularly." See *Black's Law Dictionary*, 6th ed. (St. Paul, Minn.: West Publishing Co., 1990), p. 1522. The *ultra vires* doctrine was applied successfully by state governments between 1888 and 1892 to effect the dissolution of numerous trusts. See above, Chapter 2, section 4 and note 103. However, the doctrine of *ultra vires* was also being accommodated, albeit very gradually before the turn of the century, to the changing structure of corporate ownership and management. Concerning statutory and judicial revisions of *ultra vires* during the first four decades of the twentieth century, see Henry Winthrop Ballantine, *Ballantine on Corporations*, rev. ed. (Chicago: Callaghan & Co., 1946), pp. 240–69; Clyde L. Colson, "The Doctrine of *Ultra Vires* in United States Supreme Court Decisions," *West Virginia Law Quarterly* 42 (April 1936): 179–217, 297–337; Willburt D. Ham, "Ultra Vires Contracts Under Modern Corporate Legislation," *Kentucky Law Journal* 46 (1958): 215–49; Morton J. Horwitz, "*Santa Clara* Revisited:

The Development of Corporate Theory," *West Virginia Law Review* 88 (1985): 186–88. See also note 7 above. Supreme Court decisions concerning *ultra vires* acts adhered to the traditional standard of strict accountability long after most states had adopted a liberalized interpretation or had entirely eliminated the doctrine. While this contributed to some confusion in the law, it did not greatly affect the direction of legal change. On this issue, the Court was clearly out of step with the dominant trend in state corporation law, and for that matter with legal theory expounded by leading scholars.

12. *Jacksonville Mayport, Pablo Railway & Navigation Co. v. Hooper*, 160 U.S. 514 (1896).

13. *A. P. Smith Mfg. Corp. v. Barlow*, 13 N.J. 145, 98 A.2d 681, appeal dismissed, 346 U.S. 861 (1953); *Union Pacific R.R. Co. v. Trustees*, 8 Utah 2d 201, 329 P.2d 398 (1958).

14. *Theodora Holding Corp. v. Henderson*, 257 A.2d 398 (Del.Ch., 1969).

15. Cary, *Cases and Materials*, pp. 552–56.

16. Cary notes: "One searches in vain in the decided cases for a reasoned defense of this change in legal philosophy, or for the slightest attempt to refute the powerful arguments which had been made in support of the previous rule. Did the courts discover in the last quarter of the Nineteenth Century that greed was no longer a factor in human conduct? If so, they did not share the basis of this discovery with the public; nor did they humbly admit their error when confronted with the next wave of corporate frauds arising out of the era of the formation of the 'trusts' during the 1890's and early 1900's" (ibid., p. 554).

17. *Genesee & West Virginia Railway Co. v. Retsof Mining Co.*, 36 N.Y.Supp. 896 at 901 (Sup.Ct., 1895), quoted in ibid., p. 555.

18. *United Copper Securities Co. v. Amalgamated Copper Co.*, 244 U.S. 261, 263–64 (1917); *Beveridge v. New York Elevated R.R. Co.*, 112 N.Y.1 (1889); *Briggs v. Spaulding*, 141 U.S. 132, 151–52 (1890); *Hun v. Cary*, 82 N.Y. 65 (1880); *Spering's Appeal*, Pa.St. 11, 10 Am.Rep. 684 (1872).

19. To offer one example, there have been numerous cases involving the common practice of boards of directors to appoint special litigation committees to advise them on possible corporate legal action—a method that, arguably, facilitates the dismissal of derivative suits by removing interested directors from the decision-making process: *Gall v. Exxon Corp.*, 418 F.Supp. 508 (1976); *Burks v. Lasker*, 441 U.S. 471 (1979); *Auerbach v. Bennett*, 47 N.Y.2d. 619 (1979); *Rosengarten v. ITT*, 466 F.Supp. 817 (S.D.N.Y., 1979); *Lewis v. Anderson*, 615 F.2d 778 (9th Cir., 1980); *Maldonado v. Flynn*, 485 F.Supp. 274 (S.D.N.Y., 1980). But see *Maldonado v. Flynn*, 413 A.2d 1251 (Del.Ch., 1980), and *Zapata Corp. v. Maldonado*, 430 A.2d 779 (Del.Supr., 1981), where the Delaware courts imposed a somewhat higher standard, though the discretion of the court was also enlarged in *Zapata*, where it was ruled that the court may exercise its own independent judgment and take into account the public policy served by the continuance of the suit. *Zapata*, however, was followed by several cases that decided related issues concerning judicial review of derivative suits at the intial stage of "demand" (i.e., a statutory requirement that, before instituting an action, shareholders formally demand of the directors that a suit be brought on behalf of the corporate entity or provide justification to the court, in the absence of a demand, why a demand would be futile—for example, directors' lack of independence). *Zapata* left unanswered the conditions under which demand would be deemed futile by the court. In addressing this issue in *Aronson v. Lewis*, 473 A.2nd 805 (Del.Supr., 1984), the Supreme Court of Delaware employed a business judgment standard to determine if "a reasonable doubt is created that: (1) the directors are disinterested and independent and (2) the challenged transaction was otherwise the product of a valid exercise of business judgment." The burden of proof under this test is clearly on the shareholder. See also *Pogostin v. Rice*, 480 A.2nd 619 (Del.Supr., 1984); *Grobow v. Perot* 539 A.2nd 180 (Del. Supr., 1988).

20. 418 F.Supp. 508 (1976).

21. *Shlensky v. Wrigley*, 95 Ill.App.2d 173 (1968). A similar rationale was employed in *Herald v. Seawell*, 472 F.2d 1081 (10th Cir., 1972), where the Court of Appeals upheld the board of directors' actions to defeat a takeover bid (at a loss to shareholders) on the ground that the public's interest in having a locally controlled newspaper was consistent with the corporation's duty to the shareholders and to the public. This case could stand for a broader principle if the public-interest justification were to gain wider acceptance. On the other hand, it is more likely that this decision, like *Shlensky*, represents an expansive application of the business judgment rule (guided by the principle of political autonomy) rather than a new doctrine of corporate social responsibility.

22. *Zapata Corp. v. Maldonado* (see note 19 above) appears to impose a (higher) standard of corporate social responsibility where the court *chooses* to exercise such discretion. But this ruling could be a means for preventing the total eclipse of the derivative suit rather than a method for imposing social responsibility. In any event, *Zapata*'s practical significance has been limited by *Aronson* and its progeny (see again note 19 above).

23. An exception to this dominant trend is *Smith v. Van Gorkom*, 488 A.2d 858 (Del.Supr., 1985), where the court held that the board of directors did not reach an "informed business judgment" in voting to sell the company pursuant to a cash-out merger proposal. In emphasizing that the board had not adequately informed itself or the stockholders concerning the details of the transaction before accepting the offer, the court focused on the decision-making process rather than on the result (i.e., whether or not the price was fair). Because decisions of Delaware courts often shape the direction of corporation law in numerous other states, the opinion produced considerable alarm in corporate boardrooms. See Bayless Manning, "Reflections and Practical Tips on Life in the Boardroom After *Van Gorkom*," *Business Lawyer* 41 (November 1985): 243–48. However, the Delaware legislature responded in 1986 and strongly limited the practical significance of *Van Gorkom* by providing that a corporation in its articles of incorporation may eliminate or limit the liability of directors (but not officers) to the corporation and its shareholders for money damages (Delaware General Corporation Law, Sec. 102(b)(7)). Subsequent case law has circumscribed rather than extended the holding in *Van Gorkom*. Also, following the Delaware legislature's example, forty-two states passed acts designed to achieve a similar end. See Dennis J. Block, Nancy E. Barton, and Stephen A. Radin, *The Business Judgment Rule: Fiduciary Duties of Corporate Directors*, 3rd ed. (Englewood Cliffs, N.J.: Prentice-Hall Law and Business, 1989), pp. 40–42, 60–71; William E. Knepper and Dan Bailey, *Liability of Corporate Officers and Directors*, 5th ed., 2 vols. (Charlottesville, Va.: Michie Co., 1993), 2:1–29. See also Stuart Shapiro, "Judicial Business Judgment: The Investment Banker's Role," in Arnold W. Sametz, ed., *The Battle for Corporate Control* (Homewood, Ill.: Business One Irwin, 1991), pp. 87–104.

24. Derivative suits, the traditional method under the law by which fiduciary duties are enforced, appears to be threatened with extinction in many jurisdictions. Many states have done away altogether with preemptive rights—the prerogative to purchase new issuance of stock in proportion to one's stockholdings in the enterprise. Where the right still exists, numerous exceptions have been devised to limit it with regard to various classes of stock that might be issued. Furthermore, the traditional purpose of preemptive rights in maintaining the voting power of one's proportionate share of stock has little meaning in the modern structure of the large corporation, which relies on the proxy system. And the proxy system—the method of electing directors—though subject to SEC regulations that establish procedural safeguards, is effectively controlled by the corporate oligarchy that runs the election at corporate expense, lists only its candidates on the ballots, and may count blank proxy forms as votes for the management slate. Thus, the incumbents prevail—unless a proxy fight is successfully waged by an individual or group with suffi-

cient influence (percentage of stock and independent finances) to wrest control or enforce its theoretical control.

However, under Regulation 14a-8 of the Securities Exchange Act of 1934, governing proxy solicitations, corporations are required to include, at corporate expense, shareholder proposals (with a 200 word statement) in the management proxy statement and to list the proposals in the management proxy form or ballot. In this way, proposed corporate policies concerning internal governance or social issues can be put to a general vote by shareholders. Some shareholder campaigns (e.g., Dow Chemical, General Motors) have attracted considerable public attention to corporate policies but garnered very few votes. Management may, and does, respond with its own proposals or self-promotions.

On the issue of declining stockholder rights in the twentieth century, see the sources cited in note 9 above and A. A. Berle, "Corporate Devices for Diluting Stock Participation," *Columbia Law Review* 31 (1931): 1239–65; W. H. S. Stevens, "Stockholders Voting Rights and the Centralization of Voting Control," *Quarterly Journal of Economics* 40 (May 1926): 353–92; Henry S. Drinker, "The Preemptive Right of Shareholders to Subscribe to New Shares," *Harvard Law Review* 43 (February 1930): 586–616; E. M. Dodd, "Statutory Developments in Business Corporation Law, 1886–1936," *Harvard Law Review* 50 (1936): 27–59; William L. Cary, "Federalism and Corporate Law: Reflections upon Delaware," *Yale Law Journal* 83 (March 1974): 663–705; George W. Dent, "The Power of Directors to Terminate Shareholder Litigation: The Death of the Derivative Suit?" *Northwestern Law Review* 75 (1980): 96–146; Victor Brudney, "The Independent Director: Heavenly City or Potemkin Village?" *Harvard Law Review* 95 (1982): 597–659; Daniel R. Fischel and Michael Bradley, "The Role of Liability Rules and the Derivative Suit in Corporate Law: A Theoretical and Empirical Analysis," *Cornell Law Review* 71 (1986): 261–98.

25. Tender offers, an essential strategy of the merger movement, have supplanted proxy fights as the favored means of seizing control of large corporations, though hostile takeovers often lead to proxy fights.

26. Cf. Marver Bernstein, *Regulating Business by Independent Commission* (Princeton: Princeton University Press, 1955); Grant McConnell, *Private Power and American Democracy* (New York: Knopf, 1967); Theodore J. Lowi, *The End of Liberalism* (New York: W. W. Norton & Co., 1969); Ellis W. Hawley, *The New Deal and the Problem of Monopoly: A Study in Economic Ambivalence* (Princeton: Princeton University Press, 1969); George J. Stigler, "The Theory of Economic Regulation," *Bell Journal of Economics and Management Science* 2 (Spring 1971): 3–20; James Q. Wilson, "The Politics of Regulation," in James Q. Wilson, ed., *The Politics of Regulation* (New York: Basic Books, 1980), pp. 357–94; Thomas K. McCraw, ed., *Regulation in Perspective* (Cambridge, Mass.: Harvard Business School, 1981); Fred Thompson and L. R. Jones, *Regulatory Policy and Practices* (New York: Praeger, 1982); Edward S. Herman, *Corporate Control, Corporate Power* (Cambridge: Cambridge University Press, 1981), pp. 172–86; Stephen Breyer, *Regulation and Its Reform* (Cambridge, Mass.: Harvard University Press, 1982); Alfred D. Chandler Jr. and Richard S. Tedlow, *The Coming of Managerial Capitalism: A Casebook on the History of American Economic Institutions* (Homewood, Ill.: Richard D. Irwin, 1985), pp. 624–50; Martha Derthick and Paul J. Quirk, *The Politics of Deregulation* (Washington, D.C.: Brookings Institution, 1985); David Vogel, *National Styles of Regulation: Environmental Policies in Great Britain and the United States* (Ithaca: Cornell University Press, 1986); Donald R. Brand, *Corporatism and the Rule of Law: A Study of the National Recovery Administration* (Ithaca: Cornell University Press, 1988); Cass R. Sunstein, *After the Rights Revolution: Reconceiving the Regulatory State* (Cambridge, Mass.: Harvard University Press, 1990).

My intent in discussing the relationship between corporate power and regulation is not to support or defeat a particular approach or theory to regulation. Instead, I am concerned more with exploring the dimensions of regulation as it might affect the exercise of corporate power. In this context, theories or explanations that focus on the politics of regulation have produced the most fruitful lines of inquiry for assessing the relationship between regulators and regulated corporations over the course of the twentieth century. My assumption is that regulation takes different forms, depending on who sponsors and influences the drafting of regulatory legislation, and that consequently regulation can serve different ends and interests. Regardless of the form or apparent purposes of regulation, however, its interpretation and implementation can be affected by a variety of political considerations. For a useful typology and analysis of the politics of regulation, see Wilson, "Politics of Regulation."

27. For example, Murray L. Weidenbaum made this point with regard to the dramatic increase in government regulation in the late 1960s through the late 1970s. See Weidenbaum, "The Second Managerial Revolution: The Shift of Economic Decision-Making from Business to Government," in Walter Goldstein, ed., *Planning, Politics, and the Public Interest* (New York: Columbia University Press, 1978), pp. 45–76.

28. David Vogel, *Fluctuating Fortunes: The Political Power of Business in America* (New York: Basic Books, 1989), pp. 240–89; Roger E. Meiners and Bruce Yandle, eds., *Regulation and the Reagan Era: Politics, Bureaucracy, and the Public Interest* (New York: Holmes & Meier, 1989); Thomas Ferguson and Joel Rogers, *Right Turn: The Decline of the Democrats and the Future of American Politics* (New York: Hill & Wang, 1986), pp. 130–37.

29. Robert E. Mutch, *Campaigns, Congress, and the Courts: The Making of Federal Campaign Finance Law* (New York: Praeger, 1988); Edwin M. Epstein, *Corporations, Contributions, and Political Campaigns: Federal Regulation in Perspective* (Berkeley: Institute of Governmental Studies, University of California, 1968); Louise Overacker, *Money in Elections* (New York: Macmillan, 1932); Earl R. Sikes, *State and Federal Corrupt-Practices Legislation* (Durham, N.C.: Duke University Press, 1928); Helen M. Rocca, *Corrupt Practices Legislation* (Washington, D.C.: League of Women Voters, 1928); Perry Belmont, "Publicity of Election Expenditures," *North American Review* 180 (January 1905): 166–85.

In 1907, Congress passed the Tillman Act, which prohibited corporations from making direct contributions to candidates running for federal office. By 1971, when the Federal Election Campaign Act was passed, not a single conviction had been obtained under the Tillman Act for illegal corporate contributions. The Federal Corrupt Practices Act of 1925 imposed additional constraints on labor and business campaign contributions but it was equally ineffective because it was filled with loopholes and exceptions. Herbert Alexander describes the general practice of corporate funding of candidates before the campaign financing reforms of the 1970s: "In the past business executives and politicians alike were generally secretive about campaign contributions. Neither wanted to give the public the impression that senators, representatives, governors, mayors, or even Presidents could be influenced by those who gave financial support to their campaigns. Until the 1970s federal election laws were so vague and enforcement so lax that there was usually little difficulty in hiding campaign contributions. Sometimes money was siphoned off from corporate funds and put into political campaigns. Occasionally, corporate executives were given bonuses with the explicit understanding that the aftertax balance would be contributed to campaign funds. Some few executives were assigned to work on campaigns while remaining on corporate payrolls. More often, slush funds were set up under various facades, and money was secretly dispensed from them, frequently in cash, to candidates. In general, the public did not know precisely what was going on, but the business executives and politicians did, and neither side forgot when showdowns occurred on Capitol Hill or in executive departments and agencies." See Herbert Alexander, "Corporate Political Behavior," in Thornton Bradshaw and David Vogel, eds., *Corporations and Their Critics: Issues and Answers to the Problems of Corporate Social Respsonsibiity* (New York: McGraw-Hill, 1981), p. 35.

30. The Supreme Court's decision upholding the Wagner Act (the National Labor Relations Act [NLRA]), in *NLRB v. Jones & Laughlin Steel Corp.*, 301 U.S. 1 (1937), marked the beginning of federal (statutory) regulation of industrial relations. The Wagner Act guarantees the rights of workers to organize and to strike, prohibits unfair labor practices that interfere with these rights, establishes a legal framework for collective bargaining, and promulgates rules according to which collective agreements are to be enforced in the workplace. The National Labor Relations Board was created under the NLRA to administer and enforce the provisions of the act. This dramatic turning point in labor relations also marked the end of a centuries-old method of regulating management-labor relations based on the common law of master and servant. See Karen Orren, *Belated Feudalism: Labor, Law, and Liberal Development in the United States* (Cambridge: Cambridge University Press, 1991). Under the law of master and servant, English and American courts (and to a much lesser extent legislative bodies) had developed a complex system of legal principles and remedies that governed labor contracts, the liability of employees and employers, and the duty of obedience owed by the employee (servant) to the employer (master) (ibid., esp. chaps. 3 and 4).

In terms of the conceptual framework I have employed, these legal relationships would be termed "private," in the sense that the law of master and servant as applied by courts in labor relations (much like their contemporaneous common-law doctrines regulating relations between husband and wife) was based on principles that sustained traditional forms of authority and power and thereby insulated these relationships from public regulation. Labor law, like corporation law, regulated the internal dimension of corporate power, but, unlike the law of corporations, the law of master and servant constituted an entirely separate "feudal" domain of judge-made law largely beyond the reach of legislative revision—which is to say that courts regularly overruled legislation that encroached on this domain. The labor movement's long struggle to transform or eliminate the (labor) law of master and servant successfully moved the regulation of management-labor relations into the realm of public law, and hence within the external dimension of corporate power. This was long overdue. Unlike the law of corporations and antitrust law, labor law in the early twentieth century lagged far behind changes in the firm, the economy, and society that accompanied the reconstitution of power relationships under corporate capitalism. Indeed, labor law was still catching up with the economic and social changes associated with the advent of competitive industrial capitalism.

In upholding the Wagner Act under Congress's commerce power, the *Jones & Laughlin* opinion justified the public regulation of labor disputes on the ground that this power could be employed to prevent disruptions of interstate commerce caused by labor stoppages or strikes. Thus, in jettisoning the law of master and servant, the new regulatory framework recognized the social character of the relationship between capital and labor, and by moving it from the private or internal dimension to the public or external dimension, acknowledged that this aspect of corporate power (like the marketplace and, later, political activity) must be regulated in the public interest.

31. For example, in 1965–66, Ralph Nader's *Unsafe At Any Speed* and his subsequent harassment by General Motors brought national attention to the problem of auto safety. In 1967, Senator Warren Magnuson conducted a highly publicized campaign about the dangers to children of flammable fabrics. The following year, national attention was focused on the problem of coal mine safety and black-lung disease in the aftermath of a deadly mine explosion in West Virginia. Concerning the changing public perception of big business and the rise of the consumer movement, see Vogel, *Fluctuating Fortunes*, pp. 37–58; Michael Pertschuk, *Revolt Against Regulation: The Rise and Pause of the Consumer Movement* (Berkeley and Los Angeles: University of California Press, 1982), pp. 5–45.

32. In 1972, the Labor Study Group (formed in 1965 by executives of General Electric and American Smelting & Refining to counter organized labor's attempt to repeal Section 14(b) of the Taft-Hartley Act) merged with the Construction Users Anti-Inflation Roundtable (formed in 1969 under the leadership of Roger Blough, former chairman of U.S. Steel, to combat the rising costs of labor in the construction industry) to create the Business Roundtable. In 1973, the Roundtable, which had devoted most of its attention to labor issues, merged with the March Group, an informal organization of chief executive officers from America's leading corporations. After this second merger, the political agenda of the Roundtable changed considerably to reflect the objectives of the March Group, whose leadership consisted of the more activist members of the Business Council. For more than a decade, a handful of Business Council leaders had been urging their fellow CEOs to become directly involved in politics. The events of the late 1960s and early 1970s had finally demonstrated what these business activists had claimed all along: namely, that direct political action was a necessity not a luxury. In addition to battling labor on a variety of issues, the Fortune 500 leadership of the Roundtable initiated a campaign to improve the public image of business and to enhance their political influence in Congress. Membership in the Roundtable is by invitation only. The Executive (or Planning) Committee, which consists of the Roundtable's chairman and three vice-chairmen, sets the lobbying agenda. General meetings are held once a year, and meetings of the Policy Committee (consisting of about 20 percent of the membership) are held once a month.

On the organization and activities of the Business Roundtable, See Kim McQuaid, *Big Business and Presidential Power: From FDR to Reagan* (New York: Morrow, 1982), pp. 284–310; Ferguson and Rogers, "Knights of the Roundtable," *The Nation*, December 15, 1979, pp. 620–25; Tim Smart, "Knights of the Roundtable," *Business Week*, October 21, 1988, pp. 39–44; Phillip H. Burch Jr., "The Business Roundtable: Its Make-up and External Ties," in Paul Zarembka, ed., *Research in Political Economy*, vol. 4 (Greenwich, Conn.: JAI Press, 1977), pp. 101–27; Charles Alexander, "New Voices for a New Era," *Time*, April 13, 1981, pp. 76–77; Walter Guzzardi Jr., "Business Is Learning How to Win in Washington," *Fortune*, March 27, 1978, pp. 52–58, and "Business' Most Powerful Lobby in Washington," *Business Week*, December 20, 1976, pp. 60–61.

On the new politics of business, see Perstchuk, *Revolt;* Thomas Byrne Edsall, *Power and Money: Writing About Politics, 1971–1987* (New York: W. W. Norton & Co., 1988); and Edsall, *The New Politics of Inequality* (New York: W. W. Norton & Co., 1984).

On both the Business Roundtable and the new politics of business, see Sar A. Levitan and Martha R. Cooper, *Business Lobbies: The Public and the Bottom Line* (Baltimore: Johns Hopkins University Press, 1984); Vogel, *Fluctuating Fortunes;* Irving S. Shaprio, *America's Third Revolution: Public Interest and the Private Role* (New York: Harper & Row, 1984); Ralph Nader, *The Big Boys: Power and Position in American Business* (New York: Pantheon Books, 1986); Michael Useem, *The Inner Circle: Large Corporations and the Rise of Business Political Activity in the U.S. and U.K.* (New York: Oxford University Press, 1984); William G. Domhoff, *Who Rules America Now?* (Englewood Cliffs, N.J.: Prentice-Hall, 1983); Ferguson and Rogers, *Right Turn;* Sidney Blumenthal, *The Rise of the Counter-Establishment: From Conservative Ideology to Political Power* (New York: Harper & Row, 1988), pp. 69–86; and Mark Green and Andrew Buchsbaum, *The Corporate Lobbies: Political Profiles of the Business Roundtable and the Chamber of Commerce* (Washington, D.C.: Public Citizen, 1980).

For studies that examine corporate political behavior in electoral politics, see Mark S. Mizruchi, *The Structure of Corporate Political Action: Interfirm Relations and Their Consequences* (Cambridge, Mass.: Harvard University Press, 1992); Mizruchi, "Similarity of Political Behavior Among Large Corporations," *American Journal of Sociology* 95 (September 1989): 401–21; Theodore J. Eismeier and Phillip H. Pollock III, *Business, Money, and the Rise of Corporate*

PACs in American Elections (Westport, Conn.: Quorum Books, 1988); Vallon Burris, "The Political Partisanship of American Business: A Study of Corporate Political Action Committees," *American Sociological Review* 52 (December 1987): 732–44; Dan Clawson, Alan Neuwstadtl, and James Bearden, "The Logic of Business Unity: Corporate Contributions to the 1980 Congressional Elections," *American Sociological Review* 51 (December 1986): 797–811; Ann B. Matasar, *Corporate PACs and Federal Campaign Financing Laws: Use or Abuse of Power?* (Westport, Conn.: Quorum Books, 1986); Larry J. Sabato, *PAC Power: Inside the World of Political Action Committees* (New York: W. W. Norton and Co., 1984); Marick F. Masters and Gerald D. Keim, "The Determinants of PAC Participation Among Large Corporations," *Journal of Politics* 47 (November 1985): 1158–73; Gary Andres, "Business Involvement in Campaign Finance: Factors Influencing the Decision to Form a Corporate PAC," *P.S.* 18 (Spring 1985): 213–20; Edward Handler and John R. Mulkern, *Business in Politics: Campaign Strategies of Corporate Political Action Committees* (Lexington, Mass.: Lexington Books, 1982); Stuart Rothenberg and Richard R. Roldan, *Business PACs and Ideology: A Study of Contributions in the 1982 Elections* (Washington, D.C.: Institute for Government and Politics, 1983); Herbert E. Alexander and Brian A. Haggerty, *Financing the 1984 Election* (Lexington, Mass.: Lexington Books, 1987); Herbert E. Alexander, *Financing the 1980 Election* (Lexington, Mass.: Lexington Books, 1983); Alexander, *Financing Politics: Money, Elections and Political Reform* (Washington, D.C.: Congressional Quarterly Press, 1980), pp. 67–90, 145–49; Alexander, "Corporate Political Behavior"; Edwin M. Epstein, "The Business PAC Phenomenon: An Irony of Electoral Reform," *Regulation* 3 (May–June 1979): 35–41.

33. On corporate political activism and grass-roots lobbying, see Edsall, *New Politics of Inequality*, pp. 108–12, 123–28; Vogel, *Fluctuating Fortunes*, pp. 203–13; Phyllis S. McGrath, *Redefining Corporate-Federal Relations* (New York: Conference Board, 1979). On coalition-building within the business community, see Vogel, *Fluctuating Fortunes*, pp. 148–203, 290–300.

34. Sabato, *PAC Power*, pp. 45–47, 60; Edsall, *New Politics of Inequality*, pp. 136–38; Eismeier and Pollock, *Business, Money, and PACs*, pp. 22–23, 79–85; Vogel, *Fluctuating Fortunes*, pp. 206–13. Cf. Matasar, *Corporate PACs*, pp. 71–78.

35. Vogel concludes that corporate campaign spending between 1977 and 1980 had limited impact on enhancing business influence over environmental and energy issues, but did have the effect of reducing congressional support of consumer issues, and especially of organized labor. "On balance, however, more sophisticated and intensive lobbying, and the ability of business to mobilize its supporters in the 'grass roots' proved more important than campaign contributions in strengthening the influence of business during the second half of the 1970s." See Vogel, *Fluctuating Fortunes*, pp. 210–12.

36. As a quid pro quo for convincing President Carter to adopt voluntary wage and price controls, the Roundtable agreed to support his Panama Canal Treaty. The Roundtable also played a key role in the drafting and passage of legislation that prohibited American corporations from participating in the Arab boycott of Israel. Carter regularly consulted with the Roundtable on a number of issues. According to Carter, "I was very reluctant to proceed with a decision without consulting with the leaders of the Business Roundtable. I didn't always feel constrained to take their advice, but I considered it very carefully." See Smart, "Knights of the Roundtable," p. 44; Useem, *Inner Circle*, pp. 110–11. For an informative account of the Roundtable's influence during the Carter administration, written by Irving S. Shapiro, former chairman of the board and chief executive officer of the Du Pont Company, and chairman of the Roundtable during Carter's term, see Shapiro, *America's Third Revolution*, pp. 26–51. See also McQuaid, *Big Business*, pp. 296–305.

37. Vogel, *Fluctuating Fortunes*, pp. 200–203. McQuaid, *Big Business*, pp. 303–5. On the ideological differences that separate the corporate elite from the rest of the corporate

community, see Useem, *Inner Circle*, pp. 106–15. Useem argues that the views of the corporate elite, or "inner circle," tend to be broader on social and economic issues, representing a "classwide rationality" that cannot be explained adequately in terms of an economic rationality that reduces ideological position to the profit-making imperatives of enterprise. See also notes 49 and 50 below.

38. For accounts of the extraordinary lobbying efforts behind the 1981 tax reforms, see Vogel, *Fluctuating Fortunes*, pp. 242–46; Nader, *Big Boys*, pp. 271–81.

39. Vogel, *Fluctuating Fortunes*, pp. 280–82; Useem, *Inner Circle*, pp. 108–9.

40. Ferguson and Rogers, *Right Turn*, pp. 130–37. Vogel, *Fluctuating Fortunes*, pp. 246–51, 260–70.

41. A Conference Board survey of the executives of 300 large corporations conducted by Helen Axel in 1980 revealed: "Virtually all of the responding chief executive officers believe that they should personally and actively express their views on public policy issues at high government levels. Most believe that it is part of their job to become involved in issues that affect the well-being of their companies. They believe positions which they or their companies have developed should be made known to upper echelons of government in order for business to contribute to the formulation of public policy. Not all of the respondents who feel that CEO's have this responsibility acted on their beliefs within the past year, but a substantial majority—85 percent of those responding—did." The survey also disclosed: "Chief executives from the larger corporations (those with annual sales exceeding $500 million) appear more likely to be concerned with issues of broad public policy than executives who head smaller companies. About 85 percent of the CEOs from these larger companies who have spoken out during the past year have done so on broad policy issues." See Helen Axel, *Political Activism: The Chief Executive's Role* (New York: The Conference Board, 1980), pp. 3–4.

Also, for documentation of the increasing political activism of CEOs, see David G. Moore, *Politics and the Corporate Chief Executive* (New York: The Conference Board, 1980). In *America's Third Revolution*, Shapiro makes a case for greater CEO involvement in the management of public policy. An analysis of the political and social challenges and responsibilities facing corporate leaders (written by a consultant for Shell Oil and sponsored by the Business Roundtable) is in Francis W. Steckmest, *Corporate Performance: The Key to Public Trust* (New York: McGraw-Hill, 1982). See also Robert Hessen, *In Defense of the Corporation* (Stanford, Calif.: Hoover Institution Press, Stanford University, 1979), for a response to the critics of corporate power, particularly Ralph Nader. Another indication of the politicization of the CEO is the appearance in management literature of "how to" books on political activity. See, for example, Frank Shipper and Marianne M. Jennings, *Business Strategy for the Political Arena* (Westport, Conn.: Quorum Books, 1984); Mike H. Ryan, Carl L. Swanson, and Rogene A. Buchholz, *Corporate Strategy, Public Policy and the Fortune 500* (Oxford: Basil Blackwell, 1987).

42. The initiative lists four major goals: "(1) to develop a national consensus on the vision for a world-class education system; (2) to insure acceptance for the national goals of improving student achievement and school completion rates and for the development of a sound measurement system; (3) to develop partnerships with federal and state governments, educators, parents, businesspeople, and other groups to produce a new education system; and (4) to help shape public opinion to support a restructuring of the nation's schools and to promote more direct communication between schools and the people they serve." Also consult *The Business Roundtable Participation Guide: A Primer for Business on Education* (1990) prepared by the National Alliance of Business.

43. Chris Pipho, "Coming Up: A Decade of Business Involvement," *Phi Delta Kappan*, April 1990, pp. 582–83. See also Michael Useem, *Liberal Education and the Corporation:*

The Hiring and Advancement of College Graduates (New York: Aldine de Gruyter, 1989), pp. 157–75.

44. Joan Biskupic, "Job Discrimination Legislation Roils Business Community," *Congressional Quarterly*, April 20, 1991, pp. 989–91; Biskupic, "With Business Talks Stalled, Bush Holds Best Hand," *Congressional Quarterly*, April 27, 1991, pp. 1063–64.

45. Edwin Chen and Karen Tumulty, "Business Leaders Reject Health Plan," *Los Angeles Times*, February 3, 1994, p. 1; David Ewing Duncan, "The Triumph of Harry and Sally: How the Mighty Insurance Lobby Skunked Clinton and Demolished His Health-Care Plan," *Los Angeles Times Magazine*, September 11, 1994, pp. 28–31; David Corn, "Bill of Health," *The Nation*, March 7, 1994, p. 294; Carl Mollins, "Prognosis Poor," *Maclean's*, March 14, 1994, pp. 20–21.

46. David M. Liff, Mary O'Connor, and Clarke Bruno, *Corporate Advertising: The Business Response to Changing Public Attitudes* (Washington, D.C.: Investor Responsibility Research Center, 1980), p. 2. On big business' advertising campaign to shape public opinion, see also Vogel, *Fluctuating Fortunes*, pp. 214–20; Edsall, *The New Politics of Inequality*, pp. 112–17; Useem, *Inner Circle*, pp. 129–32.

47. Studies in the early 1980s revealed that public confidence in business leaders had improved only marginally since the mid-1970s, when it reached an all-time low. See Edsall, *New Politics of Inequality*, p.117. Edsall suggests: "The success of corporate advocacy advertising has probably been to cast public doubt on the solutions offered by adversaries of business. The most consistent theme of corporate advocacy and public-interest advertising has been a sustained attack on the use of government money and regulation to solve social problems" (ibid).

48. Blumenthal, *Rise of the Counter-Establishment*, pp. 32–68. On corporate contributions to these organizations, see Edsall, *New Politics of Inequality*, pp. 117–20. On the impact of corporate efforts to influence media coverage of business, see Vogel, *Fluctuating Fortunes*, pp. 220–27. For a more general analysis of the significance of policy-planning organizations in government, see Thomas Dye, "Oligarchic Tendencies in National Policy-Making: The Role of the Private Policy-Planning Organizations," *Journal of Politics* 40 (1978): 309–31.

49. Mark S. Mizruchi has conducted the most thorough empirical investigation of business unity in American politics. Mizruchi's extensive and complex analysis of the similarity of political behavior of fifty-seven leading manufacturing companies (based on PAC contributions and testimony before Congress) advances the theoretical position that "similarity of political behavior is a function of economic interdependence among firms as well as direct and indirect social network ties." See Mark Mizruchi, *Structure of Corporate Political Action*, p. 12. It is significant that Mizruchi concludes that similarity of political behavior (i.e., similar PAC contribution patterns) is more likely among members of concentrated industries than among members of less concentrated industries and that this similar behavior is highly correlated with political influence (legislative outcomes). Moreover, 40 of the 57 firms (representing twenty different industries) were members of the Business Roundtable. See ibid., pp. 129, 190–91, 202–3. Nevertheless, Mizruchi, finds the evidence on business unity in politics to be inconclusive. Different degrees of unity indicate that such unity is variable and therefore conditional. See ibid., pp. 249–55. On this point, he appears to be in agreement with Vogel (see *Fluctuating Fortunes*, pp. 291–92). Mizruchi's approach, however, is a significant alternative to pluralist methodology, which does not take into account the complex interrelationship between the organization of corporate power in the marketplace and in politics in attempting to explain corporate political behavior. In other words, to use my own terminology, the conditional nature of business unity in politics speaks to one aspect of the external dimension of corporate power, which, to be understood fully, requires a theoretical framework that can account for findings that are consis-

tent with both pluralist and class theories of corporate political behavior. Pluralist and instrumentalist Marxist theories can explain aspects of corporate political behavior, but neither can adequately explain corporate power on a theoretical level.

Noting the decline of business unity after 1981, as compared with the previous five years, Vogel observes: "The class consciousness of American business, like that of the American working class, is limited: companies generally tend to become aware of their common interests only when they are faced with a common enemy" (ibid., p. 291). This conclusion is undoubtedly fairly accurate when applied to business as a whole, but it does not specifically address the well-documented phenomenon of class consciousness and cohesion among the hierarchy of America's leading corporations. Considerable evidence (compiled mainly by sociologists) suggests that social, organizational, and economic linkages among large corporations contribute to a classwide consciousness *outside* the political arena, which does not necessarily produce unified political action but can greatly facilitate it (on this, see note 50 below). Mizruchi's observations are to the point: "My argument is that to locate the sources of corporate political power, we should identify firms that are tied together by economic interdependence, common ownership ties, and interlocking directorates. Many of these firms, of course, will be the largest in the most concentrated industries. But it is not size or concentration *per se*, but rather corporations' economic, organizational, and social interaction that unify and empower them. Whether this unity is produced by economic leverage and implicit threat, or as a result of the social cohesion that emerges from interaction among corporate directors, the result is the same: an increased potential for concentrated political power" (ibid., p. 254).

50. In his study of the "political mobilization of business" in the United States and the United Kingdom, Michael Useem documents the organization of the "inner circle" of the corporate elite. He explains that the "classwide rationality" of the inner circle cannot be accounted for by traditional theories of the firm that view corporate (managerial) behavior strictly in terms of the economic goals and needs of a particular corporation. In other words, this anomaly gives rise to the need for a political explanation of extracorporate behavior (which includes activities that normally would be classified under the rubric of corporate social responsibility):

"This extracorporate rationality derives from the autonomous power, distinct interests, and strategic location of the inner circle. The power is autonomous in that while it arises from the nation's large corporations, it is far more than a sum of its parts; the interests are distinct in that they reflect concrete corporate concerns yet transcend their more mundane components; and the location is strategic in that its members occupy high position within a firm yet are responsive to a constituency far beyond it" (Useem, p. 117).

Drawing on personal interviews with 150 directors and senior executives of major corporations, and documentation of the political activities and careers of several thousand other corporate executives and directors of 400 large corporations, Useem (pp. 103–5) identifies five stages of movement that pave the way for entry into the inner circle: (1) company ascent (senior management position), (2) outside directorships, (3) seniormost management (CEO), (4) association leadership (e.g., Business Rountable, Business Council), and (5) government consultation (business ambassador to government). Applying these criteria, Useem concludes: "Invitation into the highly select Business Council and Business Roundtable seems almost always to require inner-circle status, as does ascent into the leadership of the Committee on Economic Development, Conference Board, and Council on Foreign Relations." He explains that the "rising corporate activism" of the 1970s and 1980s was greatly aided by "the presence of the transcorporate networks of the inner circle, the classwide social organization that had gradually developed over the years, largely for reasons unrelated to political mobilization but highly facilitating of it" (ibid., pp. 73, 171).

Mizruchi's study provides significant empirical support for Useem's thesis concerning the political influence of the inner circle and appears to build on Useem's argument in important ways: "The findings presented here suggest that [economic] concentration facilitates not only classwide organization but industry organization, and political success as well." See Mizruchi, *Structure of Corporate Political Action*, p. 203; see also pp. 31–32, 128–29, 182–87, 246–49.

51. Conceivably, this state of affairs could be altered by radical reform of campaign financing. Yet even if this occurred, corporate lobbies would still wield considerable influence simply because of the importance of corporate business in the constituencies of elected officials and the demonstrated ability of these lobbies to marshal grass-roots support for their positions. What I have termed the institutionalization of corporate influence in Congress and the electoral process complements the long-established institutionalization of corporate influence in the White House, most notably through the activities of the Business Council and the Council on Foreign Relations and through the century-old practice of appointing corporate executives to cabinet-level positions.

52. For example, see the following reports of the Business Roundtable: *Analysis of the Issues in the National Industrial Debate, Working Papers* (May 15, 1984); *International Information Flow: A Plan for Action* (January 1985); *American Excellence in a World Economy: A Report of the Business Roundtable on International Competitiveness* (June 15, 1987); *The Business Roundtable Education Initiative* (June 1989). A common theme runs through all these reports: the necessity of reshaping public opinion and of reforming government policies for the purposes of enhancing the international competitiveness of American corporations and workers and breaking down domestic and international barriers to the free trade of goods, services, and information.

53. This issue is discussed in depth in Chapter 7.

54. Justices Powell, Scalia, and Kennedy have articulated the "self-regulating political marketplace" position in majority and dissenting opinions. Chief Justice Burger and Justice O'Connor indicated their support for this view in cases in which the Court was sharply divided along ideological lines. The strongest proponents of the "market power" position, mainly in dissenting opinions, have been Chief Justice Rehnquist and Justice White, both of whom have consistently voted to uphold state and federal legislation that regulates corporate speech and political activity. Justices Marshall, Brennan, Stevens, and Blackmun have been on either side of the issue, depending on the type of corporate political activity being regulated, although Brennan and Marshall wrote the two majority opinions that advanced the "market power" position. With the exception of Chief Justice Rehnquist, all the aforementioned justices supported the extension of First Amendment rights to the corporation. Justice White has consistently maintained that the political rights of the business corporation are not on par with those of natural persons.

55. 424 U.S. 1 (1976).

56. 435 U.S. 765 (1978).

57. 425 U.S. 748 (1976); *Bates v. State Bar*, 433 U.S. 350 (1977); *Ohralik v. Ohio State Bar Association*, 436 U.S. 447 (1978); *Central Hudson Gas & Electric Corp. v. Public Service Commission*, 447 U.S. 557 (1980); *Posadas de Puerto Rico Associates v. Tourism Company*, 478 U.S. 328 (1986).

58. On corporate free speech, see Andrew Stark, "Corporate Electoral Activity, Constitutional Discourse, and Conceptions of the Individual," *American Political Science Review* 86 (September 1992): 626–37; Jill E. Fisch, "Frankenstein's Monster Hits the Campaign Trail: An Approach to Regulation of Corporate Political Expenditures," *William and Mary Law Review* 32 (1991): 587–643; Michael J. Merrick, "The Saga Continues: Corporate Political Free Speech and the Constitutionality of Campaign Finance Reform: *Austin v. Michigan*

Chamber of Commerce," Creighton Law Review 24 (1990): 195–237; Jeffrey Nesteruk, *"Bellotti* and the Question of Corporate Moral Agency," *Columbia Business Law Review* 3 (1988): 683–703; Mitchell C. Tilner, "Government Compulsion of Corporate Speech: Legitimate Regulation or First Amendment Violation? A Critique of *PG&E v. Public Utilities Commission,"* *Santa Clara Law Review* 27 (1987): 485–513; Carl E. Schneider, "Free Speech and Corporate Freedom: A Comment on *First National Bank of Boston v. Bellotti,"* *Southern California Law Review* 59 (1986): 1227–91; William G. Bernhardt, "Constitutional Law: Campaign Finance Reform and the First Amendment—All the Free Speech Money Can Buy," *Oklahoma Law Review* 39 (1986): 729-49; Edwin P. Rome and William H. Roberts, *Corporate and Commercial Free Speech: First Amendment Protection of Expression in Business* (Westport, Conn.: Quorum Books, 1985); John S. Schockley, "Direct Democracy, Campaign Finance, and the Courts: Can Corruption, Undue Influence, and Declining Voter Confidence Be Found?" *University of Miami Law Review* 39 (1985): 377–428; Lillian R. BeVier, "Money and Politics: A Perspective on the First Amendment and Campaign Finance Reform," *California Law Review* 73 (July 1985): 1045–90; Tom Scribner, ed., "Symposium: Political Action Committees and Campaign Finance," *Arizona Law Review* 22 (1980): 351–674; William Patton and Randall Bartlett, "Corporate 'Persons' and Freedom of Speech: The Political Impact of Legal Mythology," *Wisconsin Law Review* (1981): 494–512; Norman Dorsen and Joel Gora, "Free Speech, Property, and the Burger Court: Old Values, New Balances," *Supreme Court Review* (Chicago: University of Chicago Press, 1982), pp. 195–242; J. Skelly Wright, "Money and the Pollution of Politics: Is the First Amendment an Obstacle to Political Equality?" *Columbia Law Review* 82 (May 1982): 609–45. Victor Brudney, "Business Corporations and Stockholders' Rights Under the First Amendment," *Yale Law Journal* 91 (1981): 235-295.

On commercial speech, see Alex Kozinski and Stuart Banner, "Who's Afraid of Commercial Speech?" *Virginia Law Review* 76 (1990): 627–53; Steven Shiffrin, "The First Amendment and Economic Regulation: Away from a General Theory of the First Amendment," *Northwestern University Law Review* 78 (1983): 1212–83; Burt Neuborne, "The First Amendment and Government Regulation of Capital Markets," *Brooklyn Law Review* 55 (1989): 5–63; R. H. Coase, "Advertising and Free Speech," *Journal of Legal Studies* 6 (1977): 1–34; Daniel A. Farber, "Commercial Speech and First Amendment Theory," *Northwestern University Law Review* 74 (1979): 372–408; Martin H. Redish, "The Value of Free Speech," *University of Pennsylvania Law Review* 130 (1982): 591–645; Redish "Symposium: Commercial Speech and the First Amendment," *University of Cincinnati Law Review* 56 (1988): 1165–395; C. Edwin Baker, "Commercial Speech: A Problem in the Theory of Freedom," *Iowa Law Review* 62 (1976): 1–40; Baker, "Scope of the First Amendment Freedom of Speech," *UCLA Law Review* 25 (June 1978): 964–90.

59. Numerous large corporations now sell a corporate image packaged in the form of public-service announcements. Many of these announcements are really a type of political advocacy, which, under current law, corporations have a right to express. On the other hand, one could argue that issue-oriented speeches that defend corporate interests while masquerading as commercials or public-service messages should be subject to some standard of accountability, such as the standards for political ads. The prospect of such regulation has become virtually impossible with the advent of the commercial speech doctrine, which extends First Amendment protection to advertising. Barring outright fraud or deception in the selling of a product or service, it is unlikely that these types of "commercials" could be regulated on the basis of the ambiguous or misleading content. In any event, regulations of commercial speech on the basis of political content would most likely be struck down, if for no other reason than to protect rights of political speech.

60. 424 U.S. 1, 19 (1976). The Court's decision was *per curiam*. Chief Justice Burger and

Justices White, Rehnquist, Marshall, and Blackmun all wrote separate opinions concurring in part and dissenting in part.

61. Ibid., p. 47. Dissenting, Justice White found the Court's distinction between contributions and expenditures less than compelling, noting that a candidate in either case might be corrupted (ibid., pp. 260–61).

62. 435 U.S. 765, 777 (1978). At issue was the constitutionality of a Massachusetts criminal statute that prohibited banks or business corporations from making contributions or expenditures to influence "the vote on any question submitted to the voters, other than one materially affecting any of the property, business or assets of the corporation." The status of the corporation as a "person" under the Fourteenth Amendment permits the rights of speech to be extended to it. In this century, the Bill of Rights, which originally pertained only to the national government, has been applied selectively to the states by way of judicial "incorporation" through the due process clause of the Fourteenth Amendment.

63. Ibid., p. 791.

64. Ibid., pp. 809–10.

65. Ibid., pp. 825–26.

66. 475 U.S. 1 (1986).

67. Ibid., p. 16. *Bellotti*'s First Amendment guarantees were first expanded to protect corporate political advocacy outside of electoral politics in *Consolidated Edison Co. v. Public Service Commission*, 447 U.S. 530 (1980), which held that neither Consolidated Edison's corporate status nor its status as a government-regulated monopoly precluded it from asserting a First Amendment right to insert controversial messages in its billing envelope.

68. 475 U.S. 1, 33 (1986).

69. In other words, unless corporate speech is solely or preponderantly commercial in nature, the Court will not risk the possibility of diluting corporate political speech by applying the commercial speech test. (See *Central Hudson Gas & Electric Corp. v. Public Service Commission*, 447 U.S. 557 (1980), which arguably affords less protection for commercial as opposed to political speech.) In *PG&E*, the consumer advocacy group that used the extra space in the billing envelope was concerned primarily with countering the utility's efforts to justify increased utility rates. In its monthly newsletter enclosed in the billing envelope, PG&E published political editorials and information regarding rates and services designed to advance its proposed rate hikes. This is clearly a case where the distinction between commercial and political speech is essentially blurred by the interrelationship between commercial and political objectives. *PG&E* invites the conclusion that corporate political advocacy that has an essentially commercial purpose (which applies to a broad range of corporate advertising) will receive full First Amendment protection.

Justice Rehnquist has argued consistently that this new judicial creation conceals an old nemesis in a modern guise. Dissenting in *Central Hudson*, he observed that by giving commercial speech constitutional protection that is "virtually indistinguishable from that of noncommercial speech," the Court not only has obfuscated, if not erased, the line between commercial and political advertising or speech, but also has devised a weapon, all too reminiscent of the reign of substantive due process, for striking down state regulatory acts. For Rehnquist, the Court has clearly overstepped the proper bounds of the judicial function: "By labeling economic regulation of business conduct as a restraint on 'free speech' [the Court has] gone too far to resurrect the discredited doctrine of cases such as *Lochner*." Justice Rehnquist argued, moreover, that because Central Hudson Gas & Electric was a state-created monopoly, it deserved a "more wide-ranging supervision and control" than was established under the corporate free speech doctrine in *Bellotti*. He also took issue with the ideological presumptions of the majority: "There is no reason for believing that the marketplace of ideas is free from imperfection any more than there is to believe that the invisible hand will always lead to optimum economic decisions in the commercial market" (447 U.S. 557, 587, 591–92 (1980)).

70. 459 U.S. 197 (1982).

71. 2 U.S.C. sec. 441b (b)(4)(C).

72. 2 U.S.C. sec. 441b.

73. 479 U.S. 238 (1986).

74. Ibid., p. 257.

75. 494 U.S. 652 (1990).

76. Ibid., p. 660.

77. Ibid., pp. 679–95.

78. Ibid., p. 700.

79. The corporation cannot vote or hold office, nor can it claim protections afforded by the privileges and immunities clauses of Article 4, Section 2, and the Fourteenth Amendment. See *Bank of Augusta v. Earle*, 13 Peters 519 (1839); *Pembina Mining Co. v. Pennsylvania*, 125 U.S. 181 (1888). However, the Supreme Court has consistently refused to say that citizenship is a precondition for the exercise of numerous other rights granted to "the people" or to "persons" in the Bill of Rights. Political rights normally thought to be essential attributes of citizenship in a democratic political community—rights of speech, association, assembly, press, due process—extend to noncitizens and citizens alike. With the important exceptions of the rights to vote and to hold office, the constitutional status of citizenship does not bar a noncitizen (including a corporation) from exercising other constitutional rights or from otherwise participating in political activities. In addition to constitutional rights of political and commercial speech, business corporations have a First Amendment "right of petition" that allows corporations to combine and to lobby all branches of government and administrative agencies. This activity has been exempted from the reach of antitrust laws. *Eastern R.R. President's Conference v. Noerr Motor Freight*, 365 U.S. 127 (1961); *United Mine Workers v. Pennington*, 381 U.S. 657 (1965); *California Motor Transport Co. v. Trucking Unlimited*, 404 U.S. 508 (1972).

Numerous other rights have been conferred on the business corporation, including: the Fourth Amendment freedom from unreasonable warrantless regulatory searches, *Marshall v. Barlow's*, 436 U.S. 307 (1978) (exceptions established thereafter for liquor, firearms, and mining industries); the Fifth Amendment right of due process, *Noble v. Union River Logging Railroad Co.*, 147 U.S. 165 (1893); the Fifth Amendment protection against double jeopardy, *United States v. Martin Linen Supply Co.*, 430 U.S. 564 (1977); the Fifth Amendment takings clause (right of "just compensation"), *Pennsylvania Coal Co. v. Mahon*, 260 U.S. 393 (1922); the Sixth Amendment right to jury trial in a criminal case, *Armour Packing Co. v. United States*, 209 U.S. 56 (1908), and *United States v. R. L. Polk & Co.*, 438 F.2nd 377 (6th Cir. 1971); and the Seventh Amendment right to jury trial in a civil case, *Ross v. Bernhard*, 396 U.S. 531 (1970). See Carl J. Mayer, "Personalizing the Impersonal: Corporations and the Bill of Rights," *Hastings Law Journal* 41 (March 1990): 577–667; Karen Orren, "Judicial Whipsaw: Interest Conflict, Corporate Business and the Seventh Amendment," *Polity* 18 (Fall 1985): 70–97.

80. See section 2 of this chapter. Corporate political speech could be regulated under the common-law doctrine of "corporate waste," but to justify the use of corporate finances for political purposes, management must show only that the speech was plausibly related to the economic well-being of the corporation—not a very difficult task.

81. Cf. Hans B. Thorelli, *The Federal Antitrust Policy: Origination of an American Tradition* (Baltimore: Johns Hopkins University Press, 1955), pp. 604–9; Robert H. Bork, *The Antitrust Paradox: A Policy at War with Itself* (New York: Basic Books, 1975), pp. 3–11, 418–25; Thur-

man W. Arnold, *The Folklore of Capitalism* (New Haven: Yale University Press, 1937), pp. 207–29; A. D. Neale, *The Antitrust Laws of the United States of America: A Study of Competition Enforced by Law* (Cambridge: Cambridge University Press, 1970), pp. 427–32.

82. While Bork champions a less restrictive antitrust law to encourage competition, others have argued for a more restrictive policy (in some areas) to accomplish the same end. See Carl Kaysen and Donald F. Turner, *Antitrust Policy: An Economic and Legal Analysis* (Cambridge, Mass.: Harvard University Press, 1959). Cf. Richard A. Posner, *Antitrust Law: An Economic Perspective* (Chicago: University of Chicago Press, 1976).

83. See above, Chapter 2, section 5.

84. Price leadership by itself is not adequate to establish a Sherman Act violation, but it may become presumptive evidence in establishing a "conspiracy to monopolize" under Section 2 of the act. The only case supporting this view, the ambiguity of which may have been what caused some legal scholars to erroneously predict a significant change in the Court's treatment of oligopoly, is *American Tobacco Co. v. United States*, 328 U.S. 781 (1946), which apparently overruled, on this point, *United States v. International Harvester Co.*, 274 U.S. 693 (1927).

85. *Theatre Enterprises v. Paramount Film Distributing Corp.*, 346 U.S. 537 (1954); *Delaware Valley Marine Supply Co. v. American Tobacco Co.*, 297 F.2d 199 (3d Cir. 1961).

86. The precedent for this unlikely decision is the *American Tobacco* case of 1946 discussed above in note 84. To avoid semantic confusion, it should be noted that there are three possible violations under Section 2: "monopolization," "attempt to monopolize," and "conspiracy to monopolize." The bulk of case law under Section 2 concerns the offense of monopolization, which requires a showing of proof that the defendant (1) possesses monopoly power and (2) has acquired or maintained that power by monopolizing conduct (i.e., general or nonspecific intent). Both the attempt to monopolize and conspiracy to monopolize require proof of specific intent but do not require that defendant possesses monopoly power.

Because conspiracies in restraint of trade (which may be monopolistic in intent) are covered by Section 1 of the act and because Section 2 cases generally concern the actions of alleged monopolies, the prohibition of conspiracy to monopolize has not received much attention from the courts. If noncollusive oligopolistic practices (which, in effect, create a shared monopoly) were to be viewed as conspiratorial, however, the conspiracy to monopolize provision (which does not require a showing of monopoly power) could be invoked against oligopoly to effect dissolutions of highly concentrated markets.

87. A more likely tactic for the Court would be to expand the scope of Section 1 violations to reach activities that could stabilize oligopolistic markets. This would appear to be the Court's objective in *United States v. Container Corp. of America*, 393 U.S. 333 (1969), where Justice Douglas held that the reciprocal exchange of price information in the corrugated container industry (a market "dominated by relatively few sellers") had an anticompetitive effect of stabilizing prices. Chief Justice Burger's dictum in *United States v. U.S. Gypsum Co.*, 438 U.S. 422 (1978), takes this argument a step further: "Especially in oligopolistic industries such as the gypsum board industry, the exchange of price information among competitors carries with it the added potential for the development of concerted price-fixing arrangements which lie at the core of the Sherman Act's prohibitions." On the basis of this rationale, the Court could expand the per se rule against price-fixing to embrace the exchange of price information in oligopolistic industries. Such a decision would be both consistent with past methods and compatible with the judicial temperament.

88. Regardless of the dominant presumption of the Court in a given period, however, the concept of balance (political and economic) has informed the spirit and application of the law. Political balance derives from the Constitution and the concept of limited govern-

ment, whereas economic balance is the product of both classical and neoclassical political economy. The former is invoked against monopoly and market concentration to remedy the evil that concentrated power poses to individual rights and democratic institutions, while the latter justifies capitalist market activity subject to government regulation. In judicial interpretations of antitrust, these two objectives are perceived to be interdependent and to operate mutually to regulate the marketplace and hence, to maintain the principle of fair competition. Political balance, however, recognizes that corporate power extends beyond the economic sphere, or at least that it transforms the market to serve its own ends and, in doing so, attains broader social significance. Thus, the political concept of balance in antitrust law serves the same ideological function as the balance of powers within the Constitution—specifically, it identifies a legal mechanism whereby power may be checked or balanced to ensure against its arbitrary exercise.

89. Neale, *Antitrust Laws of the U.S.A.*, p. 431.

90. *United States v. Aluminum Co. of America*, 148 F.2d 416, 432 (2d Cir. 1945).

91. *United States v. U.S. Steel Corp.*, 251 U.S. 417, 451 (1920).

92. Ibid., p. 440.

93. *United States v. Aluminum Co. of America*, 148 F.2d 416, 432 (2d Cir. 1945).

94. Ibid., pp. 430–31.

95. Ibid., pp. 427–28.

96. For an analysis of the Harlan-Peckham approach, see above, Chapter 2, section 5.

97. Recent Court of Appeals decisions have considerably broadened *Alcoa*'s exceptions for nonmonopolizing conduct while making the finding of such conduct more difficult. See *Telex Corp. v. IBM*, 510 F.2d 894 (10th Cir. 1975); *Berkey Photo v. Eastman Kodak Co.*, 603 F.2d 263 (2d Cir. 1979), cert. denied, 444 U.S. 1093 (1980). Cf. *Aspen Skiing Co. v. Aspen Highlands Skiing Corp.*, 472 U.S. 585 (1985).

98. The dates are based on the analysis in Reid, *Mergers*, pp. 37–120. Analysts often divide the current merger wave into two segments (or different waves), the first ending in the early 1970s and the second beginning in 1975 and continuing through the present.

99. Phillip I. Blumberg, *The Megacorporation in American Society: The Scope of Corporate Power* (Englewood Cliffs, N.J.: Prentice-Hall, 1975), p. 74. "*Aggregate* (or overall) concentration deals with the economy as a whole and reflects the dominant position of the megacorporations as a group. It has economic, political, and social significance. It has been studied principally by economists who have been interested almost exclusively in its economic aspects. The political and social dimensions tend to receive minor consideration although they would appear to be more important" (ibid., p. 64).

100. The current merger wave peaked initially in 1968 with an unprecedented 2,407 combinations, declined considerably in the early-to-mid 1970s, and soared again in the late 1970s and throughout the 1980s. The second peak in 1989 (3,400 deals worth $230 billion) was followed by a moderate lull in 1990–91 before picking up in 1992–93. During the 1960s and 1970s, conglomerate mergers that consisted of diversified acquisitions were the most prevalent form of combination. In the 1980s, a strategy of merging with firms in related products and markets developed. This new form of conglomerate merger was accompanied by a resurgence of large horizontal combinations. Since 1981, the number of mergers (albeit quite high) has been less important in gauging the magnitude of the merger wave than has the size of mergers in terms of total assets acquired. The drama of this modern combination movement invites overstatement, but the facts speak for themselves. *Fortune*'s "Deals of the Year," which features the top fifty deals (mainly mergers and acquisitions but also securities offerings) determined by the purchase or offering price, provides a useful measure for assessing the latest trends. Here are the total prices of the top fifty deals for 1981–91: 1981 ($49.9 billion), 1982 ($48.2 billion), 1983 ($38.4 billion), 1984 ($78.5 bil-

lion), 1985 ($94.6 billion), 1986 ($92.6 billion), 1987 ($92 billion), 1988 ($111.8 billion), 1989 ($144 billion), 1990 ($72 billion), and 1991 ($76 billion). In 1992 and 1993, merger activity increased in volume and dollar amount: a total of $273 billion of assets were acquired in 5,237 mergers and acquisitions. The purchase price for 45 of these deals was more than $1 billion.

In 1983, the top 50 mergers and acquisitions accounted for more than half of a grand total of $73.1 billion representing 2,533 mergers. In 1984 alone, three horizontal mergers of oil companies totaled $29 billion. And the top 50 mergers and acquisitions for 1986 and 1987, when combined, amounted to nearly half the total of $380 billion for those two years. Between 1984 and 1993, mergers valued at $1 billion or more totaled 278, as opposed to 39 for the previous five years. Despite the stock market crash, the top 50 acquisitions for 1988 easily exceeded all previous annual highs, a total that does not include the single largest acquisition ever—the purchase of RJR Nabisco for $25 billion, which was formally completed in early 1989. In 1993, some 12 mergers accounted for $86 billion of a total $176 billion for 2,663 transactions. Of the 100 largest mergers in history, 90 occurred between 1984 and 1993, and the remaining 10 occurred between 1980 and 1983. See "Deals of the Year," *Fortune*, January 24, 1983, pp. 48–52; January 23, 1984, pp. 54–58; January 21, 1985, pp. 126–30; January 20, 1986, pp. 26–30; February 2, 1987, pp. 68–74; February 1, 1988, pp. 34–43; January 30, 1989, pp. 162–71; January 29, 1990, pp. 136–44; January 28, 1991, pp. 90–98; January 27, 1992, pp. 104–10. See also annual reports: "The Top Two-Hundred Deals," *Business Week*; and annual editions of *Mergerstat Review* (Schaumburg, Ill.: Merrill Lynch Brokerage & Valuation); Jesse W. Markham, *Conglomerate Enterprise and Public Policy* (Boston: Division of Research, Graduate School of Business Administration, Harvard University, 1973); Charles H. Berry, *Corporate Growth and Diversification* (Princeton: Princeton University Press, 1975).

The modern combination movement, like the first, is expansionist and entails a restructuring of the economic basis of corporate power. Unlike the first, however, the present movement relies on formal regulation—through the Department of Justice, Securities and Exchange Commission, and Federal Reserve Board—which is itself a product of the consolidation of corporate power in this century. In other words, the laissez-faire policy of the Reagan and Bush administrations has been implemented through the law rather than outside, or in avoidance, of it.

101. See above, Chapter 2, note 124.

102. Sklar, *Corporate Reconstruction*, pp. 162–63 (nn. 181, 182), 370–76.

103. For a description of the Clayton Act, see above, Chapter 2, note 134.

104. *United States v. Columbia Steel Co.*, 334 U.S. 495 (1948). Some 12,644 mergers were reported between 1914 and 1950, during which period the Justice Department tried only 16 cases and the FTC tried 13 under Section 7 of the Clayton Act. Reid, *Mergers*, p. 101, table 5.3.

105. Celler-Kefauver Act of 1950, 64 Stat. 1125, 15 U.S.C.A. Sec. 18 (1980). The pertinent revisions were made in Section 7; a split infinitive ("to substantially lessen") was also corrected.

106. *Brown Shoe Co. v. United States*, 370 U.S. 294 (1962).

107. Ibid., p. 313.

108. Ibid., p. 323.

109. With regard to the vertical aspect of the merger, the Court also focused on "the very nature and purpose of the arrangement," which revealed an intent on the part of Brown to force its shoes into Kinney stores, an arrangement "quite analogous to a tying clause." Moreover, the merger could not be justified by invoking the "failing company" doctrine.

110. Following *Brown Shoe*, several cases established the standard of "undue percentage

share" of the market as the basis for determining the legality of a horizontal merger. In these cases, the existing market concentration and the degree to which it would be increased by the merger was a critical factor in determining the undue share. The presumption in all these opinions is that competition declines as concentration increases. *United States v. Philadelphia National Bank*, 374 U.S. 321 (1963); *United States v. Aluminum Co. of America (Rome Cable)*, 377 U.S. 271 (1964); *United States v. Continental Can Co.*, 378 U.S. 441 (1964). Each of these cases involved markets with a significant degree of concentration. Such was not the case, however, in the most controversial of the horizontal merger decisions, *United States v. Von's Grocery Co.*, 384 U.S. 270 (1966), where the Court held that the merger, which represented 7.5 percent of a market wherein the top twelve firms accounted for 48 percent of sales, violated Section 7 of the Clayton Act. This decision was succeeded by *United States v. Pabst Brewing Co.*, 384 U.S. 546 (1966), where the Court, in holding that the merger violated Section 7, calculated the share of the market in three geographical areas—Wisconsin (23.95 percent), Wisconsin, Illinois, and Michigan (11.32 percent), and the entire United States (4.49 percent)—apparently because the majority (as separate concurrences indicate) could not agree on which market(s) produced the undue share. No opinions developed standards for quantifying the market share of an illegal foreclosure of access to a supplying firm as a result of a vertical merger.

In 1974, the Burger Court signaled its intent to draw the line on the expanding doctrine in horizontal merger cases when it held that a prima facie case based on market share percentages had been rebutted by evidence demonstrating that the market share overstated the alleged anticompetitive effect of the merger. See *United States v. General Dynamics Corp.*, 415 U.S. 486 (1974).

111. The basic premise of the theory holds that if a firm perceived to be the most likely potential entrant into a market merges with a firm that holds a significant share of that market, and if the market is not competitive, the merger will have a probable anticompetitive effect due to the loss of the "wings effect" (i.e., the most likely entrant is no longer "waiting in the wings"), a prospect that presumably encourages competition in order to keep prices and profits at reasonable levels to discourage entry. See *United States v. Penn-Olin Chemical Co.*, 378 U.S. 158 (1964). Although this case involved two corporations that formed a third corporation to perform a joint venture, the Court argued that for the purposes of Section 7 of the Clayton Act, "overall, the same considerations apply to joint ventures as to mergers." The theory established therein was later applied to conglomerate mergers. On the Burger Court's interpretation of the potential competition doctrine as it applied to market extension mergers, see note 114 below.

112. *Federal Trade Commission v. Procter & Gamble Co. (Clorox)*, 386 U.S. 568 (1967); *Federal Trade Commission v. Consolidated Foods Corp.*, 380 U.S. 592 (1965).

113. *United States v. International Telephone and Telegraph Corporation*, 324 F.Supp. 19 (D.Conn. 1970). ITT had moved from eighty-first to ninth in the Fortune 500 from 1953 to 1971, during which time it had acquired more than 100 domestic and 50 foreign corporations.

114. *United States v. Marine Bancorporation*, 418 U.S. 602 (1974); *United States v. Connecticut National Bank*, 418 U.S. 656 (1974). In *Marine Bancorporation*, Justice Powell stated: "To assume, on the basis of essentially no evidence, that the challenged merger will tend to produce a state-wide linkage of oligopolies is to espouse a per se rule against geographic market extension mergers. . . . The Court has not previously resolved whether the potential competition doctrine proscribes a market extension merger solely on the ground that such a merger eliminates the prospect for long-term deconcentration of an oligopolistic market that in theory might result if the acquiring firm were forbidden to enter except through a de novo undertaking or through the acquisition of a small existing entrant (a so-called foothold or toehold acquisition)."

115. "The current wave is pushing managers into concentration on narrower, related fields, forming more economically logical companies that they can manage more knowledgeably. In that sense, the current merger wave bears a family resemblance to the great consolidations of American industry in which the magnates such as Carnegie, Morgan, and Rockefeller rationalized the basic industries of steel, rails, and oil." See "How the Merger Boom Will Benefit the Economy," *Business Week*, February 6, 1984, p. 42. Cf. Judith H. Dobrzynski, "A New Strain of Merger Mania," *Business Week*, March 21, 1988, pp. 122–34; Michael C. Jensen, "The Takeover Controversy: The Corporate Restructuring of America," *Vital Speeches of the Day*, May 1, 1987, pp. 426–29; Betty Bock et al., *Restructuring and Antitrust* (New York: The Conference Board, 1987). The newfound power of investment bankers in the current merger wave is also reminiscent of an earlier era. See Carol J. Loomis, "The New J. P. Morgans," *Fortune*, February 29, 1988, pp. 44–51; "Icahn on Icahn," *Fortune* February 29, 1988, pp. 54–58; Sarah Bartlett, "Power Investors," *Business Week*, June 20, 1988, pp. 116–23; Ellyn E. Spragins et al., "When Power Investors Call the Shots," *Business Week*, June 20, 1988, pp. 126–30.

The trend I have projected is generally consistent with the internal "restructuring" of corporations that the current merger wave has fomented—that is, creating more efficient internal operations through reorganization, cost-cutting (often by laying off workers), and divesting firms in nonrelated market or product lines. The main economic motives to "restructure" include (1) the attempt to enhance profits, raise the value of stocks, and thereby prevent a takeover; (2) the necessity of creating economies of scale after a takeover in order to reap a decent profit (in the case of leveraged buyouts, also to pay off enormous loans); and (3) either of these factors combined with the long-term effort to improve a firm's competitive position in world markets. Political motives are less frequently addressed in the relevant literature, although among the largest firms one cannot discount market domination (as opposed to competition) as a salient factor. The fact that the era of huge, sprawling conglomerates appears to be coming to an end must therefore be analyzed in terms of the form of conglomerate that seems to be taking its place.

116. In recent years, the combination movement has become a transnational affair that includes joint ventures as well as mergers. Japanese and European companies have joined the trend with some notable acquisitions of American companies. In 1987, for example, British Petroleum acquired the remaining 45 percent of stock (the balance of which it already owned) of Standard Oil (Indiana) for $8 billion, the biggest deal of the year and the third largest ever, as of 1987. In 1988, Bridgestone Corporation, Japan's largest tire company, purchased Firestone Tire & Rubber Company for $2.6 billion; in 1989, Sony acquired Columbia Pictures Entertainment for $5 billion; and in 1990, Matsushita bought MCA for almost $7 billion. During the late 1980s, anticipating the EC agreement of 1992, American, Japanese, and European firms began to acquire European companies on an unprecedented scale. To avoid destructive competition, many of the largest corporations formed numerous joint ventures with their rivals, thus further strengthening their dominant market positions. Cf. W. Carl Kester, *Japanese Takeovers: The Global Contest for Corporate Control* (Boston, Mass.: Harvard Business School Press, 1991); Peter Fuhrman, "Getting in Bed Together," *Forbes*, May 11, 1992, pp. 86–87; Stewart Toy et al., "The Battle for Europe," *Business Week*, June 3, 1991, pp. 44–52; Blanca Riemer et al., "America's New Rush to Europe," *Business Week*, March 26, 1990, pp. 48–49; William J. Holstein et al., "The Stateless Corporation," *Business Week*, May 14, 1990, pp. 98–105; "Europe's Companies After 1992," *The Economist*, June 9, 1990, pp. 17–18; Gary Hector, "Japan Learns the Takeover Game," *Fortune*, July 31, 1989, pp. 123–28; Jack Egan et al., "Let's Make a Deal Goes Global," *U.S. News and World Report*, February 22, 1988, pp. 66–68; Peter Nulty, "Riding the Foreign Takeover Wars," *Fortune*, April 11, 1988, pp. 117–18; Blanca Riemer et al., "A Cash-Rich Europe Finds U.S. Ripe for the

Picking," *Business Week*, January 25, 1988, pp. 48–49; Richard I. Kirkland, "Merger Mania Is Sweeping Europe," *Fortune*, December 19, 1988, pp. 157–67.

The emergent oligarchy of oligopolists, moreover, will bring with it a "community of interest" facilitated by a massive network of interlocking directorates. A basic structural feature of the corporate order, interlocks have been studied in depth several times by individuals and government bodies since the first decade of this century. (See above, Chapter 1, section 4a.) Each study produces astounding evidence of the extent of this practice, although little has ever been done about it. Horizontal direct interlocks are regulated under the Clayton Act, but this provision is almost never enforced. In any event, loopholes abound and interlocks have never been a priority of antitrust enforcement, a state of affairs that suggests that officialdom is predisposed to view the power structure of the large corporation as a private internal matter.

117. The 1968 Justice Department guidelines defined the prohibited market-share percentages for both vertical and horizontal mergers—the latter correlated with the degree of market concentration. Standards for horizontal mergers were based on percentages in the Court's rulings (see the cases in note 110 above). Moreover, anticompetitive intent was listed as another basis for challenging a merger. A market percentage scheme not derived from case law was also applied to conglomerate mergers, and the theories of perceived potential entrant, market entrenchment, and reciprocity threat were all incorporated into the guidelines. As a whole, the 1968 guidelines emphasized the Warren Court's concern with increasing concentration resulting from all types of mergers. See Department of Justice, Antitrust Division, *U.S. Department of Justice Merger Guidelines*, June 14, 1968.

118. The 1982 guidelines replaced the market-percentage shares of 1968 for horizontal mergers with the Herfindahl-Hirschman Index (HHI), a method for calculating the effect that a merger would have on market concentration. The numerical standards established in the guidelines to determine the acceptable levels of postmerger concentration for horizontal mergers are comparable to those of 1968. The 1982 standards, however, are to be applied in light of a variety of "discretionary factors" that take into account the perceived competitive position of American firms in world markets. Specific market percentages for vertical mergers are eliminated, as is any mention of the effect of foreclosure. Instead, the guidelines state that a vertical merger would be challenged only when the affected market is highly concentrated (according to HHI) and when a substantial barrier to entry is created by the merger or when downstream integration facilitates horizontal collusion on prices of sellers in the upstream market. The 1982 guidelines do not contain standards for anticompetitive intent, or language concerning increasing trends toward concentration. Both the market entrenchment and the reciprocity-threat theories for conglomerate mergers have been dropped as well. The perceived potential entrant theory and the actual potential entrant theory (discussed but not approved by the Court) were adopted. The Justice Department is unlikely to challenge a conglomerate merger under these theories unless the market is highly concentrated (according to HHI) and the barriers to entry are high.

In 1984, the merger guidelines were amended to include discretionary factors affecting the significance of market shares and concentration: "changing market conditions," "financial condition of firms in the relevant market," and "special factors affecting foreign firms." See Department of Justice, *Merger Guidelines* (note 117 above), June 14, 1982, and June 14, 1984; Department of Justice and Federal Trade Commission, *Horizontal Merger Guidelines*, 62 Antitrust & Trade Reg. Rep. (BNA) No. 1559 (April 2, 1992); Margaret E. Guerin-Calvert and Janusz A. Ordover, "The 1992 Agency Horizontal Merger Guidelines and the Department of Justice's Approach to Bank Merger Analysis," *Antitrust Bulletin*, Fall 1992, pp. 667–88.

119. "New 'Anti Antitrust' Trend Could Be Pro Profit," *Los Angeles Times*, June 28, 1981, p. 1.

120. Ibid., p. 3. This attitude sums up the antitrust policy of the Reagan and Bush administrations, as witnessed by the general moratorium on enforcement. Twenty-two years after *Brown Shoe*, in 1984, the same antitrust law was interpreted by the Department of Justice to allow the mergers of Chevron with Gulf for $13.2 billion ($38.8 billion combined assets) and Texaco with Getty Oil for $10.1 billion ($46.6 billion combined assets). One is reminded of the halcyon days of the rise of the great holding companies in the two decades following the passage of the Sherman Act.

121. The transnational dimension of the federal government's antitrust policy was outlined by the Department of Justice in *Antitrust Guide for International Operations*, published in 1977. In recognizing that "American businesses enter into thousands of international transactions which raise possible antitrust issues," the guide endeavors "to help businesses plan transactions which the Department of Justice is not likely to challenge, and to see which transactions are likely to require detailed factual inquiry by the enforcement agencies" (ibid., p. 1). Under these guidelines, the Justice Department would not challenge a merger of any kind in which the foreign firm (whether acquiring or being acquired) does not directly affect the interstate or foreign commerce of the United States. If an effect on commerce is established, the merger would then be subject to the relevant test under Section 7 of the Clayton Act (ibid., pp. 15–18). Two purposes inform Justice Department enforcement policy: (1) "to protect the American consuming public by assuring it the benefit of competitive products and ideas produced by foreign competitors as well as domestic competitors"; and (2) "to protect American export and investment opportunities against privately imposed restrictions" (ibid., pp. 4–5).

122. Arnold, *Folklore of Capitalism*, p. 185.

123. Neoclassical economists have also contributed to the viability of corporate individualism. For a critique of the neoclassical school and its failure to account for the reality of capitalist development in the twentieth century, see William Lazonick, *Business Organization and the Myth of the Market Economy* (Cambridge: Cambridge University Press, 1991); see also David Campbell, "Why Regulate the Modern Corporation? The Failure of 'Market Failure,' " in Joseph McCahery, Sol Picciotto, and Colin Scott, eds., *Corporate Control and Accountability: Changing Structures and the Dynamics of Regulation* (Oxford: Clarendon Press, 1993), pp. 103–31.

124. See Richard L. Sklar, "Postimperialism: A Class Analysis of Multinational Corporate Expansion," *Comparative Politics* 9 (October 1976): 75–92; reprinted in Becker et al. *Postimperialism: International Capitalism and Development in the Late Twentieth Century*, pp. 19–40. In Chapter 7, I analyze the ideological significance of this movement in light of the writings of corporate leaders and others.

Chapter 5

1. Adolph A. Berle and Gardiner C. Means, *The Modern Corporation and Private Property*, rev. ed. (New York: Harcourt, Brace & World, 1967), pp. 309, 313.

2. The fact that Drucker is not a native of the United States should have no bearing on his status as an American political thinker—no more, for example, than it should have for Alexander Hamilton or Thomas Paine. Perhaps all three should be considered international thinkers. Still, the fact remains that each has had a significant impact on American political thought. In any event, Drucker's major studies of the corporation were conceived within the American context and for the most part addressed to an American audience. For

an account of his life and writings through the mid-1970s, see John J. Tarrant, *Drucker: The Man Who Invented the Corporate Society* (New York: Warner Books, 1976).

3. *The End of Economic Man: A Study of the New Totalitarianism* (London: William Heinemann, 1939).

4. *The Future of Industrial Man: A Conservative Approach* (New York: John Day Co., 1942); *Concept of the Corporation* (New York: John Day Co., 1946); *The New Society: The Anatomy of the Industrial Order* (New York: Harper & Brothers, 1949).

5. For an excellent biography of Berle, consult Jordan A. Schwarz, *Liberal: Adolph A. Berle and the Vision of an American Era* (New York: The Free Press, 1987).

6. *American Capitalism: The Concept of Countervailing Power* (Boston: Houghton Mifflin, 1952); *The Affluent Society* (Boston: Houghton Mifflin, 1958); *The New Industrial State* (London: Hamish Hamilton, 1967).

7. See Chapter 4, section 2.

8. Ibid., pp. 1–5, 20–24; see also Drucker's *Concept of the Corporation*, p. 25. In reconstructing Drucker's thought, I have relied heavily on *The New Society*, which provides the most systematic and synthetic account of his political theory of the corporation. This study, however, is by no means inclusive of *The Future of Industrial Man* and *Concept of the Corporation*. Each of these works contains a different focus and therefore contributes separately to the author's political study of the corporation. Because my primary focus is on Drucker's early works that concerned the political theory of the corporation, most of his later works on managerial science are not included in this study.

9. Ibid., pp. 24, 26.

10. Ibid., pp. 41–43, 203; *Industrial Man*, pp. 91–93, 242–43.

11. Ibid., pp. 35, 93, 103. "The industrial enterprise arises from the needs of industrial life rather than from the beliefs or principles underlying political organization" (ibid., p. 34). See also *New Society*, pp. 33–35.

12. Ibid., pp. 35–36.

13. *Concept of the Corporation*, p. 20.

14. *New Society*, pp. 44, 38, 50.

15. Drucker discussed these two laws in ibid., pp. 52–67.

16. Ibid., pp. 61, 63–64, 68.

17. Ibid., pp. 68, 71, 72 (emphasis in original).

18. Ibid., pp. 44, 45, 203. See also ibid., pp. 29–30; *Industrial Man*, pp. 79–80.

19. *New Society*, p. 45. See also *Concept of the Corporation*, pp. 25–26.

20. *New Society*, pp. 45–46, 99–100, 106.

21. Ibid., pp. 31–33, 47, 49; *Concept of the Corporation*, pp. 5–7, 134; *Industrial Man*, p. 74.

22. *New Society*, p. 50. See also ibid., pp. 151–56; *Concept of the Corporation*, pp. 134–43; *Industrial Man*, pp. 25–32. Drucker's political study of the corporation eventually led him in later works to pursue a more general study of organizations. In *Landmarks of Tomorrow* (New York: Harper & Brothers, 1957), pp. 210–11, he developed the concept of industrial society as an organizational society based on a "new pluralism," which consisted of "autonomous power centers within the body politic." This conception caused him to revise his concept of the corporation as the representative social institution. In *The Age of Discontinuity: Guidelines to Our Changing Times* (New York: Harper & Row, 1968), p. 175, for example, he argued that the corporation was one of several autonomous organizations in the new pluralism. Despite this revision, however, the basic assumptions and concepts of his earlier works remained unchanged. For example, see *Landmarks*, pp. 6, 15, 58–59, 62, 77–79, 98, 108–9; *Age of Discontinuity*, pp. 206, 210–11, 251, 258–60.

23. *Concept of the Corporation*, pp. 15–16; *New Society*, pp. 36–37, 50.

24. *Concept of the Corporation*, p. 17.

25. Ibid., pp. 17–19; see also *New Society*, p. 37. Drucker's conception of harmony in *Concept of the Corporation* and *The New Society* would appear to be a revision of his argument in *Industrial Man*, pp. 185–89, where he argued for a mechanical balance—that is, a check and balance between the economic and political spheres—in which the power of each was based on a "competing ethical principle."

26. *New Society*, pp. 99, 100, 106.

27. Ibid., pp. 106, 150.

28. Ibid., pp. 282–86.

29. Ibid., pp. 151–56; *Concept of the Corporation*, pp. 130–43; *Industrial Man*, pp. 25–32.

30. *Industrial Man*, pp. 150–51, 155–57.

31. *New Society*, pp. 47–49, 157–67.

32. Ibid., pp. 283–88.

33. Ibid., pp. 338, 347. See also *Concept of the Corporation*, p. 17; *Industrial Man*, pp. 265–66, 276.

34. *New Society*, p. 347.

35. *Concept of the Corporation*, p. 3.

36. In *Concept of the Corporation* and *The New Society*, Drucker argued that "federalism" constituted the new organizational principle of industrial society. Federalism, as he conceived it, allowed for decentralization of decision-making within the enterprise in an effort to accommodate a highly specialized division of labor and function. Nevertheless, responsibilities were to be delegated from the top down, thus retaining a hierarchical principle of control.

37. *New Society*, p. 67. On this point, Drucker cited Joseph Schumpeter, *Theory of Economic Development* (Cambridge, Mass.: Harvard University Press, 1934).

38. *Industrial Man*, pp. 256–64.

39. *Concept of the Corporation*, p. 21.

40. In the analysis that follows, I will draw on the entirety of Berle's publications on power and corporate power in an effort to reconstruct his political theory of the corporation. Berle's basic approach to the study of power remained quite consistent throughout these numerous works.

41. Berle, *The 20th Century Capitalist Revolution* (New York: Harcourt, Brace & World, 1954), pp. 23–24; Berle, *Modern Corporation*, p. 7.

42. *Modern Corporation*, p. 313. Although the term "non-statist political institution" was coined by Berle in later works, it was implicit in his collaborative effort with Means. See Berle's *20th Century Capitalist Revolution*, p. 60; *Power Without Property: A New Development in American Political Economy* (New York: Harcourt, Brace & World, 1959), p. 19; and *The American Economic Republic* (New York: Harcourt, Brace & World, 1963), p. 116.

43. The following analysis is based on Berle, *Modern Corporation*, pp. 47–116; and *Power Without Property*, pp. 52–76.

44. The amount of stock necessary to achieve this form of control was estimated by Berle and Means in 1932 to be 20 percent. It has since been revised downward in various studies to 10 percent and 5 percent. For a more detailed analysis of these issues, see below, Chapter 6, section 2.

45. *Power Without Property*, p. 118. Berle also referred to corporate managers as a "neutral technocracy" in *Modern Corporation*, p. 312, and as "technicians" in his *Power* (New York: Harcourt, Brace & World, 1969), p. 148.

46. *Power Without Property*, p. 55. If this shift of control occurred, Berle argued, the structure of corporate power would be significantly altered. Because the custody of trust funds was held by a handful of large banks and insurance companies, "a relatively small oligarchy of men operating in the same atmosphere, absorbing the same information,

moving in the same circles . . . and having more in common than in difference, will hold the reins" (ibid., p. 51). Theoretically, these individuals "will have no ownership relationship of any sort" and will be "essentially, non-Statist civil servants" (ibid.). Berle also discussed pension funds in his "Economic Power and the Free Society," in Andrew Hacker, ed., *The Corporation Take-Over* (Garden City, N.Y.: Anchor Books, Doubleday, 1965), pp. 93–95; and in *Economic Republic*, pp. 54–55.

47. *Modern Corporation*, pp. 219–43, 293–97.

48. Ibid., pp. 304–5; *Capitalist Revolution*, pp. 29–30; *Power Without Property*, pp. 64–69; *Economic Republic*, pp. 24–35; "Economic Power and the Free Society," pp. 89–91.

49. *Modern Corporation*, pp. 297–98.

50. Ibid., pp. 299–302.

51. Ibid., pp. 308–10. Berle and Means observed that a better understanding of the nature of corporate rule might be had "by studying the motives of an Alexander the Great, seeking new worlds to conquer, than by considering the motives of a petty craftsman in the days of Adam Smith" (ibid., pp. 307–8). In another work, Berle stated: "Toward the top of the corporate pyramid, indeed, the vested interest, or motivation, is less that of immediate financial return than that of retaining the prestige and power which goes with high corporate office." See Berle, "Corporations and the Modern State," in *The Future of Democratic Capitalism* (Philadelphia: University of Pennsylvania Press, 1950), pp. 38–39.

52. *Power*, p. 37. While Berle discussed the phenomenon of power in numerous works, his most recent and comprehensive study of the subject, *Power* (1969), may be read, for the most part, as a synthesis and refinement of earlier efforts. *Power*, however, was by no means inclusive of the author's examination of the subject, especially of his analysis of economic or corporate power.

53. Ibid., pp. 37, 39–40, 59–60. For similar definitions, see *Power Without Property*, p. 83; *Capitalist Revolution*, p. 32.

54. *Power*, pp. 37, 84, 88–92, 115–19. The third, fourth, and fifth laws described above parallel and complement Berle's conception of the "natural laws" governing the "selection of political forces" in *Natural Selection of Political Forces* (Lawrence: University of Kansas Press, 1950), esp. pp. 17–25, 35–43. Although Berle made no reference to this work in *Power*, the parallels between his theories of selection of political forces and of power are unmistakable. He did refer to *Natural Selection of Political Forces*, however, in *Power Without Property*, pp. 134–35, in the context of his analysis of the "public consensus" and economic democracy.

55. *Power*, pp. 143, 192–94, 203–9; *Capitalist Revolution*, pp. 35–42; *Economic Republic*, pp. 60–75; *Power Without Property*, pp. 27–51.

56. "Corporations and the Modern State," p. 37.

57. *Power Without Property*, pp. 81–82.

58. Ibid.; *Capitalist Revolution*, p. 32.

59. My reconstruction of this aspect of Berle's analysis of corporate power is based on his *Power*, pp. 199–214; *Capitalist Revolution*, pp. 32–34; *Economic Republic*, pp. 61–62, 83–84; and *Power Without Property*, pp. 82–83.

60. *Capitalist Revolution*, p. 35.

61. *Economic Republic*, pp. 85–91; *Power Without Property*, pp. 117–20. Berle elaborated his conception of the economic republic in *Economic Republic*, pp. 3–16, 85–185, and in *Power Without Property*, pp. 117–40.

62. *Economic Republic*, pp. 103–4, 145, 159–61; *Capitalist Revolution*, pp. 46–47.

63. *Power Without Property*, pp. 128–31; *Economic Republic*, pp. 137–43, 155–59; *Capitalist Revolution*, pp. 47–49.

64. *Economic Republic*, p. 117; and, generally, pp. 109–21.

65. Ibid., pp. 176–88; *Power*, pp. 195–98.

66. *Economic Republic*, p. 11.

67. *Power*, pp. 148–49, 155.

68. *Power Without Property*, p. 94.

69. *Economic Republic*, pp. 12–13; *Capitalist Revolution*, pp. 25–28.

70. *Power*, pp. 197–98. See also pp. 31, 100; *Economic Republic*, pp. 11–14.

71. *Power Without Property*, p. 88; *Power*, p. 155.

72. *Capitalist Revolution*, p. 66. Although Berle borrowed the term "countervailing power" from John Kenneth Galbraith's *American Capitalism: The Concept of Countervailing Power*, his interpretation of this idea was clearly his own.

73. Ibid. Berle applied the same logic to what he called the "property-power process." Power and property, according to the author, were "different phases of the same social phenomenon." Fragmented power "tends to become possessory property" just as aggregated property "increasingly sets up power." See Berle, *American Economic Republic*, p. 36. Both property and power, however, have a tendency to become concentrated. As concentration continues, it eventually becomes destructive and "begins to reconvert itself into the opposite phase." Berle concluded: "The most efficient or productive (that is to say, socially useful) phase . . . occurs when there is a balance between the propensity toward possessory property and the propensity toward power" (ibid., pp. 37–38). See also *Natural Selection of Political Forces*, p. 37, where Berle employed a similar logic and theory of balance to explain the development of political forces.

74. *Modern Corporation*, p. 310; *Power Without Property*, p. 98; *Economic Republic*, p. 42.

75. In attempting to reconstruct Berle's thought, one encounters a persistent problem. Although the author's basic concepts do not change a great deal, he has a propensity for reformulating them in each of his works. Normally this would not pose a problem, save that Berle rarely explained his reformulations in light of his past works. For example, the laws of power put forth in *Power* clearly constituted a synthesis of much of his earlier thought on that subject. Exactly how much of a synthesis, however, must be ascertained by the reader. In other words, it is often difficult to know what the author wanted to include or exclude when he reformulated or revised his concepts or terminology. To provide another example, Berle's analysis of the "property-power process" in *Economic Republic* (see note 73 above) was briefly summarized in *Power*, pp. 19–20, but no mention was made therein of how this process, which "obeys certain laws analogous, perhaps, to the laws which prevail in physical bodies" (*Economic Power*, p. 36) related, if at all, to the five laws of power. Nor, for that matter, did the author ever attempt to compare, let alone synthesize, his various conceptions of balance in *Natural Selection of Political Forces, Capitalist Revolution, Economic Republic*, and *Power*. Once again, the task is left to the analyst. It should be stressed, however, that these are primarily problems of exposition rather than logic. For the most part, Berle is quite consistent.

76. *Power Without Property*, pp. 99, 111, 134–35; *Economic Republic*, pp. 42–43.

77. Ibid., pp. 99, 104–5, 107–9.

78. Ibid., pp. 102–4, 110.

79. *Capitalist Revolution*, pp. 66–70.

80. *Power Without Property*, pp. 113, 135. See also *Capitalist Revolution*, pp. 185–88.

81. Ibid., p. 70.

82. Ibid., pp. 77–83.

83. Ibid., p. 83.

84. Ibid., pp. 104–5, 114–15. See also *Power*, pp. 373–81; *The Three Faces of Power* (New York: Harcourt, Brace & World, 1967), pp. 39–50.

85. Ibid., pp. 166–67.

86. Ibid., pp. 180–82.
87. Ibid., pp. 185–86.
88. Ibid., p. 178. Elsewhere Berle stated: "I am convinced that a philosophy or idea structure is a precondition of formation of any organization—that is, it precedes the coming into existence of power in any form or at any level." See Berle, *Power*, p. 84.
89. *Capitalist Revolution*, p. 178.
90. *Power Without Property*, pp. 96–97.
91. *Economic Republic*, p. 13.
92. *Power*, p. 149.
93. *Power Without Property*, p. 153.
94. On the compatibility of corporate power with democracy, Berle observed: "The impulse to democracy resides not in an economic organization but in the minds and hearts of men. The modern corporation and the modern state alike will be turned to the uses exacted by the controlling public opinion." See "Corporations and the Modern State," p. 57.
95. For a revisionist critique of American democracy, offered in the spirit of accommodation rather than reform, see Walter Lippmann, *Public Opinion* (1992; reprint, New York: The Free Press, 1965). Lippmann's highly influential work represented, to my knowledge, the first systematic attempt in the era of corporate capitalism (following Croly's example but without his spirit of reform) to accommodate democratic principles to oligarchic rule. Lippmann's justification of oligarchy anticipated the ideological double-think (still current in political science) that defines democracy as a condition of social stability that depends on widespread voter apathy and elite dominance of political institutions.
96. See the "Preface" of *The New Industrial State*, pp. vii–ix, for Galbraith's discussion of the relationship of *The New Industrial State* to *The Affluent Society*.
97. Galbraith, *The New Industrial State*, pp. 1, 12, 16.
98. Ibid., pp. 6–7, 20, 33.
99. Galbraith analyzed the nature of planning and the control of prices and demand in ibid., pp. 22–45, 179–97, 198–232.
100. Ibid., p. 16.
101. Ibid., p. 200.
102. Ibid., pp. 35–45.
103. Ibid., p. 43.
104. Ibid., p. 56.
105. Ibid., pp. 50–56.
106. Ibid., pp. 49–50, 57–59.
107. Ibid., pp. 63–67.
108. Ibid., p. 33.
109. Ibid., pp. 76–81, 104–8.
110. Ibid., pp. 110–13, 116, 121.
111. Ibid., pp. 130–32.
112. Ibid., pp. 138, 140–48.
113. Ibid., p. 153; see also pp. 149–58.
114. Ibid., pp. 159–61.
115. Ibid., pp. 162–63.
116. Ibid., pp. 167–70.
117. Ibid., pp. 171–72. In defining his distinction between profit maximization and growth, Galbraith argued: "Prices, sales, cost and other policies to maximize growth will differ within any given time horizon from those to maximize profits. Nor will profits be maximized if, as in the case of the technostructure, there is special reason to minimize risk" (ibid., p. 172 n. 7).

118. Ibid., pp. 173–74, 176.

119. Ibid., pp. 296–97.

120. Ibid., pp. 269–304.

121. Ibid., p. 296.

122. Ibid., p. 316. This is especially true of defense and aerospace industries, according to Galbraith.

123. Ibid., pp. 301–2.

124. Ibid., pp. 392–94, 398.

125. Ibid., pp. 277–81. Galbraith's conclusions concerning the role of labor in the industrial system constituted a significant revision of his analysis in *American Capitalism: The Concept of Countervailing Power*. In that earlier work, he argued that organized labor functioned as a countervailing power to the economic power of the large corporation. See esp. pp. 114–17.

126. Ibid., p. 323.

127. Ibid., pp. 216–18.

128. On this, see *American Capitalism*, pp. 10–31.

129. *New Industrial State*, p. 343.

130. Ibid., pp. 103–4; see also p. 396.

131. Ibid., p. 399.

132. Ibid., p. 380.

133. Ibid., pp. 282–84.

134. Ibid., pp. 370, 372.

135. Galbraith's agenda for reform also included expanding public services that were not supported by the industrial system, cultivating the aesthetic dimension of life and creating options to the normal pattern of work and leisure. See ibid., pp. 343–69. It should also be noted that he did not believe conventional economists—"the natural allies of the industrial system"—would serve the interests of emancipation (see ibid., p. 384). Galbraith observed that "economics, as it is conventionally taught, is in part a system of beliefs designed less to reveal truth than to reassure its communicants about established social arrangements" (ibid., p. 167).

136. Ibid., p. 89.

137. Ibid., p. 381.

138. "Political leadership, persuasion and action are activities of individuals; they are not readily undertaken by men who are accustomed to operating as a group. The mature corporation is run by committees. But the suborning of a legislature or even the persuasion of an electorate is accomplished, on the whole, by men working as individuals" (ibid., p. 302). Galbraith appears to have created a false dichotomy. After all, virtually all effective direct political action is accomplished by individuals who are a part of, or who work on behalf of, organizations or groups. The author's argument can easily be turned on its head. If one can judge by the tremendous proliferation of corporate political action committees in recent years, the use of the media for purposes of persuasion, and the increasing influence of such groups as the Business Roundtable, the organizational talents of corporations seem to be an asset rather than a liability.

139. Galbraith observed: "Private economic power is held in check by the countervailing power of those who are subject to it. The first begets the second. The long trend toward concentration of industrial enterprise in the hands of a relatively few firms has brought into existence not only strong sellers, as economists have supposed, but also strong buyers as they have failed to see." Because "power on one side of a market creates both the need for, and the prospect of reward to, the exercise of countervailing power from the other side," Galbraith concluded, "we can rely on countervailing power to appear as a curb on

economic power." See *American Capitalism*, pp. 111, 113. Clearly, Galbraith's theory of industrial society in *The New Industrial State* effectively refuted his earlier conception of countervailing power.

But others refuted him first: "In Professor Galbraith's analysis, countervailing power replaces competition as the regulator of the economy. Unfortunately, it will not work in times of full production and inflation, for then the opposing powers can resolve their differences at the expense of the consumer." See Melvin Anshen and Francis D. Wormuth, *Private Enterprise and Public Policy* (New York: Macmillan, 1954), p. 26. See also p. 132 n. 63, where the authors explain that, contrary to Galbraith, oligopoly does not inevitably generate oligopsony (few buyers) and thereby produce countervailing power. Indeed, most of the oligopolistic industries "are not the industries that encounter oligopsony among their customers."

140. *New Industrial State*, p. 387.

141. *Power*, p. 256.

142. Walter Lippmann, *A Preface to Morals* (New York: Macmillan, 1929), p. 20.

Chapter 6

1. See above, Chapter 3, section 4.

2. Walter E. Weyl, *The New Democracy* (New York: Macmillan, 1912), pp. 91–92.

3. Walter Lippmann, *Drift and Mastery* (1914; reprint, New York: Henry Holt & Co., 1917), pp. 45–46. Maurice Zeitlin notes that the substance of the managerial thesis concerning the separation of ownership and control (i.e., the rise of propertyless managers) was articulated at the turn of the century by Eduard Bernstein and Konrad Schmidt of the German Social Democratic Party. Zeitlin, "Corporate Ownership and Control: The Large Corporation and the Capitalist Class," *American Journal of Sociology* 79 (March 1974): 1080–81. See also Karl Marx, *Capital: A Critique of Political Economy*, vol. 3 (New York: Vintage Books, 1981), chap. 27, pp. 566–73.

4. Lippmann, *Drift and Mastery*, pp. 50, 51–55, 58–59, 63, 65. In the 1920s, the separation of ownership and control continued to be a subject of debate and speculation. See John Maynard Keynes, "The End of Laissez-Faire" (1926), in *The Collected Writings of John Maynard Keynes: Essays in Persuasion*, vol. 9 (New York: St. Martin's Press; London: Macmillan, 1972), pp. 289–90; William Z. Ripley, *Main Street and Wall Street* (Boston: Little, Brown, 1927), pp. 84–90, 127–44. Ripley's discussion included comments on a 1926 article written by Berle that anticipated Berle and Means's thesis on the separation of ownership and control. Berle and Ripley were friends and influenced one another's thinking on this issue. See Jordan A. Schwarz, *Liberal: Adolph A. Berle and the Vision of an American Era* (New York: The Free Press, 1987), p. 52.

5. On the issue of capital self-sufficiency, Philip I. Blumberg comments: "Contrary to the expectation of a number of observers several decades ago, including A. A. Berle, that major corporations would become free of dependence on capital markets, reliance on the capital markets has increased, rather than declined. Financial institutions continue to play a dominant role particularly in connection with the issuance of new security issues and the availability of credit generally." See Blumberg, *The Megacorporation in American Society: The Scope of Corporate Power* (Englewood Cliffs, N.J.: Prentice-Hall, 1975), p. 164. Vincent G. Massaro observes: "Throughout the postwar period, corporations have relied increasingly on financial institutions to meet financial requirements. And this trend is apparently continuing. In the past four years, external funds have averaged roughly 46 percent of total corporate funds, which includes internally generated and external funds. In contrast, in the preceding 30-year period, they had averaged roughly 30 percent of total corporate funds." See Massaro, *Corporate Finance and the Changing U.S. Financial Structure* (New York:

The Conference Board, 1980), p. 3. For an analysis of recent lending practices and the financing of mergers, see Sarah Bartlett, "Need a Quick Billion or Two? Just Ask Your Banker," *Business Week*, October 26, 1987, pp. 98–99. See also Vicky Cahan, "Banks Are on the Brink of Breaking Loose," *Business Week*, March 7, 1988, 99–100, concerning prospective changes in commercial banking.

6. The possible influence or control of financial institutions over industrial corporations has received increasing attention in recent years due to the large stockholdings of institutional investors. Until quite recently, institutional investors dissatisfied with the performance of companies have followed the so-called "Wall Street Rule" of selling their stock and reinvesting without challenging the powers that be. As stockholdings have grown, however, this practice has become less feasible. Perhaps more important is that poor management and/or managerial excesses (including self-serving attempts to fend off mergers) have become issues of growing importance to large institutional investors who are concerned with the putative decline in American business productivity and global competitiveness. In 1987, *Business Week* reported on what might become a long-term struggle in corporate America: "The increasingly powerful public institutional owners who banded together in the Council of Institutional Investors are spearheading a movement for change. With more than 50 pension fund members controlling $200 billion worth of investments, the CII is leading the proxy fight against antitakeover tactics in about 40 shareholder meetings this spring, from United Technologies to Control Data to J. C. Penney. Beyond that, some institutions are voicing complaints directly to management." See Bruce Nussbaum and Judith H. Dobrzynski, "The Battle for Corporate Control," *Business Week*, May 18, 1987, p. 103. With institutional stockholdings presently accounting for more than a third of all corporate stock and rising, management's prerogatives will come under increasing scrutiny. Cf. Ira Millstein, "The Responsibility of the Institutional Investor in Corporate Management," in Arnold W. Sametz, ed., *The Battle for Corporate Control* (Homewood, Ill.: Business One Irwin, 1991), pp. 67–76; John Scott, *Corporations, Classes, and Capitalism* (London: Hutchinson, 1985), pp. 49–51; John Scott, "Corporate Groups and Network Structure," in Joseph McCahery, Sol Picciotto, and Colin Scott, eds., *Corporate Control and Accountability: Changing Structures and the Dynamics of Regulation* (Oxford: Clarendon Press, 1993), pp. 291–304; Allen Kaufman and Lawrence Zacharias, "From Trust to Contract: The Legal Language of Managerial Ideology, 1920–1980," *Business History Review* 66 (Autumn 1992): 560–70. For an insightful analysis of the legal barriers that have been erected to employee control of pension funds, see Mark J. Roe, *Strong Managers, Weak Owners* (Princeton: Princeton University Press, 1994), pp. 124–45.

Berle predicted that institutional investments would eventually return majority control to shareholders represented by large financial institutions. He maintained, however, that if this control were to be exercised, it would lodge power in "non-Statist civil servants" who presumably would have no ownership interests of their own. His interpretation of this development therefore remained within the ideological parameters of the managerial thesis. See above, Chapter 5, section 3, and Chapter 5, note 46.

7. Blumberg (*Megacorporation*, p. 92) states that the voting strength necessary to achieve control will increase with each of the following four stages:

"(A) Retention of control by management or minority in the absence of any external threat.

"(B) Retention of control by management or minority owners in the face of an external threat represented by the hostile acquisition of a significant minority of shares.

"(C) Retention of control by management or minority owners in the face of an external threat represented by a tender offer for shares, typically at a substantial premium above the market.

"(D) Assumption of control in the face of management opposition by an external group through the acquisition of a minority of shares by purchase or tender offer and the institution or potential threat of institution of a proxy fight."

In fairness to Berle, however, he does take note of some of the complexities involved in exercising control. In noting that "working control" involves "the capacity to mobilize other shareholders," he emphasizes the political aspects of control—namely, the relationship of minority stockholders possessing theoretical control with the board of directors and their ability, as a consequence of this relationship, to direct the proxy machinery. Berle explains that control "is not a 'thing' but a function. It is essentially a variety of political process—non-statist and therefore, in our vocabulary, 'private,' but with substantial public responsibilities. The holder of control is not so much the owner of a proprietary right as the occupier of a power-position." See Berle, " 'Control' in Corporate Law," *Columbia Law Review* 58 (1958): 1212, 1213.

8. After reviewing the actual data in Berle and Means's study, Zeitlin concludes that the authors provided evidence that definitely confirmed management control for only 22 percent of the 200 largest corporations, as opposed to the 44 percent which they claimed. The unconfirmed balance had been "presumed" to be under management control. See Zeitlin, "Corporate Ownership and Control," pp.1081–82. Two years before Zeitlin's influential article was published, Philip H. Burch Jr. flatly challenged the accuracy of Berle and Means's study, noting that "a sizeable number of firms seem to have been placed in the wrong control category. . . . Thus, though the fact is apparently not widely recognized or conceded in academic circles, many of Berle and Means' stock ownership and control findings are of a questionable nature." See Burch, *The Managerial Revolution Reassessed* (Lexington, Mass.: D. C. Heath, 1972), p. 2.

9. Consult Raymond W. Goldsmith and Rexford C. Parmelee, *The Distribution of Ownership in the 200 Largest Nonfinancial Corporations*, Monographs of the Temporary National Economic Committee, no. 29 (Washington, D.C.: Government Printing Office, 1940); Ferdinand Lundberg, *America's Sixty Families* (New York: Vanguard, 1937); and Anna Rochester, *Rulers of America* (New York: International Publishers, 1936). The differences, however, go beyond simple interpretation of data to concepts of control. On this score, Lundberg's thesis of family control, while raising questions about the broad claims of Berle and Means, erred in the opposite direction. (For a critique of Lundberg's methods and research, see C. Wright Mills, *The Power Elite* [Oxford: Oxford University Press, 1956], p. 377.) More recent studies on the separation of ownership and control have sustained the original debate. Compare Robert J. Larner, *Management Control and the Large Corporation* (New York: Dunellen Publishing Co., 1970), which updated the Berle and Means thesis, with Don Villarejo, *Stock Ownership and the Control of Corporations* (Ann Arbor, Mich.: Radical Education Project, 1962), whose argument complemented that of Lundberg. Both Lundberg and Villarejo posited a connection between insider control and ownership of stock by financial institutions. Larner criticized this methodology for assuming what needed to be demonstrated—evidence of concerted action. Larner, on the other hand, after the fashion of Berle and Means, overstated the extent of management control (or understated minority control), while he discounted altogether the significance of institutional ownership of stock. On this, see Zeitlin, "Corporate Ownership," pp. 1082ff., and Blumberg, *Megacorporation*, pp. 87–94. Burch, who strongly criticized the methodologies of Lundberg and Villarejo, and found their conclusions highly dubious, also argued that Larner's findings seriously understated minority control. See Burch, *Managerial Revolution*, pp. 4–7, 147–57.

These studies, however, do not exhaust the possibilities. In *Corporate Control, Corporate Power* (Cambridge University Press, 1981), Edward S. Herman adds yet another twist to the debate by arguing that even though management control has largely triumphed over traditional family control, the managerial ascendancy (in Berle's sense of a neutral technocracy) clearly has not displaced capitalist (profit-oriented) management of enterprise. In what could be the most significant contribution to the empirical analysis of the separation of ownership and control (and several other aspects of corporate power) in recent decades, Herman develops the idea of "strategic control" as an explicitly political concept of internal rule. His effort to systematically analyze and weigh the various aspects of "control," including numerous constraints imposed by ownership interests, outside directors, industry and market relationships, and regulatory controls on corporate decision-making, constitutes a major advance in the political study of the corporation.

10. Zeitlin, for example, makes a strong case for advancing the empirical study of control beyond the assumptions of Berle and Means's inquiry:

"It is necessary to study the concrete situation within the corporation and the constellation of intercorporate relationships in which it is involved before one can begin to understand where control is actually located. . . . It seems advisable to conceptualize control in such a way as to link it inextricably with a method that is not reducible to a single criterion, such as a minimum percentage of stock held by a single minority bloc, but which requires instead a variety of interrelated yet independent indicators. The modalities of corporate control utilized by specific individuals and/or families and/or groups of associates differ considerably, vary in complexity, and are not easily categorized." See Zeitlin, "Corporate Ownership," p. 1090. See, generally, ibid., pp. 1085–94.

Blumberg's observation (in *Megacorporation*, p. 94) is also apposite: "Concerted action, however, need not reflect formal agreement. It may arise as an objective phenomenon produced by congruent pressures leading to common patterns of conduct. Thus, one may inquire whether the existing pattern of management control with the acquiescence and support of the institutions does not constitute a modus vivendi representing an accommodation of the interests of these groups. . . . A modus vivendi between various groups with a common social background and economic outlook accommodating their respective economic interests is, however, a radically different relationship than intentional joint action. It rests on sociological and psychological factors rather than on an economic alliance or other intentional association to achieve common objectives."

11. In addition to the obvious problem of gaining access to insider information, there are numerous methods of nondisclosure that prevent access to information concerning corporate ownership and control. For example, major institutional investors (e.g., trust departments of banks, investment companies) do not generally provide public records of who actually owns the stock that it purchases, or of the voting powers (if any) represented by the stockholdings. See Zeitlin, "Corporate Ownership," pp. 1085–86; Burch, *Managerial Revolution*, pp. 9–10; Blumberg, *Megacorporation*, pp. 124–26.

12. The empirical study of the separation of ownership from control involves a number of analytical problems that militate against glib assertions of the sort one often finds in works of social scientists who have uncritically accepted Berle and Means's ideological argument. A brief summary of the results of recent studies indicates some of these analytical difficulties and the wide differences of opinion concerning the separation of ownership from control. Using a criterion of 5 percent stock ownership or more as a measure of "working control," Villarejo (*Stock Ownership*, p. 68) concluded that between 54 percent and 61 percent of the largest 232 industrial corporations, as of 1960, were owner-controlled. Larner (*Managerial Control*, pp. 1221), who employed a standard of 10 percent stock ownership to determine minority control, found that 84 percent of the 200 largest nonfinancial corporations (and 75 percent of the 500 largest nonfinancial corporations)

were under management control in the late 1960s. Burch's study of the top 300 publicly and privately owned industrial corporations in the Fortune 500 for 1965 yielded the following: "probably management control" (40 percent), "possibly family control" (15.3 percent), and "probably family control" (44.7 percent). Burch utilized a measure of 4 to 5 percent minority ownership, combined with documentation of "inside or outside representation . . . on the part of a family on the board of directors of a company, generally over an extended period of time." See Burch, *Managerial Revolution*, pp. 29–30, 36–75.

Herman's study of the 200 largest, publicly owned, nonfinancial corporations (data for December 31, 1974), identified the following types of control: (a) Inside management, (b) inside management and outside board, (c) majority ownership, (d) minority ownership, (e) intercorporate ownership, (f) government, (g) financial, and (h) receivership. Several of these classifications contained additional subcategories. For example, "minority ownership" distinguished between 10 percent or more and 5 to 10 percent stockholdings for assessing different degrees of control that were also affected by position(s) held on the board or in management. He also categorized management-controlled corporations according to significant constraints—for example, ownership interests, financial, and regulatory. His conclusion that 82.5 percent of these corporations, accounting for 85.4 percent of total assets, were under management control, must therefore be understood within the broader analytical framework that he devised to interpret the full range and permutations of control, including an analysis of the significant constraints imposed by financial institutions. See Herman, *Corporate Control*, pp. 53–68.

13. In 1993 the twenty top-paid CEOs in America (based on salary, bonuses, and stock options) ranged from a high of $203,010,590 (Michael D. Eisner, Walt Disney) to a low of $11,278,000 (Stanley C. Gault, Goodyear Tire & Rubber). The average total compensation for a CEO of a major U.S. corporation was $3,841,273, down about $1,000 from 1992. However, if stock options and other long-term compensation are not counted, the average pay is about $2,750,000. See "That Eye-Popping Executive Pay," *Business Week*, April 25, 1994, pp. 52–56. As for the claim that technological expertise and organizational (structural) changes within the large corporation have diminished the primacy of the profit motive, Herman (*Corporate Control*, pp. 103–6) where he argues that just the opposite has occurred. The now prevalent method of internal organization by product division lines emphasizes profitability as a goal and evaluative standard within the divisional structure: "With these arrangements, a profit-maximization goal is imposed on division managers, whose compensation and promotion opportunities are heavily dependent on profit performance" (ibid., p. 105).

14. Contrary to the assertions of managerial theorists, the issue of profitability is an empirical, not a logical, issue. The great majority of comparative studies of the profitability of owner-controlled and management-controlled corporations have concluded that there is no significant difference between the profit rates of companies under these two forms of control, which would seem to indicate that success is still measured by profitability. See Herman, *Corporate Control*, pp. 85–113, 326–31; Larner, *Management Control*, pp. 25–61; David R. Kamerschen, "The Influence of Ownership and Control on Profit Rates," *American Economic Review* 58 (June 1968): 432–37; Brian V. Hindley, "Separation of Ownership and Control in the Modern Corporation," *Journal of Law and Economics* 13 (April 1970): 185–221. See also Maurice Zeitlin and Samuel Norich, "Management Control, Exploitation, and Profit Maximization in the Large Corporation: An Empirical Confrontation of Managerialism and Class Theory," in Paul Zarembka, ed., *Research in Political Economy*, vol. 2 (Greenwich, Conn.: JAI Press, 1977), pp. 33–62; Maynard S. Seider, "Corporate Ownership, Control and Ideology: Support for Behavioral Similarity," *Sociology and Social Research* 62

(October 1977): 113–28. For a study that provides evidence of higher profit rates in owner-controlled corporations, see Joseph R. Monsen Jr., J. S. Chiu, and D. E. Cooley, "The Effect of Separation of Ownership and Control on the Performance of the Large Firm," *Quarterly Journal of Economics* 82 (August 1968): 435–51.

15. Herman, *Corporate Control*, p. 28. On the role of outside directors as being one of "many constraints ideological and material, direct and indirect, that greatly influence managerial ends and behavior," see ibid., p. 48. Cf. Myles L. Mace, *Directors: Myth and Reality* (Boston: Division of Research, Graduate School of Business Administration, Harvard University, 1971), esp. chaps. 4–7 and 9; Victor Brudney, "The Independent Director: Heavenly City or Potemkin Village?" *Harvard Law Review* 95 (1982): 597–659.

16. Herman (*Corporate Control*, p. 26) maintains that in large corporations with diffused ownership "occupancy of the top positions becomes an independent source of power that can be built up by deliberate strategies and passed on to successors. . . . Strategic position typically has been attained by one of the following routes: (1) initial possession of a large stock ownership position or a major stock acquisition; (2) a role in organization and promotion (sometimes associated with the acquisition of significant stockholdings); (3) management changes or more far-reaching reorganizations following serious financial difficulties; and (4) the gradual accretion of power from within the organization."

17. This prospect gained a new dimension during the late 1980s, when investment bankers, in the tradition of J. P. Morgan, assumed the reins of control of companies recently acquired. See Carol J. Loomis, "The New J. P. Morgans," *Fortune*, February 29, 1988, pp. 44–51; Sarah Bartlett, "Power Investors," *Business Week*, June 20, 1988, pp. 116–23; Ellyn E. Spragins et al., "When Power Investors Call the Shots," *Business Week*, pp. 126–30. Whether this will become a widespread practice remains to be seen.

18. One will find a very similar conception of corporate power in the landmark *Standard Oil* and *American Tobacco* cases of 1911, and in the *U.S. Steel* case of 1920. By focusing on the intent to monopolize, the rulings in these cases identified the exercise of corporate power in the marketplace with abuse of market power, unfair practices, and predation rather than with market concentration, combination, and size. See above, Chapter 2, section 5.

19. A similar conceptual evolution, albeit slower in developing, also occurred in antitrust law and constitutional law. Beginning with Judge Hand's decision in the *Alcoa* case in 1946, the conception of corporate power in antitrust monopolization cases evinced a shift in emphasis away from intent (predation) toward market concentration and size as the source of the violation. Warren Court merger cases under the revised Clayton Act reflected a similar concern in devising methods to determine the effects of combinations on market concentration and oligopolistic (or potential) competition. These doctrinal shifts within antitrust law were consistent with recent theoretical developments in economics, but they also reflected a conception of corporate power as being rooted in control or dominance of highly concentrated markets. More recently, Supreme Court opinions in the First Amendment corporate speech cases have raised the issue of whether the aggregated wealth of large corporations might not distort the marketplace of political ideas, thereby subverting democratic processes. See above, Chapter 4, sections 4 and 5.

20. From the mid-1950s through the mid-1970s, a relative handful of political scientists did political analyses of the corporation. Of these, several tended to focus primarily on possible justifications or explanations of the internal governance of the corporation: the body politic, private government, constitutional aspects of the corporate charter. For example, see Richard Eells, *The Government of Corporations* (New York: The Free Press, 1962); Earl Latham, "The Body Politic of the Corporation," in Edward S. Mason, ed., *The Corporation in Modern Society* (Cambridge, Mass.: Harvard University Press, 1961), pp. 218–36; Scott

Buchanan, "The Corporation and the Republic," in Andrew Hacker, ed., *The Corporation Take-Over* (Garden City, N.Y.: Anchor Books, 1965), pp. 17–39; Grant McConnell, *Private Power and American Democracy* (New York: Knopf, 1967).

During the same period, however, there were a few significant case studies of corporate power in American politics. See Robert Engler, *The Politics of Oil* (Chicago: University of Chicago Press, Phoenix Books, 1967); Karen Orren, *Corporate Power and Social Change: The Politics of the Life Insurance Industry* (Baltimore: Johns Hopkins University Press, 1974). Other works analyzing political aspects of corporate power included Morton S. Baratz, "Corporate Giants and the Power Structure," *Western Political Quarterly* 9 (June 1956): 406–15; Michael Reagan, *The Managed Economy* (New York: Oxford University Press, 1963); Theodore J. Lowi, "American Business, Public Policy, Case Studies, and Political Theory," *World Politics* 16 (July 1964): 677–715; Edwin M. Epstein, *The Corporation in American Politics* (Englewood Cliffs, N.J.: Prentice-Hall, 1969); Richard J. Barber, *The American Corporation: Its Power, Its Money, Its Politics* (New York: E. P. Dutton, 1970); Richard J. Barnet and Ronald E. Müller, *Global Reach: The Power of Multinational Corporations* (New York: Simon & Schuster, 1974); and Arthur Selwyn Miller, *The Modern Corporate State: Private Governments and the American Constitution* (Westport, Conn.: Greenwood Press, 1976).

From the mid-1970s to the early 1990s, studies of corporate power in American politics still comprised a very small portion of political science publications. They include Charles E. Lindblom, *Politics and Markets: The World's Political-Economic Systems* (New York: Basic Books, 1977); Leonard Silk and David Vogel, *Ethics and Profits: The Crisis of Confidence in American Business* (New York: Simon & Schuster, 1976); David Vogel, *Lobbying the Corporation: Citizen Challenges to Business Authority* (New York: Basic Books, 1978); Vogel, "The Power of Business in America: A Reappraisal," *British Journal of Political Science* 13 (January 1983): 19–43; Vogel, "Political Science and the Study of Corporate Power: A Dissent from the New Conventional Wisdom," *British Journal of Political Science* 17 (October 1987): 385–405; Vogel, *National Styles of Regulation: Environmental Policies in Great Britain and the United States* (Ithaca: Cornell University Press, 1986); Vogel, *Fluctuating Fortunes* (New York: Basic Books, 1989); Edwin M. Epstein, "Business Political Activity: Research Approaches and Analytical Uses," in *Research in Corporate Social Performance and Policy*, vol.2 (Greenwich, Conn.: JAI Press, 1980), pp. 1–55; Lawrence B. Joseph, "Corporate Political Power and Liberal Democratic Theory," *Polity* 15 (Winter 1982): 246–67; Kim McQuaid, *Big Business and Presidential Power: From FDR to Reagan* (New York: Morrow, 1982); Robert Dahl, *A Preface to Economic Democracy* (Berkeley and Los Angeles: University of California Press, 1985); Dahl, *Dilemmas of Pluralist Democracy* (New Haven: Yale University Press, 1982); Dahl, "On Removing Certain Impediments to Democracy in the United States," *Political Science Quarterly* 92 (Spring 1977): 1–20; Dennis P. Quinn, "Investment Incentives: A Five-Country Test of the Lindblom Hypothesis," in *Research in Corporate Social Performance and Policy*, vol.10 (Greenwich, Conn.: JAI Press, 1988), pp. 87–111; Quinn, *Restructuring the Automobile Industry: A Study of Firms and States in Modern Capitalism* (New York: Columbia University Press, 1988); Dennis P. Quinn and Robert Y. Shapiro, "Business Political Power: The Case of Taxation," *American Political Science Review* 85 (September 1991): 851–74; Graham K. Wilson, *The Politics of Safety and Health* (Oxford: Clarendon Press, 1985); Wilson, "Corporate Political Strategies," *British Journal of Political Science* 20 (1990): 281–88.

Numerous recent empirical analyses of corporate PACs and lobbies are also pertinent to the political study of the corporation, but for the most part they do not address theoretical issues of corporate power. See, for example, the sources cited above Chapter 4, note 32. The contribution of other social scientists to the study of corporate power is discussed later in the present chapter.

21. For a trenchant analysis of the political, ideological, and intellectual context that

inspired Talcott Parsons's theory of structural functionalism, see in Alvin W. Gouldner, *The Coming Crisis of Western Sociology* (New York: Avon Books, 1971). The classic application of systems theory to political science is David Easton, *The Political System: An Inquiry into the State of Political Science* (New York: Knopf, 1953); and *A Framework for Political Analysis* (Englewood Cliffs, N.J.: Prentice-Hall, 1965). See also Karl W. Deutsch, *The Nerves of Government* (New York: The Free Press, 1966); Gabriel A. Almond, "A Functional Approach to Comparative Politics," in Gabriel A. Almond and James S. Coleman, eds., *The Politics of the Developing Areas* (Princeton: Princeton University Press, 1960), chap. 1; Gabriel A. Almond and G. Bingham Powell Jr., *Comparative Politics: A Developmental Approach* (Boston: Little, Brown, 1966); Morton A. Kaplan, "Systems Theory," in James C. Charlesworth, ed., *Contemporary Political Analysis* (New York: The Free Press, 1967), pp. 150–63; William Flanigan and Edwin Fogelman, "Functional Analysis," in ibid., pp. 72–85.

22. See Chapter 4, sections 3b and 3c.

23. An analysis of corporate political activity that is consistent with the premises and methods of the pluralist approach in political science is found in Edwin M. Epstein's *The Corporation in American Politics*. Epstein's effort to construct a "political theory of the firm" takes into account the expansion of government activities in the economy, which necessitates corporate involvement in politics: "The explanation manifests an awareness of the fact that corporations exist in a pluralist setting fraught with politics, and that, therefore, they must be political actors in order to survive against conflicting groups, including both other social interests and competitors" (p. 137). While Epstein claims that the corporation is not an ordinary economic interest group, his analysis of corporate power remains within the narrow confines of interest-group politics of pluralism and its ideological conception of the political marketplace.

In *Fluctuating Fortunes*, David Vogel also employs a pluralist approach to analyze corporate political activity in the United States. Elsewhere, he has argued: "My contention is not that individual companies, trade associations and interindustry coalitions do not wield significant political power; of course they do. It is rather that we do not require a distinctive methodology for measuring the political power of business in capitalist democracies. Business is not unique. There is nothing about the nature, scope or magnitude of the power wielded by business that cannot be accounted for within the framework of a sophisticated model of interest-group politics." See Vogel, "Political Science and the Study of Corporate Power," p. 408.

24. See the works cited in note 20 above.

25. Lindblom, *Politics and Markets*, p. 171.

26. Ibid., pp. 174, 179–80, 187, 194, 195–213.

27. Quinn, "Investment Incentives: A Five-Country Test of the Lindblom Hypothesis"; Quinn and Shapiro, "Business Political Power: The Case of Taxation"; David Jacobs, "Corporate Taxation and Corporate Economic Power," *American Journal of Sociology* 93 (January 1988): 852–81. For critical reviews of *Politics and Markets*, see Vogel, "Political Science and the Study of Corporate Power"; James Q. Wilson, "Democracy and the Corporation," in Robert Hessen, ed., *Does Big Business Rule America?* (Washington, D.C.: Ethics and Public Policy Center, 1981). Cf. Joseph, "Corporate Political Power and Liberal Democratic Theory"; David Marsh, "Interest Group Activity and Structural Power: Lindblom's *Politics and Markets*," *Western European Politics* 6 (April 1983): 3–13; G. William Domhoff, *The Power Elite and the State: How Policy Is Made in America* (New York: Aldine De Gruyter, 1990), pp. 187–203.

28. Barnet and Müller, *Global Reach*, pp. 244–45.

29. Ibid., pp. 49–50.

30. Ibid., p. 246.

31. Ibid., pp. 140–47.

32. Ibid., pp. 247, 252–53.

33. Ibid., pp. 162, 363.

34. Ibid., pp. 232–46.

35. Even more perplexing is Barnet and Müller's note on page 438, in which they express general agreement with Veblen's analysis of the effects of separation of ownership and control, which is based on his conception of the dominance of business (finance) over industry (technology). In any event, the authors' attempt to revive Veblen's distinction between business and industry in modern form appears to be based on a misreading of the purpose of that distinction, in its analytical and normative forms, in Veblen's social theory. Furthermore, to accept Veblen's so-called predictions without examining the problematical status of the business/industry distinction within his theory only compounds the confusion. See above, Chapter 3, section 4.

36. I will have occasion to evaluate Mills's analysis of corporate power at various points in this chapter. For the purposes at hand, it is enough to say that despite his protestations to the contrary Mills's conception of corporate power—its nature, organization, and scope—suggests a form of class domination rather than of institutional control. The Cold War context and his own disenchantment with the Left could help explain why he found it necessary continually to remind the reader that power, as conceived in his study, was based on the control of institutions. Mills's analysis of the convergence of corporate and military elites, rooted in the merger of the corporate economy and military bureaucracy ("the military-industrial complex"), however, clearly anticipated later developments that formalized this relationship in the Department of Defense. Cf. Seymour Melman, *Pentagon Capitalism: The Political Economy of War* (New York: McGraw-Hill, 1971).

Mills's view of the military ascendancy, however, seems to have been influenced by the militaristic bearing of Cold War foreign policy and the fact that a former general was then occupying the White House. Without discounting the significance of Pentagon capitalism, one need not accept the thesis of the imminent rise of the military elite to a par with the corporate rulers. This aspect of Mills's argument, which presumed an increasing politicization of the military command and posited centralization of rule within the executive branch of the federal government, leaned heavily toward a statist interpretation of the power elite and, hence, of corporate power.

37. G. William Domhoff, *Who Rules America?* (Englewood Cliffs, N.J.: Prentice-Hall, 1967); Domhoff, *The Higher Circles: The Governing Class in America* (New York: Random House, 1970); Domhoff, *The Bohemian Grove and Other Retreats: A Study in Ruling Class Cohesiveness* (New York: Harper & Row, 1974); Domhoff, "Social Clubs, Political Groups, and Corporations: A Network Study of Ruling Class Cohesiveness," *Insurgent Sociologist* 5 (Spring 1975): 173–84; Domhoff, *The Powers That Be: Process of Ruling Class Domination in America* (New York: Random House, 1979); Domhoff, *The Power Elite and the State.*

38. Zeitlin, "Corporate Ownership and Control"(note 3 above); Michael P. Allen, "Management Control in the Large Corporation: Comment on Zeitlin," *American Journal of Soiciology* 81 (January 1976): 885–94. Zeitlin, "On Class Theory of the Large Corporation: A Response to Allen," *American Journal of Sociology* 81 (1976): 894–903; Zeitlin and Norich, "Management Control" (note 14 above); Peter Mariolis, "Interlocking Directorates and Control of Corporations," *Social Science Quarterly* 56 (1975): 425–39; Thomas Koenig, Robert Gogel, and John Sonquist, "Models of the Significance of Interlocking Corporate Director- ates," *American Journal of Economics and Sociology* 38 (1979): 173–86; Johannes M. Pennings, *Interlocking Directorates: Origins and Consequences of Connections Among Organizations' Boards of Directors* (San Francisco: Jossey-Bass, 1980); Michael Useem, "The Inner Group of the American Capitalist Class," *Social Problems* 25 (February 1978): 225–40; Useem, "Classwide

Rationality in the Politics of Managers and Directors of Large Corporations in the United States and Great Britain," *Administrative Science Quarterly* 27 (June 1982): 199–226; Useem, *The Inner Circle: Large Corporations and the Rise of Business Political Activity in the U.S. and U.K.* (New York: Oxford University Press, 1984); Beth Mintz and Michael Schwartz, *The Power Structure of American Business* (Chicago: University of Chicago Press, 1985); Michael Schwartz, ed., *The Structure of Power in America: The Corporate Elite as a Ruling Class* (New York: Holmes & Meier, 1987); Mark S. Mizruchi, *The American Corporate Network, 1904–1974* (Beverly Hills, Calif.: Sage Publications, 1982); Mizruchi, *The Structure of Corporate Political Action: Interfirm Relations and Their Consequences* (Cambridge, Mass.: Harvard University Press, 1992).

39. Herman, *Corporate Control, Corporate Power*. For works by Useem and Mizruchi, see note 38 above. See also above, Chapter 1, section 4a, and Chapter 4, notes 49 and 50.

40. Nicos Poulantzas, *Political Power and Social Classes*, trans. Timothy O'Hagan (London: New Left Books, 1973), pp. 113, 193, 275–95.

41. Mills, *The Power Elite*, p. 277.

42. Ralph Miliband, *Marxism and Politics* (Oxford: Oxford University Press, 1977), pp. 54–55, 74.

43. For example, see Mills, *The Power Elite*, pp. 275–78.

44. Miliband, *The State in Capitalist Society* (New York: Basic Books, 1969).

45. For a critique on this score, see Salvador Giner and Juan Salcedo, "The Ideological Practice of Nicos Poulantzas," *European Journal of Sociology* 17 (1976): 344–65. For the debate between Miliband and Poulantzas, reprinted from *The New Left Review*, see Robin Blackburn, ed., *Ideology in Social Science: Readings in Critical Social Theory* (Glasgow: Fontana/Collins, 1977), pp. 238–64.

46. For an analysis of major contributions to this debate, see Martin Carnoy, *The State and Political Theory* (Princeton: Princeton University Press, 1984); Bob Jessop, *The Capitalist State: Marxist Theories and Methods* (Oxford: Basil Blackwell, 1982); Clyde W. Barrow, *Critical Theories of the State: Marxist, Neo-Marxist, Post-Marxist* (Madison: University of Wisconsin Press, 1993); Rianne Mahon, "From 'Bringing' to 'Putting': The State in Late Twentieth-Century Social Theory," *Canadian Journal of Sociology* 16, no. 2 (1991): 119–44.

47. See, for example, Peter Evans, Dietrich Rueschemeyer, and Theda Skocpol, eds., *Bringing the State Back In* (Cambridge: Cambridge University Press, 1985).

48. Richard L. Sklar, "On the Concept of Power in Political Economy," in Dalmas H. Nelson and Richard L. Sklar, eds., *Toward a Humanistic Science of Politics: Essays in Honor of Francis Dunham Wormuth* (Lanham, Md.: University Press of America, 1983), pp. 179–206.

49. Ibid., pp. 199–200. Richard Sklar introduced the idea of the power basis of class in an earlier essay. See Richard L. Sklar, "The Nature of Class Domination in Africa," in Richard L. Sklar and C. S. Whitaker, *African Politics and Problems in Development* (Boulder, Colo.: Lynne Rienner Publishers, 1991), p. 209; reprinted from the *Journal of Modern African Studies* 17 (December 1979): 531–52.

50. "Corporate power based upon relationships of control" (i.e., the power basis of class) is a more comprehensive idea than "power based upon property ownership" (i.e., in Marxist theory, social relations that obtain between capital and labor, which are based on the institution of private property). As I interpret it, the idea of corporate power based on relationships of control necessarily includes power based on property ownership, albeit reconceptualized to take into account the growing autonomy of the corporate oligarchy that accompanied the transition from competitive-industrial to corporate capitalism. In this sense, it is primarily a political rather than economic idea—that is, it indicates that corporate power involves relationships of domination and subordination that may or may not be a function of property ownership. What *is* certain is that this power entails *control* over the

means of production. But clearly, it is no longer tenable to argue that this control is based exclusively on economic factors or causes—for example, the argument that domination (i.e., exploitation) of labor by capital results from the declining rate of profit. A broader conception is needed to account for the essentially political or nonpecuniary apsects of corporate power and for the fact that corporate power has become socially comprehensive.

51. See Chapter 1, section 4a.

52. The corporate bourgeoisie should not be confused with the notion of a ruling class of managers that ushers in what James Burnham has dubbed the "managerial revolution"—the transition from a capitalist to a "managerial society." See Burham *The Managerial Revolution: What is Happening in the World* (New York: John Day Co., 1941). Burnham envisioned the worldwide rise of managerial classes that ruled by virtue of their control over the state, which in turn owned and controlled the means of production. Published in 1941, *The Managerial Revolution* was strongly influenced by the recent expansion of government functions under the New Deal administrations and by political developments in Europe. Albeit still under the reign of finance capitalists during this early stage of managerial society, the United States, in Burnham's view, nevertheless exhibited the same economic problems and statist tendencies as did Germany and the Soviet Union. Although he cultivated his own special version of managerial ideology, he totally misinterpreted the central thrust of corporate capitalist development in the United States. Apart from his thesis that the ruling class of the finance-capital era was destined to be supplanted by corporate managers of the state who inherited the prerogatives of control established under capitalist rule, Burnham articulated no conception of corporate power. For an insightful critique of Burnham's argument, see Hans H. Gerth and C. Wright Mills, "A Marx for the Managers," *Ethics* 52 (1941–42): 200–215.

53. C. Wright Mills's description of the "managerial reorganization of the propertied classes into the more or less unified stratum of the corporate rich" is pertinent to the conception of class domination that I have in mind:

"What has happened, I believe, is the reorganization of the propertied class, along with those of higher salary, into a new corporate world of privilege and prerogative. What is significant about this managerial reorganization of the propertied class is that by means of it the narrow industrial and profit interests of specific firms and industries and families have been translated into the *broader economic and political interests of a more genuinely class type.* Now the corporate seats of the rich contain all the powers and privileges inherent in the institutions of private property." See Mills, *The Power Elite,* p. 147 (emphasis added). Mills also stated: "Not the politicians of the visible government, but the chief executives who sit in the political directorate, by fact and by proxy, hold the power and the means of defending the privileges of their corporate world. If they do not reign, they do govern at many of the vital points of everyday life in America, and no powers effectively and consistently countervail against them, nor have they as corporate-made men developed any effectively restraining conscience" (ibid., p. 125). It is indeed difficult to square Mills's empirical analysis of corporate power with his claim that it constituted a form of institutional control.

54. Michael Useem observes that the "inner circle" of the corporate elite "constitutes a distinct, politicized business segment, if a segment is defined as a subset of class members sharing a specific location with partially distinct interests. Though members of the inner circle share with other corporate managers a common commitment to enhancing company profits, their heightened sensitivity to business interests more general than those that look solely to support individual company profits also sets them apart." See Useem, *Inner Circle,* p. 61.

55. See above, Chapter 4, section 3.

56. "Management collectively opposed hostile takeovers through the coordinated efforts of the Business Roundtable, which helped assemble business, union, and academic interests into a coalition." See Kaufman and Zacharias, "From Trust to Contract," (see note 6 above), p. 562 n. 113, and sources listed therein.

57. On the significance of "restructuring," see above, Chapter 4, note 115.

58. The collective-bargaining procedures that are the basis of modern industrial relations, established in the Wagner Act in 1935 and administered by the National Labor Relations Board, have effectively integrated labor into the corporate structure and substantially eliminated the threat of revolutionary unionism. Clearly, the legal framework that has grown out of the New Deal envisions collective bargaining as a system for drawing up rules for employment, with the unions acting as agencies for enforcing those rules. In this sense, labor leaders and management work together to ensure the viability of the capitalist system, although the adversarial aspect of the relationship is retained in the bargaining process. With this in mind, C. Wright Mills described the structure of American industrial relations as "a kind of procapitalist syndicalism from the top." See Mills, "The Labor Leaders and the Power Elite," in Arthur Kornhauser, ed., *Industrial Conflict* (New York: McGraw-Hill, 1954), p. 151. On the Wagner Act and the evolution of labor law, see above, Chapter 4, note 30.

59. Marx's analysis of class relationships is both more complex and less coherent than is often attributed to him. See Tom Bottomore, *Theories of Modern Capitalism* (London: George Allen & Unwin, 1985), pp. 14–17. "Since Marx never completed (indeed scarcely began) that part of his work which was intended to analyze class relations in capitalist society, it is impossible to know how he would have brought together, in a rigorous theoretical scheme, his divergent observations on the class structure, or precisely how he conceived its further development and the consequences this might have for political struggles" (ibid., p. 16).

60. Kevin Phillips, *The Politics of Rich and Poor: Wealth and the American Electorate in the Reagan Aftermath* (New York: Harper Perennial, 1991); Thomas Byrne Edsall, "The Return of Inequality," *The Atlantic*, June 1988, pp. 89–90, 92–94.

61. "Beginning in the late sixties, a new force emerged in American politics: the public-interest movement. An important part of this movement consisted of a wide variety of law firms, research centers, lobbying groups, membership associations, and community organizations committed to public policies that attempted to reduce the power and privilege of business. By any measure, their impact has been impressive: throughout most of the 1970s, the relationship between regulatory and corporate officials was more strained than at any time since the 1930s. . . . In sum, public-interest groups are to the last decade what the trade-union movement was to the thirties and the muckrackers were to the Progressive Era: the driving force behind increased restrictions on corporate prerogatives." See David Vogel, "The Public-Interest Movement and the American Reform Tradition," *Political Science Quarterly* 95 (Winter 1980–81): 607. See also Vogel, *Fluctuating Fortunes*, pp. 93–112.

62. Irving Kristol, *Two Cheers for Capitalism* (New York: Basic Books, 1978); Paul Weaver, "Regulation, Social Policy, and Class Conflict," *Public Interest* 50 (Winter 1978): 45–63. Cf. Vogel, *Fluctuating Fortunes*, pp. 98–100; B. Bruce-Brigges, ed., *The New Class* (New Brunswick, N.J.: Transaction Books, 1979).

63. Vogel, *Fluctuating Fortunes*, pp. 95–96. Although he has not ascribed a class consciousness to the public-interest movement of the 1970s, David Vogel has described the movement's objectives and view of itself in terms somewhat similar to those I have employed: "The central political mission of the public-interest movement is to enable those affected by corporate decisions in their roles as citizens, comsumers, and taxpayers to have the same influence over public policy as business." See Vogel, "Public-Interest Movement," p. 622.

64. The frequent charge or criticism that the leadership of the movement was "elitist" does not undermine the authenticity of the class-conscious character of its political activity. But this observation applies only insofar as one can speak óf an actual movement, as opposed to professional lobbies that represent various "public interests" in the traditional manner of interest-group politics.

65. Vogel, *Fluctuating Fortunes*, pp. 148–68. Kim McQuaid, *Big Business and Presidential Power: From FDR to Reagan* (New York: William Morrow and Co., 1982), pp. 301–3. See also above, Chapter 4, section 3b.

66. For example, see Serge Mallet, *The New Working Class* (Nottingham: Bertrand Russell Peace Foundation for Spokesman Books, 1975); Andre Gorz, *A Strategy for Labor* (Boston: Beacon Press, 1967); James O'Connor, "Some Contradictions of Advanced U.S. Capitalism," *Social Theory and Practice* 1 (Spring 1970): 1–11; Bogdan Denitch, "Is There a New Working Class?" *Dissent* 17 (July–August 1970): 351–55; Donald C. Hodges, "Old and New Working Classes," *Radical America* 5 (January–February 1971), pp. 11–32; Michael Harrington, "Old Working Class, New Working Class," *Dissent* 19 (Winter 1972): 328–343; Stanley Aronowitz, "Does the United States Have a New Working Class?" in George Fisher, ed., *The Revival of American Socialism* (New York: Oxford University Press, 1971), pp. 188–216; Harry Braverman, *Labor and Monopoly Capital* (New York: Monthly Review Press, 1974).

67. But this was not the case for all theorists who envisioned a new class structure. For some, technical knowledge and education had replaced property ownership as the basis of class domination. See Alain Touraine, *The Post-Industrial Society* (New York: Random House, 1971); Nicholas Abercrombie and John Urry, *Capital, Labour, and the Middle Classes* (London: George Allen & Unwin, 1983).

68. Martin J. Sklar's analysis of corporate liberalism succinctly conveys the adaptation of American ideology and political institutions to corporate capitalism:

"Corporate liberalism expressed the accommodation of corporate capitalism to representative government based on population, geographical district, and the American federalist tradition—it rejected syndicalism in this respect—while it afforded strong support to the shifting of the balance of decision-making initiative away from the electoral arena, party politics, and the legislative branch, to the executive and judicial branches of government and to extra-electoral bodies of experts and administrators insulated from the fluctuations of electoral politics. It gave expression to the dominant power of the capitalist class in society and in the state by validating a revised definition of property at law and by affirming a change in the rules of the market, while it embraced the political tradition of defining society as superior to the state in accordance with the doctrine of limited government under law—constitutional government. . . . To say the same things differently, the ascendancy of corporate liberalism represented an alternative to, and rejection of, the corporate state associated with European 'organicist' thought and politics of either the left or the right." See Martin Sklar, *Corporate Reconstruction*, p. 438.

69. Melman, *Pentagon Capitalism* (note 36 above), pp. 1–34.

70. Quoted in "Lewis F. Powell Jr.: His Warning Brought a New Era of Business Activism," *Nation's Business* 75 (August 1987): 66.

71. For a critique of Marxist approaches, see Richard L. Sklar, "On the Concept of Power in Political Economy," pp. 187–98; David G. Becker and Richard L. Sklar, "Why Postimperialism?" in David G. Becker et al., *Postimperialism: International Capitalism and Development in the Late Twentieth Century* (Boulder, Colo.: Lynne Rienner Publishers, 1987), pp. 1–18; David G. Becker, "Development, Democracy, and Dependency in Latin America: A Postimperialist View," in ibid., pp. 41–62; Robert Brenner, "The Origins of Capitalist Development: A Critique of Neo-Smithian Marxism," *New Left Review* 104 (1977): 25–92.

See also Richard L. Sklar, "Developmental Democracy," *Comparative Studies in History and Society* 29 (October 1987): 686–714.

Chapter 7

1. Walter E. Weyl, *American World Policies* (New York: Macmillan, 1917), p. 282.

2. Ibid., pp. 282–83.

3. On the early development of the multinational corporation, see Mira Wilkens, *The Maturing of Multinational Enterprise: American Business Abroad from 1914 to 1970* (Cambridge, Mass.: Harvard University Press, 1974). For the purposes of this analysis, a multinational or transnational corporation refers to a firm with subsidiaries located in two or more countries. Moreover, the subsidiaries of a transnational corporation are generally involved in production or in an economic activity that is not limited to trade. As it is commonly used, the term "multinational" does not necessarily describe the ownership and control of the company. For this reason, the term "transnational," which defines the enterprise by the nature of its activities, might be a more precise term. The structure and operations of the transnational or multinational corporation, however, do foster a global perspective within the enterprise, in the sense that decisions are made from the standpoint of the corporation's global activities and needs.

4. Wilkens, *Maturing*, p. 4; John Dunning and John Cantwell, *IRM Directory of Statistics of International Investment and Production* (New York: Washington Square Press, 1987), p. 254. See also DeAnne Julius, *Global Companies and Public Policy: The Growing Challenge of Foreign Direct Investment* (New York: Council on Foreign Relations Press, 1990).

5. Library of Congress study reported in Douglas Dowd, *The Twisted Dream: Capitalist Development in the United States Since 1976* (Cambridge, Mass.: Winthrop Publishers, 1977), pp. 255–56; Joseph L. Naar, *Across the Board* (New York: The Conference Board, 1980).

6. Calculations are based on "The 100 Largest U.S. Multinationals," *Forbes*, July 18, 1994, pp. 276–79; "The 100 Largest U.S. Multinationals," *Forbes*, July 25, 1988, pp. 248–50. For the top ten U.S. transnationals in 1993, the foreign revenue (as a percentage of total revenue) was 52.5 percent, and the foreign assets (as a percentage of total assets) were 44.5 percent. The companies included Exxon, General Motors, Mobil, IBM, Ford Motor, Texaco, Citicorp, E.I. du Pont de Nemours, Chevron, and Procter & Gamble. See also Eric S. Hardy, "The Forbes Foreign Rankings," *Forbes*, July 18, 1994, pp. 220–25; "The Global 1000: The World's Top Players," *Business Week*, July 11, 1994, pp. 54–56.

7. See Chapter 4, note 116.

8. A large and growing number of individuals have contributed to this ideological justification. I have chosen several authors on the basis of the representativeness and sophistication of their arguments. The group includes prominent individuals in business and academic professions, many of whom have been active in political affairs. One will also find examples of this ideological justification in television commercials that celebrate the social virtues of world capitalism. Beginning in the early 1970s, more focused (explicitly political) advocacy advertising by large corporations in television commercials and in newspaper and magazine ads and editorials conveyed messages consistent with this ideological viewpoint. Richard Barnet and Ronald Müller's discussion of "The Great Crusade for Understanding" documented examples of this effort. See *Global Reach: The Power of Multinational Corporations* (New York: Simon & Schuster, 1974), pp. 105–22. More recently, the premises and objectives of modern Free Trade ideology have been articulated by influential political leaders in the United States—among them former Secretary of State James Baker and Presidents Ronald Reagan, George Bush, and Bill Clinton.

9. See Richard L. Sklar, "Postimperialism: A Class Analysis of Multinational Corporate Expansion," in David G. Becker et al., *Postimperialism: International Capitalism and Development in the Late Twentieth Century* (Boulder, Colo.: Lynne Rienner Publishers, 1987), p. 32, (reprinted from *Comparative Politics* 9 [October 1976]: 75–92). Sklar observes: "The corporate bourgeoisie, based mainly in the industrial capitalist countries, includes a corporate international segment. The managerial bourgeoisie [i.e., the ruling stratum of the national bourgeoisie] of the newly developing, nonsocialist countries also overlaps with the corporate international bourgeoisie. These transnational extensions of, and linkages between, comparable segments of the bourgeoisie depend upon the creation and perfection of transnational institutions. The multinational corporation is probably the most effective institution for this purpose. It should, therefore, be analyzed and understood in terms of transnational class development. In this process, the bourgeoisie, true to its epoch-making tradition, has taken the lead" (ibid., pp. 31–32). See also David G. Becker, *The New Bourgeoisie and the Limits of Dependency: Mining, Class, and Power in "Revolutionary" Peru* (Princeton: Princeton University Press, 1983); Irving Louis Horowitz, "Capitalism, Communism, and Multinationalism," in Abdul A. Said and Luiz R. Simmons, eds., *The New Sovereigns: Multinational Corporations as World Powers* (Englewood Cliffs, N.J.: Prentice-Hall, 1975), pp. 120–38. Horowitz states: "By internationalizing capital relations, multinationals have also internationalized class relationships" (p. 129).

10. David Rockefeller, "Multinationals Under Siege," *International Finance*, May 19, 1975, p. 8.

11. George W. Ball, "Cosmocorp: The Importance of Being Stateless," *Columbia Journal of World Business* 2 (November–December 1967): 26.

12. Peter F. Drucker, *The Age of Discontinuity: Guidelines to Our Changing Times* (New York: Harper & Row, 1968), p. 93. See also Drucker, "Multinationals and Developing Countries: Myths and Realities," *Foreign Affairs* 53 (October 1974): 133.

13. Drucker, *Age of Discontinuity*, p. 80.

14. Raymond Vernon, a leading scholar on multinational enterprise, holds the view that the worldwide revolution in communications has created the condition for the tremendous growth of multinational corporations. See Vernon, *Storm over the Multinationals: The Real Issues* (Cambridge, Mass.: Harvard University Press, 1977).

15. A. A. Berle, *The 20th Century Capitalist Revolution* (New York: Harcourt, Brace & World, 1954), pp. 157–58.

16. Ibid., p. 159.

17. Ball, "Cosmocorp," p. 27; Ball, "The Promise of the Multinational Corporation," *Fortune*, June 1, 1967, p. 80.

18. Ball, "Cosmocorp," p. 27.

19. Ball, "Multinational Corporations and Nation States," *Atlantic Community Quarterly* 5 (Summer 1967): 249.

20. Norman McCord, *The Anti-Corn Law League 1838–1846* (London: George Allen & Unwin, 1958), p. 32.

21. John A. Hobson, *Richard Cobden: The International Man* (London: T. Fisher Unwin, 1918), esp. pp. 9–25.

22. Lord Welby, *Cobden's Works and Opinions*, p. 18, quoted in ibid., p. 20.

23. Neil H. Jacoby, "The Multinational Corporation," *Center Magazine* 3 (May 1970): 54; Jacoby, *Corporate Power and Social Responsibility: A Blueprint for the Future* (New York: Macmillan, 1973), p. 122.

24. A. W. Clausen, "The Internationalized Corporation: An Executive's View," *Annals of the American Academy of Political and Social Science* 403 (September 1972): 21.

25. Drucker, *Age of Discontinuity*, p. 101.

26. Ball, "Promise of the Multinational Corporation," p. 80.

27. Courtney C. Brown, "Prologue to a New World Symphony?" in Courtney C. Brown, ed., *World Business: Promise and Problems* (New York: Macmillan, 1970), p. 6.

28. Drucker, "Myths and Realities," p. 134. See also Drucker's *Age of Discontinuity*, pp. 100–101.

29. Brown, "Prologue," p. 7.

30. Rockefeller, "Multinationals Under Siege," p. 7. See also Jacoby, "The Multinational Corporation," p. 43.

31. Jacoby, *Corporate Power and Social Responsibility*, pp. 118–21; Jacoby, "The Multinational Corporation," pp. 53–54.

32. Clausen, "The Internationalized Corporation," p. 19.

33. Ball, "Cosmocorp," p. 28.

34. Rockefeller, "Multinationals Under Siege," p. 7.

35. Jacoby, "The Multinational Corporation," p. 46.

36. Clearly, one ideological objective of the corporate internationalists has been to obscure or deemphasize the issue of corporate power by invoking the logic of laissez-faire. Even Berle and Drucker, the two liberal thinkers most responsible for developing the concept of the corporation as a social and political institution, do not squarely face the issue of transnational corporate power. Although he argues that global corporations employ what amounts to a diplomatic staff that conducts foreign policy, Berle nevertheless maintains that the corporation in international life is "an experiment in non-national organization, pledged only to discharge certain economic functions." See Berle, *20th Century Capitalist Revolution*, p. 163. To Drucker, the multinational corporation is a "non-national institution" that "is not a political institution itself and must not be allowed to become one." Drucker, *Men, Ideas, and Politics* (New York: Harper & Row, 1971), p. 43.

37. Ball, "Cosmocorp," p. 28.

38. Richard Sklar, "Postimperialism," p. 29. Sklar first developed the doctrine of domicile in *Corporate Power in an African State: The Political Impact of Multinational Mining Companies in Zambia* (Berkeley and Los Angeles: University of California Press, 1975). On the doctrine of domicile, also consult David G. Becker, "'Bonanza Development' and the 'New Bourgeoisie': Peru Under Military Rule," in Becker et al., *Postimperialism*, pp. 63–105 (reprinted from *Comparative Political Studies* 15, no. 3 [1982]: 243–88).

39. Martin J. Sklar, *The Corporate Reconstruction of American Capitalism, 1890–1916: The Market, the Law, and Politics* (Cambridge: Cambridge University Press, 1988), p. 13. See also, on capitalism as a social movement, Richard L. Sklar, "Beyond Capitalism and Socialism in Africa," *Journal of Modern African Studies* 26 (March 1988): 1–21; David G. Becker, "Beyond Dependency: Development and Democracy in the Era of International Capitalism," in Dankwart A. Rustow and Kenneth Paul Erickson, eds., *Comparative Political Dynamics: Global Research Perspectives* (New York: Harper-Collins, 1991), pp. 98–133.

40. Brown "Prologue" (note 27 above), pp. 11–12.

41. See Chapter 4, note 52.

42. Concerning the merger wave and the transnational aspect of Justice Department antitrust policy, see above, Chapter 4, section 5, esp. notes 100, 116, 117, 118, and 121.

43. See Chapter 4, section 5.

44. Samuel Huntington, "Transnational Organizations in World Politics," *World Politics* 25 (April 1973): 341.

45. *EEC Merger Regulation*, Council Regulation (EEC) No. 4064/89. Cf. Barry E. Hawk, "The EEC Merger Regulation: The First Step Toward One-Stop Merger Control," *Antitrust Law Journal* 59 (March 1990): 195–243; Charles E. Mueller, "Antitrust and Economics: The Gulf Between Science and Policy in the U.S.," *Antitrust Law & Economics Review*, (1990): 1–

18; Horst Satzky, "New EEC Antitrust Regime for Joint Ventures," *International Business Lawyer* 18 (December 1990): 518–21.

46. Don R. Wright, "The EC Single market in 1991: Status Report," *Business America*, February 25, 1991, pp. 12–14.

47. The North American Free Trade Agreement was passed by the House on November 17, 1993, and by the Senate on November 20, 1993. NAFTA revised the U.S.-Canada Free Trade Agreement of 1988 and extended the principles of that agreement to all of North America.

Selected Bibliography

Ackerman, Robert, and Raymond Bauer. *Corporate Social Responsiveness: The Modern Dilemma*. Reston, Va.: Reston Publishing Co., 1976.

Alexander, Herbert E. *Financing Politics: Money, Elections, and Political Reform*. Washington, D.C.: Congressional Quarterly Press, 1980.

Alexander, Herbert E., and Brian A. Haggerty. *Financing the 1984 Election*. Lexington, Mass.: D. C. Heath, Lexington Books, 1987.

Allen, Michael P. "Management Control in the Large Corporation: Comment on Zeitlin." *American Journal of Sociology* 81 (January 1976): 885–94.

————. "The Structure of Interorganizational Elite Cooptation: Interlocking Corporate Directorates." *American Sociological Review* 39 (June 1974): 393–406.

Angell, Joseph K., and Samuel Ames. *A Treatise on the Law of Private Corporations Aggregate*. Boston: Hilliard, Gray, Little & Wilkins, 1832.

Appleby, Joyce. *Capitalism and a New Social Order: The Republican Vision of the 1790s*. New York: New York University Press, 1984.

Areeda, Phillip. *Antitrust Analysis*. Third edition. Boston: Little, Brown, 1981.

Arnold, Thurman W. *The Folklore of Capitalism*. New Haven: Yale University Press, 1937.

————. *The Symbols of Government*. New Haven: Yale University Press, 1935.

Ashcraft, Richard. *Revolutionary Politics and Locke's Two Treatises of Government*. Princeton: Princeton University Press, 1986.

Axel, Helen. *Political Activism: The Chief Executive's Role*. New York: The Conference Board, 1980.

Bachrach, Peter. *The Theory of Democratic Elitism: A Critique*. Boston: Little, Brown, 1967.

Bailyn, Bernard. *The Ideological Origins of the American Revolution*. Cambridge, Mass.: Harvard University Press, 1967.

Bain, Joe S. "Industrial Concentration and Antitrust Policy." In Harold F. Williamson, ed., *The Growth of the American Economy*. New York: Prentice-Hall, 1951.

Baldwin, Simeon E. "American Business Corporations Before 1789." *Annual Report of the American Historical Association* 1 (December 1902): 257–73.

Ball, George W. "Cosmocorp: The Importance of Being Stateless." *Columbia Journal of World Business* 2 (November–December 1967): 25–30.

————. "Multinational Corporations and Nation States." *Atlantic Community Quarterly* 5 (Summer 1967): 247–53.

————. "The Promise of the Multinational Corporation." *Fortune*, June 1, 1967, p. 80.

Ballantine, Henry Winthrop. *Ballantine on Corporations*. Revised edition. Chicago: Callaghan & Co., 1946.

Baltzell, E. Digby. *An American Business Aristocracy*. New York: Collier Books, 1962.

Baran, Paul A. *The Political Economy of Growth*. New York: Monthly Review Press, 1957.

Baran, Paul A., and Paul M. Sweezy. *Monopoly Capital: An Essay on the American Economic and Social Order*. New York: Monthly Review Press, 1966.

Baratz, Morton S. "Corporate Giants and the Power Structure." *Western Political Quarterly* 9 (June 1956): 406–15.

Barber, Richard J. *The American Corporation: Its Power, Its Money, Its Politics*. New York: E. P. Dutton, 1970.

Baritz, Loren. *The Good Life: The Meaning of Success for the American Middle Class*. New York: Knopf, 1988.

_____. *The Servants of Power: A History of the Use of Social Sciences in American Industry*. New York: Wiley, 1960.

Barnet, Richard, and Ronald Müller. *Global Reach: The Power of Multinational Corporations*. New York: Simon & Schuster, 1974.

Barrow, Clyde W. *Critical Theories of the State: Marxist, Neo-Marxist, Post-Marxist*. Madison, Wisc.: University of Wisconsin Press, 1993.

_____. *Universities and the Capitalist State: Corporate Liberalism and the Reconstruction of American Higher Education, 1894–1928*. Madison: University of Wisconsin Press, 1990.

Bauer, Raymond, Ithiel de Sola Pool, and Lewis A. Dexter. *American Business and Public Policy*. Chicago: Aldine, Athanon, 1963.

Becker, David G. " 'Bonanza Development' and the 'New Bourgeoisie': Peru Under Military Rule." *Comparative Political Studies* 15, no. 3 (1982): 243–88; reprinted in David G. Becker et al., *Postimperialism: International Capitalism and Development in the Late Twentieth Century* (Boulder, Colo.: Lynne Rienner Publishers, 1987), pp. 63–105.

_____. "Development, Democracy, and Dependency in Latin America: A Postimperialist View." In David G. Becker et al., *Postimperialism: International Capitalism and Development in the Late Twentieth Century*, pp. 41–62, Boulder, Colo.: Lynne Rienner Publishers, 1987.

_____. *The New Bourgeoisie and the Limits of Dependency: Mining, Class, and Power in "Revolutionary" Peru*. Princeton: Princeton University Press, 1983.

Becker, David G., Jeff Frieden, Sayre P. Schatz, and Richard L. Sklar. *Postimperialism: International Capitalism and Development in the Late Twentieth Century*. Boulder, Colo.: Lynne Rienner Publishers, 1987.

Becker, David G., and Richard L. Sklar. "Why Postimperialism?" In David G. Becker et al., *Postimperialism: International Capitalism and Development in the Late Twentieth Century*, pp. 1–18. Boulder, Colo.: Lynne Rienner Publishers, 1987.

Bellamy, Edward. *Looking Backward, 2000–1887*. New York: New American Library, 1960.

Berle, Adolph A., Jr. *The American Economic Republic*. New York: Harcourt, Brace and World, Inc., 1963.

_____. "Constitutional Limitations on Corporate Activity: Protection of Personal Rights from Invasion Through Economic Power." *University of Pennsylvania Law Review* 100 (May 1952): 933–55.

_____. "Control in Corporate Power." *Columbia Law Review* 58 (December 1958): 1212–25.

_____. "Corporate Devices for Diluting Stock Participation." *Columbia Law Review* 31 (December 1931): 1239–65.

———. "Corporate Powers as Powers in Trust." *Harvard Law Review* 44 (May 1931): 1049–79.

———. "Corporations and the Modern State." In *The Future of Democratic Capitalism*, pp. 35–62. Philadelphia: University of Pennsylvania Press, 1950.

———. "Economic Power and the Free Society." In *The Corporation Take-Over*, edited by Andrew Hacker, pp. 86–102. Garden City, N.Y.: Anchor Books, Doubleday & Co., 1965.

———. "For Whom Corporate Managers *Are* Trustees: A Note." *Harvard Law Review* 45 (June 1932): 1365–72.

———. "Legal Problems of Economic Power." *Columbia Law Review* 60 (January 1960): 4–23.

———. *Natural Selection of Political Forces*. Lawrence: University of Kansas Press, 1950.

———. *Power*. New York: Harcourt, Brace & World, 1969.

———. *Power Without Property: A New Development in American Political Economy*. New York: Harcourt, Brace and World, 1959.

———. "The Price of Power: Sale of Corporate Control." *Cornell Law Quarterly* 50 (Summer 1965): 628–40.

———. *Studies in the Law of Corporation Finance*. Chicago: Callaghan & Co., 1928.

———. *The Three Faces of Power*. New York: Harcourt, Brace & World, 1967.

———. *The 20th Century Capitalist Revolution*. New York: Harcourt, Brace & World, 1954.

Berle, Adolf A., Jr., and Roswell Magill. *Cases and Materials in the Law of Corporation Finance*. St. Paul, Minn.: West Publishing Co., 1942.

Berle, Adolf A., Jr., and Gardiner C. Means. *The Modern Corporation and Private Property*. Revised edition. New York: Harcourt, Brace, & World, 1967.

Berman, Harold J. *Law and Revolution: The Formation of the Western Legal Tradition*. Cambridge, Mass.: Harvard University Press, 1983.

Bernhardt, William G. "Constitutional Law: Campaign Finance Reform and the First Amendment—All the Free Speech Money Can Buy." *Oklahoma Law Review* 39 (Winter 1986): 729–49.

Bernstein, Irving. *The Turbulent Years*. Boston: Houghton Mifflin, 1970.

Bernstein, Marver. *Regulating Business by Independent Commission*. Princeton: Princeton University Press, 1955.

Berry, Charles H. *Corporate Growth and Diversification*. Princeton: Princeton University Press, 1975.

BeVier, Lillian R. "Money and Politics: A Perspective on the First Amendment and Campaign Finance Reform." *California Law Review* 73 (July 1985): 1045–90.

Billet, Leonard. "The Just Economy: The Moral Basis of the *Wealth of Nations*." *Review of Social Economy* 34 (December 1976): 295–315.

———. "Political Order and Economic Development: Reflections on Adam Smith's *Wealth of Nations*." *Political Studies* 23 (December 1975): 430–41.

Blackburn, Robin, ed. *Ideology in Social Science: Readings in Critical Social Theory*. Glasgow: William Collins Sons & Co., 1972.

Blackstone, William. "Of Corporations." In *Commentaries on the Laws of England*. Seventeenth edition, vol. 1, chap. xviii. London: Thomas Tegg, 1830.

Blair, John M. *Economic Concentration*. New York: Harcourt Brace Jovanovich, 1972.

Block, Dennis J., Nancy E. Barton, and Stephen A. Radin. *The Business Judgment*

Rule: Fiduciary Duties of Corporate Directors. Third edition. Englewood Cliffs, N.J.: Prentice-Hall Law and Business, 1989.

Block, Fred. *Postindustrial Possibilities.* Berkeley and Los Angeles: University of California Press, 1990.

_____. "The Ruling Class Does Not Rule: Notes on the Marxist Theory of the State." *Socialist Revolution* 33 (July–September 1977): 6–28.

Blumberg, Phillip I. *The Megacorporation in American Society: The Scope of Corporate Power.* Englewood Cliffs, N.J.: Prentice-Hall, 1975.

Blumenthal, Sidney. *The Rise of the Counter-Establishment: From Conservative Ideology to Political Power.* New York: Harper & Row, 1986.

Bock, Betty, et al. *Restructuring and Antitrust.* New York: The Conference Board, 1987.

Bork, Robert H. *The Antitrust Paradox: A Policy at War with Itself.* New York: Basic Books, 1975.

Bottomore, Tom. *Sociology and Socialism.* Sussex: Wheatsheaf Books, 1984.

_____. *Theories of Modern Capitalism.* London: George Allen & Unwin, 1985.

Bowles, Samuel, and Herbert Gintis. *Democracy and Capitalism: Property, Community, and the Contradictions of Modern Social Thought.* New York: Basic Books, 1987.

Bradshaw, Thornton, and David Vogel, eds. *Corporations and Their Critics: Issues and Answers to the Problem of Corporate Social Responsibility.* New York: McGraw-Hill, 1981.

Brand, Donald R. *Corporatism and the Rule of Law: A Study of the National Recovery Administration.* Ithaca: Cornell University Press, 1988.

Brecht, Arnold. *Political Theory: The Foundations of Twentieth-Century Political Thought.* Princeton: Princeton University Press, 1959.

Brewster, Kingman, Jr. "The Corporation and Economic Federalism." In *The Corporation in Modern Society,* edited by Edward S. Mason, pp. 72–84. Cambridge, Mass.: Harvard University Press, 1961.

_____. "Enforceable Competition: Unruly Reason or Reasonable Rules?" *American Economic Review* 46 (May 1956): 482–89.

Breyer, Stephen. *Regulation and Its Reform.* Cambridge, Mass.: Harvard University Press, 1982.

Brown, Courtney C. "Prologue to a New World Symphony?" In *World Business: Promise and Problems,* edited by Courtney C. Brown, pp. 3–12. New York: Macmillan, 1970.

Brown, Richard D. *Modernization: The Transformation of American Life, 1600–1865.* New York: Hill & Wang, 1976.

Brudney, Victor. "Business Corporations and Stockholders' Rights Under the First Amendment." *Yale Law Journal* 91 (December 1981): 235–95.

_____. "The Independent Director: Heavenly City or Potemkin Village?" *Harvard Law Review* 95 (January 1982): 597–659.

Brummer, James J. *Corporate Responsibility and Legitimacy: An Interdisciplinary Analysis.* New York: Greenwood Press, 1991.

Buchanan, Scott. "The Corporation and the Republic." In *The Corporation Take-Over,* edited by Andrew Hacker. pp. 17–39. Garden City, N.Y.: Anchor Books, 1965.

Burch, Philip H., Jr. "The Business Roundtable: Its Make-up and External Ties." In *Research in Political Economy,* edited by Paul Zarembka. 4:101–27. Greenwich, Conn.: JAI Press, 1977.

_____. *Elites in American History.* 3 vols. New York: Holmes & Meier, 1980.

_____. *The Managerial Revolution Reassessed.* Lexington, Mass.: D. C. Heath, 1972.

Burnham, James. *The Managerial Revolution: What Is Happening in the World.* New York: John Day Co., Inc., 1941.

Burris, Vallon. "The Political Partisanship of American Business." *American Sociological Review* 52 (December 1987): 732–44.

Cadman, John W., Jr. *The Corporation in New Jersey.* Cambridge, Mass.: Harvard University Press, 1949.

Carter, James Treat. *The Nature of the Corporation as a Legal Entity.* Baltimore: M. Curlander, 1919.

Cary, William L. *Cases and Materials on Corporations.* Fourth edition. Mineola: Foundation Press, 1969.

_____. "Federalism and Corporate Law: Reflections upon Delaware." *Yale Law Journal* 83 (March 1974): 663–705.

Catlin, George E. Gordon. *Systematic Politics: Elementa Politica et Sociologica.* Toronto: University of Toronto Press, 1962.

Chandler, Alfred D., Jr. "The Beginnings of 'Big Business' in American Industry." *Business History Review* 33 (Spring 1959): 1–31.

_____. *The Essential Alfred Chandler: Essays Toward a Historical Theory of Big Business.* Edited by Thomas K. McCraw. Boston, Mass.: Harvard Business School Press, 1988.

_____. *The Railroads: The Nation's First Big Business.* New York: Harcourt, Brace & World, 1965.

_____. *Scale and Scope: The Dynamics of Industrial Capitalism.* Cambridge, Mass.: Harvard University Press, Belknap Press, 1990.

_____. *Strategy and Structure: Chapters in the History of Industrial Enterprise.* Cambridge, Mass.: MIT Press, 1962.

_____. *The Visible Hand: The Managerial Revolution in American Business.* Cambridge, Mass.: Harvard University Press, Belknap Press, 1977.

Chandler, Alfred D., Jr., and Herman Daems, eds. *Managerial Hierarchies: Comparative Perspectives on the Rise of Modern Industrial Enterprise.* Cambridge, Mass.: Harvard University Press, 1980.

Chandler, Alfred D., Jr., and Richard S. Tedlow. *The Coming of Managerial Capitalism: A Casebook on the History of American Economic Institutions.* Homewood, Ill.: Richard D. Irwin, 1985.

Chayes, Abraham. "The Modern Corporation and the Rule of Law." In *The Corporation in Modern Society*, edited by Edward S. Mason, pp. 25–45. Cambridge, Mass.: Harvard University Press, 1961.

Cheit, Earl F. *The Business Establishment.* New York: John Wiley & Sons, 1964.

Clark, John Bates. *The Problem of Monopoly: A Study of a Grave Danger and of the Natural Mode of Averting It.* New York: Macmillan, 1904.

Clausen, A. W. "The Internationalized Corporation: An Executive's View." *Annals of the American Academy of Political and Social Science* 403 (September 1972): 12–21.

Clawson, Dan, Alan Neustadl, and James Beardon. "The Logic of Business Unity: Corporate Contributions to the 1980 Congressional Elections." *American Sociological Review* 51 (December 1986): 797–811.

Coase, R. H. *The Firm, the Market, and the Law.* Chicago: University of Chicago Press, 1988.

Cochran, Thomas C. *Business in American Life: A History*. New York: McGraw-Hill, 1972.

Cochran, Thomas C., and William Miller . *The Age of Enterprise: A Social History of Industrial America*. Revised edition. New York: Harper & Row, 1961.

Colson, Clyde L. "The Doctrine of *Ultra Vires* in United States Supreme Court Decisions." *West Virginia Law Quarterly* 42 (April 1936): 179–217, 297–337.

Commons, John R. *Legal Foundations of Capitalism*. New York: Macmillan, 1924.

Cook, William W. *The Corporation Problem*. New York: Knickerbocker Press, 1893.

Cooley, Thomas M. *Constitutional Limitations*. Eighth edition. Boston: Little, Brown, 1927.

Corporations: Selected Essays Reprinted from the Harvard Law Review. Cambridge, Mass.: Harvard Law Review Association, 1963.

Corwin, Edward S. "The Basic Doctrine of American Constitutional Law." *Michigan Law Review* 12 (February 1914): 247–76.

―――. "The 'Higher Law' Background of American Constitutional Law." *Harvard Law Review* 42 (December 1928), 149–85, 365–409.

―――. *The Twilight of the Supreme Court*. New Haven: Yale University Press, 1934.

Croly, Herbert. *Progressive Democracy*. New York: Macmillan, 1915.

―――. *The Promise of American Life*. New Brunswick, N.J.: Transaction, 1993.

Dahl, Robert A. *Dilemmas of Pluralist Democracy*. New Haven: Yale University Press, 1982.

―――. "On Removing Certain Impediments to Democracy in the United States." *Political Science Quarterly* 92 (Spring 1977): 1–20.

―――. *A Preface to Democratic Theory*. Chicago: University of Chicago Press, 1956.

―――. *Who Governs? Democracy and Power in an American City*. New Haven: Yale University Press, 1961.

Davis, Joseph Stancliffe. *Essays in the Earlier History of Corporations*. 2 vols. Cambridge, Mass.: Harvard University Press, 1917.

Dent, George W. "The Power of Directors to Terminate Shareholder Litigation: The Death of the Derivative Suit?" *Northwestern Law Review* 75 (March 1980): 96–146.

Dewey, John. *Democracy and Education: An Introduction to the Philosophy of Education*. New York: Macmillan, 1919.

―――. *Freedom and Culture*. New York: G. P. Putnam's Sons, 1939.

―――. "The Historic Background of Corporate Legal Personality." *Yale Law Journal* 35 (April 1926): 655–73.

―――. *Individualism Old and New*. New York: Minton, Balch & Co., 1930.

―――. *Liberalism and Social Action*. New York: G. P. Putnam's Sons, 1935.

―――. *The Public and Its Problems*. Denver: Alan Swallow, 1927.

Diggins, John P. *The Lost Soul of American Politics: Virtue, Self-Interest, and the Foundation of Liberalism*. New York: Basic Books, 1984.

Dobb, Maurice. *Theories of Value and Distribution Since Adam Smith: Ideology and Economic Theory*. Cambridge: Cambridge University Press, 1973.

Dobrzynski, Judith H. "The Battle for Corporate Control." *Business Week*. May 18, 1987, p. 103.

―――. "A New Strain of Merger Mania." *Business Week*, March 21, 1988, pp. 122–34.

Dodd, Edwin Merrick. *American Business Corporations Until 1860*. Cambridge, Mass.: Harvard University Press, 1954.

_____. "For Whom Are Corporate Managers Trustees?" *Harvard Law Review* 45 (May 1932): 1145–63.

_____. "Statutory Developments in Business Corporation Law, 1886-1936." *Harvard Law Review* 50 (November 1936): 27–59.

Domhoff, G. William. *The Bohemian Grove and Other Retreats: A Study in Ruling Class Cohesiveness*. New York: Harper & Row, 1974.

_____. *The Higher Circles: The Governing Class in America*. New York: Random House, 1970.

_____. *The Powers That Be: Process of Ruling Class Domination in America*. New York: Random House, 1979.

_____. "Social Clubs, Political Groups, and Corporations: A Network Study of Ruling Class Cohesiveness." *Insurgent Sociologist* 5 (Spring 1975): 173–84.

_____. *Who Rules America?* Englewood Cliffs, N.J.: Prentice-Hall, 1967.

Dooley, Peter C. "The Interlocking Directorate." *American Economic Review* 59 (June 1969): 314–23.

Dorfman, Joseph. *The Economic Mind in American Civilization*. Vols. 1 and 2: *1606–1865*; vol. 3: *1865–1918*. New York: Viking Press, 1946 and 1949.

_____. *Thorstein Veblen and His America*. New York: Viking Press, 1934.

_____, ed. *Thorstein Veblen: Essays, Reviews, and Reports*. Clifton, N.J.: Augustus M. Kelley Publishers, 1973.

Drinker, Henry S. "The Preemptive Right of Shareholders to Subscribe to New Shares." *Harvard Law Review* 43 (February 1930): 586–616.

Drucker, Peter F. *The Age of Discontinuity: Guidelines to Our Changing Times*. New York: Harper & Row, 1968.

_____. *Concept of the Corporation*. New York: John Day Co., 1946.

_____. *The End of Economic Man: A Study of the New Totalitarianism*. London: William Heinemann, 1939.

_____. *The Future of Industrial Man: A Conservative Approach*. New York: John Day Co., 1942.

_____. *Landmarks of Tomorrow*. New York: Harper & Brothers, 1957.

_____. *Men, Ideas, and Politics*. New York: Harper & Row, Publishers, 1971.

_____. "Multinationals and Developing Countries: Myths and Realities." *Foreign Affairs* 53 (October 1974): 121–34.

_____. *The New Society: The Anatomy of the Industrial Order*. New York: Harper & Brothers, 1949.

Dubofsky, Melvyn. *Industrialism and the American Worker, 1865–1920*. New York: Thomas Y. Crowell Co., 1975.

Dubois, Armand. *The English Business Company After the Bubble Act, 1720–1800*. New York: Commonwealth Fund, 1938.

Dunning, John, and John Cantwell. *IRM Directory of Statistics of International Investment and Production*. New York: Washington Square Press, 1987.

Dworetz, Steven M. *The Unvarnished Doctrine: Locke, Liberalism, and the American Revolution*. Durham, N.C.: Duke University Press, 1990.

Dye, Thomas. "Oligarchic Tendencies in National Policy-Making: The Role of the Private Policy-Planning Organizations." *Journal of Politics* 40 (1978): 309–31.

Eakins, David. "Policy-Planning for the Establishment." In *A New History of*

Leviathan, edited by Ronald Radosh and Murray N. Rothbard. pp. 188–205. New York: E. P. Dutton, 1972,

Edsall, Thomas Byrne. *The New Politics of Inequality*. New York: W. W. Norton & Co., 1984.

———. *Power and Money: Writing About Politics, 1971–1987*. New York: W. W. Norton & Co., 1988.

Edwards, George W. *The Evolution of Finance Capitalism*. New York: Longmans, Green, 1938.

Einhorn, Henry Adler, and William Paul Smith, eds. *Economic Aspects of Antitrust: Readings and Cases*. New York: Random House, 1968.

Ekirch, Arthur A., Jr. *The Decline of American Liberalism*. New York: Atheneum, 1976.

Engler, Robert. *The Politics of Oil*. Chicago: University of Chicago Press, Phoenix Books, 1967.

Epstein, Edwin M. "The Business PAC Phenomenon: An Irony of Electoral Reform." *Regulation* 3 (1979): 35–41.

———. "Business Political Activity: Research Approaches and Analytical Uses." In *Research in Corporate Social Performance and Policy*, vol. 2, pp. 1–55. Greenwich, Conn.: JAI Press, 1980.

———. *The Corporation in American Politics*. Englewood Cliffs, N.J.: Prentice-Hall, 1969.

Evans, George Heberton, Jr. *Business Incorporations in the United States, 1800–1943*. New York: National Bureau of Economic Research, 1948.

Ewen, Stuart. *Captains of Consciousness: Advertising and the Social Roots of Consumer Culture*. New York: McGraw-Hill, 1976.

Fairman, Charles. *Reconstruction and Reunion, Part Two*. Edited by Paul A. Freund and Stanley N. Katz. Vol 7 of *The Oliver Wendell Holmes Devise History of the Supreme Court of the United States*. New York: Macmillan, 1987.

Ferguson, Thomas, and Joel Rogers. "The Knights of the Roundtable." *The Nation*, December 15, 1979, pp. 620–25.

———. *Right Turn: The Decline of the Democrats and the Future of American Politics*. New York: Hill & Wang, 1986.

Fisch, Jill E. "Frankenstein's Monster Hits the Campaign Trail: An Approach to Regulation of Corporate Political Expenditures." *William and Mary Law Review* 32 (Spring 1991): 587–643.

Fischel, Daniel R. "From Mite to CTS: State Anti-Takeover Statutes, the Commerce Clause, and Insider Trading." In *The Supreme Court Review*, pp. 47–95. Chicago: University of Chicago, 1988.

Fischel, Daniel R., and Michael Bradley. "The Role of Liability Rules and the Derivative Suit in Corporate Law: A Theoretical and Empirical Analysis." *Cornell Law Review* 71 (1986): 261–98.

Foner, Philip. *The History of the Labor Movement in the United States*. 4 vols. New York: International Publishers, 1975.

Forcey, Charles. *The Crossroads of Liberalism: Croly, Weyl, Lippmann, and the Progressive Era, 1900–1925*. New York: Oxford University Press, 1961.

Freyer, Tony A. "The Federal Courts, Localism, and the National Economy, 1865–1900." *Business History Review* 53 (Autumn 1979): 343–63.

———. *Forums of Order: The Federal Courts and Business in American History*. Greenwich, Conn.: JAI Press, 1979.

_____. *Regulating Big Business: Antitrust in Great Britain and America, 1880–1990.* Cambridge: Cambridge University Press, 1992.

Friedman, Lawrence M. *A History of American Law.* New York: Simon & Shuster, 1973.

Galambos, Louis. *The Public Image of Big Business in America, 1880–1940.* Baltimore: Johns Hopkins University Press, 1975.

_____. *The Rise of the Corporate Commonwealth: United States Business and Public Policy in the Twentieth Century.* New York: Basic Books, 1988.

Galbraith, John Kenneth. *The Affluent Society.* Boston: Houghton Mifflin, 1958.

_____. *American Capitalism: The Concept of Countervailing Power.* Boston: Houghton Mifflin, 1952.

_____. *The New Industrial State.* London: Hamish Hamilton, 1967.

Giddens, Anthony. *Capitalism and Modern Social Theory: An Analysis of the Writings of Marx, Durkheim, and Max Weber.* Cambridge: Cambridge University Press, 1971.

_____. "Classical Social Theory and the Origins of Modern Sociology." *American Journal of Sociology* 81 (January 1976): 703–29.

Gillman, Howard. *The Constitution Besieged: The Rise and Demise of Lochner Eva Police Powers Jurisprudence.* Durham, N.C.: Duke University Press, 1993.

Gilpin, Robert. *The Political Economy of International Relations.* Princeton: Princeton University Press, 1987.

_____. *U.S. Power and the Multinational Corporation: The Political Economy of Foreign Direct Investment.* New York: Basic Books, 1975.

Ginger, Ray. *The Bending Cross.* New Brunswick, N.J.: Rutgers University Press, 1949.

Goldman, Eric F. *Rendezvous with Destiny.* New York: Vintage Books, 1955.

Goldsmith, Raymond W., and Rexford C. Parmelee. *The Distribution of Ownership in the 200 Largest Nonfinancial Corporations.* Monographs of the Temporary National Economic Committee, no. 29. Washington, D.C.: Government Printing Office, 1940.

Gouldner, Alvin W. *The Coming Crisis of Western Sociology.* New York: Avon Books, 1971.

Graham, Howard Jay. "The Conspiracy Theory of the Fourteenth Amendment." *Yale Law Journal* 47 (January 1938): 371–403.

_____. "Justice Field and the Fourteenth Amendment." *Yale Law Journal* 52 (September 1943): 851–89.

Green, Mark J., and Andrew Buchsbaum. *The Corporate Lobbies: Political Profiles of the Business Roundtable and the Chamber of Commerce.* Washington, D.C.: Public Citizen, 1980.

Gutman, Herbert G. "The Worker's Search for Power: Labor in the Gilded Age." In *The Gilded Age,* edited by H. Wayne Morgan, pp. 38–68. Syracuse: Syracuse University Press, 1963.

Hacker, Andrew. "Politics and the Corporation." In *The Corporation Take-Over,* edited by Andrew Hacker, pp. 239–62. Garden City: Anchor Books, 1965.

Haines, Charles G. "Judicial Review of Legislation in the United States and the Doctrine of Vested Rights and of Implied Limitations on Legislatures." *Texas Law Review* 3 (December 1924): 1–43.

Hamilton, Alexander, John Jay, and James Madison. *The Federalist.* New York: Modern Library, 1937.

Hamilton, Robert W. *Cases and Materials on Corporations*. St. Paul, Minn.: West Publishing Co., 1981.

Hamilton, Walton H. "The Path of Due Process of Law." In *American Constitutional Law: Historical Essays*, edited by Leonard W. Levy, pp. 129–54. New York: Harper & Row, 1966.

———. *The Politics of Industry*. New York: Alfred A. Knopf, 1957.

Handler, Edward, and John R. Mulkern. *Business in Politics: Campaign Strategies of Corporate Political Action Committees*. Lexington, Mass.: Lexington Books, 1982.

Handlin, Oscar, and Mary F. Handlin. "Origins of the American Business Corporation." *Journal of Economic History* 5 (May 1945): 1–23.

Hart, H.L.A. *The Concept of Law*. Oxford: Clarendon Press, 1961.

Hartz, Louis. *Economic Policy and Democratic Thought: Pennsylvania, 1776–1860*. Chicago: Quadrangle Books, 1948.

———. *The Liberal Tradition in America: An Interpretation of American Political Thought Since the Revolution*. New York: Harcourt, Brace & World, 1955.

Hawley, Ellis W. *The New Deal and the Problem of Monopoly: A Study in Economic Ambivalence*. Princeton: Princeton University Press, 1966.

———. "The Study and Discovery of a 'Corporate Liberalism.' " *Business History Review* 52 (Autumn 1978): 309–20.

Heilbroner, Robert. *An Inquiry into the Human Prospect*. New York: W. W. Norton & Co., 1974.

———. *21st Century Capitalism*. New York: W. W. Norton & Co., 1993.

Henderson, Gerard Carl. *The Position of Foreign Corporations in American Constitutional Law: A Contribution to the History and Theory of Juristic Persons in Anglo-American Law*. Cambridge, Mass.: Harvard University Press, 1918.

Herman, Edward S. *Corporate Control, Corporate Power*. Cambridge: Cambridge University Press, 1981.

Hessen, Robert. *In Defense of the Corporation*. Stanford, Calif.: Hoover Institute Press, 1979.

———, ed. *Controlling the Giant Corporation: A Symposium*. Rochester, N.Y.: Center for Research in Government Policy and Business, 1982.

———, ed. *Does Big Business Rule America?* Washington, D.C.: Ethics and Public Policy Center, 1981.

Hill, Christopher. *The Century of Revolution, 1603–1714*. New York: W. W. Norton & Co., 1961.

Hindley, Brian V. "Separation of Ownership and Control in the Modern Corporation." *Journal of Law and Economics* 13 (April 1970): 185–221.

Hobson, John A. *Richard Cobden: The International Man*. London: T. Fisher Unwin, 1918.

Hofstadter, Richard. *The Age of Reform: From Bryan to F.D.R.* New York: Vintage Books, 1955.

———. *The American Political Tradition*. New York: Vintage Books, 1948.

———. *Social Darwinism in American Thought*. New York: George Braziller, 1955.

———. "William Leggett: Spokesman of Jacksonian Democracy." *Political Science Quarterly* 58 (December 1943): 581–94.

Horowitz, Irving Louis. "Capitalism, Communism, and Multinationalism." In *The New Sovereigns: Multinational Corporations as World Powers*, edited by Abdul A. Said and Luiz R. Simmons, pp. 120–38. Englewood Cliffs, N.J.: Prentice-Hall, 1975.

Horwitz, Morton J. "*Santa Clara* Revisited: The Development of Corporate Theory." *West Virginia Law Review* 88 (Winter 1985): 173–224.

_____. *The Transformation of American Law, 1780–1860*. Cambridge, Mass.: Harvard University Press, 1977.

_____. *The Transformation of American Law, 1870–1960: The Crisis of Legal Orthodoxy*. New York: Oxford University Press, 1992.

Hunt, B. C. *The Development of the Business Corporation in England, 1800–1867*. New York: Russell & Russell, 1936.

Huntington, Samuel. "Transnational Organizations in World Politics." *World Politics* 25 (April 1973): 333–68.

Hurst, James Willard. *Law and Markets in U.S. History*. Madison: University of Wisconsin Press, 1981.

_____. *Law and Social Order in the United States*. Ithaca: Cornell University Press, 1977.

_____. *Law and the Conditions of Freedom in the Nineteenth-Century United States*. Madison: University of Wisconsin Press, 1956.

_____. *The Legitimacy of the Business Corporation in the Law of the United States, 1780–1970*. Charlottesville: University Press of Virginia, 1970.

Hymer, Stephen. "The Multinational Corporation and the Law of Uneven Development." In *Economics and World Order from the 1970s to the 1990s*, edited by Jagdish N. Bhagwati, pp. 113–40. New York: Macmillan, 1972.

Jacoby, Neil H. *Corporate Power and Social Responsibility: A Blueprint for the Future*. New York: Macmillan, 1973.

_____. "The Multinational Corporation." *Center Magazine* 3 (May 1970): 37–55.

Jensen, Michael C. "The Takeover Controversy: The Corporate Restructuring of America." *Vital Speeches of the Day*, May 1, 1987, pp. 426–29.

Jessop, Bob. *The Capitalist State: Marxist Theories and Methods*. Oxford: Basil Blackwell, 1982.

Joseph, Lawrence B. "Corporate Political Power and Liberal Democratic Theory." *Polity* 15 (Winter 1982): 246–67.

Julius, DeAnne. *Global Companies and Public Policy: The Growing Challenge of Foreign Direct Investment*. New York: Council on Foreign Relations Press, 1990.

Kahn, Herman, ed. *The Future of the Corporation*. New York: Mason & Lipscomb, 1974.

Kairys, David, ed. *The Politics of Law: A Progressive Critique*. Revised edition. New York: Pantheon Books, 1990.

Kaufman, Allen and Lawrence Zacharias. "From Trust to Contract: The Legal Language of Managerial Ideology, 1920–1980." *Business History Review* 66 (Autumn 1992): 524–72.

Kaysen, Carl, and Donald F. Turner. *Antitrust Policy: An Economic and Legal Analysis*. Cambridge, Mass.: Harvard University Press, 1959.

Keynes, John Maynard. "The End of Laissez-Faire." *The Collected Writings of John Maynard Keynes*, vol. 9: *Essays in Persuasion*. New York: St. Martin's Press, London: Macmillan, 1972.

Kindleberger, Charles P., ed. *The International Corporation*. Cambridge, Mass.: MIT Press, 1970.

Kipnis, Ira. *The American Socialist Movement*. New York: Greenwood Press, 1968.

Kirkland, Edward Chase. *A History of American Economic Life*. New York: F. S. Crofts & Co., 1941.

————. *Industry Comes of Age: Business, Labor, and Public Policy, 1860–1897*. Chicago: Quadrangle Books, 1961.

Knepper, William E., and Dan Bailey. *Liability of Corporate Officers and Directors*. Fifth edition. 2 vols. Charlottesville, Va.: The Michie Co., 1993.

Kolko, Gabriel. *Railroads and Regulation, 1877–1916*. Princeton: Princeton University Press, 1965.

————. *The Triumph of Conservatism*. New York: The Free Press, 1963.

Kotz, David. *Bank Control of Large Corporations in the United States*. Berkeley and Los Angeles: University of Calif. Press, 1978.

Kristol, Irving. *Two Cheers for Capitalism*. New York: Basic Books, 1978.

Kuhn, Thomas S. *The Structure of Scientific Revolutions*. Second edition. Chicago: University of Chicago Press, 1970.

Kutler, Stanley I. *Privilege and Creative Destruction: The Charles River Bridge Case*. Philadelphia: J. B. Lippincott, 1971.

Kyd, Stewart. *Treatise on the Law of Corporations*. London: 1793–94.

Lamoreaux, Naomi R. *The Great Merger Movement in American Business, 1895–1904*. Cambridge: Cambridge University Press, 1985.

Larner, Robert J. *Management Control and the Large Corporation*. New York: Dunellen Publishing Co., 1970.

Laski, Harold J. *The Rise of Liberalism: The Philosophy of Business Civilization*. New York: Harper & Brothers., 1936.

Laslett, John H. M. *Labor and the Left: A Study of Socialist and Radical Influences Within the Labor Movement, 1881–1924*. New York: Basic Books, 1970.

Latham, Earl. "Anthropomorphic Corporations, Elites, and Monopoly Power." *American Economic Review* 47 (May 1957): 303–10.

————. "The Body Politic of the Corporation." In *The Corporation in Modern Society*, edited by Edward S. Mason, pp. 218–36. Cambridge, Mass.: Harvard University Press, 1961.

Latty, Elvin R. "Why Are Business Corporation Laws Largely 'Enabling'?" *Cornell Law Quarterly* 50 (1965): 599–619.

Lazonick, William. *Business Organization and the Myth of the Market Economy*. Cambridge: Cambridge University Press, 1991.

Letwin, William. *Law and Economic Policy in America: The Evolution of the Sherman Antitrust Act*. Edinburgh: University Press, 1966.

Levitan, Sar A., and Martha R. Cooper. *Business Lobbies: Public Good and the Bottom Line*. Baltimore: Johns Hopkins University Press, 1984.

Levy, David W. *Herbert Croly of "The New Republic": The Life and Thought of an American Progressive*. Princeton: Princeton University Press, 1985.

Levy, Leonard W. "Chief Justice Shaw and the Formative Period of American Railroad Law." *Columbia Law Review* 51 (March 1951): 327–48, 852–65.

Lichtheim, George. "The Concept of Ideology." *History and Theory* 4, no. 2 (1965): 164–95.

————. "Power and Ideology." *Partisan Review* 30 (Summer 1963): 241–55.

Lindblom, Charles E. *Politics and Markets: The World's Political-Economic Systems*. New York: Basic Books, 1977.

Link, Arthur S. *Wilson: The New Freedom*. Princeton: Princeton University Press, 1956.

Lippmann, Walter. *Drift and Mastery*. New York: Henry Holt & Co., 1917.

————. *A Preface to Morals*. New York: Macmillan, 1929.

_____. *Public Opinion*. New York: The Free Press, 1965.

Lofgren, Charles A. *The Plessy Case: A Legal-Historical Interpretation*. New York: Oxford University Press, 1987.

Lowi, Theodore J. "American Business, Public Policy, Case Studies, and Political Theory." *World Politics* 16 (July 1964): 677–715.

_____. *The End of Liberalism*. New York: W. W. Norton & Co., 1969.

Lundberg, Ferdinand. *America's Sixty Families*. New York: Vanguard, 1937.

_____. *The Rich and the Super-Rich*. New York: Lyle Stuart, 1968.

Lustig, R. Jeffrey. *Corporate Liberalism: The Origins of Modern American Political Theory, 1890–1920*. Berkeley and Los Angeles: University of California Press, 1982.

Lynd, Robert S. "Power in American Society as Resource and Problem." In *Problems of Power in American Democracy*, edited by Arthur Kornhauser, pp. 1–45. Detroit: Wayne State University Press, 1959.

Mace, Myles L. *Directors: Myth and Reality*. Boston: Division of Research, Graduate School of Business Administration, Harvard University, 1971.

Maine, Sir Henry Sumner. *Ancient Law: Its Connection with the Early History of Society and Its Relation to Modern Ideas*. London: John Murray, Albemarle Street, W., 1906; reprint ed., 1930.

Mannheim, Karl. *Ideology and Utopia: An Introduction to the Sociology of Knowledge*. New York: Harcourt, Brace & World, 1939.

Mariolis, Peter. "Interlocking Directorates and Control of Corporations." *Social Science Quarterly* 56 (December 1975): 425–39.

Mark, Gregory A. "The Personification of the Business Corporation in American Law." *University of Chicago Law Review* 54 (1987): 1441–83.

Markham, Jesse W. *Conglomerate Enterprise and Public Policy*. Boston: Division of Research, Graduate School of Business Administration, Harvard University, 1973.

Marx, Karl. *Capital*. Vols. 1–3. New York: Random House, 1906.

_____. *The Grundrisse*. Edited and translated by David McLellan. New York: Harper & Row, 1971.

_____. *Karl Marx: Early Writings*. Edited and translated by T. B. Bottomore. New York: McGraw-Hill, 1963.

_____. *The Marx-Engels Reader*. Edited by Robert C. Tucker. New York: W. W. Norton & Co., 1972.

_____. *The Poverty of Philosophy*. New York: International Publishers Co., 1963.

_____. *Pre-Capitalist Economic Formations*. Edited by Eric J. Hobsbawm. New York: International Publishers Co., 1965.

Marx, Karl, and Frederick Engels. *The German Ideology*. Edited by C. J. Arthur. New York: International Publishers Co., 1970.

Mason, Edward S., ed. *The Corporation in Modern Society*. Cambridge, Mass.: Harvard University Press, 1961.

Massaro, Vincent G. *Corporate Finance and the Changing U.S. Financial Structure*. New York: The Conference Board, 1980.

Masters, Marick F., and Gerald D. Keim. "The Determinants of PAC Participation Among Large Corporations." *Journal of Politics* 47 (November 1985): 1158–73.

Matasar, Ann B. *Corporate PACs and Federal Campaign Financing Laws: Use or Abuse of Power?* Westport, Conn.: Quorum Books, 1986.

McCahery, Joseph, Sol Picciotto, and Colin Scott, eds. *Corporate Control and Accountability: Changing Structures and the Dynamics of Regulation*. Oxford: Clarendon Press, 1993.

McConnell, Grant. *Private Power and American Democracy*. New York: Alfred A. Knopf, 1967.

McCord, Norman. *The Anti-Corn Law League, 1838–1846*. London: George Allen & Unwin, 1958.

McCraw, Thomas K. *Prophets of Regulation*. Cambridge, Mass.: Harvard University Press, Belknap Press, 1984.

McCurdy, Charles W. "American Law and the Marketing Structure of the Large Corporation, 1875–1890." *Journal of Economic History* 38 (September 1978): 631–49.

———. "Justice Field and the Jurisprudence of Government-Business Relations: Some Parameters of Laissez-Faire Constitutionalism, 1863–1897." *Journal of American History* 61 (1975): 970–1005.

———. "The *Knight* Sugar Decision of 1895 and the Modernization of American Corporation Law, 1869–1903." *Business History Review* 53 (Autumn 1979): 304–42.

McQuaid, Kim. *Big Business and Presidential Power: From FDR to Reagan*. New York: Morrow, 1982.

Means, Gardiner C. *The Corporate Revolution in America: Economic Reality vs. Economic Theory*. New York: Crowell-Collier, 1962.

Melman, Seymour. *Pentagon Capitalism: The Political Economy of War*. New York: McGraw-Hill, 1971.

Merrick, Michael J. "The Saga Continues—Corporate Political Free Speech and the Constitutionality of Campaign Finance Reform: *Austin v. Michigan Chamber of Commerce*." *Creighton Law Review* 24 (December 1990): 195–237.

Michels, Robert. *Political Parties: A Sociological Study of the Oligarchical Tendencies of Modern Democracy*. Translated by Eden and Cedar Paul. Introduction by Seymour Martin Lipset. New York: The Free Press, 1962.

Miliband, Ralph. *Marxism and Politics*. Oxford: Oxford University Press, 1977.

———. *The State in Capitalist Society*. New York: Basic Books, 1969.

Miller, Arthur Selwyn. *The Modern Corporate State: Private Governments and the American Constitution*. Westport, Conn.: Greenwood Press, 1976.

Mills, C. Wright. "The Labor Leaders and the Power Elite." In *Industrial Conflict*, edited by Arthur Kornhauser, pp. 144–52. New York: McGraw Hill, 1954.

———. *The Power Elite*. New York: Oxford University Press, 1956.

———. *Sociology and Pragmatism: The Higher Learning in America*. Edited by Irving Louis Horowitz. New York: Oxford University Press, 1966.

———. *White Collar: The American Middle Classes*. New York: Oxford University Press, 1951.

Milner, Helen. *Resisting Protectionism: Global Industries and the Politics of International Trade*. Princeton: Princeton University Press, 1988.

Mintz, Beth. "The President's Cabinet, 1897–1972." *Insurgent Sociologist* 5 (Spring 1975): 131–48.

Mintz, Beth, and Michael Schwartz. *The Power Structure of American Business*. Chicago: University of Chicago Press, 1985.

Mizruchi, Mark S. *The American Corporate Network, 1904–1974*. Beverly Hills, Calif.: Sage Publications, 1982.

_____. "Similarity of Political Behavior Among Large Corporations." *American Journal of Sociology* 95 (September 1989): 401–21.

_____. *The Structure of Corporate Political Action: Interfirm Relations and Their Consequences.* Cambridge, Mass.: Harvard University Press, 1992.

Mizruchi, Mark S., and Michael Schwartz, eds. *Intercorporate Relations: The Structural Analysis of Business.* New York: Cambridge University Press, 1987.

Montgomery, David. *Workers Control in America.* Cambridge: Cambridge University Press, 1979.

Moody, John. *The Truth About the Trusts: A Description and Analysis of the American Trust Movement.* 1904. Reprint. New York: Greenwood Press, 1968.

Moore, David G. *Politics and the Corporate Chief Executive.* New York: The Conference Board, 1980.

Naar, Joseph L. *Across the Board.* New York: The Conference Board, 1980.

Nader, Ralph. *The Big Boys: Power and Position in American Business.* New York: Pantheon Books, 1986.

Nader, Ralph, and Mark J. Green, eds. *Corporate Power in America.* New York: Grossman Publishers, 1973.

Natural Resources Committee. Appendix 13: "Interest Groupings in the American Economy." In *The Structure of the American Economy, Part 1: Basic Characteristics,* pp. 306–17. Washington, D.C.: Government Printing Office, 1939.

Neale, A. D. *The Antitrust Laws of the United States of America: A Study of Competition Enforced by Law.* Cambridge: Cambridge University Press, 1970.

Nelson, Ralph L. *Merger Movements in American Industry, 1895–1956.* Princeton: Princeton University Press, 1959.

Nesteruk, Jeffrey. "*Bellotti* and the Question of Corporate Moral Agency." *Columbia Business Law Review* 3 (1988): 683–703.

Noble, David. *America by Design: Science, Technology, and the Rise of Corporate Capitalism.* New York: Alfred A. Knopf, 1977.

O'Connor, James. *The Corporations and the State.* New York: Harper & Row, 1974.

Orren, Karen. *Belated Feudalism: Labor, the Law, and Liberal Development in the United States.* Cambridge: Cambridge University Press, 1991.

_____. *Corporate Power and Social Change: The Politics of the Life Insurance Industry.* Baltimore: Johns Hopkins University Press, 1974.

Parrington, Vernon L. *Main Currents in American Thought.* Vols. 1 and 2. New York: Harcourt, Brace & World, 1927.

Parrini, Carl P., and Martin J. Sklar. "New Thinking About the Market, 1896–1904: Some American Economists on Investment and the Theory of Surplus Capital." *Journal of Economic History* 43 (September 1983): 559–78.

Pateman, Carole. *Participation and Democratic Theory.* Cambridge: Cambridge University Press, 1970.

Patton, William and Randall Bartlett. "Corporate 'Persons' and Freedom of Speech: The Political Impact of Legal Mythology." *Wisconsin Law Review* 1981, no. 3 (1981): 494–512.

Paul, Arnold. *Conservative Crisis and the Rule of Law: Attitudes of Bar and Bench, 1887–1895.* Ithaca: Cornell University Press, 1960.

Pelling, Henry. *American Labor.* London: Macmillan, 1965.

Pennings, Johannes. *Interlocking Directorates: Origins and Consequences of Connections Among Organizations' Boards of Directors.* San Francisco, Calif.: Jossey-Bass, 1980.

Penrose, Edith T. *The Theory of the Growth of the Firm*. Second edition. White Plains, N.Y.: M. E. Sharpe, 1980.

Perlmutter, Howard V. "The Multinational Firm and the Future." *Annals of the American Academy of Political and Social Science* 403 (September 1972): 139–52.

———. "The Tortuous Evolution of the Multinational Corporation." In *World Business: Promise and Problems*, edited by Courtney C. Brown, pp. 66–82. New York: Macmillan, 1970.

Pertschuk, Michael. *Revolt Against Regulation: The Rise and Pause of the Consumer Movement*. Berkeley and Los Angeles: University of California Press, 1982.

Phillips, Kevin. *The Politics of Rich and Poor: Wealth and the American Electorate in the Reagan Aftermath*. New York: Harper Perennial, 1991.

Posner, Richard A. *Antitrust Law: An Economic Perspective*. Chicago: University of Chicago Press, 1976.

Potter, David. *People of Plenty: Economic Abundance and the American Character*. Chicago: University of Chicago Press, 1954.

Poulantzas, Nicos. *Political Power and Social Classes*. Translated by Timothy O'Hagan. London: New Left Books, 1973.

Pound, Roscoe. *The Formative Era of American Law*. Boston: Little, Brown, 1938.

———. "Liberty of Contract." *Yale Law Journal* 18 (May 1909): 470–78.

Quinn, Dennis P. "Investment Incentives: A Five-Country Test of the Lindblom Hypothesis." In *Research in Corporate Social Performance and Policy* 10: 87–111. Greenwich, Conn.: JAI Press, 1988.

———. *Restructuring the Automobile Industry: A Study of Firms and States in Modern Capitalism*. New York: Columbia University Press, 1988.

Quinn, Dennis P., and Robert Y. Shapiro. "Business Political Power: The Case of Taxation." *American Political Science Review* 85 (September 1991): 851–74.

Radice, Hugo. *International Firms and Modern Imperialism*. Harmondsworth, Middlesex: Penguin Books, 1975.

Radosh, Ronald. "The Corporate Ideology of American Labor Leaders from Gompers to Hillman." *Studies on the Left* 6 (November–December 1966): 66–87.

Radosh, Ronald, and Murray N. Rothbard, eds. *A New History of Leviathan: Essays on the Rise of the American Corporate State*. New York: E. P. Dutton, 1972.

Reagan, Michael D. *The Managed Economy*. New York: Oxford University Press, 1963.

Reich, Robert B. *The Work of Nations: Preparing Ourselves for 21st-Century Capitalism*. New York: Knopf, 1991.

Reid, Samuel Richardson. *Mergers, Managers, and the Economy*. New York: McGraw-Hill, 1968.

———. *The New Industrial State: Concentration, Regulation, and Public Policy*. New York: McGraw-Hill, 1976.

Rezneck, Samuel. "The Rise and Early Development of Industrial Consciousness in the United States, 1760–1830." *Journal of Economic and Business History* 4 (November 1931–August 1932): 784–811.

Rhodes, Robert I., ed. *Imperialism and Underdevelopment*. New York: Monthly Review Press, 1970.

Ripley, William Z. *Main Street and Wall Street*. Boston: Little, Brown, 1927.

Roche, John P. "Entrepreneurial Liberty." In *The Shaping of Twentieth Century America*, edited by Richard M. Abrams and Lawrence W. Levine, pp. 128–53. Boston: Little, Brown, 1965.

———. "Entrepreneurial Liberty and the Commerce Power: Expansion, Contraction, and Consistency in the Age of Enterprise." *University of Chicago Law Review* 30 (Spring 1963): 680–703.

———, ed. *Origins of American Political Thought*. New York: Harper & Row, 1967.

Rochester, Anna. *Rulers of America*. New York: International Publishers, 1936.

Rockefeller, David. "Multinationals Under Siege." *International Finance*, May 19, 1975, pp. 7–8.

———. "Prospects for New World Monetary and Trade Patterns." *The Atlantic Community Quarterly* 6 (Winter 1968–69): 549–55.

Roe, Mark J. *Strong Managers, Weak Owners: The Political Roots of American Corporate Finance*. Princeton: Princeton University Press, 1994.

Roll, Erich. *A History of Economic Thought*. New York: Prentice-Hall, 1939.

Rome, Edwin P., and William H. Roberts. *Corporate and Commercial Free Speech: First Amendment Protection of Expression in Business*. Westport, Conn.: Quorum Books, 1985.

Rothenberg, Stuart, and Richard R. Roldan. *Business PACs and Ideology: A Study of Contributions in the 1982 Elections*. Washington, D.C.: Institute for Government and Politics, 1983.

Sabato, Larry J. *PAC Power: Inside the World of Political Action Committees*. New York: W. W. Norton and Co., 1984.

Said, Abdul A., and Luiz R. Simmons, eds. *The New Sovereigns: Multinational Corporations as World Powers*. Englewood Cliffs, N.J.: Prentice-Hall, 1975.

Sametz, Arnold W., ed. *The Battle for Corporate Control*. Homewood, Ill.: Business One Irwin, 1991.

Schlesinger, Arthur M., Jr. *The Age of Jackson*. Boston: Little, Brown, 1945.

Schneider, Carl E. "Free Speech and Corporate Freedom: A Comment on *First National Bank of Boston v. Bellotti*." *Southern California Law Review* 59 (September 1986): 1227–91.

Schockley, John S. "Direct Democracy, Campaign Finance, and the Courts: Can Corruption, Undue Influence, and Declining Voter Confidence Be Found?" *University of Miami Law Review* 39 (May 1985): 377–428.

Schumpeter, Joseph. *Theory of Economic Development*. Cambridge, Mass.: Harvard University Press, 1934.

Schwartz, Michael, ed. *The Structure of Power in America: The Corporate Elite as a Ruling Class*. New York: Holmes & Meier, 1987.

Schwarz, Jordan A. *Liberal: Adolph A. Berle and the Vision of an American Era*. New York: The Free Press, 1987.

Scott, William R. *The Constitution and Finance of English, Scottish and Irish Joint-Stock Companies to 1720*. 3 vols. Cambridge: Cambridge University Press, 1910–12.

Scribner, Tom, ed. "Symposium: Political Action Committees and Campaign Finance." *Arizona Law Review* 22 (1980): 351–674.

Seavoy, Ronald E. *The Origins of the American Business Corporation, 1784–1855: Broadening the Concept of Public Service During Industrialization*. Westport, Conn.: Greenwood Press, 1982.

Seliger, Martin. *Ideology and Politics*. New York: The Free Press, 1976.

———. *The Marxist Conception of Ideology: A Critical Essay*. Cambridge: Cambridge University Press, 1977.

Shannon, David A. *The Socialist Party of America*. Chicago: Quadrangle Books, 1955.

Shannon, H. A. "The Coming of General Limited Liability." *Economic History* 2 (January 1931): 267–91.

Shapiro, Irving. *America's Third Revolution: Public Interest and the Private Role.* New York: Harper & Row, 1984.

Shiffrin, Steven. "The First Amendment and Economic Regulation: Away from a General Theory of the First Amendment." *Northwestern University Law Review* 78 (December 1983): 1212–83.

Silk, Leonard, and David Vogel. *Ethics and Profits: The Crisis of Confidence in American Business.* New York: Simon & Schuster, 1976.

Sklar, Martin J. *The Corporate Reconstruction of American Capitalism, 1890–1916: The Market, the Law, and Politics.* Cambridge: Cambridge University Press, 1988.

――――. *The United States as a Developing Country: Studies in U.S. History in the Progressive Era and the 1920s.* Cambridge: Cambridge University Press, 1992.

――――. "Woodrow Wilson and the Political Economy of Modern United States Liberalism." *Studies on the Left* 1 (Fall 1960): 17–47.

Sklar, Richard L. *Corporate Power in an African State: The Political Impact of Multinational Mining Companies in Zambia.* Berkeley and Los Angeles: University of California Press, 1975.

――――. "Developmental Democracy." *Comparative Studies in History and Society* 29 (October 1987): 686–714.

――――. "The Nature of Class Domination in Africa." *Journal of Modern African Studies* 17 (December 1979): 531–52.

――――. "On the Concept of Power in Political Economy." In *Toward a Humanistic Science of Politics: Essays in Honor of Francis Dunham Wormuth,* edited by Dalmas H. Nelson and Richard L. Sklar, pp. 187–88. Lanham, Md.: University Press of America, 1983.

――――. "Postimperialism: A Class Analysis of Multinational Corporate Expansion." *Comparative Politics* 9 (October 1976): 75–92; reprinted in David G. Becker et al., *Postimperialism: International Capitalism and Development in the Late Twentieth Century* (Boulder, Colo.: Lynne Rienner Publishers, 1987), pp. 19–40.

Skowronek, Stephen. *Building a New American State: The Expansion of National Administrative Capacities, 1877–1920.* New York: Cambridge University Press, 1982.

Smith, Adam. *An Inquiry into the Nature and Causes of the Wealth of Nations.* 2 vols. Edited by Edwin Cannan. New Rochelle, N.Y.: Arlington House, 1966.

Smith, Rogers M. *Liberalism and American Constitutional Law.* Cambridge, Mass.: Harvard University Press, 1985.

Snowiss, Sylvia. *Judicial Review and the Law of the Constitution.* New Haven: Yale University Press, 1990.

Solberg, Winton U., ed. *The Federal Convention and the Formation of the Union of the United States.* Indianapolis: Bobbs-Merrill, 1958.

Spencer, Herbert. *On Social Evolution: Selected Writings.* Edited by J.D.Y. Peel. Chicago: University of Chicago Press, 1972.

Stark, Andrew. "Corporate Electoral Activity, Constitutional Discourse, and Conceptions of the Individual." *American Political Science Review* 86 (September 1992): 626–37.

Steckmest, Francis W. *Corporate Performance: The Key to Public Trust*. New York: McGraw-Hill, 1982.

Stevens, W.H.S. "Stockholders Voting Rights and the Centralization of Voting Control." *Quarterly Journal of Economics* 40 (May 1926): 353–92.

Sumner, William Graham. "The Concentration of Wealth: Its Economic Justification." In *Selected Essays of William Graham Sumner: Social Darwinism*, pp. 150–59. Englewood Cliffs, N.J.: Prentice-Hall, 1963.

————. *What Social Classes Mean to Each Other*. Caldwell, Idaho: Caxton Printers, 1974.

Susman, Warren. *Culture as History: The Transformation of American Society in the Twentieth Century*. New York: Pantheon Books, 1973.

Sutton, Francis X., Seymour E. Harris, Carl Kaysen, and James Tobin. *The American Business Creed*. Cambridge, Mass.: Harvard University Press, 1956.

Swisher, Carl B. *The Taney Period, 1836–1864*. Edited by Paul A. Freund. Vol. 5 of *The Oliver Wendell Holmes Devise History of the Supreme Court of the United States*. New York: Macmillan, 1974.

Taft, Philip. *The AF of L in the Time of Gompers*. New York: Octagon Books, 1970.

Thompson, John B. *Studies in the Theory of Ideology*. Berkeley and Los Angeles: University of California Press, 1984.

Thorelli, Hans B. *The Federal Antitrust Policy: Origination of an American Tradition*. Baltimore: Johns Hopkins University Press, 1955.

Tilner, Mitchell C. "Government Compulsion of Corporate Speech: Legitimate Regulation or First Amendment Violation? A Critique of *PG&E v. Public Utilities Commission*." *Santa Clara Law Review* 27 (1987): 485–513.

Tocqueville, Alexis de. *Democracy in America*. Translated by Henry Reeve. Introduction by John Stuart Mill. 2 vols. New York: Schocken Books, 1967.

Twiss, Benjamin R. *Lawyers and the Constitution*. Princeton: Princeton University Press, 1942.

Unger, Roberto Mangabeira. *Law in Modern Society: Toward a Criticism of Social Theory*. New York: The Free Press, 1976.

U.S. Department of Commerce, Bureau of the Census. *1987 Census of Manufactures: Concentration Ratios in Manufacturing*. Washington, D.C.: U.S. Government Printing Office, 1987.

————. *Statistical Abstracts of the United States, 1993*. Washington, D.C.: Government Printing Office, 1993.

U.S. Department of Justice, Antitrust Division. *Antitrust Guide for International Operations*, March 1, 1977; revised January 26, 1977.

————. *U.S. Department of Justice Merger Guidelines*. June 14, 1968; June 14, 1982; June 14, 1984.

U.S. Department of Justice and Federal Trade Commission. *Horizontal Merger Guidelines*. 62 Antitrust & Trade Reg. Rep. (BNA) No. 1559 (April 2, 1992).

U.S. Federal Trade Commission. *Report on Interlocking Directorates*. Washington, D.C.: Government Printing Office, 1951.

U.S. House of Representatives, Committee on Banking and Currency, Subcommittee on Domestic Finance. *Commercial Banks and Their Trust Activities: Emerging Influence on the American Economy*. Washington, D.C.: Government Printing Office, 1968.

U.S. House of Representatives, Committee on the Judiciary. *Hearings on Trust Legislation*. 2 vols. Washington, D.C.: Government Printing Office, 1914.

U.S. House of Representatives, Committee on the Judiciary, Antitrust Subcommittee. *Interlocks in Corporate Management*. Washington, D.C.: U.S. Government Printing Office, 1965.

U.S. Senate, Committee on Governmental Affairs, Subcommittee on Reports, Accounting, and Management. *Interlocking Directorates Among the Major U.S. Corporations*. Washington, D.C.: Government Printing Office, 1978.

Useem, Michael. "Classwide Rationality in the Politics of Managers and Directors of Large Corporations in the United States and Great Britain." *Administrative Science Quarterly* 27 (June 1982): 199–226.

———. *The Inner Circle: Large Corporations and the Rise of Business Political Activity in the U.S. and U.K.* New York: Oxford University Press, 1984.

———. "The Inner Circle and the Political Voice of Business." In *The Structure of Power in America: The Corporate Elite as a Ruling Class*, edited by Michael Schwartz. New York: Holmes & Meier, 1987.

———. "The Inner Group of the American Capitalist Class." *Social Problems* 25 (February 1978): 225–40.

———. *Liberal Education and the Corporation: The Hiring and Advancement of College Graduates*. New York: Aldine de Gruyter, 1989.

Veblen, Thorstein. *Absentee Ownership and Business Enterprise in Recent Times*. New York: B. W. Huebsch, 1923.

———. "The Beginnings of Ownership." In *Essays in Our Changing Order*, edited by Leon Ardzrooni, pp. 42–49. New York: Viking Press, 1934.

———. *The Engineers and the Price System*. New York: Viking Press, 1932.

———. *The Higher Learning in America: A Memorandum on the Conduct of Universities by Businessmen*. New York: B. W. Huebsch, 1913.

———. *The Instinct of Workmanship and the State of the Industrial Arts*. New York: B. W. Huebsch, 1918.

———. *The Place of Science in Modern Civilization*. New York: B. W. Huebsch, 1919.

———. "The Preconceptions of Economic Science II." *Quarterly Journal of Economics* 13 (July 1899): 396–426.

———. "Some Neglected Points in the Theory of Socialism." *Annals of American Academy of Political and Social Science* 2 (November 1891): 57–74.

———. *The Theory of Business Enterprise*. New York: Mentor Books, 1958.

———. *The Theory of the Leisure Class: An Economic Study of Institutions*. New York: Mentor Books, 1953.

———. *The Vested Interests and the Common Man*. New York: Viking Press, 1933.

Vernon, Raymond. *The Economic and Political Consequences of Multinational Enterprise: An Anthology*. Boston: Division of Research, Graduate School of Business Administration, Harvard University, 1972.

———. *Sovereignty at Bay: The Multinational Spread of U.S. Enterprise*. New York: Basic Books, 1971.

———. *Storm over the Multinationals: The Real Issues*. Cambridge, Mass.: Harvard University Press, 1977.

Villarejo, Don. *Stock Ownership and the Control of Corporations*. Ann Arbor: Radical Education Project, 1962.

Viner, Jacob. "Adam Smith and Laissez-Faire." In *Essays in Economic Thought: Aristotle to Marshall*, edited by Joseph J. Spengler and William R. Allen, pp. 305–29. Chicago: Rand McNally, 1960.

Vogel, David. *Fluctuating Fortunes*. New York: Basic Books, 1989.

_____. *Lobbying the Corporation: Citizen Challenges to Business Authority*. New York: Basic Books, 1978.

_____. *National Styles of Regulation: Environmental Policies in Great Britain and the United States*. Ithaca: Cornell University Press, 1986.

_____. "Political Science and the Study of Corporate Power: A Dissent from the New Conventional Wisdom." *British Journal of Political Science* 17 (October 1987): 385–405.

_____. "The Power of Business in America: A Reappraisal." *British Journal of Political Science* 13 (January 1983): 19–43.

_____. "The Public-Interest Movement and the American Reform Tradition." *Political Science Quarterly* 95 (Winter 1980–81): 607–27.

Von Halle, Ernst. *Trusts or Industrial Combinations and Coalitions in the United States*. New York: Macmillan, 1895.

Walker, Albert H. *History of the Sherman Law of the United States*. New York: The Equity Press, 1910.

Ware, Norman. *The Industrial Worker, 1840–1860*. New York: Quadrangle / New York Times Book Co., 1964.

_____. *The Labor Movement in the United States, 1860–1895*. New York: Appleton-Century-Crofts, 1929.

Warner, W. Lloyd, and D. B. Unwalla. "The System of Interlocking Directorates." In *The Emergent American Society: Large Scale Organizations*. Edited by W. Lloyd Warner, D. B. Unwalla, and J. H. Trimm. New Haven: Yale University Press, 1967.

Warren, Charles. *The Supreme Court in United States History*. 3 vols. Boston: Little, Brown, 1922.

Warren, Edward H. *Select Cases and Other Authorities on the Law of Private Corporations*. Cambridge, Mass.: Harvard University Press, 1916.

Weaver, Paul. "Regulation, Social Policy, and Class Conflict." *Public Interest* 50 (Winter 1978): 45–63.

Weinstein, James. *The Corporate Ideal in the Liberal State, 1900–1918*. Boston: Beacon Press, 1968.

_____. *The Decline of Socialism in America, 1912–1925*. New York: Monthly Review Press, 1967.

Weyl, Walter E. *American World Policies*. New York: Macmillan, 1917.

_____. *The New Democracy: An Essay on Certain Political and Economic Tendencies in the United States*. New York: Macmillan, 1912.

White, G. Edward. *The American Judicial Tradition: Profiles of Leading American Judges*. New York: Oxford University Press, 1988.

_____. *The Marshall Court and Cultural Change, 1815–1835*. Edited by Paul A. Freund and Stanley N. Katz. Vols. 3 & 4 of *The Oliver Wendell Holmes Devise History of the Supreme Court of the United States*. New York: Macmillan, 1988.

Wiebe, Robert H. *Business and Reform: A Study of the Progressive Movement*. Cambridge, Mass.: Harvard University Press, 1962.

_____. "The House of Morgan and the Executive, 1905–1913." In *The Shaping of Twentieth Century America*, edited by Richard M. Abrams and Lawrence W. Levine, pp. 254–68. Boston: Little, Brown, 1965.

Wilkens, Mira. *The Maturing of Multinational Enterprise: American Business Abroad from 1914 to 1970*. Cambridge, Mass.: Harvard University Press, 1974.

Williams, William Appleman. *The Contours of American History*. Chicago: Quadrangle Books, 1966.

Williston, Samuel. "History of the Law of Business Corporations Before 1800." *Harvard Law Review* 2 (October–November 1888): 105–24, 149–66.

Wilson, James Q., ed. *The Politics of Regulation*. New York: Basic Books, 1980.

Wood, Gordon S. *The Creation of the American Republic, 1776-1787*. New York: W. W. Norton & Co., 1972.

Wormuth, Francis D. *The Origins of Modern Constitutionalism*. New York: Harper, 1949.

———. "A Typology of Revolution and Ideology." In *Essays in Law and Politics: Francis Dunham Wormuth*, edited by Dalmas H. Nelson and Richard L. Sklar, pp. 177–99. Port Washington, N.Y.: Kennikat Press, 1978.

Wormuth, Francis D., and Hobert P. Sturm. "The International Power Elite." In *Essays in Law and Politics: Francis Dunham Wormuth*, edited by Dalmas H. Nelson and Richard L. Sklar, pp. 215–19. Port Washington, N.Y.: Kennikat Press, 1978; reprinted from *Monthly Review* 11 (December 1959): 282–87.

Wright, Benjamin Fletcher, Jr. *The Contract Clause of the Constitution*. Cambridge, Mass.: Harvard University Press, 1938.

Wright, J. Skelly. "Money and the Pollution of Politics: Is the First Amendment an Obstacle to Political Equality?" *Columbia Law Review* 82 (May 1982): 609–45.

Zeitlin, Maurice. "Corporate Ownership and Control: The Large Corporation and the Capitalist Class." *American Journal of Sociology* 79 (March 1974): 1073–119.

Zeitlin, Maurice, and Samuel Norich. "Management Control, Exploitation, and Profit Maximization in the Large Corporation: An Empirical Confrontation of Managerialism and Class Theory." In *Research in Political Economy*, edited by Paul Zarembka, 2:33–62. Greenwich, Conn.: JAI Press, 1977.

Table of Cases

A number in parentheses following a note indicates the page in the text where the note appears.

Index

Adams, John, 267
administered markets. *See* corporate capitalism
administrative law, 128
AFL-CIO, 143
Alexander, Herbert E., 352n.29, 355n.32
Althusser, Louis, 263
American Business Conference, 146, 147
American Council for Capital Formation (1973), 150
American Enterprise Institute (1970), 150
American Revolution, 7–8, 38–39
American Smelting & Refining Company, 354n.32
American Sugar Refining Company, 329n.116
anarchism, 77
Anti-Corn Law League, 293
antimonopoly tradition
    and corporate power, 5–6, 27, 49–51, 61–63, 334n.135
    early nineteenth century, 5, 49, 61, 318n.55
    and general incorporation acts, 50–51, 61, 70
    laissez-faire argument (Adam Smith), 320n.64
    late nineteenth century, 5, 59, 61–63, 76–78, 143, 274–75
    and liberalism, 5–6, 51, 70
    mid-nineteenth century (anticharter movement), 49–51, 70
    and regulatory commissions, 5–6
antitrust law. *See also* antitrust policy; Clayton Antitrust Act; Federal Trade Commission Act; mergers; Sherman Antitrust Act
    Alcoa's impact on, 173–74
    antitrust activism, periods of, 171, 174
    "antitrust majority" on Supreme Court, 177
    balance in, 67, 363n.88
    and the Burger Court, 174, 177–80
    and commerce clause: authority under, 63; manufacturing/commerce distinction, 329n.116
    common-law interpretation of Sherman Act, 64–66
    conspiracy, doctrine of, 169
    conscious parallel action, 170
    constitutional rules of, 16, 68–69, 168, 169–70, 181
    and corporate autonomy, 71–72, 140, 154
    and corporate liberalism, 13, 37, 67, 68–69, 71–72
    and corporate political speech, 129–30, 154–55, 164, 166–67

and corporate power, 12, 23, 37–38, 68–69, 137, 170, 171, 174–75, 178–80
and economic theory, 68, 172, 333n.133
enforcement of and first great merger wave, 60, 175, 331n.124
equal opportunity to compete, 37–38, 67–68, 137, 169, 170
fair competition, 16, 23, 37–38, 67–68, 73, 169, 170, 173, 181, 333n.132
and federalism, 64, 71–72
freedom to contract (liberty of contract), 37–38, 64, 66, 67–68, 169, 171, 330nn.118, 119
and global marketplace, 130, 171
Hand-Warren interpretation of potential competition, 171–74, 176–80
Harlan-Peckham interpretation of Sherman Act, 64–65, 173, 330nn.118, 119, 121, 331n.124
ideological significance, 168–69, 170, 182
and judicial policy-making, 169
limited government in, 67, 170, 363n.88
market concentration, 171, 176–78
monopoly, 64, 66, 168–73, 179, 325n.103, 332n.129, 363n.86
normal methods of industrial development, 68, 172, 173
oligarchy of oligopolists, 179–80, 301, 367nn.115, 116
oligopolistic competition, transnational conception of, 180
oligopolistic practices sanctioned, 169–70
oligopoly, 23, 71–72, 140, 169, 173, 174, 177
per se violations, 68, 333n.132
political character of, 168–69
potential competition, 67, 140, 171, 173, 177, 180, 181
and price leadership, 169–70
and regulating the marketplace, 67–69, 140
restraints of trade, 62, 63–66, 67–68, 169, 330nn.118, 119, 121, 331n.124
right to compete, 64, 330n.118
rule of reason, 63–69, 170, 172, 173
shared monopoly, 169–70, 363n.86
and transnational corporations, 180, 369n.121
White-Holmes interpretation, 64–69
antitrust policy. *See also* antitrust law
    Bush administration, 140–41, 171, 174, 180
    Carter administration, 147, 174
    Cleveland administration, 175, 331n.124
    Harrison administration, 331n.124
    McKinley administration, 175, 331n.124